Cognition Within and Between Organizations

Organization Science

Series Editor: Arie Y. Lewin

Books from Sage Publications, *Organization Science*, and the Institute for Operations Research and the Management Sciences

The Sage Publications **Organization Science** book series reprints expanded Special Issues of *Organization Science*. Each individual volume is based on the original Special Issue that appeared in *Organization Science*. It includes all-new introductions by the editors as well as several chapters that did not appear in the original Special Issue. These new chapters may include reprints of papers that appeared in other issues of *Organization Science*, relevant papers that appeared in other journals, and also new original articles.

The book series is published by Sage Publications in partnership with INFORMS (the Institute for Operations Research and Management Sciences) the publisher of *Organization Science*. The Series Editor is Arie Y. Lewin, the Editor in Chief of *Organization Science*.

Organization Science was founded in 1989 as an international journal with the aim of advancing the field of organization studies by attracting, then publishing innovative research from across the social sciences. The term "Science" in the journal's title is interpreted in the broadest possible sense to include diverse methods and theoretical approaches. The editors of *Organization Science* believe that creative insight often occurs outside traditional approaches and topic areas, and that the role of *Organization Science* is to be broadly inclusive of the field by helping to integrate the diverse stands of organizational research. Authors are expected to describe theoretical concepts that give meaning to data, and to show how these concepts are relevant to organizations. Manuscripts that speculate beyond current thinking are more desirable than papers that use tried and true methods to study routine problems.

Initial books in this series:

Longitudinal Field Research Methods: Studying Processes of Organizational Change
Edited by George P. Huber and Andrew H. Van de Ven

Organizational Learning
Edited by Michael D. Cohen and Lee S. Sproull

Cognition Within and Between Organizations
Edited by James R. Meindl, Charles Stubbart, and Joseph F. Porac

For information on subscriptions to *Organization Science*, please contact INFORMS at 940-A Elkridge Landing Road, Linthicum, MD 21090-2909, 800-446-3676. For submission guidelines, contact INFORMS at 290 Westminster Street, Providence, RI 02903, 800-343-0062.

of several individuals or groups; the problem of raw data conversion to achieve the necessary comparability and pragmatic compression; and finally, the need of a rigorous and efficient computerized platform for the comparative analysis. The approach presented in this chapter offers realistically accessible tools that—in the presented form or adapted in innovative ways—can help solve such tasks in future MOC research.

NOTES

1. A computer program (*CMAP2*) to support the method is obtainable from the author. It is a character-based DOS application, running on normal PCs with hard disk. However, many of the described operations can be performed using some of the so-called relational database programs, such as dBase, FoxPro or Paradox.

2. The constructs used include, e.g., cognitive and/or cause maps (Axelrod 1976, Eden et al. 1979, Huff 1940, Lee et al. 1992, Sevón 1984, Weick and Bougon 1986), dominant logic (Prahalad and Bettis 1986), schema (Bartunek and Moch 1987, Huff 1990, Rumelhart 1984), mental mode (Johnson-Laird 1983, 1988), mental map (Morecroft 1992), interpretive scheme (Bartunek 1984), worldview and ideology (Nystrom and Starbuck 1984, Salancik and Porac 1986, Starbuck 1982), recipe (Schutz 1962, Spender 1989), belief patterns (Donaldson and Lorsch 1983, Nystrom and Starbuck 1984).

3. Sometimes, cause maps are called *cognitive* maps, usually traced to Axelrod and his colleagues, who used them for analyzing the decisions of politicians and decision-making bodies (Axelrod 1976). In organizational contexts, early landmark studies are those by Bougon, Weick, and Binkhorst (1977), and Edén and his colleagues (Eden et al. 1979). We would prefer the term *cause map/mapping* because it is the *phenomenological* (concept base) and the *causal belief dimensions* in Ss' thinking that are being represented (cf. Huff 1990, Laukkanen 1990), whereas some other aspects of human cognitions, e.g., connotative and temporal relations also linking subjective constructs, are not explicitly covered.

4. This resembles the critical decision method (CDM) in Expert Systems' knowledge acquisitions (KA) (Klein 1992).

5. A useful form example has 50 numbered rows, one column for the NLUs and one for the causal link from an NLU to another on the sheet, indicated by the row number of the effect-NLU entered on the cause-NLU's row in the column. If the respondents, Ss, and the pages have codes/numbers, this enables a *unique code* for each NLU entry (e.g., 091025 = respondent 9's raw data sheet 10, row 25). This is necessary for computer entry and for maintaining the audit trail. The CMAP2 program creates the code automatically during data entry.

6. In CMAP2, the ST-use-file generation calculates the *indegree-* and *outdegree-*values of the ST-concepts. An indegree tells how many causal influence links flow into a concept; an outdegree, how many go from it into other concepts. They or their sums are sometimes used as an index for concept centrality (Axelrod 1976, Hart 1977).

7. The CMAP2-program calculates *cluster* incidence, a cluster referring to a predefined group of the respondents, and locates *core-SCUs.* Also, simple quantitative measures are provided, such as the *weight of core STs* or *core SCUs,* or the map's *density* (cf Hart 1977).

8. A report of the study (Laukkanen 1989) can be obtained from the author upon request.

9. For example, we could envision adding notation for types or classes of concepts, e.g., attributes of variable phenomena, or new types of links, such as connotative, nonlinear, ratchet-

type, time related, or attributes of the links, like firing clauses or conditions, levels of certainty, etc. (cf. Axelrod 1976).

10. See note 1.

REFERENCES

Allison, G. T. (1971), *The Essence of Decision: Explaining the Cuban Missile Crisis,* Boston: Little, Brown.

Argyris, C. and D. A. Schön (1978), *Organizational Learning,* Reading, MA: Addison-Wesley.

Axelrod, R. (Ed.) (1976), *Structure of Decision: The Cognitive Maps of Political Elites,* Princeton, NJ: Princeton University Press.

Bandura, A. (1986), *Social Foundations of Thought and Action,* Englewood Cliffs, NJ: Prentice Hall.

Bartunek, J. M. (1984), "Changing Interpretive Schemes and Organizational Restructuring: The Example of a Religious Order," *Administrative Science Quarterly,* 29.

——— and M. K. Moch (1987), "First-Order, Second-Order, and Third-Order Change and Organizational Development Interventions," *Journal of Applied Behavioral Science,* 23, 4.

Bonham, G. M., M. J. Shapiro, and D. Heradstveit (1988), "Group Cognition: Using an Oil Policy Game to Validate a Computer Simulation," *Simulation & Games,* 19, 4, Dec.

Bougon, M. G. (1983), "Uncovering Cognitive Maps: The Self-Q Technique," in G. Morgan (Ed.), *Beyond Method: Strategies for Social Research,* Beverly Hills, CA: Sage.

——— G. N. Baird, J. M. Komocar, and W. Ross (1990), "Identifying Strategic Loops: The Self-Q Interviews," in A. S. Huff (Ed.), *Mapping Strategic Thought,* Chichester, UK: Wiley.

——— K. E. Weick, and D. Binkhorst (1977), "Cognition in Organizations: An Analysis of the Utrecht Jazz Orchestra," *Administrative Science Quarterly,* 22, 606-639.

Brehmer, B. (1980), "In One Word: Not from Experience," *Acta Psychologica,* 45.

Collins, A. and D. Gentner (1987), "How People Construct Mental Models," in D. Holland and N. Quinn (Eds.), *Cultural Models in Language and Thought,* Cambridge, UK: University of Cambridge Press.

Cooke, N. J. (1992), "Modeling Human Expertise in Expert Systems," in R. R. Hoffman (Ed.), *The Psychology of Expertise: Cognitive Research and Empirical AI,* New York: Springer-Verlag.

Cossette, P. and M. Audet (1992), Mapping of an Idiosyncratic Schema. *Journal of Management Studies,* 29, 3.

Cropper, S., C. Eden, and F. Ackermann (1990), "Keeping Sense of Accounts Using Computer-Based Cognitive Maps," *Social Science Computer Review,* 8, 3, Fall.

deGeus, A. P. (1992), "Foreword: Modelling to Predict or to Learn?" *European Journal of Operational Research,* 59, 1.

Diffenbach, J. (1982), "Influence Diagrams for Complex Strategic Issues," *Strategic Management Journal,* 3.

DiMaggio, P. J. and W. W. Powell (1983), "The Iron Cage Revisited: Institutional Isomorphism and Collective Rationality in Organizational Fields," *American Sociological Review,* 48.

Donaldson, G. and J. W. Lorsch (1983), *Decision Making at the Top: The Shaping of Strategic Direction,* New York: Basic Books.

Douglas, M. T. (1986), *How Institutions Think,* Syracuse, NY: Syracuse University Press.

Eden, C. (1989), "Using Cognitive Mapping for Strategic Options Development," in J. Rosenhead (Ed.), *Rational Analysis for a Problematic World,* Chichester, UK: Wiley.

———(1991), "Working on Problems Using Cognitive Mapping," in S. C. Littlechild and M. Shutler (Eds.), *Operations Research in Management,* London: Prentice Hall.

——— (1992), "On the Nature of Cognitive Maps," *Journal of Management Studies,* 29, 3, May.

——— F. Ackermann, and S. Cropper (1992), "The Analysis of Cause Maps," *Journal of Management Studies,* 29, 3, May.

——— S. Jones, and D. Sims (1979), *Thinking in Organizations,* London: Macmillan.

Evans, J. St. B. T. (1987), "Human biases and computer decision making," *Behaviour and Information Technology,* 6.

——— (1988), "The Knowledge Elicitation Problem: A Psychological Perspective," *Behaviour and Information Technology,* 7.

Fahey, L. and V. K. Narayanan (1989), "Linking Changes in Revealed Causal Maps and Environmental Change," *Journal of Management Studies,* 26, 4, July.

Fiol, C. M. (1990), "Explaining Strategic Alliances in the Chemical Industry," in A. S. Huff (Ed.), *Mapping Strategic Thought,* Chichester, UK: Wiley, 227-249.

Fiol, C. M. and M. A. Lyles (1985), "Organizational Learning," *Academy of Management Review,* 10, 4, 12.

Gammack, J. G. and R. M. Young (1984), "Psychological Techniques for Eliciting Expert Knowledge," in M. A. Bramer (Ed.), *Research and Development in Expert Systems,* Cambridge, UK: Cambridge University Press.

Gordon, S. E. (1992), "Implications of Cognitive Theory for Knowledge Acquisition," in R. R. Hoffman (Ed.), *The Psychology of Expertise: Cognitive Research and Empirical AI,* New York: Springer-Verlag.

Grant, R. M. (1988), "On dominant Logic, Relatedness, and the Link Between Diversity and Performance," *Strategic Management Journal,* 9, 10.

Hage, P. and F. Harary (1983), *Structural Models in Anthropology,* New York: Cambridge University Press.

Hall, R. I. (1984), The Natural Logic of Management Policy Making: Its Implications for the Survival of an Organization. *Management Science,* 30, 8.

Hart, J. (1977), "Cognitive Maps of Three Latin American Policy Makers," *World Politics,* Oct., 1.

Hedberg, B. (1981), "How Organizations Learn and Unlearn," in P. C. Nystrom and W. H. Starbuck (Eds.), *Handbook of Organizational Design,* Vol. 1. New York: Oxford University Press.

Hogarth, R. M. (1985), *Judgment and Choice: The Psychology of Decision,* Bury St. Edmunds, UK: Wiley.

Holland, D. and N. Quinn (Eds.) (1987), *Cultural Models in Language and Thought,* Cambridge, UK: University of Cambridge Press.

Huff, A. S. (1990), *Mapping Strategic Thought,* Chichester, UK: Wiley.

Isenberg, D. J. (1986), "Thinking and Managing: A Verbal Protocol Analysis of Managerial Problem Solving," *Academy of Management Journal,* 29, 4, 775-788.

Janis, I. L. (1982), *Groupthink: Psychological Studies of Policy Decisions and Fiascoes,* Boston: Houghton Mifflin.

Johnson-Laird, P. N. (1983), *Mental Models,* Cambridge, MA: Harvard University Press.

——— (1988), *The Computer and the Mind: An Introduction to Cognitive Science,* Cambridge, MA: Harvard University Press.

Kidd, A. L. (1987), *Knowledge Acquisition for Expert Systems: A Practical Handbook,* New York: Plenum.

Klein, G. A. (1992), "Using Knowledge Engineering to Preserve Corporate Memory," in R. R. Hoffman (Ed.), *The Psychology of Expertise: Cognitive Research and Empirical AI,* New York: Springer-Verlag.

Langfield-Smith, K. (1992), "Exploring the Need for a Shared Cognitive Map," *Journal of Management Studies,* 29, 3.

Laukkanen, M. (1989), *Understanding the Formation of Managers' Cognitive Maps: A Comparative Case Study of Context Traces in Two Business Firm Clusters,* Helsinki, Finland: Helsinki School of Economics Publications, A-65.

——— (1990), "Describing Management Cognition: The Cause Mapping Approach," *Scandinavian Journal of Management,* 3.

——— (1992), *Comparative Cause Mapping of Management Cognitions: A Computer Database Method for Natural Data,* Helsinki, Finland: Helsinki School of Economics Publications, D-154.

Lee, S., J. F. Courtney Jr., and R. M. O'Keefe (1992), "A System for Organizational Learning Using Cognitive Maps," *Omega,* 20, 1.

Lenz, R. T. and J. L. Engledow (1986), "Environmental Analysis: The Applicability of Current Theory," *Strategic Management Journal,* 7.

Lord, R. G. (1991), "Memory: Theory and Measurement," paper presented at the Annual Academy of Management Meeting, August, 1991, Miami Beach, FL.

Mintzberg, H. (1983), "An Emerging Strategy of 'Direct' Research," in J. Van Maanen (Ed.), *Qualitative Methodology,* 105-116.

Morecroft, J. D. W. (1992), "Executive Knowledge, Models, and Learning," *European Journal of Operational Research,* 59, 9-27.

Nozicka, G., G. M. Bonham, and M. J. Shapiro (1976), "Simulation Techniques," in R. Axelrod (Ed.), *Structure of Decision: The Cognitive Maps of Political Elites,* Princeton, NJ: Princeton University Press.

Nystrom, P. C. and W. H. Starbuck (1984), "Managing Beliefs in Organizations," *Journal of Applied Behavioral Science,* 20, 3.

Orton, J. D. and K. E. Weick (1990), "Loosely Coupled Systems: A Reconceptualization," *Academy of Management Review,* 15, 2.

Pfeffer, J. (1981), "Management as Symbolic Action: The Creation and Maintenance of Organizational Paradigms," in L. L. Cummings and B. M. Staw (Eds.), *Research in Organizational Behavior,* Greenwich, CT: JAI, 3, 1-52.

Porac, J. F. and H. Thomas (1989), "Managerial Thinking in Business Environments," *Journal of Management Studies,* 26, 4, July.

———, ——— and C. Baden-Fuller (1989), "Competitive Groups as Cognitive Communities: The Case of Scottish Knitwear Manufacturers," *Journal of Management Studies,* 26, 4, July.

Potter, J. and M. Wetherell (1990), *Discourse and Social Psychology: Beyond Attitudes and Behaviour,* Beverly Hills, CA: Sage Publications, Ltd.

Prahalad, C. K. and R. A. Bettis (1986), "The Dominant Logic: A New Linkage Between Diversity and Performance," *Strategic Management Journal,* 7.

Ramaprasad, A. and E. Poon (1985), "A Computerized Interactive Technique for Mapping Influence Diagrams (MIND)," *Strategic Management Journal,* 6.

Read, S. J. (1987), "Constructing Causal Scenarios: A Knowledge Structure Approach to Causal Reasoning," *Journal of Personality and Social Psychology,* 52, 2.

Regoczei, S. and E. P. O. Plantinga (1987), "Creating the Domain of Discourse: Ontology and Inventory," *International Journal of Man-Machine Studies,* 27.

Regoczei, S. B. and G. Hirst (1992), "Knowledge and Knowledge Acquisition in the Computational Context," in R. R. Hoffman (Ed.), *The Psychology of Expertise: Cognitive Research and Empirical AI,* New York: Springer-Verlag.

Roos, L. L. Jr. and R. I. Hall (1980), "Influence Diagrams and Organizational Power," *Administrative Science Quarterly,* 25.

Rosenhead, J. (Ed.) (1989), *Rational Analysis for a Problematic World,* Chichester, UK: Wiley.

Rouse, W. B. and N. M. Morris (1986), "On Looking into the Black Box: Prospects and Limits in the Search for Mental Models," *Psychological Bulletin,* 100, 3.

Rumelhart, D. E. (1984), "Schemata and the Cognitive System," in R. S. Wyer and T. K. Srull (Eds.), *Handbook of Social Cognition,* Vol. 1. Hillside, NJ: Lawrence Erlbaum, 161-188.

Salancik, G. R. and J. F. Porac (1986), "Distilled Ideologies: Values Derived from Reasoning in Complex Environments," in H. P. Sims, Jr. and D. A. Gioia (Eds.), *The Thinking Organization,* San Francisco: Jossey-Bass.

Schön, D. A. (1983), *The Reflective Practitioner: How Professionals Think in Action,* New York: Basic Books.

Schutz, A. (1962), *Collective Papers I: The Problem of Social Reality,* Edited and introduced by M. Natanson, The Hague, The Netherlands: Martinus Nijhoff.

Schwenk, C. S. (1988), "The Cognitive Perspective on Strategic Decision Making," *Journal of Management Studies,* 25, I, January.

——— (1989), "Can We Believe What They Say? The Use of Public Statements in Studying Managerial Cognitions," paper in Working Conference on Managerial Thought and Cognition, Washington, DC.

Scribner, S. (1986), "Thinking in Action: Some Characteristics of Practical Thought," in R. J. Sternberg and R. K. Wagner (Eds.), *Practical Intelligence,* New York: Cambridge University Press.

Sevón, G. (1984), "Cognitive Maps of Past and Future Economic Events," *Acta Psychologica,* 56.

Sims, H. P. Jr. and D. A. Gioia (Eds.) (1986), *The Thinking Organization,* San Francisco: Jossey-Bass.

Smircich, L. and Stubbart, C. (1985), "Strategic Management in an Enacted World," *Academy of Management Review,* 10, 4.

Sowa, J. F. (1984), *Conceptual Structures: Information Processing in Mind and Machine,* Reading, MA: Addison-Wesley.

Spender, J. C. (1989), *Industry Recipes: An Enquiry into the Nature and Sources of Managerial Judgement,* Oxford, England: Blackwell.

Sproull, L. S. (1981), "Beliefs in Organizations," in P. C. Nystrom and W. H. Starbuck (Eds.), *Handbook of Organizational Design,* Vol. 2. New York: Oxford University Press.

Starbuck, W. (1982), "Congealing Oil: Inventing Ideologies to Justify Acting Ideologies Out," *Journal of Management Studies,* 19, 1.

Stubbart, C. I. (1989), "Managerial Cognition: A Missing Link in Strategic Management Research," *Journal of Management Studies,* 26, 4, July.

——— and A. Ramaprasad (1988), "Probing Two Chief Executives' Schematic Knowledge of the U.S. Steel Industry Using Cognitive Maps," *Advances in Strategic Management,* Vol. 5. Greenwich, CT: JAI.

Tesch, R. (1989), "The Many Ways Researchers Work With Text: A Survey of Qualitative Research Methods," Paper presented at the Eighth International Human Science Research Conference, August, Aarhus, Denmark.

Weick, K. E. (1977), "Enactment Processes in Organizations," in B. M. Staw and G. R. Salancik (Eds.), *New Directions in Organizational Behavior,* Chicago: St. Clair.

——— and M. G. Bougon (1986), "Organizations as Cognitive Maps: Charting Ways to Success and Failure," in H. D. Sims Jr. and D. A. Gioia (Eds.), *The Thinking Organization,* San Francisco: Jossey-Bass.

Yin, R. K. (1991), *Case Study Research: Design and Methods,* Newbury Park, CA: Sage.

2

Reasoning in the Executive Suite

The Influence of Role/Experience-Based Expertise on Decision Processes of Corporate Executives

NANCY PAULE MELONE

This study investigates the effect of high-level executives' professional experience, expertise, and role in a specific functional area such as finance or corporate development on their reasoning pro-cesses when making managerial decisions. Chief Financial Officers (CFOs) and Vice-Presidents of Corporate Development (VPs) in the diversified foods industry were tape recorded as they thought aloud while evaluating four restaurant chains which were candidates for corporate acquisition. The experiment was designed so that these four acquisition candidates varied with respect to key financial and profitability data and such measures of a firm's strategic business position as product concept, markets, distribution channels, labor relations, and managerial expertise and loyalty. The attributes of financial performance and strategic position embedded in the descriptions of candidate firms were validated by an expert panel. The executives also provided rating-scale evaluations of the strategic, financial, and overall desirability of the four candidate firms.

The taped thought processes (verbal protocols) were analyzed to determine whether CFOs and VPs differed when evaluating the overall desirability of the acquisition candidates in their use of such lines of reasoning as assessments of the candidate's competitive environment, financial strength, management, operations, and the potential financial, managerial, and operational synergies offered by the proposed acquisition. The probability of generating these assessments during the evaluation process did not appear to be related to expertise based on experience or organizational role.

This chapter originally appeared in *Organization Science,* Vol. 5, No. 3, August 1994.

When the protocols were analyzed with respect to specific business issues identified by CFOs and VPs when evaluating acquisition candidates, however, there was a role/experience effect. Overall ratings of candidate-firm desirability were straightforward functions of the executive's ratings of the candidate's strategic position and financial performance. On average, VPs tended to be more optimistic in their evaluations than CFOs.

There is modest statistical evidence that VPs and CFOs differ in the emphasis they place on strategic and financial ratings in evaluating a candidate's overall promise. VPs tend to take a balanced view in forming their overall ratings, whereas CFOs place the predominant weight on financial matters.

The similarity in lines of reasoning used by CFOs and VPs presents evidence of shared expertise at the corporate level. The difference in the attention that CFOs and VPs place on specific business issues suggests that collectively these different perspectives constitute an adaptive survival mechanism which evolves in successful organizations. The mechanism complements the shared expertise and protects organizations from making flawed strategic decisions. Analyzing these role/experience-based differences has value in developing an understanding of how organizations do and should integrate recommendations from executive officers of various functional areas.

(MANAGERIAL COGNITION; STRATEGIC DECISION MAKING; REASONING; EXPERTISE; CORPORATE ACQUISITION; PROTOCOL ANALYSIS)

INTRODUCTION

Stubbart (1989) observes that the capacities and constraints characterizing executives' thinking have largely been ignored in management research and notes the following:

> Most strategic management scholars would probably agree that the rationality of managers is often limited, their knowledge often incomplete, and their attention often overloaded. Yet, simultaneously, many managers are skilled at strategy making, adept organizational experts, and ingenious innovators. Nor do all managers think alike in terms of their vision, expertise, risk-profiles, motivations, or goals. These conflicting views leave the field in a quandary regarding managerial cognition. (p. 326)

In contrast to Stubbart's observation about management, much is known about cognition in other domains such as medicine (Johnson et al. 1982, Elstein and Bordage 1979), physics (Larkin 1981, Chi et al. 1981), and software design (Jeffries et al. 1981). A primary objective of this study is to investigate how organizational role and expertise (e.g., experience in a functional role such as finance or marketing) influence managerial cognition and strategic decision making.

In their classic study of managerial cognition, Simon and Dearborn (1958) found that subjects who were asked to read a case and to make a problem diagnosis tended to see problems from their own areas of responsibility and expertise rather than from a broader, corporate perspective. While that study does not permit statistical inference, it suggests that organizational role influences managerial cognition. More recently, Walsh (1988) reexamined Simon and Dearborn's conclusions using middle-level managers drawn from several firms and focusing on the relationship between work histories, belief structures and three indices of information processing. This study did not replicate Simon and Dearborn's earlier findings of functionally biased information processing. The current study reconsiders these inconsistencies.

While expertise in cognition has been studied extensively, the effect of role on expert cognition has received far less attention. For example, one might conjecture that because high-level executives would have developed a broad view of the organization, they would consider strategic decisions requiring their functional-area expertise in a more integrated and holistic fashion. On the other hand, as executives advance in their professions, adaptation to their responsibilities and roles may lead to a deeper but narrower understanding of corporate decisions.

This study focuses on the reasoning processes of high-level corporate executives (chief financial officers and vice presidents of corporate development) as they evaluate candidates for corporate acquisition. Within large organizations this task involves executives from different functional areas. Hence, this task offers a forum for examining managerial cognition. At the individual level, executives occupying different roles are likely to attend to different issues, employ different approaches in processing information, and combine (weight) information differently. Decision making at the organizational level involves integration—considering *all* the issues raised by executives in various roles, considering *all* the lines of reasoning that might be generated, and deciding how best to combine the collective knowledge and beliefs. To understand how an executive's role/experience-based expertise influences the evaluation of candidates for corporate acquisition, the study addresses these broad questions:

- Do differences in roles/experience result in the use of substantively different content-based (macro) lines of reasoning?

- How does the executive's specialized role/experience influence the specific business (micro) issues generated in the course of evaluating a candidate for corporate acquisition?

- How do executives of differing specialties (within the same industry) integrate strategic (nonquantitative) information with financial information in arriving at their evaluations and action recommendations?

PAST RESEARCH

Considerable attention has been directed to the general topic of expertise and excellence in management. For example, Schön (1983) has discussed expertise in the context of "knowing-in-action." Such "knowing" is analogous to the "tacit knowing" discussed in Polanyi's work (1973) and Buckley's "body of operative knowledge" (1984). Similarly, Dreyfus and Dreyfus (1986) refer to the "intuition" possessed by experts. Given the present study's focus on understanding the process by which highly skilled executives make strategic decisions, it is appropriate to discuss briefly the structures hypothesized that underlie their so-called "intuition."

While various writers in business and the professions have labeled the expertise phenomenon "intuition," cognitive psychologists have taken a different approach in explaining performance by highly skilled individuals. Individuals who possess such "intuition" are said to be in the autonomous and most advanced stage of knowing (Anderson 1983, Fitts and Posner 1967). At this stage, skilled performers have developed a declarative encoding of productions (i.e., condition-action rules) tailored to the specific task. These well-honed knowledge structures enable the skilled performer to achieve dramatic increases in speed and accuracy in task performance. Individuals at this stage also often lose their ability to describe the knowledge from which their skill originates. In the context of the declarative/procedural viewpoints, the autonomous stage can be seen as emergence (i.e., a theory of doing) and elaboration (i.e., movement into automaticity) of procedural knowledge (see Anderson 1983). Years of practice are a necessary but not sufficient condition for the acquisition of such skill.

Idiographic process-tracing approaches have been applied to tasks performed by various middle managers, including auditors (Biggs and Mock 1983; Bouman 1978, 1983; Johnson et al. 1991; Isenberg 1986). Rarely have these approaches been applied to tasks performed by very high-level executives making strategic-level decisions. One reason may be the time commitment required of the executive.

Although corporate acquisitions have been studied extensively from the larger economic or smaller "deal-making" perspectives, only recently has attention been paid to the thought processes employed by individuals in making such evaluations (Jemison and Sitkin 1986). A small number of investigators has begun to develop cognitive models of candidate-evaluation behavior. The most notable are those of behavioral decision theory (e.g., linear models) and human information processing (i.e., verbal protocol analysis). These studies have explored expertise and biases in decision makers. For example, in an exploratory study, Duhaime and Schwenk (1985) examined the use of cognitive simplifying procedures (i.e., reasoning by analogy and illusion of control). Stahl and Zimmerer (1984) and Pechtel (1985) also conducted empirical studies of decision processes in acquisition-related tasks. The first of these studies, using a behavioral decision theory framework, traded realism for control by employing a strategy in which information could be controlled so that policy differences could be revealed. In this study, subjects were given a set of attributes of the firms (e.g., cash flow) and the associated evaluations ("excellent" or "adequate"). They were asked to indicate the extent to which they would strongly recommend acquisition or strongly be against acquisition of the candidate. The second study (Pechtel 1985) analyzed verbal protocols to elucidate the reasoning strategies used by attorneys in structuring (in contrast to evaluating) acquisitions. In this case, the level of control exhibited in Stahl and Zimmerer's policy-capturing study was sacrificed for greater realism.

METHOD

Subjects

Eight high-level diversified foods industry executives participated in the study. None was known to the investigator prior to the study. To select the subjects a list of 12 very large, publicly-owned firms in this industry was prepared. The 24 potential subjects who occupied the position of either CFO or Vice President of Corporate Development/Planning in these firms were identified. Each potential subject was sent a packet of printed materials informing him of the research goals, the time (approximately four hours) and tasks that would be required of him, and benefits from participation. The packet also contained the researcher's vita and listed the recognized experts who served as advisers to the research study. An invitation to participate and subsequent willingness to do so was *not* a guarantee of participation. To qualify, executives were required to have a minimum of five years of executive-level experience and at least three years of experience in their specialty. Furthermore, executives were required to have evaluated at least three acquisition candidates within the last five years. Additional evidence of experience-based knowledge (e.g., prior positions, experience, education, authorship, relevant service) was also required.

Although 11 male subjects (five CFOs and six VPs of Corporate Development/ Planning) qualified and consented to participate, two of the CFOs did not participate. The firm of one of these CFOs was acquired, and the acquirer would not disclose his new location; and the other assumed the presidency of his firm. Of the remaining nine subjects, eight provided usable protocols.[1] Five executives were VPs and three were CFOs.

Experimental Materials

The demand for task veridicality to suitably engage this level of subject required assistance in developing the experimental materials. Six collaborating executives (CFOs and VPs) experienced in acquisitions worked with the investigator over a 12-month period to construct the experimental tasks. Interactions with the collaborating experts were numerous but brief (approximately 20-40 minutes). The initial meetings focused on understanding the nature of task expertise as these practitioners defined it. A major objective during this period was to determine the particular context and phase of the corporate acquisition process that could be converted to experimental tasks that were complex enough to engage experts. The task selected for study was candidate evaluation. In subsequent discussions, the collaborators addressed such questions as what aspects of this task require specialized expertise, what is the form of that expertise, what expertise is transferable across industries, and what is industry specific. The collaborating experts uniformly agreed that some knowledge generalizes across industries, but that skilled performers were distinguished from average performers by their ability to integrate the specific knowledge of one's industry, functional business specialization, and role within the organization. From these discussions, a decision was made to base the experimental task on a single industry (the diversified foods industry) and candidate firms that might reasonably be acquired by a large corporation within that industry (restaurants). This decision dictated that subjects with extensive acquisition experience in diversified foods would be recruited.

Subsequent meetings with the collaborators were shorter and focused on: (1) determining the particular variables (cues) to be used in depicting the parent firm and the four candidates in the task materials; (2) ensuring that the cue values embodied the desired experimental manipulations; and (3) confirming that these cue values were coherent, consistent, and believable within the context of practice. To maximize efficiency of the continuing interactions with the collaborators during the task "tuning" process, a method of summarizing the cues and cue values on one large sheet of paper was developed. Only when the cue values remained stable over several meetings were the collaborators asked to read the full text within which were embedded the cue values. All interactions with the collaborators were extremely well focused and organized to *the minute*. According to the collaborators, this and their interest in the topic were major reasons why they gave frequent access.

The experimental materials consisted of the description of a large diversified foods company (i.e., Severson Corporation) for whom the subject was to assume he worked, descriptions of four restaurant chains (i.e., Greens, Etc., Hacienda, Health Club, and Sweet Potato Pie) presented as potential acquisitions, and a mid-task and post-task questionnaire that accompanied each candidate description. The description of each firm was presented in a separate-bound notebook.

The description of the candidate firms was conceived as consisting of a strategic position (operational and managerial) component and a financial performance component. The four restaurant cases were created by manipulating cues within each of these components, so as to represent one of two possible conditions: (1) meets the minimum threshold of acceptability based on the acquiring firm's business, geographic, and financial criteria stated in the description of the acquiring firm, and (2) exceeds the threshold. These components (factors) were crossed to make up the four experimental cases. The facts comprising the strategic business position component of the task included such items as a description of product concept, markets, distribution channels, facility design, labor relations, managerial expertise, and willingness of executives to remain with the acquired firm. The financial performance component consisted of quantitatively-oriented information presented on the balance sheet and income statement, and other facts related to profitability, risk, and growth useful in determining economic value to the shareholder. Each cue statement was numbered and presented on a separate sheet of paper bound within a notebook describing one of the restaurant chains. In all cases the strategic information was presented before the financial performance information. This is the ordering of information typically used by investment bankers in presenting prospective acquisition candidates to executives. A diagram of the experimental cases and the manipulations is shown in Figure 2.1.

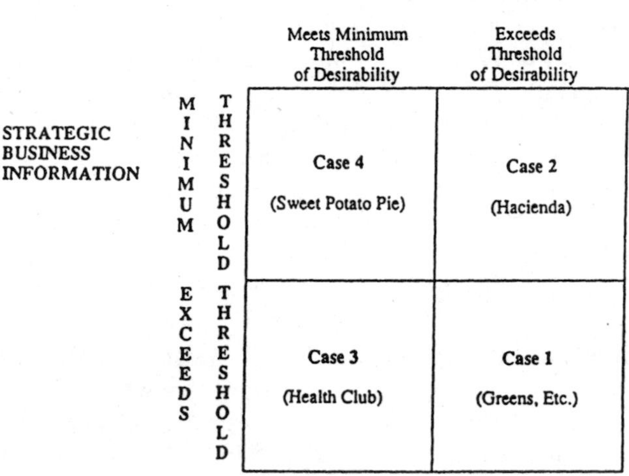

Figure 2.1. Experimental Manipulations

Design and Procedure

The research was conducted as a field experiment using a 2 × 2 × 2, repeated-measures design (i.e., strategic business position × financial performance × subject role/experience-based expertise—CFO or VP of Corporate Development). The first two factors were crossed to make up the four experimental cases (i.e., candidate firms). The dependent measures were the occurrence and frequency of specific business issues (knowledge states) and lines of reasoning (patterns of issues generated in the decision process), rating-scale judgments of financial, strategic, and overall desirability of the candidate firms, recommendations to pursue or terminate interest in each of the candidates, and retrospective discussion of the analysis process.

For each subject, the execution of the study consumed approximately two hours for each of two sessions. All data were collected within a twenty-four-month period. Data from individual subjects were generally collected within one month of the initial session.

Each executive read a set of instructions describing the procedures to be used in the experiment and was given the opportunity to ask questions about the procedures. The instructions required that the executive assume he was to give a professional opinion in the evaluation of several acquisition candidates. Although each candidate was presented independently, the instructions stated that more than one candidate could be recommended for acquisition or that none could be recommended. Each executive was told to assume that the facts and information presented in the cases were accurate, reasonably complete, and the best available. The executive was asked to read out loud the number preceding the cue statement and the statement's content and to think out loud about what the statement meant in the evolution of his recommendation. If the information was irrelevant or not useful, he was told to say so and go to the next statement. If needed information was absent, he was told to state what information would be needed. When the thoughts related to a statement had been expressed, the executive was to read the next statement. The executives were not permitted to skip ahead, but could return to earlier statements. To simplify the determination of the potential acquisition's cost, subjects were told that a cash transaction was the preferred method. They were free, however, to suggest other methods. Likewise, to reduce the uncertainty and complexity in hostile takeovers, the executive was told that this overture was considered to be "friendly."

Once questions about the instructions were answered, the executive was given an opportunity to "practice" thinking out loud using the description of the acquiring company. While this practice session was tape recorded (for realism), none of these data were analyzed. Following this practice, the subject was given the first candidate description and asked to provide thinking aloud protocol as he evaluated the firm. Specifically, the subject was asked to describe his thoughts as they came to him in the course of determining (1) the business issues involved in the situation, (2) the desirability of this firm as an acquisition, and (3) the action that should be taken. The session was tape recorded. During the entire process, the experimenter remained silent unless an unusual amount of time passed (approximately 3-5 seconds) in which the subject failed to speak. If such a situation arose, the subject was prompted to "please talk more."

Midway through and at the end of the experiment, the executive provided rating-scale evaluations of strategic position and financial performance. At the conclusion, he provided an overall evaluation of candidate desirability and an action recommendation. After all four candidates were evaluated, the executive was debriefed.

Procedure for Scoring Protocol Data

Eight executives generated 32 usable protocols which were tape-recorded, transcribed, and coded for subsequent analyses. Every typed transcript was verified against the recording to clarify words that the typist was unable to understand, to correct spelling, and to insert syntactical markings. The corrected transcript was the transcript used for coding. Two trained coders scored the data. The first coder scored all 32 protocols. The second coder, who was naive about the intent of the study, scored nine out of the 32 protocols. The protocols were selected such that each subject and each case were represented at least once in the protocols scored by both coders. The overall interrater agreement for knowledge-state data as indicated by Cohen's Kappa (Cohen 1960) was 0.83, ranging from 0.78 to 0.88. Overall reliabilities for scoring of cognitive operations (inferred processes) was 0.77. Typical reliabilities for protocol data are between 0.75 and 1.0 (perfect agreement), with most falling around 0.80 (Pechtel 1985). To control for differences in the total number of comments generated across subjects, normalized data were used in subsequent analysis.

The protocols were coded at three levels: knowledge states (verbalized business topics), cognitive conceptual operations, and lines of reasoning. In this study, there are four basic knowledge state categories: (1) issues and hypotheses related to the candidate firm's management, financial, or operating status; (2) strategies which the candidate or acquirer might pursue in the future; (3) issues related to the "fit" between the candidate firm and the acquiring firm; and (4) other data descriptions. During the first reading of the protocol the coder underlined verbatim references (a word or group of words) that seemed to fall into one of the basic categories. During a second reading the coder labeled the underlined references according to the codes summarized in Appendix A. For example, in the first reading, the coder underlines the following phrase: "What's a food company wanna get into the restaurant business for when it *doesn't fit* anything we now have?" In the second reading, the coder classifies the underlined phrase by selecting the appropriate knowledge state from the list in Appendix A. The phrase is labeled as "AS," a comment on the acquisition strategy.

The second level of coding identified conceptual operations. While these are not relied upon heavily in this chapter, the coding description is provided for completeness. The coding of conceptual operations is complicated because they cannot be directly observed in the subject, but must be inferred using a set of rules for recognizing their occurrence in the protocol. The rules typically consist of a definition of the operation's objective or goal, a list of key words that signal the use of an operation, a description of particular situations in which the operation is likely to be used, and examples. Protocols were examined for instances of seven basic operations: (1) data acquisition (ACQ); (2) data exploration (EXP); (3) generation (GEN) of issues, hypotheses, or strategies; (4) analysis (ANAL); (5) discrepancy processing (QUAL); (6) summarization (SUM); and (7) metareasoning (META). A basic operation may be further categorized. For example, within the ANAL operation there are three suboperations: computation (calc), association (assoc), and analogy (analog). Any operation coded as *calc* must conform to the following rule:

Computation (calc). The subject performs an explicit mathematical calculation such as the computation of a ratio, a difference, a trend, or a percentage. The distinguishing feature of this calculus is the production of a *numerical* result (e.g., margin growth in 1981 is 17%) rather than a qualitative statement (e.g., high, low). For the latter see the rule for Compare (comp) operations.

The complete set of rules is contained in Melone (1987). A general discussion of the protocol analysis methodology is found in Ericsson and Simon (1984).

A third level of coding identifies lines of reasoning (LOR) that are hypothesized as mechanisms around which the task would be executed. The six lines of reasoning represent "macro strategies" or scripts that guide the process by which the executive evaluates the acquisition candidate. Lines of reasoning represented in the coding are: (1) strategy confirmation/criteria screen; (2) competitive environment assessment; (3) management assessment; (4) financial assessment; (5) operations assessment; and (6) synergy proposal. The structure of these lines of reasoning is shown in Appendix B. The coding scheme incorporates the hypothesized goal structure in Figure 2.2. This structure accommodates concepts discussed in the literatures of finance, planning/corporate development, and psychology.

LOR coding is done by creating a matrix work sheet within which the specific subject's knowledge states are recorded. Along the top of the matrix are the broad knowledge categories. Along the left side are the numbers corresponding to the statement numbers of the experimental task (in order of presentation to the subject). The coder records the knowledge states generated by the subject within the cells. Thus, by looking down the column of the matrix, the coder can quickly see, for example, if the subject screened on all, some, or none of the acquisition criteria, at what point in the presentation of the task statements this was done, and how it was done. Where appropriate, how the subject evaluated certain generated knowledge is indicated with a "+" (supportive of acquisition) or "–" (not supportive). Following the recording process, each of the columns for each of the subjects is examined to identify any sequences that are associated with the LOR described in Appendix B. The scoring of LOR is essentially a matching task.

RESULTS

We start with the big picture by examining the protocol data to detect if content-based lines of reasoning (LOR) are present. Then, to obtain a more detailed understanding of how specialized knowledge influences the generation of business issues and synergies, we examine knowledge-state data from the taped and coded protocols. Finally, rating-scale and judgment data are

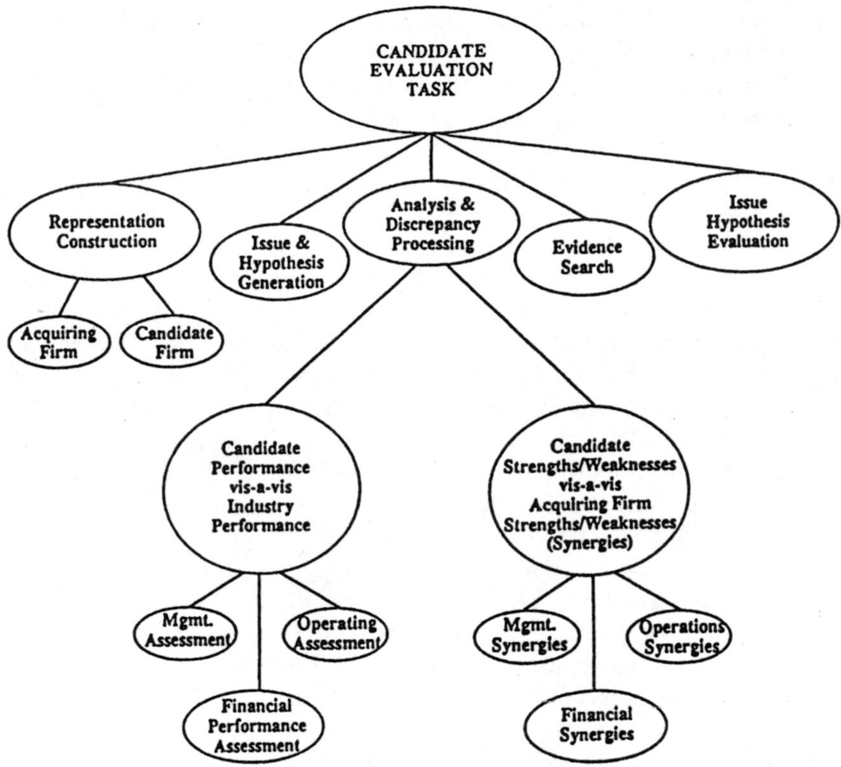

Figure 2.2. Summary of Candidate Evaluation Goal Structure

analyzed to determine how the executives combine their strategic and financial assessments into an overall evaluation.

Lines of Reasoning (LOR)

The analysis of results presented in this section addresses whether differences in role/experience-based expertise result in the use of substantively different content-based reasoning strategies (i.e., lines of reasoning) to guide the evaluation of candidates for corporate acquisition. The protocols were examined for the six lines of reasoning (LOR) characterized in Appendix B. Table 2.1 displays the LORs found in the protocols. Given the amount of data relative to the number of potential interaction effects, statistical tests would not be meaningful and hence have not been performed.

TABLE 2.1 Lines of Reasoning (LOR), by Executive Specialty, by Case

Subject	*S/C*	*CE*	*MGMT*	*FIN*	*OP*	*SYN*
Corporate Development Executives						
CD1	1***	1234	1***	1*34	****	123*
CD2	*2**	1234	***4	1**4	****	12**
CD3	1234	1234	12**	1***	****	*2**
CD4	****	1234	123*	*2*4	****	*2**
CD5	*23*	1234	1234	1234	****	*23*
No. of Cases in which LOR was used by CDs	8	20	11	12	0	9
Percentage of Cases LOR was used by CDs	40%	100%	55%	60%	0%	45%
Chief Finance Officers						
CF01	1***	1234	****	1*34	1***	**34
CF02	1***	1234	*23*	1234	***4	*2**
CF03	1***	1234	123*	1**4	****	12**
No. of Cases in which LOR was used by CFOs	3	12	5	9	2	5
Percentage of Cases LOR was used by CFOs	25%	100%	42%	75%	17%	42%

A number indicates use of an LOR for that case. * indicates that the executive did not use LOR for that case.

1 = Greens, Etc. (F +, S +)
2 = Sweet Potato Pie (F –, S –)
3 = Health Club (F –, S +)
4 = Hacienda (F +, S –)

S/C = Strategy Confirmation / Criteria Screen
CE = Competitive Environment
MGMT = Management Assessment
FIN = Financial Assessment
OP = Operations Assessment
SYN = Synergy Proposal

One LOR found in several subjects' protocols began by questioning the diversification strategy and, if the strategy was accepted, the screening of the candidate firm against stated acquisition criteria of the parent firm. The following CFO's protocol illustrates how such questioning unfolds. Unlike most subjects, he then generates a strategy that focuses on another business (distribution), emphasizing the potential for financial synergies.

> I can only speak from my own experience. . . . I am not a majority figure on this one. . . . Ah, I think for a company to get into a business where it hasn't had prior experience or . . . has had experience, but yet is not a major factor . . . this is a very major strategic shift.

At this point, he proposes his own strategy.

> Ah, in my judgment, there is a much greater opportunity for a food processing company to get into distribution . . . to get into distribution rather than the

> retail-end of products . . . not as capital intensive . . . much greater ease of entry . . . much lower risk . . . you can go into the food distribution business, make an acquisition (there are 2,500 firms out there) right now! The vast majority of them are undercapitalized. . . .

Another LOR suggested by task analysis and revealed in the protocols involved the assessment of the candidate's management. The typical chain of cognitive events evaluated the degree of expertise possessed by key management and, to the extent management was perceived as being knowledgeable, the likelihood of retaining such individuals:

> Certainly the fact that they have a willingness to stay on is critical. That is certainly the most significant thing I've seen . . . we've had some unhappy experiences with a couple, where a key manager did not stay on and it was totally destructive . . . so I would say it is about as important as anything I've seen . . . after profitability and the growth potential.

To the extent the candidate's management was considered lacking in skill or likely to leave, the reasoning strategy typically identified compensating characteristics of the acquiring firm's management. Usually, the subject acknowledged the parent firm's substantial expertise in general management and control, but complete lack of expertise in restaurant operations. This deficiency disturbed most subjects. Other issues considered in the management strategy included incentives and compensation. In many cases, these were related to retaining management.

Often LORs assessed the financial performance of the candidate firm as well as its competitive environment. Somewhat surprisingly, as can be seen in Table 2.1, only two subjects examined operations. This is an interesting contrast to the rather detailed chain of reasoning used to examine the competitive environment. The following excerpt illustrates a segment from a VP of Corporate Development's LOR:

> Ah, the location strategy would appear to be an excellent one. . . . The expansion program, particularly with the thought as to moving this format into an east coast state, would have to be looked at carefully because the ah . . . preferences of ah . . . people that lived in the states in which these restaurants operate could be quite different than the preferences and ahm . . . ah . . . expectations of people on the east coast . . . Specifically, the ah . . . focus on self service, ah . . . could be a problem. . . .

Every subject, regardless of specialization, addressed a rather detailed set of questions relating to the maturity of the product concept, the saturation of existing markets, and the exportability of the concept to new markets. The unanimity with which all subjects generated this LOR was not expected prior to actual scoring:

> Ah . . . my first reaction is you probably . . . you've already achieved most of the market penetration possible.
>
> I'd certainly want to test that somehow.
>
> I don't know how, but maybe go into Arkansas . . . perhaps Oklahoma and Texas . . . up to Kentucky . . . Virginia and West Virginia.
>
> But my initial reaction is the food is so . . . ah, much of this is a sectional menu and since you operate in most of those sectional menu markets . . . my suspicion is that market growth is going to come from the states that you're already in—greater penetration of existing markets rather than geographical expansion.

CFOs are more likely to generate the financial assessment LOR than are corporate development officers (75% versus 60%) and less likely to generate the strategy confirmation/criteria screen (25% versus 40%), the management assessment LOR (42% versus 55%), and the synergy proposal line of reasoning (42% versus 45%).

The data summarized in Table 2.1 were examined to reveal whether particular experimental manipulations (e.g., candidate cases) trigger particular LORs. For Greens, Etc. (manipulation = finance and strategic positions better than threshold criteria stated by the acquirer) five of the eight executives generated a strategy/confirmation screen LOR. A second case-effect occurs for the two cases in which the financial manipulation clearly exceeds the threshold (i.e., Greens, Etc. and Hacienda). In these cases subjects were considerably more likely to generate financial LOR. In fact, seven out of eight subjects generated a financial LOR for each of these cases. This compares to two and four respectively, out of eight executives for Sweet Potato Pie and Health Club (where financial manipulations just equal the minimum threshold established by the acquirer).

Two other case-effects are present for Hacienda and Sweet Potato Pie in the use of the synergy LOR. For Hacienda, only one of the eight executives generated a synergies LOR, whereas for Sweet Potato Pie, the synergy LOR was generated by seven out of eight of the executives. Again, the manipulation in Sweet Potato Pie is for the financial data to equal but not exceed the minimum threshold set by the acquirer. This contrast to Hacienda, where the financials clearly exceed the threshold.

One explanation may be that stronger financials fail to trigger the synergy LORs because there is less need for the executive to convince others that the firm is healthy, well-managed (as reflected by the financials), and a good candidate for acquisition. When acquiring a new line of business, a healthy, well-managed and profitable candidate may be more palatable than one founded on less certain nonfinancial synergies. Arguing on the basis of synergies may be what one does when there is no other choice. Similarly, executives may generate synergies only in the less promising situations to give the candidate the benefit of the doubt. In the case of Sweet Potato Pie, although a number of synergies were generated. the probability of realizing them was not considered high. Even with a mediocre candidate, the executive may still desire to fully examine the synergy possibilities before rejecting the candidate.

In summary, the following can be said about the existence of the general reasoning used in evaluating candidates for corporate acquisition:

- Evidence was presented for the existence of LOR supporting the goal structure consisting of an initial screen of criteria, an assessment of the management, financial, and, to a much lesser extent, operations, and a search for possible synergies.
- There is no strong evidence of a role/experience-based expertise effect.
- Examination of data reveal that different LOR have different likelihoods of generation, but these do not appear to be functions of executive role/ experience-based expertise.

Generation of Business Issues and Synergies (Knowledge States)

Much of the practitioner literature suggests that decisions related to the evaluation of candidates for corporate acquisition are influenced by the participants' education, training, and experience (e.g., O'Connor 1975). Empirical evidence supporting this contention is not readily available. In this section we analyze protocol data to evaluate the question of whether such role/experience-based differences exist and, if so, how they manifest themselves. Results are organized around testing the general hypothesis that role/experience-based specialization influences both the number and types of issues and synergies generated by an executive.

Since there is not a formal, theoretical model for predicting issue generation, a panel of six experts was assembled for this purpose. The panel consisted of three CEOs or former CEOs, two very senior executives, and a professor of strategy. Four of the six panel members had extensive experience on boards of firms other than their own.[2] Predictions were generated by presenting each panel member with a list of issue categories and their definitions and asking him to indicate whether he believed that knowledge states associated with these issues would be generated equally by CFOs and VPs of Corporate Development or if they would be generated with differing frequency as a result of role/experience-based expertise. If the panel member judged that there would be differential knowledge-state generation, then he was to indicate on a seven-point Likert scale which role/experience-based expert would be more likely to engage in deeper discussion of the issue (i.e., generate more knowledge states relevant to this issue). The panel of experts was considered to have made a prediction if the median of the six responses was three or less or five or more.[3] The data were analyzed using the panel's predictions. The issues and the panel's predictions are shown in Table 2.2, where a "–" indicates a panel prediction that the VPs of Corporate Development are likely to generate more of these issues, a "+" indicates a panel prediction that CFOs are likely to generate more of these issues, and a "?" indicates no predicted difference.

Analysis of Individual Issues by Specialization. This analysis focuses on isolating the specific issues on which the two specializations differed in terms of frequency of generation. Data were normalized by dividing each single issue total by the total number of issues generated for each subject so that the relative frequency distributions for the two specialities could be compared. These data were analyzed by regressing the issue proportion on the area of role/experience-based expertise (finance = 1, corporate development = 0) and a set of case dummy variables. Results of the analysis are displayed in Table 2.2.[4]

Fifteen of the 21 predictions of sign are supported ($p = 0.039$). Furthermore, where the results are significant, no predictions are contradicted. Indeed the most significant beta for the six issues for which the estimated sign is *not* in the direction predicted by the panel has a two-tailed p-value of only 0.388; 10 of the 15 coefficients with signs in the predicted direction have better p-values (the worst of which is 0.224).

These arguments can be appreciated graphically by examining Figure 2.3.[5] The graph below the 45-degree line in Figure 2.3 shows the cumulative frequency of the 15 estimated coefficients with the predicted sign plotted against the "significance" of the estimate (one minus its p-value). If there were no relationship between issue generation and expertise, these points would tend to lie on the 45-degree line. As the relationship gets stronger, the cumulative frequency plot falls increasingly below the 45-degree line. Similarly, the graph above the 45-degree line in Figure 2.3 shows the cumulative frequency of the six estimated coefficients with signs in the opposite direc-

TABLE 2.2 Results of Analysis of Individual Issues

Business Issues	*Constant*	*Average Beta*	*Pred. Sign*	*t-stat.*	*2-tailed p-value*	*Adjusted* R^2
Criteria Match	3.2%	0.0077	–	1.704	0.547	5.9%
Acquis. Strategy	5.4	–0.0355	–	2.285	0.030	12.5
Saturation	3.5	–0.0064	–	0.583	0.565	25.3
Location Strategy	9.3	0.0017	–	0.118	0.907	4.0
Concentration	1.9	–0.0018	?	0.219	0.828	–10.1
Product	7.5	–0.0411	–	2.394	0.024	9.6
Customer Demographics	10.9	–0.0260	–	1.244	0.224	5.0
Mgmt. Expertise	5.2	–0.0016	–	0.118	0.907	–10.8
Retention of Mgmt.	3.7	0.0017	–	0.137	0.892	–2.2
Mgmt. Culture	0.8	–0.0084	–	1.380	0.179	–1.1
Why Selling	1.6	–0.0156	?	2.770	0.010	15.7
Labor Availability	1.8	0.0019	–	0.206	0.838	–10.4
Labor Relations	3.3	0.0214	?	2.125	0.043	3.2
Antitrust	0.2	0.0005	?	0.194	0.848	–6.9
Operations	2.9	0.0055	?	5.58	0.575	14.6
Profitability	12.7	0.0486	+	2.465	0.020	30.7
Capital Reqrmts.	3.2	0.0049	+	0.383	0.705	–2.7
Leverage	2.2	0.0211	+	1.889	0.070	12.2
Leases	1.0	0.0061	+	0.814	0.423	0.0
Tax Policy	1.1	0.0170	+	2.322	0.028	8.2
Stock Value	2.4	0.0125	+	1.304	0.203	7.7
Interest Expense	0.9	–0.0046	+	0.824	0.417	–7.3
Acquisition Premium	3.4	0.0031	+	0.224	0.825	6.8
Dilution	0.5	–0.0030	+	0.877	0.388	2.9
Dividend Policy	0.2	0.0120	+	2.002	0.055	8.5
Equity Position	0.7	0.0069	?	1.302	0.204	16.2
Mgmt. Synergies	6.2	–0.0206	–	1.336	0.193	30.8
Operations Syn.	2.7	–0.0052	?	0.471	0.641	–10.8
Financial Synergies	1.7	–0.0026	?	0.353	0.727	4.9

tion from that predicted. Figure 2.3 therefore strongly suggests that the coefficients with signs opposite from those predicted are less significant than would arise by chance. The null hypothesis that coefficients with the predicted sign and those with the opposite from the predicted sign are drawn from the same population is rejected at less than the 0.05 level by a two-tailed Wilcoxon rank sum test. This result suggests that an executive's role/experience-based expertise does influence the type of knowledge states (business issues) that he generates when evaluating an acquisition candidate.

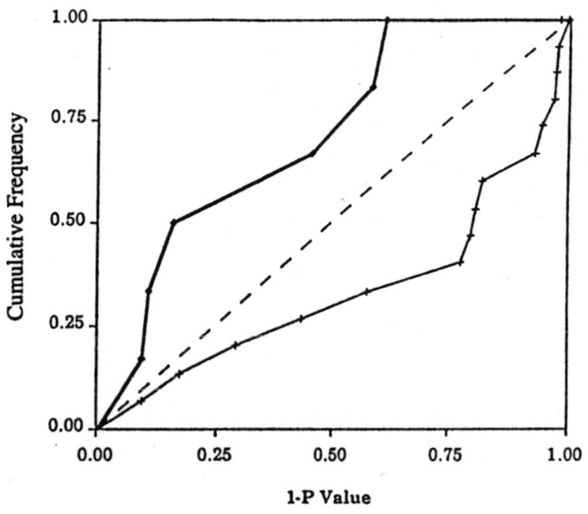

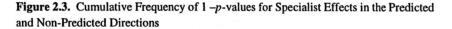

Note:

—+— Represents the 6 values not in the predicted direction.
—+— Represents the 15 values in the predicted direction.

Figure 2.3. Cumulative Frequency of 1 $-p$-values for Specialist Effects in the Predicted and Non-Predicted Directions

The Integration of Strategic Position and Financial Performance Information

The results reported in this section address how executives of differing role/experience-based expertise integrate information about strategic position and financial performance in their evaluations of the candidate firms and their development of recommendations. The presentation first addresses the issue of a general rating bias as a function of expertise and then the issue of differential weighting of strategic versus financial evaluations as a function of expertise in determining an overall rating of desirability.

Rating Biases as a Function of Specialization. The executive's knowledge may have one of several effects on his rating of the strategic position and financial performance components. One possible effect of the role/experience based specialization is the biasing of the executive's evaluation. The explanation for such a bias may reside in the way in which the executive

TABLE 2.3 Average Rating of Strategic Issues

CASE	*By Corp. Dev. Exec.*	*By CFOs*	*Difference*	*t-stat for Difference*
Case 1 (F + S +) (Greens, Etc.)	4.6	3.3	1.3	1.21
Case 2 (F +, S –) (Hacienda)	4.0	3.5	0.5	0.40
Case 3 (F –, S +) (Health Club)	5.4	4.5	0.9	0.75
Case 4 (F –, S –) (Sweet Potato Pie)	2.2	1.0	1.2	1.15

views his or her corporate responsibility. Based on informal interviews, the CFO and the VP of Corporate Development clearly see themselves as having distinctly different organizational responsibilities in the evaluation of candidates for corporate acquisition. Executives in charge of corporate development may view generating a large number of prospective candidates as their primary responsibility. CFOs may assume responsibility for protecting the financial integrity of the acquiring firm. Both may believe that they serve as "counter balances" to the optimism or conservatism of the other group.

These differing views of responsibility provide a basis for hypothesizing that financial officers may have a conservative bias in evaluating acquisition candidates. The corresponding hypothesis suggests that corporate development executives may have a somewhat more optimistic bias. Analysis of the rating scale data indicates that CFOs systematically value (rate) strategic issues lower than do corporate development executives (see Table 2.3). These data suggest that VPs tend to evaluate strategic characteristics of candidate firms relatively more optimistically than CFOs.

There is no evidence of a subject-within-specialty effect based on the rating data for all subjects who provided ratings for all cases. Consequently, executives' ratings of the strategic aspects of the candidate (STRATRATE) were regressed on a constant, a finance-specialist effect (F), and case effects, again parameterized as deviations from average.[6] On average, the CFOs rate strategic factors a point lower than do the corporate development executives ($p = 0.067$). The direction of these average differences holds for all four cases, as shown in Table 2.3. The specialist effects across the four cases do not differ significantly ($p = 0.0906$). This consistency across cases supports the hypothesis that a specialist effect in rating strategic issues is a general phenomenon and not case specific.

This empirical support for the bias attributable to specialization, however, is seen only in evaluations of the strategic aspects of the candidate. There is no evidence of a functional specialist bias in financial ratings. The explanation may relate to the existence of relatively more well-defined and agreed-upon procedures for evaluating financial performance and, conversely, less well-defined procedures for evaluating strategic potential or liability. The protective orientation of the CFO and the lack of well-accepted procedures for assessing strategic position and potential may explain the systematic, relative downward biasing of ratings of the four candidates' strategic positions. The current research design does not allow inference about whether the corporate development executives' ratings are biased upward or the CFOs' ratings are biased downward.

In contrast to the specialist effects, the case effects in the model without interactions are highly significant ($p < 0.001$). As can be seen in Table 2.3, both corporate development executives and CFOs found the Health Club case to be the most attractive from the strategic viewpoint. The Greens, Etc. case was considered the second strongest case with regard to strategic position by the corporate development executives and was virtually tied with the Hacienda case for second strongest case by CFOs. Since the Health Club and Greens, Etc. cases were intended to be the strongest cases on strategic position grounds in the manipulation, the significance of the case effect is consistent with the design of the experiment.

An effort was made to find a simpler (lower-order) explanation for the case effects. One potential hypothesis is that the ratings are additive functions of a financial condition effect and a strategic condition effect, a financial-strategic interaction, and a specialist effect. The data in Table 2.4 suggest that such a model would not represent the data well, since the average ratings of Greens, Etc. and the Health Club are not in the expected order for either financial or strategic specialists. Hence, there is little basis for simplifying the case effects.

Weighting Biases as a Function of Specialization. An executive's role and experience may influence the weight or emphasis he or she places on the evaluation of the strategic and financial desirability of the candidate in forming an overall impression. Depending on background and experience, one class of information about the candidate firm may be more salient and concrete than another. The existence of analogies (i.e., experiences in other firms) may make certain information more vivid in the mind of the executive. Thus, we ask if there is a specialist effect in the weighting of the strategic and financial ratings to form an overall rating of desirability.

To investigate this question, a sequential strategy for analyzing the data was adopted. The analysis proceeded by evaluating first the feasibility of a general linear model, next the feasibility of a model with the intercept and financial specialist effect constrained to 0, and finally, that of a model fur-

TABLE 2.4 Weighting of Strategic and Financial Components

	(1) General Model	*(2)* Intercept & Specialists Deleted	*(3)* & Weights Sum to 1	*(4)* & Equal Weights
Variable Intercept	–0.51			
(*t*-stat.)	(0.70)			
STRATRATE	0.58	0.56	0.55	0.5
(*t*-stat.)	(5.09)	(5.12)	(5.48)	
FINRATE	0.54	0.46	0.45	
(*t*-stat.)	(3.37)	(4.39)	(5.48)	0.5
F (Fin'l. Specialist)	1.45			
(*t*-stat.)	(1.32)			
F × STRATRATE	–0.22	–0.25	–0.26	
(*t*-stat.)	(0.84)	(0.98)	(1.71)	
F × FINRATE	0.05	0.25	0.26	
(*t*-stat.)	(0.16)	(1.33)	(1.71)	
R^2	0.73			
Sum of Squared Residuals	15.86	17.11	17.19	18.64
Degrees of Freedom	23	25	27	29
F against Previous Model		0.91	0.05	1.14

ther constrained by the restriction that the weights on the individual strategic and financial ratings must sum to one. The estimated models are shown in Table 2.4, where STRATRATE is the executive's rating of the candidate's strategic desirability, FINRATE is his rating of the financial desirability, and the financial specialist dummy variable (F) is defined as previously.

There is no evidence to reject any of the restrictions imposed. Hence, the most constrained model (3) is the preferred summary of the data. Indeed, even the financial specialist effect is only barely significant by a two-tailed test ($p = 0.098$). However, since the sign is in the predicted direction (CFOs use a weight of 0.72 on the financial rating and only 0.28 on the strategic rating) this effect is stronger by a one-tailed test.

An even simpler model is that executives weight the financial and strategic ratings equally, independent of specialty. Clearly, this hypothesis is not rejected for corporate development executives. For CFOs, the two-tailed $t(10)$-statistic for testing this hypothesis is not significant ($p = 0.114$) Similarly, the joint hypothesis that both CFOs and corporate development executives weight both the financial and strategic ratings equally (0.5) is not rejected ($F(2, 25) = 1.14$). However, since the sign is in the predicted direction (CFOs weight the financial rating more heavily), the one-tailed test

($p = 0.057$) offers suggestive although certainly inconclusive evidence of a role/experience-based expertise effect.

To explore the robustness of these results, the model was reestimated using the minimum sum of absolute error (MSAE) criterion rather than the least squares criterion. The optimal estimate of β (the weight on the strategic rating) for CFOs is exactly 0; that is, the best predictor of a CFO's overall rating is his financial rating. Hence, the more robust MSAE criterion estimates the weight on the financial rating for CFOs at the endpoint of the [0,1] range, a more extreme value than the least squares estimate of 0.72.

In contrast, the MSAE estimates of the weights on the strategic and financial ratings for corporate development executives are equal (0.5). This is very similar to the least squares estimate of 0.5469 on the strategic rating (or 0.4531 on the financial rating). These results strengthen the evidence for the hypothesis that CFOs weight financial factors more heavily than strategic factors, whereas corporate development executives are more balanced in weighting these factors.

Analysis of Recommendations. Consistent with earlier hypotheses regarding the influence of role/experience-based expertise on overall ratings, this analysis considers the influence of specialization on recommendations (i.e., terminate interest in or pursue the candidate). The original intent of the analysis was to use PROBIT analysis to relate the recommendations of the corporate development executives and the CFOs to their separate ratings of strategic and financial attractiveness of the candidate firms. Statistical analysis proved to be impossible, because the recommendations of both groups are predicted perfectly by this class of models when we allow separate models for the two groups of specialists, as suggested by the analysis of the formation of overall ratings.

The three CFOs all recommended against pursuing acquisition of the Sweet Potato Pie case (relatively negative descriptions of both the strategic and financial components); their other seven recommendations (one CFO did not give ratings for two cases) were all in favor of pursuing the candidates. The three CFOs also were unanimous in giving the Sweet Potato Pie case a strategic rating of one (i.e., undesirable); in all other cases they rated the strategic attractiveness above one. Hence, we can predict the recommendations of the CFOs with a very simple model. For any constant K between (but not including) one and two

Predicted Recommendation

$$= \begin{cases} \text{pursue if strategic rating} > K \in (1,2) \\ \text{do not pursue if strategic rating} < K \in (1,2). \end{cases}$$

TABLE 2.5 Critical Observations for the Corporate Development Group

Subject	*Case*	*Strategic Rating*	*Financial Rating*	*Recommendation*
4	Greens (F +, S +)	3	6	Pursue
5	Greens (F +, S +)	3	5	Do Not Pursue
5	Health (F –, S +)	4	3	Do Not Pursue
5	Hacienda (F +, S –)	4	4	Pursue

Given the experimental design and the requirement that financial performance even in the worst case meet a threshold of acceptability, this result is not a surprise. Had the financial manipulation in the worst case been below the minimum criteria established by the acquiring firm, the subject would have immediately terminated any further evaluation. Execution of the experiment required a subject's complete evaluation of each case, because even the worst case had to meet a threshold value. The result further confirms that the intent of the experimental design was achieved.

In analyzing the responses by the corporate development executives, only four of the 19 (one corporate development executive did not rate one case) observations are critical in determining the set of weight pairs (W_S, W_F) which will yield perfect predictions of the recommendations of this group in the following normalized prediction function (where W_S is the weight on the strategic rating and W_F is the weight on the financial rating).

$$X = W_S\,(\text{STRATRATE}) + W_F\,(\text{FINRATE}) - 1,$$

$$\text{Predicted Recommendation} = \begin{cases} \text{pursue if } X > 0 \\ \text{do not pursue if } X < 0. \end{cases}$$

The four critical observations are shown in Table 2.5.

The strategic and financial ratings of all other recommendations to pursue the candidate dominate either three and six or four and four, respectively, while the strategic and financial ratings of all other recommendations not to pursue the candidate are dominated by either three and five or four and three, respectively.

Hence the recommendations of corporate development executives can be predicted perfectly with any set of weights from just over half to just under

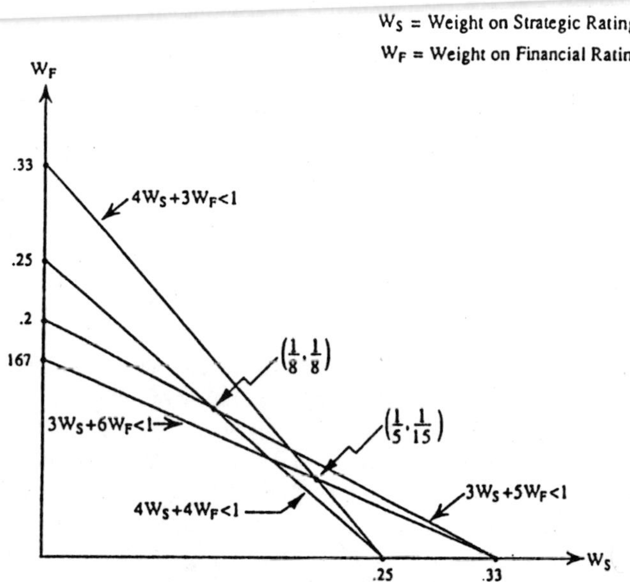

Figure 2.4. Analysis of Recommendations of Corporate Development Executives

three-quarters on the strategic rating, with the cutting point (i.e., region) being chosen appropriately, this is illustrated in Figure 2.4. This range of relative weights is consistent with the estimated weights used by corporate development executives to form their overall ratings.

These ratings may be explained by the corporate development executive's relative lack of expertise in analyzing the financial performance of a firm. If the corporate development executive does not have a well-developed and refined set of financial norms with which to make comparisons, financial ratings are likely to be more variable than those of CFOs.

The analysis presented in this section can be summarized in the following manner:

- The overall ratings of executives are straightforward functions of their ratings of the strategic position and financial performance of the candidate.

- There is modest statistical evidence that corporate development executives and CFOs differ in the weights they assign to strategic and financial ratings in arriving at their overall evaluations.

- Corporate development executives tend to take a "balanced" view of strategic and financial ratings in forming their overall ratings.

- CFOs place the predominant weight on financial matters in deciding upon their overall ratings.

DISCUSSION

This study finds effects of role/experience-based expertise that are somewhat more complex than were suggested in Simon and Dearborn (1958). While the protocol data do not reveal differences in macro lines of reasoning, they do reveal differences in the attention to and generation of business issues as a function of expertise. Furthermore, there appear to be differences in the ways in which the two types of executives evaluate the same candidates. VPs of Corporate Development tend to evaluate the strategic potential of the corporate candidates more optimistically than do CFOs, whereas there is no difference in optimism between CFOs and VPs in the evaluation of the financial characteristics. Finally, while CFOs appear to place greater emphasis on their evaluation of the candidate's financial characteristics in forming their overall evaluation, VPs place approximately equal emphasis on their evaluations of the strategic and financial characteristics in forming their summary judgment.

These findings are consistent with other work in cognition and extend it by using subjects who are well adapted to a complex management task. The executives' problem-solving behaviors support the general hypothesis that skilled performers rely on their strategic knowledge and basic action knowledge when establishing goals and subgoals of problem solving and in determining the appropriate sequence of actions (Anderson 1983, 1985; Chase and Simon 1973; Chi et al. 1981; de Groot 1965; Elstein and Bordage 1979). The protocols also reveal that an executive's representation of knowledge in memory allows for the generation of default values when critical information is missing and for the storage and recall of prototypes and analogies for use in problem solving (Abelson 1976, Cantor et al. 1982, Rumelhart and Ortony 1977, Rumelhart and Norman 1981, Shank and Abelson 1977). Unlike Pechtel (1985) and Walsh (1988), we find evidence for specialty-based differences in (micro) issue generation, suggesting differences in knowledge bases. The existence and survival of differences in the attention CFOs and VPs place on specific business issues suggest an adaptive survival mechanism that may evolve in successful organizations to protect them from "cognitive myopia."

Despite the specialty-based differences at the micro-level (i.e., issue generation), experts in both specialties share a subset of macro-level structures called lines of reasoning, suggesting that some form of shared cognition exists at the organizational level. This finding is consistent with those of Walsh (1988). Indeed, in the two organizations for which both the CFO and the VP were subjects, each correctly anticipated what his colleague would say without knowing the other was a subject in the experiment. This supports Weick's (1979) notion of organizational cognition as sets of thinking practices used by the organization. Similarly, that all subjects clearly understood the limits of their expertise suggests the possession of "dominant rules for combining cognitions" at the organizational level based on various sources of expertise. These men were highly skilled in evaluating the candidates from the perspectives of their functional areas, their organizations, and their industry. Once outside these areas of expertise, they were quick to acknowledge their lack of knowledge and to defer to other specialists.

In studying a task as complex as the evaluation of candidates for corporate acquisition, one must find ways of making the task experimentally tractable. In doing this, certain important aspects of the task may be lost. The decision to make the candidate an unrelated acquisition may have forced the executives to attend to certain issues that would not receive consideration in related acquisitions. Thus, generalizability of conclusions to such situations may not be possible. Likewise, the task was given to individuals whose industry expertise was in diversified foods rather than restaurants. This may be why they generated a relatively lower number of issues relating to operations. To keep executives at this level engaged in the evaluation of all candidates to the completion of the experiment, including those candidates that were relatively less attractive, the financial descriptions of candidates had to meet a minimum threshold value. This may have resulted in the apparent reluctance of subjects to terminate interest in a few of the less desirable cases. Certainly, one would hope that the findings of this study are generalizable to other areas of strategic decision making involving individuals with specialized knowledge. Unfortunately, the study's focus on a single task does not provide evidence upon which to base that generalization. This empirical question should be addressed in a future study. Finally, the small sample size, which is unavoidable in data-intensive studies using verbal protocols of high-level executives, is a limitation. The tradeoff in this study was made in favor of developing a detailed understanding of a few, highly-skilled specialists who are generally not well represented in academic research.

Suggestions for future work naturally flow from the analysis of data and the limitations of the current work. The data reveal a bias in ratings and difference in the weightings placed on the financial performance and strategic business position components between CFOs and VPs of Corporate Development. While the study offers evidence for a bias in weightings, its design does not pinpoint in which specialist group(s) the bias is present. Future studies might locate the bias and in addition direct attention at understanding the nature of the tradeoff between strategic position and financial performance in cases where manipulations of the components are free to range from poor (below threshold) to exceptional. Given the preliminary nature of the proposed lines of reasoning, additional work on developing the model and goal structures identified in the protocols should be attempted. This may involve studies with novices as well as experts in other industries.

The strengths of the current work are its use of practicing, high-level professionals, the realism of the tasks, the structuring of the experiment within the complex context of strategic management, and the illustration and use of a nontraditional methodology, protocol analysis, combined with more traditional methods. In conclusion, it would appear that studying these role/experience-based differences has value in developing our understanding of how organizations do and should integrate recommendations from their various executive officers.[7]

NOTES

1. The executive who was dropped found it difficult to "think aloud" while being tape recorded.

2. None of these panel members was associated with any other aspects of this experiment (i.e., they were not involved in the development of the experimental materials, nor did they serve as subjects, nor were they at the time associated with the firms whose members served in any of these capacities).

3. Results of the analyses are not sensitive to whether one uses this criterion applied to the mean or the median or to whether the critical values are 2.5 and 5.5 rather than 3 and 5.

4. Casual inspection of the results in Table 2.2 reveals that the adjusted R^2 are generally "small"; indeed in nine cases they are negative. Negative adjusted R^2 can occur because, unlike unadjusted R^2, the lower bound is not zero but rather $(p-1)/(N-p)$, where p is the number of regression-function parameters estimated (including the intercept). For the regressions in Table 2.2, $p = 5$ and $N = 32$, so the lower bound on the adjusted R^2 is –0.148. While one generally prefers a higher R^2 to a lower one, the low R^2 for this analysis are not per se a problem. The goal of this analysis is to estimate the extent to which specialization affects the generation of issues in predicted ways. Hence, it is the signs and precisions of the estimated specialist effects which are critical. The adjusted R^2 are important to the extent that the significance of the specialist effects imply upper bounds on the adjusted R^2.

5. I am indebted to Raymond E. Willis for suggesting this graphical analysis.

6. The parameter estimates are based only on 29 rather than 32 (eight subjects times four cases) observations, because the second CFO did not provide ratings for the Health Club and Hacienda cases and the third corporate development executive did not rate the Hacienda case.

7. I wish to thank the special issue editor and the two anonymous reviewers for their helpful comments. I am indebted to my dissertation chairman, Paul E. Johnson, who gave me the freedom and support to pursue this topic. I am especially grateful for the suggestions and comments on the statistical analysis provided by Raymond E. Willis and Timothy W. McGuire. Special thanks to Eugene Borgida, Gary Dickson, P. George Benson, William F. Wright, Gerald Salancik, Dennis Epple, and Chester Spatt for their comments and suggestions. I owe the greatest debt to the CFOs and the Vice Presidents of Corporate Development in the diversified foods industry who participated as experimental subjects. Credit for the realism of the experimental tasks must be given to Jerry Levin, then Vice President of Acquisition for Pillsbury, and John Danielson, then Vice President of Strategic Planning, First Bank Minneapolis, and President of the Minneapolis Chapter of the NASCP. Similarly, I wish to thank the members of my expert panel: Benno Bernt, Richard M. Cyert, Robert Dalton, John "Jack" Thorne, Roland D. Sullivan, and Jeffrey Williams. Many thanks to Gail McGuire for her editorial suggestions.

This research was funded, in part, by an IBM Doctoral Fellowship, a McKnight Grant, and a Doctoral Dissertation Special Grant from the University of Minnesota. Additional support was provided by Carnegie Mellon University.

Appendix A
Description of Business Issues (Knowledge States)

AC = Acquisition Criteria	Match criteria and candidate characteristics.
AS = Acquisition Strategy	Comment on strategy.
CE = Competitive Environment	
CE-SAT	Saturation of market.
CE-LOC	Location of facilities, including location strategy.
CE-CON	Concentration of units in a region to attain critical mass.
CE-PROD	Product concept or format (e.g., position in life cycle, attractiveness, relative success).
CE-CUST	Customers, demographics.
MGT = Management Skills/Capabilities	
MGT-EXP	Expertise or knowledge of the industry.
MGT-RET	Ability to retain quality management.
MGT CULT	Corporate culture.
MGT-MOT	Motivation for selling.
L = Labor Issues	
L-AVAIL	Availability of labor, skills.
L-REL	Labor relations, unionization.
LEGAL = Antitrust Issues	
FIN = Financial	
FIN-PROFIT	Profitability.
FIN-CAP	Capital requirements.
FIN-LEV	Leveraging.
FIN-TAX	Tax policy.
FIN-FRANCHISE	Treatment of franchises and leases.
FIN-STK	Price of candidate's stock.
FIN-INT	Interest expense.
FIN-PRICE	Price of acquisition plus any premium.
FIN-DILU	Dilution effect.
FIN-DIV	Dividend policy.
FIN-OWNER	Equity position of owners.
OP = Operations	
S = Synergies	
S-MGT	Synergies related to management skills.
S-FIN	Synergies related to financial capabilities.
S-OP	Synergies related to operations (e.g., distribution).

Appendix B
Description of Lines of Reasoning

Line of Reasoning	*Script*
Strategy Confirmation/ Criteria Screen	Recognize diversification strategy. Generate risks associated with diversification. Generate alternatives to diversification. Conclude that to exceed growth rate of 4% may require diversification. Match criteria (location, growth, business) to characteristics of the candidate firm.
Competitive-Environment Assessment	Determine extent of market saturation (if any). Identify maturity of product concept/format. Consider potential for economies of scale based on concentration (e.g., advertising, distribution).
Management Assessment	Determine performance to assess degree of knowledge about restaurant business. Consider motivation for selling. Generate probability of retaining skilled personnel after sale. Determine likelihood that existing culture could be changed or maintained.
Financial Assessment	Compare profitability of this firm to others in industry. Determine the magnitude of investment required to maintain or improve profitability. Consider franchise/lease arrangements. Consider past tax policy. Assess equity position of owners. Estimate likelihood of premium. Project impact on stockholders.
Operations Assessment	Consider extent to which operation is computerized. Consider extent to which facilities are designed to support work flow and traffic patterns. Consider age of facilities.
Synergy Proposal	Generate/evaluate management synergies—general knowledge of Severson and business knowledge of candidate. Generate/evaluate financial synergies—unused funds of Severson and candidates' needs for capital to expand. Generate/evaluate operations synergies—use of existing distribution channels to distribute to restaurants.

REFERENCES

Abelson, R. P. (1976), "Script Processing in Attitude Formation and Decision Making," in J. S. Carroll and J. W. Payne (Eds.), *Cognition and Social Behavior,* Hillsdale, NJ: Lawrence Erlbaum.

Anderson, J. R. (1983), *The Architecture of Cognition,* Cambridge, MA: Harvard University Press.

——— (1985), *Cognitive Psychology and Its Implications,* 2nd Ed., San Francisco: Freeman.

Biggs, S. and T. Mock (1983), "An Investigation of Auditor Decision Processes in Internal Control and Audit Scope Decisions," *Journal of Accounting Research,* 21, 334-355.

Bouman, M. J. (1978), "Financial Diagnosis: A Cognitive Model of the Processes Involved," Unpublished Ph.D. dissertation, Carnegie Mellon University, Pittsburgh, PA.

——— (1983), "Human Diagnostic Reasoning by Computer," *Management Science,* 29, 653-672.

Buckley, W. F. (1984), *Airborne: A Sentimental Journey,* New York: Little.

Cantor, N., W. Mischel, and J. C. Schwartz (1982), "A Prototype Analysis of Psychological Situations," *Cognitive Psychology,* 14, 45-77.

Chase, W. G. and H. A. Simon (1973), "Perception in Chess," *Cognitive Psychology,* 4, 55-81.

Chi, M., P. Feltovich, and R. Glaser (1981), "Categorization and Representation of Physics Problems by Experts and Novices," *Cognitive Science,* 5, 121-152.

Cohen, J. (1960), "A Coefficient of Agreement for Nominal Scales," *Educational and Psychological Measurement,* 20, 37-46.

de Groot, A. (1965), *Thought and Choice in Chess,* The Hague: Mouton.

Dreyfus, H. L. and S. E. Dreyfus (1986), *Mind over Machine,* New York: Macmillan.

Duhaime, J. M. and C. R. Schwenk (1985), "Conjectures on Cognitive Simplification in Acquisition and Divestment Decision Making," *Academy of Management Review,* 10, 287-295.

Elstein, A. S. and F. Bordage (1979), "Psychology of Clinical Reasoning," in G. Stone, P. Cohen, and N. Adler (Eds.), *Health Psychology,* San Francisco: Jossey-Bass, 333-367.

——— (1980), "Verbal Reports as Data," *Psychological Review,* 87, 255-271.

Ericsson, K. A. and H. A. Simon (1984), *Protocol Analysis: Verbal Reports as Data,* Cambridge: MIT Press.

Fitts, P. M. and M. I. Posner (1967), *Human Performance,* Belmont, CA: Brooks Cole.

Isenberg, D. (1986), "Thinking and Managing: A Verbal Protocol Analysis of Managerial Problem Solving," *Academy of Management Journal,* 29, 775-788.

Jeffries, R., A. Turner, P. Polson, and M. Atwood (1981), "The Processes Involved in Software Design," in J. R. Anderson (Ed.), *Cognitive Skills and their Acquisition,* Hillsdale, NJ: Lawrence Erlbaum, 255-284.

Jemison, D. and S. B. Sitkin (1986), "Corporate Acquisitions: A Process Perspective," *Academy of Management Review,* 11, 145-163.

Johnson, P. E., F. Hassebrock, A. Duran, and J. Moller (1982), "A Multimethod Study of Clinical Judgment," *Organizational Behavior and Human Performance,* 30, 201-230.

——— K. Jamal, and R. G. Berryman (1991), "Effects of Framing on Auditor Decisions," *Organizational Behavior and Human Decision Performance,* 50, 75-105.

Larkin, J. (1981), "Enriching Formal Knowledge: A Model for Learning to Solve Textbook Physics Problems," in J. R. Anderson (Ed.), *Cognitive Skills and Their Acquisition,* Hillsdale, NJ: Lawrence Erlbaum, 311-334.

Melone, N. P. (1987), "Expertise in Corporate Acquisitions: An Investigation of the Influence of Specialized Knowledge on Strategic Decision Making," Unpublished Ph.D. dissertation, University of Minnesota, Minneapolis.

O'Connor, R. (1975), *Managing Corporate Development,* New York: The Conference Board.

Pechtel, B. J. (1983), "The Role of Experience and Specialization in Lawyer Problem Solving," Unpublished Ph.D. dissertation, University of Minnesota, Minneapolis.

Polanyi, M. (1973), *The Tacit Dimension*, Garden City: Doubleday.

Rumelhart, D. E. and D. A. Norman (1981), "Analogical Processes in Learning," in J. R. Anderson (Ed.), *Cognitive Skills and Their Acquisition*, Hillsdale, NJ: Lawrence Erlbaum.

——— and A. Ortony (1977), "Representation of Knowledge in Memory," in R. C. Anderson, R. J. Spiro and W. E. Montague (Eds.), *Schooling and the Acquisition of Knowledge*, Hillsdale, NJ: Erlbaum.

Schön, D. (1983), *The Reflective Practitioner: How Professionals Think in Action*, New York: Basic Books.

Shank, R. C. and R. P. Abelson (1977), *Scripts, Plans, Coals, and Understanding*, Hillsdale, NJ: Lawrence Erlbaum.

Simon, H. A. and D. C. Dearborn (1958), "Selective Perception: Identifications of Executives," in H. A. Simon, *Administrative Behavior: A Study of Decision Making in Administrative Organization* (3rd Ed.), New York: Free Press, 1976, 309-314. Reprinted with minor revisions from *Sociometry*, 21, 140-144.

Stahl, M. J. and T. W. Zimmerer (1984), "Modeling Strategic Acquisition Policies: A Simulation of Executives' Acquisition Decisions," *Academy of Management Journal*, 27, 369-383.

Stubbart, C. I. (1989), "Managerial Cognition: A Missing Link in Strategic Management Research," *Journal of Management Studies*, 26 (July), 325-345.

Walsh, J. P. (1988), "Selectivity and Selective Perception: An Investigation of Managers' Belief Structures and Information Processing," *Academy of Management Journal*, 31, 873-896.

Weick, K. E. (1979), "Cognitive Processing in Organizations," in *Research in Organizational Behavior* (Vol. 1), Greenwich, CT: JAI.

3

The Formulation Processes and Tactics Used in Organizational Decision Making

PAUL C. NUTT

One hundred and sixty-three decision cases were explored to determine how managers carry out formulation during organizational decision making. Four types of formulation processes were identified (called idea, issue, objective-directed, and reframing) as well as the tactics decision makers apply to carry out each process type. Decision adoption, merit, and duration were used to determine the success of each process and tactic. The implications of these findings for decision makers and researchers are discussed.

(ORGANIZATIONAL DECISION MAKING; FORMULATION; STRATEGIC DECISION-MAKING PRACTICE AND THEORY)

INTRODUCTION

Consider a Toyota dealer who has been getting disturbing signals after a long period of sales growth. Declines in the closing ratio (a measure of lost sales) were noted and profit had leveled off. The dealer judged these performance indicators to be important signals and linked them to staffing problems. Growth was thought to have forced the addition of sales people who were not enculturated into the dealer's approach to the car business. A sales manager position was created to train and supervise the sales force.

This chapter originally appeared in *Organization Science,* Vol. 4, No. 2, May 1993.

After a year, the closing ratio and profit continued to fall. The sales manager was fired and the dealership was back to square one.

This case, drawn from the data base developed for this study, indicates how formulation influences decision making. Consistent with the literature on strategic decision making, *formulation* is defined as a process that begins when signals, such as performance indicators, are recognized by key people and ends when one or more options have been targeted for development (e.g., Ansoff 1984). During formulation individuals interpret signals that capture their attention by making claims. The claim indicates beliefs and values (e.g., we must improve our closing ratio) that call for action. To act, the decision maker sets a *direction* that guides subsequent activity. The importance of formulation stems from the pivotal role that these directions play in determining what will be considered and what will be excluded. The Toyota dealer linked declines in the closing ratio to sales force quality. The remedy was seen in terms of training. Given this direction no other option could be considered.

This research attempts to identify and describe the formulation procedures used by managers during organizational decision making addressing two questions. First, do managers use distinct types of procedures to carry out formulation? Second, do the results produced by these practice-based procedures differ? Answering these questions demands field settings in which a combination of descriptive and quantitative tools can be applied (Kolb 1983, Schön 1987). To carry out this research, 163 decision cases were analyzed to identify the formulation procedures used by managers in decision making. The cases were classified to identify procedural types. Adoption rates, merit, and duration were used to determine the success of each type of formulation procedure.

FORMULATION AND DECISION MAKING

Decision researchers agree that the early, formative steps in decision making are crucially important because they guide the search for solutions (e.g., Cyert and March 1963, Soelberg 1967, Bower 1972, Witte 1972, Mintzberg et al. 1976, Quinn 1981, Lyles 1981, Nutt 1984, 1986, Pettigrew 1985, Hickson et al. 1986). Although a variety of terms are used, each study suggests that decision makers interpret signals and provide direction. Decision makers are exposed to many signals, such as how key people interpret cost increases and innovations by competitors, and must determine which signal merits attention. After claims based on these signals have been sorted out by a decision maker, a direction is offered. Directions can be expressed as problems to be overcome (Pounds 1969), boundaries that circumscribe what can be done (Maier 1970), ideals to be met (Nutt and Backoff 1992), strategies to be followed (Schendel and Hofer 1979), issue agendas to be managed (Ansoff 1984), idealized solution targets (Nadler 1981), a preferred solution (Cohen, March, and Olsen 1976), and objectives (Locke et al. 1981). Qualifications can also be imposed such as stakeholders to be involved (Freeman 1983), urgency (Kolb 1983), and core values to be preserved (Quinn 1988).

One of the most important acts in decision making is deriving directions from claims based on signals thought to be important (Slovic, Fischhoff and Lichtenstein 1977, MacCrimmon and Taylor 1976). However, as Mintzberg et al. (1976) and Fredrickson (1985) point out, little is known about how managers carry out formulation. Furthermore, studies of organizational decision making seldom address outcomes to distinguish between good and less desirable practice (Schendel and Hofer 1979).

This research was undertaken to identify the formulation procedures used by managers during organizational decision making and to assess these practices by addressing two questions:

1. *Procedural types.* Determine how managers carry out formulation, identifying procedural types that have unique steps and step sequences.
2. *Procedural success.* Determine whether formulation procedure influences decision-making success.

THEORETICAL FRAMEWORK

A *decision process* is made up of a stream of action-taking steps that begins with claims by stakeholders drawn from signals that seem important and ends when a decision has been adopted. This research is concerned with the action-taking steps of decision makers as they respond to seemingly important claims and establish directions that guide development, called *formulation.* Formulation is defined as a procedure carried out by a responsible agent (a manager) that begins by responding to the claims made by key people ends when an option or options have been targeted for development.

To carry out this research each of action-taking steps in a decision is identified. Identifying each of the steps in a decision process before formulation procedures are identified has two benefits. First, viewing all decision-making steps makes it easier to recognize and appreciate the steps that are related to formulation. Second, this treatment of the data makes no assumptions about which decision activity involves formulation. As a result, arbitrary distinctions that determine what constitutes a formulation procedure are avoided during data collection.

Identifying Decision-Making Procedure

The action-taking steps that make up a decision-making process can be identified by imposing a framework or from an examination and comparison of cases. Soelberg (1967), Bower (1972), Witte (1972), and Mintzberg, Raisinghani, and Theoret (1976) popularized an "emergent theme" approach which immerses the researcher in raw data describing each case to find key decision-making activities. This approach becomes unwieldy when large databases are assessed. The mass of detail makes it difficult to analyze the data. As a result, researchers using the emergent theme approach have been forced to examine a limited number of cases, making the generalizability of their conclusions suspect. Researchers using a small case database may fail to discover important action-taking steps or fail to recognize the idiosyncratic nature of the steps that are discovered.

An alternative to this approach imposes a framework on the data. The researcher can fit the decision case to the framework and then look for action-taking steps. Both reliability and generalizability improve when patterns emerge that have the same steps and step sequences in a large number of cases. However, imposing a framework has the disadvantage of creating the appearance of orderliness in what may be a chaotic process. Also, imposing a framework may result in losing important messages that do not fit the framework. The advantages of systematic description of decisions and using a large case database outweigh the disadvantages of matching to an overly neat set of steps and the possibility of lost information.

Using a framework to find patterns in decision-making steps is similar to the "etics and emics" classification approach, from phonetics and phonemics, applied by linguists (Pike 1967). An emic representation applies a minimal set of conceptual components to describe the object being analyzed (e.g., a decision procedure). Components of the thing being described (decision making) are used to identify elements in the classificatory framework. This kind of framework allows the researcher to look for similarities and differences. The etic describes how the framework is used to profile an object (e.g., decision case), drawing on the thing being classified (the case) as a point of reference. Such a classification is phyletic (McKelvey 1978), because it attempts to identify and explain the origin of types.

The Classification Framework

The framework shown in Figure 3.1 pulls together the phases and routines identified in studies of organizational decision making, planning and design (e.g., Nadler 1981), innovation (e.g., Zaltman, Duncan, and Holbek 1973), policy formation (e.g., Dunn 1981), organizational change (e.g., Hage and

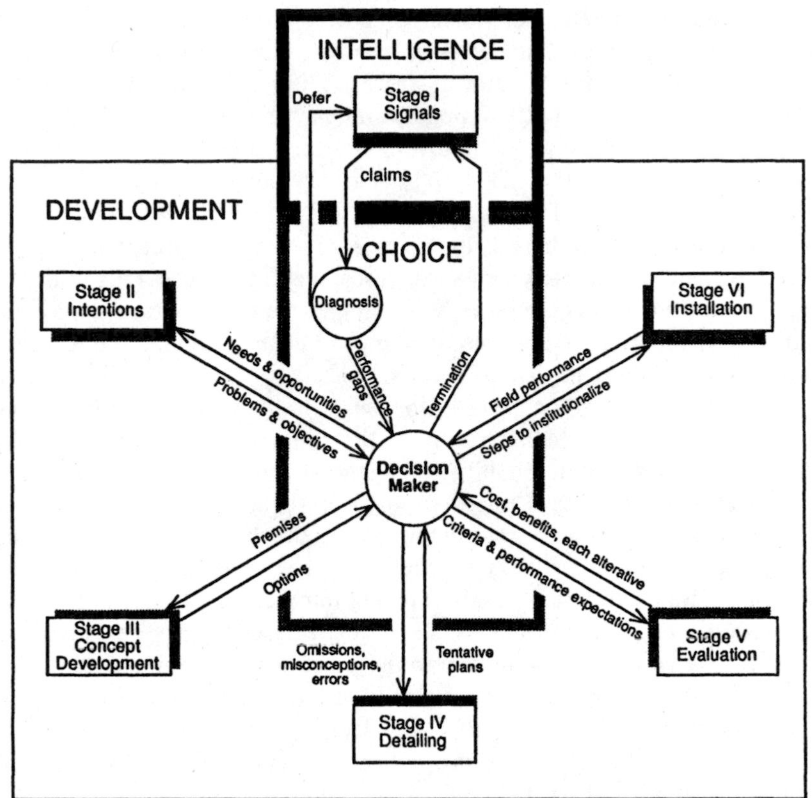

Figure 3.1. The Transactional Representation of Decision Making

Aiken 1970), planned change (e.g., Beyer and Trice 1978), and organization theory (Simon 1977, March 1981). To create the framework, process phases identified in these studies were systematically compared. The synthesis which emerged drew together recommendations for the staging of activity and monitoring by a decision maker, providing a prescriptive view of decision making that has broad support in literature. Including monitoring in the prescriptions captures the transactional nature of decision making, identifying the key choices called for by a decision maker as the decision process unfolds.

The decision-making process shown in Figure 3.1 has three major blocks of activity: intelligence, choice, and development, drawn in part from Simon's (1977) intelligence, design, and choice typology. The boxes in Figure 3.1

represent decision-making *stages* which identify the types of information that should be collected. The circles identify where *choices* are made by a decision maker to monitor information gathering. The arrows in Figure 3.1 indicate decision-making steps which identify actions called for by the decision maker and others involved in the decision process.

In the intelligence block, signals (Stage 1) that stem from sources such as liaison, management information systems, and industry reports are interpreted by interested parties. This interpretation is used to fashion claims that call for action. A decision process is activated when key people make claims. This activism forces a decision maker to make a diagnosis that assesses the importance of each claim and reconciles competing claims, determining if the claims suggest an important performance gap. Many decisions would be deferred at this point. If not deferred, a performance gap would be recognized. Beginning with Downs (1967), the notion of a performance gap has been widely accepted as the trigger of decision-making activity. When a performance gap seems substantial, decision makers specify needs and opportunities which activate development. The *choice* block identifies key judgments that are made by the decision maker. The *development* block identifies the staging of information gathering activity carried out to fashion and implement the decision. The blocks are linked by a series of transactions. The arrows in Figure 3.1 indicate how information flows between a decision maker making choices and a support team that is carrying out development. Support teams are made up of technical staff, other managers, or even the decision maker acting as his/her own technical adviser and periodically change.

Development begins in Stage II, intentions, when the decision maker specifies needs or opportunities suggested by claims. A support team clarifies these needs and opportunities by offering problems or objectives. In Stage III, concept development, the decision maker states premises, which identify ways to deal with the problems or respond to the objectives identified in Stage II. A support team responds by offering options. In Stage III the decision maker tests the options for omissions, misconceptions, and errors. Alternatives that can be modified to overcome the decision maker's objections are subjected to an evaluation in Stage V. The decision maker identifies criteria and the support team applies them to assess the merits of alternatives that survive Stage IV. During installation (Stage VI) the decision maker applies tools such as rewards and incentives, personnel selection and promotion, resource allocation, sanctions, coordination, and delegation to implement the preferred option. The decision process ends when field performance is judged to be adequate and the decision maker terminates surveillance. The actions suggested by support staff can lead to cycling in a stage as the decision maker gathers information to explore possibilities.

The transactional framework goes beyond a linear unfolding of steps that is typically used to describe decision making (e.g., Mintzberg et al. 1976, Kolb 1983). First, the transactions recognize that dialogues about possibilities between members of a support team and the decision maker are essential for successful decision making to occur (Churchman 1975, Nutt and Backoff 1986). Second, the framework captures both the concepts required to understand decision making *and* the steps required to make a decision. By capturing both the meta and focal level of decision making as well as the dialogue in which crucial actions are uncovered, a decision process can be represented with more precision and a greater depth of understanding. The framework identifies decision-making stages that should be activated to gather information, but may be latent for a given decision.

Capturing Types of Decision-Making Processes

To profile a decision-making process, key transactions are identified that trace action-taking steps. There are two types of traces. The *normative trace* identifies what should take place in a decision-making process, indicating choices that should be made, as shown by the arrows in Figure 3.1. The *descriptive trace* describes how a decision maker carries out a particular decision-making process by taking steps to interpret claims, establish intentions, guide the selection and development of options, assess options, and install a preferred option. For a particular decision, decision makers may delegate some of the analysis or design activities to a support staff. To describe the stream of choices in a particular decision, each action-taking step is shown by an arrow that connects one of the stages to the choice block. The profile of these steps captures the sequence of events in a decision case.

A Case Profile

A solar energy decision by a firm will be described to illustrate how the framework is used to trace the action-taking steps of a decision. Figure 3.2 provides a profile of the key steps in this decision.

A solar heat pump idea was devised during the mid-seventies when the escalating cost of energy was thought likely to continue indefinitely (signals). The CEO of an air conditioning manufacturer was approached by a developer of a solar heat pump who offered the firm a license for its manufacture (a claim, see Step 1, Figure 3.2). Exploration of the idea (diagnosis) revealed growth and diversification potential (Step 2). A 30% increase in sales was thought to be possible (performance gap) through a new heating and cooling device that could be sold to homes. The firm's CEO signed a new heating and cooling device that could be sold to homes. The

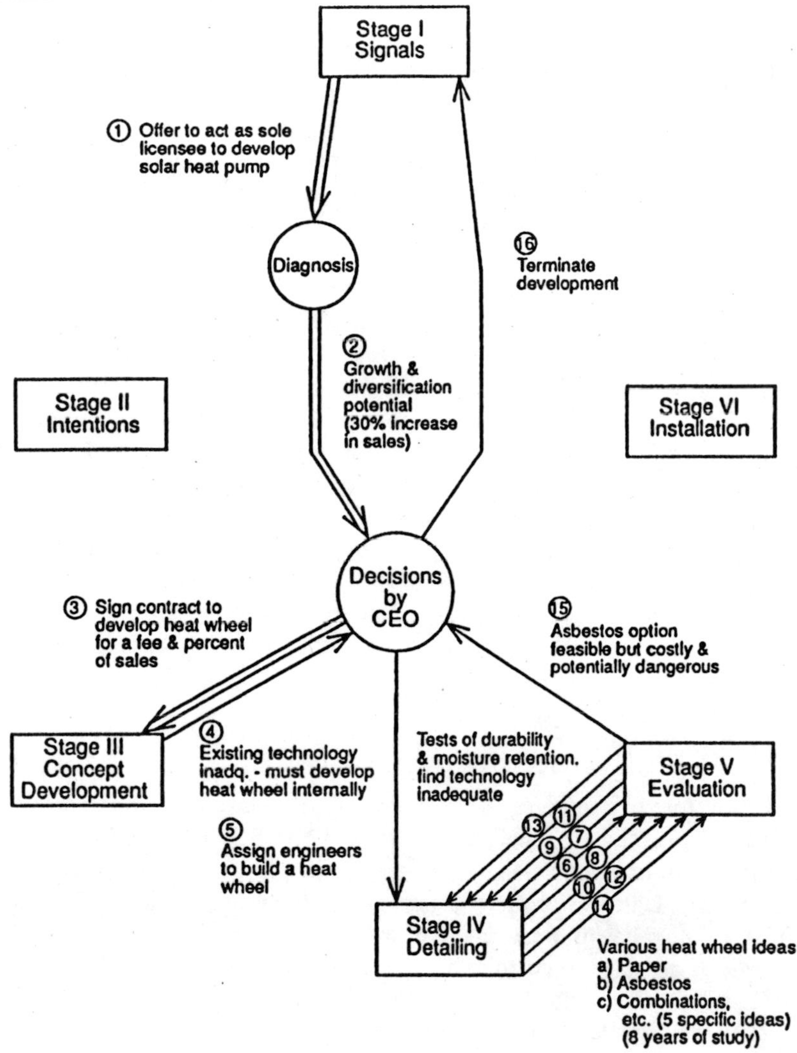

Figure 3.2. Profile of the Solar Energy Case

firm's CEO signed a contract to develop a heat wheel, an integral part of the solar heat pump that the licensure had yet to develop, for a fee and a percentage of the ultimate sales (Step 3). A search revealed that existing technology was inadequate and that the firm must develop the heat wheel internally (Step 4). In Step 5, the firm's CEO assigned engineers to build the heat wheel. This resulted in an eight-year effort in which the engineers devised five specific heat wheel ideas and tested them for durability and moisture retention without the CEO's involvement (Steps 6 to 14). The first four of these ideas lacked either durability or moisture retention or both. After eight years, an asbestos heat wheel was created that met the durability and moisture retention requirements and was presented to the CEO (Step 15). However, the material was also found to be costly and potentially dangerous. Recently disclosed environmental studies had linked asbestos to health hazards. The CEO terminated development in Step 16.

METHODS

Several activities are carried out to create a profile for a decision case and determine outcomes. First, interviews are conducted with people intimately involved with the details of each decision. In the interview, the informants are asked to identify action-taking steps and the order that these steps were carried out. Second, the steps and their ordering are transcribed, as in Figure 3.2, and the steps related to formulation isolated. Third, a search is then mounted to find cases with similar and dissimilar formulation procedures by comparing the nature and sequence of the formulation steps in each case and naming distinct procedural types. Lastly, indicators of success are collected for each case.

Data Collection

Cases for this research were collected from organizations across the United States and Canada. A top executive (CEO, CFO, COO) in each organization was contacted and asked to supply a case and identify key participants. Data were collected through interviews with the decision maker and two others who were familiar with the decision. The second set of interviews are used to corroborate the recall of the primary informant (Yin 1981, 1985). The data that emerged from these interviews were used to identify the steps taken during decision making and the dependent variables (success measures).

Table 3.1 offers a description of the decision cases, types of organizations providing the cases, and the informants who provided information about the decisions. The prime informant (decision maker) was a top manager (CEO, COO, or CFO) in two-thirds of the cases. The most frequently observed decisions in the cases involved services (e.g., hospitals initiating burn care) or products (e.g., the heat pump case), closely followed by support services and space renovations. In all, 14 types of decisions were included in the case (Table 3.1). This diversity of decisions and organizations suggests that a

TABLE 3.1 Organizations, Decision Types, and Informants

Case Characteristics	*Number*	*Percentage*
Decision Types		
Service/product	33	20
Support services[a]	28	17
Space renovation	19	12
Planning	12	7
Construction	11	7
Financial management	11	7
Personnel policy[b]	11	7
Equipment purchases	10	6
Mergers	4	2
Staffing	4	2
Public relations	3	2
Organizational restructuring	3	2
Marketing	2	1
TOTAL	163	100
Organizations		
Public	42	26
Private	26	16
Third-sector	95	58
TOTAL	163	100
Primary Informant		
CEO	55	34
COO	40	25
CFO	6	4
Middle Management	62	37
TOTAL	163	100
Secondary Informant		
Subordinates	73	45
Staff	78	48
Task force member	12	7
TOTAL	163	100

a. Material management, parking, telephone, records, purchasing, laboratory, etc.
b. Time off compensation, wage and salary, retirement, dismissal, etc.

broad range of decision practice is represented in the cases, which makes the study's finding broadly descriptive of organizational decision making.

Profiling a Decision Case

To minimize memory distortion and memory failure, the two most common errors in reconstructing events (Bartlett 1954), separate interviews with the decision maker and the other informants were conducted by the author. Each informant was asked to spell out the sequence of actions taken during decision making. Informants were cued by asking "what happened first" and then "what happened next" to elicit action steps as the decision process was reconstructed for a case (Nutt 1984). The information from each interview was transcribed as a narrative and then fit to Figure 3.1 using the rules for coding transactions, described in the previous section of the chapter. The profile was presented to each informant to verify that it captured the steps that were used, modifying the steps until they were acceptable. The profiles from each informant were then compared and differences identified. If differences persisted, others involved in the decision were interviewed (Huber and Power 1985). This, along with other data sources, such as reports and records, were used to determine which version of events seemed most plausible. A case was retained for the classification phase of the study if there was agreement on the action-taking steps and sufficient detail to understand what was done. Twelve cases failed to meet these tests and were discarded. For two cases some of the key documentation was lost and could not be reconstructed.

Identifying Formulation Procedures

To identify the formulation procedure used in a decision, the sequence of action-taking steps that began with what informants said happened first and ended with one or more options being targeted for development as highlighted by a double line in the case profile (see Figure 3.2). The profiles were then sorted by the author, placing each case profile in a pile that used similar steps until a set of groupings emerged that had distinct action-taking steps and step sequences (Campbell and Fiske 1959). A code number was placed on the back of each case profile and the sorting process repeated. Each case with an ambiguous classification was carefully reviewed, attempting to create a new category or to match it with an existing one. To improve intrarater reliability this process was repeated several times for all cases, without reference to past sorts. A second rater was asked to re-sort a sample of the case narratives to get an indication of interrater reliability. The two raters agreed on the classifications for 81% of the cases. A sort of a sample of the case profiles (e.g., Figure 3.2) by the same rater produced 100% agreement.

Measures of Success

Success was determined by measuring each decision's adoption, merit, and duration. These measures are conceptually independent. Good decisions may not be implemented and vice versa, and adopted as well as meritorious decisions can be time consuming. Decisions may be adopted, but only after an extended time period implying considerable effort and have marginal effect. To avoid self-serving assessments by the decision maker, the adoption, merit, and duration measures were collected with a questionnaire given to the two secondary informants for each case.

Pragmatics suggests adoption as a success measure. Success for a manager is bound up in implementation. If a decision is used, it meets this test. In the questionnaire, the informants were asked to apply a "put to use" criterion to determine initial decision adoption. For example, a burn center would be adopted if it were opened, an MIS would be adopted if the organization stopped using the old system, and a merger would be adopted if it were completed.

Changes in decision status were traced by adding additional categories to the initial adoption measure. The secondary informants were asked in a follow-up questionnaire to classify each decision as an adoption, ultimate adoption, partial adoption, failure, or ultimate failure. Differences were resolved by discussion immediately after the questionnaire was filled out. An "ultimate adoption" occurred if, for example, a merger met with initial resistance, which held up adoption, but ultimately was carried out. A "partial adoption" occurred when a part of the decision was adopted. For example, some departments may refuse to participate in an MIS or all departments may use some of the capability of an MIS, ignoring other features. "Ultimate failures" depict decisions that were initiated, but later withdrawn. For instance, a new product can be withdrawn after performance monitoring. Delays in use, proportion of use, and terminated use suggest important adoption qualifications. To capture these qualifications, at least two years transpired before assessments were finalized. The "unqualified adoption" measure puts all qualifications (ultimate adoption, partial adoption, and ultimate failure) in the failure category, creating a stringent test of use.

Decision merit provides another indicator of success that may not agree with what was pragmatic. Objective data, describing the economic returns or benefits of a decision, offer ideal indicators of merit but proved to be difficult to collect. Most organizations were either unwilling or unable to provide information that linked the decision to factors such as money lost or gained. As a consequence, merit was determined subjectively by having the secondary informants rate decision merit in a questionnaire. The rating scale for merit in the questionnaire had five anchors: 5 = outstanding, defined as making a decisive contribution, 4 = good, defined as being useful in several ways, 3 = adequate, defined as meeting some needs, 2 = disappointing, defined as having several residual problems, and 1 = poor, defined as having no redeeming features. The secondary informants were told to review these definitions and to check anywhere along a scale with these anchors to reflect their views, creating interval scale properties in the merit assessment. Informants then met and reviewed their initial ratings, discussing and exploring differences. After discussion, new ratings were made in which informants made changes that seemed appropriate. These steps improve recall and reliability (Nutt 1992). Averaging the ratings of informants provides a balanced assessment, closer to the organization's perspective of merit.

Decision makers want fast answers and minimal use of resources in making decisions. This suggests man-hours and duration as success measures. Estimates of man-hours or indeed any process-related measure of cost were not collectible, for reasons similar to those cited for merit. Duration was determined by the time, measured in months, required to make a decision. The secondary informants for each decision made initial estimates of decision duration and reconciled these estimates using the steps described for the merit measure. The time in months averaged over the informants final estimates were used to measure duration for each case.

Analysis

Statistical analysis of the data treated formulation procedures as a factor, with categories for each procedural type, to be linked with the success measures. One-way ANOVAs were carried out using formulation procedures as an independent variable with multiple levels and one of the measures of success as the dependent variable.

The dependent variables are scaled in several ways which calls for care when using parametric statistical methods, such as ANOVA. The decision merit measure was collected with an anchored rating scale to create interval scale properties in the ratings. However, the two adoption measures have binary values and a nominal scale. This calls for both parametric and nonparametric tests to be used in an ANOVA format applying F tests and Kruskal-Wallis Chi-square tests, respectively. To ensure that statistical tests give an accurate picture, the more conservative significant level from these tests is reported. The results are described using a parametric format so the relative merits of the formulation procedures can be determined by the average adoption rates, merit ratings, and duration. Nonparametric methods would be limited to reporting results by a ranking of formulation types.

A Duncan Multiple Range Test (DMRT) is used to isolate differences in the success measures by comparing the types of formulation procedures, two at a time. The DMRT accounts for the number of comparisons being made, identifying categories (in this case, types of formulation procedures) that are different at a 0.05 level of significance.

TABLE 3.2 Dependent Variables Correlations

	Merit	*Initial Adoption*	*Unqualified Adoption*
Duration	–0.16 (ns)	–0.10 (ns)	–0.03 (ns)
Merit		0.64 ($p \leq 0.0001$)	0.51 ($p \leq 0.0001$)
Initial Adoption			0.70 ($p \leq 0.0001$)

Correlations between the dependent variables are shown in Table 3.2. Duration (time in months) had no correlation with the adoption measures nor the decision merit measure. In the case data, long duration decisions could be high or low merit and are not linked to decisions that are more or less likely to be adopted. The merit and adoption measures are positively related. As merit increased, the prospect of an adoption and an unqualified adoption also increases. This correlation confirms what one would predict. The adoption and unqualified adoption measures are also strongly related, but had to have this relationship given how each is defined.

THE NATURE AND SUCCESS OF FORMULATION PROCEDURES

Study of the cases revealed four procedural types, called formulation processes, each using two distinct tactics. These processes and tactics are summarized in Table 3.3, which lists their salient features and frequency of occurrence. The steps used in these formulation procedures are listed in Table 3.4. Figure 3.3 describes the simplest trace of steps that was highlighted for each formulation procedure. More complex traces typically involved repeats of the steps, following the same pattern.

The formulation processes and tactics were found to have several distinctive differences and a few similarities. Similarities stemmed from steps that were applied in several of the processes and tactics. Steps that considered claims and articulated some form of a performance gap appeared in each formulation procedure. A step that identified a need or an opportunity appeared in many of the procedures and, less frequently, a problem solving or an idea analysis step was observed. However, the problem solving and idea analysis steps had different purposes and produced different rationales

TABLE 3.3 Formulation Types

Process Type/Tactic	*Number*	*Frequency**	*Salient Features*
Idea Process	54	33.1%	*Idea* ultimately used available at outset.
a. Inferred problem tactic	40	(24.5%)	Analysis used to link problems to idea before fine tuning.
b. Concept tactic	14	(8.6%)	Process used to fine tune idea.
Issue Processes	43	26.5%	*Issues* uncovered and used to identify solutions.
a. Inferred solution tactic	31	(19.0%)	Problem analysis used to infer solution.
b. Arena search tactic	12	(7.4%)	Arena identifies topics that guide solution search.
Objective-directed Processes	47	28.8%	*Objectives* used to guide development.
a. Specific objectives tactic	32	(19.6%)	Objectives have specific targets.
b. General objectives tactic	15	(9.2%)	Objectives have general targets.
Reframing Process	19	11.7%	A *Demonstration* of needs or opportunities.
a. Solution intervention tactic	4	(2.4%)	Demonstration of feasible idea, followed by analysis to link them to problems.
b. Problem intervention tactic	15	(9.2%)	New norms created to define problems before analysis used to infer solutions.
TOTAL	163	100.0%	

*Percentage of all cases.

for action. Differences were also noted in the number, nature, and sequence of steps in a formulation procedure. These procedures called for very different types of actions to guide development, suggesting that distinct procedural types emerged from the analysis.

Tables 3.5 and 3.6 summarize the results of statistical tests that determined the success of decisions guided by each of the formulation processes and tactics. The DMRT identifies formulation processes and tactics that produce different results ($p \leq 0.05$). Processes and tactics with similar success indicators have the same letter code, those that differ have a different letter code in Tables 3.5 and 3.6. The statistical analyses suggest that formulation procedure has a significant impact on decision-making success. The nature of these formulation procedures and their success record is presented by beginning with the simplest procedure and moving progressively to the more complex.

(text continues on page 98)

TABLE 3.4 The Nature and Sequence of Steps in the Formulation Procedures

	Step Sequence						
Process/Tactic	*1*	*2*	*3*	*4*	*5*	*6*	*7*
Idea							
• Inferred Problem	Claim	Performance gap	Idea	Idea analysis	Inferred need or opportunity		
Example (NASA program program)	Demonstrate cost consciousness	Increase Utilization	Give hyperbaric oxygen program	Program value for the hospital to a hospital	Opportunity to provide service and enhance prestige		
• Concept	Claim	Performance gap	Idea				
Example (Income tax check-off for natural areas and wildlife protection	Can transport Minnesota tax rules to Ohio	Lack of state funding	Tax check-off idea introduced in Ohio legislature				
Issue							
• Inferred Solution	Claim	Performance gap	Need or opportunity statements	Problem solving	Inferred solution		
Example (Social Security benefit appeals	Volume calls for change in procedure	18 months too long	Need to reduce backlog	Assess problems causing backlog	Pool similar cases for mass handling		
• Arena Search	Claim	Performance gap responses	Arena of search	Arena bound			
Example (Salary	Unequal salaries for males and females	Equity required	Overhaul compensation system	List changes			

(continued)

TABLE 3.4 Continued

	Step Sequence						
Process/Tactic	*1*	*2*	*3*	*4*	*5*	*6*	*7*
Objectives-directed							
• Specific Objectives	Claim	Performance gap	Identify needs or opportunities	Objectives with specific targets	Search for options		
Example (Blue Cross reimbursement	Reduce reimbursement rates due to overstaffing	Hospital overstaffed	Need to cut nursing hours per patient day	Expected labor cost reduction	Search for ways to cut labor cost		
• General Objectives	Claim	Performance gap	Identify needs or opportunities	Objectives with general targets	Search for options		
Example (Revenue enhancement)	Changes in reimbursement policy cut revenues	Lost revenue	Need to increase revenue	Find services with revenue potential	Search for revenue producing serviceds		
Reframing							
• Solution Intervention	Claim	Performance gap	Demonstrate feasible solutions	Reframe with new norms suggested by the solutions	Suggest ideas	Analysis	Infer needs
Example (Materials management)	Problems caused by stockouts	Nature and frequency of stockouts	Examine materials management systems	Most stockouts preventable	Inventory control procedures	Extent of preventahle stockouts	Need to reduce stockouts
• Problem Intervention	Claim	Performance gap	Demonstrate need to act	Reframe with new norms	Specify needs new ideas	Problem solving	Derive ideas
Example (Reorganization)	Most boards have fewer responsibilities	Nature & scope of duties	Clarify expectation	Trimmed list of duties	Need to increase delegation	Consultants develop ideas	Reorganization plan

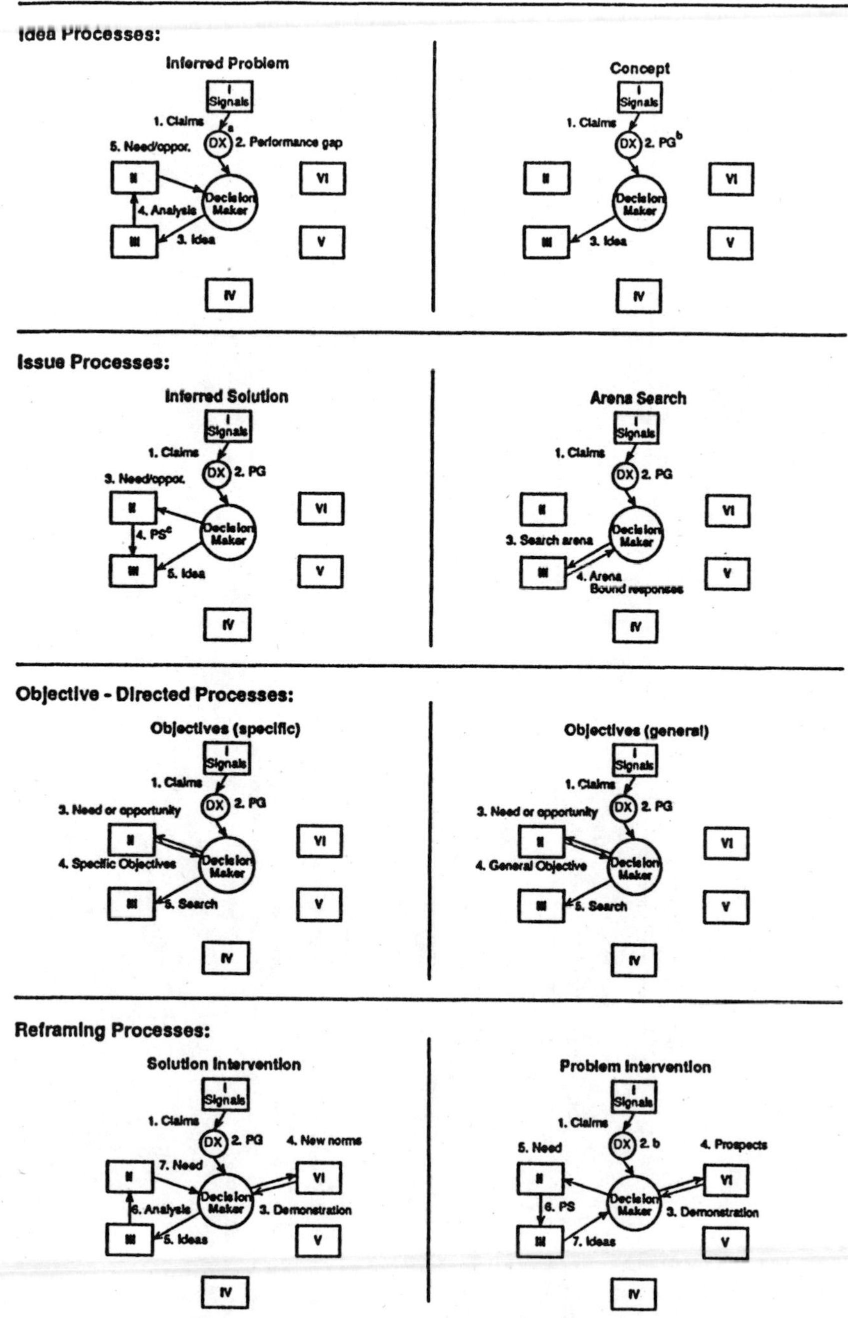

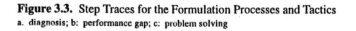

Figure 3.3. Step Traces for the Formulation Processes and Tactics

a. diagnosis; b: performance gap; c: problem solving

TABLE 3.5 The Success of Formulation Processes

Process	*Total Cases*	*Use Rate*	*Initial Decision Adoption*	*DMRT* [a]	*Unqualified Adoption Decision*	*DMRT*	*Decision Merit*	*DMRT*	*Decision Duration*	*DMRT*
Idea	54	33	67% [b]	B	50% [c]	C	4.0 [d]	B	12.0 [e]	B
Issue	43	26	57%	C	39%	D	3.4	C	11.4	B
Objective-directed	47	29	71%	B	60%	B	3.9	B	8.6	A
Reframing	19	12	100%	A	79%	A	4.5	A	8.5	A
Totals	163	100%								
Statistical Significance [f]				$p \leq 0.008$		$p \leq 0.02$		$p \leq 0.01$		$p \leq 0.10$

a. Duncan Multiple Range Test. Letters identify categories that are significantly different ($p \leq 0.05$).
b. Percentage of initially adopted decisions.
c. Percentage of decisions adopted without qualifications.
d. Scale increments: 5 = outstanding, 4 = good, 3 = adequate, 2 = disappointing, 1 = poor.
e. Decision time in months.
f. From a one-way ANOVA.

TABLE 3.6 The Success of Formulation Tactics

Process/Tactic	Total Cases	Use Rate	Initial Decision Adoption	DMRT	Unqualified Decision Adoption	DMRT	Decision Merit	DMR	Decision Duration	DMRT
Idea Process										
a. Inferred problem tactic	40	24.5	61%	D	47%	C	4.1	B	9.1	C
b. Concept Tactic	14	8.6	85%	B	57%	B/C	3.7	B	30.5	E
Issue Process										
a. Inferred solution tactic	31	19.0	56%	D	45%	C	3.4	C	11.2	C
b. Area search tactic	12	7.4	59%	D	25%	D	3.4	C	11.9	C
Objective-directed Processes										
a. Specific objectives tactic	32	19.6	73%	C	62%	B	4.0	B	5.0	A
b. General objectives tactic	15	9.2	67%	C	53%	C	3.9	B	14.5	D
Reframing Process										
a. Solution intervention tactic	4	2.5	100%	A	75%	A	4.5	A	9.5	C
b. Problem intervention tactic	15	9.2	100%	A	80%	A	4.4	A	7.5	B
Totals	63	100%								
Statistical Significance				$p \leq 0.05$		$p \leq 0.05$		$p \leq 0.07$		$p \leq 0.07$

Idea Processes

Idea formulation processes provide direction with a solution (Table 3.3). The decision maker imposes a solution idea on the decision-making process. In the cases, solution ideas emerge from several sources, including the decision maker's visions and beliefs, educational activities, the media, the literature, vendors, joint venture opportunities, the notions of key people, and staff proposals. Development is concerned with certifying the idea's virtues, determining the reactions of key stakeholders to the idea, and suggesting idea refinements. The key features of the idea do not change much during development. Such an approach limits innovation but reduces uncertainty about what will be done. Risk for the decision maker is lowered because surprises that can mobilize unexpected oppositions are unlikely. Also, decision makers' time is not taken up in the idea finding, just idea refining.

Idea formulation processes are related to the work of Cohen et al. (1976) and others who have found that solutions are used to direct a decision-making process. According to Brunsson (1982) and Starbuck (1983), decision makers prefer to use existing ideas because they can quickly provide a way out of the traps posed by seemingly out of control situations.

Idea formulation was observed in 33% of the cases, making it the most frequently observed formulation process. Idea processes had 67% initial adoptions, which fell to 50% when qualifications were considered, produced decisions judged to be "good," and took an average of 12.0 months to carry out (Table 3.5), suggesting that this process is not very successful. Two tactics were used to carry out idea processes, called "concept" and "inferred problem."

Inferred Problem Tactics. The inferred problem tactic matches problems to available ideas. This tactic has steps of claims, performance gap, idea, analysis, and needs or opportunities inferred from the idea analysis (see Figure 3.3). Soelberg (1967) also found evidence that a search for problems follows the selection of a solution. Decision makers applying the inferred problem tactic conduct an analysis to link problems to their idea before development begins. For example, responding to claims calling for cost consciousness, NASA sought ways to increase the use of their hyperbaric oxygen treatment program that provides pressurized oxygen for the decompression of astronauts (Table 3.4). A performance gap of increased utilization was identified. A Florida hospital would be offered NASA's program with the condition that NASA would have priority use during a space flight (the idea). NASA studied hyperbaric oxygen treatment to determine its value to a hospital. The prospect of enhancing a hospital's prestige through a joint venture with NASA made the idea seem salable.

When an inferred problem tactic is used, the decision maker offers an idea and calls for a study to determine problems it could solve. This type of study suggests that difficulties with the idea should be ignored or downplayed, making the decision maker seem manipulative and self-serving. This may explain why the inferred problem tactic is less successful than other tactics (see Table 3.6). Initial adoptions for the inferred problem tactic were 61%, which fell to 47% when qualifications were considered. Decisions were judged to be good and took an average of 9.1 months to carry out. Despite the limited success of this tactic it was applied in nearly 25% of the cases, making it the most frequently used tactic observed in the study.

Concept Tactics. The concept tactic merely imposes an idea, refining it in subsequent process steps. The tactic employs three steps: claims, performance gap, and imposing an idea. The idea directs activity during development. For example, the Department of Natural Resources in Ohio came across an idea, developed by the state of Minnesota, in which taxpayers would check a box on their income tax forms to send a dollar of their refund to support "natural areas" and "wildlife protection" programs. Claims were based on the apparent transportability of the Minnesota program. The lack of state funding for preservation programs identified a performance gap to the DRN Director. The tax check-off idea prompted developmental steps to insure passage of the required legislation. The solar energy case, shown in Figure 3.2, also applied the concept tactic.

The concept tactic had an 8.6% use rate and produced both good and bad results (Table 3.6). This tactic had a very high initial adoption rate of 85%, which fell dramatically (57%) when adoption qualifications were considered. Decision merit was judged to be "somewhat below good." The process took almost 31 months to carry out, which is nearly three times that required by the next most timely tactic ($p \leq 0.05$). This extended time period seems to result because the idea must be tailored to fit its new application (Nutt 1984) and because this tactic produces resentment, producing more opposition than the other tactics. Tactics which appear self-serving and manipulative reduce decision-making success.

Issue Processes

In this type of formulation process an issue is analyzed to produce options for the decision process to consider. This notion of an issue differs from the broader and more general view of an issue in strategic management (e.g., Ansoff 1984, Dutton et al. 1983, Dutton and Jackson 1987). The narrower and more concrete notion of a process that deals with a "matter under dispute" is intended.

The issue identifies a concern or difficulty. Problems implied by the concern or difficulty are explored to extract solution clues. Decision makers then become problem solvers, attempting to tease solutions from the problem analysis (e.g., Maier 1970). This approach can be effective if problems become clear following analysis. If not, symptoms may be attacked and the decision process may fail to deal with important concerns that lie behind the symptoms (Kolb 1983).

Issue processes were observed in 26% of the cases. Dealing with issues was the least effective process observed in the study ($p \leq 0.05$). Issue processes produced decisions with the lowest rate of initial adoption (57%) and the lowest unqualified adoption rate (39%), decisions with the least merit (judged to be between adequate and good), and took as long to carry out as any of the other processes (Table 3.5). Two tactics were observed as attempts were made to extract solutions from a problem assessment called "inferred solution" and "arena search."

Inferred Solution Tactics. The inferred solution tactic extracts a solution from a problem statement. The steps are claims, performance gaps, statement of needs or opportunities, analysis of needs or opportunities, and seeking a solution that deals with the needs or opportunities (Figure 3.3). For example, claims were made that the "appeals process" in a state department providing social security benefits could not deal with the volume of eases without a change in procedure (Table 3.4). After considerable debate, a backlog of 18 months in dispositions was termed excessive, creating a performance gap. The need to reduce the backlog led to problem solving which came up with a pooling idea that grouped similar cases for mass handling.

The inferred solution tactic was used in 19% of the cases. For this tactic initial adoptions were 56%, unqualified adoptions were 45%, decision merit was between adequate and good, and the process took 11.2 months to carry out (Table 3.6). Limiting a solution search to the vicinity of a presumed problem seems to restrict ideas which lower success.

Arena Search Tactics. The arena search tactic identifies an arena instead of a problem to guide the search for solutions. The steps are claims, performance gap, arena of search, and arena bound responses (see Figure 3.3). For example, key people in a firm claimed that inequities in salaries between males and females in comparable jobs would create charges of discrimination (Table 3.4). The need for equity became the performance gap. A search for ways to overhaul the compensation system was then mounted. The arena, overhaul the compensation system, directed developmental activities to make changes in the compensation procedures. Rather than a problem to be overcome, as in the inferred solution tactic, the arena identifies where to search for solutions.

The arena search tactic was comparatively rare, occurring in just 7.4% of the cases. This tactic had fewer unqualified adoptions than the inferred solution tactic but was similar in timeliness and merit (Table 3.6). Initial adoptions for arena searches were 59%, which plummeted to 25% when qualifications were considered. Decisions were judged to be adequate to good and took an average of 11.9 months to complete.

Objective-Directed Processes

Objective-directed formulation processes use expectations (e.g., missions, aims, or goals) to guide developmental activities. Intentions are stated in terms of desired results, such as reduce cost or increase capacity. A remedy is not suggested or implied. There is considerable freedom to search for a way to meet stated aims during development. This may encourage innovations and increase decision-making cost.

Objective-directed formulation processes were observed in 29% of the cases. Direction setting with objectives was the second most successful process type in the study. These decisions had a 71% initial adoption rate and an unqualified adoption rate of 60%, produced outcomes judged to be "good," and were quite timely, taking significantly less time to carry out than all but one other formulation process (Table 3.5). The tactics that decision makers use to set objectives call for a general target (e.g., reduce cost) or a specific target (e.g., reduce costs by 20%).

Specific Objectives Tactics. Steps of claims, performance gap, identify needs or opportunities, statement of objective with specific targets, and an unrestricted search for options are used in the specific objectives tactic (see Figure 3.3). For example, a hospital responded to Blue Cross claims of overstaffing and threats to reduce reimbursement rates by identifying excessive labor cost as the performance gap, suggesting the need to cut nursing hours per patient day (Table 3.4). Objectives targeted the required amount of labor cost reduction and a search was mounted to find ways to cut labor cost. Other examples of specific objectives include making internal operations self-supporting and identifying specific expectations for profit or utilization.

The specific objectives tactic was used in 20% of the cases. This tactic led to 73% initial adoptions, 62% ultimate adoptions producing "good" decisions in an average of 5 months (Table 3.6). Decisions made using specific objectives had very good outcomes.

General Objectives Tactics. The general objectives tactic had the same steps as the specific objectives tactic (Figure 3.6) but created expectations such as the needs to improve cost and profit performance that did not specify a target amount of cost or profit. For example, key people in a hospital claimed that declining revenues were caused by changes in the reimbursement policies of Medicaid and insurance carriers (see Table 3.4). The changes limited patient revenues to actual cost and not institutionally set charges, sharply reducing hospital revenue. The performance gap identified lost revenues. The need to increase revenue led to an objective of funding new services with a revenue enhancement potential. Suggestions were systematically reviewed to determine their revenue prospects.

General objectives was used in 9.2% of the cases. This tactic had 67% initial adoptions and 53% ultimate adoptions, producing "good" decisions in 14.5 months (Table 3.6). Both specific and general objectives lead to good decisions. These findings give *some* support to laboratory studies reported by Locke et al. (1981), who found that a specific objective improves results. In real decisions considered in this study, this distinction does *not* hold for merit or initial adoptions. However, specificity does shorten the decision process and results in decisions that are more apt to be sustained. With general objectives, a demonstration that aims have been met may take longer because the information to support such a demonstration can be argumentative, which can lengthen the decision process.

Reframing Processes

Decision makers who apply a reframing formulation process are careful to justify the need to act, using either solutions or problems as the focus of a demonstration that calls for action. Reframing was the most successful formulation process, but was infrequently used, being observed in less than 12% of the cases. As shown in Table 3.5, *all* of the decisions made using this formulation process were initially adopted, in the shortest time period (8.5 months), with some of the best results. The average time period was three or more months shorter than issue and idea formulation processes and decisions were rated between good and outstanding, compared to the next highest rated formulation process that produced "good" results. Finally, a 79% unqualified rate of adoption, treating adoption delays and incomplete adoptions as failures, had almost 20% more adoptions than the next best formulation process. Two tactics emerged from an analysis of the cases called solution intervention and problem intervention.

Solution Intervention Tactics. This tactic uses potential solutions to demonstrate opportunities for action. The solution intervention tactic's steps are claims, performance gap, solution demonstrations, norms determined from expected performance using these solutions, ideas, ideas analyses, and inferred needs from the idea analysis (Figure 3.3). Each of these steps occurred before idea development was attempted. To illustrate, claims in one of the cases called attention to supply item stockouts (see Table 3.4). The nature and frequency of the stockouts suggested a performance gap. Material management programs were described by the firm's vice president who demonstrated that stockouts seldom occur in organizations that have up-to-date management procedures. The inventory control procedures in the material management systems were analyzed to identify expected stockout frequency. This led to an agreement that stockouts could be prevented and that new inventory management practices should be developed.

Decision makers who use the solution intervention tactic are careful to deal with negative impressions that can be created by imposing ideas on a decision process. The decision maker establishes norms, shows that performance is subpar, and then demonstrates new ways to act that can cope with these performance shortfalls. These ideas are subjected to careful study, matching their attributes to needs identified by the performance failure. The decision maker steers the decision process using these steps, making action seem essential by offering several ideas that can be modified or even discarded during development.

The additions of norming and need demonstration steps distinguish the solution intervention tactic from the concept and inferred problem tactics. Demonstrating the need for action removes many of the self-serving and manipulative features found in the idea formulation process and its tactics which stress expediency. Solution intervention tactics stress tact and diplomacy. Also, a means is not imposed. Instead options are provided for further study. The search for solutions, however, is more restricted than with tactics using objectives. The options offered during solution intervention become the focus of study which seldom ventures beyond the type of solutions that are implied. For example, decisions that examine inventory control system options do not shift their focus to consider new topics, such as revenue enhancement options.

The solution intervention tactic was applied in 2.4% of the cases, making it the least frequently used tactic observed in the study. However, the solution intervention tactic produced some of the most successful decisions in the study. The solution intervention tactic had a 100% initial adoption rate, the third shortest decision duration of 9.5 months, and a decision merit rating of between good and outstanding (Table 3.6). Seventy five percent of the decisions that apply the solution intervention tactic were adopted without qualifications. This increase in success, compared to the inferred problem and concept tactics, is attributed to the justification steps in the solution intervention tactic which diplomatically demonstrated the need for action.

Problem Intervention Tactics. The problem intervention tactic is similar to the solution intervention tactic, except that solutions are inferred. Demonstrations center on needs, showing that change is necessary, but do not offer specifics about what to do. The decision maker norms the situation, terming performance subpar. After demonstrating a performance shortfall a study of the needs implied by this low performance is carried out and solution ideas are elicited by problem-solving activity. Steps are claims, performance gap, demonstrations, identify new expectations, specify needs, problem solving, and derive ideas (Figure 3.6). For example, a corporate reorganization decision was initiated by members of a firm's board of directors who had become frustrated with the scope of their responsibilities (Table 3.4). They claimed that most boards have much less to do. The nature and scope of these responsibilities became a performance gap. The board justified the need for action by listing what was and was not expected of a board member in other companies. A trimmed list of responsibilities was drawn from these practices to set new norms, justifying the need for action. The need to increase delegation to top management was then specified. Consultants were hired to propose solutions that reduced the board's oversight responsibilities through delegation, retaining only fiduciary responsibilities for the board.

Decision makers who apply the problem intervention tactic help the organization see the value of exploring new practices by demonstrating the need for and feasibility of action. Norms are selected that heighten expectation drawing on the performance of competitors, previous work experiences, and innovations. The norm is applied to indicate performance shortfalls that call for action. Because key people see the range of possibilities being considered, they can shed preconceptions which limit search during problem solving. In contrast, the inferred solution and arena search tactics focus attention on narrowly construed statements of dysfunctions to be overcome. The norm step helps decision makers using the problem intervention tactic to open the decision process to possibilities before the narrowing that occurs during problem solving. This is like steps advocated to promote creativity such as the red light-green light dictums of Guilford (1967), the convergence-divergence approach of de Bono (1973), and Maier's (1970) focus in-focus out suggestions. Steps that broaden and then narrow distinguish problem intervention tactics from other tactics.

The problem intervention tactic was used in 9.2% of the cases. This tactic had a success record much like the solution intervention tactic, but took less time. The problem intervention tactic produced more adoptions and higher decision merit than any of the other tactics. As noted in Table 3.6, this tactic had a 100% initial adoption rate and a 80% unqualified adoption rate, required 7.5 months to complete, and produced decisions judged to be between good and outstanding.

CONCLUSIONS

The formulation practices of organizational decision makers were found to have qualitative differences in procedure and quantitative differences in their success. Several types of formulation procedures were identified. Reframing demonstrates the need for and feasibility of new practices. Objectives provide targets that encourage an unrestricted search for solutions. Issues infer solutions from problems and concerns. Ideas push preconceived solutions. The nature, number, and sequence of the steps in these formulation procedures produced different decision-making directions, rationales, and success. Reframing is far more successful than any other formulation procedure. Objectives are also quite successful, although not as good as reframing. Success falls when preconceived ideas or problem solving are used. Both reframing and objectives produce better and more timely decisions. These findings will be used to offer advice to decision makers, extend decision-making theory, theory build, and suggest further research needs.

Several ways to improve decision-making practice can be suggested. First, formulation procedures have rates of use and success records that fail to match. The most successful tactics are infrequently used and the least successful are frequently used. Replacing formulation by issues and ideas with reframing or objectives should improve success. Second, the search for ideas can be carried out using problem analysis or objectives. Analysis of problems prompts a restricted search which is less successful than using objectives which mount an open, unrestricted search. For instance, a decision process can be directed to deal with training, such as "the problem with this organization is poor training," as in the Toyota dealer case. This limits search to training solutions. By implying a type of solution, search becomes narrow and overly focused (Nutt 1989). Objectives provide a more useful direction and analysis a less useful direction during decision making. Third, the cases suggest that problem solving is prone to failure. This may stem from the defensive behavior evoked in people who see themselves as responsible for the problem. Fourth, combining the demonstration and norming steps in reframing with specific objectives seems desirable. Demonstrating the need to act appears to be the crucial step which distinguishes reframing from the less successful formulation procedures. The specific objectives tactic could incorporate demonstration and norming steps without altering the logic of objective setting and the norm would suggest an attainable target for the objective.

Extensions to decision-making theory can be drawn from the logic applied by the most successful process: reframing. Reframing seems to work because it adheres to steps called for in learning and development (Pettigrew 1985). When formulation quickly narrows to dysfunctions or displaces to ideas, little learning can occur. By opening up the decision process to new possibilities, stakeholders are more apt to recognize the value of new ideas. This opening up allows people to move away from stereotyped responses and traditional ways of acting.

Other extensions to decision-making theory can be made by comparing the results of this study with other descriptions of formulation procedure (e.g., Soelberg 1967, Bower 1972, Witte 1972, Mintzberg et al. 1976, Pettigrew 1985.) For example, Mintzberg et al. (1976) found that formulation has recognition and diagnostic steps but say little about how these steps are carried out. This study provides additional detail, identifying the type of information that is collected and the action-taking steps that are carried out to set the directions that guide development. These findings have use at two levels. At the meta level, the findings of the study describe the types of directions and justifications for action that will be more and less successful. At the focal level, the study offers a detailed listing of steps making formulation procedure explicit as well as providing evaluation of each procedure's success. The classification framework and the method of profiling decisions using the framework allowed both concepts and procedural specifics to be identified. This approach can be used by other researchers to carry out process studies of decision making.

Themes of power, ambiguity, politics, uncertainty, and paradox can be inferred from the findings of the study suggesting ideas for theory building. Powerful decision makers often impose their ideas on a decision process. Also, solutions cropped up which seduced decision makers. Seizing such "opportunities" is viewed as a pragmatic way to take decisive action. However, imposing a solution frequently leads to failure. This suggests that sense making (Weick 1979) and garbage can models (Cohen et al. 1976) and the like describe what decision makers *prefer* to do but do *not* capture what decision makers *should* do, again pointing out the tendency to mix description with prescription in the decision literature. Preconceived solutions and the constraints on search that they impose led to poor results.

When decision makers impose "an answer" they create a clarity of purpose that is misleading. Important sources of ambiguity and uncertainty are swept aside. Consider the heat pump case (Figure 3.2). After the heat pump concept had been accepted by the company CEO, no one was prepared to challenge its merit. The expectation of 30% increase in sales was never validated or even discussed with anyone in the organization as the decision process unfolded. Also, decisions formulated by an idea seldom go beyond that idea. People become fixated with the idea and do not ask reframing questions, such as "how do we find a product that complements our air-conditioning business" or pose objectives, such as "how do we increase sales." The merits of concepts were never questioned in the cases. Decisions made in haste with poor information were not reviewed to verify the information. People also seem reluctant to carry bad news (the idea does not work), as eight years of repeated failure in the heat pump case suggests.

As Wildavsky (1979) points out, managers do not know what they want until they can see what they can get. Having an answer sweeps away this ambiguity and uncertainty. However, beginning with an answer can be rash because decision making is not based on a clear understanding of what is needed. Instead, the decision process explores the virtues of an idea and reactions of key people to it. The more blatant this behavior becomes the more time decision makers seem to spend defending the idea. Decision makers who take steps to justify the need to act, using solution intervention or problem intervention tactics, cut the duration of the decision process by 300%. Managing the politics of the situation with these steps greatly improves the prospect of decision success. Ideas can be helpful when used to illustrate the benefits of new practices. These benefits are lost if the options considered are limited to the initial set of ideas. Treating ideas as possibilities, as in solution intervention tactics, improves the adoption prospects and merit of a decision.

Interest in formulation has been prompted by the *paradoxes* associated with the identification and verification of ways to direct a decision process (Rumelt 1978, Nutt 1979, Volkema 1983). By selecting a direction one sets aside an array of potentially relevant directions. Post-decision review often reveals that attending to some of the directions that were set aside would have created significant opportunities and advantages. As a result, managers are admonished to avoid solving the "wrong problem," which Raiffa (1968) calls the "error of the third kind." However, neither Raiffa nor his followers have provided tests to determine if the directions under consideration will misdirect a decision process. Consider the Toyota dealer case. The linkage of lost sales and declining profits to sales force training and inculturation proved to be incorrect, but what tests could have been applied to find a more appropriate direction for this decision process?

Although this question poses problems of logic that may never be fully answered, directions can be tested. One approach examines directions that are both narrower and broader in scope than the preferred direction, before committing to a direction. Consider the Toyota case. The cultural training direction adopted by the car dealer could have been expanded and narrowed in useful ways. A narrower view, for example, could focus on the behavior of salespersons, attempting to identify things that are turning off customers. Action would be limited to modifying undesirable behavior. A broader view could look for ways to expand profits bringing into view options such as promotions, buyer incentives, cost cutting, and pricing policy. The direction is broadened by considering ways to increase profits. These directions have a hierarchical relationship. The decision maker must solve the behavioral problem to do training and training must be adequate before promotions, cost-cutting, and the like can work. Examining directions in this way can bring to light hidden difficulties that have eluded the decision maker's attention and must be dealt with to ensure good results. Because none of the decision makers in the cases developed directions in this way the cases cannot be used to evaluate the suggested test. Further research will be required to verify its merit.

Several limitations to this research should be noted. These limitations stem from the database, decision adoption rates, the nature of decisions examined, and the influence of context. Each suggests future research efforts.

Only 16% of the cases were carried out in firms. As a result, the database may not fully capture decision making in the private sector. The sector distinctions noted by Rainey et al. (1976), among others, suggest that differences among sectors may arise. Sector differences should be explored in subsequent research.

The initial adoption rates of 70% in the cases may overstate the number of decisions that are implemented by organizations. Allowing the contact person to select a case makes it easier to get a case but also makes it unlikely that failed decisions and particularly bad practice would be suggested. As a result, the rate of decision failure may be understated, suggesting that *more* than 30% of the decisions made by organizations fail. It also suggests that the worst examples of decision practice may have been excluded from the cases. However, there is no practical way to determine the "true" rate of failure or to insure that a representative number of decision "debacles" have been included in a case data \base.

Intervening variables of problem type and context are likely to influence a decision process and its effectiveness, suggesting conditions under which a formulation tactic can be best used. In addition to sector, intervening factors include urgency, extent of support (e.g., budget and staff), type of decision (internal operations, products, etc.), and political factors (decision-maker level, leverage, savvy, etc.). A preliminary assessment of politics and organizational level suggests that the conclusions cited in this chapter hold for both top managers (CEOs, COOs, and CFOs) and middle managers, no matter how well they handle implementation. Laying out the qualifications that these factors offer goes beyond what can be accomplished in a single chapter. Future research will be needed to determine how each of these factors influences formulation. In such an effort, factors such as "interests" (Hickson et al. 1986), "idea champions" (Bower 1972), and implementation (Nutt 1986) should be considered.

Another needed study would explore the action-taking steps that were common to all of the formulation tactics. For instance, claims derived from industry reports may be handled differently during formulation than those derived from an MIS or liaison arrangements, and with different results. Performance gaps can be clearly articulated, such as reaching for an industry leader's profit, or vague, such as improving image. Alternatives can be single or multiple, specific or general, etc. Differences in the basis for claims made, performance gap clarity, and the nature of alternatives may add important qualifications to the success of formulation procedures.

ACKNOWLEDGMENTS

The helpful comments of Robert Backoff, David Landsbergen, Dick Daft, and the anonymous referees are gratefully acknowledged.

REFERENCES

Ansoff, H. I. (1984), *Implanting Strategic Management,* Englewood Cliffs, NJ: Prentice Hall.

Bartlett, F. C. (1954), *Remembering: A Study in Experimental and Social Psychology,* Cambridge, MA: Harvard University Press.

Beyer, J. M. and H. M. Trice (1978), *Implementing Changes: Alcoholism Policies in Work Organizations,* New York: Free Press.

Billings, R. S., T. W. Milburn, and M. Shaalman, (1980), "A Model of Crisis Perception: A Theoretical & Empirical Analysis," *Administrative Science Quarterly,* 25, 300-316.

Bower, J. L. (1972), *Managing the Resource Allocation Process: A Study of Corporate Planning and Investment,* Homewood, IL: Irwin.

Brunsson, N. (1982), "The Irrationality of Action and Action Rationality: Decisions, Ideologies, and Organizational Actions," *Journal of Management Studies,* 19, 29-44.

Campbell, D. T. and D. W. Fiske (1959), "Convergent and Discriminant Validation by the Multitrait-Multimethod Matrix," *Psychological Bulletin,* 56, 81-105.

Churchman, C. W. (1975), "Theories of Implementation," in R. L. Schultz and D. P. Slevin (Eds.), *Implementing Operations Research/Management Science,* New York: Elsevier.

Cohen, M. D., J. P. March, and J. P. Olsen (1976), "A Garbage Can Model of Organizational Choice," *Administrative Science Quarterly,* 17, 1-25.

Cyert, R. M. and J. G. March (1963), *A Behavioral Theory of the Firm,* Englewood Cliffs, NJ: Prentice Hall.

de Bono, E. (1973), *Lateral Thinking,* New York: Harper.

Downs, A. (1967), *Inside Bureaucracy,* Boston: Little, Brown, 63.

Dunn, W. N. (1981), *Public Policy Analysis*, Englewood Cliffs, NJ: Prentice Hall.

Dutton J. E., L. Fahey, and V. K. Narayanan (1983), "Toward Understanding Strategic Issue Diagnosis," *Strategic Management Journal*, 4, 307-323.

——— and S. E. Jackson (1987), "Categorizing Strategic Issues: Links to Organizational Action," *Academy of Management Review*, 12, 76-90.

Fredrickson, J. W. (1985), "Effects of Decision Motive and Organizational Performance Level on Strategic Decision Processes," *Academy of Management Journal*, 28, 821-843.

Freeman, R. E. (1983), *Strategic Management: A Stakeholder Approach*, New York: Pitman.

Guilford, J. P. (1967), *The Nature of Human Intelligence*, New York: McGraw-Hill.

Hage, J. and M. Aiken (1970), *Social Change in Complex Organizations*, New York: Random House.

Hickson, D, R. Butler, D. Gray, G. Mallory, and D. Wilson (1986), *Top Decisions: Strategic Decision Making in Organizations*, San Francisco: Jossey-Bass.

Huber, G. P. and D. Power, (1985), "Retrospective Reports of Strategic Level Managers: Guidelines for Increasing Their Accuracy," *Strategic Management Journal*, 6, 171-180.

Kolb, D. A. (1983), "Problem Management: Warning from Experience," in S. Srivastra (Ed.), *The Executive Mind*, San Francisco: Jossey-Bass, 109-143.

Locke, E. A., K. N. Shaw, L. M. Saari, and G. P. Latham (1981), "Goal Setting and Task Performance 1969-1980," *Psychological Bulletin*, 90, 125-152.

Lyles, M. A. (1981), "Formulating Strategic Problems: Empirical Analysis and Model Development," *Strategic Management Journal*, 2, 61-75.

MacCrimmon, K. R. and R. N. Taylor (1976), "Decision Making and Problem Solving," in M. Dunnette (Ed.), *Handbook of Industrial and Organizational Psychology*, Chicago: Rand McNally.

Maier, N. R. F. (1970), *Problem Solving and Creativity: In Individuals and Groups*, New York: Brooks-Cole.

March, J. G. (1981), "Footnotes to Organizational Change," *Administrative Science Quarterly*, 26, 4, 563-577.

McKelvey, B. (1978), "Organizational Systematics: Taxonomic Lessons from Biology," *Management Science*, 24, 13, 1428-1449.

Mintzberg, H., D. Raisinghani, and A. Theoret (1976), "The Structure of Unstructured Decision Processes," *Administrative Science Quarterly*, 21, 2, 246-275.

Nadler, G. (1981), *The Planning and Design Approach*, New York: John Wiley.

Nutt, P. C. (1979), "Calling Out and Calling Off the Dogs: Managerial Diagnosis in Organizations," *Academy of Management Review*, 4, 2, 203-214.

——— (1984), "Types of Organizational Decision Processes," *Administrative Science Quarterly*, 29, 3, 414-450.

——— (1992), *Managing Planned Change*, New York: Macmillan.

——— (1986), "The Tactics of Implementation," *Academy of Management Journal*, 29, 2, 230-261.

——— (1989), *Making Tough Decisions*, San Francisco: Jossey-Bass.

——— and R. B. Backoff (1987), "A Strategic Management Process for Public and Third Sector Organizations," *American Journal of Planning* (Winter), 44-59.

——— and ——— (1986), "Mutual Understanding and Its Impact on Formulation During Decision Making," *Technological Forecasting and Social Change*, 29, 13-31.

——— and ——— (1992), *The Strategic Management of Public and Third Sector Organizations*, San Francisco: Jossey-Bass.

Pettigrew, A. (1985), *The Awakening Giant: Continuity and Change at ICI*, Oxford: Blackwell.

Pike, R. L. (1967), *Language in Relation to a Unified Theory of the Structure of Human Behavior*, The Hague: Mouton.

Pounds, W. (1969), "The Process of Problem Finding," *Industrial Management Review* (Fall), 1-19.

Quinn, J. B. (1981), "Managing Strategic Change," *Sloan Management Review* (Spring), 19-34.

Quinn, R. A. (1988), *Beyond Rational Management,* San Francisco: Jossey-Bass.

Raiffa, H. (1968), *Decision Analysis,* Reading, MA: Addison-Wesley.

Rainey, H. G., R. W. Backoff, and C. H. Levine (1976), "Comparing Public and Private Organizations," *Public Administration Review* (March/April), 233-244.

Rumelt, R. P. (1978), "Evaluation of S Strategy: Theory & Models," in D. Schendel and C. Hofer (Eds.), *Strategic Management,* Boston: Little, Brown.

Schendel, D. E. and C. W. Hofer (1979), *Strategic Management,* Boston: Little, Brown.

Schön, D. A. (1987), *Educating the Reflective Practitioner,* San Francisco: Jossey-Bass.

Simon, H. A. (1977), *The New Science of Management Decision,* Englewood Cliffs, NJ: Prentice Hall.

Slovic, P., Fischhoff, S., and S. Lichtenstein (1977), "Behavioral Decision Theory," *Annual Review of Psychology,* 6, 649-744.

Soelberg, P. O. (1967), "Unprogrammed Decision Making," *Industrial Management Review* (Spring), 19-29.

Starbuck, W. H. (1983), "Organizations as Action Generations," *American Sociological Review,* 48, 91-102.

Volkema, R. (1983), "Problem Formulation in Planning and Design," *Management Science,* 29, 6, 639-652.

Weick, K. (1979), *The Social Psychology of Organizing* (2nd ed.), Reading, MA: Addison-Wesley.

Wildavsky, A. (1979), *Speaking Truth to Power,* Chapter 5, "Between Planning and Politics: Intellect vs. Interaction as Analysis," Boston: Little, Brown.

Witte, E. (1972), "Field Research on Complex Decision-Making Process—The Phase Theory," *International Studies of Management and Organization,* 156-182.

Yin, Robert (1985), *Case Study Research: Design and Methods,* Beverly Hills, CA: Sage.

——— (1981), "The Case Study Crisis: Some Answers," *Administrative Science Quarterly,* 26, 1, 58-65.

Zaltman, G. R. Duncan, and J. Holbeck (1973), *Innovations in Organizations,* New York: Wiley-Interscience.

4

Executive Judgment, Organizational Congruence, and Firm Performance

RICHARD L. PRIEM

Contingency theory suggests that a match among business-level strategy, organizational structure, and the competitive environment is necessary for high performance. This research asks whether manufacturing firm chief executives judge as "good" those strategy-structure-environment matches recommended by contingency theory. Knowledge of executive judgment is particularly important for two reasons. First, judgment—defined as an individual's understanding of relationships among objects—governs the strategic choices made by top managers. Second, prescriptive strategy theories recommend the judgments that executives "should" use, but there is little evidence specifically tying executive judgment to firm performance.

Part of this research is essentially a "laboratory" study of executive judgment that was conducted in the field. Manufacturing firm chief executives' beliefs about cause-and-effect relationships among business-level strategy, structure, environment and performance were ascertained through a judgment task. The second part of the study was a field survey wherein other top executives of each firm reported on their firm's actual strategy, strategy-making processes, structure, competitive environment, and performance. Both the chief executives' judgments and the actual alignments were compared to the matches recommended as "best" by contingency theory. The hypotheses tested link the two parts of the study. Some predict relationships between judgment policies, realized alignments, and firm performance. Others attempt to identify factors that may lead to differences in executives' judgments.

This chapter originally appeared in *Organization Science,* Vol. 5, No. 3, August 1994.

Results indicate that chief executive judgment is strongly related to the actual organizational alignment. Further, judgment policies that favor the strategy-structure-environment matches recommended by contingency theory produce higher performance than do other judgment policies. No support was found for either executive experience or quality of the firm's strategy-making process as factors leading to executive judgment. These results suggest that the judgment of top executives is important to both organizational alignment and firm performance.

(CHIEF EXECUTIVE; MANAGERIAL JUDGMENT;
CONJOINT ANALYSIS; CONTINGENCY THEORY;
STRATEGIC CHOICE; BUSINESS-LEVEL STRATEGY)

Hambrick and Mason's (1984) "upper echelons" perspective has renewed research interest in top managers and top management teams, and in their influence on organizations. Studies are successfully linking top management characteristics to organizational outcomes, providing considerable support for the efficacy of the upper echelons approach (e.g., Eisenhardt and Schoonhoven 1990, Finkelstein and Hambrick 1990, Norburn and Birley 1988, Thomas et al. 1991, Wiersema and Bantel 1992). Top managers *do* appear to matter. Recent studies of top managers, however, are insufficiently precise to provide evidence as to *how* they may matter. Top managers may influence organizations through judgment and choice, as suggested by Hambrick and Mason (1984). Alternately, top managers may exert influence through their ability to organize, or their charisma, or their skill at delegation, as well as *or instead* of through their judgment.

Judgment, defined as an individual's understanding of relationships among objects, is particularly important for two reasons. First, executive judgment guides the strategic choices that are central to the strategy concept (Child 1972). Schoemaker (1990), for example, argues that executive judgment represents an important source of sustainable competitive advantage. Penrose asserts similarly that an executive's "knowledge of the external world" is a key productive resource for the firm (1959, p. 79). Second, the normative theories that result from strategy content or process studies are actually recommended judgments; they prescribe beliefs about causal relationships that managers "should" adopt in making strategic choices. Executive judgment is thus fundamental to both descriptive and prescriptive strategy theory.

Part of the research presented in this chapter is essentially a "laboratory" study of executive strategic judgment that was conducted in field settings. Chief executive officers (CEOs) of manufacturing firms were individually presented with the same judgment task. The task involves evaluating the desirability of different combinations of strategy, structure, and environment for manufacturing firms. Each CEO completed the task in the presence of the researcher, following identical instructions, in the CEO's office. The task was designed to allow the researcher to ascertain the *judgment policy* employed by each executive in evaluating different strategy-structure-environment alignments. An analogous situation would be one wherein a military officer is asked to perform a combat simulation exercise offering numerous alternatives, and then his or her understanding of key causal relationships associated with victory is evaluated based on decisions made during the exercise. As would be expected in a laboratory study, this portion of the research exhibits relatively high precision (McGrath 1982). The second part of the study was a field survey wherein *other* top executives at each manufacturing firm reported on the firm's *actual* strategy, strategy-making processes, structure, competitive environment, and performance on scales frequently used in organization research (e.g., the Aston studies). This portion of the research is higher on the contextual realism dimension (McGrath 1982).

The hypotheses tested link the two parts of the study. Some hypotheses predict relationships between CEO judgment policies and tangible firm outcomes. Others predict relationships between possible judgment antecedents and CEO judgment. Thus, this chapter takes a first step toward evaluating the degree to which the *judgments* of top managers matter to firm outcomes, and the degree to which those judgments may be predicted by executive- or firm-level characteristics. The following section explores judgment and choice. Contingency theories are suggested as particularly effective platforms from which to study managerial judgment. Then, possible antecedents to managerial judgment are discussed. Next, details of the method, data analysis, and results of the field research are presented. Finally, implications are suggested for future strategic management research.

THEORETICAL BACKGROUND AND RELEVANT RESEARCH

The Hambrick and Mason model suggests that observable characteristics of top managers are "determinants of strategic choices and, through these choices, of organizational performance" (1984, p. 197). However, strategic choices are represented in this model by organizational *outcomes* such as the degrees of product innovation, diversification, or plant newness. Executive judgment and choice are unmeasured variables that are assumed to intervene between executive demographic characteristics and tangible firm-level outcomes.

This study, however, separates executive judgment from organizational outcomes. This separation parallels Mintzberg and Waters' (1985) distinction between intended and realized strategies. Intended strategies are those intentionally sought by decision makers based on their judgment, realized strategies are the tangible strategic outcomes. The intentions of decision makers may *or may not* be realized. The separation of judgment from achieved outcomes is a necessary first step in including judgment as a key variable in models of organizations.

Executive Judgment and Contingency Theory

Conceptual and empirical work on managerial cognitions has focused on cognitive biases, categorizations, or perceptions (e.g., Dutton et al. 1989, Dutton et al. 1983, Jackson and Dutton 1988, Schwenk 1988). Less attention has been paid to the cognitive structures (i.e., judgment policies) that reflect cause-and-effect relations seen by executives (Fahey and Narayanan 1989, Schoemaker 1990, and Stubbart 1989 are exceptions). One base for evaluating executives' judgment policies is the cause-and-effect relationships previously identified through organizational research.

Since contingency theories have long been influential in strategy and organization studies (Tosi and Slocum 1984, Venkatraman 1989), one would expect that executives may frequently be required to make decisions based on contingent judgment policies. Early contingency theories focused on how the fit between two variables might influence firm performance. These bivariate contingency theories, at the business-level, emphasized variously structure-environment alignment (e.g., Burns and Stalker 1961, Lawrence and Lorsch 1967, Thompson 1967), strategy-structure alignment (e.g., Miller 1986, Porter 1980), or strategy-environment alignment (Miller 1988, White 1986). More recently, multivariate or configuration approaches have been advocated (e.g., Miller and Mintzberg 1984, Miller 1986), and studies have examined the influence of simultaneous strategy-structure-environment alignments on firm performance (Lenz 1980, Miller 1987, 1988, Miller et al. 1988).

Both the bivariate and multivariate contingency research suggests that certain business-level strategy-structure-environment alignments are associated with high performance. Cost leadership strategies have been suggested to be most effective when implemented through structures that emphasize formalization, centralization, and specialization (Porter 1980). Stable environments encourage the realization of efficiency-based competitive advantage (Kim and Lim 1988, Miller 1988) and are appropriate settings for such mechanistic structures (Burns and Stalker 1961, Child 1975, Tung 1979). On the other hand, differentiation strategies are more effective in dynamic environments and are best implemented through organic structures. These extreme alignments are representative of the *many* high performance alignments that are theoretically possible in contingency formulations. For example, an appropriate alignment of strategy and structure may be found for any level of environmental uncertainty.

Executive Judgment, Organizational Design Outcomes, and Firm Performance

The contingent strategy-structure-environment relationships with performance suggest that effective strategists must make decisions while taking into account the overarching constraints of contingency theory. However, all strategists may not see these relationships in the same way. Some executives' judgment policies may match the prescriptions of contingency theory; other executives' judgments may be different from, or even counter to, the theory.

For example, one strategist may make alignment choices based on the judgment that an organic structure is *always* superior to a mechanistic structure. Since this judgment policy is not contingent, it cannot be considered to be consistent with the prescriptions of contingency theory (e.g., Burns and Stalker 1961). Another strategist may make alignment choices based on the judgment that organic structures are appropriate in stable environments, but mechanistic structures are appropriate in dynamic environments. This second judgment policy is contingent, but is directly *opposite to* the prescriptions of contingency theory. Finally, a third strategist may make alignment choices based on the judgment that stable environments call for more mechanistic structures, while dynamic environments call for more organic structures. This last judgment is consistent with contingency theory. Strategists' judgments can similarly be evaluated for the strategy-structure and strategy-environment contingencies.

The strategic choice perspective suggests that choices made by top managers influence organizational design outcomes. This perspective has long been advanced by strategy scholars (Andrews 1971, Ansoff 1965, Bourgeois 1984, Child 1972), and has recently found additional support in the empirical work of organization researchers (e.g., Oliver 1988, Thomas 1988). One would therefore expect that CEO judgment policies will be related to organizational outcomes (Gioia and Poole 1984, Lord and Kernan 1987), and that the firms of those CEOs whose judgment policies are consistent with normative contingency theory should indeed exhibit a strategy-structure-environment alignment that would be deemed appropriate by contingency theories (i.e., an alignment exhibiting good fit). Thus, the following descriptive hypothesis may be advanced.

H1. *CEO judgment policies for business-level strategy-structure-environment alignment will be related to the firm's actual strategy-structure-environment fit.*

H1a. *Firms with CEOs who employ judgment policies that are consistent with normative contingency theory will be more likely to exhibit a strategy-structure-environment alignment with good fit than will firms with CEOs who employ other decision rules.*

Further, contingency theory suggests that firms which exhibit the appropriate fit among strategy, structure and environment variables will achieve optimum performance. Firms may be equally successful using differing combinations; the key is that a match must exist among the contingency variables. Following from H1 above, one would expect that the use of contingency-theory-consistent judgment policies by a CEO would result in an appropriate strategy-structure-environment alignment and, therefore, high performance. Thus, the following normative hypothesis may be advanced.

H2. *Firms with CEOs whose judgment policies are consistent with normative contingency theory will outperform firms with CEOs who employ other decision rules.*

Antecedents to Executive Judgment

How do executives develop their understanding of cause-and-effect relationships and, thus, their judgment policies? Organization scholars have suggested that top managers learn about action-outcome relationships (Duncan and Weiss 1979) through their own and others' interactions with the environment (Daft and Weick 1984, Walsh and Ungson 1991). Exposure to such learning opportunities may be related to the length and breadth of the manager's experience, and to the quality of the strategic analysis that occurred during that experience.

Executive Experience. Executives' career experiences have been posited to influence their choices (Hambrick and Mason 1984), organizational adaptation (Cyert and March 1963), and organizational growth (Penrose 1959). Empirical work has frequently found relationships between top managers' experience and firm performance (e.g., Govindarajan 1989, Gupta and Govindarajan 1984, Norburn and Birley 1988). Few studies, however, have examined potential intervening constructs in the experience-performance relationship. Executives implementation skills (e.g., Brodwin and Bourgeois 1984) may improve with experience, thereby influencing performance. Top managers' judgments may also improve with experience. For example, executive understanding of relationships among strategy, structure, and environment variables has been argued to be reflected in their judgment policies for strategy-structure-environment alignment. CEOs with longer and broader experience may be more likely to perceive accurately the contingent action-outcome relationships in their environment and, therefore, employ judgment policies consistent with normative contingency theory. Thus:

H3. *Length of CEO experience will be associated with the use of judgment policies that are consistent with normative contingency theory and*

H4. *Breadth of CEO functional experience will be associated with the use of judgment policies that are consistent with normative contingency theory.*

Strategy-Making Process Rationality. Rationality in the strategy-making process, represented by the degrees of scanning and analysis and the futurity of planning (Miller 1987) associated with strategy making in a firm, may reflect the *quality* of the experience obtained by the executive. Ghoshal (1988), for example, notes that environmental scanning is both an early step in rational strategy models (e.g., Schendel and Hofer 1979) and a prerequisite for adaptation when organizations are viewed as interpretation systems (e.g., Daft and Weick 1984). Executives may gain understanding of key action-outcome relationships through their interactions with the competitive environment during the scanning process (Daft et al. 1988). The intensity of analysis that occurs may also increase their understanding of such relationships. These ideas are consistent with Walsh and Ungson's assertion that "individuals acquire information in (during their) problem-solving and decision-making activities" (1991, p. 61). Similarly, the length of the planning horizon (i.e., future orientation) may be related to recognition of longer-term action-outcome relationships. Therefore, planning may also be related to executive understanding of long-term, cause-and-effect relationships. One might expect from these arguments that executives of firms employing high levels of scanning, analysis, and planning (futurity) in the strategy-making process would be most likely to perceive the contingent action-outcome relationships of contingency theory. Thus,

H5. *Rationality in the strategy-making process will be positively associated with the use by the CEO of judgment policies that are consistent with normative contingency theory.*

H1 and H5 together suggest that rationality in the strategy-making process will be positively related to firm performance *through* executive judgment. This assertion is consistent with the normative stance of the dominant rational strategy models (e.g., Andrews 1971, Ansoff 1965, Schendel and Hofer 1979).

METHOD

A multi-method, multiple respondent approach encompassing several levels of analysis was used in this research. First, CEOs of manufacturing firms completed judgment tasks designed to identify their beliefs about key cause-and-effect relationships involving strategy, structure, the environment, and performance. These judgment policies may be expected to form the basis for their strategic intentions. Second, each CEO identified two *other* top managers who participate in strategy making at their firm. These other top executives responded to questionnaires containing multi-item scales used for assessing *actual* organizational-level strategy, structure, environment, and performance. Pilot tests of the judgment task and questionnaire were conducted using three firms that were not included in the sample. The judgment task was also piloted on a group of advanced MBA students. Finally, normative contingency theory provided the "ideal" strategy-structure-environment-performance relationships against which both the CEO judgments of these relationships, and the fit of the strategy-structure-environment alignment actually achieved by the firm, could be compared. The sections that follow first provide an overview of the sample criteria and experimental procedures, and descriptive data for the sample. Then, details are provided for the operationalizations of CEO judgment policies, the realized organizational-level strategy-structure-environment fit, firm performance, and judgment antecedents, and for the data analysis procedures.

Sample and Procedures

One hundred and six autonomous, nondiversified manufacturing firms were selected from a southwestern state's *1989 Survey of Manufacturers.* These firms represented all manufacturers within the researcher's geographical reach that could be identified as meeting the following criteria. First, each manufacturing firm must have been an independent business rather than a subsidiary, a division of another firm, or a unit of a conglomerate. This criterion ensured that neither the CEO's judgment policy nor the firm's realized strategy, structure and environment could be influenced by a parent firm, thus controlling for firm autonomy (Child 1973). Without this control, a firm's realized strategy-structure-environment fit could be attributed to decisions made by parent-firm executives rather than to the strategic choices of the focal firm's CEO. Second, the firm must have been a single business firm, indicated by operation in only one four-digit SIC code. This helped to ensure that the responses of the two other top executives focused only on the business-level strategy, structure, and environment of the primary business, rather than on the potential multiple strategies, structures, and environments associated with diversified firms. This criterion was relaxed in several cases to ensure adequate sample size, but only where it was clear that the firm participated in two four-digit SICs that could be considered in the same industry. For example, a firm that manufactured both women's blouses (SIC 2331) and women's slacks (SIC 2339) was included in the sample. Finally, firms in the sample were required to have had more than 100 production employees, to help ensure that multiple executives were aware of and involved in the firm's strategy, structure, and competitive environment. This was important so that the CEO, who performed a task to reveal his/her judgment policy, would not also be providing information on the realized strategy, structure, and environment of his/her firm, thereby minimizing any common method variance problems. Also, it was deemed to be important to have multiple respondents in each organization concerning realized organizational outcomes, since different executives may perceive outcomes differently (Bourgeois 1985, McCabe 1990) or attend to different sectors of the environment (Daft et al. 1988). Thus, multiple respondents could be expected to increase the reliability of the organization-level data.

A letter requesting participation was sent to the CEO of each firm and followed up with telephone calls. Sixty-three top executives were reached personally via telephone; the remainder declined participation through return letter or via an assistant, citing company policy against participation in academic research, time pressures, and so on. Thirty-eight of the contacted CEOs agreed to participate. In all cases these individuals were the top executive in their firm, with titles of either CEO, President, or President and CEO. Usable responses to the firm-level questionnaires were received from both of the other key strategy-making executives identified by the CEOs for 25 firms, and from one of the CEO-identified key executives for eight firms. Thus, the final sample consisted of 33 firms, representing a 31% overall response rate and a 52% response rate for those chief executives actually reached by telephone. The average participating firm had 354 employees (s.d. = 433). Thirty-one of the 33 firms were privately held. Not more than two firms participated in any one 4-digit SIC industry. The products manufactured ranged in technological complexity from plastic dinner plates to electronic switches used in the space shuttle. No statistically significant differences were found between responding and nonresponding firms using the categorical annual sales or number of employees variables that were available for both responding and nonresponding firms ($\chi^2 = 2.02$, $p = 0.37$, $n = 98$, and $\chi^2 = 2.28$, $p = 0.52$, $n = 105$, respectively).

All of the CEOs were males. All except one had at least one college degree, 16 had received degrees in business administration, and one held a Ph.D. in physics. The average CEO was 47.9 years old (s.d. = 8.3) at the time of the interview and had spent 7.3 years (s.d. = 6.6) as the top executive of his firm.

Operationalization of Variables

CEO Judgment Policies. During the field interview each CEO was first provided with definitions of differentiation and cost leadership business-level strategies (Porter 1980), dynamic and stable environments (Duncan 1972), and organic and mechanistic structures (Burns and Stalker 1961). The mechanistic and organic structures were labeled "Type A" and "Type B," respectively, to avoid any negative connotations associated with the word "mechanistic." The CEO was encouraged to refer to these definitions as necessary during the judgment exercise that followed. Then, the CEO was presented simultaneously with all eight strategy-structure-environment combinations that result from the three variables at two levels each, representing eight otherwise equal manufacturing firms. He was asked to assign 100 points to the combination (or each of the combinations—ties were permitted throughout the exercise) he deemed most desirable. Each remaining combination was then rated on a 0-100 point scale relative to the preferred combination(s), with all ratings based on the likelihood of success for a manufacturing firm exhibiting each combination. Thus, each CEO was asked to judge the desirability of eight possible strategy-structure-environment alignments for manufacturing firms, all other things being equal. Next, the CEO was given a demographics questionnaire that functioned as a filler task to reduce carryover effects. Finally, the CEO was asked to complete a second judgment task incorporating the same variables and combinations. This replication allowed evaluation of the test-retest reliability of each CEOs responses. The order of presentation of the variables and combinations for both tasks was varied between and within CEOs to minimize any order effects and carryover effects.

Use of a judgment task rather than simply asking the CEOs to explain their beliefs provides an important advantage. Respondents are asked to actually *make* strategy-structure-environment judgments rather than just explain how they *would* make such judgments. This distinction is particularly important since individuals' espoused theories are frequently incompatible with their theories-in-use (Argyris and Schön 1974, Brunsson 1989). Espoused theory is the understanding of relationships that one is willing *and able* to express to others. Theory-in-use actually controls one's actions. An example of incompatibility between espoused theory and theory-in-use would be someone expressing values supporting charitable contributions without actually contributing. Brunsson (1989) found similarly that the ideas expressed in organizations may differ widely from the actions undertaken. Even when they are willing, managers are generally unable to accurately describe their own judgment policies (Stahl and Zimmerer 1984, Viswesvaran and Barrick 1992). Thus, a judgment task such as the one used in this research may provide more information about judgment policies than executives would otherwise be willing or able to provide.

CEO Characteristics. CEO background characteristics were determined by a questionnaire administered between replications of the judgment task. This questionnaire asked the CEO to report age, length of time with the firm, length of time in the industry, length of time as CEO, functional areas in which the CEO had previous experience, and level and types of educational experience.

Firm Characteristics. The questionnaire that was filled out by the two other top-level executives at each firm addressed perceptions of the existing strategy, structure, environment, and strategy-making process of the firm. Multiple questions were used to assess each construct, and each scale had been used in prior research. The strategy section is from Miller (1988), with scales assessing the degree of emphasis on cost leadership, innovative differentiation, and marketing differentiation (the marketing differentiation scale was ultimately eliminated from the analysis due to low scale reliability). The structure variables are from the Aston studies (Inkson et al. 1970) and Miller (1983). The Aston scales for formalization, decentralization, and specialization ask for fairly objective self-report data (e.g., number of documents used, who makes which decisions), while the control and liaison devices scales are more judgment-based. The questions concerning the environment are from Miller and Droge (1986). Their combined uncertainty scale measures both the rate and unpredictability of environmental change, reflecting the dynamism (Dess and Beard 1984) in the firm's competitive environment. Three scales from Miller (1987) address perceptions of the firm's existing scanning, analysis, and planning processes, representing the degree of rationality in the firm's strategy making.

Operationalization of the concept of congruence (or, "fit") has long been problematic in strategy and organization research (Drazin and Van de Ven 1985, Schoonhoven 1981). Multivariate fit may be conceptualized and evaluated as gestalts, profile deviation, or covariation (Venkatraman 1989). Venkatraman notes that evaluation of fit using the profile deviation perspective "allows a researcher to specify an ideal profile and to demonstrate that adherence to such a profile has systematic implications for effectiveness" (1989, p. 434).

The prescriptions of contingency theory, however, do not result in only *one* preferred, "baseline" profile; different combinations of the variables of interest may be equally appropriate. There may be *many* ideal profiles, but to be ideal each must reflect prescribed levels of strategy-structure-environment variables relative to *each other* rather than to one particular baseline. Assume, for example, that data on environmental dynamism and structural centralization, standardization, and formalization have been gathered from a group of firms with the intent of evaluating their environment-structure fit. Following Burns and Stalker's (1961) prescriptions, firms facing relatively dynamic environments would exhibit good fit with more organic structural characteristics, while firms facing stable environments could exhibit equally good fit with more mechanistic structures. To measure relative fit, the scales used must first be aligned so that high scale values represent high centralization, standardization and formalization, *and* the stable end of the stable-dynamic environmental continuum. Thus, firms that score relatively high on all of the scales, or relatively low on all of the scales, each would exhibit good fit. After standardizing each variable used in the fit calculation across firms, for example, a hypothetical firm that scored one standard deviation above the mean on each scale would exhibit theoretically ideal relative fit, as would also a hypothetical firm that scored one standard deviation below the mean on each scale. Thus, the important factor is the relationship of the variables to each other rather than to a single ideal profile. The fit index used in this research was computed as follows:

$$FIT = -\left\{\frac{\Sigma_{j \in A}(ENV - STRA_j)^2}{A} + \frac{\Sigma_{k \in B}(ENV - STRU_k)^2}{B} + \frac{\Sigma_{jk \in C}(STRA_j - STRU_k)^2}{C}\right\},$$

where ENV represents the standardized (across firms) scores for environmental uncertainty (1 variable), STRA represents standardized scores for the strategy variables ($j = 2$: cost leadership and innovative differentiation), and STRU represents standardized scores for the structure variables ($k = 5$:

formalization, centralization, specialization, controls, and liaison devices). *A, B,* and *C* represent the number of pairs of environment-strategy (2 pairs), environment-structure (5 pairs), and strategy-structure (jk = 10 pairs) relationships in each component of the fit index. The raw score for each component of the index is divided by the number of pairs used in forming that component so that the same relative misfit within each component will have the same contribution to the overall index. This is actually an index of misfit, so the total is made negative to convert to an index of fit. As an example of the normative alignments, strong pursuit of a cost leadership strategy would be appropriately aligned with relatively low environmental uncertainty (Kim and Lim 1988, Miller 1988) and with structural centralization, formalization, specialization, controls, and relatively little use of liaison devices (Burns and Stalker 1961, Porter 1980). To achieve the alignment specified by contingency theory, the innovative differentiation, environmental uncertainty, decentralization, and liaison devices scales were reversed after standardization but prior to the fit calculation. This fit index, based on the conceptual work of Venkatraman (1989) and similar to the indices employed by Thomas et al. (1991) and Miller (1992), results in a measure of fit that does not rely on specification of an ideal baseline. The index does, however, reflect the relationships posited by contingency theory, with equal weighting for strategy-structure, strategy-environment, and structure-environment fit.

Firm Performance. The CEO and the two non-CEO respondents were also asked firm performance questions based on Dess and Robinson (1984). Each was asked to rank his/her firm's performance compared to other similar firms on sales growth, after tax return on sales, after tax return on total assets, and overall performance/success, all for the previous five-year period. Several practical and theoretical issues guided the selection of these subjective, self-reported measures of performance. First, five-year averages were sought to minimize the influence of short-term variations on the reported performance of the firm. Second, since many of the firms in the sample were expected to be closely held, their executives were expected to be unwilling to provide detailed accounting data. Third, the comparison to other similar firms provides a form of control for differences in performance that may be due to industry (Dess, Ireland, and Hitt 1990) and strategic group (Hatten et al. 1978) effects. Finally, multiple measures of performance were used to reflect the multidimensionality of the performance construct (Cameron 1978, Chakravarthy 1986). Subjective, self-reported performance measures such as those used in this study have been found to be highly correlated with objective measures of firm performance (Dess and Robinson 1984, Venkatraman and Ramanujam 1987).

Data Analysis

A number of analytical techniques are available for identifying judgment policies (also frequently called decision rules or composition rules) after a decision process has taken place. Each of these techniques is said to "decompose" a series of judgments (Arkes and Hammond 1986, p. 7). Decomposition techniques such as conjoint analysis and policy capturing have seen some use in the strategy literature (e.g., DeSarbo et al. 1987, Hitt and Tyler 1991). The current research design was developed for use of metric conjoint analysis techniques (Louviere 1988), due in part to the ability of metric conjoint to evaluate contingent judgments. Nonmetric conjoint analysis, for example, asks respondents to *rank order* objects and typically requires the assumption that the respondents' judgment policies are additive (i.e., any interactions in the judgment model are not statistically significant—DeSarbo et al. 1987, Green and Wind 1973). This limits the usefulness of nonmetric techniques for studying the contingent judgment policies prescribed by strategic management theories. Metric conjoint analysis involves *rating* objects, making it easier to examine contingent (interactive) judgments statistically, at either individual or aggregate levels (Louviere 1988). Metric conjoint generally focuses on a smaller number of variables than are typical in policy capturing studies (e.g., Hitt and Tyler 1991), but uses full factorial designs that facilitate the study of contingent judgments.

Metric conjoint analysis is based on the Information Integration Theory of Anderson (1981, 1982). The major theorem states that:

> Marginal response means from a factorial experimental design constitute an interval scale estimate of the unknown part-worth utilities of each attribute if some subset of the multilinear model is correct. . . . This result for the marginal means also holds for any set of regression coefficients that represent these means. (Louviere 1988, p. 23)

Thus, the data analysis plan first called for regressing each CEO's ratings from the judgment task on the strategy, structure, and environment variables from that task, and their interactions. This was done twice, once for each replication of the task. Orthogonal polynomial effect codes were used for the independent variables to establish the baseline relationships posited by normative contingency theory. The differentiation strategy, organic structure, and dynamic environment each received 1 as their code. Cost leadership, mechanistic and stable each were coded –1. Through this coding, it can be concluded that a CEO whose judgment model shows a positive regression coefficient for the strategy variable uses a judgment policy that favors differentiation strategies, while a CEO whose judgment model shows a negative regression coefficient for the strategy variable uses a judgment policy that favors cost leadership strategies, and so on for the structure and environment judgments. Large main effect regression coefficient values would be generally *in*consistent with contingency theory prescriptions. The effect codes similarly align the double interactions in the judgment models with contingency prescriptions. For example, CEOs whose judgments favor combinations that contain organic structure and dynamic environments together ($1 \times 1 = 1$), *and* combinations that contain mechanistic structure and stable environment together ($-1 \times -1 = 1$), would produce a judgment model with a positive regression coefficient for the structure-environment interaction. and so on for the strategy-structure and strategy-environment interactions. Thus, CEOs whose judgment models contain positive coefficients on the interactions are making contingent judgments consistent with contingency theory prescriptions, while CEOs whose judgment models show negative coefficients on the interactions are making contingent judgments that are directly opposite to normative theory. The three-way interaction is *not* perfectly aligned with multivariate contingency prescriptions, but *does* represent consideration by the CEO of simultaneous alignments of strategy-structure-environment in forming judgment policy.

The mean parameters (i.e., regression coefficients) from the two judgment regressions represent each CEO's judgment policy regarding causal relationships among strategy, structure, the environment, and firm performance. However, the patterns of the coefficients may vary among the CEOs. For example, two CEOs may have judgment policies that each are consistent with contingency theory, although one of the CEOs may emphasize strategy-structure contingencies while the other may emphasize structure-environment contingencies. Therefore, CEOs were next clustered based on the mean regression parameters in their judgment models, in order to group CEOs who use similar judgment policies. These procedures allow hypothesis testing with correlation and regression techniques using the regression parameters from the judgment models, and with multiple analysis of variance techniques using the cluster analysis results. More information on decomposition techniques for the analysis of individual judgments can be found in Arkes and Hammond (1986). The statistical basis for metric conjoint analysis is described in detail in Louviere (1988). Priem (1992) provides a strategy-related example of individual-level judgment analysis using metric conjoint techniques.

The sample size for this research was expected to be small due to the time-intensiveness of interview-based field research and the difficulty in obtaining CEO participants whose firms meet the criteria for inclusion. Effect size was expected to be relatively small due to the many factors other

TABLE 4.1 Mean CEO Judgment Model Parameters

	Mean	SD	*1*	*2*	*3*	*4*	*5*	*6*	*7*
1. INTERCEPT	66.4	11.5							
2. STRATEGY	6.5	6.6	−25						
3. STRUCTURE	5.6	10.7	−37	06					
4. ENVIRONMENT	0.1	9.3	−20	23	10				
5. STRA × STRUC	2.7	5.8	15	−18	−12	−01			
6. STRA × ENV	3.2	6.7	01	−11	−20	−12	46		
7. STRUC × ENV	2.7	6.6	−30	−26	−01	−04	11	07	
8. STRA × STRUC × ENV	0.8	3.4	13	−07	−56	−15	16	03	14

Correlations of 0.29 are significant at $p < 0.1$, 0.34 at $p < 0.05$, and 0.44 at $p < 0.01$.

than the CEO that may influence organization design and performance outcomes. The hypotheses to be tested were developed from the strong theory base of contingency theory. Small sample size, small effect size, and a coherent underlying theory all suggest that it is appropriate to use a less conservative criterion for statistical significance in order to provide a better prospect for uncovering existing relationships (Sauley and Bedeian 1989, Skipper et al. 1967). Thus, 0.1 was selected a priori as the level of significance which would provide an indication of reliable relationships in this research.

RESULTS

Descriptive statistics and correlations among the CEO judgment model (regression) parameters are presented in Table 4.1. Interpreted based on the effects coding discussed earlier, these results indicate that the CEOs in the sample favor differentiation strategies and organic structures, and that they are cognizant of the double interactions suggested by bivariate contingency theories. The median test-retest reliability for the CEOs' replications of the judgment task was 0.93 ($Q_3 = 0.97$, $Q_1 = 0.75$). The relatively large standard deviations for the parameter values, however, indicate that considerable variance exists in judgment across CEOs. Cluster analysis was therefore used to group like-thinking CEOs based on their judgment policies.

First, the regression parameter values were standardized (mean = 0, s.d. = 1) across the CEOs in the sample to ensure that each judgment variable and interaction would have equal potential for contributing to the cluster solution. The intercept from each CEO's individual regressions was included in the cluster analysis and subsequent analyses because, since each CEO's most-preferred alignment was anchored at 100, this parameter provides

TABLE 4.2 Cluster Analysis Results

	Ward's				*K-Means*			
	Cluster 1 (n = *24)*		*Cluster 2* (n = *9)*		*Cluster 1* (n = *23)*		*Cluster 2* (n = *10)*	
	Mean	SD	*Mean*	SD	*Mean*	SD	*Mean*	SD
INTERCEPT	0.37	0.78	–0.98	0.88	0.36	0.83	–0.82	0.89
STRA	–0.26	0.96	0.71	0.76	–0.31	0.95	0.70	0.75
STRUC	–0.20	0.66	0.54	1.5	–0.43	0.70	1.0	0.86
ENV	–0.42	0.77	1.1	0.58	–0.25	0.80	0.58	1.2
STRA × STRUC	0.23	0.76	–0.61	1.3	0.29	0.69	–0.66	1.3
STRA × ENV	0.23	1.0	–0.63	0.64	0.25	1.0	–0.59	0.64
STRUC × ENV	0.04	1.1	–0.12	0.79	0.03	1.1	–0.08	0.68
STRA × STRUC × ENV	0.21	0.98	–0.55	0.89	0.31	0.94	–0.71	0.76

information on the variance and range of the CEO's preferences across all eight combinations. The correlation between intercept and variance was –0.86, and the correlation between intercept and range was –0.82.

Then, Ward's minimum variance technique, a hierarchical agglomerative clustering method, was employed (Hair et al. 1987). Both the Pseudo-F and Pseudo-T criteria indicated a two-cluster solution. The cubic clustering criterion suggested either two or five clusters. The two-cluster solution was selected for interpretation because it was suggested by all three criteria and it is the most parsimonious.

Although the goal in cluster analysis is generally to identify structure in data, as is the case here, cluster algorithms are "structure-seeking" (Aldenderfer and Blashfield 1984, p. 16), making validation of cluster results extremely important. The sample size in this research precluded replication using a holdout sample. Two separate methods were used, however, to validate the Ward's cluster solution. First, the clustering was repeated using the *K*-means iterative partitioning method, a technique quite different from Ward's. The *K*-means solution matched the Ward's classification for all but 3 of the 33 observations, indicating consistent results across the two techniques. The correlation between group membership using Ward's and *K*-Means was 0.78 ($p < 0.001$). Second, the tests of Hypothesis 2 (see below) indicate that the cluster solutions are significantly different on variables other than those used to form the clusters—another recommended validation method (Aldenderfer and Blashfield 1984). Means and standard deviations for both the Ward's and *K*-means groupings of CEOs by their judgment are presented in Table 4.2. Since the regression parameter values were standardized prior to clustering, the cluster results must be interpreted as standardized variables relative to the actual means shown in Table 4.1.

For each cluster technique, Cluster 2 CEOs exhibit strong preferences for differentiation strategies, organic structures, and dynamic environments (i.e., the main effects). and below average recognition of bivariate contingencies (i.e., the two-way interactions) and multivariate configurations (i.e., the triple interaction). Cluster 1 CEOs, on the other hand, exhibit below average preference strengths for particular strategies, structures and environments, but above average recognition of the bivariate contingencies and multivariate configurations suggested by contingency and configuration theories. Thus, Cluster 1 represents those CEOs whose judgment policies are consistent with aspects of normative contingency theory, while Cluster 2 represents those CEOs whose judgment policies are generally based on universal preferences for particular strategies, structures and environments. These thought patterns were labeled "contingent" and "noncontingent," respectively.

Means, standard deviations and correlations for the firm-level data gathered from the other strategy-making executives concerning each firm's realized strategy, structure. environment, strategy-making process and performance are presented in Table 4.3. Cronbach's alpha scale reliabilities and interrater reliabilities are shown on the diagonals. The marketing differentiation scale exhibited unacceptable reliability (Van de Ven and Ferry 1980). Therefore, it was deleted from further analyses. The reliability of the cost leadership scale was unacceptable until two items from the Aston control scale, involving use of cost centers and fixing standard costs and included as part of cost leadership by Miller (1988), were removed. Univariate analyses indicated that both the size and fit variables departed significantly from normality (Shapiro-Wilk $W = 0.55$, $p < 0.01$ and $W = 0.86$, $p < 0.01$, respectively). Therefore, these variables were transformed using the natural logarithm and are called Log Size ($W = 0.94$, $p = 0.07$) and Log Fit ($W = 0.97$, $p = 0.624$). All structure variables (decentralization, formalization, specialization, controls, and liaison devices) and strategy-making process variables (scanning, analysis and planning) were controlled for Log Size (Blau and Schoenherr 1971, Pugh et al. 1969, Lindsey and Rue 1980). Given their high intercorrelations, and consistent with previous work (Miller 1987), the scanning, analysis and planning variables were summed to produce an aggregate rationality variable for use in subsequent analyses. Similarly, the highly-correlated return on assets and return on sales variables were combined to form an aggregate return variable for subsequent MANOVAs.

TABLE 4.3 Descriptive Statistics and Pearson Correlations

n = 33	*Mean*	SD	*1*	*2*	*3*	*4*	*5*	*6*	*7*	*8*	*9*	*10*	*11*	*12*	*13*	*14*	*15*	*16*	*17*	*18*	*19*	*20*	*21*	*22*
Firm Variables																								
1) Log Size	5.5	0.74																						
2) Env. Uncertainty	4.0	0.97	04	(81	37)																			
Strategy:																								
3) Cost Leadership	4.4	2.3	14	−14	(56)																			
4) Differentiation via Marketing	3.9	0.85	03	13	−14	(17	48)																	
5) Product Innovation	4.4	0.78	−27	20	−27	48	(62	50)																
Structure:																								
6) Decentralization	2.4	0.37	00	−21	04	−33	−04	(78	42)															
7) Formalization	9.2	3.6	00	02	−31	24	37	05	(67	56)														
8) Specialization	9.4	3.6	00	29	−35	44	37	−16	42	(NA	53)													
9) Control	4.9	1.1	00	22	−22	45	50	−31	36	51	(70	61)												
10) Liaison Devices	4.1	1.0	00	11	−48	40	59	14	27	29	42	(81	44)											
11) Log Fit	−1.6	0.68	17	07	−16	00	31	07	34	25	−10	06												
Strategy Making Process:																								
12) Scanning	3.8	0.98	00	01	11	55	35	−31	24	23	27	50	−06	(87	07)									
13) Analysis	3.6	0.96	00	−10	−14	62	62	−06	40	38	62	65	−06	61	(75	54)								
14) Planning	4.0	1.0	00	07	04	63	44	−14	29	50	43	67	−11	64	83	(87	53)							
15) Composite Rationality	0.0	2.6	00	−01	00	68	53	−19	35	42	49	68	−09	84	91	93	(NA	NA)						
Performance:																								
16) Return on Assets	3.3	1.1	21	−32	22	13	21	01	−22	04	15	15	12	34	31	35	38	(NA	88)					
17) Return on Sales	3.3	1.1	18	−34	28	15	13	−00	−24	−04	11	10	10	28	30	36	35	96	(NA	90)				
18) Sales Growth	3.7	0.97	06	02	−13	26	48	−23	−15	22	35	34	30	37	31	35	38	53	45	(NA	77)			
19) Overall Performance	3.7	1.1	02	−13	12	19	46	−05	−16	09	30	26	14	36	36	45	44	77	72	83	(NA	88)		
CEO Experience Variables:																								
Tenure:																								
20) In Industry	20.6	10.3	10	−03	46	02	−18	13	27	−04	06	03	−25	−11	08	23	07	−04	04	−36	−16			
21) With Firm	13.5	10.9	−16	15	43	18	−02	−06	−15	10	05	−09	−15	08	−01	24	12	10	19	−02	10	47		
22) In Job	7.3	6.6	−37	01	15	19	24	35	03	−01	22	06	−20	03	14	28	17	02	10	−01	22	28	61	
Breadth:																								
23) Of Functional Exper.	3.6	1.4	−27	−33	06	−07	−23	02	−20	−23	−24	−04	−48	−06	−24	−08	−16	−18	−01	−41	−14	31	19	22

Correlations of 0.29 are significant at $p < 0.1$, 0.34 at $p < 0.05$, and 0.44 at $p < 0.01$. Cronbach alpha scale reliabilities and interrater reliabilities, where appropriate, are presented in parentheses on the diagonal. Decimal points are omitted for correlations and reliabilities. Structure variables no. 6 - 10 and strategy process variables no. 12 - 16 have been controlled using the natural log of size in number of employees; thus, the correlations for these variables are partials/semi-partials.

TABLE 4.4 Log Fit Hierarchical Regression on CEO Judgment Model Parameters

Hierarchical Regression Models	R-*square*	*Adjusted* R-*square*	F *for Change in Adjusted* R-*square*
Model I Included			
INTERCEPT			
STRATEGY			
STRUCTURE	0.43	0.35	
ENVIRONMENT			
Model II Added			
STRA × STRUC			
STRA × ENV	0.59	0.47	3.2*
STRUC × ENV			
Model III Added			
STRA × STRUC × ENV	0.63	0.51	3.01^{+}

$^{+}p < 0.1$; $^{*}p < 0.05$

Hypothesis Tests

Hypothesis 1, which suggests that CEO judgment policies will be related to the firm's actual strategy-structure-environment fit, was tested using hierarchical multiple regression analysis. Hierarchical regression was used because the individual beta weights in a standard regression would be unstable with this sample size, and because the hierarchical technique allows statistical evaluation of the contribution of the groups of independent variables (i.e., main effect judgments versus contingent judgments) that are the focus of this research. The results of this analysis are presented in Table 4.4. The first regression equation included only the Intercept and the Strategy, Structure and Environment main effect variables, representing noncontingent preferences in the CEOs' judgment policies. These variables alone explained significant variance in Log Fit ($F = 5.29$, $p < 0.01$). Addition of the double interaction variables in the next equation, representing contingent judgments by the CEOs, resulted in a significant improvement in variance explained. The incorporation of the triple strategy-structure-environment interaction, representing configural thinking, in the final regression equation also contributed significantly to variance explained. The final regression equation, including all CEO judgment model parameters, was quite effective in explaining variance in fit ($F = 5.11$, $p < 0.001$). Thus, Hypothesis 1 receives strong support.

TABLE 4.5 CEO Judgment Model-Firm Performance Correlations

	Return on Assets	*Return on Sales*	*Sales Growth*	*Overall Performance*
INTERCEPT	–0.05	–0.04	0.18	–0.01
STRATEGY	0.03	–0.00	–0.33⁺	–0.08
STRUCTURE	–0.13	–0.18	–0.16	–0.16
ENVIRONMENT	–0.02	–0.13	–0.15	–0.10
STRA × STRUC	–0.03	–0.06	0.10	–0.06
STRA × ENV	–0.07	–0.09	–0.09	–0.11
STRUC × ENV	–0.05	0.03	0.11	0.08
STRA × STRUC × ENV	0.21	0.31⁺	0.34*	0.20

⁺$p < 0.1$; *$p < 0.05$

Hypothesis 1a proposes that CEOs' use of judgment policies that are consistent with multivariate contingency theory will be positively associated with the realized strategy-structure-environment fit of their firms. ANOVAs examining Log Fit means across the Ward's and *K*-means clusters ($F = 0.01$, $p = 0.94$; $F = 0.89$, $p = 0.35$) did not indicate reliable relationships. Thus, these data do not support Hypothesis 1a. However, the partial correlation of the triple interaction parameter with Log Fit, controlling for the other CEO judgment factors, indicated the expected positive relationship (partial $r = 0.33$, $p = 0.06$), suggesting that the simultaneous consideration of multiple variables in a judgment model may be important to realized fit.

Hypothesis 2 states that CEOs' use of judgment policies that are consistent with contingency theory will be positively related to firm performance. This hypothesis was tested using correlation, multiple analysis of variance, and regression techniques. Correlations among the CEO judgment model parameters and the within-industry performance variables are presented in Table 4.5.

Only the triple interaction from the CEOs' judgment models is positively correlated with all performance measures, achieving statistical significance in two of the four cases. Further, although not individually significant, 11 of the 12 correlations between the main effect judgment variables and performance are negative, suggesting that noncontingent preferences for particular strategies, structures, and environments hinder performance. Finally, none of the two-way interactions from the CEOs' judgment models show reliable relationships with performance. Although not explicitly considered in the current research hypotheses, the fit (outcome rather than cognitions)-performance relationships found in earlier research (Miller 1988) receive some support from the Log Fit-performance correlations in Table 4.3.

TABLE 4.6 CEO Judgment Model-Experience Correlations

	Industry Tenure	*Firm Tenure*	*Tenure as CEO*	*Functional Breadth*
INTERCEPT	−0.22	0.10	−0.06	−0.21
STRATEGY	0.02	−0.12	0.08	0.18
STRUCTURE	−0.04	−0.06	0.09	0.07
ENVIRONMENT	−0.07	−0.28	-0.29^{+}	0.03
STRA × STRUC	-0.30^{+}	−0.04	−0.16	0.06
STRA × ENV	0.02	0.05	0.06	0.17
STRUC × ENV	0.27	0.15	−0.01	0.04
STRA × STRUC × ENV	−0.01	−0.05	−0.02	0.31^{+}

$^{+}p < 0.1$; $^{*}p < 0.05$

As a further test of Hypothesis 2, MANOVAs were conducted to examine performance differences across the "contingent-thinking" and "noncontingent-thinking" clusters of CEOs. First, however, the Return on Assets and Return on Sales variables were combined for this and subsequent multivariate performance analyses to avoid problems due to their high intercorrelation ($r = 0.96$). The composite variable was labeled Return. The clusters were found to differ significantly on the performance variables (Wilks's Lambda $F = 2.89$, $p < 0.05$ and $F = 3.51$, $p < 0.05$ for the Ward's and K-means clusters, respectively), with the contingent-thinking CEO clusters' firms outperforming those of the noncontingent thinkers in each case. Finally, the triple interaction from the CEOs' judgment models was regressed on the performance measures, yielding an R^2 of 0.24 ($F = 3.0$, $p < 0.05$). Thus, the correlation, regression, and MANOVA results provide support for Hypothesis 2.

Hypothesis 3 suggests that CEO experience will be positively associated with use of judgment policies that are consistent with the prescriptions of contingency theory. Hypothesis 4 suggests that the use of such judgment policies may be positively related to the breadth of the past functional experience of the CEO. Correlations between CEO judgment model parameters and CEO experience and breadth are presented in Table 4.6. Neither the CEO length-of-experience nor breadth-of-experience variables show significant relationships with the CEO judgment variables. Further, canonical correlation between the experience and judgment variables is not significant (Wilks's Lambda $F = 0.67$, $p = 0.86$).

Hypothesis 5 proposes that rationality in the firm's strategy-making process will be positively associated with the CEO's use of judgment policies that are consistent with the prescriptions of contingency theory. Correlations among the strategy-making rationality variables and the CEO judgment

TABLE 4.7 CEO Judgment Model-Strategy Process Correlations

	Scanning	*Analysis*	*Planning*	*Composite Rationality*
INTERCEPT	0.07	–0.05	–0.02	0.00
STRATEGY	0.34+	0.25	0.19	0.29+
STRUCTURE	–0.21	–0.08	–0.13	–0.16
ENVIRONMENT	–0.16	–0.20	–0.26	–0.23
STRA × STRUC	0.19	0.09	–0.08	0.07
STRA × ENV	0.06	0.10	0.14	0.11
STRUC × ENV	0.12	0.16	0.19	0.18
STRA × STRUC × ENV	0.37*	0.35*	0.36*	0.40*

+$p < 0.1$; *$p < 0.05$.

model parameters are presented in Table 4.7. The triple interaction judgment parameter, representing thinking consistent with the multivariate nature although not the precise prescriptions of contingency and configuration theory, is positively correlated with each of the scanning, analysis, and planning variables, and with the composite rationality variable. CEO preference for differentiation strategies is positively correlated with scanning and composite rationality. Neither the remaining main effect judgment variables nor the two-way interactions show reliable relationships with strategy-making rationality.

As a further test of Hypothesis 5, MANOVAs were conducted to examine differences in scanning, analysis and planning across the clusters representing contingent and noncontingent judgment models. The clusters did not differ on the rationality variables (Wilks's Lambda $F = 1.01$, $p = 0.4$ and $F = 0.78$, $p = 0.51$ for the Ward's and *K*-means clusters, respectively). Thus, the correlation and MANOVA results do not support Hypothesis 5. The Correlations in Table 4.3 do show a positive relationship between each of the strategy-making process rationality variables and each of the firm performance variables. The influence of rationality on performance is not, however, through CEO judgments of business-level strategy-structure-environment contingencies.

The lack of support for the experience- and process-based hypotheses could lead one to speculate that completion of a degree in business administration may be a more important influence on CEO cognitions of configural strategy-structure-environment relationships than length, breadth, or quality of experience. Therefore, a MANOVA was performed to examine the relationship between completion of a degree in business and use of particular judgment policies. Again, no significant relationship was found (Wilks's Lambda $F = 0.57$, $p = 0.87$).

DISCUSSION AND IMPLICATIONS

This study found that the judgment policies used by CEOs of manufacturing firms in making strategy-structure-environment alignment decisions are strongly related to the realized strategy-structure-environment fit of the firm. This result indicates that top managers' judgments *do* influence organization design outcomes, supporting the strategic choice perspective of organizational adaptation (Child 1972). Recent studies have offered support for the key role of strategic choice in determining organizational outcomes through examination of interorganizational networks (Oliver 1988), leader succession (Thomas 1988), founding team characteristics (Eisenhardt and Schoonhoven 1990), and top management team tenure (Finkelstein and Hambrick 1990, Wiersema and Bantel 1992). The current study, however, may provide the most *direct* test of the role of strategic choice by examining the individual judgments of top managers and the resulting organizational fit.

This study also found that CEOs whose judgments are more consistent with contingency theory prescriptions are associated with higher performing firms, providing support for the efficacy of normative contingency theory. Non-contingent preferences for particular strategies, structures, or environments were found to be marginally negatively related to performance, while bivariate contingent preferences, individually, exhibited no reliable relationships with performance. The triple interaction in the CEOs' judgment models exhibited the strongest and most consistent relationships with performance, strategy-making processes, and realized fit. Thus, the degree to which a CEO considers *simultaneous* relationships among multiple variables appears to be important to realized fit and performance outcomes.

The idea that judgment consistent with the prescriptions of contingency theory is associated with realized organizational fit, however, is not supported by these data. The statistical tests for the CEO judgment-realized fit hypothesis may have lacked power or, perhaps more intriguingly, CEOs may see strategy-structure-environment contingencies somewhat differently than do the academic theorists. This remains an issue for future research.

No support was found for CEO experience as an antecedent to configural judgment. Neither tenure as CEO, tenure with the firm, tenure in the industry, nor breadth of functional experience exhibited reliable relationships with CEO decision rules. It may be that any such relationships are simply too weak to be identified with these data. The lack of results is consistent, however, with Hitt and Tyler's (1991) recent finding that executive experience explains less than 3% of the variance in managers' acquisition decisions.

This study found rationality in the strategy-making process, represented by the levels of scanning, analysis and planning reported by top managers of manufacturing organizations, to be positively related to firm performance. This result, although not an explicit hypothesis in this research, is consistent with the prescriptions of rational models of strategy formulation (e.g., Andrews 1971, Ansoff 1965, Schendel and Hofer 1979). Little support was found for the idea that process rationality may influence firm performance *through* CEO judgment policies for strategy-structure-environment alignment. Rationality in strategy making was not related to either CEOs' simple main effect judgments, the interaction parameters in their judgment models, or judgment policy patterns represented by contingent-thinking and non-contingent-thinking CEO clusters. Process rationality was, however, related to the triple interaction in the CEOs' judgment models, providing at least a suggestion that rationality in strategy making may be related to use of more complex judgment policies. Thus, although rationality in the strategy-making process appears to have been beneficial for the manufacturing firms in the sample, the benefits were not achieved via CEOs' judgments of strategy-structure-environment relationships with performance.

Limitations

This study has a number of limitations. First, the sample was limited to manufacturing firms located in a major southwestern metropolitan area. The threat to external validity from the restriction in geography can be expected to be low, but the results may not be generalizable to service firms. Second, the limited research budget and the demands of interview-based field research combined to restrict sample size. Thus, these results must be viewed as preliminary pending support from future research.

Third, the data are cross-sectional, making causal inferences difficult. The discussion leading to Hypothesis 1, however, clearly implies a causal sequence. CEO judgment concerning strategy-structure-environment relationships with performance is posited to influence the firm's realized alignment. Alternate arguments can be made which reverse the causal direction. For example, one might argue that a CEO's intended alignment may be a reflection of the realized alignment of the firm; a CEO may simply adjust his/her intentions to match whatever outcome is realized (Mintzberg and Waters 1985). This argument suffers when one considers that the nondiversified firm may only exhibit one alignment at a time. Although a CEO may adjust the intended alignment to reflect the realized alignment, it is unlikely that a CEO could develop the *contingent* judgments that are the focus of this research based on only *one* realized alignment. That is, there is no basis from which the CEO can interpret contingent, causal strategy-structure-environment relationships with performance given only one combination of strategy, structure, and the environment. Thus, the use of fit as the dependent variable, rather than realized strategy or structure, strengthens this research.

Implications

Our results indicate that logical-empirical judgment (Etzioni 1992) plays an important role in strategic decision making. Executive judgment consistent with contingency theory is important to firm performance. Although rational decision models have often been criticized (e.g., Zey 1992) and the influence of individual biases noted (e.g., Schwenk 1988), for complex strategic problems logical-empirical models may provide baselines from which the influence of values and emotions may be productively examined (Lewin and Stephens 1994).

Future research might examine other contingency-based theories from the perspective of top manager judgment. For example, contingent judgment policies for strategy-making process fit (Miller 1987) or for functional area capabilities fit (Galbraith and Nathanson 1979) could be evaluated using similar conjoint techniques. Such research may indicate which fit relationships CEOs are most cognizant of and can most influence, ultimately complementing strategy content and process research and informing prescription.

These approaches, as in the current study, require a priori specification of the decision factors of interest. They are appropriate for supporting existing theory via CEO cognition research. Other research might focus on theory *building* by using, for example, perceptual mapping techniques to identify those variables that may be viewed as most important by CEOs making alignment decisions. Such variables, and their perceived relationships, may or may not be the same as those identified by current contingency theories. Theory-building research, with no a priori specification of key decision variables, may provide a means for extending contingency theory based on the cognitions of practicing strategic managers. Thus, additional work on top manager judgment may warrant high research priority. Executive judgment remains, although relatively unexplored, the essence of the strategic management field.

ACKNOWLEDGMENTS

The author wishes to thank Greg Dess, David Harrison and Abdul Rasheed, Guest Editors James R. Meindl, Joseph F. Porac, and Charles Stubbart, and the anonymous *Organization Science* reviewers for their helpful comments on earlier drafts of this chapter.

REFERENCES

Aldenderfer, M. S. and R. K. Blashfield (1984), *Cluster Analysis,* Sage University Paper Series on Quantitative Applications in the Social Sciences, 44, Beverly Hills, CA: Sage.

Anderson, N. H. (1981), *Foundations of Information Integration Theory,* New York: Academic Press.

——— (1982), *Methods of Information Integration Theory,* New York: Academic Press.

Andrews, K. R. (1971), *The Concept of Corporate Strategy,* Homewood, IL: Dow Jones-Irwin.

Ansoff, I. H. (1965), *Corporate Strategy,* New York: McGraw-Hill.

Argyris, C. and D. A. Schön (1974), *Theory in Practice: Increasing Professional Effectiveness,* San Francisco: Jossey-Bass.

Arkes, H. R. and K. R. Hammond (Eds.) (1986), *Judgment and Decision Making: An Interdisciplinary Reader,* Cambridge, UK: Cambridge University Press.

Blau, P. and R. Schoenherr (1971), *The Structure of Organizations,* New York: Basic Books.

Bourgeois, L. J. III (1984), "Strategic Management and Determinism," *Academy of Management Review,* 9, 586-596.

——— (1985), "Strategic Goals, Perceived Uncertainty, and Economic Performance in Volatile Environments," *Academy of Management Journal,* 28, 548-573.

Brodwin, D. R. and L. J. Bourgeois III (1984), "Five Steps to Strategic Action," *California Management Review,* 26, 176-190.

Brunsson, N. (1989), *The Organization of Hypocrisy: Talk, Decisions and Actions in Organizations,* New York: John Wiley.

Burns, T. and G. M. Stalker (1961), *The Management of Innovation,* London: Tavistock.

Cameron, K. (1978), "Measuring Organizational Effectiveness in Institutions of Higher Education," *Administrative Science Quarterly,* 23, 604-632.

Chakravarthy, B. (1986), "Measuring Strategic Performance," *Strategic Management Journal,* 6, 437-458.

Child, J. (1972), "Organization Structure, Environment, and Performance: The Role of Strategic Choice," *Sociology,* 6, 1-22.

——— (1973), "Strategies of Control and Organizational Behavior," *Administrative Science Quarterly,* 18, 1-17.

——— (1975), "Managerial and Organizational Factors Associated with Company Performance—Part II," *Journal of Management Studies,* 12, 12-27.

Cyert, R. and J. G. March (1963), *A Behavioral Theory of the Firm,* Englewood Cliffs, NJ: Prentice Hall.

Daft, R. I., J. Sormunen, and D. Parks (1988), "Chief Executive Scanning, Environmental Characteristics, and Company Performance: An Empirical Study," *Strategic Management Journal,* 9, 123-139.

——— and K. E. Weick (1984), "Toward a Model of Organizations as Interpretation Systems," *Academy of Management Review,* 9, 284-295.

DeSarbo, W., I. C. MacMillian, and D. L. Day (1987), "Criteria for Corporate Venturing: Importance Assigned by Managers," *Journal of Business Venturing,* 2, 329-350.

Dess, G. G. and D. W. Beard (1984), "Dimensions of Organizational Task Environments," *Administrative Science Quarterly,* 29, 52-73.

———, R. D. Ireland, and M. A. Hitt (1990), "Industry Effects and Strategic Management Research," *Journal of Management,* 16, 7-27.

——— and R. B. Robinson (1984), "Measuring Organizational Performance in the Absence of Objective Measures: The Case of the Privately-held Firm and the Conglomerate Business Unit," *Strategic Management Journal,* 5, 265-273.

Drazin, R. and A. H. Van de Ven (1985), "Alternative Forms of Fit in Contingency Theory," *Administrative Science Quarterly,* 30, 514-539.

Duncan, R. B. (1972), "Characteristics of Organizational Environments and Perceived Environmental Uncertainty," *Administrative Science Quarterly,* 17, 313-327.

——— and A. Weiss (1979), "Organizational Learning: Implications for Organizational Design," in B. Staw (Ed.), *Research in Organizational Behavior (Vol. 1),* Greenwich, CT: JAI, 75-123.

Dutton, J. E., L. Fahey, and V. K. Narayanan (1983), "Toward Understanding Strategic Issue Diagnosis," *Strategic Management Journal,* 4, 307-323.

———, E. J. Walton, and E. Abrahamson (1989), "Important Dimensions of Strategic Issues: Separating the Wheat from the Chaff," *Journal of Management Studies,* 26, 379-396.

Eisenhardt, K. M. and C. B. Schoonhoven (1990), "Organizational Growth: Linking Founding Team, Strategy, Environment, and Growth among U.S. Semi-conductor Ventures, 1978-1988," *Administrative Science Quarterly,* 35, 504-529.

Etzioni, A. (1992), "Normative-Affective Factors: Toward a New Decision-Making Model," in M. Zey (Ed.), *Decision Making: Alternatives to Rational Choice Models,* Newbury Park, CA: Sage, 89-111.

Fahey, L. and V. K. Narayanan (1989), "Linking Changes in Revealed Causal Maps and Environmental Change: An Empirical Study," *Journal of Management Studies,* 26, 361-378.

Finkelstein, S. and D. C. Hambrick (1990), "Top-Management-Team Tenure and Organizational Outcomes: The Moderating Role of Managerial Discretion," *Administrative Science Quarterly,* 35, 484-503.

Galbraith, J. R. and D. A. Nathanson (1979), "The Role of Organizational Structure and Process in Strategy Implementation," in D. E. Schendel and C. W. Hofer (Eds.), *Strategic Management: A New View of Business Policy and Planning,* Boston: Little, Brown.

Ghoshal, S. (1988), "Environmental Scanning in Korean Firms: Organizational Isomorphism in Action," *Journal of International Business Studies,* 19 (Spring), 69-86.

Gioia, D. A. and P. P. Poole (1984), "Scripts in Organizational Behavior," *Academy of Management Review,* 9, 449-459.

Govindarajan, V. (1989), "Implementing Competitive Strategies at the Business Level: Implications of Matching Managers to Strategies," *Strategic Management Journal,* 10, 251-269.

Green, P. E. and Y. Wind (1973), *Multiattribute Decisions in Marketing: A Measurement Approach,* Hinsdale, IL: Dryden.

Gupta, A. K. and V. Govindarajan (1984), "Business Unit Strategy, Managerial Characteristics, and Business Unit Effectiveness at Strategy Implementation," *Academy of Management Journal,* 27, 25-41.

Hair, J. F., Jr., R. E. Anderson, and R. I. Tatham (1987), *Multivariate Data Analysis,* New York: Macmillan.

Hambrick, D. C. and P. A. Mason (1984), "Upper Echelons: The Organization as a Reflection of Its Top Managers," *Academy of Management Review,* 9, 193-206.

Hatten, K. J., D. E. Schendel, and A. C. Cooper (1978), "A Strategic Model of the U.S. Brewing Industry," *Academy of Management Journal,* 21, 592-610.

Hitt, M. A. and B. B. Tyler (1991), "Strategic Decision Models: Integrating Different Perspectives," *Strategic Management Journal,* 12, 327-351.

Inkson, J. H. K., D. S. Pugh, and D. J. Hickson (1970), "Organization, Context, and Structure: An Abbreviated Replication," *Administrative Science Quarterly,* 15, 318-329.

Jackson, S. E. and J. E. Dutton (1988), "Discerning Threats and Opportunities," *Administrative Science Quarterly,* 33, 370-387.

Kim, L. and Y. Lim (1988), "Environment, Generic Strategies and Performance in a Rapidly Developing Country: A Taxonomic Approach," *Academy of Management Journal,* 31, 802-827.

Lawrence, P. R. and J. F. Lorsch (1967), *Organization and Environment,* Boston, MA: Harvard Graduate School of Business Administration.

Lenz, R. T. (1980), "Environment, Strategy, Organizational Structure, and Performance: Patterns in One Industry," *Strategic Management Journal,* 1, 209-226.

Lewin, A. Y. and C. U. Stephens (1994), "CEO Attitudes as Determinants of Organization Design: An Integrated Model," *Organization Studies,* 15, 183-212.

Lindsey, W. M. and L. W. Rue (1980), "Impact of the Organization Environment on the Long-Range Planning Process: A Contingency View," *Academy of Management Journal,* 23, 385-404.

Lord, R. G. and M. C. Kernan (1987), "Scripts as Determinants of Purposeful Behavior in Organizations," *Academy of Management Review,* 12, 265-277.

Louviere, J. L. (1988), *Analyzing Decision Making: Metric Conjoint Analysis,* Sage University Paper Series on Quantitative Applications in the Social Sciences, 67, Newbury Park, CA: Sage.

McCabe, D. L. (1990), "The Assessment of Perceived Environmental Uncertainty and Economic Performance," *Human Relations,* 43, 1203-1218.

McGrath, J. E. (1982), "Dilemmatics: The Study of Research Choices and Dilemmas," in J. E. McGrath, J. Martin, and R. A. Kulka (Eds.), *Judgment Calls in Research,* Beverly Hills, CA: Sage, 69-102.

Miller, D. (1983), "The Correlates of Entrepreneurship in Three Types of Firms," *Management Science,* 29, 770-791.

——— (1986), "Configurations of Strategy and Structure: Towards a Synthesis," *Strategic Management Journal,* 7, 233-249.

——— (1987), "Strategy Making and Structure: Analysis and Implications for Performance," *Academy of Management Journal,* 30, 7-32.

——— (1988), "Relating Porter's Business Strategies to Environment and Structure: Analysis and Performance Implications," *Academy of Management Journal,* 31, 280-308.

——— (1992), "Environmental Fit Versus Internal Fit," *Organization Science,* 3, 159-178.

——— and C. Droge (1986), "Psychological and Traditional Determinants of Structure," *Administrative Science Quarterly,* 31, 539-560.

———, ———, and J. M. Toulouse (1988), "Strategic Process and Content as Mediators between Organizational Context and Structure," *Academy of Management Journal,* 31, 544-569.

——— and H. Mintzberg (1984), "The Case for Configuration," in G. Morgan (Ed.), *Beyond Method,* Beverly Hills, CA: Sage, 57-73.

Mintzberg, H. and J. A. Waters (1985), "Of Strategies, Deliberate and Emergent," *Strategic Management Journal,* 6, 257-272.

Murray, A. I. (1988), "A Contingency View of Porter's 'Generic Strategies,' " *Academy of Management Review,* 13, 390-400.

Norburn, D. and S. Birley (1988), "The Top Management Team and Corporate Performance," *Strategic Management Journal,* 9, 225-237.

Oliver, C. (1988), "The Collective Strategy Framework: An Application to Competing Predictions of Isomorphism," *Administrative Science Quarterly,* 33, 543-561.

Penrose, E. T. (1959), *The Theory of the Growth of the Firm,* New York: John Wiley.

Porter, M. E. (1980), *Competitive Strategy,* New York: Free Press.

Priem, R. L. (1992), "An Application of Metric Conjoint Analysis for the Evaluation of Top Managers' Individual Strategic Decision-making Processes," *Strategic Management Journal,* 13 (Summer Special Issue), 143-151.

Pugh, D. C., D. J. Hickson, R. Hinings, and C. Turner (1969), "Dimensions of Organization Structure," *Administrative Science Quarterly,* 13, 65-105.

Sauley, K. S. and A. G. Bedeian (1989), ".05: A Case of the Tail Wagging the Distribution," *Journal of Management,* 15, 335-344.

Schendel, D. E. and C. W. Hofer (Eds.) (1979), *Strategic Management: A New View of Business Policy and Planning,* Boston: Little, Brown.

Schoemaker, P. J. H. (1990), "Strategy, Complexity, and Economic Rent," *Management Science,* 36, 1178-1192.

Schoonhoven, C. B. (1981), "Problems with Contingency Theory: Testing Assumptions Hidden within the Language of Contingency 'Theory,' " *Administrative Science Quarterly,* 26, 319-377.

Schwenk, C. R. (1988), "The Cognitive Perspective on Strategic Decision Making," *Journal of Management Studies,* 25, 41-55.

Skipper, J. K., Jr., A. L. Guenther, and G. Nass (1967), "The Sacredness of .05: A Note Concerning the Uses of Statistical Levels of Significance in Social Science," *American Sociologist,* 2, 16-18.

Stahl, M. J. and T. W. Zimmerer (1984), "Modeling Strategic Acquisition Policies: A Simulation of Executives' Acquisition Decisions," *Academy of Management Journal,* 27, 369-383.

Stubbart, C. I. (1989), "Managerial Cognition: A Missing Link in Strategic Management Research," *Journal of Management Studies,* 26, 325-347.

Thomas, A. B. (1988), "Does Leadership Make a Difference to Organizational Performance?" *Administrative Science Quarterly,* 33, 388-400.

Thomas, A. S., R. J. Litschert, and K. Ramaswamy (1991), "The Performance Impact of Strategy-Manager Coalignment: An Empirical Examination," *Strategic Management Journal,* 12, 509-522.

Thompson, J. D. (1967), *Organizations in Action,* New York: McGraw-Hill.

Tosi, H. L., Jr. and J. W. Slocum. Jr. (1984), "Contingency Theory: Some Suggested Directions," *Journal of Management,* 10, 9-26.

Tung, R. S. (1979), "Dimensions of Organizational Environments: An Exploratory Study of Their Impact on Organization Structure," *Academy of Management Journal,* 22, 672-693.

Van de Ven, A. H. and D. L. Ferry (1980), *Measuring and Assessing Organizations,* New York: John Wiley.

Venkatraman, N. (1989), "The Concept of Fit in Strategy Research: Toward Verbal and Statistical Correspondence," *Academy of Management Review,* 14, 423-444.

——— and V. Ramanujam (1987), "Measurement of Business Economic Performance: An Examination of Method Convergence," *Journal of Management,* 13, 109-122.

Viswesvaran, V. and M. R. Barrick (1992), "Decision-Making Effects on Compensation Surveys: Implications for Market Wages," *Journal of Applied Psychology,* 77, 588-597.

Walsh, J. P. and G. R. Ungson (1991), "Organizational Memory," *Academy of Management Review,* 16, 57-91.

White, R. E. (1986), "Generic Business Strategies, Organizational Context, and Performance: An Empirical Investigation," *Strategic Management Journal,* 7, 217-231.

Wiersema, M. F. and K. Bantel (1992), "Top Management Team Demography and Corporate Strategic Change," *Academy of Management Journal,* 35, 91-121.

Zey, M. (1992), *Decision Making: Alternatives to Rational Choice Models,* Newbury Park, CA: Sage.

Part II

COGNITION OF GROUPS IN ORGANIZATIONS

5

Integrating Organizational and Individual Information Processing Perspectives on Choice

PATRICIA DOYLE CORNER
ANGELO J. KINICKI
BARBARA W. KEATS

Existing information processing theories of strategic choice focus on either the organizational or individual level of analysis. This single level focus makes these theories incomplete representations of how strategic decisions are actually made in organizations. We believe an integration of these two levels is necessary for a comprehensive view of choice. This chapter thus proposes a parallel process model of strategic decision making that integrates organizational and individual level information processing perspectives. The integrated, comprehensive view afforded by the proposed model enhances understanding of strategic decision making by identifying (1) multiple ways in which bias can enter into choices and (2) dual level influences on decision activities such as information gathering and alternative generation.

The proposed model portrays strategic decision making as complex, multilevel information processing and choices as emergent outcomes of that processing. The model is developed as follows. First, the individual level of the model is generated by recognizing that people process information in stages. The notion of stages is used because it depicts the basic structure of information processing and is widely supported by empirical research. Second, the organizational level of the model is articulated by acknowledging organizations (1) process information in stages and (2) exhibit information processing activities analogous to those at the individual level. Third, a series of linking mechanisms connecting individual information

---

This chapter originally appeared in *Organization Science,* Vol. 5, No. 3, August 1994.

processing stages to analogous organizational level ones is proposed. These linking mechanisms thus conceptually operationalize the integration of the two levels. Fourth, three contingency variables are presented to flesh out the model and formulate propositions. Contingency variables specifically acknowledge differences in information processing across organizations. A final section of the chapter explains how key variables in the proposed model can be operationalized and outlines a test for the presence of multiple levels of information processing in a strategic choice context.

(ORGANIZATIONAL INFORMATION PROCESSING; INDIVIDUAL INFORMATION PROCESSING; FRAMES; STRATEGIC DECISION MAKING)

Information processing theories of strategic choice reflect either an organizational or individual level of analysis. The single level focus of these theories makes them incomplete representations of how strategic decisions actually are made in organizations. For example, an individual level model cannot capture the big car mindset that was shared by and influenced the choices of General Motors' top managers in the late seventies and early eighties. Nor can an organizational level model adequately capture the influence of a Harold Geneen on the decision making of an International Telephone and Telegraph. We thus believe an integration of the two levels is necessary for a comprehensive view of choice.

The purpose of this chapter is to propose a parallel process model of strategic decision making that integrates organizational and individual level information processing perspectives. We conceptually operationalize this integration by proposing a series of linking mechanisms that connect individual level information processing stages with organizational level ones. The value of the model for research is highlighted through a series of propositions and the description of an initial empirical test.

AN OVERVIEW OF THE PARALLEL PROCESS MODEL

The parallel process model is grounded in concepts established in the individual and organizational level information processing literatures. The individual level of the model reflects the idea that people process information in stages. The concept of stages is used because it depicts the basic structure of information processing and is extensively supported by empirical research. The parallel process model thus holds that individual decision makers first pay attention to information about a choice situation. This information is then assigned a meaning. Meaning assignment is called encoding and is referred to as interpretation or sense making in the organizational literature. Encoded information is stored in a person's memory and retrieved when he or she is faced with a choice. A choice is made and outcomes occur which then are available for the decision maker's attention.

Concepts for the organizational level were more difficult to select. The literature here is scant when compared to that available for individual level information processing. Nevertheless, the organizational level was articulated by recognizing that organizations (1) process information in stages and (2) exhibit information processing activities analogous to those seen at the individual level (Finney and Mitroff 1986, Gioia 1986, Levitt and March 1988). The parallel process model thus depicts organizational level information processing as the following set of stages: attention, encoding, storage/retrieval, choice, and outcomes. These stages are similar in function to those at the individual level but different in that an implicitly shared consensus underlies them (Daft and Weick 1984). The organizational level is viewed as the context within which individual level information processing takes place.

In summary, the parallel process model offers an integrated, comprehensive information processing approach to the study of strategic choice. This model advances research on decision making in three ways. First, it provides a comprehensive framework for identifying biases that affect strategic decisions at both processing levels. Second, it enhances our understanding of decision-making activities such as information gathering and problem solving through an explicit recognition of the dual level influences on them: Table 5.1 summarizes these influences. For example, information gathering is believed to be affected by both organizational level procedures for data collection and the idiosyncratic knowledge structures of the individuals involved (see Table 5.1).

Perhaps most important, the current model provides a new way of thinking about the strategy process. This process is viewed as a very complex, multilevel process of sense making. This conceptualization of the strategy process suggests that important influences on the process are missed if singular level models are used to understand it (see Table 5.1).

A PARALLEL PROCESS MODEL OF STRATEGIC DECISION MAKING

Organizations are strategic information processing *systems* encompassing information processing activities on both the individual and organizational

TABLE 5.1 A Comparison of the Multilevel Parallel Process Model to Singular Level Information Processing Models of Choice

Issue	*Organization Level Approaches*	*Individual Level Approaches*	*Multilevel Parallel Process Model Approach*
Levels of Information Processing	Explicitly acknowledge organizational level processing only. Assume away or don't deal with individual level information processing.	Acknowledge only individual level processing effects, organizational level effects not considered.	Explicitly acknowledges both individual and organizational level effects and suggests mechanisms linking the two levels.
Strategic Choice	View choice as a function of collective, shared context such as established decision premises (Cohen et al. 1972), procedures (March and Simon 1958), frames of references (Shrivastava and Schneider 1984), and routines (Nelson and Winter, 1982).	View choice as a function of individual level cognitive processing, which is controlled by decision maker's knowledge structures.	View choice as a function of both collectively shared context and individual cognitive processing.
Information Gathering	Collective context specifies what information is important. In choice situations this information is collected routinely.	Individual decision maker's knowledge structure determines what information is important and tailors information gathering to a particular choice situation.	Allows for both routinized information collection as specified by collective context and specialized information gathering done by individuals.
Problem Solving	This process is specified by collective context and is somewhat standardized.	A unique problem solving process is designed for each choice situation encountered.	Reflects a dynamic changing balance between standardized and specialized problem solving.
Alternative Development	Collective context likely specifies standard alternatives.	Decision maker seen as developing alternatives that are idiosyncratic to choice situation.	Incorporates the potential for *both* standardized and idiosyncratic alternatives in a particular choice situation.
Alternative Evaluation	Alternatives evaluated against standard criteria embodied in collective context.	Alternatives evaluated against criteria uniquely generated for specific situation.	Alternative evaluation criteria standardized if entrenched frame invoked, unique if new frame constructed.
Illustrative Examples	Cohen et al. 1972 Nelson and Winter 1982 Shrivastava and Schneider 1984	Child 1972 Schwenk, 1986, 1988 Dutton and Jackson, 1987 Mintzberg et al. 1976 Fredrickson 1984	Corner, Kinicki, & Keats

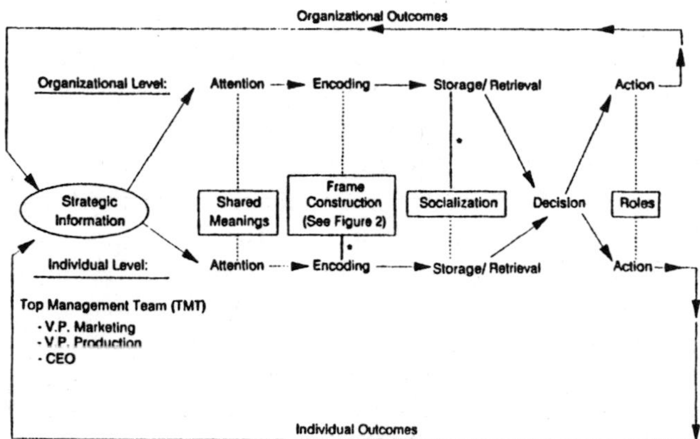

Figure 5.1. A Parallel Process Model of Strategic Decision Making
*Solid line indicates specific causal sequence.

levels. Figure 5.1 specifies how these two process levels interact. Two important boundary conditions apply to the model (Dubin 1978). At the organizational level, the model applies to ongoing, established organizations rather than emerging ones. At the individual level, it focuses only on members of the top management team (TMT) since they are responsible for strategic decision making. These assumptions do not appear to overly restrict the model's usefulness since (1) the bulk of organizations are beyond the initial emerging phase and (2) TMT members are the only individuals whose information processing has a direct influence on strategic decisions.

Strategic information (left side of the Figure) is processed sequentially through the parallel stages shown horizontally across the Figure. The following sections comprehensively explain the model stages. For each stage, the individual level of analysis is presented first. This is followed by a development of the analogous organizational level stage. Finally, we discuss a mechanism that links the individual and organizational levels of information processing.

Attention

Attention is a focus on information. It is the first stage in the model because information about a strategic decision must capture top managers' attention before it can be processed and infused with meaning. Attention is limited at both the individual and organizational level. Attentional limits filter or screen incoming information such that a great deal of data pertinent to a strategic decision may never get processed by TMT members. The following section describes factors affecting attention at the individual and organizational level and details a mechanism linking these levels.

Individual Level. Selective attention is the focus of consciousness at any point in time and is limited to approximately 7 items of information (Lord 1985, Schneider and Shiffrin 1977). As already stated, limited attentional capacity "filters" strategic information such that TMT members are unable to attend to all relevant information. This filtering reduces the amount of information available for further processing and decision making (Hambrick and Mason 1984, Kiesler and Sproull 1982). An underlying factor controlling members' selective attention is processing mode: automatic or controlled.

Processing mode controls the flow of information in consciousness at any given time (Ilgen and Feldman 1983, Isen and Daubman 1984, Schneider and Shiffrin 1977, Sinclair 1988). The automatic or default mode allows team members to direct attention to multiple strategic information items simultaneously. Members engaged in this mode are more likely to make impressionistic interpretations of strategic information and less likely to differentiate across types and sources of information. They thus are unlikely to distinguish a strategic issue from its environmental background unless it is sharply different from that background.

Controlled processing is a sequential series of thought patterns requiring a team member's effortful, conscious control (Schneider and Shiffrin 1977, Ungson et al. 1981). It completely absorbs cognitive resources and facilitates the differentiation of strategic information from its environmental background. TMT members thus are more likely to discern important strategic issues embedded within ambient environmental information when in this mode.

Organizational Level. Organizational or group attention is defined as the focus of a TMT's environmental scanning and it determines which data are available for interpretation by the group. Similar to an individual, a group has a limited capacity for attention (Levitt and March 1988, March and Shapira 1982). Attentional capacity is limited by a TMT's routines for gathering and sharing information.

Organizational attention, like individual attention, exhibits one of two processing modes: surveillance (March and Shapira 1982) or motivated search (Cyert and March 1963, Mintzberg et al. 1976). Surveillance is the default mode analogous to individual level automatic processing. It reflects a broad, routine scan of a firm's domain: A team in this mode attends to information only when it is congruent with its data collection routines.

Motivated search is the organizational analog of controlled processing. It reflects an intensive, narrowly focused environmental exploration intended to yield in-depth information about one portion of a firm's domain. Lant and Mezias (1990, 1992) see this mode as the search for previously unnoticed opportunities capable of enhancing firm performance. Unfortunately, their recent simulation suggests that motivated search results in improved performance only under special conditions since it requires a great expenditure of resources (Lant and Mezias 1990). For example, a firm following an industry leader's strategy can benefit from motivated search after a time of upheaval if its managers are unsure about what factors lead to good performance.

Linking Mechanism. Meanings shared among or held in common by members of the TMT provide for a consensus view that links individual and organizational level attention processes (see Figure 5.1). The result is an implicit consensus or commonly shared "definition" of information appropriate for TMT members' attention. A shared definition enables a TMT to separate *information* (potentially meaningful data that deserves attention) from extraneous data (March and Shapira 1982, Feldman and March 1981). For example, Ginsberg (1990) suggests that shared meanings determine which acquisition targets are noticed and considered by a TMT.

An important point regarding shared meanings is that all meanings do not have to be shared in order for individual and organizational attention to be linked. Even one or two shared meanings provide a common perspective or shared attentional focus for TMT members.

Encoding

Encoding is interpreting or understanding information. It occurs when an individual or team, in an effort to gain information processing efficiencies, compares information about a phenomenon to existing knowledge of that phenomenon. Bias can result from this comparison because pieces of existing knowledge get included in the understanding of the new information. Encoding thus results in biased decisions: choices grounded in an understanding of information that is actually different from initially observed information. The following section describes how encoding introduces bias and suggests a particular sequence for encoding: Individual level encoding precedes organizational level encoding and provides the medium from which collective meanings emerge. This sequence is shown in Figure 5.1 by the solid line connecting the antecedent of individual encoding to the linking mechanism of frame construction (D'Andrade 1981, Weick 1979).

Individual Level. Strategic information surpassing a person's selective attention filter is given meaning through encoding. Encoding is the transformation of strategic information into an abstract internal representation which is then infused with meaning (Fiske and Taylor 1984). It is important for two reasons. First, encoding determines what information is readily retrievable from memory for decision making. Second, encoding is the critical "point of entry" for cognitive biases and thus can help explain some of the strategic choice biases identified in the literature (Duhaime and Schwenk 1985, Schwenk 1984, 1988).

Meaning infusion is accomplished through a feature matching process governed by structures known as categories (Cantor and Mischel 1979, Higgins and Bargh 1987, Rosch 1978). A category is a "fuzzy set" of equivalent things most often designated by a name like "competitor" or "stakeholder." Categories encompass prototypes or idealized examples of a category member. Feature matching is best seen through an example. Consider a TMT member such as the VP of Marketing who is considering a potential acquisition target. Two characteristics of this target—"large number of employees" and "strong markets"—surpassed attention and are available for encoding. The VP of Marketing then recalls a "good acquisition target" category from memory. The feature matching process involves comparing characteristics of the target to features of the category prototype and generating a final encoded representation suitable for storage in memory. There are four important outcomes of this process.

First, acquisition target characteristics like "strong markets" that match prototype features are included in the final-encoded representation of the target (Cantor and Mischel 1979). Second, target characteristics that *do not* match category prototype features (e.g., "large number of employees") are excluded from the final encoded representation. Third, prototypical features not reflected by the original target tend to be falsely included in the final encoded representation because observed information is processed as an example of a category (Wyer and Srull 1980). As cognitive satisficers, TMT members minimize cognitive effort by including prototypical features in the encoded version of the acquisition target (Cantor and Mischel 1979). A prototypical feature such as "reliable suppliers" thus is falsely included in the final representation of the original information. Fourth, TMT members make inferences during encoding and store them along with information retained from the feature matching process (Wyer and Srull 1980). In the example, the vice president combines "strong markets" with "reliable suppliers" and infers attractiveness of the target because it reflects a few key features of a good acquisition.

As a result, the encoded representation of the acquisition target is an information "bundle" that includes the following information: strong markets, reliable suppliers, and the inference of good acquisition target. This "bundle" of information is stored in memory and ultimately retrieved when needed. Two important aspects of this information "bundle" should be noted. The information stored in memory is not accurate and it is biased toward the category prototype. This type of cognitive bias is hypothesized to affect strategic issue diagnosis (Dutton et al. 1983), decisions regarding divestitures (Duhaime and Schwenk 1985) and competitive positioning (Porac and Thomas 1990, Reger 1988).

Relative category accessibility is an important factor in the feature matching process. Category accessibility is the availability of a stored category for selectively attending to and interpreting information (Bargh et al. 1986). TMT members' experience leads them to develop chronically (always) accessible categories that regulate encoding and determine what information is available for strategic decision making (Kelly 1955, Hambrick and Mason 1984).

Organizational Level. Organizational encoding is a TMT's socially interactive interpretation of information. A TMT interactively interprets information because the complexity of many strategic decisions it faces exceeds the cognitive limits of any given member (Jacobs and Jaques 1987, Schweiger et al. 1989). Organizational encoding determines the information preserved by a team and available for decision making. As at the individual level, organizational encoding also provides a "point of entry" for bias as illustrated in the following example.

Consider again the acquisition target example used to describe individual encoding. At this level however, the three TMT members listed on Figure 5.1 interact to make sense of the target. Team members bring to this interaction their individual understandings of the target. These are reflected in the information bundles generated by each members' individual cognitive processing. Each bundle contains an information item reflecting an originally observed characteristic of the acquisition. For example, the VP of Marketing's information bundle includes the "strong markets" item that survived his or her cognitive processing.

Information contained in these bundles invokes a frame or group knowledge structure. Frames are analogous to categories and thereby function as integrative structures providing holistic interpretations of information (Shrivastava and Schneider 1984). They serve two broad roles in the current model: meaning assignment and linking mechanism. (Because we are concerned only with the meaning assignment function in this section, details of frames as linking mechanisms are presented in the next section). Frames encompass images: the collective analog of individual level prototypes (Mitchell and Beach 1990). Images are shared representations of an ideal choice, such as an ideal acquisition candidate. Images enable TMT members to visualize, articulate, and use frames collectively to assign meaning to strategic information.

Organizational encoding of strategic information occurs through an interactive feature matching process in which TMT members collectively match information contained in bundles against image features. Returning to the example, assume the TMT utilizes a "success is achieved through marketing excellence" frame to make sense of the acquisition target. Embedded in this frame is the image of a previous acquisition whose marketing resources and skills contributed to an increase in the firm's return on investment. This acquisition's idiosyncratic features serve as the image features against which information items contained in bundles are matched. There are four possible outcomes of this feature matching process.

First, bundles' information items may match a corresponding image feature and thus be included in a final understanding of a target. For example, the VP of Marketing's bundle reflects "strong markets" and is included in the final understanding since the prior acquisition also had strong markets. The CEO's bundle includes a "related business" item that survived encoding. This bundle also is included since the previous acquisition was a related one.

Second, items that do not match a corresponding image feature are not included in a team's final understanding of a target. For instance, the VP of Production's information bundle includes "functional organizational structure" as an information item which survived encoding. The comparison acquisition had a divisional structure so there is *not* a match. This bundle thus is not included in the team's final understanding of the target.

Third, image features that characterize the example acquisition but do not correspond to bundle items also may be included in the final understanding of the target. This is because the bundle information is processed as if it were an instance of the frame. In the example, the prior acquisition had a "customer-oriented culture" and this feature is likely included as an implicitly assumed characteristic in the final understanding of the target.

Finally, judgments are made during organizational encoding (Isabella 1990). In this case, the "strong markets" and "related business" bundles are combined with "customer-oriented culture" to produce a "good potential acquisition" judgment about the acquisition target. The final organizational understanding of the target includes the following: "strong markets," "related business," "customer-oriented culture" and "good potential acquisition." This information may not all be of equal importance in the frame. Information's relative importance is determined by the power (defined below) of the TMT member espousing it (Walsh and Fahey 1986) (this point is elaborated on in a later, contingency variables section of the chapter). There are two interesting things to note about the information encompassed in this collectively generated understanding.

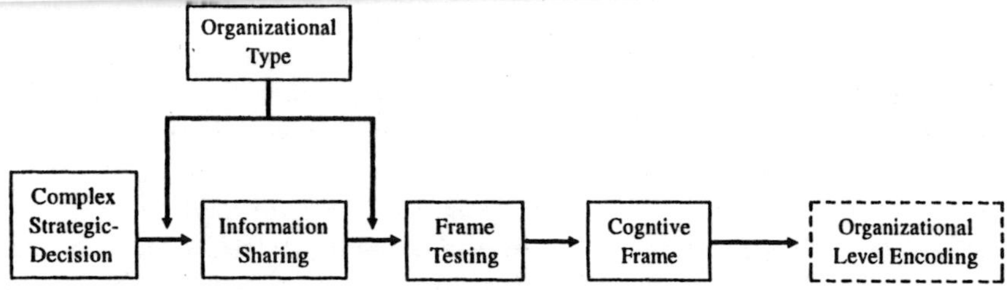

Figure 5.2. A Model of the Frame Construction Process

First, the organizational understanding of the acquisition target reflects more originally observed information items (i.e., "strong markets" and "related business") than does any individual cognitive representation of this information (these reflect only one item, such as "strong markets" in the case of the VP of Marketing). The TMT thus partially overcame the cognitive limitations of its individual members by providing a richer, more detailed interpretation of the target. This echoes Walsh, Henderson, and Deighton's (1988) point that a team's information processing structure includes or "covers" more of the information in a particular domain than does the processing structure of a single individual within the group. Second, the organizational interpretation of the acquisition target reflects biases from two sources: those resulting from individual processing and those induced by group information processing such as information originating from the frame. Thus, strategic information processing by a top management team may be a two-edged sword. The enhanced information increases the potential for bias. This concern is an important focal point for studies directed toward enhanced decision quality.

Linking Mechanism. Frame construction is the mechanism linking individual and organizational encoding. Frames are constructed when TMT members share and discuss alternative interpretations of information (Daft and Weick 1984, Frost and Morgan 1983, Levitt and March 1988). During the process of frame construction, TMT members' individual cognitions are woven into a collectively shared frame that is used to encode strategic information. Individual encoding thus is the antecedent of frame construction as indicated by the solid line in Figure 5.1. A model of frame construction is presented in Figure 5.2.

As already stated, strategic decisions are complex and require socially interactive information processing *in addition* to individual cognitive processing (Jacobs and Jaques 1987, Schweiger et al. 1989). The necessity of making such a decision engenders the following stages of a socially interactive frame construction process.

Information sharing is the first stage of interactive frame construction. This stage involves TMT members reporting and discussing decision data that they or their staffs have gathered (Daft and Weick 1984, D'Andrade 1981). Members thus ante data into an information "pool" during this sharing phase of frame construction.

This "pool" of information is a puzzle the TMT seeks to solve by imposing order upon it. Order imposition is achieved in the frame testing phase of the process (see Figure 5.2). Frame testing involves suggesting an integrative structure that provides a holistic interpretation of the morass of information contained in the "pool." TMT members may take turns suggesting interpretive frames (Frost and Morgan 1983). Once a member suggests a frame, others test it by "trying it on for size" to see if it helps make sense of the mass of data contained in the "pool" (Frost and Morgan 1983).

Eventually, members agree that one particular frame provides a suitable integrative meaning and a consensus frame is established (Daft and Weick 1984, Frost and Morgan 1983). The consensus frame then serves as a collective knowledge structure, analogous to an individual level category, that infuses information with meaning during encoding at the organizational level. It is important to note that a consensus frame does not imply that TMT members share all meanings. Instead it suggests members are able to agree on one or several meanings and thus come to some shared understanding of information. For example, Donnellon, Gray, and Bougon (1986) found that a group in a behavioral simulation agreed on a metaphor for a choice situation and was able to unanimously agree on a choice even though group members' interpretations had nothing in common but the metaphor.

Established consensus frames are one of two types: emergent or entrenched. An emergent frame is constructed in an ad hoc fashion to deal with a novel problem or issue. Constructing an emergent frame is a lengthy process because each stage requires extensive cognitive energy and time on the part of TMT members. Once a consensus frame has been achieved, there is substantial inertial and process efficiency value in retaining it to interpret future issues (Weick 1979). Emergent frames thus become entrenched over time and the frame construction portion of the process occurs more quickly as TMT members apply a repeatedly used frame to new data.

An entrenched consensus frame regulates organizational encoding in the same way a chronic category controls individual level encoding and is analogous to the concept of dominant logic espoused by Prahalad and Bettis (1986). A frame can become so deeply entrenched that a TMT invokes it automatically when interpreting strategic information, whether it is appropriate or not. In this case a TMT may have to unlearn a frame before a new one can be constructed (Hedberg 1981).

As indicated in Figure 5.2, organizational type, or variation in collective information processing styles (Daft and Weick 1984), moderates two relationships in the frame construction process. In the interest of logical flow, the role of this concept is merely noted here to acknowledge its placement in the figure. An expanded definition and discussion of this contingency variable is reserved for a later ("contingency variables") section of the chapter.

Storage/Retrieval

Storage is the preservation of interpreted information. Information is retrieved when a strategic decision is required (Finney and Mitroff 1986). Information about a decision that surpassed attention and survived encoding could be lost here due to imperfections in storage mechanisms. This further dilutes the information in which a strategic choice is grounded. This section outlines storage/retrieval at the individual and organizational level and suggests a mechanism linking them.

Individual Level. A strategic decision opportunity triggers a search of memory for information (Mintzberg et al. 1976). Strategic information is stored in memory within an associative network of nodes in which each node contains an item of information. Connections between nodes reflect relationships between items (Hastie 1980) that become stronger with repeated use (Hastie 1980) and learning (Langer 1978). Strategic information is retrieved in the memory search phase through a "spreading activation" mechanism. Activation spreads from node to node via the connections between them so that related events and ideas tend to be recalled together (Fiske and Taylor 1984). Experience and learning thus produce a rich network of informational connections that aid a TMT member in accessing complex "bundles" of information when making strategic decisions.

Organizational Level. An organization also searches its (collective) memory for applicable information when presented with a strategic choice opportunity (Levitt and March 1988, Walsh and Ungson 1991). Collective memory is a meaning structure resulting from experience that is sustained despite employee turnover (Walsh and Ungson 1991). Experience-based knowledge is stored in routines or organizationally legitimized patterns of response (Nelson and Winter 1982). Routines include forms, rules, procedures, conventions, strategies, technologies, culture, and frameworks; any of which can be retrieved from collective memory and applied to newly noticed problems or issues. The knowledge included in these routines can be retrieved from collective memory and applied to a choice. Knowledge stored in frequently used routines is most likely to be extracted and incorporated into decisions since these are most available (Nelson and Winter 1982).

Linking Mechanism. Socialization links individual and organizational storage (see Figure 5.1). Socialization is the process by which an individual acquires the social wisdom and skills necessary to assume an organizational role (Van Maanen and Schein 1979). Veteran TMT members subtly influence newcomers to learn and preserve accepted knowledge and routines by filtering out information that contradicts preserved knowledge and by acknowl-edging as credible only those who accept organizational routines (Feldman 1981). We suggest that established routines lead to socialization (see solid line in Figure 5.1) which, in turn, integrates individuals into a firm's collective storage pattern.

Decision

Strategic decisions are based on information retrieved from storage (Mintzberg et al. 1976, Nutt 1984). Decisions are shown as a single level stage in Figure 5.1 because a strategic choice is a collective phenomenon in most organizations (Cyert and March 1963, Ginsberg 1990, Prahalad and Bettis 1986, Thompson 1967, Walsh and Fahey 1986). Decisions also are depicted as outcomes of previous process stages. According to this information processing view, decisions are not so much *"made"* in organizations as they are developed in a context of meaning (March 1987, Smircich and Stubbart 1985). This view of decisions is consistent with Mintzberg's (1978) notion of strategic decisions as emergent phenomena. It's also consistent with the interpretive view of strategy process, which is gaining momentum in the literature (Fredrickson 1984, Huff 1982, Smircich and Stubbart 1985, Quinn 1980). We thus suggest that not all strategic decisions are rationally constructed choices. Many may be emergent outcomes of complex sense making that publicize or celebrate an organization's interpretations and function as a signal for organizational action (March 1987, Quinn 1980).

Action

Action is the enactment of a strategic decision at both the individual and organizational level. In this section, we explain action at the two levels and discuss the link between them.

Individual Level. Individual action is a TMT member's contribution to (or role in) a plan of concerted action. A member's action is the enactment of the strategic decision within his or her sphere of responsibility (e.g., functional department). Individual action thus includes much of what is traditionally considered in the area of implementation (Galbraith and Kazanjian 1986).

Organizational Level. Collective action is the concerted effort required to implement a strategic decision. For instance, a firm is taking collective action when it enters new markets with an expanded product line because the coordinated action of a number of people is required to accomplish entry.

Linking Mechanism. Organizational and individual level actions are linked through TMT members' roles. Roles provide for integrated individual behavior patterns capable of achieving a concerted action. Consider again the new market entry example. Each vice-president (see Figure 5.1) has a role to perform in accomplishing this particular concerted action. The VP of Marketing, for example, may develop a new product while the VP of Production assembles the product in mass quantities. Both actions—new product creation and mass assembly—must occur in order to achieve successful market entry.

Outcomes

Outcomes are the results of decision enactment. Outcomes are experienced at both the individual level (i.e., performance evaluations) and the organizational level (i.e., competitors' reactions, financial returns, market penetration, government fines, etc.). Individual outcomes result from role performance in the context of a collective action. Organizational level outcomes are the consequences of collective action. Outcomes, like all environmental response data, can become strategic information or feedback if they capture attention. Feedback creates the potential for learning at both process levels (see Figure 5.1).

We offer a final comment on the model presented in Figure 5.1. Action and outcomes were included even though their links with decision are very complex and a full exploration of them is beyond the scope of the chapter. They were included in order to present a comprehensive picture of the parallel process and to suggest avenues for future conceptual research.

PARALLEL PROCESS CONTINGENCIES

Contingency variables are incorporated into the proposed model in order to illustrate potential differences in parallel processing across organizations. Three variables are important in a strategic decision context. These are power

(Pfeffer 1981, Walsh and Fahey 1986) organizational types (Daft and Weick 1984) and TMT demographic characteristics (Bantel and Jackson 1989, Hambrick and Mason 1984, Murray 1989). There probably are additional contingencies but these were chosen because they are specifically identified as information processing contingencies in the literature. The three variables their importance and their effect on the parallel process are all discussed in the following sections. A summary of this discussion is presented in Table 5.2.

Power

Power is the capability of a social actor to overcome resistance in achieving a desired objective or result (Pfeffer 1981). It is an important contingency because it determines the extent to which the organizational level of the parallel process is either (1) a true combination of TMT members' ideas and knowledge or (2) a reflection of the most powerful members' ideas and knowledge. This tradeoff is illustrated by the differences power can produce at attention and encoding (see Table 5.2).

At attention, powerful TMT members can shape the content of shared meanings which link individual and organizational levels (see Figure 5.1). Such shaping occurs when a powerful TMT member limits participation in discussion so that his or her interpretations are ultimately adopted (Thomas and McDaniel 1990, Walsh and Fahey 1986). Shared meanings are predictable in this case since they likely mirror those included in powerful TMT members' chronic categories. Chronic categories preserve meanings acquired through education and experience (Higgins and King 1981). For example, efficiency-oriented meanings are probably preserved in the technical categories developed by those with engineering backgrounds. Over time, these efficiency meanings become shared and shape a team's attention as less powerful vice presidents begin to espouse them. This idea is summarized in the following proposition.

P1. *There will be a strong positive correlation between a TMT member's power and the number of shared meanings that originated in the member's individual category.*

At encoding, a powerful TMT member can exert observable, tangible influence during the frame construction process that links individual and organizational encoding. For instance, a powerful team member can propose the first framework considered during frame testing (see Figure 5.2) and press for a commitment to it, thereby constraining the suggestions of others. He or she may ignore any frameworks suggested by others so that they never get a sufficient "test" (see Figure 5.2). Empirical evidence supports this notion of powerful TMT members controlling frameworks for information interpretation (Eisenhardt and Bourgeois 1988). In such cases, the consensus frame used to encode information is probably identical to the most powerful TMT member's chronic category (see Table 5.2).

Chronic categories evolve from and thus mirror functional experience (Dearborn and Simon 1958, Ireland et al. 1987). For instance, a powerful, finance-oriented TMT member with a chronic "portfolio" category can induce acceptance of the "portfolio" framework by (1) pressing for a commitment to this perspective and (2) ignoring the "product differentiation" framework suggested by the marketing vice-president. The "portfolio" thus emerges as a consensus frame and information about potential opportunities is encoded relative to it as reflected in the following proposition.

P2. *The consensus frame generated by a team is more likely to be grounded in the functional background of the most powerful team member than in the functional background of any other team member.*

Organizational Type

Daft and Weick (1984) proposed four organizational types to account for differences in interpretation across firms. These types are important for the proposed model because they suggest standard forms that the parallel process might take across organizations. Organizational types reflect two underlying dimensions: (1) firms' assumptions about the analyzability of the environment—unanalyzable or analyzable—and (2) firms' intrusiveness relative to the environment—passive or active. (Organizational types are described in summary form here, and the reader is referred to the original article for further information.) Enacting organizations (unanalyzable; active) are "action-based" sense makers because they take action to generate information which they interpret retrospectively. Discovering organizations (analyzable; active) are "analytical" sense makers because preserved interpretations are consistently reanalyzed to reflect new, aggressively pursued environmental information. Conditioned viewing organizations (analyzable; passive) are "history-based" sense makers. These organizations apply historical interpretations of the environment to any newly acquired strategic information. Finally, undirected viewing organizations (unanalyzable; passive) are "accidental" sense makers. These firms interpret strategic issues only if pointed out by an outsider.

Organizational types produce parallel process differences at attention and encoding (see Table 5.2). At attention, differences are due to variation in the number of meanings shared by TMT members across organizational types.

TABLE 5.2 Parallel Process Contingencies

Contingency	*Stage at which Contingency Applies*	*Impact on the Parallel Process*	*Outcomes Resulting From Impact of Contingency Variables*
Power	Attention	Most powerful TMT members shape the content of shared meanings	TMTs attend to information consistent with content of teams' most powerful members' chronic categories & schemes.
	Encoding	Most powerful TMT members shape consensus frames	Consensus frames reflect the chronic categories of a TMT's most powerful member.
Organizational Type	Attention	Determines number of shared meanings that link the individual and organizational level	Given few shared meanings, TMTs attend to a wide variety of information. As number of shared meanings increases, variety in noticed information decreases.
	Encoding	Modifies the relationship between complex strategic decision and information sharing in the frame construction process (see Figure 5.5)	The amount of information compiled in response to the necessity to make a complex strategic decision differs according to organizational type.
		Modifies the relationship between information sharing in the frame testing in the frame construction process (see Figure 5.5)	Frame testing process and the number of frames tested differs according to organizational type.
Age Heterogeneity of TMT	Encoding	TMTs low in age heterogeneity use an entrenched frame to make sense of choice information	TMTs low in age heterogeneity make strategic decisions more quickly than do TMTs high in age heterogeneity.
Tenure Heterogeneity of TMT	Encoding	TMTs low in tenure heterogeneity use an entrenched frame to make sense of choice information.	TMTs low in tenure heterogeneity make strategic decisions more quickly than do TMTs high in age heterogeneity.

This variation is best seen by ordering organizational types along a continuum ranging from few shared meanings to many shared meanings (Ginsberg 1990, Weick and Bougon 1986).

Enacting organizations fall at one end of the continuum since few meanings are shared in these firms (Weick and Bougon 1986). Few shared meanings suggest enacting TMTs have scant a priori specified attention targets to guide attention. They thus are likely to attend to a great variety of information. Conditioned viewing organizations fall at the other end of the spectrum because members share many meanings (Ginsberg 1990, Weick and Bougon 1986). Teams in these firms have an extensive set of a priori specified attention targets directing attention. As such, there probably is little variation in the kinds of information attended to by conditioned viewing teams. Thomas and McDaniel's (1990) results support this conclusion. Their findings indicate that TMTs with many specified attention targets (data collection procedures) use less variety of information for environmental analysis than do TMTs with few specified attention targets.

Discovering organizations anchor the middle of the continuum because they share a moderate number of meanings. These organizations thus are expected to attend to a semicomprehensive set of specified attention targets that falls in between that of enacting and conditioned viewing organizations. Finally, undirected viewing organizations cannot be located on the spectrum because teams here don't share meanings. What meanings team members once shared have disintegrated and a state of interpretational chaos reigns (Weick and Bougon 1986). The following proposition summarizes the contingency effect of organizational type at attention.

P3. *TMTs sharing few meanings will collect and discuss a greater variety of choice information than will TMTs sharing many meanings.*

Organizational type is a contingency at encoding in two ways (see Table 5.2). First, organizational type moderates the complex strategic decision/information sharing relationship within the frame construction process (see Figure 5.2). Enacting TMTs don't have entrenched frames specifying information to be collected and shared during decision making. This produces ambiguity regarding the sharing of choice information and results in TMT members collecting and sharing a vast amount of information about a strategic choice (Thompson 1967). In contrast, conditioned viewing organizations have entrenched frames dictating the kind and amount of choice information that is collected and shared. TMT members therefore are expected to limit information sharing to that dictated by the frame. Discovering TMTs fall somewhere in between conditioned viewing and enacting teams since they are likely to have moderately entrenched frames that remove some of the ambiguity about information sharing. These firms thus collect a moderate amount of information. A prediction for undirected viewing firms is again impossible because of the state of interpretational chaos that reigns. Information sharing patterns among TMT members of different organizational types suggest the following proposition.

P4. *TMTs with entrenched frames will collect and discuss less information about a strategic choice than will TMTs without entrenched frames.*

Organizational type also moderates the information sharing/frame testing relationship (see Figure 5.2). Conditioned viewing organizations automatically tend to impose entrenched frames (dominant logics) on any accumulated information, thereby engaging in a "rubber stamp" sort of frame testing. For these firms, dominant logic predetermines the frame that will be tested and ultimately used as the consensus frame. Frame testing is more random in undirected viewing organizations where it resembles a garbage can process (Cohen et al. 1972). Suggested frames randomly intermingle with sets of strategic information. A particular frame and a specific set of strategic information become prominent simultaneously, are linked together, and emerge from the garbage can as a consensus frame.

Frame testing in enacting and discovering organizations possesses elements of both the "rubber stamp" process seen in conditioned viewing firms and the more random process observed in undirected viewing organizations. Frame testing is a process of guided discovery for these firms, guided by either an acknowledged leader in an enacting organization or a shared set of analytical procedures in a discovering organization. The leader or analytical procedure sets the constraints within which the random component of frame testing is allowed to operate. This discussion is summarized in the following proposition.

P5. *TMTs with entrenched frames will generate fewer explanatory scenarios or frameworks than will TMTs without entrenched frames.*

Yet another proposition is suggested by the role of organizational type in the frame construction process. Frame construction is a lengthy, time-consuming process in undirected viewing organizations since TMT members extensively share information and entertain multiple frames before developing a consensus frame. TMTs in conditioned viewing organizations engage in very limited information sharing and consider only the entrenched frame during frame testing. Frame construction thus takes less time than it does in undirected viewing firms. The time involved in frame construction for enacting and discovering organizations falls somewhere in between that of undirected and conditioned viewing organizations. Time differences in frame construction are likely to affect the length of time needed to make a decision as suggested by the following proposition.

P6. *TMTs with entrenched frames will take less time to make strategic decisions than will TMTs without entrenched frames.*

Demographic Characteristics of TMT Members

Characteristics of team members such as age and organizational tenure are believed to influence teams' information processing (Hambrick and Mason 1984). Similar age cohorts are likely to share many meanings since the same social, political, and economic environments shaped their respective individual categories. An extensive set of shared meanings suggests teams with relatively homogeneous ages use entrenched frames to make sense of choice information. As already stated, use of an entrenched frame means quick decision making. Alternately, teams with relatively heterogeneous ages probably share few meanings due to members' very different backgrounds. Few shared meanings suggests the need to negotiate a consensus frame for every strategic decision. Such negotiation is a lengthy process indicating slow decision making. These ideas are summarized in the following propositions.

P7. *TMTs high in age heterogeneity will share fewer meanings than teams low in age heterogeneity.*

P8. *TMTs high in age heterogeneity will take longer to make strategic decisions than teams low in age heterogeneity.*

Similarly, TMTs whose members have similar lengths of organizational tenure are more likely to share meanings. This occurs because similar tenure lengths suggest a common organizational history and corresponding understanding of the firm and its environment. Again, extensively shared meanings indicates the presence of an entrenched frame for decision making and less time needed to make choices. TMTs whose members have very heterogeneous tenure lengths are likely to share few meanings due to a lack of common experience and history. Few shared meanings indicate the need to construct new consensus frames for every choice and lengthy decision making. The following propositions formally state these ideas.

P9. *TMTs whose members have heterogeneous lengths of organizational tenure will share fewer meanings than teams whose members have homogeneous lengths of organizational tenure.*

P10. *TMTs whose members have heterogeneous lengths of organizational tenure will take a longer time making strategic decisions than teams whose members have homogeneous lengths of organizational tenure.*

Parallel process contingencies have implications for strategic decision making other than those presented in the propositions above. These implications are addressed in a series of additional propositions presented in Table 5.3. These propositions serve as an illustration of the effects of parallel processing on strategic decision making, not as an exhaustive list of propositions potentially derivable from the model.

IMPLICATIONS AND TESTING THE MODEL

The parallel process model presents a unified conceptualization of the multilevel information processes shaping strategic decisions. It thus contributes to the understanding of choice because it enables us to conceptualize strategic decision making differently. Decisions in this context are thought of as emergent outcomes of complex sense making, not as the rationally or consciously constructed deductions suggested by tradition. The model also offers a view of the strategic decision process that facilitates a comprehensive identification of the multiple biases inherent in that process. In this section, we discuss two important implications of the parallel process model for research and outline an initial test of the model.

Implications

One implication is that the traditional domain of strategy "content" is too narrow. Conventional wisdom views a strategy's content as the set of economic and structural elements that collectively represent a "cost leadership," or "differentiation" strategy, for example (Porter 1980). However, our model suggests the importance of including the rhetorical elements of decisions as significant components of a strategy's content (March 1987). For instance, a cost leadership strategy may be communicating (1) a TMT's decision to compete on the basis of cost to other firms in the industry and (2) a message of cost cutting and efficiency to firm members.

Another implication is that information processing levels dynamically interact with each other. The importance of this interaction is very straightforward: One process level cannot be studied in the absence of the other.

TABLE 5.3 Additional Propositions Suggested by the Model and the Contingency Variables

Attention	
P11:	Individual TMT members in a controlled processing mode will identify more opportunities within the environment than will individual TMT members in an automatic processing mode.
P12:	A TMT in a motivated search mode will identify more opportunities within the environment than will a TMT in a surveillance mode.
P13:	There will be a strong association between the content of shared meanings and the content of choice information collected and discussed by a TMT.
P14:	A transcript of a TMTs discussion of a strategic choice situation will contain more of the originally available choice information than will an individual member's description of a choice situation.
P15:	TMTs with entrenched frameworks will share more meanings than TMTs without entrenched frameworks.
P16:	There will be a strong negative correlation between the number of meanings shared by TMT members and the number of explanatory frameworks forwarded in a discussion about a choice.
P17:	TMTs whose members exhibit a high level of functional background heterogeneity share fewer beliefs than teams with a low level of functional background heterogeneity.
P18:	TMTs whose members exhibit a high level of functional background heterogeneity take longer to make decisions than teams with a low level of functional background heterogeneity.
P19:	There will be a strong negative correlation between the number of meanings shared among TMT members and the number of contingency plans developed to back up strategic choices.
P20:	TMTs that share few meanings will discuss a greater number of information items pertaining to a choice than will TMTs sharing many meanings.

Future research is clearly needed to examine both the interdependencies and resulting outcomes of individual and organizational level information processing. The following section suggests a way to pursue this objective.

Testing the Model

Operationalizing "Meanings." The proposed model suggests TMT members use meanings stored in individual or group knowledge structures to make sense of choice information. The first step is thus to operationalize meanings. This can be done by measuring TMT members' beliefs (Walsh et al. 1988). Beliefs are units of knowledge representing an association between two things, most often a cause and effect association (Ajzen and Fishbein 1980, Axelrod 1976). In the case of an acquisition choice for example, a TMT member might believe that an acquisition target's technologically advanced production facilities can lead to cost savings for the parent firm. Beliefs can be identified using Fishbein's procedure (see Ajzen and Fishbein 1980). Specifically, the literature can provide a list of 10 acquisition outcomes (i.e., enhanced market presence) and 10 acquisition characteristics leading to such outcomes (i.e., large market share). Beliefs about acquisitions are then obtained by asking team members to identify the 5 most important outcomes and characteristics.

Beliefs *shared* by members are used to tap into organizational level information processing. Specifically, shared beliefs are captured by counting the number of pairwise overlaps in TMT members' beliefs. The number of pairwise overlaps in a team's beliefs is calculated by first figuring the number of overlaps for each possible belief. These overlaps are then summed across all possible beliefs.

Testing for a Parallel Process. We envision an initial test designed to confirm the occurrence of information processing at both levels in an acquisition choice situation. The initial experiment involves TMTs that never made an acquisition so that teams with entrenched frames for choosing acquisitions are avoided.

TMT members' beliefs about acquisitions would first be elicited following the Fishbein procedure described above. Teams then participate in an acquisition choice exercise. Teams are required to discuss ideas and information pertaining to the available candidates. TMTs then select an acquisition and members' beliefs about acquisitions are assessed again. An increase in the number of pairwise overlaps in members' beliefs in the after-choice condition as compared to the before-choice condition indicates that organizational level information processing took place. Specifically, the increase implies members identified beliefs to share—created a consensus frame—and used this to make their choice. The addition of beliefs to individuals' belief sets indicates that individual level information processing also took place (Ward and Reingen 1990). These changes could be confirmed by making transcripts of team meetings and identifying the meanings (1) discussed by individual members and (2) agreed on by the team as essential to decision making.

The proposed test and formulated propositions are not intended as a comprehensive treatment of parallel process research but rather as a suggested starting place for empirical work on the proposed model. Initial experiments should suggest new avenues of research as well as contribute to knowledge of strategic decision making.

ACKNOWLEDGMENTS

We are indebted to James Corner, Richard Gooding, Michael Hitt, and Hugh O'Neill for their insightful comments on earlier drafts of this chapter.

REFERENCES

Ajzen, I. and M. Fishbein (1980), *Understanding Attitudes and Predicting Social Behavior,* Englewood Cliffs, NJ: Prentice Hall.

Axelrod, R. (1976), *Structure of Decision,* Princeton, NJ: Princeton University Press.

Bantel, K. and S. Jackson (1989), "Top Management and Innovations in Banking: Does the Composition of the Top Management Team Make a Difference?" *Strategic Management Journal,* 10, 108.

Bargh, J. A., R. N. Bond, W. J. Lombardi, and M. E. Tota (1986), "The Additive Nature of Chronic and Temporary Sources of Construct Accessibility," *Journal of Personality and Social Psychology,* 50, 5.

Cantor, N. and W. Mischel (1979), "Prototypes in Person Perception," in L. Berkowitz (Ed.), *Advances in Experimental Social Psychology,* New York: Academic Press, 3-52.

Child, J. (1972), "Organizational Structure, Environment, and Performance: The Role of Strategic Choice," *Sociology* 6, 1.

Cohen, M., J. March, and J. Olsen (1972), "A Garbage Can Model of Organizational Choice," *Administrative Science Quarterly,* 17, 1.

Cyert, R. and J. G. March (1963), *A Behavioral Theory of the Firm,* Englewood Cliffs, NJ: Prentice Hall.

Daft, R. and K. E. Weick (1984), "Toward a Model of Organizations as Interpretation Systems," *Academy of Management Review,* 9, 2.

D'Andrade, F. (1981), "The Cultural Part of Cognition," *Cognitive Science,* 5, 1.

Dearborn, D. C. and H. A. Simon (1958), "Selective Perception: A Note on the Department Identification of Executives," *Sociometry,* 21, 1.

Donnellon, A., B. Gray, and M. Bougon (1986), "Communication, Meaning, and Organized Action," *Administrative Science Quarterly,* 31, 43.

Dubin, R. (1978), *Theory Building,* New York: The Free Press.

Duhaime, I. M. and C. R. Schwenk (1985), "Conjectures on Cognitive Simplification in Acquisition and Divestment Decision Making," *Academy of Management Review,* 10, 2.

Dutton, J. E., L. Fahey, and V. K. Narayanan (1983), "Toward Understanding Strategic Issue Diagnosis," *Strategic Management Journal,* 4, 4.

——— and S. Jackson (1987), "Categorizing Strategic Issues: Links to Organizational Action," *Academy of Management Review,* 12, 76.

Eisenhardt, K. and L. Bourgeois (1988), "Politics of Strategic Decision Making in High-Velocity Environments: Toward a Midrange Theory," *Academy of Management Journal,* 31, 737.

Feldman, D. C. (1981), "The Multiple Socialization of Organizational Members," *Academy of Management Review,* 8, 2.

Feldman, M. and J. G. March (1981), "Information in Organizations as Signal and Symbol," *Administrative Science Quarterly,* 26, 1.

Finney, M. and I. Mitroff (1986), "Strategic Plan Failures," in H. P. Sims and D. Gioia (Eds.), *The Thinking Organization,* San Francisco: Jossey-Bass, 317-335.

Fiske, S. T. and S. E. Taylor (1984), *Social Cognition,* New York: Random House.

Fredrickson, J. (1984), "The Comprehensiveness of Strategic Decision Processes: Extension, Observations, Future Directions," *Academy of Management Journal,* 27, 445.

Frost, P. and G. Morgan (1983), "Symbols and Sense Making: The Real-ization of a Framework," in G. Morgan, P. Frost and L. Pondy (Eds.), *Organizational Symbolism,* Greenwich, CT: JAI, 207-236.

Galbraith, J. and R. Kazanjian (1986), *Strategy Implementation: Structure, Systems, and Process,* St. Paul, MN: West.

Ginsberg, A. (1990), "Connecting Diversification to Performance: A Sociocognitive Perspective," *Academy of Management Review,* 15, 3.

Gioia, D. A. (1986), "Symbols, Scripts, and Sensemaking: Creating Meaning in the Organizational Experience," in H. P. Sims, D. A. Gioia, and Associates, *The Thinking Organization: Dynamics of Organizational Social Cognition,* San Francisco: Jossey-Bass, 49-74.

Hambrick, D. C. and P. A. Mason (1984), "Upper Echelons: The Organization as a Reflection of Its Top Managers," *Academy of Management Review,* 9, 2.

Hastie, R. (1980), "Memory for Behavioral Information That Confirms or Contradicts a Personality Impression," in R. Hastie et al. (Eds.), *Person Memory: The Cognitive Basis of Social Perception,* Hillsdale, NJ: Lawrence Erlbaum, 155-177.

Hedberg, B. (1981), "How Organizations Learn and Unlearn," in P. Nystrom and W. Starbuck (Eds.), *Handbook of Organizational Design,* Oxford, UK: Oxford University Press, 3, 27.

Higgins, E. T. and J. A. Bargh (1987), "Social Cognition and Social Perception," *Annual Review of Psychology,* 38, 2.

Higgins, E. T. and G. A. King (1981), "Accessibility of Social Constructs: Information Processing Consequences of Individual and Contextual Variability," in N. Cantor and J. Kihlstorm (Eds.), *Personality, Cognition, and Social Interaction,* Hillsdale, NJ: Lawrence Erlbaum, 69-121.

Huff, A. (1982), "Industry Influences on Strategy Reformulation," *Strategic Management Journal,* 3, 119-131.

Ilgen, D. R. and J. M. Feldman (1983), "Performance Appraisal: A Process Focus," in L. L. Cummings and B. M. Staw (Eds.), *Research in Organizational Behavior,* Greenwich, CT: JAI, 141-197.

Ireland, R. D., M. A. Hitt, R. A. Bettis, and D. A. De Porras (1987), "Strategy Formulation Processes: Differences in Perceptions of Strength and Weaknesses Indicators and Environmental Uncertainty by Managerial Level," *Strategic Management Journal,* 8, 5.

Isabella, L. A. (1990), "Evolving Interpretations as a Change Unfolds: How Managers Construe Key Organizational Events," *Academy of Management Journal,* 33, 1.

Isen, A. M. and K. A. Daubman (1984), "The Influence of Affect on Categorization," *Journal of Personality and Social Psychology,* 47, 1206-1217.

Jacobs, T. O. and E. Jaques (1987), "Leadership in Complex Systems," in J. Zeidner (Ed.), *Human Productivity Enhancement,* New York: Praeger, 7-65.

Kelly, G. A. (1955), *The Psychology of Personal Constructs,* New York: Norton.

Kiesler, S. and L. Sproull (1982), "Managerial Response to Changing Environments: Perspectives on Problem Sensing from Social Cognition," *Administrative Science Quarterly,* 27, 3.

Langer, E. J. (1978), "Rethinking the Role of Thought in Social Interaction," in J. Harvey, W. Ickes, and R. Kidd (Eds.), *New Directions in Attributional Research,* Hillsdale, NJ: Lawrence Erlbaum, 35-58.

Lant, T. and S. Mezias (1990), "Managing Discontinuous Change: A Simulation Study of Organizational Learning and Entrepreneurship," *Strategic Management Journal,* 11, 147.

——— and ——— (1992), "An Organizational Learning Model of Convergence and Reorientations," *Organization Science,* 3, 47.

Levitt, B. and J. G. March (1988), "Organizational Learning," in W. R. Scott and J. Black (Eds.), *Annual Review of Sociology,* Palo Alto, CA: Annual Reviews, 319-340.

Lord, R. (1985). "An Information Processing Approach to Social Perceptions, Leadership and Behavioral Measurement in Organizations," in B. Staw and L. L. Cummings (Eds.), *Research in Organizational Behavior,* Greenwich, CT: JAI, 87-128.

March, J. and H. Simon (1958), *Organizations,* New York: John Wiley.

March, J. G. (1987), "Ambiguity and Accounting: The Elusive Link Between Information and Decision Making," *Accounting, Organizations, and Society,* 12, 153-168.

——— and Z. Shapira (1982), "Behavioral Decision Theory and Organizational Decision Theory," in G. Ungson and D. Braunstein (Eds.), *Decision Making: An Interdisciplinary Inquiry,* Boston: Kent, 92-115.

Mintzberg, H. (1978), "Patterns in Strategy Formation," *Management Science,* 24, 8.

———, D. Raisinghani, and A. Theoret (1976), "The Structure of 'Unstructured' Decision Process," *Administrative Science Quarterly,* 21, 2.

Mitchell, T. and L. Beach (1990), " '. . . Do I Love Thee? Let Me Count . . .' Toward an Understanding of Intuitive and Automatic Decision Making," *Organizational Behavior and Human Decision Processes,* 47, 1.

Murray, A. (1989), "Top Management Group Heterogeneity and Firm Performance," *Strategic Management Journal,* 10, 125.

Nelson, R. and S. Winter (1982), *An Evolutionary Theory of Economic Change,* Cambridge, MA: Belknap Press of Harvard University Press.

Nutt, P. (1984), "Types of Organizational Decision Processes," *Administrative Science Quarterly,* 29, 2.

Pfeffer, J. (1981), *Power in Organizations,* Cambridge, MA: Ballinger.

Porac, J. and H. Thomas (1990), "Taxonomic Mental Models in Competitor Definition," *Academy of Management Review,* 15, 2.

Porter, M. (1980), *Competitive Strategy,* New York: Free Press.

Prahalad, C. K. and R. A. Bettis (1986), "The Dominant Logic: A New Linkage Between Diversity and Performance," *Strategic Management Journal,* 7, 6.

Quinn, (1980), *Strategies for Change: Local Incrementalism,* Homewood, IL: Irwin.

Reger, R. (1988), "Competitive Positioning in the Chicago Banking Market: Mapping the Mind of the Strategist," doctoral dissertation, University of Illinois, University Microfilms International, Order Number 8823231.

Rosch, E. (1978), "Principles of Categorization," in E. Rosch and B. B. Lloyd (Eds.), *Cognition and Categorization,* Hillsdale, NJ: Lawrence Erlbaum, 27-48.

Schneider, W. and R. M. Shiffrin (1977), "Controlled and Automatic Human Information Processing: 1. Detection, Search, and Attention," *Psychological Review,* 84, 1.

Schweiger, D., W. Sandberg, and P. Rechner (1989), "Experiential Effects of Dialectical Inquiry, Devil's Advocacy, and Consensus Approaches to Strategic Decision Making," *Academy of Management Journal,* 32, 4.

Schwenk, C. R. (1984), "Cognitive Simplification Processes in Strategic Decision Making," *Strategic Management Journal,* 5, 2.

——— (1986), "Information, Cognitive Biases, and Commitment to a Course of Action," *Academy of Management Review,* 11, 298.

——— (1988), "The Cognitive Perspective on Strategic Decision Making," *Journal of Management Studies,* 25, 1.

Shrivastava, P. and S. Schneider (1984), "Organizational Frames of Reference," *Human Relations,* 37, 10.

Sinclair, R. C. (1988), "Mood, Categorization Breadth, and Performance Appraisal: The Effects of Order of Information Acquisition and Affective State on Halo, Accuracy, Information Retrieval, and Evaluations," *Organizational Behavior and Human Decision Processes,* 42, 1.

Smircich, L. and C. Stubbart (1985), "Strategic Management in an Enacted World," *Academy of Management Review,* 10, 724.

Thomas, J. and R. McDaniel (1990), "Interpreting Strategic Issues: Effects of Strategy and the Information Processing Structure of Top Management Teams," *Academy of Management Journal,* 33, 286.

Thompson, J. D. (1967). *Organizations in Action,* New York: McGraw-Hill.

Ungson, G. R., D. N. Braunstein, and P. Hall (1981), "Managerial Information Processing: A Research Review," *Administrative Science Quarterly,* 26, 1.

Van Maanen, J. and E. Schein (1979), "Toward a Theory of Organizational Socialization," in B. Staw (Ed.). *Research in Organizational Behavior,* Greenwich, CT: JAI, 209-264.

Walsh, J. and L. Fahey (1986), "The Role of Negotiated Belief Structures in Strategy Making," *Journal of Management,* 12, 3.

———, C. Henderson, and J. Deighton (1988), "Negotiated Belief Structures and Decision Performance: An Empirical Investigation," *Organizational Behavior and Human Decision Processes,* 42, 194.

——— and G. Ungson (1991), "Organizational Memory," *Academy of Management Review,* 16, 1.

Ward, J. and P. Reingen (1990), "Sociocognitive Analysis of Group Decision Making Among Consumers," *Journal of Consumer Research,* 17, 1-18.

Weick, K. (1979), *The Social Psychology of Organizing,* New York: Random House.

——— and M. Bougon (1986), "Organizations as Cognitive Maps," in H. P. Sims and D. Gioia (Eds.), *Thinking Organizations,* San Francisco: Jossey-Bass, 102-135.

Wyer, R. S. and T. K. Srull (1980), "The Processing of Social Stimulus Information: A Conceptual Integration," in R. Hastie et al. (Eds.), *Person Memory: The Cognitive Basis of Social Perception,* Hillsdale, NJ: Lawrence Erlbaum, 227-300.

6

Consensus, Diversity, and Learning in Organizations

C. MARLENE FIOL

Organizational learning, like individual learning, involves the development of new and diverse interpretations of events and situations. Unlike individual learning, however, collective learning also involves developing enough consensus around those diverse interpretations for organized action to result. Traditional measures of organizational consensus are unable to capture the multiplex nature of collective agreement that encompasses both unity and diversity. Traditional wisdom thus suggests that to achieve unity in groups, one must sacrifice diversity.

This study breaks the notion of consensus into two component parts: consensus around interpretations embedded in the content and in the framing of communications. Communicated content consists of the labels people use to convey their "pictures" of reality, e.g., pictures of issues as threats or as opportunities. The framing of communications refers to the form people use to construct a picture, regardless of its content, e.g., rigid or flexible perceptions of an issue. People may hold very different pictures of reality and still agree on the way they frame them. It is thus possible for groups to simultaneously agree and disagree, an essential component of collective learning.

Simultaneous agreement and disagreement is especially important in corporate innovative efforts. Successful corporate innovation requires that decision makers develop a collective understanding that incorporates the new and the different. This [chapter] describes the changing pictures and frames communicated in a new-venture development process in a large financial institution over a two-year period. Several linguistic analyses show how the venture team members devel-

This chapter originally appeared in *Organization Science*, Vol. 5, No. 3, August 1994.

oped unified ways of framing their arguments, while at the same time maintaining diversity through differences in the content of team members' interpretations. The results reveal one way that organizations manage to combine the unity and diversity needed for collective learning. The managerial implications present a challenge for anyone wishing to promote learning as a community: Managers must actively encourage the development of different and conflicting views of what is thought to be true, while striving for a shared framing of the issues that is broad enough to encompass those differences.

(ORGANIZATIONAL LEARNING;
CONSENSUS; UNIFIED DIVERSITY;
CORPORATE INNOVATION; COMMUNICATION)

> One sensible operating rule is that whenever organizations adopt one prescription, they should adopt a second prescription which contradicts the first. Contradictory prescriptions remind organizations that each prescription is a misleading simplification that ought not be carried to excess. (Starbuck et al. 1978, p. 123)

In late 1984, a mid-level manager of a Fortune 100 financial services firm introduced Project X as a new-venture idea during a seminar at corporate headquarters. The venture represented a significant departure from the company's business. Despite widespread resistance to the idea, the division's CEO appointed an 11-member venturing team to analyze the feasibility of the project. The team was torn by conflicts during early stages of the two-year venture development process that ensued. Even those on the team that opposed the idea did not agree about their reasons for resistance. Ultimately, after extensive conflict and negotiations, the Project X team unanimously supported the venture and successfully managed its implementation. Interviews with team members indicated that the powerful elite did not "force" a consensus. The composition of the new-venture team remained the same. The venture concept was recast a number of times, but emerged at the end of the process almost identical to the idea that was initially proposed by its champion. What appeared to have changed was not the ultimate definition of the venture, nor its relationship to the environment, nor the people involved with the venture, but rather the cognitive frames of reference through which people understood the venture. The Project X team learned as a group: They converged around an innovative idea that required a fundamental shift in their collective understanding to be successfully implemented.

How does collective learning occur? The answer may lie in the balance of two apparently contradictory prescriptions: (1) generate diversity and (2) build consensus. The seeming contradiction mirrors a much broader debate about the conditions for progressive development of social knowledge. Minds as diverse as John Dewey (1954) and Thomas Kuhn (1970) have argued that all knowledge development rests on *unity* of interpretations—even the confirmation and explanation of new scientific "facts." Yet learning, or the development of new knowledge, is also based on *diversity* of interpretations (Bower and Hilgard 1981). To remain viable in the face of change, organizations have to maintain both prescriptions in balance. To learn as a community, organizational members must simultaneously agree and disagree.

Though current management theories of organizational learning encompass this apparent contradiction (Fiol and Lyles 1985, Huber 1991), we know very little about how organizations actually manage to resolve it. I argue that this is because we have tended to view consensus as a unidimensional phenomenon that is either present or absent. To begin to describe and explain how organizations manage "unified diversity" (Eisenberg 1984), we need to recognize the multidimensional nature of consensus building.

This study unpacks the notion of consensus. It describes two interpretive dimensions along which consensus may develop: consensus around interpretations embedded in the content and in the framing of communications. It traces the interplay of these two dimensions of understanding among the managers involved in the two-year development of Project X. The results suggest that the content and the framing of communications both play critical and distinct roles in organizational processes of developing unified diversity.

THE APPARENT ORGANIZATIONAL LEARNING PARADOX

Learning involves developing new understanding. Research in the area of cognitive and behavioral sciences at the individual level describes this process as involving the acquisition and interpretation of knowledge (Lindsay and Norman 1977). The process need not be conscious or intentional (Bower and Hilgard 1981), nor need it necessarily increase the learner's effectiveness or visibly change the learner's behaviors (Friedlander 1983). Rather, learning is the process of modifying one's "cognitive maps or understandings" (Friedlander 1983, p. 194), thereby changing the range of one's potential behaviors (Huber 1991).

Learning thus may have more to do with a change in one's interpretation of events and actions than with the events or actions themselves. Daft and Weick (1984) defined interpretation as the process through which people give meaning to information.[1] A person learns through developing different interpretations of new or existing information, that is, through developing (consciously or unconsciously) a new understanding of surrounding events.

Organizational learning, like individual learning, also involves the development of diverse interpretations (Fiol and Lyles 1985, Huber 1991). However, learning in organizations is not simply the sum of the learning of its employees (Cohen and Levinthal 1990). As Nelson and Winter (1982) noted, organizational capabilities are not embedded in any single person, but in the links across diverse individual capabilities. Learning in organizations entails not only the acquisition of diverse information, but the ability to share common understanding so as to exploit it. The apparent paradox is that collective learning, by definition, encompasses both divergence and convergence of the meanings that people assign to their surroundings.

Previous research has suggested several ways of dealing with the apparent paradox. One is to view the relationship between unity and diversity as one of necessary trade-offs. According to Cohen and Levinthal (1990, p. 134), "The observation that the ideal knowledge structure for an organizational subunit should reflect only partially overlapping knowledge complemented by nonoverlapping diverse knowledge suggests an organizational trade-off between diversity and commonality of knowledge across individuals." In this view, to achieve more diversity, organizations must sacrifice commonality and vice versa. The only way to achieve both is to emphasize each of them at different times.

A second view is that the sharing of meanings is not necessary for collective learning and organized action (Weick 1979). Eisenberg (1984), for instance, argued that ambiguity in group processes facilitates collective action in that it allows for consensus despite multiple interpretations. Donnellon et al. (1986) similarly argued that organized action can occur despite differences of interpretation among organizational members. They suggested that members use a number of communication techniques for broadening ideas to encompass multiple interpretations that are consistent in their behavioral implications. Thus, they argued, parties can agree to take action despite differences in the meanings they assign to the action.

Finally, a third view, developed in this chapter, suggests that "meaning" is not a unidimensional construct, but rather encompasses multiple dimensions. If we unpack the construct, we may find that meanings can be simultaneously diverse and shared across individuals. Consensus may develop around one dimension of meaning and not around another. This third view further develops and refines the argument of the second view, that organized action can occur despite differing interpretations of group members: It argues that organized action can occur in the face of dissension around one dimension of meaning, as long as there is consensus around another.

First, meaning resides in the *content* of communications, which is reflected in the categories or labels that define *what* is expressed. People make sense of isolated "bits" of information by categorizing them in a way that associates them with a body of more generalized beliefs (Kiesler and Sproull 1982). In organizational work groups, such categories are often institutionalized and legitimated through the use of labels. Once solidified in this way, they become pictures that are highly resistant to change. If new stimuli are inconsistent with existing pictures, people will tend to ignore them, attending to only those stimuli that conform. There is considerable support in the management literature for the notion that organizational decision makers persistently use cognitive categories to make sense of surrounding events (Bartunek 1984, Gray et al. 1985, Lakoff 1987, Neisser 1987). For example, organizations commonly incorporate the category labels "threat" and "opportunity" in formal planning processes and managers use them in their everyday vocabulary. These labels paint a cognitive picture that serves to organize bits of information. Assumptions buried in these labels are opposite with respect to perceptions of an issue as negative or positive (overtly judgmental elements of a picture) and as uncontrollable or controllable (apparently "objective" elements of a picture) respectively (see Dutton and Jackson 1987, Jackson and Dutton 1988).

Meaning also resides, however, in the *framing* of communications, which is reflected in *how* something is expressed (Bartunek 1984, Gray et al. 1985). "Framing" refers to the way people construct their argument or viewpoint, regardless of its content. In particular, researchers have noted differences in the breadth and the rigidity of people's framing of their views (Bartunek et al. 1983, Holsti 1976, Weick and Bougon 1986). Research suggests that the breadth of a frame (e.g., the number or scope of issues attended to) positively relates to decision effectiveness, particularly in novel decision situations during early stages of the process (Walsh et al. 1988). The rigidity of a frame (e.g., the degree of certainty conveyed) indicates how fixed a position is, and thus relates to possibilities for change (Putnam 1985) If decision makers proceed with confidence and certainty, they leave little room for resolving differences of viewpoint that are likely to arise in ill-defined decision contexts (Bettenhausen and Murnighan 1985). In contrast, if decision makers proceed with less certainty during early stages of ambiguous decision processes, they open the way for achieving a common basis for their interactions. Both the breadth and the rigidity of issue framing thus convey important meanings in collective decision processes without relating directly to the content of communications. In fact, Weick and Bougon (1986, p. 114) have

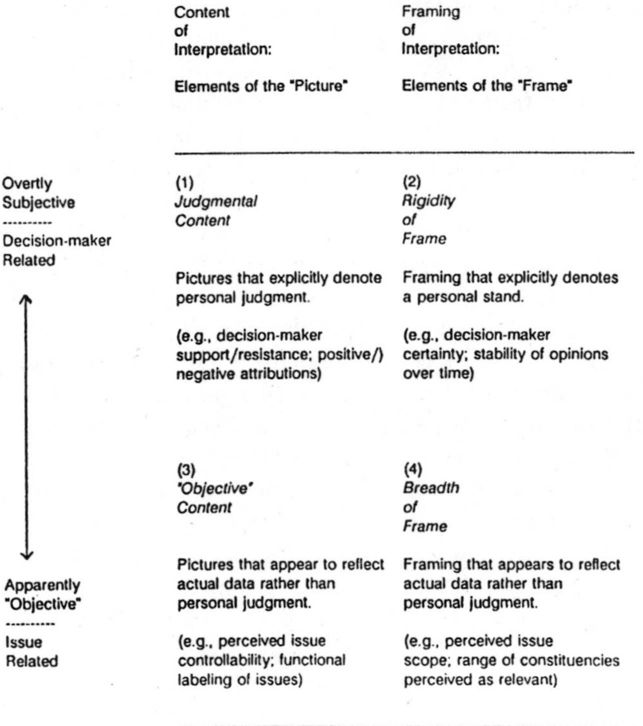

Figure 6.1. Content and Framing of Interpretation

argued that content-free analyses that examine how issues are framed can tell us more about the meanings underlying communication than studies of the content itself.

Figure 6.1 summarizes the constructs that previous research has identified as signalling the *content* and the *framing* of interpretations. It further distinguishes between interpretations that are more explicitly linked to the decision maker and to the decision issue. Statements of personal value and certainty are *overtly subjective* and have thus received the greatest attention in previous studies of meaning making in organizations. In contrast, expressions of perceived issue controllability or perceived scope of relevant issues are often couched in *"objective"* language, thus appearing to be less interpretive in nature. Though less explicitly linked to one's personal values, such "objective" expressions nevertheless reflect one's understanding of an issue.

The important point is that meaning resides not only in the content of the pictures we convey in our communications,but also in the way we frame them. Consensus or dissensus may develop around either the content or the frame. Consider as an example a group of organizational members who are discussing whether to purchase a new computer system. They may disagree about their interpretation of this acquisition as either "good" or "bad" (judgmental content of communication). Alternatively, they may disagree about their interpretations as to whether the acquisition has "uncertain ramifications for the entire firm" (broad, flexibly-framed argument) or "a relatively certain impact on IS efficiencies" (narrow, rigidly-framed argument). Achieving agreement about the frame or the content within it does not automatically imply agreement about the other.

This third view of the apparent learning paradox encourages us to question the need for trade-offs, given that it encompasses the possibility for unity and diversity of interpretation to unfold simultaneously in organizations. Furthermore, this view subsumes and reframes the assertion of the second view, that collective learning can occur in the absence of shared meaning. For broad and ambiguous ideas to effectively "unify" people around multiple meanings of issues or events (Donnellon et al. 1986, Eisenberg 1984), people must *share* that broad framing of the issues. In other words, people may disagree about their interpretive pictures, while converging around a frame that is broad enough to encompass those differences.

FROM THEORY TO PRACTICE

The previous discussion suggests the following research proposition: *One can achieve unified diversity by embracing diverse pictures of what is thought to be true within a unifying frame.* What does this theoretical and abstract claim mean in practical terms? How does one recognize and manage the elements of unified diversity? Previous research has identified many of them. The challenge lies in becoming more sensitive to their role in processes of collective learning.

Huber (1991, p. 103) recently admonished that "with regard to the relationships among clarity of communication, information interpretation, and organizational effectiveness, it seems important to move from speculation to empirical research." The point is well taken. In our attempts to move toward empirical validity, however, we should not oversimplify our models for the sake of unambiguous results.

Most empirical research on consensus in strategic decision making has examined managers' personal preferences and level of certainty regarding organizational objectives. The research has failed to take into account the less explicitly subjective interpretations that may accompany those preferences. Not surprisingly, the results have been conflicting. In a study of the role of consensus about means for corporate innovation, for example, De-Woot et al. (1978) found that more efficient decisions resulted from groups that expressed frequent disagreement on the objective of innovation. Similarly, Bourgeois (1985) found a negative relationship between top managers' consensus around preferred objectives and firm performance. In contrast, other studies have shown a positive relationship between top management consensus around preferences and performance (Dess 1987, Hrebiniak and Snow 1982). None of these researchers specified potential differences in the less explicitly subjective interpretations that may have existed. It is possible that the effects of shared preferences on performance depend on the extent of agreement around the less blatantly subjective meanings accompanying those preferences.

Another body of research has begun to examine the less overtly subjective meanings that managers convey in their communications. Researchers interested in the content of decision makers' interpretations have examined "objective" labels people use to define an issue or event. For example, Walsh (1988) identified managers' functional labels of issues. Jackson and Dutton (1988) extracted managers' labels of situations as either controllable or uncontrollable. Researchers interested in the framing of decision makers' interpretations have examined the breadth of issues reflected in communications. They have identified the number of concepts and the relationships among the concepts that people use to describe a situation or event (Bartunek et al. 1983, Weick and Bougon 1986).

Several simplifying tendencies of this body of empirical research have limited its contributions to understanding consensus-building processes in organizations. First, researchers have tended to examine the content and framing of interpretations as independent constructs, and have ignored how they may function together in the same situation. In fact, Weick and Bougon (1986, p. 114) have argued that we should maintain this separation and do content-free analyses that examine how people frame their arguments. They support Holsti's (1976) assertion that it may not be very fruitful to assume direct linkages between the content of decision-maker interpretations and decision outcomes. Yet assuming no linkage may be as fruitless as assuming a direct linkage between the content of meaning and decision outcomes. We do not yet know the extent to which the content and framing of interpretations may interact in decision processes.

Second, most empirical research on how the content and framing of interpretations relate to decision making has been conducted with the individual as the unit of analysis, assuming that what is organizationally meaningful is somehow an aggregation of meanings at the individual level (e.g., Bougon et al. 1977, Walsh et al. 1988). In contrast, studies of group behavior suggest that the common "expectations" (Opp 1982), "rules" (Feldman

1984), or "behavior patterns" (Bettenhausen and Murnighan 1985) that emerge in group processes are distinct from those of group members. Group thinking does not equal the sum of its individual parts.

Finally, previous studies have tended to portray static snapshots of managerial interpretations linked to a particular event or situation, neglecting the temporal dimension of meaning making in organizations (Blackburn and Cummings 1982, Bougon et al. 1977, Jackson and Dutton 1988, Reger and Huff 1993, Walton 1986). Yet organizational task forces are rarely involved in a single, isolated decision (Mintzberg and Waters 1985). Static snapshots say very little about the linkages over time between consensus-building efforts and ongoing group decisions and actions.

CURRENT RESEARCH SETTING: A NEW FINANCIAL SERVICES VENTURE

Research Questions

This study explored the dynamics characterizing collective patterns of interpretation as they reflected innovative efforts over a two-year period in one large organization. The aim was to inductively describe and explain the nature of consensus that was associated with the Project X team's transition from conflict to collaboration. Since the study advances a new way of thinking about and managing the nature of consensus in collective learning processes, it was impossible to formulate specific hypotheses. Previous research, however, suggested the following questions to guide the exploration: *Did the learning process in the Project X team build on diversity of interpretive content? Did the Project X team converge around interpretive frames that were broad enough to encompass multiple interpretations of issue content?*

Managing unified diversity is especially important to managers involved in developing corporate new ventures. Diversity of viewpoints is the norm rather than the exception for corporate new-venturing teams, and formal control mechanisms and routines often do not exist to shape collective action. Moreover, the diversity of such teams is a critical ingredient for success (Hage and Aiken 1970). However, as Van de Ven and his associates (1989) pointed out, diversity of new-venture participants can only lead to success if the boundaries that separate them are sufficiently "permeable" for "boundary crossing" or intersection of interests. Though this point is central to their analysis of new-venturing processes, the authors did not specify how such an intersection of interests might occur.

Knowing how the content and framing of interpretations interact, and how consensus patterns along each dimension of meaning may develop and change in groups over time, is critical to an understanding of how collaboration becomes possible or impossible during corporate innovation processes. Though we believe that a person who views issues surrounding a new-venture idea as controllable (content of a communication) is likely to commit greater efforts to it than someone who views them as uncontrollable (Dutton and Jackson 1987), this tells us little about the outcome of the new-venturing process. For it is not an individual, but a team, that is usually involved in such decisions; it is not only the substantive content of an argument, but also how it is framed, that is likely to influence outcomes; and innovative efforts do not usually involve a discrete decision point, but a process of managing meanings over time.

Internal and External Environment

Project X took place in a Fortune 100 financial services firm with several diverse operating units. The company has elaborate control and planning systems. It makes extensive use of structural integration devices (primarily meetings) to coordinate a high level of interdepartmental differentiation. The organization thus has a history of attempting to explicitly manage and contain high levels of internal diversity.

The mid-1980s in the U.S. banking industry was a period marked by significant technological, economic, social, and legal changes. Technologically, major advances included new systems capabilities leading to increased ease and speed of credit and other decisions. Economically, a healthy investment climate had created a cache of available investment resources. Predictions of a recession, however, coupled with increasing consumer spending power (due, in part, to a rise in two-income families), led banks to move toward consumer services as the area of greatest profit potential. "Full-service" regulatory barriers were being lowered, allowing entry into areas previously closed to some firms. The dynamic environment increased the likelihood that managers within the same company would differ in the meanings they assigned to their own role in the organization and to the organization's role in the environment.

The New-Venture Team

The new-venture team consisted of 11 managers, ranging in formal hierarchy from Division CEO to Group Vice President; and ranging across functions of Systems, Operations, Law, Marketing, and Finance. The group as a whole had not previously worked together on a project. However, stable

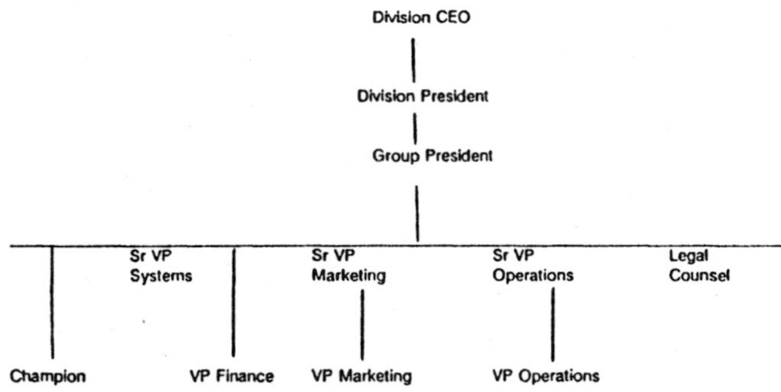

Figure 6.2. Partial Organization Chart

subgroupings developed early in the process between pairs of managers who had worked together in the past.

The Champion of the new venture had the least formal authority of all group members. Prior to the development of the new venture, he had been sent to run a "dog" business that the company had recently acquired. The position was considered by most to be a dead-end and far from the power centers of the company. The partial organization chart in Figure 6.2 shows the hierarchical and functional positions of the new-venture team members.

The Communication Log

To monitor progression on this controversial project, the Division CEO required that all major transactions among these 11 individuals be recorded in a new-venture log, a procedure that has become the norm in this division's subsequent venturing processes. Team members submitted all key issues raised in meetings or written communications to the office of the Division CEO. His staff entered them in the log under predetermined categories of "Milestones" and "Closed/Open Issues." Top management stated that the log was required in order to monitor the process and avoid "sloppy errors" that had been made in the past. Lower-level venture-team members saw the log entries as a means of protecting themselves should the venture fail after launch, a means of going back and saying, "You see, I warned that this might happen." In any case, the record-keeping process was taken seriously, and interviews with the organizational members gave reason to believe that the entries reflected sincere concerns.

The log consisted of three separate volumes, marking three distinct phases of the project, each built around a different conceptualization of the new venture. The phase breaks occurred as a natural outcome of the group's

TABLE 6.1 Subgroups of the Project X Team

Subgroup 1	*Subgroup 2*	*Subgroup 3*	*Subgroup 4*
Sr VP Marketing	Group President	Div CEO	Sr VP Systems
Product Champion	VP Marketing	Div President	Sr VP Operations
			VP Finance
			VP Operations
			Legal Counsel

process, rather than as a result of retrospective labeling. The first phase ended after six months, when the task force discontinued discussions and meetings, presuming the project had died. When the project was resurrected, entries were filed in a new volume. Phase II ended seven months later, when the Division CEO tentatively approved a recasting of the aim of the search effort from a product extension to a new business. Subsequent entries were, once again, filed in a new volume.

Every log entry included the names of the participants and dates of a particular communication. The entries originated from subgroups of managers rather than from individuals. Team members explained that this was because there was "a lot of paranoia in this company about sticking your neck out by yourself" at least until it was clear that the activity met with top management's approval. In fact, five of the eleven team members (subgroup 4) went on record as opposing the venture in any form (it was "disruptive to operations") until the final phase. Table 6.1 lists the managers in each subgroup, as defined by the joint log entries.

The log was clearly not the sole communication device for this project team. In particular, it does not reflect much of the informal communication among subgroup members who worked together on this and other projects. According to participants, however, the log does reflect most communications across subgroups as the different subgroups did not see or work with each other on a regular basis. This is critical since consensus building *across* subgroups was the focus of this study.

The Story of Project X

Here is the new-venture story as the log told it.

Phase I. The first volume had "X Product Enhancement" scrawled on its cover and included communications of the first six months of the process. At first, communications occurred between the Champion and his earliest supporter, Senior VP Marketing (subgroup 1). They focused primarily on the need for improvements in the current product mix. The Group President and VP Marketing (subgroup 2) then communicated to the Champion that his proposed improvements were needed, but they disapproved of the ideas offered because too many internal specifications were lacking ("What is needed is a much more detailed study of the way this is supposed to be integrated into our current systems and how it is to be financed"). Finally, the top management representatives, the Division CEO and President (subgroup 3), raised the question, "What does this . . . potentially add to our existing product?" In short, in Phase I the team failed to see a need for the new venture. The idea appeared to have been abandoned, the volume closed.

Phase II. Three months after the close of Volume One, the Champion re-initiated the process. Discussions with team members suggested that he gained a second chance because he managed to uncouple the new-venture idea from the division's existing products. The second volume was not labeled and included communications of the subsequent seven months of the process. Again, the earliest communications occurred between the Champion and Senior VP Marketing. Their discussions revolved around redefining the nature of the project to address concerns about the potential contribution of the new venture. Questions, rather than solutions, marked the tone of these discussions. As the idea of a totally new business began to emerge, the Champion again approached the Group President and VP Marketing. Input of the latter consisted mostly of questions about a broad range of potential ramifications. With these questions in hand, the Champion reintroduced the project as a new business to the two top management representatives. Their tentative support apparently legitimated the new version, for this log was closed and a third one opened that was confidently framed as a "New Business Proposal."

Phase III. Labeled "New Business Proposal," the third volume covered the final nine months of the development process. Interestingly, the "New Business" concept that emerges from the third notebook is almost identical to the idea the Champion had presented more than a year earlier and that had been soundly rejected. Once again, the same communication flows marked the beginning of this phase, with the Champion and Senior VP Marketing first meeting alone, the Champion then consulting with the Group President and VP Marketing, and finally with the top management representatives. However, these subgroup processes were condensed, lasting only several weeks. With the tentative support of top management, the final eight months accounted for in the new-venturing log involved active participation of all four subgroups, the discussions revolving around putting the operational pieces of the project together.

METHOD

The study traced the group's communication process over the two-year period to look for consensus building around the content and framing of the meanings they attached to the venture idea.

Data Source

The detailed log of communications among the 11 managers of the new-venturing team, consisting of over 2,000 pages, provided a source of data that could be interpreted within an observable context, traced over time, and cross-validated with multiple research methods. The communication patterns disclosed in the log provided a unique opportunity to explore the nature of group-level consensus that developed in the stormy progression from venture initiation to launch.

Theoretical Constructs and Operationalizations

To explore the dynamics of cognitive development during Project X, I analyzed the language of the communication log. I coded 60 randomly chosen entries myself. An independent researcher then carried out the entire analysis. An "entry" consisted of the whole set of arguments entered in the log at one time by one subgroup. The total number of entries was 1,128. We coded each entry along four dimensions (see Figure 6.1):

1. Decision-maker *Support/Resistance* as an indicator of the judgmental content of communications.
2. Decision-maker *Certainty* vis-à-vis the project idea as an indicator of the rigidity of issue framing.
3. Perceived issue *Controllability* as an indicator of "objective" content of communications.
4. Perceived issue *Scope* as an indicator of the breadth of issue framing.

Decision-maker Support/Resistance. The Project X experience provided an extreme case of a corporate decision group shifting from a state of debilitating conflict to successful collaboration. Pre-study discussions with members of the venturing team as well as several abrupt discontinuities in the venturing log provided ample evidence of the difficulty in achieving a working consensus on this project. Initial communications of most group members indicated overt resistance to the venture champion's idea. Final expressions reflected full support. Though expressed support of the idea may reveal little about the less overtly subjective meanings people assign to it (e.g., perceived control over issues), it was included as a means of tracing signals of open conflict or collaboration within the group.

The new-venture team members evaluated the merits of Project X in their judgmental statements either supporting or resisting the project idea. Cumulative statements over time revealed patterns of stable or changing value judgments. To the extent that patterns across subgroups progressively converged, there was increasing consensus around the *judgmental content* of their interpretations.

A "Support/Neutral/Resist" code was assigned to each entry by counting the number of positive, neutral, and negative arguments, and giving the entire entry a single code that reflected the overall tone. Thus, a neutral code for an entire entry meant that it contained no clear positive or negative reactions to the project, or alternatively, that there were as many positive as negative reactions. For example, the following were both considered neutral entries: (1) "We need to assess systems requirements . . ." and (2) "Our customers will welcome such a product . . . [later in the same entry] . . . the product does not fit with our current offerings." Though the former indicates no value judgment at all, the latter provides an equally neutral evaluation in its equivocality.

Decision-maker Certainty. The new-venture team members expressed differing levels of certainty regarding their positions vis-à-vis Project X. To the extent that patterns of certainty across subgroups progressively converged, there was increasing consensus around the level of *rigidity of their framing* of events.

A "Certain/Neutral/Uncertain" code was assigned to each entry based on linguistic qualifiers such as "I think," "I am sure," "maybe," and so forth. Again, a neutral code for an entry meant that it contained no explicit qualifiers, or that there was an equal number of qualifiers indicating certainty and uncertainty.

Perceived Issue Controllability. Drawing on previous research on the content of interpretations, this study examined one of the key attributes underlying perceptions of threat and opportunity: perceived issue controllability (Jackson and Dutton 1988). This attribute was appropriate in the context of this study, as successful new venturing revolves around the extent to which one perceives control over that which is unknown and uncertain (Block and

MacMillan 1985). To the extent that patterns of these control attributes progressively converged across subgroups, there was increasing consensus around an *"objective"* aspect of their labeling of issues.

A "Controllable/Neutral/Uncontrollable" code was assigned to each entry by noting the extent to which it revealed no obstacles or the extent to which obstacles were countered with measures for overcoming them. For example, the following is an entry that I coded as indicating uncontrollability: "This was supposed to be a product enhancement to existing customers. The product as it now stands would require major changes in the system. It's impossible, given current levels of support." In contrast, this is an example of an entry indicating issue controllability (as well as negative judgment): "The product does not fit with our current offerings. . . . It will be difficult to make customers aware of Product X features. The meeting . . . should focus on how to tie advertising to new customer campaign for the existing product." We gave each entire entry a single code that reflected the perceived controllability of issues in that entry. Again, overall neutrality of an entry sometimes meant there was no indication of controllability. Alternatively, it sometimes meant that it raised an equal number of controllable and uncontrollable issues.

Perceived Issue Scope. Again consistent with earlier research, I measured the issue-related framing of interpretations in terms of the scope of the arguments that the managers presented (e.g., Kiesler and Sproull 1982, Walsh et al. 1988). The measure was appropriate in the context of this study because of the cross-functional and hierarchical makeup of the project team that suggested the likelihood of critical differences in focus. Scope was operationalized by identifying the number of different functional areas included in the arguments. To the extent that patterns in the scope of the arguments progressively converged across subgroups, there was increasing consensus around the *breadth of their framing* of events.

A "Broad/Medium/Narrow" Scope code was assigned to each entry by counting the number of different functional topic areas included in a single entry. My preliminary analysis indicated a range from 1-9 topic areas, including a direct focus on customers, marketing, competition, systems, finance, operations, personnel, economic environment, and legislative environment. Each entry was coded as: broad (6-9 areas), medium (3-5 areas), or narrow (1-2 areas).

Reliance on textually-salient coding dimensions resulted in high interrater reliability. For the 60 entries that both researchers coded, there was 92 percent agreement in coding Support/Resistance, 90 percent in coding Controllability, 89 percent in coding Certainty, and 100 percent in coding Scope.

We discussed and reconciled all areas of disagreement. The codes provided the data for the analyses described below.

ANALYSIS

Content Analysis

The purpose of a content analysis is to identify the manifest content of a communication (Berelson 1952). It entails counting the number of references to a recurring set of ideas in a particular discourse. Major assumptions underlying this type of analysis are that (1) clusters of related words indicate themes of importance and (2) changes in word use can be taken as indicators of changing attention. Limitations often associated with content analysis include (1) its focus on broad themes, missing potentially important nuances, and (2) its focus on manifest content, thereby not explaining the logic behind apparent shifts in content (Huff 1990).

In this study, I content-analyzed the process log to identify the content of group members' interpretations: decision-maker support/resistance and perceived issue controllability.

Structural Analysis

The purpose of a structural analysis is to identify the way people frame their arguments (Weick and Bougon 1986). Major assumptions underlying this type of analysis are that (1) juxtaposition of words can be taken as an indicator of mental connection between concepts, and (2) those connections indicate how an actor frames the context of a communication (Huff 1990). Structural language analysis, with its focus on argument structure rather than themes, compensates for some of the limitations of thematic content analysis. By identifying the way themes are connected to each other, it reveals patterns of meaning across multiple and possibly changing themes. However, it is limited by its focus on structural components in a content vacuum.

In this study, I structure-analyzed the log entries to identify the framing of group members' interpretations: decision-maker certainty and perceived issue scope.

Analysis of Means and Confidence Intervals

To identify patterns of divergence and convergence along the four coded dimensions for the manager subgroups over time, I divided each project phase into three equal temporal segments. For each segment, I calculated mean coding scores for each subgroup. Consecutive means across the nine segments allowed me to trace a trajectory of each subgroup along the four coded dimensions. The trajectory revealed cognitive "distances" and changes in those distances among the subgroups over time.

I calculated confidence intervals around each mean score to assess the extent of convergence of multiple entries of a single subgroup during a segment of time. The 95 percent confidence intervals were all relatively small, ranging from +/–0 to +/–0.1 on a scale of 1 to 3. The small intervals suggested that the mean coding score of a segment was a fair representation of the individual entries within that segment.[2]

Discriminant Analysis

To determine the statistical significance of the differences among the manager subgroups as well as the shifting importance of each of the four variables in differentiating the three subgroups, I conducted a series of discriminant analyses. The objective of discriminant analysis is to maximize the ratio of between-group variation to within-group variation when that variation is measured on the derived discriminant scores. While the most common use for discriminant analysis is to classify persons or objects into various groups, it can also be used to analyze known groups to determine the relative influence of specific factors for determining into which group various cases fall. The latter use was of interest here.

The known groups were the three subgroups of managers. The fourth subgroup was unimportant for this analysis since these team members did not actively participate until the final phase of the process. A Bayesian approach assigned prior probability estimates to each of the nine time periods (three segments within each of the three phases of the project) to overcome problems caused by the different number of entries per time period and per subgroup.

The discriminating variables were decision-maker support/resistance and certainty, and issue controllability and scope. The procedure allows one to identify the mean and the within- and between-group variance around the mean of each of the four discriminating variables for each subgroup. One can then assess the relative influence of this study's measures of interpretive content and framing in differentiating the subgroups. I performed the analysis separately for each of the nine time periods, allowing me to assess changes over time in (1) the ability to discriminate among the manager subgroups, and (2) the discriminating variable(s) that accounted for most of the variance among the subgroups.

RESULTS

The trajectory of mean coding scores graphically depicts the cognitive dynamics accompanying the group's shift from conflict to collaboration. The graphs in Figure 6.3 show the paths of mean subgroup scores for each of the four coded dimensions. The paths show the changing nature and shape of the arguments used by the manager subgroups over time. Vertical axes of the graphs list the range of coding scores. Horizontal axes list the project phases and segments.

One can read the graphs as follows: Phase I began with the product Champion and Sr VP Marketing (subgroup 1) expressing support for the venture idea with a moderate degree of certainty, and perceiving a moderate number of issues (scope included questions of marketing, finance, and systems) as controllable. While the managers in subgroup 2 (Group President and VP Marketing) shared the Champion's view of the scope of relevant issues, they aligned themselves with the top management team (subgroup 3) in expressing overt resistance to the venture idea and in perceiving the issues to be uncontrollable. The top management representatives in subgroup 3 resisted the idea within a far more restricted context (narrow scope of arguments) and with greater certainty. Their arguments focused exclusively on the potential impact of the proposed new product on current customers.

The second segment of Phase I was marked by little change in the subgroups' support/resistance to the project and in their perceptions of controllability, but an abrupt shift in the scope of the arguments of subgroups 1 and 2. The Champion and his early supporter shifted toward top management's relatively narrow view. Subgroup 2 moved toward the opposite extreme.

A particularly interesting set of shifts occurred during the first segment of Phase II. In terms of personal support/resistance, the Champion (subgroup 1) moved from a highly supportive to a neutral position. At the same time, subgroups 2 and 3 moved from a predominantly resistant to a neutral position. The scope of their arguments also converged around a middle range of issues deemed relevant. Along the dimension of perceived controllability, the subgroups followed a similar but more extreme pattern, the two opposing camps actually trading positions. While subgroup 1 (Champion) began to view the issues as less controllable, the other two subgroups began to view them as more controllable. Throughout the second phase of the process, subgroups 1 and 2 continued to express moderate levels of certainty in their arguments. The top managers (subgroup 3), however, vacillated between fairly extreme positions of certainty and uncertainty.

At the end of Phase II, the subgroups shifted back toward their original positions regarding support/resistance and perceptions of controllability.

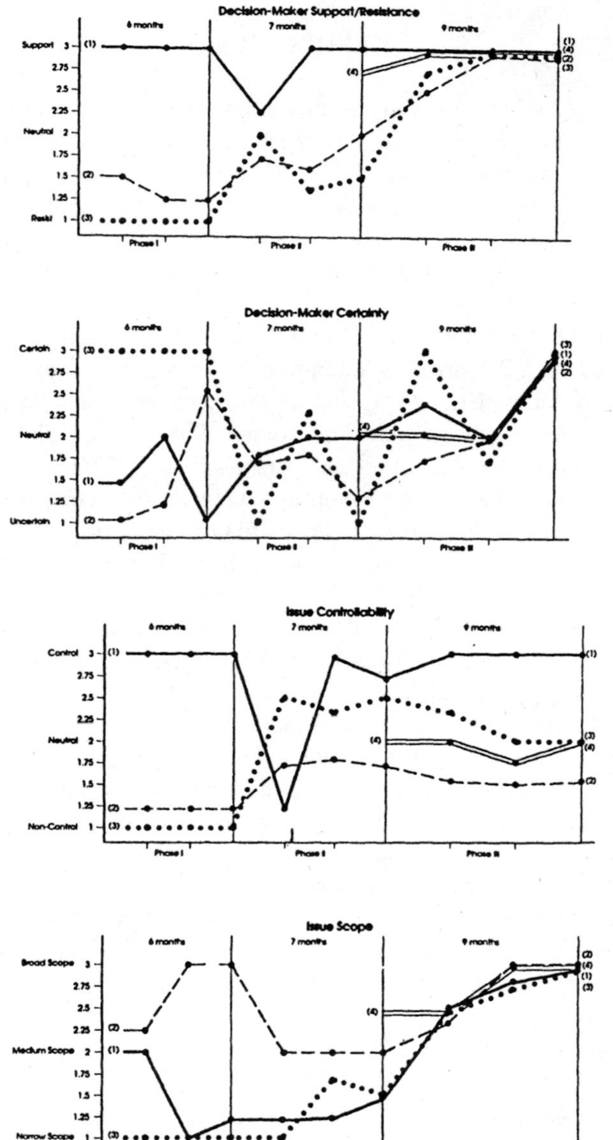

Figure 6.3. Support/Resistance, Certainty, Controllability, and Scope
NOTE: Subgroup (1) ——— ; Subgroup (2) - - - - - - - ; Subgroup (3) ··········; Subgroup (4) ═════ .

Only the scope of their arguments continued to converge. Though returning toward original differences about whether or not to support the project, and differences in their perceptions of the controllability of the issues, the subgroups continued to communicate within an increasingly shared issue context.

In Phase III, the managers of subgroup 4, previously opposed to and uninvolved in the process, began to submit log entries. Apparently pulled along by the momentum, they now aligned themselves with the more positive views emerging in the process. In this phase, all of the managers' communications abruptly converged around project support, while their perceptions of the controllability of the issues remained divergent. Subgroups 2 and 3 still perceived less control over possible project outcomes than the Champion (subgroup 1). Subgroup 4 aligned itself with the powerful in subgroup 3. Again, the scope of their arguments continued to converge until all entries reflected a similarly broad range of issues.

Overall, the support/resistance paths show extreme and consistent divergence in Phase I between the project initiators in subgroup 1 and the managers in subgroups 2 and 3. Though the paths appear to converge at the beginning of Phase II, the temporary convergence is followed by a retreat toward original positions until the abrupt convergence during the final phase.

The certainty paths reveal a general progression from less to greater certainty as the process unfolded. However, it is important to note the sharp swings of the top managers between their initial expressions of relative certainty and periods of extreme uncertainty.

The "objective" content of the subgroups' labeling of Project X issues, measured in terms of perceived issue controllability, reveals a pattern similar to that of support/resistance, though here the shifts are more extreme. Rather than converging in Phase II, the paths actually cross each other and exchange places, the managers now opposing each other from opposite ends of the spectrum. As subgroup 1 moved toward emphasizing areas of less control, subgroups 2 and 3 moved toward emphasizing areas of more control. At the end of Phase II, the issue controllability paths return toward their original positions and never converge.

The paths of perceived issue scope reveal the most consistent and progressive patterns toward convergence among the manager subgroups. If one thinks of the shared scope of an argument as indicating a shared language used to argue a position, subgroups 1 and 2 initially were close to sharing the same language. Their entries reflected a similar focus on internal systems, customer needs, and marketing issues. Yet their paths of support/resistance and perceived issue controllability indicate that they were sharing a language to argue opposing positions in this task. Sharp movements toward the use of different languages followed almost immediately (second segment of Phase I). The two subgroups maintained those language differences throughout the first phase, subgroup 1 arguing that the new venture filled a marketing gap, and subgroup 2 arguing more broadly that the venture was too risky because of a host of potential ramifications.

Only when the managers traded positions in terms of the content of their communications (Phase II), did they begin to re-converge toward sharing a common language. Even top managers in subgroup 3 who had remained fixed on a single concern—the potential effects on current customers—showed signs at the end of Phase II of sharing more of the language of subgroup 2. This point marked the beginning of consistent progression of all subgroups toward an increasingly broad scope of arguments.

Appendix 6.1 summarizes the results of the discriminant analyses, which are consistent with the patterns described above. During all three segments of Phase 1, the subgroups were most easily discriminated (over 90 percent of the variance) along the content of their communications (both personal support/resistance and perceived issue controllability—Function 1). Though both functions were significant in distinguishing the subgroups, the measures of argument framing (personal certainty and perceived scope of the issues—Function 2) explained less than 10 percent of the between-subgroup variance.

During the first segment of Phase II, interpretive content continued to differentiate the subgroups (explaining 76 percent of the variance), but the differences among them were not significant. In the next two time periods, perceived issue controllability ceased to account for much of the between-subgroup variance, with expressions of personal support/resistance and certainty distinguishing among significant subgroupings (Function 1).

During the last phase, the issue-related measures of interpretation (perceived issue scope and controllability—Function 1) accounted for most of the variance between the subgroups. In the final segment of Phase III, only perceived issue controllability remained a significant discriminator among them.

Taken together, these discriminant analyses indicate changes in the strength and nature of the differences among the manager subgroups. Across the project phases, it was increasingly difficult to differentiate among the subgroups. (Eigenvalues are highest in Phase I and lowest in Phase III.) However, the groups were more easily differentiated at the end of Phases I and II than during earlier periods of the phases. The nature of the differences among the subgroups also shifted over time: Both the judgmental and the "objective" content of their arguments (decision-maker support/resistance and issue controllability) accounted for most of the differences early on; the more overtly subjective, person-related dimensions of argument content and framing (decision-maker support/resistance and certainty) accounted for most of the differences in the second phase; and only the "objective," issue-related dimension of argument content (perceived issue controllability) was an important discriminator at the end. Phase II appears to have been the most politically heated part of the two-year process, with explicitly subjective and person-related dimensions of interpretation (support/resistance and certainty) accounting for most of the differences between subgroups. In sum, the results of the discriminant analyses show that the interpretive dimensions of these managers' arguments continued to be significantly differentiable throughout the two-year process (with the exception of the first segment of Phase II). The most critical differences began and ended with interpretive content and shifted from the overtly subjective dimensions of interpretation to those couched in an "objective" garb.

DISCUSSION

Comparisons of the beginning and end points of the Project X experience reveal that the group began with a lack of consensus around their personal support/resistance and degree of certainty, and around their perceptions of issue controllability and scope. In the end, they achieved consensus around personal certainty and support, and around the scope of their arguments. They maintained their differing views of issue controllability.

There are several reasons to suspect ultimate group consensus around personal support and certainty as indicators of a "common mind" or shared understanding (Huber 1991, p. 30) that enabled the group to collaborate. First, the patterns of consensus-building around personal support/resistance revealed in the Project X log suggest a great deal of instability. The timing of the log entries by subgroups, discussed earlier, is important here. Subgroup 1 made the first set of entries during each phase of the process, thus setting the tone for subsequent entries. Having fought resistance to the venture idea throughout the six months of the first phase, subgroup 1 communicated doubts about the merits of the venture idea (see Phase II of support/resistance paths in Figure 6.3). Immediately following the decreased level of support of subgroup 1, subgroups 2 and 3 found reasons to be less resistant to the idea. Similarly, the increased certainty of subgroup 1 at the beginning of the second phase was followed by reversals of the certainty levels of the two opposing subgroups (see Phase II of the certainty graphs in Figure 6.3). All three subgroups, however, reverted toward their original preferences and levels of certainty before abruptly converging around project support and certainty at the end. The instability of these patterns sheds doubt on the validity of the final positions as a stable indicator of shared understanding.

A possible explanation of the unstable patterns of support/resistance and certainty lies in their overtly subjective nature. As noted earlier (Figure 6.1), expressions of preference and certainty cannot be easily couched in objective terms, leaving one vulnerable to personal attack or liability. They may thus reflect symbolic behaviors rather than converging thought processes.

Another reason to suspect ultimate consensus around overt project support as an indicator of shared understanding is that the subgroup support/resistance paths (Figure 6.3) run roughly parallel to the controllability paths during early phases of the process, and the latter never converge. Though personal support/resistance and perceived issue controllability are not equivalent cognitive constructs as measured here, they are hypothesized to be related attributes that underlie perceptions of threat and opportunity (Dutton and Jackson 1987). The results of this study partially support that hypothesis. During early phases of this venturing process, the support/resistance paths tended to parallel the paths indicating perceived controllability. Ultimately, however, perceptions of controllability were stickier in that they reverted back toward original positions. Despite vacillation during the two-year process, the subgroups emerged at the end of it with close to their original views of issue controllability. Given the close parallel of personal support/resistance and perceived issue controllability of these subgroups throughout the beginning of the process, and given the sharp swings and lack of progressive overlap in both, one is led to question the extent to which either explains the cognitive shifts associated with shared understanding.

The perceived issue scope paths in Figure 6.3 tell a different story. The subgroups do not appear to have entered the process with fixed and stable initial positions. Rather, differing views of the relevant scope seem to have grown out of the dynamics of Phase I. The greatest divergence occurred in the second segment of Phase I when the Champion and his early supporter narrowed the scope of their arguments and subgroup 2 broadened its scope. The beginning of Phase II marked a return to more of a shared framing of their arguments. Thereafter, the subgroups followed a stable, progressive process of converging around an increasingly broad range of issues.

Top management's reduced certainty and the reversal of perceptions of controllability of the subgroups in Phase II may have allowed the subgroups to move toward more commonality in the way they framed their arguments. As Putnam (1985, p. 138) noted, "trading issues" is one strategy for simplifying issues in group negotiations. When the Champion's subgroup began to verbalize doubts about the viability of the proposed new venture, its two opponents (perhaps following the tone of conflict that was becoming a norm for the group) found reasons for being less resistant to it. At the same time, their perceptions of issue controllability reversed themselves. This reversal did not spell the beginning of neutrality from which to resolve differences. Perceptions of controllability reversed themselves once again before the group achieved collaboration. The first reversal did, however, spell the beginning of the use of a shared language in framing their arguments. Though the managers continued to disagree about the viability of Project X, they did so within a progressively shared issue context.

The claim, then, based on the results of this study, is that convergence around a broad frame of interpretations provided the common understanding needed to move toward collective action despite the persistence of divergent content of interpretations. The claim is consistent with this study's proposition (see "From Theory to Practice"). However, there are at least two alternative explanations for the success of Project X. One is that ultimate collaboration was simply the result of increased access to more information. The increasingly broadened scope of the arguments of all group members in Phase III suggests that they were processing increasing levels of relevant data. However, subgroup 2 provided the group with a broad scope of data throughout most of Phase I. Group conflict continued to worsen. The process of this group provides some evidence that more information, alone, does not lead to effective collective action. More information became useful only after the group members (in Phase II) began to share a common view of what sorts of data were relevant.

Another alternative explanation of this group's trajectory is that ultimate collaboration was the product of power relations among the group members. Of the three subgroups, the top management representatives in subgroup 3 held the most formal or positional power. Given their powerful status, their approval was of central concern to the Champion's subgroup. This might explain why the Champion reframed his arguments early in the process to match the focused concerns of the top management subgroup. The managers in subgroup 2, already following top management's lead in resisting the venture, did not need to frame their arguments to fit those of top management. Their position was sufficiently invulnerable to allow them to generate their own language. One might thus explain the abrupt convergence around project support in Phase III on the basis of top management's legitimation of the idea. As numerous researchers have suggested (e.g., Burgelman 1983, Gray et al. 1985), the influence of the powerful often shapes the beliefs of subordinates, overriding their individual, role-based beliefs.

Though top management input was clearly a trigger, explaining the successful development of Project X based solely on the influence of the powerful is unsatisfactory in light of the cognitive patterns reflected in the log. First, top managers continued to stress the uncontrollable aspects of issues related to the new-venture idea, suggesting that they were not wholehearted champions of the venture even at the end. Second, the top management certainty paths provide a further check against the claim that the powerful may have molded the group's cognitive development. The certainty paths reflect the level of ambiguity surrounding the task of this group. Subgroups 1 and 2 both began the process with great uncertainty, and despite a few dips, gradually gained more confidence. Top management in subgroup 3 initially resisted the project with a high level of certainty, but subsequent sharp swings indicate that even for the "powerful," the task came to represent an ill-defined and ambiguous decision context. The degree of top managers' expressed uncertainty throughout the process suggests that they were not forcefully pushing their views on their subordinates. Finally, as argued earlier, even if top managers "forced" a consensus around expressed preferences, the successful collaboration of this group required some level of shared understanding of this novel project. The results of this study suggest that such shared understanding can derive from a common view of the scope of relevant issues, even in the face of differing views of issue content.

Limitations of the Study

The study analyzed a single venturing process. One must question the limits of its generalizability. The Project X experience may have been unique in at least two respects. First, distinct subgroups maintained different but remarkably clear cognitive pictures and frames through which they evaluated the project. Is such a clear division of perspectives unique to this organization or even to Project X? Informal discussions with the 11 managers suggested that the subgroups existed long before Project X began. There was a general expectation that the subgroups would always "team up" with predictable kinds of arguments.

Are such consistent subgroup differences unique to this organization? Previous research on ambiguous and ill-defined organizational decision processes (Bower 1970, Burgelman 1983, Dougherty 1992) provides evidence of consistent subgroup-level perspectives in other organizations. Unlike previous research, however, this study suggests that the different perspectives are not clearly determined by either organizational function or hierarchy. Future research should continue the search for the sources of a person's or group's frames of reference.

Second, the communication log, used as the primary source of data in the study, was certainly a unique aspect of this venture. One might argue that the mere existence of such a log potentially altered the venturing process. The log itself may be seen as part of a larger frame around the group's argumentative process, providing bounds that may have prevented the polarized beliefs from exploding. One might then argue that neither the content nor the framing of the arguments of these managers would have converged without the artificial control mechanism provided by the log. Future research should study the cognitive dynamics of less bounded group processes to determine whether the results are generalizable beyond such a setting.

Finally, this study examined only a limited number of interpretive dimensions of the project team's communications. Future research must continue to apply others. It is important to note that the interpretive dimensions relevant to group consensus building are not always obvious to those involved in the process. In discussing the results of this study with the Project X team, I learned that decision-maker certainty and support/resistance were dimensions of meaning that team members were consciously aware of during their negotiations. The less openly subjective interpretations of issue controllability and scope, in contrast, were not obvious to the participants until they observed the patterns revealed in this study. This informal finding underscores the need to identify "objective," issue-related as well as more openly subjective, person-related dimensions of meaning in decision processes.

CONCLUSION

The study offers a cognitive framework for studying collective processes of negotiating toward shared understanding of new and diverse information. It contributes toward furthering our efforts to move from "speculation" to "empirical research" (Huber 1991, p. 103) in the area of organizational consensus building and learning by (1) distinguishing between openly subjective and apparently "objective" expressions of meaning, (2) examining consensus building along different dimensions of meaning, allowing for possible interactions of the content and framing of interpretations, and (3) tracing the links between subgroup and group-level understanding over time.

First, the results highlight the need to distinguish between personal, openly judgmental expressions of meaning and those couched in more "objective" terms. As noted earlier, previous research on consensus in strategic decision making has focused exclusively on expressed personal certainty of preferences (e.g., Bourgeois 1985, Dess 1987). The inconsistent results may have reflected differences in the less overtly subjective meanings those managers assigned to their preferences.

Second, the results begin to clarify the role of consensus along different dimensions of meaning in novel and ambiguous group decision processes.

The content and framing of communications both reflect "meaning," but they are not equivalent constructs. Group consensus around one does not necessarily imply consensus around the other.

Interpretive content represents people's labeling of facts as they see them. Whether those labels reflect beliefs about issues as controllable or uncontrollable, or another set of labels, they represent mapping devices that are used to simplify and make sense of new information. Such content labels tend to portray well-defined extremes that are resistant to change (Dutton and Jackson 1987). The Project X subgroups temporarily "traded" their pictures of issue controllability, but they never moved to a neutral place from which to proceed together toward a shared view.

In contrast, the interpretive framing of these manager-subgroups was reflected in the language of the stories that connected the polarized pictures of the new-venture idea. The language of the managers converged around ways to frame their arguments that were broad enough to encompass multiple viewpoints. They shared this frame despite divergent pictures about the degree of controllability associated with the change efforts.

The differences uncovered in this study between the development of the content and the framing of interpretations support Weick and Bougon's (1986) argument that it is possible to understand how meaning is shared by doing content-free analyses of argumentation. Yet the results of this study also suggest important reasons for not ignoring the content of communication. Though the eventual movement toward collaboration may have grown out of the shared language that reflected consensus around the framing of issues, the substantive content or pictures within those frames appeared to be an important factor in shaping the direction of early conflict. The content of early arguments revealed the extreme positions that Putnam (1985, p. 137) suggested are characteristic of initial stages of issue development in group negotiations. If one wishes to explain the source of conflict in early stages of an ambiguous project, content-free analyses of argument frames may reveal very little until the group begins the process of packaging and repackaging the issues to move away from polarized extremes.

If one wants to explain why particular argument frames emerge in groups, one must understand the tensions arising from different content labels of reality. The way the subgroups framed their arguments did not emerge as clearly conflictive at the start of Project X, but appeared to pull apart as they began to air their content differences. The reversal of positions of support/resistance and of perceptions of controllability in Phase II of the negotiations appeared to play a role in the re-emergence of a shared language. If one's research objective is to understand *what* argument frames emerge, one may not need to examine the substantive content of argumentation. If, however, the objective includes an understanding of *why* argument frames in groups develop and change over time, one must pay attention to labels of argument content.

Finally, this study also contributes to an understanding of the links between subgroup and group-level understanding over time. On the basis of the support/resistance paths (Figure 6.3), it appears that in late 1987 the Project X group achieved a "common mind." But the dynamics along different dimensions of understanding suggest that what we are capturing at such a moment is the convergence of the *language* used to construct group-wide meanings. There was progressive agreement about how to tell the story, not about the underlying content or moral of the story. The converging language of the story, as it unfolded, became sufficiently shared to give the *appearance* of a unitary moral.

The practical implications of these results for managers seem clear. Successful corporate innovation requires not only that overt decisions embrace something new, but that decision makers develop a new collective understanding that allows them to collaborate in implementing the innovation (Van de Ven et al. 1989). Collective learning involves such a change in understanding in decision-making groups. Expressed certainty of project support or resistance may reveal initial sources of conflict and final decisions, but may say very little about the more implicit dimensions of learning that form the basis of collaborative innovation. The Project X team learned by embracing diverse interpretive pictures within a collectively shared interpretive frame. It was not necessary to trade off unity and diversity of interpretations in the group's learning process. The results reveal one way that organizations manage to combine the unity and diversity needed for collective learning. If further research on consensus building supports these findings, we may have an important message for managers: To promote learning as a community, managers must actively encourage the development of different and conflicting views of what is thought to be true, while striving for a shared framing of the issues that is broad enough to encompass those differences.

ACKNOWLEDGMENTS

I gratefully acknowledge the helpful comments of Howard Aldrich, Graham Astley, Jean Bartunek, Joel Baum, Jane Dutton, Anne Huff, Frances Milliken, Jim Walsh, Ray Zammuto, the co-editors of this special issue, and the anonymous reviewers.

Appendix 6.1 Discriminant Analysis Results Discriminate Among Subgroups of Managers

Function		*Important Variables of Function*	*Eigenvalue*	*Percent of Variance Explained*	*Canonical Correlation*	*Significance*
Phase I						
Segment 1	1	S/R & CONTR	5.07	92	0.91	0.00
	2	SCOPE & CERT	0.46	8	0.56	0.00
Segment 2	1	S/R & CONTR	3.9	92	0.89	0.00
	2	CERT	0.34	8	0.5	0.00
Segment 3	1	S/R & CONTR	32.5	98	0.99	0.00
	2	SCOPE & CERT	0.55	2	0.6	0.00
Phase II						
Segment 1	1	S/R & CONTR	2.8	76	0.86	0.21
	2	SCOPE & CERT	0.9	24	0.69	0.31
Segment 2	1	S/R	12.5	97	0.96	0.00
	2	CONT & SCOPE & CERT	0.45	3	0.56	0.1
Segment 3	1	CERT & S/R	29	97	0.98	0.00
	2	SCOPE & CONTR	0.86	3	0.68	0.2
Phase III						
Segment 1	1	SCOPE & CONTR	3.5	93	0.88	0.00
	2	CERT&S/R	0.25	7	0.45	0.02
Segment 2	1	CONTR	1.6	90	0.78	0 00
	2	SCOPE & CERT & S/R	0.17	10	0.38	0.11
Segment 3	1	CONTR	2.8	98	0.85	0.00
	2	SCOPE & CERT & S/R	0.04	2	0.21	0.29

S/R = Decision maker Support/Resistance CERT = Decision-maker Certainty
CONTR = Perceived Issue Controllability SCOPE = Perceived Issue Scope
Eigenvalue is the ratio of between-subgroup to within-subgroup sum of squares.
Percent of Variance is the percent of between-subgroup variance that is explained by the variables.
Canonical Correlation is a measure of the degree of association between the discriminant scores and the subgroups. When squared, it is the proportion of total variability explained by the between-subgroup differences.

Appendix 6.2 Standardized Canonical Discriminant Coefficients (Asterisk Indicates Importance of Variable in Contributing to Discriminant Function)

Variables	*Phase I*					
	Segment 1 *Fn1/Fn2*		*Segment 2* *Fn1/Fn2*		*Segment 3* *Fn1/Fn2*	
Support/Resistance	0.4*	–0.37	0.39*	–0.36	–0.63*	0.51
Certainty	0.1	0.93*	0.45	0.92*	0.62	–0.51*
Issue Controllability	0.86*	0.08	0.73*	–0.04	–0.28*	0.2
Issue Scope	–0.32	–0.23*	Failed Tolerance Test		0.65	0.76*
	Phase II					
	Segment 1 *Fn1/Fn2*		*Segment 2* *Fn1/Fn2*		*Segment 3* *Fn1/Fn2*	
Support/Resistance	–1.1	–0.38*	0.98*	0.53	1.1*	0.37
Certainty	–0.36	0.28*	–0.3	–0.41*	0.82*	–0.19
Issue Controllability	1.1	–0.32*	0.82	–0.51*	0.99	–0.77*
Issue Scope	0.72	0.92*	–0.06	0.73*	0.33	0.75*
	Phase III					
	Segment 1 *Fn1/Fn2*		*Segment 2* *Fn1/Fn2*		*Segment 3* *Fn1/Fn2*	
Support/Resistance	0.28	–0.37*	–0.2	–0.19*	–0.29	0.23*
Certainty	0.53	0.83*	0.17	0.47*	–0.21	–0.21*
Issue Controllability	0.93*	–0.24	0.99*	0.27	1.1*	0.11
Issue Scope	0.2*	0.03	–0.35	0.72*	–0.14	0.94*

NOTE: *Canonical Discriminant Coefficients* show the contribution of variables to the discriminant function. When these coefficients are standardized, variables with larger coefficients contribute more to the overall function. The interpretation of the coefficients is similar to that in multiple regression. Since the variables are correlated, it is not possible to assess the importance of an individual variable. The value of the coefficient for a particular variable depends on the other variables included in the function.

NOTES

1. Because they all refer to the way people make sense of information, the terms "interpretation," "meaning," and "understanding" are used interchangeably throughout this hapter.

2. I calculated the standard error of the mean (SE_M), which is $SD_x / \sqrt{n}$, where n is the number of entries. The 95-percent confidence interval for the mean is then from $M - 1.96(SE_M)$ to $M + 1.96(SE_M)$ (see Schmidt and Hunter 1989).

REFERENCES

Bartunek, J. M. (1984), "Changing Interpretive Schemes and Organizational Restructuring: The Example of a Religious Order," *Administrative Science Quarterly,* 29, 355-372.

———, J. R. Gordon, and R. P. Weathersby (1983), "Developing 'Complicated' Understanding in Administrators," *Academy of Management Review,* 8, 273-284

Berelson, B. (1952), *Content Analysis in Communications Research,* Glencoe, IL: Free Press.

Bettenhausen, K. and J. K. Murnighan (1985), "The Emergence of Norms in Competitive Decision-Making Groups," *Administrative Science Quarterly,* 30, 350-372.

Blackburn, R. and L. L. Cummings (1982), "Cognitions of Work Unit Structure," *Academy of Management Journal,* 25, 836-854.

Block, Z. and I. MacMillan (1985), "Growing Concern: Milestones for Successful Venture Planning," *Harvard Business Review,* Sept-Oct.

Bougon, M., K. Weick, and D. Binkhorst (1977), "Cognition in Organizations: An Analysis of the Utrecht Jazz Orchestra," *Administrative Science Quarterly,* 22, 606-639.

Bourgeois, J. (1985), "Strategic Goals, Perceived Uncertainty, and Economic Performance in Volatile Environments," *Academy of Management Journal,* 28, 548-573.

Bower, G. H. and E. R. Hilgard (1981), *Theories of Learning,* Englewood Cliffs, NJ: Prentice Hall.

Bower, J. L. (1970), *Managing the Resource Allocation Process,* Cambridge, MA: Harvard University Press.

Burgelman, R. A. (1983), "A Process Model of Internal Corporate Venturing in the Diversified Major Firm," *Administrative Science Quarterly,* 28, 223-244.

Cohen, W. M. and D. A. Levinthal (1990), "Absorptive Capacity: A New Perspective on Learning and Innovation," *Administrative Science Quarterly,* 35, 128-152.

Daft, R. L. and K. E. Weick (1984), "Toward a Model of Organizations as Interpretation Systems," *Academy of Management Review,* 9, 284-295.

Dess, G. (1987), "Consensus on Strategy Formulation and Organizational Performance: Competitors in a Fragmented Industry," *Strategic Management Journal,* 8, 259-278.

Dewey, J. (1954), *The Public and Its Problems,* Chicago: Swallow.

DeWoot, P., A. Heyvaert, and F. Martou (1978), "Strategic Management: An Empirical Study of 168 Belgian Firms," *International Studies of Management and Organization,* 7, 60-75.

Donnellon, A., B. Gray, and M. G. Bougon (1986), "Communication, Meaning, and Organized Action," *Administrative Science Quarterly,* 31, 43-55.

Dougherty, D. (1992), "Interpretive Barriers to Successful Product Innovation in Large Firms," *Organization Science,* 3, 179-202.

Dutton, J. and S. Jackson (1987), "Categorizing Strategic Issues: Links to Organizational Action," *Academy of Management Review,* 12, 76-90.

Eisenberg, E. M. (1984), "Ambiguity as Strategy in Organizational Communication," *Communication Monographs,* 51, 227-242.

Feldman, D. C. (1984), "The Development and Enforcement of Group Norms," *Academy of Management Review*, 9, 47-53.

Fiol, C. M. and M. A. Lyles (1985), "Organizational Learning," *Academy of Management Review*, 10, 803-813.

Friedlander, F. (1983), "Patterns of Individual and Organizational Learning," in S. Srivastva and Associates (Eds.), *The Executive Mind: New Insights on Managerial Thought and Action*, San Francisco: Jossey-Bass.

Gray, B., M. Bougon, and A. Donnellon (1985), "Organizations as Constructions and Destructions of Meaning," *Journal of Management*, 11, 83-98.

Hage, J. and M. Aiken (1970), *Social Change in Complex Organizations*, New York: Random House.

Holsti, O. R. (1976), "Foreign Policy Formation Viewed Cognitively," in R. Axelrod (Ed.), *Structure of Decision*, Princeton, NJ: Princeton University Press.

Hrebiniak, L. and C. Snow (1982), "Top Management Agreement and Organizational Performance," *Human Relations*, 35, 1139-1158.

Huber, G. P. (1991), "Organizational Learning: An Examination of the Contributing Processes and the Literatures," *Organization Science*, 2, 88-115.

Huff, A. (1990), "Mapping Strategic Thought," in A. Huff (Ed.), *Mapping Strategic Thought*, New York: John Wiley.

Jackson, S. and J. Dutton (1988), "Discerning Threats and Opportunities," *Administrative Science Quarterly*, 33, 370-387.

Kiesler, S. and L. Sproull (1982), "Managerial Response to Changing Environments: Perspectives on Problem Sensing from Social Cognition," *Administrative Science Quarterly*, 27, 548-570.

Kuhn, T. S. (1970), *The Structure of Scientific Revolutions*, Chicago: University of Chicago Press.

Lakoff, G. (1987), "Cognitive Models and Prototype Theory," in U. Neisser (Ed.), *Concepts and Conceptual Development: Ecological Conceptual Factors in Categorization*, Cambridge, UK: Cambridge University Press.

Lindsay, P. H. and D. A. Norman (1977), *Human Information Processing*, Orlando, FL: Academic Press.

Mintzberg, H. and J. A. Waters (1985), "Of Strategies, Deliberate and Emergent," *Strategic Management Journal*, 6, 257-272.

Neisser, U. (1987), "Introduction: The Ecological and Intellectual Bases of Categorization," in U. Neisser (Ed.), *Concepts and Conceptual Development: Ecological and Conceptual Factors in Categorization*, Cambridge: Cambridge University Press.

Nelson, R. R. and S. Winter (1982), *An Evolutionary Theory of Economic Change*, Cambridge, MA: Harvard University Press.

Opp, K. D. (1982), "The Evolutionary Emergence of Norms," *British Journal of Social Psychology*, 21, 139-149.

Porter, M. E. (1980), *Competitive Strategy: Techniques for Analyzing Industries and Competitors*, New York: Free Press.

Putnam, L. (1985), "Bargaining as Organizational Communication," in R. D. McPhee and P. K. Tompkins (Eds.), *Organizational Communication: Traditional Themes and New Directions*, Beverly Hills, CA: Sage.

Reger, R. K. and A. S. Huff (1993), "Strategic Groups: A Cognitive Perspective," *Strategic Management Journal*, 14, 2, 103-124.

Schmidt, F. L. and J. E. Hunter (1989), "Interrater Reliability Coefficients Cannot Be Computed When Only One Stimulus Is Rated," *Journal of Applied Psychology*, 74, 368-370.

Starbuck, W. H., A. Greve, and B. L. T. Hedberg (1978), "Responding to Crises," *Journal of Business Administration,* 9, 111-137.

Van de Ven, A. H., S. Venkataraman, D. Polley, and R. Garud (1989), "Processes of New Business Creation in Different Organizational Settings," in A. H. Van de Ven, H. L. Angle, and M. S. Poole (Eds.), *Research on the Management of Innovation,* New York: Harper Collins, Ballinger Division.

Walsh, J. P. (1988), "Selectivity and Selective Perception: An Investigation of Managers' Belief Structures and Information Processing," *Academy of Management Journal,* 31, 873-896.

———, C. M. Henderson, and J. Deighton (1988), "Negotiated Belief Structures and Decision Performance: An Empirical Investigation," *Organizational Behavior and Human Decision Processes,* 42, 194-216.

Walton, E. J. (1986), "Managers' Prototypes of Financial Terms," *Journal of Management Studies,* 23, 679-698.

Weick, K. E. (1979), *The Social Psychology of Organizing,* (2nd ed.), Reading, MA: Addison-Wesley.

——— and M. G. Bougon (1986), "Organizations as Cognitive Maps: Charting Ways to Success and Failure," in H. Sims, Jr. and D. Gioia (Eds.), *The Thinking Organization,* San Francisco: Jossey-Bass.

7

Symbolism and Strategic Change in Academia

The Dynamics of Sensemaking and Influence

DENNIS A. GIOIA
JAMES B. THOMAS
SHAWN M. CLARK
KUMAR CHITTIPEDDI

This study investigated the uses of sensemaking, influence, and symbolism in launching a strategic change effort at a university. It employed an ethnographic/interpretive approach in examining the ways that symbols, metaphors, and various subtle influence processes were used to lend meaning to concepts and possible courses of action by a task force instrumental to the strategic change process. Two distinct researcher perspectives were used: an "insider" perspective employing several informants along with an active participant-observer and an "outsider" perspective employing several researchers. Both perspectives were brought to bear as a means of countering the "researcher arrogance" that typifies organizational study by lending balanced voice to both insider and outsider interpretations of events. The findings showed that sensemaking and influence emerged as fundamental processes in the instigation of strategic change. Both processes were symbolically based and varied in directionality over the life of the task force (internally directed in the embryonic phases, and externally directed in the mature phases). Contrary to common wisdom, sensemaking and influence emerged as frequently coincident, interdependent processes that were difficult to distinguish from each other. The discovery of the common symbolic base for sensemaking and influence also indicated that symbols served both expressive and instrumental roles: suggesting that the accepted view of symbols as predominantly expressive devices does not present a complete picture of their dynamic nature. The use of

This chapter originally appeared in *Organization Science,* Vol. 5, No. 3, August 1994.

symbolism also was shown simultaneously to reveal and conceal different aspects of the change process, thus providing task force members the means to circumvent resistance while accomplishing desired action. Symbols and metaphors thus facilitated both cognitive understanding and intended action in attempting to "reinstitutionalize" a major public university via the strategic change process. Overall, the study suggests that efforts to stabilize an organizational system in flux from the systematic upheaval represented by strategic change can be understood as the symbolic interplay between sensemaking and influence.

(INFLUENCE; INSTITUTIONALIZATION;
SENSEMAKING; STRATEGIC CHANGE;
SYMBOLISM; SYMBOLS)

INTRODUCTION

To effectively compete, or even survive, in market environments that have become complex and turbulent after years of relative stability (e.g., health care, higher education) frequently requires organizations to undertake a process of dramatic, and often traumatic, strategic change. Increasingly, this type of change is seen not just as a shift in norms, structures, processes, and goals (cf. Ginsberg 1988), but as a form of "second-order change" (Bartunek 1984) involving a fundamental alteration in the social construction of reality (Berger and Luckmann 1967). This view suggests that strategic change involves, at its essence, a *cognitive* reorientation of the organization (Gioia and Chittipeddi 1991): one that reflects an acceptance of perceptual, structural, and contextual discontinuities that occurs through the shifting interplay of deliberate and emergent processes (Mintzberg and Waters 1985, Tichy 1983).

From this cognitive perspective, the success of strategic change efforts depends not only on the organization's ability to undergo a significant shift in direction, vision, and values, but also the ability of stakeholders to understand and accept a new conceptualization of the organization (Smircich 1983). The impetus for this kind of change often lies with top management who typically are key actors in articulating the need for, and intended nature of the impending change (Smircich and Morgan 1982, Quinn 1980). It is in this attempt to forge understanding and acceptance of an alternative strategic reality among organizational stakeholders that influence (Pfeffer 1981b), sensemaking (Gioia and Chittipeddi 1991, Smircich and Stubbart 1985, Weick 1979), and symbolism (Morgan et al. 1983, Pfeffer 1981a) are likely to be critically important (cf. also Powell and DiMaggio 1991).

Although the role of strategic change in affecting organizational outcomes has been well-documented, the processes involved in promoting cognitive understanding, acceptance, and institutionalization of a new organizational reality during strategic transitions have not been adequately studied. The purpose of this project was to study the dynamics involved in constructing new understandings in the embryonic stages of a strategic change effort. We tracked, from inception, the proceedings of a task force instrumental to the change process in a university, and studied the means by which the members of the task force came to understand not only their roles, but also the constraining and facilitating factors that affected their ability to instigate strategic change.[1] We used a grounded approach (Glaser and Strauss 1967) to "discover" dimensions and nuances involved in the strategic change initiation process. The general research question guiding the study was framed as follows: In an organization where strategies and structures have been long established, what processes characterize the development and acceptance of new realities associated with the launching of strategic change?

In the past, academic institutions have not had to be overly concerned with "strategic" change per se. Enrollments were more or less stable and operating funds were more or less guaranteed either by state and federal governments or other traditional private sources (Keller 1983, Mortimer and Tierney 1979). The modern academic environment, however, has brought a disquieting trend toward declining enrollments, reduced funding, and external competition. Thus, many higher-education institutions have entered a period of reorientation, requiring nontraditional types of change to deal with the new, competitive environment (Milliken 1990). It is in such an institution that we studied the dynamics of the early phases of a strategic change effort.

Strategic Change

Strategic change involves either a redefinition of organizational mission and purpose or a substantial shift in overall priorities and goals to reflect new emphases or direction. It is usually accompanied by significant changes in patterns of resource allocation and/or alterations in organizational structure and processes to meet changing environmental demands. As Ginsberg (1988) notes, strategic change has been discussed in terms of changes in strategy *content* as well as transformations in strategy *process*. Changes in content typically involve alterations in competitive decisions within particular product/market domains such as price or quality (see also Rumelt, 1974). Change in terms of strategy-making processes involve shifts in organizational culture (e.g., Tushman and Romanelli 1985), formal management systems (e.g., Ansoff 1979), and/or structures (e.g., Chandler 1962). Snow and Hambrick (1980) view strategic change as capturing both dimensions, i.e., as an alteration of an organization's alignment with its environment and an attendant modification in processes to conform to the new alignment.

Tushman and Romanelli (1985) argue that this degree of change (i.e., simultaneous shifts of strategy, structures, and processes) constitutes a pronounced discontinuity in the life of the organization. Such a reorientation, as opposed to incremental changes that simply adjust an organization's existing stance, requires top management to confront the difficult task of not only developing a vision of the intended reorientation, but also disseminating an "abstract" of the transformed organization to key stakeholders (cf. Gioia and Chittipeddi 1991, Greiner and Bhambri 1989). Further, given that changes of this nature are seldom brought about by mandate, a process of negotiated social construction occurs (Berger and Luckman 1967). Such a process might include attempts to influence perceptions of the need for, or the nature of, strategic change (Walsh and Fahey 1986) through the use of symbols or symbolic actions (Frost and Morgan 1983, Pfeffer 1981a). This perspective suggests that to understand and manage strategic change, it is necessary to examine symbolism, sensemaking, and influence processes that serve to create and legitimate the meaning of the change (Dutton and Duncan 1987).[2]

Symbolism, Sensemaking, and Influence

Much of human understanding occurs through the use of symbolic processes (Axley 1984, Spradley and McCurdy 1983). A symbol can be any sign (an act, event, logo, etc.) that represents some concept; thus, the representation of the concept becomes the symbol's "meaning" (Geertz 1973). The most pervasive medium of symbolism is language. In particular, the use of metaphor, wherein one concept is understood in terms of another concept already known (Ortony 1975), is key to understanding (Daft 1983, Daft and Wiginton 1979, Frost and Morgan 1983, Pondy and Mitroff 1979). Indeed, Lakoff and Johnson (1980) argue that not only our language but also our conceptual systems are fundamentally metaphorical in nature. When we try to understand a new experience or concept, we do so by trying to ascribe meaning to it, and the meaning is often most effectively grasped through symbolic or metaphorical representation (cf. Chen and Meindl 1991). Thus, symbols and especially language symbols (such as visionary images and metaphors), are basic to the process of sensemaking (Donnellon et al. 1986, Morgan 1986).

When people are called upon to enact some change in their existing patterns of thinking and acting, the proposed change must make sense in a way that relates to previous understanding and experience (Bartunek 1984, Gioia 1986, Louis 1980, Ranson et al. 1980). Symbols and metaphors are key to this process (Huff 1983, Johnson 1990), in part because their inherent ambiguity provides a bridge between the familiar and the strange, thus fostering a sense of continuity while simultaneously facilitating change (Pondy 1983). In this sense symbols both conceal and reveal facets of change. They conceal threatening aspects within the camouflage of the known (Meyer and Rowan 1977), yet reveal those aspects that emphasize difference; but, differences are rendered in terms that echo the familiar (cf. Meyer 1984). When a strategic change is proposed, different symbolic language is used to herald the change and to articulate its nature. Our focus, therefore, often is on the language used by organizational actors during the attempt to launch the strategic change process.

Sensemaking, however, involves not only "pure" cognitive interpretation processes, but interpretation in conjunction with action (Thomas et al. 1993, Weick 1979). In organizations, people take into consideration the realized or likely outcomes of their own actions or those of other significant stakeholders in trying to understand what to do next. Not only is language symbolic, but action itself is symbolic (Feldman and March 1981, Pfeffer 1981a), perhaps especially in organizations. In particular, symbolic action is central to the institutional legitimacy of the espoused changes (cf. March and Shapira 1982), perhaps as a way of making proposed new arrangements subjectively plausible (Berger et al. 1973).

Symbolic actions are frequently used by management to legitimate decisions and strategies that affect perceptions of the organization by members and other stakeholders (Pfeffer 1981a). In attempting to launch strategic change in institutions that are unfamiliar with such a process, it is arguably necessary first to formulate a strategy to facilitate acceptance of the new strategy. Such a "meta-strategy" (Allaire and Firsirotu 1985) depends on symbolic procedures to legitimize the transition process and its likely outcomes (Langley 1989, Quinn 1980). Gaining insight into the symbolic meaning structures of organizations (whether language-nor action-based), and especially into the origins and manipulations of these meaning structures, allows an understanding of the creation and maintenance of alternative organizational realities (Mumby 1988).

Symbols, metaphors, and actions, however, are not the only means for making sense of organizational experience. Both sensemaking and action-taking are affected by the context in which they occur (e.g., Thomas and McDaniel 1990, Thomas et al. 1993, Weick 1979). In organizations, context often is defined by influence relationships and political structures, an observation that applies to universities as much as to any other organization (see Pfeffer and Salancik 1974, Pfeffer and Moore 1980). The construction of organizational reality, therefore, is in some significant measure also likely to be influence-based. When sense must be made of observed events or proposed changes, people account for influence relationships in deciphering or ascribing meaning to the situation (Dutton et al. 1983). Yet, influence in organizations is often more covert than overt; subtlety is its hallmark, because powerholders seldom flaunt their influence ability (Frost 1987). One of the few occasions that influence is likely to be manifested in visible ways, however, is during change efforts (Pfeffer 1981b). Even then, however, influence is likely to be subtle, i.e., couched in symbolic representations (Das 1988, Frost 1987, Lukes 1974). Thus, influence processes are likely to occur in concert with symbolism, which suggests a potentially complex interrelationship among symbolism, sensemaking, and influence. This perspective also suggests that symbols have influential capacity, which in turn implies that they can have an instrumental role in accomplishing strategic change in addition to their long-noted expressive role (Edelman 1964). Symbols, therefore, not only constitute a medium for sensemaking, but for a medium for influence as well.

Realistically speaking, we also must recognize that the symbols, visions, and constructions of some actors are more powerful than those of others (Ranson et al. 1980, Riley 1983), and therefore exert greater influence over the meanings attributed to various actions and events. Even in universities, which are ostensibly egalitarian organizations, the accomplishment of strategic change implies the influence of certain constructions of reality over others. Leaders of such change efforts must find some means for proposing a new vision of the organization's meaning and value system and facilitating its acceptance.

BACKGROUND: THE UNIVERSITY SETTING

The university under study is a comprehensive public research university with 17 branch campuses that serve as feeders for the main campus and also as the delivery system for the university's continuing education programs. At the time of this research, the university was on the threshold of a strategic change effort envisioned by a new president who was faced with daunting fiscal and demographic trends. Not only were fiscal policies tightly coupled to enrollment and tuition, but the university also depended to a significant extent on state appropriations for its operating budget. Yet while these appropriations were increasing, they were doing so at a decreasing rate. Further, because of the retrenchment stance of the previous administration, he was confronted with a legacy devoid of long-range vision or plans for the institution. Although there had been earlier attempts to develop university-wide plans, these all were held to be ineffective. In the words of the new president, they were: "Bureaucratic exercises! Nothing but window dressing.

They made up these elaborate plans, bound them in blue [a school color] . . . and put them on the shelf."

The new president arrived in a university community that presented a paradox; it was steeped in tradition, yet outwardly espoused a receptivity to change. Old guard members of the institution were, however, wary of possible radical moves by a new leader. Past attempts to restructure the university had faced entrenched power and political structures that had contributed to their failure. The history of failures had made long-standing members of the university community skeptical of new efforts to implement significant change.

The avowed goal of the new President was ". . . to make this a 'Top-10' public university." Toward that end he publicly called for "strategic change": a new, ambiguous term for members of the university and one that was never specifically defined except by examples of intended action (e.g., "We cannot continue to be all things to all people. . . . We need to identify pockets of excellence and reallocate our resources towards the development of those pockets"). *Strategic planning* (another initially undefined term introduced by the president) would, in his opinion, enable the university to pursue a path of selective excellence. The President first broached the subject of strategic planning at a special retreat with key members of the university during his first months in office. He stated that the focus on strategic change and planning was a necessary first step in changing the philosophy, values, and "mindset" of the university. Within four months he formally initiated the process by announcing the appointment of a university-wide task force, known as the Strategic Planning Task Force (SPTF), which was charged with designing a strategic planning process that would make the university competitive in the future academic and economic environment. A "Special Assistant to the President" was nominated to chair this task force. This group was assigned to analyze the external environment, assess institutional strengths and weaknesses, and recommend necessary changes in the mission and goals, and structures.

The primary initial charge of the task force was to recommend mechanisms and procedures that would institutionalize strategic planning at the university. Specifically, the task force was to identify the most effective strategic planning units (SPUs) for the university (an SPU was intended to be analogous to an SBU, or strategic business unit, in the business policy field). The top management team recognized that the actions of this task force were likely to influence the existing power bases in the university, especially if they recommended reorganization into strategic units that differed appreciably from the current structure. To preclude undue influence by representatives of the existing structure, they intentionally avoided appointing members to the task force who had vested interests in the status quo (most notably the Council of Academic Deans or the Faculty Senate). SPTF's specific charge was:

> To examine the alternative levels of analysis for conducting strategic planning and to identify those units, both organizational and those not implied by existing structures, that will develop strategic plans. . . . Recommend a methodology for dealing with [the planning process] including a brief rationale for each planning unit.

The net effect of the formation of the SPTF was the creation of a group that had little precedent on which to base its deliberations and recommended actions. Few of the ten members (professors, administrators, and staff) even had knowledge of the concepts of strategic planning and strategic change. Those who did were confined to knowledge of such processes in business organizations and expressed little confidence that they could be translated directly into the academic domain. Thus, the task force was in the position of constructing the reality with which it would try to deal (cf. Weick 1977). In this sense, we viewed SPTF's situation as a close-to-ideal setting for studying the evolution of processes involved in launching a strategic change effort in a previously unstudied context. We were able to study the work of this key task force from its inception to its disbanding.

METHOD

An Interpretive Approach to Understanding Strategic Change

We approached this study with two basic assumptions: first, that organizational reality is essentially socially constructed (Berger and Luckmann 1967), and second, that attempts to change that reality should be studied in a way that taps into processes used to fashion understanding by the participants themselves, to avoid the imposition of alien meanings upon their actions and understandings (Vidich 1970). Therefore, we deemed an interpretive approach to research (Rabinow and Sullivan 1979) to be most appropriate, i.e., an approach that attempted to represent the experience and interpretations of informants, without giving precedence to prior theoretical views that might not be appropriate for their context. This research approach was driven, in part, because "strategic change" in the context of the university studied was an unfamiliar concept requiring grounded exploration.

In this work we have adopted a purist stance toward interpretive research. To be interpretive in this sense does *not* mean that we as researchers have engaged in deeper and deeper levels of subjective interpretation. Rather, we have tried to represent the informants' experiential structure and subjective understanding in terms that are adequate at their level of meaning (Rabinow and Sullivan 1979, Weber 1947). Our research reporting tries to maintain the interpretations and experiences of the informants in the foreground. This is not a matter of granting precedence to the sensemaking experience of the actors, but rather is a matter of resisting the temptation to downplay it. Too often we organizational researchers have adopted an "arrogant" stance toward our subjects of study. Because we are usually theory-driven in our approaches, we often presume to know what is going on in a given setting, and consequently are too hasty in moving to an abstract level. Thus, we tend to discount first-hand experience and interpretation in favor of a purely theoretical view, a stance that is not only elitist, but also potentially misleading. In this study, we take seriously our responsibilities as researchers to articulate how the informants' views are informative. In that vein, we give uncommon attention to the insiders' "commonsense" representations of their experience and interpretive worldview. The voice given to the actors, however, is not some fawning attempt to take whatever the actors say at face value without looking at the deeper structure of their interpretations and actions; the presentation of their view is based on a qualitatively rigorous analysis.[3]

Clearly, however, sole dependence on either an informant or a researcher perspective presents an incomplete picture. Informant and researcher views each tend to reveal and conceal different aspects of phenomena under study. Although informant views can reveal the rich means or methods by which members construct reality (cf. Garfinkel 1967), they usually do not address the deep structure of experience. Similarly, although researcher views tend to gloss the richness of lived experience, they place in *bas-relief* the dimensions or structure of phenomena. Because the knower and known are interdependent in this process of understanding, however, the most desirable approach is to triangulate insider and outsider views. In this study, we juxtapose the first-hand account with a grounded theoretical analysis aimed at uncovering the underlying dimensions of the dynamics involved in the case. The result is a narrative account and accompanying theoretical analysis that gives balanced voice to multiple perspectives and provides the potential for insight into the dynamics of launching a strategic change effort.

The Role of the Researchers

One of the authors was nominated as a member of the Strategic Planning Task Force and was granted permission to tape all deliberations. Thus, the authors acquired a distinctive vantage for studying the processes by which strategic change was initiated in the university. Because the basic nature of the study was ethnographic, the role of the author who held membership on the task force might usually be described as a participant-observer. That is, he was an "insider" (Evered and Louis 1981) who participated in the ongoing activities of the group, used informants, kept field notes, etc. Yet, because he also was a bona fide member of the task force and engaged in the deliberations, decisions, and actions of the group, we have chosen to label his more comprehensive role as that of *"actor-observer"* to connote the more involved dual nature of his participatory and scholarly observer status. The nature of the actor-observer role gives virtually literal meaning to Morgan's (1983) argument that research should be treated as a process of engagement.

The actor-observer's role allowed him to get as close as possible to the data, so that he had direct experience with the knowledge structures of the participants; it provided information, meanings, and perspectives unattainable otherwise. His role, however, might be questioned under the traditions of classical participant-observation because he was not "naive" enough (see Spradley 1980). Therefore, the other authors adopted the role of outside researchers, treating the actor-observer as only one of several informants and data sources in the study. With this multiple researcher, insider/outsider approach, we thus attempted to achieve the desired pluralist perspectives on the study of the means used to facilitate strategic change (cf. Gioia and Pitre 1990, Jick 1979). Use of the multiple researchers also served to counter one of the main criticisms of ethnographic research in organizations: no matter how carefully and faithfully done, the study always represents the interpreting perspective of only a single observer, and is thus subject to idiosyncrasies. Using two perspectives helped to mitigate this problem.

Data

The actor-observer used five primary sources of data: (1) his field notes, in the form of a diary and meeting summaries; (2) the tapes and transcripts of the SPTF meetings; (3) tapes of interviews with SPTF members and other important players (including top management team members); (4) all documentation relating to the actions of the task force; and (5) his own "self-debriefing" tapes consisting of reflections on the proceedings of the SPTF. The outside researchers had access to virtually all the same data (with the exception of a minimal amount of documentation and tapes/transcripts that were confidential). In addition, they also had tapes and notes from debriefing the actor-observer.

The actor-observer employed conventional ethnographic analysis techniques in that he used his membership in the organization as well as his interviews, notes, and documentation to infer the subjective interpretations associated with the SPTF experience. The outside researchers relied mainly on the language used by the participants during their interactions to try to infer the meanings and experiential understandings (cf. Huff 1983). Overall, multiple interviews (one to two hours on average) were conducted with the ten members of SPTF over a six-month period. In addition, other interviews with officers familiar with the work of SPTF (e.g., the Director of Planning) were also conducted. These interviews, coupled with the tape recordings of the SPTF meetings provided a rich database with which to examine the launching of strategic change in the university. The following sections provide more detail on the specific analytic techniques used.

The Actor-Observer's Analysis

Over time, the actor-observer established close relationships with the principal participants (including the President, the Executive Vice President, and the Chair of the SPTF) and acquired a sensitivity to the context and forces that might bear on the task force's deliberations. In his analysis, the actor-observer used procedures based on the tenets of a grounded-theory approach (Glaser and Strauss 1967), which typically involves simultaneous data gathering and analysis. Initial data gathering was guided by the central research question: What processes are involved in developing and instilling new organizational realities during the initiation of strategic change? More specific questions emerged from the progression of the task force's experience.

The heart of the initial stage of the grounded approach is the method of *constant comparison* (Conrad 1982, Glaser and Strauss 1967, Strauss 1987), wherein data from the many different sources (e.g., multiple informants) or from different points in time are repeatedly compared to discern major categories, dimensions, themes, or processes. Data from the transcripts, field notes, interviews, and documents were repetitively reviewed, coded, categorized, and studied for content and meaning until patterns emerged (Agar 1986, Miles and Huberman 1984, Spradley 1980). In this study, a range of *first-order* informant codes (i.e., terms used by the actors; see Van Maanen 1979) were developed by the actor-observer. These are shown in the far left and right columns of Exhibit 7.1. The actor-observer then assimilated these codes into a set of summary analytical codes (i.e., labels induced by the researcher that were still meaningful to the informants). These are also shown in Exhibit 7.1.[4] Based on these codes the actor-observer also began the process of inducing more general themes or dimensions in the data. Two tentative dimensions, "meaning construction" and "influence and politics" emerged, which began to serve as guides for more focused data gathering and analysis (a process termed *theoretical sampling* by Glaser and Strauss 1967).

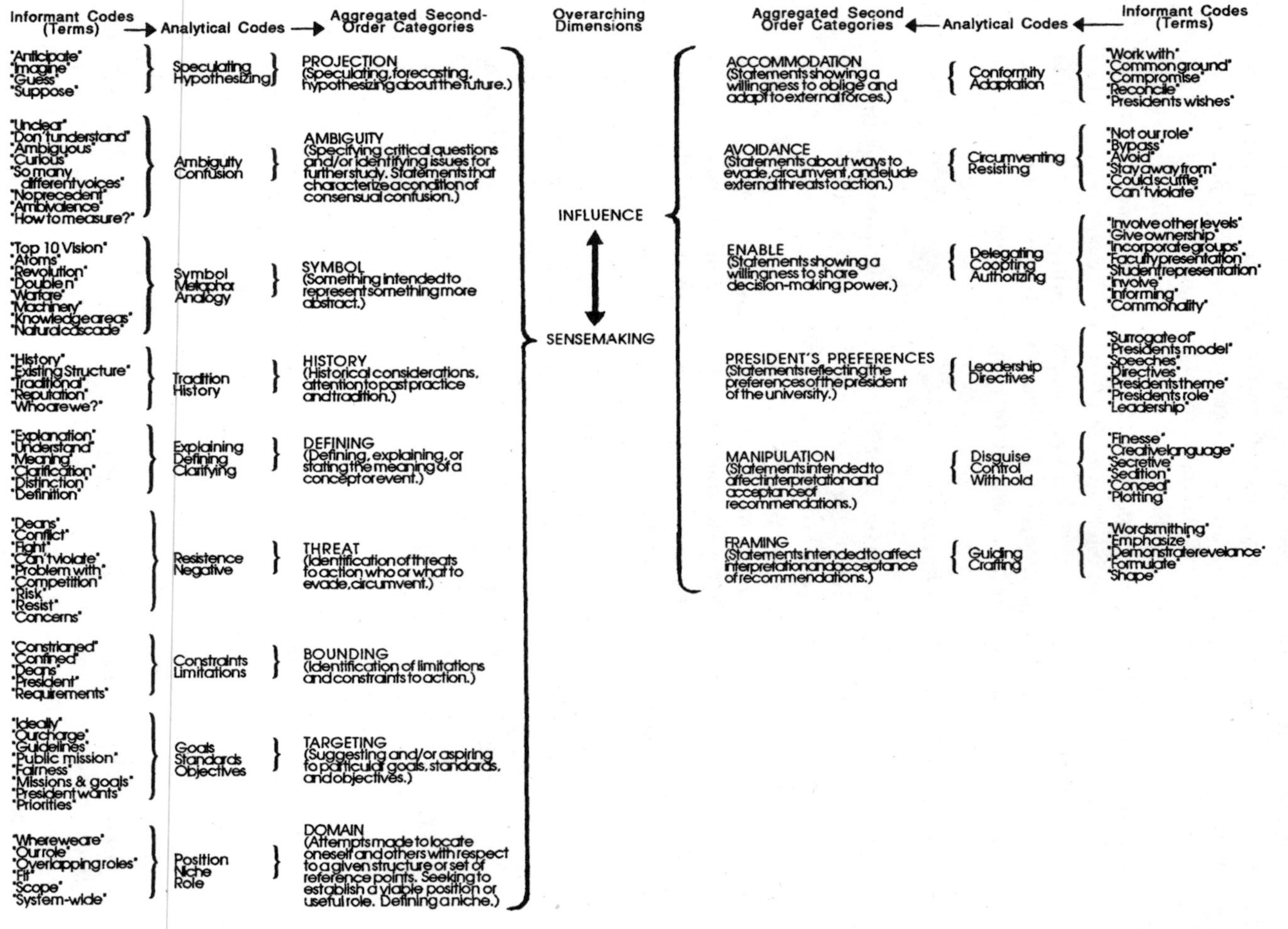

Exhibit 7.1. Emergent Analytical Codes, Categories, and Dimensions

The Outside Researchers' Analyses

The analytical task facing the outside researchers was similar to that of the actor-observer, except that they did not have the benefit of the immersion in the process enjoyed by the actor-observer. The outside researchers therefore focused on performing a more fine-grained analysis of the available data (mainly meeting transcripts, supplemented by interviews with committee members and the actor-observer, and the public documentation), which was initially independent of the insider. The two outside researchers also did their initial coding independently of each other using techniques based on Miles and Huberman (1984).

First, each researcher made repeated readings of the verbatim transcripts while listening to the tapes of the meetings to get a sense of the task force's understanding of its charge and its sequence of activities. During these readings, the tapes and transcripts were "location coded" (i.e., emerging codes were cross-referenced according to tape footage and transcript pages). Using techniques of constant comparison they identified a range of independent first-order codes in the data. Next, the outside researchers met to compare and contrast coding systems. After a series of consultations, they generated a consensual, "outsider" coding system that allowed them to assign descriptive summary labels for related groups of first-order terms (not shown).

Insider-Outsider Integration and Analysis

The insider and outsiders then met to compare coding systems. There was a high degree of convergence in coding content (86% agreement between the insider and outsider analyses); differences occurred mainly in the choices of summary labels for the code groupings. Negotiation led to agreements on representative labels and the elimination of categories that did not emerge from both analyses. Precedence was given primarily to the actor-observer's labels at this stage because he was more closely grounded in the context and experience of the informants. The outcome of this negotiation process was a set of summary "analytical codes" shown in Exhibit 7.1 (columns 2 and 6).

After this stage of the analysis was complete, the insider and outsiders again met to examine the coded data for possible further aggregation into second-order categories and dimensions (Spradley 1980). This process led to the assimilation and labeling of the code groupings at a more theoretical level as a means of discerning general patterns in the data (also shown in Exhibit 7.1, along with a succinct description). The main outcome of this stage was the emergence and formal labeling of two overarching dimensions of analysis: "sensemaking" and "influence" (which converged with those tentatively induced by the actor-observer, differing only by chosen labels, i.e., "sensemaking" vs. "meaning construction" and "influence" vs. "power and politics"). All relevant quotes, exchanges, decisions, and actions were noted in the data by coding passages using both the aggregated second-order categories and these two overarching dimensions. These codings were then used to guide further analysis in another iteration of theoretical sampling (Conrad 1982, Glaser and Strauss 1967, Strauss 1987) until categories were saturated. For instance, a focus at this point was on further data that had bearing on either sensemaking or influence. Guiding questions included: What means are used by the members for engaging in and communicating about attempts to make sense of their experience? How is influence accomplished? Does the nature of sensemaking or influence processes change over time? Theoretically sampled data were examined for commonality across members, time, and events. Finally, these higher-order codes were used as inputs for a computer-assisted analysis of the data.

The "Ethnograph" Analysis

The "Ethnograph" (Seidel and Clark 1984) is a set of interactive, menu-driven programs designed to assist in the categorization and analysis of qualitative data. The "Ethnograph" allowed not only complex coding of the data, but also facilitated the manipulation and management of coded statements for further analysis. Transcripts were first entered into a word processor and converted into data files; these text files were then printed and used for "code mapping" (Seidel and Clark 1984). The aggregated second-order labels were used as code words for identifying and tagging segments of text. The code map of the printed document was then entered back into the data files for analysis. The program's search procedure allowed us to locate all of the occurrences of a particular code or set of codes and retrieve them with original text segments. Using multiple code searches, it was possible to analyze and confirm previously discovered patterns, which served as a form of reliability assessment on the foregoing analyses. It also was possible to investigate category nestings and overlaps, thus enabling us to discern whether and when the main sensemaking and influence dimensions might subsume each other or co-occur. In particular, the "Ethnograph" analysis allowed a detailed look at the nature of interactions occurring between sensemaking and influence as they related to strategic change.

This multistage process of independent, comparative, and collaborative analysis ultimately generated a narrative of the SPTF's experience of the strategic change initiation process that was credible at the level of meaning of the participants (Weber 1947). These findings in narrative form were submitted to several of the informants for review and comment (a process of "member checking," Spradley 1980). A number of presentational changes were made to the narrative, but the essence of the findings was affirmed. Disputed findings (i.e., those reported by one perspective, but not corroborated independently by the other) are not included in the Findings section.[5] Finally, the existing data and narrative were used to construct a conceptual model of the strategic change process, using the second-order constructs and dimensions that emerged from the study.

FINDINGS

An Overview of the SPTF Deliberations

The SPTF met for several months to develop their recommendations. One of the SPTF members provided a retrospective synopsis of the task force's life cycle that serves as a foreshadowing overview of the narrative that follows:

> The initial meeting indicated no agreement as to purpose, required action, or vocabulary, leading to the development of a modest sense of desperation over the next several meetings. Soon, however, the committee leadership provided a way out of the quandary by invoking the ostensive preferences of a higher authority figure (the President), who suggested a symbolic framework for initiating strategic change. This symbol became the construct for rallying around a unified direction that eventually led to substantive action.

Because the findings are woven into the rather complex narrative that follows, it is helpful to preview not only the events that transpired, but also the main theoretical concepts that subsequently were generated from the study. As noted earlier, two primary dimensions emerged: *sensemaking* and *influence*. Both dimensions were symbolically based and served as running themes over the life of the SPTF. The task force progressed through four phases from its formation to its dissolution. During these phases the nature of the sensemaking and influence attempts underwent transitions, both in terms of the symbols and metaphors used to communicate understanding and action, and in terms of the "directionality" of the processes (i.e. whether they were directed inward toward the task force, or directed outward by the task force toward others). Exhibit 7.2 presents a descriptive summary of these phases, including representative quotes.

	Interpretation →	Definition →	Legitimation →	Institutionalization
Description	"Who are we?" and "What is our charge?" are key questions posed during this stage. Attempts are made to interpret experience using outside models and historical referents. The task force becomes increasingly aware of external influences that have the potential to constrain thought and action.	Top management attempts to define strategic change issues for key stakeholders by using the task force as a conduit. The task force becomes aware that they are being used by top management as a symbol for change. In response, the task force begins to define its role as facilitator of top manangement's plans for change. The task force tries to avoid provoking resistance from influential stakeholders.	Top management preferences continue to influence the task force. To legitimize itself, the task force begins to align with top management. The task force also develops its own concepts and terms for "giving" sense to top management and stakeholders and considers ways to exert influence on stakeholders using tactics of inclusion and cooptation.	Both the task force and top management attempt to institutionalize change and planning processes. The task force crafts a formal statement to influence and create the desired meaning for stakeholders. The task force and top management concurrently signify the content and direction of strategic change.
Quotes	-"We have a charge from the President which I didn't understand then and I still don't now." -"What are 'planning units'? I don't understand 'strategic' either." -"It's not clear who is going to make the real decisions or even make recommendations on the planning units." -"I hope they give us some guidelines for this process." -"Let's look at the planning process of this university over the last five years." -"We have to account for the dean's preferences."	-"He (the President) just won't take the deans on face-to-face." -"This is the President's model we're peddling." -"If being top-10 is the President's goal, then it should be ours." -"He is going to deny leadership and make us assume ownership of this plan." -"The deans are trying to set premises and usurp our prerogatives. We have to deal with that." -"We must be careful not to suggest that we have a final formulation of the planning organization - which people will immediately start shooting down."	-"We are creating terms that are relatively value-free, then we give them meaning for others to use." -"Hopefully we can convince the President that this is a fairly interesting idea...If he's not taking our advice, he's just fooling around." -"He's trying to influence us with that plan again." -"We need to include 'public service' in the mission statement. The word 'service' is what people like." -"We have to make them comfortable with this or we are in a political war."	-"We are going to institutionalize the strategic mission and goals in this process." -"This is the general statement of the strategic planning machinery." -"This is basically a radical solution but we can sell it by calling it 'creative.'" -"We have got to have a statement right at the beginning that clearly divorces this apparatus from the universities planning guide." -"What we are doing is clearly and rationally articulating the function of UPACT so we're in with the president."

Exhibit 7.2. Emergent Stages of Strategic Change: Description and Representative Quotes

The Interpretation Phase of the Task Force

The early meetings of the Strategic Planning Task Force (SPTF) were distinguished by the attempts of the members to construct some identity for themselves and some interpretation of their charge. These attempts were floundering, trial-and-error efforts to answer the fundamental questions: Who or what are we? What are we supposed to do? Given the lack of historical analogues, such apparently simple questions turned out to be very difficult indeed. Members described their situation as "having no precedents," "being at ground zero," and saw the first meetings as ones fraught with "mayhem" and "confusion." The following exchange captures their nascent state and the effort to arrive at some interpretation of their task:

> Chair: Our charge is to examine the alternative levels of analysis. We are conducting strategic planning. (pause) I don't understand what that means. (pause) I don't understand "alternative levels" either.
>
> Second Member: We were hoping you would explain!
>
> Third Member: I just don't understand. What are we supposed to do?

Clearly "strategic planning" was intended to be a meaningful, action-oriented metaphor in this scenario, but the members did not have a workable definition of it. Even after lengthy discussions, the issue repeatedly surfaced:

> Chair: Again I think the main thing we need to do is identify the meaning of "strategic planning."
>
> Member: You know I didn't understand this term before and I still don't.

Primarily, the early meetings consisted of repeated attempts at figuring out their purpose and role, as well as efforts devoted to negotiating the meaning of key terms (which occurred on at least eleven separate occasions during the first meeting alone). The multiple discussions surrounding the central notion of strategic planning were based on such metaphorical representations as: strategic planning units as "constituent parts or atoms," "planning machinery," "centers of excellence"; all of which were proposed and discussed, but were never established as defining metaphors.

At these early meetings, the Chair alluded to the President's suggestion that emulating another university's planning model might be a possible way to help define their own situation. ("He wants us to have a look at the Texas model; thinks it might give us some ideas.") Although that model was dismissed at this point (but revisited later), the influence of top management and other stakeholders on the task force's efforts now was evident. As this initial phase of SPTF's development progressed, members became aware of the effect of the actions and desires of others on their own thinking and possible action, which engendered considerable indignation and affective reaction by other members who argued for autonomy in deciding how they might frame the change problem and what they could and should do to address it. Nonetheless, there were several attempts to infer "what the President wants," a reference to his implied power to define the situation in terms of his stated "Top 10 university" vision ("It's his theme to be Top 10. Let's go back to him on this and see what that means to him").

The Definition Phase of the Task Force

As the task force continued to flounder, a sense of powerlessness and resignation settled in. ("It seems to me that you're either a surrogate of the President or you're nowhere.") In addition, the SPTF members began to suspect that they were being used as a symbolic device in top management's attempts to sway other stakeholders, especially faculty members, to "buy into" the strategic change notion. For one thing, the mere existence of the prominent task force signified a serious (albeit nebulous) intent to change. The SPTF members also began to see that the President's public statements limited their range of possible thinking and acting and made them pawns in some larger game:

> He's done it again. . . . He's made an end run on us. . . .
>
> You know, if I work backwards from the real politik, it is still not clear to me who is going to make the real decisions in this process. I don't think it's who we think it is. Who makes the hard decisions? Not us. We're a smokescreen.
>
> Part of what the President is going to have to do when he delivers his plan is deny leadership of it and make us have the ownership. I think he's already doing that, in fact.
>
> Did you see the CDT [the local paper] yesterday? He said we are the ones deciding how to make us top 10. Now if I were a dean I would be paying attention to that.

During this phase of the task force's evolution there were several pronounced allusions to the strong symbolic implications of *not* taking certain actions, e.g., of not defining a strategic planning unit to include some specific constituent groups, especially those coveted by multiple factions. ("If we recommend that alignment, what would that say? That would lead to warfare.") This tactic prefigured a running theme in the deliberations: overt attempts to anticipate the meaning of decisions and actions (to themselves and others) as a way of avoiding trouble. Avoidance, in the form of considered nonaction, was a proactive tactic. Of particular importance, the members were very sensitive about signaling any impending drastic actions:

> I think it would be unwise to stray too far from the existing organization structure. . . .

> Let's keep a traditional structure and use proper consultation. That way we avoid any scare stuff in proposing strategic planning units.

Most notably, there were multiple attempts to avoid provoking the deans, who were seen as potentially crippling adversaries in launching any changes:

> I am extremely nervous about bypassing the classic dean structure. . . . On this point maybe the best action is no action.

> I don't see how to reconfigure this place in any way that ignores them, because they are essentially all-powerful.

> Actually, I think the deans have taken the lead already. That's where all this stuff is coming from in my judgment. They see what this committee can do and they are already trying to usurp us. We have to deal with that.

Eventually the SPTF members defined a role for themselves as facilitators in helping to launch the change effort. Still, they failed to develop a framework for envisioning specific processes to be used, and their lack of consensus and inaction invited external intervention.

A crystallizing event then occurred that reframed the approach to thinking about change initiation and allowed the SPTF members to envision the nature of the strategic planning process and to design a way to facilitate it. It also revealed the power structure and political dynamics in the process for them. The Chair introduced "the President's 'Double W' Model," a diagrammatic depiction of the way the strategic planning process might work. We have replicated that model in Figure 7.1. The introduction of this symbolic framework removed ambiguity from the committee's understanding of the process whereby strategic planning could be accomplished, and allowed the deliberations to enter a qualitatively different phase.

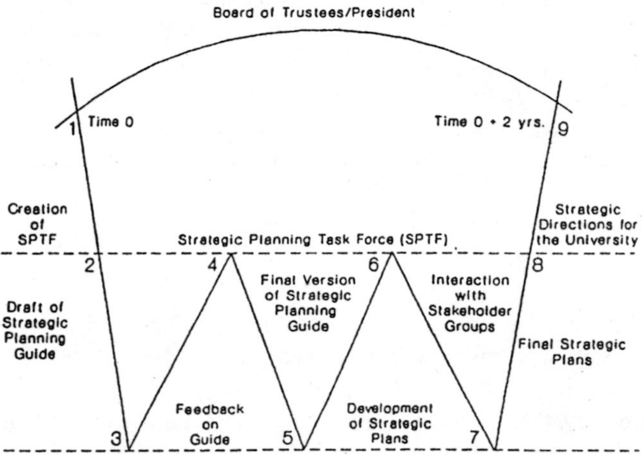

Figure 7.1. The Double "W" Strategic Planning Process Model

The Legitimation Phase of SPTF

If the earlier SPTF deliberations were aimed at answering the questions "Who are we?" and "What should we do?" subsequent events were focused on a related but different series of questions: "How can we be perceived as legitimate agents of strategic change?" "How can we exert influence (without bringing on conflict and countervailing influence)?" "How can we accommodate the President in disseminating the Top 10 vision?" By far the greatest direct influence on the SPTF was the President himself who supplied the specific charge for the committee, shaped their framework for strategic planning, and (either intentionally or unintentionally) affected SPTF's actions via his public declarations. Although the members recognized his influence tactics ("He's snookered us again!") and chafed about them ("I think politically we're driven to do what he wants"), they ultimately accepted them as legitimate. ("He is, after all, the President.") Consequently, SPTF aligned themselves with the President as a way of obtaining surrogate legitimization for themselves.

> Ultimately this is the President's strategic plan. We need to present ourselves as implementors of the President's wishes.

In addition to the President, other individuals and groups held considerable sway, including other top managers (e.g., the head of the planning office), other university committees which attempted to claim jurisdiction over their work, and other stakeholders (e.g., the Faculty Senate, who argued that their "traditional role" was being ignored). Concern over the reactions of these groups, in particular the Council of Academic Deans, continued to receive attention. The members continued to be wary of this presumed nemesis whom they assumed would try to sabotage the change process. Therefore, they kept working to avoid a confrontation:

> [We need to] recognize that these people will feel they're being undermined or excluded and will try to do something about it.
>
> You can pick your sides, marshal your troops and hope you win. But I don't see the sense in making a war out of it.

The symbolic importance of allowing potentially recalcitrant factions to play a role became a key issue affecting not only the credibility of the task force, but its viability as a change agent as well. The tactic adopted was one of inclusion and co-optation:

> There have to be deans, department heads, other administrative mid-level people, and faculty that have to feel a sense of ownership of the plan all up and down the line.
>
> We should also give appropriate representation to students, minorities, and even people outside the university who have a strong stake in this.

In the latter part of this phase, however, SPTF began to move toward an influencing stance of its own. Although members couched their attempts at influence in terms of trying to communicate "what the President wants," they also tried to develop themselves into a force to be reckoned with. ("Let's not ask for advice; if we ask for advice, we'll get it.") Attention again focused on the "Double W" model and the requirements for operationalizing it. Following its implied (although never fully articulated) acceptance, the task force devoted more effort to identifying or creating the strategic planning units (SPUs) of the university. Three major planning concepts evolved, and although they had somewhat mundane names they nonetheless became descriptive symbols used to envision and communicate proposed actions:

Aggregate Strategic Planning Units (ASPUs): the major campuses or components of the total university system;

Individual Strategic Planning Units (ISPUs): specific colleges or programs that were to be subsumed under the ASPUs; and

Study Groups: task forces designed to evaluate the plans of the ASPUs and render opinions on possible reorganizational configurations.

In particular, the ASPU/ISPU distinction was seen as significant because it formed a "natural cascade" (a consensual metaphor) whereby the central administration could set missions and goals for the main strategic planning units. Those units could then identify their own individual constituents with self-set missions and goals, thus rendering a reasonable degree of autonomy to the lower levels. More importantly perhaps, the ASPU/ISPU "centerpiece" conveyed an affirmation of respect for the traditional structures of the university, which represented an anchor of normalcy in the face of espoused radical change. ASPUs and ISPUs amounted to little more than a new nomenclature that paralleled the existing university structure, an outcome with important symbolic overtones because it conveyed to currently powerful factions that "radical sedition was not forthcoming from this task force" as a way of accomplishing strategic change. Indeed, one of the main reasons for support of the "Double W" model of the strategic change process among SPTF's members was because it implied change ". . . without rending apart the institution and redirecting it": a feature judged to be necessary to allay fears and disarm resistance or even attempted sabotage of the process. [The members recognized the paradox that in order to create the context for strategic change, which implies radical redirection, they had to avoid the appearance of proposing radical change]. In actuality, they viewed the ASPU/ISPU design as a smokescreen that concealed the real change vehicle from those that might undermine the process. It was instead the innocuous "Study Groups" that contained the potential for triggering substantive change.

> This is just a way to finesse the real teeth in the new mission and goals thing [Top 10 status] without suggesting that we have a final planning formulation. This way, there won't be any consternation with this stuff that will cause people to want to shoot you down.

The role of the study groups was described with the rich metaphor, "prisms transmitting a spectrum of inputs." Taken collectively, the study groups were variously, but convergently, described as "beads on a necklace" and "pearls on a chain" to connote their role as components of the strategic change effort and associated planning "system" that would generate strategic change.

The Institutionalization Phase of the Task Force

In the final work of SPTF, attention turned toward the construction of an influential statement that would explain and give rationales for their recommendations to outside constituencies. There was a keen awareness on the part of the members that the language of this report was very important to convey the desired meaning to outsiders as well as to top management. ("They [SPTF's recommendations] have meaning in this context; they do not yet have meaning beyond it.") In the attempt to create the desired meaning, multiple instances of "wordsmithing" were noted by writers, i.e., labels and language intentionally selected to convey the "right message." The final report itself was an overtly symbolic document cast in metaphorical and rhetorical terms. (e.g., "We are trying to identify a dominant chord from amid the cacophony of individual planning documents.") It attempted to describe not only the need for strategic planning, but the approach to be taken by the university. It defined ASPUs, ISPUs, and study groups, and described the "Double W" model. Furthermore, it provided rationales for adopting the proposed strategic planning process and became the primary statement of the direction of the strategic change effort.

In this final phase of the task force's life their attempts to exert their own influence increased as did their attempts to lend permanency to their vision and proposed actions; these were mainly efforts by the task force to influence their constituencies to accept their way of thinking while avoiding conflicts that might undermine the delicate process. These discussions were rife with metaphorical description, with a marked preference for war metaphors (e.g., "I know we have to bite the bullet, but I don't want to immerse this thing in a huge struggle"). Once again, the idea of vesting power in the ASPUs to decide their own ISPUs (anticipated to be defined as the existing colleges) was affirmed, thus averting a likely rebellion by the Council of Academic Deans. ("This should get it past the deans, who could scuttle this whole thing completely. . . .") As a result, SPTF began a series of attempts to "co-opt" or "draft" stakeholders. These attempts ranged from stressing how the "public-service mission" of the university would be enhanced if the SPTF recommendations were adopted, to the adoption of a political strategy that focused on aligning the SPTF with the President as a means of garnering support. They also attempted to engineer the appointment of the executive vice president of the university as head of the planning effort for the main campus because he had "sufficient clout to make sure the thing will work out."

As a more overt form of influence, the committee culminated their efforts by attempting to forge the final document into an instrument of lasting impact. Of critical importance to the task force was the goal of "internalizing" the change effort through SPTF's recommendations:

> What we are trying to institutionalize here is that both missions and goals are locked in right at the top: in the Office of the President and in our recommendations.
>
> What we're suggesting to be implemented becomes part of the general strategic planning process. We'll put it in a planning guide that the President can push.
>
> We want to enculturate the university community toward the concept and associated structures of strategic planning.

These efforts were deemed to be a necessary step toward a major strategic change. Indeed, the president declared that strategic planning and change would be the lasting legacy of his administration.

Second-Order Findings

Contained within the first-order narrative are a number of substantive findings about the nature and uses of symbolism, sensemaking, and influence processes. But, to tease out their deeper structure requires not only reference to the "story," but also analysis from a second-order level. Such an analysis does not discount the first-order findings (which are adequate at the level of meaning of the informants; cf. Weber 1947), but employs an alternative view to gain insights using a more "theoretical" perspective. At this level of analysis, we began by treating the first-order findings as data. We first attended to the insights generated from the case itself, as well as the ethnographer's interpretation of it, focusing in particular on key terms and events (Isabella 1990). We then employed the procedures described in the Method section to aggregate the first-order codes and categories, assign them second-order thematic labels, and then induce the overarching dimensions of *sensemaking* and *influence* (see Exhibit 7.1). We begin by summarizing the significant events in the narrative.

First, an examination of the narrative progression, as well as the codes and categories, reveals a pervasive use of symbols and metaphors in SPTFs attempts to make sense of their experience. "Top 10" quickly became the overarching visionary symbol and the "Double W model" soon became the dominant operational symbol. "Strategic planning" emerged as an ambiguous, ill-defined, but nonetheless guiding metaphor in this context (i.e., in an institution that, unlike most businesses, had not previously employed this specific concept). An array of supporting metaphors and other rich language infused every phase and aspect of the task force's attempts at framing, defining, interpreting, and acting upon issues (see Exhibit 7.2 for a representative summary). In addition to the many considerations of symbolic actions involving the task force, the symbolic implications of *not* taking some apparently logical actions played a significant role, mainly as a way of avoiding countervailing influence.

Secondly, an examination of the first-order narrative and the attendant analytical codes also showed that various forms of influence permeated the experience of SPTF. Indeed, it became evident from these analyses that both the understanding of influence and consideration of its use were rooted mainly in symbolic expression (as made most evident by the overlaps between symbolism and influence codes in the Ethnograph program categorizations). For example the influence of the President was manifested in an explicit fashion via his metaphorical framing of the task force's charge and his interjection of the basic Double W process model; it was manifested implicitly in his preemptive public statements that short-circuited SPTF's possible actions and co-opted them as an influential symbol of change. Other important forms of influence emerged in the task force's awareness of and careful attendance to the existing power structure, expressed in terms of a range of evocative conflict metaphors and symbols. SPTF's own attempts to act as influencing agents were accomplished in several ways: by adopting a surrogate role aligning them with the powers-that-be; by disguising the genuine power of the "study group" notion to allay the fears of wary powerholders; and by using potent rhetorical devices as their primary means for influencing stakeholders to accept their recommendations and to institutionalize an orientation toward strategic change.

Taken together, the many symbols and metaphors played a central role not only in the task force's attempt to make sense of their experience by socially constructing their identity and purpose while dealing with external influence attempts (which characterized the early phases), but also in their attempts to construct ways to avoid resistance, legitimize themselves, and exert lasting influence on the thinking of other stakeholders (which characterized the later phases). These observations suggest another dimension to the analysis that becomes evident from the second-order level: There were subtle, but important, transitions in the directionality of the sensemaking and influence attempts over the interpretation, definition, legitimation, and institutionalization phases of the task force's life cycle. In the early, developmental stages, attention was focused on what might be called internal sensemaking; in the latter stages attention was focused on what could be called external sensemaking in that they were trying to affect the understanding and actions of crucial external actors (a process termed *sensegiving* by Gioia and Chittipeddi 1991).

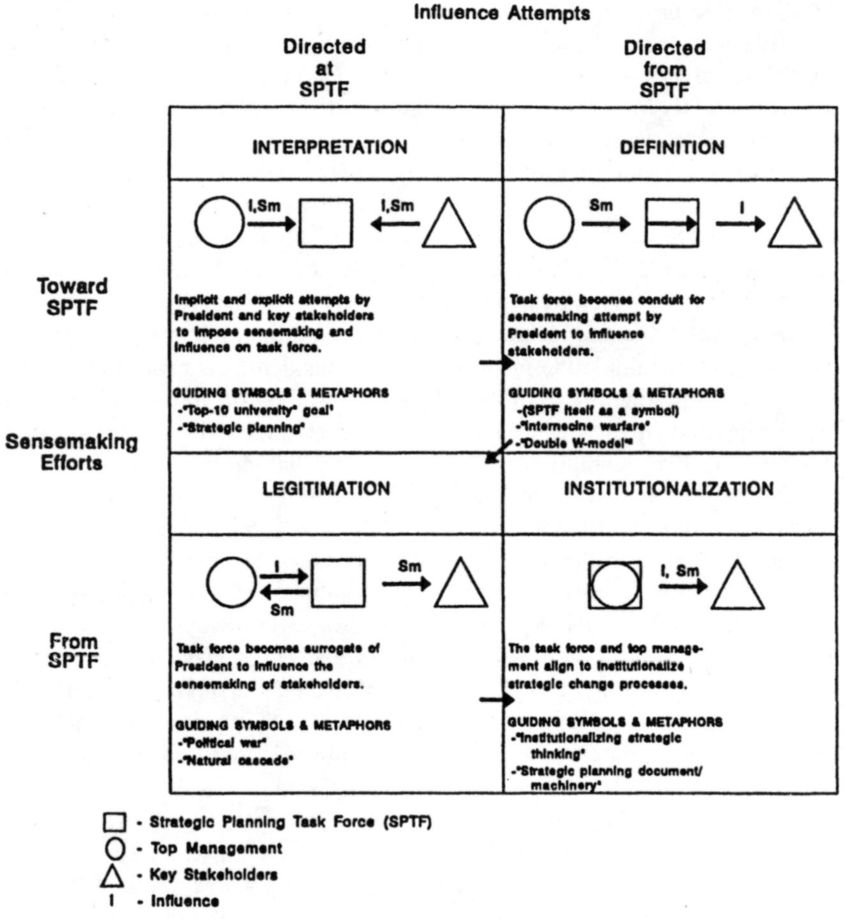

Exhibit 7.3. Sensemaking, Influence, and Guiding Symbols/Metaphors Across Stages of Strategic Change

[1] This was the overarching voluntary symbol that was also used in subsequent stages.

[2] This was the overarching operational symbol that was also used in subsequent stages.

The major findings of the second-order analysis are shown in Exhibit 7.3, which includes the main dimensions of sensemaking and influence in terms of the guiding symbols and metaphors used, as well as the directionality of these dominant processes. This depiction is grounded in the data in that it represents an integration of the major findings presented in the preceding narrative, but takes a more theoretical perspective on events. It portrays not only the major players in the strategic change initiation process (top management, the SPTF, and key stakeholders), but also the manner in which sensemaking and influence evolved and were directed over the task force's existence. To this point we have treated the sensemaking and influence findings as distinct, although it is evident from both the first-order narrative findings and the second-order analysis that they indeed converge across all stages of SPTF's life cycle. Therefore, the exhibit is presented in matrix form to emphasize the interplay between sensemaking and influence.

As a postscript to the case, the change effort subsequently has resulted in the addition of a new college and the restructuring of two others, as well as a reorientation toward market competitiveness in the academic arena. It also has led the administration to develop some new profit-seeking ventures of a type that had not previously been identified with the university. As of this writing, acceptance of the strategic change effort in terms of the Top 10 notion has met some resistance, particularly from faculty members. Although academic pursuits seem to have changed only moderately, the level of "encouragement" to seek external funding has gone up dramatically. Also, there are some signs of serious intent to "enforce Top-10 standards" at the individual-faculty level. Most notably, academic records that previously would have received tenure and promotion are now being denied. Such actions have carried strong symbolic overtones that have instilled anxiety in the faculty ranks and led to substantial faculty turnover. As further evidence, recruiting committees now routinely invoke a "Top 10" standard in deciding upon interview candidates ("Is this a Top-10 profile?"). The final outcome of the strategic change effort, however, will require more time to assess.

DISCUSSION

Studies concerning deliberate strategic change typically have investigated the impact of various demographic and economic factors on different aspects of change. Although these studies have established statistically significant relationships among key change-related variables (e.g., senior management, structure, and effectiveness), they have not provided fundamental descriptions or explanations about *how* such dramatic changes are accomplished (Greiner and Bhambri 1989). The dynamics of the strategic change process, perhaps especially concerning the precarious period when strategic change is just being instigated, have not been well studied. Understanding this initial period is particularly relevant for organizations where *strategic* change is a relatively new and problematic concept. In this light, the overarching contribution of this research is the insight provided into processes involved in launching strategic change, and especially in managing its acceptance and institutionalization (cf. DiMaggio and Powell 1991).

The focus on these aspects of strategic change suggests a notably different view of the process itself: Strategic change can be understood not only as a change in the position and fit of an organization in its environment, but perhaps more fundamentally as a change in the *cognitive perspective* represented by a new strategy. Strategy as cognitive perspective (cf. Ginsberg 1988, Mintzberg 1987) emphasizes the set of assumptions through which the problems and issues of the organization are identified and interpreted by top managers and key stakeholders (Hedberg and Jonsson 1978). The alteration of this "conceptual lens" represents a fundamental shift in the organization's belief structure, value system, and identity (Bartunek 1984, Dutton and Dukerich 1991, Gioia and Chittipeddi 1991, Walsh 1988). Indeed, reorienting strategic systems, structures, and commitments requires efforts to legitimize not only the new social order represented by the change (Zucker 1987), but also how the legitimization process itself will occur (Scott 1991).

Efforts to stabilize a social system in flux from the systemic upheaval represented by strategic change can be understood as the symbolic interplay of sensemaking and influence. These processes emerged in the attempt to develop a consensual *redefinition* of social reality in the face of an induced discontinuity in the existing perspective of the institution and its stakeholders. In the process of trying to develop a strategy for instigating strategic change (a "meta-strategy") (Allaire and Firsirotu 1984), the task force members had to make sense of their situation for themselves and others, while simultaneously acting as both influenced and influencing actors. In the midst of the uncertainty, ambiguity, and political tension that marked these attempts, key metaphors and symbols emerged that simultaneously heralded, represented, and facilitated the change. Indeed, symbols and metaphors dominated the experience of the task force as it progressed through the interpretation, definition, legitimation, and institutionalization phases of its life cycle.

Symbols

Key symbols and metaphors were central to the construction of meaning and the communication of understanding, and also acted as an impetus for influence and action. Symbols became the primary means by which participants grounded their perceptions and articulated their preferences concerning many of the aspects of strategic change. Specifically, symbolism became the language for understanding change, while the interplay of sensemaking and influence captured the specific actions associated with attempts to redefine and legitimize the new social reality. For example, SPTF remained stalled *until* a symbolic operational framework (the Double W model) was suggested. This model was based on another university's process and served as a mimetic symbol that helped define and legitimize the change process itself (cf. Scott 1987). It was the primary means by which the task force itself arrived at a consensual validation of what was plausible and legitimate. Furthermore, the model's external origination and alleged success in a related environment seemed to have the effect of elevating SPTF, and the goals espoused in its final report, to a "rulelike status in [the university's] social thought and actions" (Meyer and Rowan 1977, p. 341). In this sense, the model was the means for executing what might more accurately be termed a *reinstitutionalization* process surrounding the strategic change effort. Reinstitutionalization implies an accepted reorientation in the dominant belief structure of the organization.

In broader view, this process of attempted reinstitutionalization involved both substantive action and expressive representation for its accomplishment. Yet, it is clear from the findings that both action and expression took symbolic forms at various times. Pfeffer (1981a), Edelman (1964) and others have implied that the role of management can be divided into more-or-less separate "substantive" and "expressive" functions. Symbolism is usually cast only as a medium of expression, thus suggesting that the symbolic aspects of management have little to do with instrumental action. This study has revealed not only the pervasiveness of symbolism in the initiation and acceptance of strategic change, but also that symbols are one of the main means by which management accomplishes substantive action. Thus, the two functions appear more closely related than previous portrayals would cast them. The instrumental aspects of management are often symbolically communicated, and the symbolic aspects are often instrumental to action.

Symbols central to the case took several forms in addition to those already noted. In particular two manifest forms, *symbolic action* and *symbolic nonaction,* played major roles. Actions, such as the specification of ASPUs, ISPUs, and study groups, carried significant symbolism, both within the committee and to external targets of intended influence. Less obvious, but also of importance, was the symbolically significant avoidance of certain actions, often to circumvent probable countervailing influence by others (Dutton and Dukerich 1991). This concern with studied nonaction by the committee members revealed a phenomenon that had an anticipatory character about it: the conscious and intentional consideration of the probable future impact of certain actions, and especially nonactions, on the meaning construction processes of themselves and others. We eventually came to label this process as "prospective sensemaking," mainly in recognition of its future-oriented focus. Prospective sensemaking was a frequent influence on the consensual understandings reached and decisions made by the task force.[6] Their repeated attempts to infer the future consequences of proposed actions as a way of understanding their present situation showed the committee members to be both proactive and prospective information seekers (Louis 1980, Donnellon et al. 1986).

Symbols were also influential in suggesting changes in structural arrangements without implying loss of image or status for those affected by the change, a point noted by Trice and Beyer (1984). The effective use of symbols is essential for organizations that are susceptible to environmental changes (a category that now prominently includes universities). In the case of the SPTF, its recommendation to designate "strategic study groups" was based mainly on the need to insure organizational flexibility for change without provoking the deans by signaling that their traditional power was being diluted. This finding affirms Pondy's observation that, "In organizing, the use of metaphor simultaneously facilitates change and reinforces traditional values" (1983, p. 164). In our terms, symbols facilitate change because they simultaneously *reveal* and *conceal* important features of change.

Sensemaking and Influence

The often blurred distinction between sensemaking and influence processes found in this study suggests that they were interdependent and reciprocal processes during the launching of strategic change. (Indeed, 41% of the passages in the transcripts that were coded as sensemaking coincided with those coded as influence). Thus, the usual conceptualization of sensemaking and influence as separate processes disguises their interrelationship.

Sensemaking and influence, however, varied in terms of their source and directionality over the life cycle of the task force. For example, as the SPTF evolved from the early to mature phases, it moved from being the *conduit* (Axley 1984) for sensemaking and influencing efforts by others to being a *source* of sensemaking and influence for key stakeholders. Overall, sensemaking and influence efforts were directed primarily inward toward the task force during the interpretation and definition stages and mainly outward from the task force during the legitimation and institutionalization stages. That is, in the early stages the critical issue for the SPTF members was how to interpret the alternative change processes and concepts they confronted. Their sensemaking efforts were susceptible to the influence of external actors (especially the President and other top managers who were perceived by SPTF members to be engaged in "political" behavior). Over time, they shifted to identifying or constructing means to influence the sensemaking processes of others (cf. Gioia and Chittipeddi 1991, Whetten 1984).

These findings suggest that strategic change efforts instigated by new leadership (in this case, a new president) might effectively begin with attempts to legitimize a structural component of the organization (e.g., SPTF) to convey to stakeholders that the message and process of change is being institutionalized. Indeed, the SPTF became a key symbol of the change process. The existence, size, composition, and charge of the SPTF were symbolic indicators to the university community of the commitment to strategic change (cf. Feldman and March 1981).

In the case of this university, symbolic actions were taken to disguise an intended second-order change and make it appear as a less threatening first-order change (Bartunek 1984). The affirmation of existing structures in the form of ASPUs and ISPUs, while simultaneously embodying the potential for radical change in the "study groups," was an instantiation of the power of symbolic action both to emphasize the comforting features of a change while de-emphasizing the threatening features. This influencing feature of symbols converges with Lukes' (1974) view of influence as the ability to prevent conflict by affecting perceptions, cognition, and preferences of recalcitrant parties. It also constitutes a manifestation of Pfeffer's (1981b) argument that influence is concealed in the ability to affect decision premises.

Future Research

These findings raise a number of interesting research questions. For example: Is the degree to which stakeholders accept the discontinuity associated with strategic change related to the source and type of symbolism used to introduce the change? What characteristics of the top management team or new ad hoc organizational structures facilitate the acceptance of symbols of change? How is the use of symbolism tied to the performance effectiveness of strategic change efforts? What are the cross-level and/or multilevel manifestations of the symbolism-effectiveness relationship? What is the role of structural symbols (e.g., a visible task force) as catalysts for institutionalizing strategic change? Cognitive structures in an organization are most often the product of vested interests (Mumby 1988), which suggests that certain groups or organizations will want to reproduce dominant belief systems while others will want to create or import other belief systems (Scott 1991) that would facilitate change rather than perpetuate the status quo. Understanding the role of symbolism across this spectrum of change processes and goals would provide further insight into the initiation of effective strategic change.

CONCLUSION

Cohen and March (1972) portrayed universities as organizations steeped in conservative academic tradition, giving their presidents little leeway for instituting radical change. They argued that the power of the university presidency is confined mainly to the invocation of symbolism in the creation of meaning for organization members. Our findings suggest a somewhat revised portrayal and interpretation, perhaps as a consequence of changing times and context. First, this study seems to have caught the university at a time of substantive transition; universities in general now have found themselves in a bona fide competitive market that has forced them to act in a more "business-like" manner. The immediate upshot of this environmental change was a need to "think and act strategically." This orientation, which was historically unnecessary, and therefore essentially unfamiliar, forced consideration of more radical changes at a faster pace than previously experienced. The key to such changes in this tradition-bound institution was still symbolism, but the domain of symbolism appears to have broadened in scope, such that it now constitutes a medium not only of meaning construction and expression, but of action as well.

The grounded, interpretivist approach we used to explore symbolic processes represents an attempt to give balanced voice to both insider and outsider views and to allow insights to emerge without force-fitting them into prior theoretical perspectives. The fact that a number of the findings align with prior theory merely affirms that we are not entirely reinventing the wheel and that previous views have some reasonable credibility. Yet, the emergence of some nonobvious findings, as well as revised portrayals of some symbolic phenomena, suggest that plausible, alternative ways of understanding the dynamics of strategic change are available only by suspending accepted views and pursuing alternative modes of study.

A brief recap of the major insights available from this approach include the following observations: (1) Symbols are not only an expressive medium, as most existing portrayals imply, but also a medium for substantive action. (Symbolism, therefore, not only captures the thoughts and feelings of organization members, but is action- and outcome-oriented as well); (2) Symbols are the medium for both sensemaking and influence and these two key processes are inextricably intertwined. (Although symbols often have been acknowledged as central to interpretation processes, their use as a means of influence has been underrepresented); (3) Symbolic processes associated with the instigation of change involve evolutionary shifts in directionality (They are primarily internally directed in the early, embryonic stages and externally directed in later, more mature stages); (4) Symbolic processes simultaneously occur at multiple levels of understanding (Symbols were the medium of operation of the change-agent task force, but the task force was itself a symbol); (5) Symbolic *non*-action can be important to change initiation (Not doing something was as important a symbolic harbinger as overt action); and finally, (6) strategic change might usefully be cast as a process of *reinstitutionalization* of cognitions, actions, and practices.

These observations also perhaps suggest that what distinguishes strategic change in university settings from change in other types of organizations is the increased necessity to instill a *cognitive* reorientation through the use of symbolism as a precursor to change implementation. The university studied here was enmeshed in the dilemma of having a strong tradition, with an entrenched strategy and structure, in the face of a newly complex and turbulent environment demanding change. That description fits many modern universities, as well as other organizations. Symbolic processes appear to possess the subtlety needed to execute the dynamics involved in launching strategic change in such precarious environments.

ACKNOWLEDGMENTS

We would like to thank Jean Bartunek, Mary Jo Hatch, Gareth Morgan, and Linda Smircich for inspiration and assistance during the development of this work. We also would like to thank the special issue editors and several anonymous reviewers for being provocatively helpful during the review process.

NOTES

1. In a sense, this study represents a companion piece to the study by Gioia and Chittipeddi (1991). Both studies focused on a strategic change effort in a university. Gioia and Chittipeddi (1991) presented a study of the top management team and its efforts to manage and manipulate the acceptance of change by its constituencies. The present chapter is a study of the struggles and evolution of the task force charged with designing and recommending ways to implement the change process. Thus, the two works are related, but have a markedly different focus and derive from different databases using different informants (except for the actor-observer, who worked on both projects).

2. In the sections that follow we have used the theoretical concepts that emerged mainly from the analyses. In the interpretive research approach used, the conceptual framework is grounded in, and emerges from, the data and analyses (rather than being derived mainly from prior theory that drives data collection and analysis). However, rather than ask the reader to work through a lengthy qualitative data presentation before discovering the contributions of the study (cf. Daft 1985), we have elected to preview the major findings and conceptual frameworks that, in fact, emerged from the study. We have, however, woven in some literature that became relevant after the form of the findings became clear.

3. In one sense, this study provides an empirical demonstration of Derrida's (1978) thesis that multiple readings of a "text" are viable. Derrida has assailed the assumption that the writer's (actor's) meaning should necessarily be given precedence in interpreting a text; rather readers' (researchers') alternative readings are also valid (cf. Cooper 1989). In an intriguing twist on this thesis, we believe that organizational science has made the opposite error of assigning excessive weight to researchers' theoretical views at the expense of actors' interpretations. This stance is tantamount to presuming that the reader/interpreter (researcher) has an advantage over the writer/actor (informant) when it comes to interpreting the writer's works. A *different* perspective perhaps, but it is presumptuous to assume that it is a *superior* perspective. In addition, the actors in our case were academics; they were not unsophisticated viewers of their own experience.

4. Although Exhibit 7.1 actually reveals findings that emerged from the study itself, we present it here not only as a demonstration of the progression of the analysis, but also as a way of providing an advance framework for understanding the first-order narrative and second-order inferences that follow.

5. As previously noted, there were disputed findings not reported here because of a lack of corroboration between the two researcher perspectives. Some examples of the excluded findings and the reasons for their exclusive might be informative, however. For instance, in the fine-grained analysis of the transcripts, the outside researchers noted that on several occasions the committee members used a "blood-to-the-cell" metaphor to argue for including as many constituencies as possible in the strategic planning process, all bringing blood (information) to the cell (the study groups). The actor-observer argued that although this metaphor was repetitively used, in his participating experience it did not become a consensual symbol for understanding how the strategic planning process was to be accomplished. Thus, this rich metaphor is not reported because it was not seen as a rallying metaphor for shared understanding by a person experiencing it.

6. We chose the label "prospective sensemaking" primarily as a descriptor of everyday phenomenology, although this process might have been a special case of retrospective sensemaking (Weick 1979), wherein people reflect on possible courses of action *as if* they had already occurred.

REFERENCES

Agar, M. H. (1986), *Speaking of Ethnography,* Beverly Hills, CA: Sage.

Allaire, Y. and M. Firsirotu (1985), "How to Implement Radical Strategies in Large Organizations," *Sloan Management Review,* 26, 3 (Spring), 19-34.

Ansoff, H. I. (1979), *Strategic Management,* London: Macmillan.

Axley, S. R. (1984), "Managerial and Organizational Communication in Terms of the Conduit Metaphor," *Academy of Management Review,* 9, 428-437.

Bartunek, J. M. (1984), "Changing Interpretive Schemes and Organizational Restructuring: The Example of a Religious Order," *Administrative Science Quarterly,* 19, 355-372.

Berger, P. L., B. Berger, and H. Kellner (1973), *The Homeless Mind: Modernization and Consciousness,* New York: Random House, Vintage Books.

——— and T. Luckmann (1967), *The Social Construction of Reality: A Treatise in the Sociology of Knowledge,* Garden City, NY: Doubleday.

Chandler, A. D. (1962), *Strategy and Structure,* Cambridge: MIT Press.

Chen, C. C. and J. R. Meindl (1991), "The Construction of Leadership Images in the Popular Press: The Case of Donald Burr and People Express," *Administrative Science Quarterly,* 36, 521-551.

Cohen, M. D. and J. C. March (1972), *The American College President,* New York: McGraw-Hill, Carnegie Commission on The Future of Higher Education.

Conrad, C. F. (1982), "Grounded Theory: An Alternative Approach to Research in Higher Education," *The Review of Higher Education,* 5, 259-269.

Cooper, R. (1989), "Modernism, Postmodernism and Organizational Analysis 3: The Contribution of Jacques Derrida," *Organization Studies,* 10, 479-502.

Daft, R. L. (1983), "Symbols in Organizations: A Dual-Content Framework for Analysis," in L. R. Pondy, P. J. Frost, G. Morgan, and T. C. Dandridge (Eds.), *Organizational Symbolism,* Greenwich, CT: JAI, 199-206.

——— (1985), "Why I Recommend That Your Manuscript Be Rejected and What You Can Do about It," in L. L. Cummings and P. J. Frost (Eds.), *Publishing in the Organizational Sciences,* Homewood, IL: Irwin, 193-209.

——— and J. C. Wiginton (1979), "Language and Organization," *Academy of Management Review,* 4, 179-192.

Das, H. (1988), "Reference of Symbolic Interactionist Approach in Understanding Power: A Preliminary Analysis," *Journal of Management Studies,* 25: 251-267.

Derrida, J. (1978), *Writing and Difference,* Chicago: University of Chicago Press.

DiMaggio, P. J. and W. W. Powell (1991), "The Iron Cage Revisited: Institutional Isomorphism and Collective Rationality in Organization Fields," in W. W. Powell and P. J. DiMaggio (Eds.), *The New Institutionalism in Organizational Analysis,* Chicago: University of Chicago Press, 63-82.

Donnellon A., B. Gray, and M. G. Bougon (1986), "Communication, Meaning and Organized Action," *Administrative Science Quarterly,* 31, 43-55.

Dutton, J. E. and J. M. Dukerich (1991), "Keeping an Eye on the Mirror: Image and Identity in Organizational Adaptation," *Academy of Management Journal,* 34, 517-554.

——— and R. B. Duncan (1987), "The Creation of Momentum for Change Through the Process of Strategic Issue Diagnosis," *Strategic Management Journal,* 8, 279-295.

———, L. Fahey, and U. K. Narayanan (1983), "Toward Understanding Strategic Issue Diagnosis," *Academy of Management Review,* 12, 76-90.

Edelman, M. (1964), *The Symbolic Uses of Politics,* Urbana: University of Illinois Press.

Evered, R. and M. R. Louis (1981), "Alternative Perspectives in the Organizational Sciences: 'Inquiry from the Inside' and 'Inquiry from the Outside,' " *Academy of Management Review,* 6, 385-395.

Feldman, M. S. and J. G. March (1981), "Information in Organizations as Signal and Symbol," *Administrative Science Quarterly,* 26, 171-186.

Frost, P. J. (1987), "Power, Politics, and Influence," in F. M. Jablin, L. L. Putnam, K. H. Roberts, and L. W. Porter (Eds.), *Handbook of Organizational Communication: An Interdisciplinary Perspective,* London: Sage, 503-548.

Frost, P. J. and G. Morgan (1983), "Sensemaking: The Real-ization of a Framework," in L. R. Pondy, P. J. Frost, G. Morgan, and T. C. Dandridge (Eds.), *Organizational Symbolism,* Greenwich, CT: JAI.

Garfinkel, H. (1967), *Studies in Ethnomethodology,* New York: Prentice Hall.

Geertz, C. (1973), *The Interpretation of Cultures,* New York: Basic Books.

Ginsberg, A. (1988), "Measuring and Modelling Change in Strategy: Theoretical Foundations and Empirical Directions," *Strategic Management Journal,* 9, 559-575.

Gioia, D. A. (1986), "Symbols, Scripts, and Sensemaking: Creating Meaning in the Organizational Experience," in H. P. Sims, D. A. Gioia, and Associates, *The Thinking Organization: Dynamics of Organizational Social Cognition,* San Francisco: Jossey-Bass, 49-74.

——— and K. Chittipeddi (1991), "Sensemaking and Sensegiving in Strategic Change Initiation," *Strategic Management Journal,* 12, 433-448.

——— and E. Pitre (1990), "Multiparadigm Perspectives on Theory Building," *Academy of Management Review,* 15, 584-602.

Glaser, B. G. and A. L. Strauss (1967), *The Discovery of Grounded Theory: Strategies for Qualitative Research,* Chicago: Aldine.

Greiner, L. E. and A. Bhambri (1989), "New CEO Intervention and Dynamics of Deliberate Strategic Change," *Strategic Management Journal,* 10, 67-86.

Hedberg, B. and S. Jonsson (1978), "Designing Semi-confusing Information Systems for Organizations in Changing Environments," *Accounting, Organizations and Society,* 3, 47-64.

Huff, A. S. (1983), "A Rhetorical Examination of Strategic Change," in L. R. Pondy, P. J. Frost, G. Morgan, and T. C. Dandridge, (Eds.), *Organizational Symbolism,* Greenwich, CT: JAI:

Isabella. L. A. (1990), "Evolving Interpretations as a Change Unfolds: How Managers Construe Key Organizational Events," *Academy of Management Journal,* 33, 7-41.

Jick, T. D. (1979), "Mixing Qualitative and Quantitative Methods," *Administrative Science Quarterly,* 24, 602-611.

Johnson, G. (1990), "Managing Strategic Change: The Role of Symbolic Action," *British Journal of Management,* 1: 183-200.

Keller, G. (1983), *Academic Strategy,* Baltimore, MD: Johns Hopkins University Press.

Lakoff, G. and M. Johnson (1980), *Metaphors We Live By,* Chicago: University of Chicago Press.

Langley, A. (1989), "In Search of Rationality: The Purpose Behind the Use of Formal Analysis in Organizations," *Administrative Science Quarterly,* 39, 598-631.

Louis, M. R. (1980), "Surprise and Sensemaking: What Newcomers Experience in Entering Unfamiliar Organizational Settings," *Administrative Science Quarterly,* 25, 225-251.

Lukes, S. (1974), *Power: A Radical View,* London: Macmillan.

March, J. G. and Z. Shapira (1982), "Behavioral Decision Theory and Organizational Decision Theory," in G. Ungson and D. Braunstein (Eds.), *Decision Making: An Interdisciplinary Inquiry,* Boston: Kent, 92-115.

Meyer, A. D. (1984), "Mingling Decision Making Metaphors," *Academy of Management Review,* 9, 6-17.

Meyer, J. W. and B. Rowan (1977), "Institutional Organizations: Formal Structure as Myth and Ceremony," *American Journal of Sociology,* 83, 340-363.

Miles, M. D. and A. M. Huberman (1984), *Qualitative Data Analysis: A Sourcebook of New Methods,* Beverly Hills, CA: Sage.

Milliken, F. J. (1990), "Perceiving and Interpreting Environmental Change: An Examination of College Administrators' Interpretation of Changing Demographics," *Academy of Management Journal,* 33, 42-63.

Mintzberg, H. and J. A. Waters (1985), "Of Strategies Deliberate and Emergent," *Strategic Management Journal,* 6, 257-272.

——— (1987), "Five Ps for Strategy," *California Management Review,* 30, 11-24.

Morgan, G. (1983), "Research as Engagement: A Personal View," in G. Morgan (Ed.), *Beyond Method: Strategies for Social Research,* Beverly Hills, CA: Sage.

——— (1986), *Images of Organization,* Beverly Hills, CA: Sage.

———, P. J. Frost, and L. R. Pondy (1983), "Organizational Symbolism," in L. R. Pondy, P. J. Frost, G. Morgan, and T. C. Dandridge (Eds.), *Organizational Symbolism,* Greenwich, CT: JAI.

Mortimer, K. P. and M. Tierney (1979), "The Three 'R's" of the Eighties: Reduction, Reallocation and Retrenchment," *ASHE-ERIC/Higher Education Research Report,* Washington, D.C., 4.

Mumby, D. K. (1988), "Ideology and Organization Cultures," *Communication and Power in Organizations: Discourse, Ideology, and Domination,* Norwood, NJ: Ablex, 71-94.

Ortony, A. (1975), "Why Metaphors Are Necessary and Not Just Nice," *Educational Theory,* 25, 45-53.

Pfeffer, J. (1981a), "Management as Symbolic Action: The Creation and Maintenance of Organizational Paradigms," in L. L Cummings and B. M. Staw (Eds.), *Research in Organizational Behavior,* 3, 1-52.

——— (1981b), *Power in Organizations,* Cambridge, MA: Ballinger.

——— and W. L. Moore (1980), "Power and Politics in University Budgeting: A Replication and Extension," *Administrative Science Quarterly,* 25, 637-653.

——— and G. R. Salancik (1974), "Organizational Decision Making as a Political Process: The Case of a University Budget," *Administrative Science Quarterly,* 19, 135-151.

Pondy, L. R. (1983), "Union of Rationality and Intuition in Management Action," in S. Srivastva (Ed.), *The Executive Mind,* San Francisco: Jossey-Bass.

——— and I. Mitroff (1979), "Beyond Open Systems Models of Organization," in B. M. Staw (Ed.), *Research in Organizational Behavior,* Vol. 1, Greenwich, CT: JAI.

Powell, W. W. and P. J. DiMaggio (1991), *The New Institutionalism in Organizational Analysis,* Chicago: University of Chicago Press.

Quinn, J. B. (1980), *Strategies for Change: Logical Incrementalism,* Homewood, IL: Irwin.

Rabinow, P. and W. M. Sullivan (1979), *Interpretive Social Science,* Berkeley: University of California Press.

Ranson, S., B. Hinings, and R. Greenwood (1980), "The Structuring of Organizational Structures," *Administrative Science Quarterly,* 25, 1-17.

Riley, P. (1983), "A Structurationist Account of Political Culture," *Administrative Science Quarterly,* 28, 414-437.

Rumelt, R. P. (1974), *Strategy, Structure, and Economic Performance,* Boston: Harvard Business School, Division of Research.

Scott, W. R. (1987), "The Adolescence of Institutional Theory," *Administrative Science Quarterly,* 32, 493-511.

——— (1991), "Unpacking Institutional Arguments," in W. W. Powell and P. J. DiMaggio (Eds.), *The New Institutionalism in Organizational Analysis,* Chicago: University of Chicago Press, 164-182.

Seidel, J. V. and J. A. Clark (1984), "The Ethnograph: A Computer Program for the Analysis of Qualitative Data," *Qualitative Sociology,* 7, 110-125.

Smircich, L. (1983), "Organizations as Shared Meanings," in L. R. Pondy, P. Frost, G. Morgan, and T. Dandridge (Eds.), *Organizational Symbolism,* Greenwich, CT: JAI, 55-65.

Smircich, L. and G. Morgan (1982), "Leadership: The Management of Meaning," *Journal of Applied Behavioral Science,* 18, 257-273.

——— and C. Stubbart (1985), "Strategic Management in an Enacted World," *Academy of Management Review,* 10, 724-736.

Snow, C. C. and D. C. Hambrick (1980), "Measuring Organizational Strategies: Some Theoretical and Methodological Problems," *Academy of Management Review,* 5, 527-538.

Spradley, J. P. (1980), *Participant Observation,* New York: Holt, Rinehart & Winston.

——— and D. W. McCurdy (1983), *Conformity and Conflict: Readings in Cultural Anthropology,* Boston: Little Brown.

Strauss, A. S. (1987), *Qualitative Analysis for Social Scientists,* Cambridge, UK: Cambridge University Press.

Thomas, J. B., S. M. Clark, and D. A. Gioia (1993), "Strategic Sensemaking and Organization Performance: Linkages Among Scanning, Interpretation, Action, and Outcomes," *Academy of Management Journal,* 36, 239-270.

——— and R. R. McDaniel (1990), "Interpreting Strategic Issues: Effects of Strategy and Top Management Team Information Processing Structure," *Academy of Management Journal,* 33, 286-306.

Tichy, N. (1983), *Managing Strategic Change,* New York: John Wiley.

Trice, H. M. and J. M. Beyer (1984), "Studying Organizational Culture Through Rites and Ceremonials," *Academy of Management Review,* 9, 653-669.

Tushman, M. L. and E. Romanelli (1985), "Organizational Evolution: A Metamorphosis Model of Convergence and Reorientation," *Research in Organizational Behavior,* Greenwich, CT: JAI, 171-222.

Van Maanen, J. (1979), "The Fact of Fiction in Organizational Ethnography," *Administrative Science Quarterly,* 24, 539-550.

Vidich, A. J. (1970), "Participant Observation and the Collection and Interpretation of Data," in W. J. Filstead (Ed.), *Qualitative Methodology,* Chicago: Markham.

Walsh, J. P. (1988), "Selectivity and Selective Perception: An Investigation of Managers' Belief Structures and Information Processing," *Academy of Management Journal,* 31, 873-896.

——— and L. Fahey (1986), "The Role of Negotiated Belief Structures in Strategy Making," *Journal of Management,* 12, 325-338.

Weber, M. (1947), *The Theory of Social and Economic Organization,* New York: Oxford University Press.

Weick, K. E. (1977), "Enactment Processes in Organizations," in B. M. Staw and G. R. Salancik, *New Directions in Organizational Behavior,* Chicago: St. Clai, 267-300.

——— (1979), *The Social Psychology of Organizing,* 2nd ed., Reading, MA: Addison-Wesley.

Whetten, D. A. (1984), "Effective Administrators: Good Management on the College Campus," *Change,* November-December, 38-43.

Zucker, L. G. (1987), "Instructional Theories of Organizations," *Annual Review of Sociology,* 13, 443-464.

8

Designing Information Technology to Support Distributed Cognition

RICHARD J. BOLAND, JR.
RAMKRISHNAN V. TENKASI
DOV TE'ENI

Cognition in organizations is a distributed phenomenon, in which individual members of an organization reflect upon their experience, make plans, or take action. Organizational learning or organizational cognition are familiar terms, but it is only the individual persons in an organization who create interpretations and test understandings, as they think and learn in their organizational setting. Coordinated outcomes emerge in organizations when individuals think and act in ways that take others in the organization and their interdependencies into account.

We argue that much of the effort to design information technology to support cognition in organizations has not addressed its distributed quality. Such systems have tended to focus either on the individual as an isolated decision maker, or on the group as a producer of a decision or policy statement in common. In distributed cognition, by contrast, the group is a set of autonomous agents who act independently yet recognize that they have interdependencies. To guide the design of information technology, we propose that distributed cognition be viewed as a hermeneutic process of inquiry, emphasizing the importance of individual interpretation and group dialogue.

Hermeneutics provides a theory of the interpretive process through which an individual gives meaning to organizational experience. Inquiry systems provide a theory of how a community of inquirers build and test knowledge representations through dialogue. Together, hermeneutics and inquiry systems are used to propose a set of design principles to guide the development of information

This chapter originally appeared in *Organization Science,* Vol. 5, No. 3, August 1994.

technology that supports distributed cognition. The design principles we describe in the chapter are ownership, easy travel, multiplicity, indeterminacy, emergence, and mixed forms.

Applications of information technology which embody these design principles would support distributed cognition by assisting individuals in making interpretations of their situation, reflecting on them, and engaging in dialogue about them with others. The objective is to refine their own understanding of the situation and better appreciate the understandings of others, enabling them to better take their interdependencies into account in their individual actions. A project to develop such a system is discussed, along with some implications for research.

(DISTRIBUTED COGNITION;
HERMENEUTICS; INQUIRING SYSTEMS;
ORGANIZATIONAL LEARNING; COGNITIVE MAPS)

Information technologies have been applied with considerable success to the core tasks of organizations, as evidenced by computer systems for on-line reservations, order entry, or integrated manufacturing. But information technologies have been applied with less success in systems that go beyond these transaction processing tasks to support the cognition and decision making of managers (Feldman and March 1981, Preston 1991, Silver 1991). This lack of success becomes most evident in turbulent environments (Emery and Trist 1965) where the need for interpreting new situations and adjusting existing practices is increased (Nonaka 1988, Hedberg et al. 1976).

We argue that the decision theoretic, choice-making image of managers that has traditionally guided the design of information technologies in organizations is in part to blame. It has portrayed managers as analyzers of data who solve problems that are presented to them and has encouraged the design of systems that provide them with decision models and a pipeline of data (Boland 1979). We propose instead that a more active, sense-making image be used to guide the design of systems that support managers as interpreters and enactors of a stream of events in their organization (Weick 1979). Recently, developments in formatted electronic mail systems such as coordinator (Flores et al. 1988) or information lens (Malone et al. 1989) and groupware such as Amsterdam Conversation Environment (Dykstra and Carasik 1991) and Post Mechanistic Groupware (Johnson-Lenz and Johnson-Lenz 1991) suggest such alternatives are beginning to emerge. In this chapter we propose that viewing cognition in organizations as a hermeneutic process of inquiry provides a theoretical basis for designing systems that support interpretation and sense making.

Organizational cognition is a distributed cognition. As Simon (1991) reminds us, organizations do not think or learn, people do. He portrays cognition in an organization as a set of individuals exchanging information among themselves within a system of roles, or prescribed decision premises.

> Roles tell organization members how to reason about the problems and decisions that face them: where to look for appropriate and legitimate information premises and goal (evaluative) premises, and what techniques to use in processing these premises. (Simon 1991, pp. 126-127)

Simon correctly warns against our habit of reifying organizations as when we speak of them "thinking" or "learning." But he himself appears to reify the concept of role as he speaks of a role "telling" people how to select and use decision premises. We will try to avoid this anthropomorphic usage that is so common when speaking of learning, memory, and related phenomena in an organizational setting (Walsh and Ungson 1991) by focusing our attention on distributed cognition.

Distributed cognition is the process whereby individuals who act autonomously within a decision domain make interpretations of their situation and exchange them with others with whom they have interdependencies so that each may act with an understanding of their own situation and that of others. To use Simon's role image, it is the process whereby individuals construct and reconstruct a system of roles through self-reflection, dialogue, and action.

When distributed cognition works well, the managers' individual actions take each other and their interdependencies into account in a way that yields a coordinated outcome. Dougherty (1992), for example, found that successful product innovators were distinguished from unsuccessful ones in that they created collaborative mechanisms that encouraged appreciation of each other's perspectives and their mutual interdependencies. Taking each other into account requires a process of surfacing and examining individual understandings. Weick (1990) has argued that in this process, managers should attempt to portray and re-examine rich displays of their thinking in order to complicate the familiar and make new interpretations possible. We propose that information technology can support distributed cognition by enabling individuals to make rich representations of their understanding, reflect upon those representations, engage in dialogue about them with others, and use them to inform action (see Figure 8.1).

Organizational participants do not do particularly well at actively and openly reflecting upon their understanding of a situation or the theories-in-

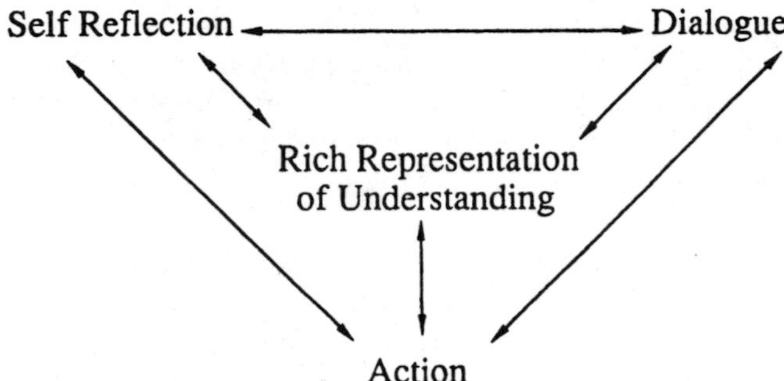

Figure 8.1. Role of Rich Representation in Supporting Distributed Cognition

use in their practices (Argyris 1982, Schön 1983, Argyris and Schön 1978). Weick (1990) suggests that because of this, managers have a tendency to operate on increasingly impoverished views of the world. In a similar vein, scholars concerned with organizational design (Clark 1975, Kilmann et al. 1976) have noted that organizations seldom have mechanisms for generating new structures that help to complicate the thinking of members. Complicating the thinking of managers is sometimes necessary to change interpretations and understandings that are no longer appropriate (Bartunek et al. 1983, Starbuck and Hedberg 1977).

In a series of influential papers, Starbuck and colleagues (Starbuck and Milliken 1988, Nystrom and Starbuck 1984, Starbuck 1983, Starbuck and Hedberg 1977) posit that a major contributory cause for organizational decline and failure is the oversimplified belief structures and stereotypes organizational actors use in dealing with the environment. Others such as Janis (1989) have traced major governmental policy fiascoes to the simple decision rules relied upon by the policymakers involved. A visible and accepted difference in "mind sets" (Janis 1989) allows members to be skeptical about each others' key presumptions, particularly those affecting the way the problem is formulated, the types of alternatives that are excluded at the onset, and the way cogent information about positive and negative consequences is interpreted. Likewise, Eisenhardt's (1989) case study findings suggest that faster and higher quality decision making occurs in teams that use more, not less information, and consider more, not fewer alternatives. Investing in multiple problem-solving strategies and debating competing hypothesis (Eisenhardt 1989) obviates the possibility of oversimplification and premature decision closure (Imai et al. 1985).

Complicating the thinking of managers is not an end in itself. Managers may find that a new, much simpler way of understanding their situation proves more effective in diagnosing and responding to events. But such a new, simpler understanding seldom comes from merely eliminating features from an existing interpretation. It comes instead from disturbing a familiar interpretive structure and adopting a perhaps simpler model but at a different level of understanding (Vygotsky 1962) or integration (Streufert and Swezey 1986, Schroeder et al. 1967).

In spite of the increasing attention being paid to more flexible organizational forms capable of dealing with unexpected and turbulent future environments (Huber 1984, Malone et al. 1987, Drucker 1988, Schein 1989), not much attention has been directed to information systems that are intended to support the examination and possible change of underlying assumptions and understandings (Orlikowski and Gash 1991). The possibility of significant change in understandings requires the capacity for organization members to regularly reflect on existing assumptions, processes, and structures (Bartunek and Moch 1987). It requires a self-diagnostic capacity for organization members to become aware of the perspectives from which they are operating, and "the capacity to change one's point of view, and therefore to explore one's situation through a different light" (Smith 1984, p. 290). Bartunek et al. (1983) submit that establishing mechanisms that enable members to engage different perspectives is one way to induce such change. Making representations of various perspectives enables organization members to recognize the different ways in which they understand a specific problem and to develop a working appreciation for other available alternatives (Bartunek and Moch 1987).

Efforts to create more open, self-reflective processes in organizations may, however, encounter several kinds of difficulty. Political efforts to gain power and dominance may lead to the suppression or distortion of communication in organizations in order to manipulate or confuse colleagues (Eisenberg and Phillips 1991). Information technologies intended to enhance performance may in fact lead to a passive, unreflective use by those adopting them (Orlikowski 1991) and the actual effect of information technologies intended to enhance group performance will be mediated by the ways in which they are appropriated by the group using it (Poole and DeSanctis 1990). We will discuss some of these organizational issues with the use of information technologies later in the chapter, but for now we will assume a situation in which organization leaders and members are open to and supportive of attempts to create less bureaucratic, hierarchical mechanisms and more network, marketlike arrangements for coordinating their actions through mutual adjustment (Huber 1984, 1990; Malone et al. 1987).

We will first review the traditional approach to designing management information systems and contrast it with the requirements of distributed cognition. We will then develop a set of design principles for systems that would support distributed cognition as a hermeneutic process of inquiry. Finally, we will describe an action research project that attempts to embody these design principles in an organizational system.

DISTRIBUTED COGNITION AS HERMENEUTIC INQUIRY

Images That Have Traditionally Guided Information System Design

Theory and research on information systems design has traditionally followed a model-based approach, viewing decision making as choice making, both at the individual and the organizational level (March 1978). Ackoff (1967) is a clear and frequently cited advocate of this framework but the foundational work of Anthony (1965), Simon (1977), and Feltham and Demski (1970) is equally important. In its simplest form, the model-based approach represents how the organization works in input-output terms. The objective is to solve the model and define the conditions necessary for optimum (or satisfactory) performance. The information required by the model is, or should be, the information required by the decision maker. Information system design is then the process of building a pipeline that will deposit the required data at the proper time to the appropriate decision maker. Advances in information technology enabling managers to interrogate a wide range of data, both internal and external to the firm, and explore a large repertoire of analytic models are the latest, high-tech version of this same basic image of information technology support. Weick and Meader (1991) criticize the research on Group Support Systems for a similar emphasis on answers and decisions at the expense of questions and interpretations. Huber's (1990) extensive review of computer-aided and decision-aiding technologies does not identify any applications or design variables outside this framework.

We hold that the presumption of an obdurate, "simply given" world where information analysts can rely on a technical language to provide a valid statement of a manager's information requirements (Demski 1980, Davis and Olson 1985) denies that individuals are importantly sense makers (Weick 1979) who use information in action, searching for meaning and understanding of their organizational context (Boland 1979).

On the contrary, this objectification of information fosters an image of the world in which the human meaning of social organization and action are framed as unproblematic, predefined, and prepackaged. It presupposes a one-for-one mapping between words in an information system and objects or conditions in the world, and overlooks the fact that words are symbols whose meanings are always multiple and ambiguous (Lyytinen 1985, 1987; Stamper 1987). The information system is an unfamiliar text that is read, interpreted and made meaningful by those who use it in ways that will always surpass any clear picture the system's creators had in mind (Boland 1991). Sense making is importantly an active process of making an organization and a self. In making their interpretation, the readers bring the world into being differently, and bring themselves into being differently as well (Rorty 1982). The passive choice maker pictured by model-based approaches to information system design fails to appreciate the truly dynamic quality of organizational life.

From an action and sense-making perspective, the task of information systems is to support human inquiry as a process of subjective, interpretive, meaning making. This is a hermeneutic process of inquiry. The need is for facilities of self-indication, reflection, and interpretation by organizational participants (Blumer 1969): an environment for making sense of their situation as opposed to a pipeline of data. This is a call for a movement beyond "procedural rationality" (Simon 1978) to information systems that support reflexive dialogue. The designers of distributed cognition systems would try to use information technologies to create an environment for acting out interpretations in conversation with others. As an environment for active sense making, the information in a distributed cognition system would not be the data structures or decision models made by an analyst, but would be representations made by individuals of their changing understandings of the organization and its environment. The issues considered by such an active approach to information system design would then be: how can individuals represent an understanding of the world, how can individuals reflect upon and exchange these interpretations with others, and how can individuals grow in their understanding of the world?

Our thesis is that a distributed cognition system that improves a group's ability to represent their interpretations, to reflect upon them, to engage in dialogue about them, and to inform action with them will provide the conditions for surfacing and challenging important assumptions (Argyris 1982, Schön 1983), for complicating their thinking (Weick 1990), and for enabling significant change when it is required (Bartunek and Moch 1987, Orlikowski and Gash 1991).

Designing for Distributed Cognition

Relatively little work has been done on distributed cognition, especially as it relates to how new problem representations are developed and exchanged in organizational dialogue (Simon 1991, Cheng et al. 1992). Simon suggests in this regard that our research should attend to:

> . . . the contents of important organizational memories, the ways in which those contents are accessed (or ignored) in the decision-making process, and the ways they are acquired by organizations and transmitted from one part of an organization to another. Among the contents of organizational memories, perhaps the most important are the representation of the organization itself and its goals. . . . (Simon 1991, p. 133)

We agree with the general thrust of these remarks, but as suggested above, we will argue for an approach that emphasizes enhancing an individual's ability to make these kinds of representations, explore them in dialogue with others, reflect about their implications, and incorporate them in action. Walsh and Ungson (1991) provide an extensive review of issues surrounding organizational memory, but they pay little attention to the dynamic process of dialogue among individuals as they create, draw upon, and exchange memory structures through distributed cognition.

A distributed cognition system supports interpretation and dialogue among a set of inquirers by providing richer forms of self-reflection and communication. We do not mean richer as discussed by Daft and Lengel (1984), because they take richness to be a media characteristic. For example, face-to-face communication is richer than a written memo because of the nonverbal gestures that are available. Instead of media richness, we are concerned with communication richness. We seek to increase richness of communication with self and other by increasing the ability to represent and travel among layers of context, regardless of media. A system to support distributed cognition as a hermeneutic process of inquiry should enable actors to better identify, discuss, and elaborate upon their understanding of context. Context, as a layering of assumptions and preferences that stand behind our views, is what makes meaning and communication possible (Levinson 1983, Givon 1989).

Our way of identifying better distributed cognition is similar in some respects to the work of Huber on organizational learning when he argues that organizational learning is increased "when more and varied interpretations are developed," and "when more organizational units develop uniform comprehensions of the various interpretations" (Huber 1991, p. 90). We doubt that individual managers who actively interpret and make sense of their situation ever develop uniform comprehensions with other managers, but we recognize their felt need to communicate their understandings as effectively as possible. The environment used as interpretive context by an individual is not a presented one, that can be uniformly shared among sense makers, but is a personally constructed, symbolic, and malleable one (Giddens 1979, Weick 1991, Boland 1993). A system to support distributed cognition should enable a person to easily represent context in the process of constructing interpretations, and to exchange those representations in dialogue with others.

The theoretical views we will be drawing upon to describe our understanding of distributed cognition are hermeneutics and inquiring systems. Using these two as a basis, we will propose design criteria to guide the development of information technology to support distributed cognition. Together, hermeneutics and inquiring systems provide a framework for thinking about the organization task and environment as both multivariant and multivocal, and for emphasizing an action-based and dialogical approach to supporting distributed cognition.

Hermeneutics

Hermeneutics is the study of interpretation. It originally referred to the problem of interpreting ancient religious texts. Because the writer, the language, and the culture behind these texts is quite obviously alien and unfamiliar to us, it is easy to see the need for interpretation. But today, hermeneutics is seen as a universal interpretive problem each of us faces every day in achieving human understanding in our social and organizational lives (Taylor 1971, Gadamer 1975, 1976, 1981). Our interpretation of the world is an historic act, grounded in our traditions. Gadamer calls the traditions we draw upon in interpreting the world our prejudices and celebrates prejudice as a positive, not a negative, element in our ability to understand the world.

> It is not so much our judgments as our prejudices that constitute our being. (Gadamer 1976, p. 9)

Our prejudice cannot disappear, nor should we want it to. Our prejudice is the way we are "open to" the world, and the search for meaning through interpretation is a dialogue in which we push to the horizon of our tradition and attempt to open ourselves to the horizon of others in active reciprocity. Understanding of the world is not an end point that we reach when our prejudice is stripped away, but is rather a moving dialectic process of dialogue that always takes place anew at the horizon of our prejudice. As new understandings emerge, new questions arise. Our horizon may change, but the process of interpretation continues. There is no fixed or final interpretation of a text or a situation to be "got right." The attitude of play is important for hermeneutics (Gadamer 1975). It is an attitude of engagement, yet openness: an appreciation for self-renewal and learning through interpretation (Starbuck and Webster 1991) and an enjoyment in playing the game again and again.

The process through which we come to an understanding of the world is an interplay of our tradition and the world-as-a-text, an interplay known as the hermeneutic circle. The hermeneutic circle is the recognition that in understanding a text, we depend on a comprehension (or anticipation) of the whole in order to identify and understand the parts, and, at the same time, we depend on a knowledge of the parts to guarantee our comprehension of the whole. We know the details we attend to in light of a theory, but we hold the theory as valid because of our knowledge of the details we attend to. Gadamer is careful to point out that the hermeneutic circle is not something that disappears once a situation is "perfectly" understood. It is not simply a method, but is the essential underlying structure of understanding.

> Thus the circle of understanding is not a "methodological circle," but describes an ontological structural element in understanding. (Gadamer 1975, p. 261)

Tacking back and forth between theory and details, comprehensions and particulars, is a phenomenological description of how we create and sustain understanding. Tacking back and forth, setting layer upon layer of reciprocally validating relation between the overall grasp and the immediate instance is the play dynamic in hermeneutics that characterizes management cognition (Pondy 1983). It is not just a technique for gaining an understanding, but is constitutive of our understanding.

Hermeneutics emphasizes that we should stop searching for objective, ultimate foundations to our knowledge of the social world and accept that humankind both makes and knows itself and its world through social practice. Accepting the hermeneutic, conversational quality of social practice helps us to see "man as a self-changing being, capable of remaking himself by remaking his speech" (Rorty 1985, p. 104).

Hermeneutic Implications for Supporting Distributed Cognition

Hermeneutics provides a starting point for understanding some structural features of distributed cognition and a starting point for saying in general terms what kind of activity we are trying to support. First, our focus should not be on the individual as a decision maker, as in most attempts to design decision support systems (Keen and Scott Morton 1978, Silver 1991) but on the individual as a conversation maker. Decision support systems have traditionally focused on the individual decision maker as she interacts with decision models and databases. Here we wish to focus on the individual's interpretive conversation with self and others.

The traditional image of the lonely decision maker has recently been supplemented by attempts to support decision-making groups (DeSanctis and Gallupe 1987), but that work has primarily been oriented toward aiding the process of group meetings, and includes features to help the group conduct brainstorming, create ranked lists of priorities, or allocate resources among competing projects. It is a discrete group decision that is being supported, not the continuous individual sense making of distributed cognition (Weick and Meader 1991). A hermeneutic perspective directs our attention to the ongoing, day-to-day, sense-making dialogue among organization members. To date, this aspect of organization life is only minimally supported by information technology through free form electronic mail (Sproull and Kiesler 1986, Eveland and Bikson 1987) or through systems to keep track of promises and commitments among group members (Winograd and Flores 1986). Only recently has there been a first attempt at designing information technology to support the interweaving of individual and group decision-making processes (Sengupta and Te'eni 1994). Early work suggestive of the kind of system we are proposing (Bush 1945) has largely been ignored.

From a hermeneutic perspective, a system to support distributed cognition should recognize the tradition-bound nature of individual understanding. The system should not try to remove bias, but should have facilities that help people push to the horizon of their understanding by making their assumptions visible. The standard of success for such a system should not be achieving the most accurate and true picture of a situation, as in a model-building approach to knowing the organization, but in achieving an understanding that is useful to the individual in making interpretations and taking action. The point is not to simulate a world, but to bring a world and a self into being differently through reflexivity and a dialogue of self-discovery. Traditional decision support systems are built to operate a decision model, with facilities for changing the model as the need arises. For a hermeneutic support system, in contrast, the interest is to allow for easy ways to configure and dynamically reconfigure understandings of a situation, in dialogue with others.

To support the hermeneutic circle, the system should allow for several levels of representation (from most global comprehension to most minute detail) to be at work simultaneously. The premises and assumptions of a user should be easily added layer upon layer as a dialogue of discovery proceeds, and the user should be able to move freely back and forth among these layers of context.

A hermeneutic support system for distributed cognition should not have a termination, as a meeting support system does. In a hermeneutic system, action and decision interrupts the discourse but it does not close the conversation. The conversation supported by such a system should be open as to its starting point and data inputs, and should have no set termination, except as the participants themselves change the conversation.

Finally, such a system must be truly dialogical. All participants should be equally enabled to make independent representations. It is when the separate horizons of those in dialogue are opened to each other that a hermeneutic understanding can develop. A hermeneutic support system does not try to support a "group mind" and sees "shared understanding" as an especially elusive condition to achieve. In distributed cognition, it is recognized that only the individual participants have understandings of a situation. A hermeneutic system should help them to represent and exchange their individual understandings in as rich and flexible a way as possible, but it does not intend to provide a shared understanding, as many shared editor systems would.

Shared editor systems, such as Cognoter (Tatar et al. 1991) or ShrEdit (Olson and Olson 1991) allow for flexible participation by many individuals in creating a single representation, and this type of group process is important to support. But because they are a shared writing space in which a single document is produced in common, the individual is not supported in representing, pushing to the horizon of, and exchanging their own complex understanding of the situation with others. Instead, each is supported in making modifications to an evolving, group representation. The same is true of the SODA cognitive mapping tool as described by Eden (1988). This type of group work, based on an image of a group mind being represented, is quite distinct from the needs of distributed cognition.

Inquiring Systems

Hermeneutics provides us with a description of the process of interpretation and with guidelines for some features of distributed cognition systems that would tend to support that process. But our discussion of hermeneutics leaves open the epistemological question of how we judge the validity and limits of our interpretations (Mitroff and Pondy 1974). For this we look to Churchman's (1971) review of foundational concepts of epistemology as they apply to designing an inquiring system. Inquiry is the act of producing knowledge, not as a mere collection of facts, but as a potential for acting purposively: seeking goals in light of an understanding of a situation, with the ability to adjust behavior as circumstances change. Churchman determines how to design an inquiring system by reviewing the ideas of Locke, Leibniz, Kant, Hegel, and Singer, among others, as if they were answering that question. We will first review the way he progressively builds the requirements for an inquiring system by playing these writers one against the other. We will then summarize the implications for designing an information system to support distributed cognition.

Churchman begins with Leibniz, and reads him as saying that an inquiring system should be able to produce fact nets that represent contingent truths. The Leibnizian inquirer is always testing new statements for internal consistency within an existing fact net but the source of new statements that feed the growing fact net is internal and innate to the inquiring system (Churchman 1971, p. 95).

In contrast, Churchman argues, the Lockean inquirer denies the existence of innate ideas, and insists that all factors or entities of interest to an inquirer must be received as an input to the system. Thus, the Lockean inquirer identifies as a significant problem the question of how factors are labeled and what those labels mean. Churchman argues that the Lockean inquirer solves this labeling and meaning problem by recognizing the importance of a community of inquirers and the role of consensus within the community in guaranteeing its knowledge.

Churchman then uses Kant to argue that any Lockean inquirer capable of receiving and classifying input presupposes a formal, internal structure for doing so. In a sense, what order we find in the world we have placed there ourselves. Churchman interprets the Kantian inquirer as one that moves beyond consensus to involve a dialogue among inquirers who view the same situation with several different sets of presuppositions.

A Hegelian inquirer is then introduced to dramatize and radicalize the multiperspective Kantian inquiring system. The Hegelian inquiring system recognizes no data as meaningful except as it is seen through the inquirer's unique Weltanschauung, which in addition to Kantian perceptual primitives includes an individual's values, beliefs, and emotional commitments. Also, inquiry proceeds not through the convergence of multiple perspectives, but through the dialectic confrontation of thesis and antithesis in strong debate.

Churchman, however, does not accept Hegel's optimistic view that a synthesis with better understanding inevitably results from a dialectic process. Churchman uses Singer, his own mentor, to problematize Hegel's uni-directional image. A Singerian inquiring system emphasizes that the direction and style of inquiry change frequently and dramatically. Convergence of measurements and opinions that might signal progress to the Liebnizian, Lockean, or Kantian inquirers are a signal to the Singerian inquirer that the interpretive scheme giving rise to the consensus must be somehow challenged or disturbed. Finding an answer to the current question becomes less important than finding a better question. A principle technique Singer suggests for doing so is to "sweep in" concepts and elements from outside the currently accepted ways of understanding a situation.

As in a hermeneutic circle, Singer proposes a kind of tacking back and forth from images that simplify the view of a situation to ones that complicate; from greater scrutiny of details, instrumentation, and measurements to a rethinking of basic categories, concepts, and theories. Churchman characterizes this endless process as a type of heroic journey, and enriches the image of inquiry by "sweeping in" considerations of love, ethics, culture, and religion. Thus, an individual's desires, preferences, moral norms, and aesthetic judgment are as important to "sweep into" the inquiring system as are assumptions about key economic indicators or competitor activities.

Inquiring System Implications for Designing Distributed Cognition Support

This sketch of inquiring systems gives us insights into a slightly more detailed set of requirements for supporting distributed cognition than the general overview provided by hermeneutics. First, the Leibnizian inquiring system points out the need for individuals to construct networks of contingent truths. We will take this to mean constructing displays of the relations among a set of factors or entities including causal relations, along with the normally unstated assumptions and presuppositions that support an individual's belief in these contingent truths. This gives us a clearer image of the hermeneutic requirement to allow for building up layers of context and moving back and forth between layers of assumptions.

Commercially available systems, such as Teamfocus from IBM, Hypercard from Macintosh or Lotus Notes, allow for the design of applications that manage the construction of such networks and the movement within them. We see great potential for using these and other similar software environments for realizing the possibilities of hermeneutic inquiry in a wide variety of ways. But what design requirements does an inquiring system perspective add to this basic image of contingently linked elements in a "fact net?"

The idea of a Lockean inquiry system adds the requirement that there should be an identifiable community of inquirers, or a recognized group in distributed cognition, for whom the evolving image of contingent truths is significant. This community of inquirers are engaged in a process of structuration (Giddens 1979) in which they instantiate in action the organization that they are trying to understand.

The Kantian inquiring system highlights the need for multiple ways to depict understandings of the organization, based on different underlying approaches to representing, or imposing order upon, a situation. We will take this requirement to mean that spatial, visual, and graphic modes of representation (Meyer 1991) should be supported equally to numerical, procedural, and analytic modes of representation. The effort to develop spreadsheets and word processing tools should be balanced with equivalent efforts to develop tools for representing understandings with pictorial, spatial formats such as cognitive maps (Huff 1990).

The Hegelian inquiring system highlights the importance of openness to strong disagreement among the inquirers, going so far as to invite "deadly enemy" confrontations. This requires that members of the community be able to make representations of the organizational situation with complete control over the premises, assumptions, and context used to portray their version of what the situation is and what its implications are.

Finally, the Singerian inquiring system gives us a more refined understanding of how the hermeneutic circle might be realized in a system to support distributed cognition. First and foremost is the importance of being able to "sweep in" the widest range of context. Inquirers should be able to represent not only traditional economic, environmental, and strategic data and assumptions, but also less traditional types of data, such as subjective preferences, ethical positions, and aesthetic judgments.

In keeping with a hermeneutic sensibility, we take the Singerian inquiring system to emphasize that each representation made by an inquirer is partial and inherently incomplete. The situation is never understood by an inquirer from a total, world-encompassing view, but, in a series of partial and limited ways, the inquirer is trying to sweep in new ways of seeing the situation including different levels of abstraction, different breadths of view, and different contexts of concern.

The Singerian inquiring system also enriches our understanding of the hermeneutic circle by emphasizing that it is not just a movement back and forth through layers of context between theory and detail, but is also importantly a process of alternately simplifying and complicating. When the Singerian inquirer is satisfied with the level of theoretic generality being used, its focus is on refining the precision of measurements, the distinctions among entities and factors, and the elaboration of causal interdependencies. However, when refining of detail has been pushed to new limits, the Singerian inquirer increasingly focuses on creating new groupings of entities and measures, looking for more general patterns of relationships and a greater simplicity of theoretical frameworks. Thus, a support system for distributed cognition designed as an inquiring system should have facilities for elaborating new levels of detail by taking any existing element or factor and "exploding" it into more refined descriptors and measures and also for collapsing several existing factors and interrelations into a new, more abstract and general construct.

Most importantly, an inquiring system to support distributed cognition must facilitate a dialogue among the organization's community of inquirers. Each individual should have the capacity to create and modify their own representations. They should be able to exchange representations with others in the community, sending and receiving reactions, challenges, and comments about each others' representations. A method to manage these representations and the messages exchanged about them is important in making such a system truly conversational and useful in inquiry.

DESIGNING SYSTEMS FOR DISTRIBUTED COGNITION

Overview

A hermeneutic process of inquiry involves actors who make interpretations of their situation and reflect upon their action and their interpretations in order to push to the horizons of their understanding. They open themselves to their horizon of understanding and to those of others through an ongoing process of surfacing and discussing the multiple levels of assumptions and preferences that are the tradition within which they make their interpretations. *Actors, interpretations* and *action* are the core elements of a distributed cognition system. Interpretations, in turn, are composed of multiple levels of assumptions and preferences.

In order to create a physical system with these elements that has a quality of hermeneutic inquiry, six design principles are proposed. These design principles are intended to guide the application of information technologies so that they support the creation and exchange of the rich forms of representation that are central to distributed cognition systems as depicted in Figure 8.1. Individuals should have *ownership* of an interpretation so that their horizon of context may be opened to that of other actors in dialogue. This requires a *multiplicity* of interpretations, at least one per individual. The hermeneutic circle requires *easy travel* between theory and detail, foreground and background assumption. This easy travel for tacking back and forth between developing greater precision of measures and rethinking of the concepts being measured is also required for a Singerian inquiry component. As in a Singerian system, the representations will be partial, tentative, and have a quality of *indeterminacy.* Because of the dynamic, evolving quality of the hermeneutic circle and Singerian inquiry, the system should support the *emergence* of new categories, constructs, and levels of abstraction. Finally, to allow for a hermeneutic openness to new modes of representation and a Kantian recognition of more than one valid way of structuring an interpretation, a distributed cognition system should support *mixed forms* of representation.

The design principles do not define any specific technology or feature, but are rather an expression of the ideals to be achieved by the selection of specific technologies and the development of particular features in distributed cognition systems. We discuss the implications and the basis for each element and design principle below, and in the next section describe one attempt to realize them in an actual system.

Elements of Distributed Cognition Systems

The three elements of a distributed cognition system are described below. Their interactions constitute a process of hermeneutic inquiry.

Actors. The system is oriented toward an individual person, and not toward a group or a role because only individual persons have hermeneutic understanding and meaning to represent. It is the individual in dialogue with others that is the locus of inquiring systems.

Interpretations. The system is oriented toward an actor's interpretation of his or her situation taken as an integral, whole unit of understanding; not toward a database of facts or decision models. An actor's interpretation includes an understanding of the factors at work in a situation and their relationships. Relationships among factors may often, but not always, be understood as causal influences, and we will be using cognitive maps extensively to represent this kind of understanding (Axelrod 1976, Bougon et al. 1977, Stagner 1977, Weick and Bougon 1986, Eden et al. 1979, Eden 1988, 1992). Although an individual may incorporate a simulation or analytic model as part of an interpretation, such models are not the primary focus of a distributed cognition system. It is the interpretation and its levels of context that is the primary focus.

Hermeneutic inquiry involves surfacing the assumption for each aspect of an interpretation. The context or background assumption is part of the tradition of prejudgments through which we make an interpretation, and of the horizon of our own understanding in a hermeneutic sense. No data is meaningful to a Kantian or Hegelian inquiring system except as seen through an image of the world that must itself be questioned as a basis for Singerian learning.

Hermeneutic inquiry is a process of continuously elaborating levels of text and context, foreground and background, statement and assumptions. Any part of an interpretation that is in focal awareness is attended to from a set of background assumptions and preferences, or tacit understandings (Polanyi 1967). When focal awareness shifts to one of those assumptions or preferences another set of background assumptions and preferences is drawn upon in understanding it. These multiple levels of context are the essential basis for a hermeneutic circle. Moving through levels of context brings the actor closer to her horizon of understanding and being able to discuss that horizon with others. Multiple levels of context are also required for a Singerian inquiry system to alternate between a successive refinement of details and a reexamination of basic questions being asked.

A Singerian inquiry system tries to "sweep in" as preferences the nonrational, noncausal, more emotive aspects of an individual's understanding. The horizon of a person's hermeneutic understanding includes not only presumptions of the way the world is, but also desires, hopes, and fears for the way it may be.

Action. The system is oriented toward the actions which punctuate the ongoing process of distributed cognition. Action taken by actors who have interdependencies defines the set of managers that will participate in a distributed cognition system, and defines the domain they will make interpretations of. From both a hermeneutic and inquiring systems perspective, it is action that lends a cyclical character to the individuals' interpretations, providing an opportunity for them to review, modify, and further exchange the multiple levels of assumptions and preferences in their interpretations.

Design Principles for Distributed Cognition

The six principles of design for a hermeneutic inquiry system are described below. We do not claim to be the originator for all these principles. Each individually has been mentioned or used in some proposed or real system in the past. Our contribution here is twofold. We derive these principles from theory in the context of distributed cognition, and, in the next section, we show how these principles can be applied comprehensively in one application.

Ownership. An interpretation is always owned by an actor who is responsible for creating and maintaining it. This includes the responsibility of sharing any part of the representation with others through a mail system at the owner's discretion. Similarly, when those others respond with ideas, critiques or alternatives, it is up to the owner to decide if they will be incorporated in her understanding of the situation. From a hermeneutic perspective, an interpretation must belong to an individual if it is to give access to her context of tradition and horizon of understanding. As an inquiring system, the dialogue or dialectic among different underlying images of the world requires an owner who truly believes in them.

Let us introduce an example that will demonstrate this and future design principles. Say an organization has two major actors, one in Engineering and one in Production. Each actor has to make decisions about volume planning of specific products. Looking top down, at the left portion of Figure 8.2, we see Engineering's preference for building novel technology, which applies to the factor "functionality" in Engineering's interpretation of the problem situation. An example of an assumption (a lower level of context) is the anticipated trend for purchases of home computers. The action that follows from this combination of interpretation and context is a forecast of the types and quantity of products to be developed. Note that some assumptions may be adopted from other owners without transfer of ownership. For example, the assumption that consumer confidence lags behind GNP is owned and will continue to be maintained by the organization's economist, but it is an open reference for others to use. (In Figure 8.2, this is denoted by multiple copies of the box denoting Economic Assumption.)

Easy Travel. An individual's interpretation should display a hypertext-like structure in which any element can be linked to any other, and the links can be followed quickly and easily. Easy travel between text and context is required by the hermeneutic circle and the Singerian inquirer. There are two types of travel: one is within an interpretation across levels of reference and the other is across interpretations. Looking back at the left-hand side of Figure 8.2, we notice directed relationships between Engineering's preference, cognitive maps, assumptions, and actions. Directionality is all-important. For example, the arrow from a factor within the cognitive map to an assumption means that the assumption explains the factor. Similarly, a preference evaluates factors pointing at it. The directed paths between entities within a representation constitute layers of context. Ease of travel is the quality of a system which most directly supports the hermeneutic circle, allowing actors to tack back and forth from overviews to underlying assumptions, from theories to details (Te'eni 1992).

The Hypertext model (Conklin 1987) demonstrates well what we mean by easy travel through associations. It also shows some of its potential problems. For example, as the collection of representations grows, it becomes increasingly difficult to navigate through the collection and appropriate help is needed. (This is a price one will need to pay for richer communication.)

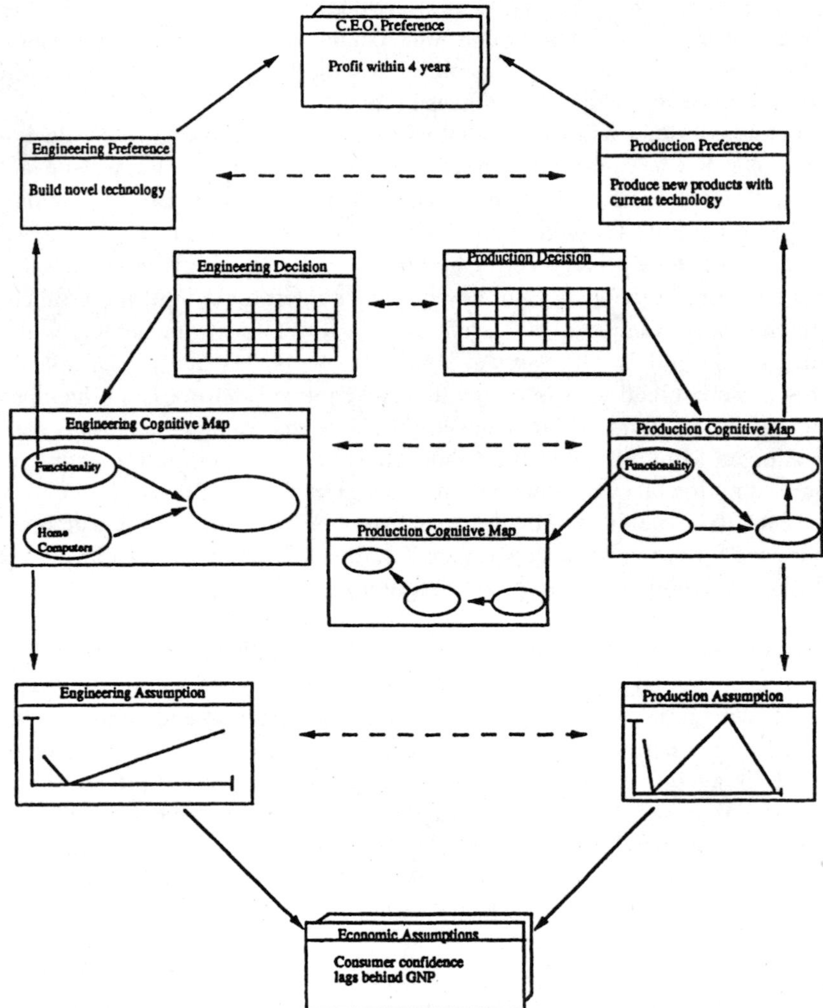

Figure 8.2. Two Interpretations of the Same Situation

The second type of travel is across interpretations. Users may wish to travel along time paths or along content paths across different contexts.

Multiplicity. Each actor involved in distributed cognition should make her own interpretation and be able to participate in the exchange and critique of representations. The possibility of a hermeneutic fusion of horizons presupposes each actor has her own understanding and horizon. Actors can also maintain multiple interpretations of the same situation. This may be the result of uncertainty, ambiguity, contingency, or any other reason, and is left completely to the actor's discretion.

Multiple interpretations are needed to support individual reflective thought as well as group dialogue. But allowing multiple interpretations may be counterproductive if the different interpretations are hard to distinguish. The system should therefore help actors to compare and contrast interpretations. At the very least, different interpretations should be viewed in parallel to facilitate manual comparison. A higher level of support can be given with facilities for automatically detecting and highlighting similarities or differences. Figure 8.2 demonstrates two representations, one of Engineering and the other of Production. The bidirectional, broken-lined arrows between the two models represent possible areas for comparison. Multiplicity also implies room for both redundancy and indeterminacy with regard to naming; both should be identified with the system's support but resolved by the users.

These first three principles (ownership, multiplicity, and easy travel) partially determine communication within distributed cognition. Communication must take place in order to exchange representations among individuals. In other words, Engineering cannot travel into Production's interpretations without Production's communicative actions. Communication can be either synchronous or asynchronous. Production can send a representation, or part of it, to Engineering and await her reply. An individual can communicate information to the entire world by announcing it in the public domain, e.g., the economist publishing an economic assumption. Most importantly, communication can occur not only at different levels of context but can encompass several levels of context.

Indeterminacy. Interpretations are not required to be comprehensive, complete, or precise. Actors are necessarily tentative, vague, and equivocal about parts of their understanding. From a hermeneutic perspective, there is no final or stable understanding to be achieved, only a continuing interpretive process. As in a Singerian inquiring system, understanding is always taken to be partial and limited with a continuing need to "sweep in" more context. For example, cognitive maps should allow for incomplete maps, fuzzy areas, and correlationals rather than directed relationships. Indeterminacy as a design principle explicitly leaves room for conversation, as elements from each of the separate views in a representation do not fit precisely and tightly in a logical monolith.

Emergence. New, more abstract constructs and concepts will be developed during the process of interpretation. The hermeneutic circle involves a playful experimentation with new concepts, categories, and levels of representation. Lockean, Hegelian, and Singerian inquiring systems all emphasize induction, synthesis, and movement beyond apparent categories. Inquiry should alternate between complicating and simplifying an interpretation. New constructs, relationships, and theories should be easily added to and incorporated within a set of representations. The system should not only allow for expansion through additional links to new assumptions as a view becomes more elaborate and finely detailed, the system should also allow for new, more general or higher-level entities to emerge as a synthesis of an existing set of relations. In a cognitive mapping tool, for instance, authors should not only be able to link elements in a map to documents that provide more detailed context for understanding them, they should also be able to merge several elements together into a synthetic construct that uses the previous set of factors as its context.

Mixed Form. Actors have sometimes radically different modes of expressing their understandings, ranging from text, pictures, and graphs to perhaps audio or video. In order to allow a Kantian inquirer to represent an understanding fluidly, the system should be as open as possible to the actors' preferred mode of expression. The actors should be able to choose how to represent an element by using a variety of visual modes as well as auditory or other sensory modes. Being able to communicate with multiple (redundant) modes concurrently is sometimes necessary for effective communication. Let us concentrate on the more traditional distinction between different forms of visual representation. Figure 8.2 shows a cognitive map linking to textual, graphic, and tabular information. Recent psychological theories provide guidance on how to implement this principle. The theory of dual coding (Paivio 1986) differentiates the spatial, parallel representation enabled by graphs from the linear, sequential representations enabled by numbers and text. The theory views interpretation and decision as mediated by the joint activity of spatial and textual systems, with the relative contribution of each system depending on characteristics of the task and the decision maker's cognitive abilities and habits. Mixed form is also the basis for using technology to achieve the engaging, playful interaction (Te'eni 1990) that should characterize a hermeneutic process.

A PROJECT WITH BUSINESS UNIT PLANNERS

In an attempt to physically realize these design principles in a working information system, we are developing Spider, a software environment for distributed cognition. We are working with business unit planners from a large international manufacturing company. These managers display distributed cognition because each has interdependencies with other business units which should be taken into account in their individual actions. The managers will use Spider to represent their understanding of the market for their products and to exchange and critique those representations among themselves in a hermeneutic process of inquiry.

Project members from the company come from engineering, marketing, sales, and manufacturing departments. Each company participant is involved in making quarterly sales forecasts of the company's major products over a three-year time horizon in units and dollars. The departments are different worlds, and actors from these unique environments find that effective communication is very difficult to achieve. It requires substantial effort in representing their own context of assumptions and understandings and in exchanging those representations with others in a meaningful dialogue. In this action research, we are drawing upon the design principles discussed above, and are presenting the project here as but one way the principles could be realized. At this point, our interest is primarily an engineering one to see if a system for distributed cognition can be constructed and used.

Spider reflects the design criteria for distributed cognition in that it is oriented toward an individual *actor* (a planning manager) and is a tool for enabling the actor to build and reflect upon an *interpretation* of the market. Even though each actor is concerned with the subset of products which his or her planning *actions* affect directly, these managers have interdependencies which, if taken into account in their separate actions, would yield a more coordinated outcome. At the end of each quarterly period, when new forecasts are made and actual results are received, a new cycle of reflection, interpretation, and dialogue begins.

An interpretation is represented by creating a linked set of spreadsheets, cognitive maps, notes, or graphs. These four are an initial set of document types, but one aim of the action research is to identify other possible tools for depicting understandings that can be developed and added to Spider. We believe that even this initial set of tools, though, is an innovative use of cognitive maps. Traditionally, a researcher has constructed a decision maker's cognitive map for the researcher's own purposes, and has taken it to be a rather static representation (Axelrod 1976, Huff 1990). Our use of cognitive maps is unique in that these managers are constructing their own maps, exchanging them, critiquing them, modifying them, and generally making them their own representation and communication device.

Assumptions are a central focus of the system, and when the actor declares a link from one document to another it indicates the link to an assumption or a context for that part of the interpretation. In addition to enabling links among layers of context, the system provides dialog boxes for clarifying assumptions and preferences. The system explicitly allows the actors to state preferences by distinguishing what they believe to be the case in the existing and future marketplace, from a separate indication of how the individual would like to see it change.

Actors can begin their interpretation with any of the document types. In this project, the central document of their representations is often a cause map showing the market factors that are important to take into account and their causal influence on each other. "The cause map contains the structure, the process, and the raw materials from which agreements and conflicts are built when people coordinate actions" (Weick and Bougon 1986, p. 132). Each factor in a map, or the entire map, can be linked to another map, a spreadsheet, a note, or a graph that serves as an assumption or a context for it. Each of those documents can in turn be linked to other document types in which their assumptions or context can be represented. Thus, an interpretation is composed of multiple levels of context.

A Brief Example

A sample top-level screen in Spider is shown in Figure 8.3. This example includes several document types, including a matrix of sales forecasts and a cognitive map for a family of products. Clicking on the bubbles in the cognitive map or the rows in the spreadsheet will travel links to other windows. In these windows, underlying assumptions, general views, and preferences are depicted with appropriate document types. Managers reflect upon their understanding of their situation by moving back and forth between elements in a map, calculations in a spreadsheet, and other layers of assumptions. Their interpretation builds as they add elements to their map, group elements into higher-level constructs, and elaborate on the web of contextual assumptions and preferences. Below we give a brief example of how Spider might be used in a business unit setting.

Figure 8.3 shows the screen of a hypothetical marketing manager (Mark) who has received a message from a manufacturing manager (Paula). She has sent him her production plans for a new product (product A) over the next two years in the form of a spreadsheet, along with a line graph showing the volume trends. Her representation also includes her cognitive map of product A in the marketplace, indicating her plan to introduce a new production technology. Mark has surfaced some of Paula's assumptions for product A by following a link to her more detailed map of "new production technology." While he was exploring her maps, he noticed that the new technology enables a more compact assembly, which is a requirement that has been voiced to him by several major clients. This triggers an idea for a new promotion initiative that will become part of his marketing effort.

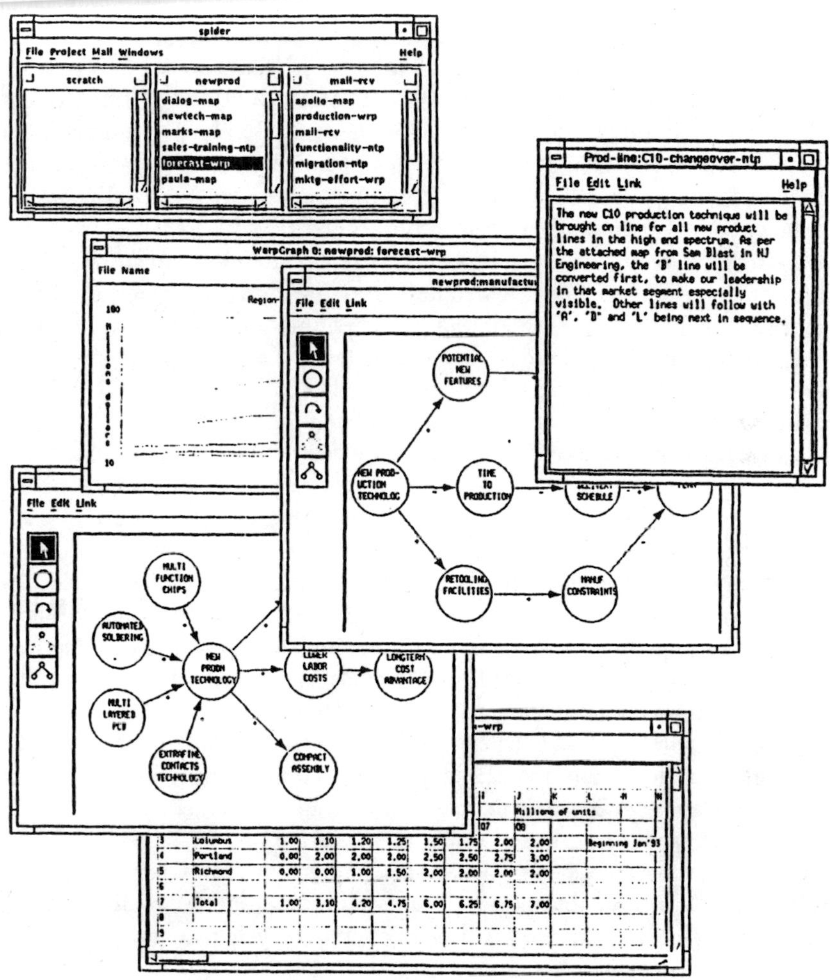

Figure 8.3. A Sample Screen from Spider Showing Multiple Documents of a Representation

From her detailed map and related notes he also discovers that the new production technology will first be introduced for product B, because Engineering believes that being first in the marketplace with that product innovation will be an important technical coup for the company. Historically, the firm has been recognized as the leader in product B innovations.

Mark disagrees with this assumption and wonders if Engineering or Manufacturing has considered the possibility that the company's speed in developing new versions of product B may actually be undermining their market. His own customers seem to just now be settling in with the last improvements to product B, and no competitor products are on the horizon. He wonders if moving up the conversion of the "A" line, and putting off that of the "B" line, might not be more advantageous. He plans to augment his representation, showing how, from his perspective, speeding up product B may be counterproductive, whereas speeding up product A may allow them to meet some important new competitors. First he will create a new map, showing how product lifespan is positively related to a new construct he will call "customer integration," which he will define as a customer's ability to gain full advantage from integrating a product into their operations. He will link the product lifespan factor to a spreadsheet he already has showing the shortening of the life cycle for B over the last 5 years, and will link the customer integration factor to a memo he recently received from a regional sales manager discussing this integration effect at one of their customer's plants.

Then he will go back to his own representation for product A and expand the section of his map that deals with product competitiveness, showing specific new products developed by competitors and their estimated announcements. He will then send these representations to Paula and to Engineering, guiding them to these new sections in his map and urging them to rethink the priority of product B and consider new ways of shortening the production time line for product A in light of the competition.

This example illustrates the central dynamic of distributed cognition and how information technology can support it. Rich forms of representation of the understandings of each manager are being exchanged, reinterpreted, revised, and used to inform action. Assumptions are surfaced and questioned, new constructs emerge, and a dialogue among different perspectives is supported. Below we discuss in more detail how Spider embodies each of the six design principles for distributed cognition systems.

How Spider Embodies the Design Principles

In Spider, *ownership* is defined at the point of creation and cannot be changed. Furthermore, a user can only mail an interpretation (or part of it) that he or she owns. Spider does not provide for a shared understanding, i.e., a general representation that is owned by the community of actors. However, to facilitate certain organizational functions, such as chief economist, an actor can make her representations available to all users by posting it on a bulletin board. Items on the bulletin board remain the responsibility of the owner to change or update.

Multiplicity in Spider is facilitated by a window-based environment which allows users the ability to maintain and display several interpretations concurrently. The data structures contain sufficient information for comparing interpretations semiautomatically in terms of the overall structure (concepts and relationships in the cognitive maps) and labels used. We are planning several research projects using pattern recognition techniques in order to detect and highlight similarities and differences between maps automatically.

Easy travel is possible through links that are user-defined. Any element within an interpretation can be linked to any document or set of documents. Users create and travel links by selecting objects and clicking with a mouse to bring up the document it is linked to. A problem representation can become large and complex, making navigation within such a space quite difficult. To support navigation, a roadmap of the user's problem representation will be provided, showing an overview of the links among levels of assumptions.

In Spider, *emergence* takes several forms. First, the system provides all the necessary facilities to incorporate elements from other problem representations (owned or received in mail) into one's own and edit them. Such editing would typically involve adding, updating, and deleting parts, rearranging them, and rebuilding their links. Moreover, when a document is added to a representation, it brings along all its properties including links to its context. Second, a set of existing factors in a cognitive map can be selected and merged into a new, higher-level construct. This enables the actor to better engage in the hermeneutic circle by adding not only more detail and assumptions, but also more abstract and general understandings while tacking back and forth.

Spider is built to allow for *indeterminacy:* There is no requirement that cognitive maps be complete or that the elements in any one document be in a measure or on a scale that is compatible with that of other documents. The direction of causal influence among factors in a cognitive map can be indicated or omitted, and preferences can be declared or not. Similarly, confidence in beliefs about the current situation can be stated or not.

Support of *mixed forms* of representation are becoming common in learning and decision related software design. All modern spreadsheets provide an easy transition from tabular to graphic presentation of the same numeric data. In Spider we go one step further by letting users sketch graphic patterns and interpolate them into tabular form. Thus, users can choose to represent information in structured or free form, graphic or verbal forms, and process this information in parallel by displaying these different forms simultaneously thorough different windows on the same screen.

We regard Spider as an enabling tool for richer communication, but it is also an important tool for better self-understanding by an individual actor.

Most of the understanding represented in the multilayered web of links among the cognitive maps, spreadsheets, text, and graphs is usually held by an individual tacitly. It is not readily available as a well-formulated set of "reasons why" that are used in making a particular forecast. People "know more than they can say" (Polanyi 1967). We have found that it takes a great deal of effort to systematically construct a cognitive map of a product line situation and to unpack the underlying factors and assumptions used in making spreadsheet entries.

The intellectual effort and careful self-examination required to interactively construct a cognitive map, its related spreadsheet, and its layers of assumptions is a source of new understanding for the managers involved. This in itself is an important learning experience. Nonetheless, the principle benefit of Spider as a collaborative technology should come when individuals exchange their representations, compare their own layered context descriptions with those of others, and communicate new understanding and inquiries back to their colleagues.

SUMMARY DISCUSSION

We have proposed a theoretical basis for understanding distributed cognition as a hermeneutic process of inquiry. Implications from that theoretical position were used to develop a set of design principles for information systems that would support distributed cognition in an organizational setting. A physical system called Spider that would realize these design principles was presented. Several levels of research are suggested by this type of hermeneutic inquiring system. These include understanding the conditions where we can expect distributed cognition to be genuinely open, self-reflective, and honest; understanding how information technologies for supporting distributed cognition will be appropriated by organization members; and understanding the consequences of such technologies on individuals and organizations.

Orlikowski and Robey (1991) propose a structurational model which emphasizes the recursive interaction between information technology use and social structures. Information technology mediates human activities, but human actors draw upon interpretive schemes, moral norms, and understandings of power from a broader institutional context in their action. When using information technology, actors produce and reproduce organizational structures, and may either sustain them or change them. As a process of structuration, the use of information technology is subject to the same level of indeterminacy as any other human action and will result in both intended and unintended consequences.

Poole and DeSanctis (1990) propose that through a process of structuration, the intended use of a technological system is read and appropriated by its users. Depending on the reading of the user, appropriation can be "faithful" or "ironic." Ironic appropriation means using the system in a manner that violates or is inconsistent with the intentions of its designer. A faithful appropriation of the intended use of a hermeneutic support system such as Spider, at least as conceived by the designers, presupposes values such as trust, self-disclosure, and cooperation among a community of reflective, willing users, who are interested in performing better distributed cognition (Habermas 1981). Under conditions of faithful appropriation we expect that Spider will be an environment for enhancing an individual's ability to make interpretations, exchange them in dialogue with others, reflect about their implications, and incorporate them in action. However, we do recognize that users develop their own unique readings, and that "ironic" appropriations of a hermeneutic support system are possible. The hermeneutic support system, like any other organizational process, can become an arena for acting out strategic power games.

Possible adverse implications of this sort from a hermeneutic support system are highlighted by Orlikowski's (1991) insightful analysis of information technology and forms of organization and control. By making transparent hitherto implicit understanding and thought processes, users of a hermeneutic inquiry system may make themselves vulnerable for a deeper, more repressive and embedded means of control, through electronic surveillance of their knowledge representations. Furthermore, the rules for reflection embodied in Spider in the form of creating cognitive maps could become reified and taken for granted as a fixed routine. It could lead to a situation where users cannot effectively engage in reflection without utilizing the reflection tool and hence without invoking these particular rules and routines of reflection. This fusion of rules and means of production can routinize the very act of reflection, leading to an inner contradiction. This can serve to reinforce existing structures of legitimation, and actually inhibit the sense making that a hermeneutic support system is designed to encourage.

Individual and group characteristics can also influence the appropriation process. Factors such as individual cognitive styles (Hunt et al. 1989), and information overload (Schroeder et al. 1967) can affect how the system is used, or what features are used. We began this chapter with the observation that people in organizations are induced to oversimplify their cognition, and proposed that the structured layers of interpretation in a hermeneutic support system can enable richer forms of cognition and communication. But, users may not be able to create cognitive maps. They may get overwhelmed by the information processing burden involved in scanning multiple cognitive maps, may stop updating their cognitive maps or exchanging them, or may decide to selectively use only a few features of the system and leave its full potential unrealized.

The creation and exchange of cognitive maps in this environment of layered context opens up a wide array of research possibilities. One interesting area of exploration centers around complicating the thinking practices in organizations, and the need to overcome inertial forces of "schema perseverance." Schemas are hypothesized as cognitive structures (Bartlett 1932, Markus 1977, Taylor and Crocker 1981) and cognitive maps can be viewed as a form of schema representations (Weick 1990, Weick and Bougon 1986). Schemas are often portrayed as relatively enduring structures, impervious to change and disproof (Ross 1977, Scotland and Cannon 1972) that can result in dysfunctional consequences such as groupthink (Janis 1972) and organizational decline (Barr et al. 1992). There have been repeated calls for organizations to find new structures and mechanisms to help reduce schema perseverance (Clark 1975, Kilmann et al. 1976), and complicate managers' thinking practices so that they develop multiple and richer views of their environments (Weick 1990).

A principal research question would then be: Can the creation and exchange of cognitive maps overcome the problem of schema perseverance and result in complexification of understanding as expressed in higher levels of integrative complexity (Schroeder et al. 1967) or tolerance for ambiguity (Lorsch and Morse 1974)? A related question would be: Under what conditions will actors change their old problem representations and create, maintain, and apply more complex representations signifying a complexification of understanding (Weick 1990)? Such conditions can be examined at the individual and/or the group level, can entail factors such as cognitive styles and cognitive modes (Hammond 1988), or can include affective considerations in the form of trust and cooperation (Gibb 1978, Zand 1972).

Another major question is whether individuals can in fact create interpretations of their situation using cognitive maps. Our experience to date suggests that only about a third of the managers in our project feel fluid and comfortable in creating them from scratch as a way of representing their thoughts. Some guidance from more experienced map makers who interview managers and help them to create initial maps that the managers can start working with may be necessary.

Ultimately, the real test of success for a hermeneutic inquiring system is the ability of the actors in a distributed cognition community to coordinate their independent actions toward organizationally beneficial outcomes. In the Spider project, we hope to track the process of distributed cognition and assess the actors' ability to coordinate the product planning process and to improve the quality and accuracy of their forecasts. The Spider system is but one interpretation of the design principles we have developed. We invite others to make their interpretations so that we might open our horizons to theirs.

Information technology has for too long been used to replicate familiar features and functions of organizations. If we are to truly take advantage of the possibilities of information technologies for supporting new forms of organizing, decision making, and managing, there is a need for invention of alternatives. Business schools will need to adopt more of the laboratory orientation of engineering schools. Such a laboratory orientation would legitimize invention, using emerging information technologies to construct and experiment with new organizational forms. We see our work on distributed cognition as one example of the efforts at invention we have in mind, and look forward to a varied and increased set of other efforts in the future.

ACKNOWLEDGMENTS

This work has been supported by National Science Foundation Grant #IRI-9015526 and Digital Equipment Corporation Grant #1111. The authors are equal contributors to this chapter and gratefully acknowledge the helpful suggestions by Scott Poole, Jim Meindl, and two anonymous reviewers.

REFERENCES

Ackoff, R. L. (1967), "Management Misinformation Systems," *Management Science*, 14, 4, 147-156.

Anthony, R. N. (1965), *Planning and Control: A Framework for Analysis*, Cambridge, MA: Harvard GSBA.

Argyris, C. (1982), *Reasoning, Learning, and Action*, San Francisco: Jossey-Bass.

——— and D. Schön (1978), *Organizational Learning: A Theory of Action Approach*, Reading, MA: Addison Wesley.

Axelrod, R. (1976), *Structure of Decision: The Cognitive Maps of Political Elites*, Princeton, NJ: Princeton University Press.

Barr, P. S., J. L. Stimpert, and A. S. Huff (1992), "Cognitive Change, Strategic Action, and Organizational Renewal," *Strategic Management Journal*, 12, 15-36.

Bartlett, F. C. (1932), *Remembering: A Study in Experimental and Social Psychology*, London: Cambridge University Press.

Bartunek, J. M., J. R. Gordon, and R. P. Weathersby (1983), "Developing Complicated Understanding in Administrators," *Academy of Management Review*, 8, 273-284.

——— and M. K. Moch (1987), "First-Order, Second-Order, and Third-Order Change and Organization Development Interventions: A Cognitive Approach," *Journal of Applied Behavioral Science*, 23, 4, 483-500.

Blumer, H. (1969), *Symbolic Interaction: Perspective and Method*, Englewood Cliffs, NJ: Prentice Hall.

Boland, R. J. (1979), "Control, Causality, and Information System Requirements," *Accounting, Organization, and Society*, 4, 259-272.

——— (1991), "Information System Use as a Hermeneutic Process," in H. E. Nissen, H. K. Klein, and R. Hirscheim (Eds.), *Information Systems Research: Contemporary Approaches and Emergent Traditions,* Amsterdam, The Netherlands: North-Holland—Elsevier Science.

——— (1993), "Accounting and the Interpretive Act," *Accounting, Organizations, and Society,* 18, 2/3, 125-146.

Bougon, M. K., K. E. Weick, and D. Binkhorst (1977), "Cognition in Organizations: An Analysis of the Utrecht Jazz Orchestra," *Administrative Science Quarterly,* 22, 606-639.

Bush, V. (1945), "As We Think," *Atlantic Monthly,* 176: 101-108.

Cheng, C., C. W. Holsapple, and A. B. Whinston (1992), "Reputation, Learning and Coordination in Distributed Decision-Making Contexts," *Organization Science,* 3, 2, 275-297.

Churchman, C. W. (1971), *The Design of Inquiring Systems,* New York: Basic Books.

Clark, P. (1975), "Organizational Design: A Review of Key Problems," *Administration and Society,* 7, 213-256.

Conklin, J. (1987), "Hypertext: An Introduction and Survey," *IEEE Computers,* 20, 17-41.

Daft, R. L. and R. H. Lengel (1984), "Information Richness: A New Approach to Managerial Behavior and Organization Design," in L. L. Cummings and B. M. Staw (Eds.), *Research in Organizational Behavior,* 6, Greenwich, CT: JAI, 191-233.

Davis, G. B. and M. H. Olson (1985), *Management Information Systems,* New York: McGraw-Hill.

Demski, J. (1980), *Information Analysis,* Reading, MA: Addison-Wesley.

DeSanctis, G. and R. B. Gallupe (1987), "A Foundation for the Study of Group Decision Support Systems," *Management Science,* 33, 589-609.

Dougherty, D. (1992), "Interpretive Barriers to Successful Product Innovation in Large Firms," *Organization Science,* 3, 2, 179-202.

Drucker, P. (1988), "The Coming of the New Organization," *Harvard Business Review,* January-February, 45-53.

Dykstra, E. A. and R. P. Carasik (1991), "Structure and Support in Cooperative Environments: The Amsterdam Conversation Environment," *International Journal of Man-Machine Studies,* 34, 419-434.

Eden, C. (1988), "Cognitive Mapping," *European Journal of Operations Research,* 13, 1-13.

——— (1992), "On the Nature of Cognitive Maps," *Journal of Management Studies,* 29, 3, 261-265.

———, C. Jones, and D. Sims (1979), *Thinking in Organizations,* New York: Macmillan.

Eisenberg, E. M. and S. R. Phillips (1991), "Miscommunications in Organizations," in N. Coupland, H. Giles, and J. M. Wiemann (Eds.), *Miscommunications and Problematic Talk,* Newbury Park, CA: Sage, 244-258.

Eisenhardt, K. M. (1989), "Making Fast Strategic Decisions in High-Velocity Environments," *Academy of Management Journal,* 32, 3, 543-576.

Emery, F. E. and E. L. Trist (1965), "The Causal Texture of Organizational Environments," *Human Relations,* 18, 21-32.

Eveland, J. D. and T. K. Bikson (1987), "Evolving Electronic Communication Networks: An Empirical Assessment," *Office, Technology, and People,* 3, 103-128.

Feldman, M. S. and J. G. March (1981), "Information in Organizations as Signal and Symbol," *Administrative Science Quarterly,* 26, 171-186.

Feltham, G. and J. Demski (1970), "Use of Models in Information Review," *Accounting Review,* 623-640.

Flores, F., M. Graves, B. Hartfield, and T. Winograd (1988), "Computer Systems and the Design of Organizational Interaction," *ACM Transactions on Office Information Systems,* 6, 153-172.

Gadamer, H. G. (1975), *Truth and Method,* New York: Seabury.

——— (1976), *Philosophical Hermeneutics,* Berkeley: University of California Press.

——— (1981), *Reason in the Age of Science,* Cambridge, MA: MIT Press.

Gibb, R. (1978), *Trust: A New View of Personal and Organizational Development,* Ramona, CA: Guild of Tutors Press.

Giddens, A. (1979), *Central Problems in Social Theory,* London: Macmillan.

Givon, T. (1989), *Mind, Code and Context: Essays in Pragmatics,* Hillsdale, NJ: Lawrence Erlbaum.

Habermas, J. (1981), *The Theory of Communicative Action,* Boston: Beacon.

Hammond, K. (1988), "Judgement and Decision Making in Dynamic Tasks," *Information and Decision Technologies,* 14, 3-14.

Hedberg, B.L.T., P. C. Nystrom, and W. H. Starbuck (1976), "Camping of Seesaws: Prescriptions for a Self-Designing Organization," *Administrative Science Quarterly,* 21, 41-65.

Huber, G. P. (1984), "The Nature and Design of Post-Industrial Organizations," *Management Science,* 30, 928-951.

——— (1990), "A Theory of the Effects of Advanced Information Technologies on Organizational Design, Intelligence, and Decision Making," *Academy of Management Review,* 15, 47-71.

——— (1991), "Organizational Learning: The Contributing Processes and the Literatures," *Organization Science,* 2, 88-115.

Huff, A. S. (1990), *Mapping Strategic Thought,* Chichester, UK: Wiley.

Hunt, R. G., F. J. Krzystofiak, J. R. Meindl, and A. M. Yousry (1989), "Cognitive Style and Decision Making," *Organizational Behavior and Human Decision Processes,* 44, 436-453.

Imai, K., I. Nonaka and H. Takeuchi (1985), "Managing the New Product Development Process: How Japanese Companies Learn and Unlearn," in K. Clark, R. Hayes, and C. Lorenz (Eds.), *The Uneasy Alliance,* Boston: Harvard Business School.

Janis, I. L. (1972), *Victims of Groupthink,* Boston: Houghton Mifflin.

——— (1989), *Crucial Decisions,* New York: Free Press.

Johnson-Lenz, P., and T. Johnson-Lenz (1991), "Post-Mechanistic Groupware Primitives: Rhythms, Boundaries, and Containers," *International Journal of Man-Machine Studies,* 34, 395-417.

Keen, P.G.W. and M. S. Scott Morton (1978), *Decision Support Systems: An Organizational Perspective,* Reading, MA: Addison-Wesley.

Kilmann, R. H., L. R. Pondy, and D. P. Slevin (Eds.) (1976), *The Management of Organization Design,* New York: North-Holland.

Levinson, S. C. (1983), *Pragmatics,* New York: Cambridge University Press.

Lorsch, J. W. and J. J. Morse (1974), *Organizations and Their Members: A Contingency Approach,* New York: Harper & Row.

Lyytinen, K. (1985), "Implications of Theories of Language for Information Systems," *MIS Quarterly,* 9, 1, 61-74.

——— (1987), "A Taxonomic Perspective of Information Systems Development: Theoretical Constructs and Recommendations," in R. J. Boland and R. A. Hirscheim (Eds.), *Critical Issues in Information Systems Research,* Chichester, UK: Wiley.

Malone, T., J. Yates, and R. Benjamin (1987), "Electronic Markets and Electronic Hierarchies," *Communications of the ACM,* 26, 430-444.

Malone, T. W., K. R. Grant, K. Lai, R. Rao, and D. A. Rosenblitt (1989), "The Information Lens: An Intelligent System for Information Sharing and Coordination," in M. H. Olson (Ed.), *Technological Support for Work Group Collaboration,* Hillsdale, NJ: Lawrence Erlbaum.

March, J. G. (1978), "Bounded Rationality, Ambiguity, and the Engineering of Choice," *Bell Journal of Economics,* 587-608.

Markus, H. (1977), "Self-Schemata and Processing Information about the Self," *Journal of Personality and Social Psychology,* 35, 63-78.

Meyer, A. D. (1991), "Visual Data in Organizational Research," *Organization Science,* 2, 218-236.

Mitroff, I. I. and L. R. Pondy (1974), "On the Organization of Inquiry: A Comparison of Radically Different Approaches to Policy Analysis," *Public Administration Review,* 471-479.

Nonaka, I. (1988), "Creating Organizational Order out of Chaos: Self-Renewal in Japanese Firms," *California Management Review,* Spring, 57-74.

Nystrom, P. C. and W. H. Starbuck (1984), "To Avoid Organizational Crises, Unlearn," *Organizational Dynamics,* 12, 4, 53-65.

Olson, G. M. and J. R. Olson (1991), "User-Centered Design of Collaboration Technology," *Journal of Organizational Computing,* 1, 61-83.

Orlikowski, W. J. (1991), "Integrated Information Environment or Matrix of Control? The Contradictory Implications of Information Technology," *Accounting, Management, and Information Technologies,* 1, 9-42.

——— and D. C. Gash (1991), "Changing Frames: Understanding Technological Change in Organizations," *Academy of Management Best Paper Proceedings,* 51st Annual Meeting, Miami Beach, FL, August.

——— and D. Robey (1991), "Information Technology and the Structuring of Organizations," *Information Systems Research,* 2, 143-169.

Paivio, A. (1986), *Mental Representations: A Dual Coding Approach,* New York: Oxford University Press.

Polanyi, M. (1967), *The Tacit Dimension,* Garden City, NJ: Doubleday.

Pondy, L. R. (1983), "Union of Rationality and Intuition in Management Action," in S. Srivastava (Ed.), *The Executive Mind,* San Francisco: Jossey-Bass, 169-191.

Poole, M. S. and G. DeSanctis (1990), "Understanding the Use of Group Decision Support Systems," in C. Steinfeld and J. Fulk (Eds.), *Organizations and Communication Technology,* Newbury Park, CA: Sage, 175-195.

Preston, A. M. (1991), "The 'Problem' in and of Management Information Systems," *Accounting, Management, and Information Technologies,* 1, 43-69.

Rorty, R. (1982), *Consequences of Pragmatism,* Minneapolis, MN: University of Minnesota Press.

——— (1985), "Epistemological Behaviorism and the Detranscendentalization of Analytic Philosophy," in R. Hollinger (Ed.), *Hermeneutics and Praxis,* Notre Dame, IN: University of Notre Dame Press, 89-121.

Ross, L. (1977), "The Intuitive Psychologist and his Shortcomings: Distortions in the Attribution Process," in L. Berkowitz (Ed.), *Advances in Experimental Social Psychology,* 10, New York: Academic Press.

Schein, E. (1989), "Reassessing the 'Divine Rights' of Managers," *Sloan Management Review,* 30, 63-68.

Schön, D. A. (1983), *The Reflective Practitioner,* New York: Basic Books.

Schroeder, H. M., M. J. Driver, and S. Streufert (1967), *Human Information Processing: Individuals and Groups Functioning in Complex Situations,* New York: Holt, Rinehart & Winston.

Scotland, E. and L. K. Cannon (1972), *Social Psychology: A Cognitive Approach,* Philadelphia: W. B. Saunders.

Sengupta, K. and D. Te'eni (1994), "Cognitive Feedback in Group Decision Support Systems," *MIS Quarterly.*

Silver, M. S. (1991), *Systems that Support Decision Makers: Description and Analysis*, Chichester, UK: Wiley.

Simon, H. A. (1977), *The New Science of Management Decision*, 2nd rev., Englewood Cliffs, NJ: Prentice Hall.

——— (1978), "Rationality as a Process and as Product of Thought," *American Economic Review*, 68, 1-16.

——— (1991), "Bounded Rationality and Organizational Learning," *Organization Science*, 2, 125-139.

Smith, K. K. (1984), "Rabbits, Lynxes, and Organizational Transitions," in J. R. Kimberly and R. E. Quinn (Eds.), *Managing Organizational Transitions*, Homewood, IL: Irwin, 267-294.

Sproull, L. and S. Kiesler (1986), "Reducing Social Context Cues: Electronic Mail in Organizational Communication," *Management Science*, 32, 1492-1512.

Stagner, R. (1977), "New Maps of Deadly Territories," *Contemporary Psychology*, 22, 547-549.

Stamper, R. (1987), "Semantics," in R. J. Boland and R. A. Hirscheim (Eds.), *Critical Issues in Information Systems Research*, Chichester, UK: Wiley, 43-78.

Starbuck, W. H. (1983), "Organizations as Action Generators," *American Sociological Review*, 48, 91-102.

——— and B. L. T. Hedberg (1977), "Saving an Organization from a Stagnating Environment," in H. Thorelli (Ed.), *Strategy + Structure = Performance*, Bloomington, IN: Indiana University Press.

——— and F. J. Milliken (1988), "Executives' Perceptual Filters: What They Notice and How They Make Sense," in D. Hambrick (Ed.), *The Executive Effect: Concepts and Methods for Studying Top Managers*, Greenwich, CT: JAI.

——— and J. Webster (1991), "When Is Play Productive?" *Accounting, Management, and Information Technologies*, 1, 71-90.

Streufert, S. and R. W. Swezey (1986), *Complexity, Managers, and Organizations*, Orlando, FL: Academic Press.

Tatar, D. G., G. Foster, and D. G. Bobrow (1991), "Design for Conversation: Lessons from Cognoter," *International Journal of Man-Machine Studies*, 34, 185-209.

Taylor, C. (1971), "Interpretation and the Sciences of Man," *Review of Metaphysics*, 3-51.

Taylor, S. E. and J. Crocker (1981), "Schematic Bases of Social Information Processing," in E. T. Higgins, C. P. Herman, and M. P. Zanna (Eds.), *Social Cognition: The Ontario Symposium in Personality and Social Psychology*, Hillsdale, NJ: Lawrence Erlbaum.

Te'eni, D. (1990), "Direct Manipulation as a Source of Cognitive Feedback: A Human-Computer Experiment with a Judgment Task," *International Journal of Man-Machine Studies*, 33, 453-466.

——— (1992), "Analysis and Design of Process Feedback in Information Systems: Old and New Wine in New Bottles," *Accounting, Management, and Information Technologies*, 2, 1-18.

Vygotsky, L. S. (1962), *Thought and Language*, edited and translated by E. Hanfmann and G. Vakar, Cambridge: MIT Press.

Walsh, J. P. and G. R. Ungson (1991), "Organizational Memory," *Academy of Management Review*, 16, 57-91.

Weick, K. E. (1979), *The Social Psychology of Organizing*, (2nd ed.), Reading, MA: Addison-Wesley.

——— (1990), "Cognitive Processes in Organizations," in L. L. Cummings and B. M. Staw (Eds.), *Information and Cognition in Organizations*, Greenwich, CT: JAI.

——— (1991), "The Nontraditional Quality of Organizational Learning," *Organization Science*, 2, 116-124.

——— and M. K. Bougon (1986), "Organizations as Cognitive Maps: Charting Ways to Success and Failure," in H. Sims and D. Gioia (Eds.), *The Thinking Organization,* San Francisco: Jossey-Bass.

Weick, K. and D. Meader (1991), "Sense Making and Group Support Systems," in L. Jessup and L. Valacich (Eds.), *Group Support Systems,* New York: Macmillan.

Winograd, T. and F. Flores (1986), *Understanding Computers and Cognition: A New Foundation for Design,* Norwood, NJ: Ablex.

Zand, D. E. (1972), "Trust and Managerial Problem Solving," *Administrative Science Quarterly,* 229-239.

Part III

COGNITION AND ORGANIZING

9

Organizational Culture and Individual Sensemaking

A Schema-Based Perspective

STANLEY G. HARRIS

Organizational culture encompasses both individual- and group-level phenomena. However, to date, the individual-level dynamics of organizational culture have remained relatively neglected. This chapter addresses this neglect by focusing on culture's manifestation in individuals' sensemaking structures and processes. Building off the social cognition literature, I propose that organizational culture's influence on individual sensemaking is revealed in the operation of a patterned system of organization-specific schemas. Schemas refer to the cognitive structures in which an individual's knowledge is retained and organized. In addition to being knowledge repositories, schemas also direct information acquisition and processing. They guide answering the questions central to sensemaking efforts: "What or who is it?" "What are its implications; what does it mean?" and "How should I respond?"

After a brief review of schema theory, the categories of schema knowledge relevant to understanding sensemaking in organizations and the cultural influences on their emergence are examined. The conscious and unconscious operation of these schemas in the actual process of making sense of organizational stimuli is framed within a schema-directed, intrapsychic, mental dialogue perspective on social cognition. Specifically, I propose that in the social setting of organizations, individuals make sense out of their experiences based in large part on the outcomes of contrived mental dialogues between themselves (e.g., "I think it means this and I would be inclined toward this response") and other contextually

This chapter originally appeared in *Organization Science,* Vol. 5, No. 3, August 1994.

relevant (past or present; real or imagined) individuals or groups (e.g., "What would my boss and peers think about this? What would they want me to do?"). The content of the argument provided for others is guided by the individual's schemas for those others. I close the chapter by discussing the ways in which this schema-based perspective enhances our understanding of the individual experiences of cultural sharing, subcultural boundaries, and psychological attachment.

(ORGANIZATIONAL CULTURE; SCHEMA; SENSEMAKING; MENTAL DIALOGUE)

> As the social world under any aspect whatsoever remains a very complicated cosmos of human activities, we can always go back to the "forgotten man" of the social sciences, to the actor in the social world whose doing and feeling lies at the bottom of the whole system. (Schutz 1964, pp. 6-7)

Schutz's observation has important implications for the present status of organizational culture theory and research. Generally defined as the shared beliefs, values, and assumptions that guide sensemaking and action in organizations (Ott 1989), organizational culture encompasses both individual- and group-level phenomena (Louis 1985a). As Van Maanen and Barley (1985) observed, "While a group is necessary to invent and sustain culture, culture can be carried only by individuals" (p. 35). However, the bulk of scholarly attention has been devoted to organizational culture's group-level manifestations while its individual-level manifestations have remained relatively neglected. Examples of group-level topics receiving a great deal of attention include symbolic mechanisms such as language, stories, myths, and ceremonies by which an organization's culture is expressed and maintained (e.g., Martin 1982, Trice and Beyer 1984); the demarcation of organizational subcultures (e.g., Louis 1985b, Van Maanen and Barley, 1985); organizational culture as a form of control (e.g., Ouchi 1980, Ray 1986); culture strength (e.g., Kilmann et al. 1985); culture's implications for organizational performance (e.g., Denison 1984, Saffold 1988); and the management and change of organizational culture (e.g., Lundberg 1985, Sathe 1985b). The individual-level dynamics implied by these group-level topics (e.g., culture as a mechanism of control ultimately implies the control of individual behavior) generally remain unexamined and rarely are they explicitly examined in their own right. Notable exceptions include the literatures on organizational entry and socialization (e.g., Louis 1980; Van Maanen 1976), the influence of founders' and leaders' beliefs, values, and cognitive styles on the emergence, maintenance, and change of cultures (e.g., Kets de Vries and Miller 1986, Schein 1985), and individual acts of nonadherence to cultural norms (Golden 1992).

Given that organizational culture is ultimately manifested in and maintained by the sensemaking efforts and actions of individuals, neglecting its individual-level manifestations hobbles efforts to fully understand and appreciate the concept. A perspective which provides a clearer specification of the dynamics involved in culture's shaping of *common* sensemaking *across* a set of *individuals* is needed. Questions such as "How does organizational culture influence the sensemaking activities of individuals?" "How are cultural meanings manifested at the individual level?" and "How is cultural 'sharing' experienced by individuals?" demand more attention. Exploring the nature of the individual-level dynamics and experiences of organizational culture is the purpose of this chapter.

The facilitation of shared sensemaking and social cognition within the organization context lies at the heart of most treatments of organizational culture (Barley 1983). Therefore, it follows that social cognition theory and research, with its focus on individuals' interpretations of the social world, offers a useful perspective from which to explore the cultural influences on individual sensemaking. Building off this literature, I propose that the individual-level manifestations and experiences of organizational culture are revealed in the operation of a patterned system of organization-specific schemas held by organizational members. Specifically, I suggest that individuals' organization-specific schemas are the repository of cultural knowledge and meanings and the source of the consensual sensemaking characteristic of culture. In addition, I suggest that the activation and interaction of these schemas in the social context of the organization creates the cultural experience for individuals. This perspective serves to locate sensemaking phenomena at the individual level yet connects them back into the sociocultural reality of the organization. The remainder of this chapter is devoted to articulating this perspective.

AN OVERVIEW OF SCHEMA THEORY

In their intensive review of the social cognition literature, Markus and Zajonc (1985) conclude that schema theory is the most useful and pervasive perspective on the mechanics of social cognition. Not surprisingly, many organizational scholars (e.g., Gioia and Poole 1984, Lord and Foti 1986, Martin 1982, Weick 1979b) have employed schema theory to frame examination of cognitive issues within organizational settings. Some scholars have even recognized, albeit cursorily, the advantages of viewing organizational culture in terms of schemas. For example, Bartunek and Moch (1987) refer to "organizational schemas" as the essence of culture. Similarly, Louis and Sutton (1991) define culture as "shared schemas." However, none of these applications of schema theory to the context of organizations explicitly articulate in any detail the schematic nature of culturally influenced sense-making in organizations. Before offering this articulation, the definition, functions, and dynamic nature of schemas are reviewed.

Schemas Defined

Schemas refer to the dynamic, cognitive knowledge structures regarding specific concepts, entities, and events used by individuals to encode and represent incoming information efficiently (Markus 1977). Schemas are typically conceptualized as subjective theories derived from one's experiences about how the world operates (Markus and Zajonc 1985) that guide perception, memory, and inference (Fiske and Taylor 1984). For example, one's "college class" schema would include knowledge regarding typical attributes (e.g., professor, students, classroom, reading material, and tests) and the relationships between those attributes (e.g., the professor assigns reading material and administers tests to the students) (e.g., Fiske and Taylor 1984).

The Functions of Schemas

Schemas serve as mental maps which enable individuals to traverse and orient themselves within their experiential terrain (Louis 1983, Weick 1979a) and guide interpretations of the past and present and expectations for the future. As Neisser (1976) and Weick (1979b) observed, schemas guide the search for, acquisition of, and processing of information and guide subsequent behavior in response to that information. Lord and Foti (1986) note that "schemas help reduce the information-processing demands associated with social activities by providing a ready-made knowledge system for interpreting and storing information about others" (p. 38). Summarizing research in the area, Taylor and Crocker (1981) identified seven functions of schemas: They (1) provide a structure against which experience is mapped, (2) direct information encoding and retrieval from memory, (3) affect information processing efficiency and speed, (4) guide filling gaps in the information available, (5) provide templates for problem solving, (6) facilitate the evaluation of experience, and (7) facilitate anticipations of the future, goal setting, planning, and goal execution. The following example drawn from the research of Bransford and Johnson (1972) highlights several of these functions:

> The procedure is actually quite simple. First, you arrange things into different groups. Of course, one pile may be sufficient depending on how much there is to do. . . . It is important not to overdo things. That is, it is better to do too few things at once than too many. In the short run this may not seem important, but complications can easily arise. A mistake can be expensive as well. At first the whole procedure will seem complicated. Soon, however, it will become just another facet of life. (p. 722)

What was the passage about? How much of it can you recall? Now reread the passage knowing that its title was "Washing Clothes." When provided with this title, a "washing clothes schema" is evoked and individuals more easily understand the passage and are better able to recall it later. As an interesting contrast, reread the passage considering the title "Organizing Receipts for Tax Purposes." As a result of cuing a different schema, the meaning distilled is vastly different.

As this example demonstrates, the perceptions and interpretations of events and information are shaped by the schemas applied to them. As Taylor and Crocker (1981) note, "When a stimulus configuration is encountered in the environment, it is matched against a schema, and the ordering and relations among the elements of the schema are imposed on the elements of the stimulus configuration" (p. 94). Schemas have been conceptualized as outlines of expectations with certain ranges of acceptability for the values of those expectations (e.g., Rumelhart 1984). If information is missing (e.g., nothing in the clothes washing passage from Bransford and Johnson mentioned choosing water temperature), default values may be inserted (e.g., individuals may recall water temperature information where none existed). This feature of schema-based sensemaking serves to "fill in [information] when there is too little and allow the perceiver to go beyond the information given" (Markus and Zajonc 1985, p. 143) so as to offer a more "complete" experience than would otherwise be possible. However, it also increases the potential for making incorrect assumptions about the stimulus. So while schemas make sensemaking possible, they also may lead to perceptual mistakes.

Schema Dynamism

In addition to guiding the processing of information, schemas may be modified as a result of that information. Schemas are expanded and elaborated as they incorporate new information. This type of schema change has been labeled "first-order" change by Bartunek and Moch (1987). Over time, as more stimulus-relevant information is encountered, the schema for that stimulus becomes more complex, abstract, and organized (Fiske and Taylor

1984). The development of expertise in the form of highly elaborate schemas resulting from the incorporation of information from many experiences with a particular issue or area of concern is one example of this form of schema modification (e.g., Prietula and Simon 1989). Sometimes, however, information is confronted which conflicts with the knowledge in a person's schemas. Information conflicting with a schema will either be ignored as an aberration, be cognitively recast to fit current schemas, or generate either schema modification or the addition of a schema subcategory (Lord and Foti 1986). Bartunek and Moch (1987) have labeled the fundamental alteration of a schema "second-order" change.

It is important to recognize that the schema-directed nature of the perceptual process lessens the frequency with which schema-inconsistent information is discovered and made conscious. The very nature of schemas act to ensure that drastic challenges to their validity seldom arise. Since schemas direct searches for information, it is likely that the information uncovered will reinforce those schemas. In addition, because schemas represent general knowledge, "No single example fits the schema perfectly, but most fit well enough" (Fiske and Taylor 1984, p. 171). While schemas emerge to facilitate making sense of the world, they can also blind individuals to features of the world that threaten the validity of those schemas or operate outside their purview (Krefting and Frost 1985). Lorsch (1985) refers to this phenomenon as "strategic myopia."

THE MANIFESTATION OF CULTURE IN INDIVIDUAL SENSEMAKING

The brief summary of schema theory offered above should demonstrate that it has important implications for expanding our understanding of sensemaking in organizations and the role of organizational culture in guiding that sensemaking. In the sections that follow, a schema-based perspective on culturally guided sensemaking is developed. Specifically, I outline the categories of schemas central to cultural concerns, examine the process by which those schemas come to be similar across organizational members, examine the cultural influences on schema salience, and suggest that much of the individual experience of culture is a product of an intrapsychic mental dialogue between self and culturally relevant others.

Culturally Relevant Schemas

Given that knowledge about any stimulus can be schematized (Rumelhart 1984), individuals have at their disposal myriad schemas. Which of these are relevant to understanding organizational culture? Because social knowledge is generally contextually bound (Holyoak and Gordon 1984), organization-context-specific schemas will obviously be of most relevance. In their discussion of schemas about other individuals, Cantor et al. (1982) noted that those schemas can have context specific variants (e.g., a schema about a friend versus a schema about a friend out with the guys) which are more elaborate, vivid, and concrete than their noncontext-specific counterparts. These "in-situation" schemas represent a merger of the schema for the stimulus domain with the schema for the situation or context in which it is encountered (e.g., Lord and Foti 1986). Following this line of reasoning, I propose that "in-organization" forms of individuals' schemas are particularly central to developing a schema-based understanding of organizational culture. Within the organizational context, individuals encounter social entities (e.g., themselves, others, and organizational groupings), events and situations, and nonsocial objects and concepts that must be perceived and responded to. Building off the categorization schemes of others (Lord and Foti 1986, Taylor and Crocker 1981), five categories of in-organization schemas seem to capture the range of knowledge needed for these sensemaking efforts: self, person, organization, object/concept, and event.

Self Schemas. Self-in-organization schemas refer to individuals' theories and generalizations regarding aspects of themselves in the organizational context such as personality, values, roles, and behavior (e.g., "I am a white female accountant who is honest and hardworking and who values a balanced life between work and family") (Fiske and Taylor 1984, Markus 1977). As Mead (1934) noted, much of what an individual comes to define as self is a reflection of the reactions of others to the individual. Therefore, while focused inward, these schemas also are social creations. Self schemas help direct individuals' reactions to organizational stimuli and decide upon responses consistent with self. For example, an accountant who viewed herself as being honest would refer to this schema knowledge when deciding how to react to a client's request to help "cook the books."

Person Schemas. Person-in-organization schemas are organized memories, impressions, and learned expectations regarding the traits, goals, behaviors, and preferences of particular individuals (e.g., "my boss is very independent, supportive, intelligent, and extroverted"), groupings of people (e.g., "management can't be trusted"), and organizational roles (e.g., "labor leaders should work to maximize benefits for their constituents") (Fiske and Taylor 1984, Lord and Foti 1986). Developing schemas of others is important because their behavior shapes the reality one is trying to understand. Therefore, in addition to guiding the assignment of individuals into appropriate schematic categories (e.g., "she is in management") much of the content of person schemas will be devoted to summarizing knowledge regarding the beliefs, values, and likely behaviors of others (i.e., educated guesses regarding the schemas by which others' own sensemaking and behavior is determined). Others likely to be particularly influential in organizations, and therefore schematized, are important role senders (Katz and Kahn 1978) and shapers of an individual's experiences including organizational leaders, peers, and subordinates.

Organization Schemas. A subset of person schemas, organization schemas, are particularly central to understanding how the culture of an organization is embodied cognitively in individuals. For example, Mead (1934) made consideration of the attitudes of "other" a central feature of his theory of the development of self. Of particular importance to Mead's argument is an individual's perspective on the attitudes of "generalized others": the communities or social groups within which the individual is embedded. Knowledge regarding this generalized other corresponds to organization schemas (cf. Bartunek and Moch 1987), and are particularly central to the perspective being developed here. Organization schemas refer to knowledge and impressions regarding organizational groupings (or subgroupings) as entities (e.g., "headquarters") somewhat abstracted from their individual members (e.g., "the executives at headquarters"). While individuals have schemas for organizations of which they are not members (e.g., "McDonald's values service consistency"), of particular interest here are individuals' schemas for the organizations and organized social groups of which they are members. These organization schemas correspond most closely to an individual's knowledge of his or her organization's culture (or subunit's subculture) (cf. Bartunek and Moch 1987).

Object/Concept Schemas. Object/concept-in-organization schemas refer to knowledge about stimuli which are not inherently social such as big offices with corner windows or the meaning of "quality" or "participation." These schemas are relevant for understanding culture because they guide the interpretation of physical and verbal cultural artifacts (cf. Lundberg 1985). Since organizational communication is central to sensemaking efforts, concept schemas facilitate this communication by providing a framework within which verbal terms can be understood.

Event Schemas. Event-in-organization schemas capture knowledge about social contexts, situations, encounters, and events such as departmental parties, firings, and customer complaints. Scripts are the most frequently studied form of event schemas. Scripts contain knowledge of expected event sequences and appropriate behavior in specific situations (Gioia and Manz 1985, Gioia and Poole 1984, Lord and Kernan 1987, Martin 1982). For example, one's script for a staff meeting might specify the following: one should arrive on time, greet participants, pleasantly joke until the boss takes charge and starts the meeting, listen to presentations, answer questions, ask polite questions, and pleasantly bid farewell after the boss adjourns the meeting.

In addition to capturing scripted knowledge, event schemas also serve to guide interpretation of behavioral artifacts such as ceremonies and rituals. Such artifacts are cultural expressions which serve to reinforce certain meanings. For example, a weekly staff meeting could be interpreted as a control maneuver or as a team building opportunity. The schemas attached to such events are an important aspect of any examination of organizational culture.

Finally, it is important to note that these event schemas can be overlaid on other schema categories to create more specific in-situation schemas (e.g., "In private, my boss is very receptive to bad news but he hates to get it during the weekly staff meeting") than the in-organization ones described earlier. Organizational situations for which in-situation schemas are likely to exist include those circumstances captured in event schemas (e.g., staff meetings, sales calls, strikes, etc.).

Taken together, the schemas described above capture the range of information individuals use to make sense out of organizational life. From a cultural perspective, they serve as individuals' repository for organizational culture knowledge including the values and beliefs attributed to various individuals and collectivities, appropriate behaviors for various situations, traditional ways of doing things, reinforcement contingencies, peer and normative pressures, role knowledge, the meaning ascribed to verbal, physical, and behavioral artifacts, and the defining characteristics of the organization and its subgroups. However, the actual presence of culture requires more than sharing categories of schemas; it requires that the content and relative salience of those schemas be similar across organizational members. The process by which members' schemas come to bear a resemblance to one another is addressed next.

The Emergence of Schema Similarity

How do an individual's schemas come to resemble those of other organizational members? In part, the answer rests on realizing that all members of the community have a vested interest in the establishment of common meanings so that a predictable social order is possible. Individuals value the ability to predict and understand their circumstances that a shared conception of reality makes possible (cf. Sutton and Kahn 1987). As Schein (1985) notes: "The bulk of the content of a given culture will concern itself primarily with those areas of life where objective verification is not possible and where, therefore, a social definition becomes the only basis for judgment" (pp. 90-91).

Individuals' schemas become similar as a result of shared experience and shared exposure to social cues regarding others' constructions of reality. Since schemas are summaries of experiential knowledge, sharing experiential space and time and the challenges posed by communicating, interacting and solving common problems facilitates and encourages the development of similar schemas (e.g., Schein 1985). Given that members of organizational subgroups are likely to share more immediate experiences with each other than with members of the entire organization, it is not surprising that the schemas which emerge in such subgroups (subcultures) tend to be more specific, more well-defined, and more generally shared than those emerging across an organization's entire membership (e.g., Louis 1985b, Van Maanen and Barley 1985).

Schema similarity is also shaped by the social construction of reality (Berger and Luckman 1966) that occurs through the processing of social information (Salancik and Pfeffer 1978). Through social comparison, individuals gain important information regarding reality by observing the responses of others sharing that reality (Berger and Luckman 1966). For example, an individual's schema for the event of a complaining customer is influenced by witnessing how others construct similar events. In summarizing the social information processing perspective, Salancik and Pfeffer (1978) note that the social environment "provides a direct construction of meaning through guides to socially acceptable beliefs, attitudes, and needs, and acceptable reasons for action" and "focuses an individual's attention on certain information, making that information more salient, and provides expectations concerning individual behavior and the logical consequences of such behavior" (p. 227).

Similarly, Mead (1934) suggests that meaning emerges through social communication. This communication can either be explicit and direct (e.g., "Hey buddy, you can't trust management as far as you can throw them") or symbolic and indirect (e.g., a new hire is ostracized at breaks because of fraternizing with management). Over time and through social information processing, organizational members come to develop similar schemas. As individuals' schemas become more similar, the social information they provide others becomes more focused, clear, consistent, and persuasive. As a result, the group's shared schema knowledge becomes somewhat self-perpetuating.

It is important to note another way social information processing influences schema acquisition. In the process of providing social cues to others, individuals indirectly reveal themselves to those others. In the process of receiving cues about the meaning of organizational stimuli from others, knowledge about those others *and* about their preferred constructions of reality (i.e., their schemas) is gained and used to build and elaborate a schematic representation of them (cf. Pfeffer 1981, Pondy 1983). For example, watching a coworker deal very pleasantly with an irate customer would lead one to infer that customers, regardless of their demeanor, should be treated well. However, hearing the coworker complain after the encounter that "I would have liked to punch that guy's lights out," would shape one's schema of the coworker: "He treats customers well because he feels he has to, rather than wants to."

Culturally Influenced Schema Salience and Activation

In addition to schema similarity, organizational culture implies that some schemas are more salient and more likely to be activated (cued for use) than others. At the most basic level, the interpretation of organizational stimuli—concepts, events, people, and groups—is guided by the schemas specific to those stimuli. The appropriate schema is activated because the key aspects of the stimulus match a schema's main attributes (e.g., seeing people in suits sitting around a conference table has key elements which match most people's "business meeting" schema and therefore that schema is activated). However, many organization stimuli have many possible meanings and may have features that match diverse schemas. For example, depending upon one's perspective, a given strategic event can be perceived as either a threat or an opportunity (cf. Dutton and Jackson 1987). In such circumstances, schemas that are salient are more likely to be cued for sensemaking use (e.g., a person looking for threats is more likely to find them). Schema salience and activation is determined in several culturally sensitive ways.

First, given that schemas can be nested in or cross-reference other schemas (Taylor and Crocker 1981), schemas currently activated can increase the likelihood that others will be salient or activated. For example, one's schema for the event of a meeting would direct activation of schemas for the other meeting participants. Some schemas, particularly context-specific schemas such as organizational schemas and event schemas, are likely to be influential in cuing other schemas (Markus and Zajonc 1985). This is particularly important for understanding culture. For example, one's organization schema is likely to make salient other schemas seen as being of central concern to the organization (e.g., quality, customers, etc.). In fact, one of the main ways culture is reflected in the individual act of sensemaking may be the pattern of schema salience across organizational members: To what do they attend and toward what interpretations are they biased?

Second, social information, particularly labels offered by others, has a profound impact on schema activation (Dutton and Jackson 1987, Lord and Maher 1991, Salancik and Pfeffer 1978). In this sense, verbal artifacts such as slogans to which people are exposed may encourage schema salience (e.g., signs throughout a workplace with safety information and messages will likely make safety-related schemas salient).

Third, one's motives and goals serve to make certain schemas more salient than others (Fiske and Taylor 1984). These motives and goals are captured in self schemas and shaped by the reinforcement contingencies summarized in person schemas and influenced by the culture of the organization. Several writers have recognized that reinforcement contingencies are an important artifact of an organization's culture (e.g., Ulrich 1984). Such contingencies hold sway over sensemaking because they shape schema salience. For example, a person in an organization which rewards quality craftsmanship is more likely to be attuned to quality-relevant issues.

A Mental Dialogue Perspective on Culturally Based Sensemaking

One major question regarding the application of schema theory to culturally based individual sensemaking remains unaddressed: How does schema-driven sensemaking occur? Schemas guide organizational sensemaking on two fundamental levels. First, they facilitate answering the question: "What or who is it?" (Taylor and Crocker 1981). In other words, schemas are used to categorize and thus identify stimuli (e.g., "it is a quality problem," "this is an informal performance evaluation session," or "she is a customer"). After categorization, the next step involves determining what the stimulus means so that a response can be formulated. In general, this search for meaning is egocentric (cf. Gray et al. 1985, Schutz 1964): "What should *I* pay attention to?" "Once noticed, what does this situation or event mean for *me?*" "What should *I* expect to happen next?" "Does anyone else have a stake in *my* reaction?" "What would any relevant others expect or want *me* to do?" "How would those relevant others respond in *my* situation?" and "What should *I* do in response?"

It is important to note that schema-guided sensemaking can occur relatively unconsciously or consciously (e.g., Gioia and Poole 1984, Louis and Sutton 1991). In relatively unconscious, automatic processing, schemas drive perception with little conscious intervention, choice, or required schema reconciliation (when more than one schema is activated). In conscious processing, some conscious schema manipulation, reflection, and reconciliation is required. The degree of conscious processing required is largely determined by the extent of experience with the stimulus domain: More experience is likely to facilitate more unconscious, tacit processing. Conscious, reflective processing is generally required in response to novel stimuli (e.g., a new boss), novel features of familiar stimuli (e.g., a new work-team member), or schema-inconsistent information (e.g., an accepted business practice leads to failure) (e.g., Louis and Sutton 1991). Given their inexperience in the organizational setting, organizational newcomers are particularly likely to engage in conscious, reflective sensemaking. However, over time, conscious, reflective sensemaking makes unconscious processing possible. This occurs as a result of elaborating the schema for the stimulus with information regarding the outcome of previous reflective cognition making it less necessary to engage in such cognition later on. I propose that this reflective, conscious cognition in process or as part of schematic memory reveals the schema-based dynamics of sensemaking.

The social cognition literature on schema theory has been most concerned with categorization issues and the structure of schemas. Little attention has been devoted to understanding the dynamics of social sensemaking, particularly the influence the social context has on that process (Schneider 1991). Therefore, to understand how schemas are consciously manipulated to make sense of organizational experiences, we must look beyond traditional schema theory. I propose employing a "mental debate" perspective. This perspective is articulated below.

Consistent with the social information processing (Salancik and Pfeffer 1978) and social construction of reality (Berger and Luckman 1966) views described earlier, Louis (1983) suggests that meaning is negotiated in organizations through "bargaining among alternative meanings differentially preferred by the various parties to an interaction" (p. 44). This negotiation occurs directly and indirectly. As Fiske and Taylor (1984) note, "Other people can influence a person's actions without even being present . . . our perceptions of others actually present and our imagination of their presence both predict behavior" (p. 8). While one's efforts to decide how to react to a customer's complaint will be directly shaped by the customer's actions and the actions of coworkers and supervisors present at the exchange (e.g., a supervisor may come over and offer assistance if an inappropriate response is made), it is the intrapsychic act of evoking the perspectives of others to guide cognition that is central to understanding individual sensemaking. Interestingly, several theorists (e.g., Mead 1934, Weick 1979a) have recognized the sensemaking centrality of individuals' ability to take the perspectives of others to guide intrapsychic debate regarding the construction of reality and behavioral decisions.

Mead (1934) argued that individuals define themselves and make behavioral decisions relative to the social world by engaging in internalized conversations between self and others. Such conversations require taking the perspectives of others. Of particular importance to Mead were the internalized conversations which individuals hold with generalized others: the community or social groups within which the individual is embedded. The generalized other's dialogue is directed by the individual's abstracted knowledge regarding the attitudes of the social group. As demonstrated in the following argument, Mead's theory is particularly relevant to understanding cultural influences on individual sensemaking:

> It is in the form of the generalized other that the social process influences the behavior of the individuals involved in it and carrying it on, i.e., that the community exercises control over the conduct of its individual members; for it is in this form that the social process or community enters as a determining factor into the individual's thinking. . . . And only through the taking by individuals of the attitude or attitudes of the generalized other toward themselves is the existence of a universe of discourse, as that system of common or social meanings which thinking presupposes at its context, rendered possible. (Mead 1934. p. 155)

Similarly, Weick (1979a) suggests that social cognition in organizations often involves contriving implicit conversations with "phantom others" (p. 67). He offered the following quote from Lofland (1976) to support this assertion:

> All encounters involve people in immediate interaction, but not all interactants need be in separate bodies. By means of memory, consciousness, and symbolization, humans summon particular past humans (more accurately, a residue composite of one) and composite categories of persons ("them," "my family," "the government," etc.) into the forefront of consciousness, taking account of what are projected to be their belief and action when dealing with a situation. No other person need physically be present for there to be social interaction in this sense. It is *social* interaction in that the individual is taking other person into account when constructing his own action. (p. 100)

This "mental dialogue" mode of social cognition offers a useful perspective on the process by which the broader cultural context of the organization manifests itself in the sensemaking efforts of organizational members. Specifically, I propose that in the social setting of organizations, individuals enact their experiences and choose to behave in response to those experiences based in large part on the outcomes of contrived mental dialogues between themselves and other contextually relevant (past or present, real or imagined) individuals or groups. This "mental dialogue" perspective on social cognition is consistent with the intersubjective weighing of personal attitudes and perceptions of norms in the creation of behavioral intentions described by Ajzen and Fishbein (1980). According to them, individuals' intentions to behave are based on a reconciliation of their personal attitudes with the perceived normative expectations of contextually relevant others. From a mental dialogue perspective, the arguments supplied for each of the parties to the conversation are basically the verbalization of normative and cultural pressures.

I also propose that an individual's schemas make it possible to take the various perspectives required to craft mental dialogues. The "I" perspective is supplied by an individual's self schemas. The perspectives of relevant others—S/he, They, My Organization, or My Subgroup—are abstracted from the person schemas specific to them. Consistent with social information processing models, this "mental conversation" treatment of social cognition helps identify how the normative pressures arising from the behaviors of others (resulting from their own organizational schemas) in an organization can influence an individual member's schema-driven cognition.

This mental dialogue process is likely to influence sensemaking in a relatively conscious and reflective manner when novel or unexpected social stimuli are encountered. The reflective dynamics of this process are most likely evident in the sensemaking endeavors of organizational newcomers (e.g., Louis 1980). Newcomers enter organizations with a wealth of schemas based upon their previous experiences. Through anticipatory socialization activities, they will also have some very general organization-specific schemas. Upon entering the organization, the newcomer's "newcomer" event schema will direct him or her to define relevant social actors and social groupings (i.e., "who is important here?") and to consider broadly the perceived social definitions and normative pressures emanating from them (i.e., "what do they believe, value, and want from me?") so as to inform person and self-schema creation and elaboration. The resultant schemas provide the perspectives from which mental dialogue-based introspection regarding meaning and action occurs. For example, a newcomer may hit upon an idea that would boost productivity. To determine how to act with regard to this idea, he will be compelled to consider his preferences (I) and the preferences of workgroup members (My Subgroup), supervisor (She), management (They), and the organizational entity (My Organization). This intrapsychic dialogue can reveal both agreement ("My supervisor would agree with me that this idea should be made public") and disagreement ("But my peers would be against such a pro-management activity, particularly one that would upset the status quo"). Such dialogue outcomes serve to elaborate the schema for the stimulus under consideration. For example, the newcomer's schema for production-improvement ideas would be elaborated by indicating that the supervisor's perspective agrees with his own while that of coworkers does not. In addition, the individual's mental resolution of any conflicts will also become part of schema knowledge (e.g., "Since I am the new kid on the block, I decided to keep the idea quiet in deference to my coworkers"). Many forms of conflict resolution are possible, even altering self schemas to create consonance with the perceived preferences of influential Others (Mead 1934).

As the newcomer gains more experience with various stimulus domains in the organization, develops more elaborate in-organization schemas, and conducts more mental dialogues, sensemaking for these domains begins to require less conscious effort. Conscious mental dialogue need not be evoked under several circumstances. For familiar or routine stimuli, the results of previous, conscious dialogues (conducted when the stimulus was not familiar or routine) which have been incorporated into the schema for the stimulus inform sensemaking in a relatively tacit, unconscious, and "effortless" manner. In particular, dialogue need not occur when previous dialogues regarding the stimulus have resulted in agreement between I and the other party or parties to the mental dialogue and that agreement has been included in the schema for the stimulus. I propose that these agreements generally lead to a "We" experience for that stimulus domain and that this "We" experience is used to elaborate the active schema. This treatment of We is similar to that of Schall (1983):

> As interacting participants organize by communicating, they evolve shared understandings around issues of common interest, and so develop a sense of the collective "we" (Harris and Cronen 1979), that is, of themselves as distinct social units doing things together in ways appropriate to those shared understandings of the "we." (p. 560)

Unconscious, tacit sensemaking is also possible for stimulus domains where previous mental dialogues resulted in disagreement. That disagreement must have been fully and permanently resolved and notation of this resolution added to the schema for the stimulus. Any remaining tension or conflict between mental parties, such as for "one time only" resolutions, will cue future dialogue. For example, in the example of the newcomer with an innovative idea, he chose to withhold it because of his newcomer status. As a result of this tentative resolution, any new ideas he has will have to be processed consciously. However, if his resolution had been less tentative ("I believe in improvements and will always share them with others even if they resist"), then making sense of new ideas would require relatively less conscious mediation.

Many organizational scholars have argued that organizational cultures are manifested along hierarchical levels demarcated by degrees of visibility and conscious awareness (e.g., Ott 1989, Sathe 1985a, Schein 1985). Most scholars employing a levels perspective suggest that the most fundamental level of organizational culture comprises the set of basic assumptions about organizational reality. It is clear from Schein's (1985) discussion of these basic assumptions that they correspond very well to the in-organization schemas whose sensemaking guidance has, over time, become more tacit and unconscious:

> When a solution to a problem works repeatedly, it comes to be taken for granted. What was once a hypothesis, supported by only a hunch or a value, comes gradually to be treated as a reality. . . . Basic assumptions . . . have become so taken for granted that one finds little variation within a cultural unit. . . . What I am calling basic assumptions are congruent with what Argyris has identified as "theories-in-use," the implicit assumptions that actually guide behavior, that tell group members: how to perceive, think about, and feel about things. . . . (p. 18)

It is important to note that conscious dialogue can be cued again for stimulus domains which were previously resolved and operating unconsciously. Such is the case when discrepant information becomes salient or when the context introduces new salient features (e.g., a new person who is outside the bounds of previous agreements or dispute resolutions). For example, a visitor observing a small group interact will make conversation and interaction within that group more effortful than was normally the case. Topics and communication styles which had previously been schematized will now be forced into consciousness and engaged in dialogue against the other (e.g., "how should we act with her around?").

IMPLICATIONS FOR THE EXPERIENCE OF CULTURE

I have proposed that organizational culture is reflected in the emergence of congruent schemas, which are similarly salient, and which shape, and are shaped by the social sensemaking process of intrapsychic mental dialogue between self and others. This perspective has important implications for our understanding of the ways in which organizational culture is experienced by individuals. Several of these implications are explored below.

The Experience of (Sub)Cultural Sharing

Although most organizational scholars agree that the sharing of beliefs and values (captured in schemas) is a prerequisite for the existence of culture in organizations, there is no agreement on exactly what sharing means, how much is required, or how it should be measured (e.g., Martin et al. 1985). For example, Bartunek (1984) talks about shared assumptions but doesn't define what those are or how this sharing is manifested at the individual level. In these cases, questions such as "Does sharing require that the parties to that sharing be aware of its existence?" are problematic.

The existence of sharing is not necessarily the same as the individual-level experience of sharing. It is possible for individuals to share a schema without being aware of that commonality. However, since organizational culture is bound up in notions of the community, it seems reasonable to assume that the *psychological experience* of sharing is of importance in its own right. This is consistent with Schein's (1985) observation that " 'Shared' understanding means that the members of the group recognize a particular feeling, experience, or activity *as common*" (p. 168). Efforts to treat sharing as simply a group-level aggregation of the number of individuals holding particular beliefs and values neglects the fact that such an approach may not capture the extent to which individuals experience sharing.

I propose that cultural sharing can be experienced at two levels: directly and indirectly. The direct experience of sharing results from the realization of agreement between I and Other in schema-based mental dialogues. This agreement generates the experience of "We" (cf. Harris and Cronen 1979, Schall 1983) for the particular stimulus being considered. In this sense, sharing can be experienced on a stimulus-by-stimulus basis. An individual may experience sharing in certain contexts and not others or may experience sharing with one group in one context and with another in a different context. Obviously, the experience of sharing is enhanced to the degree that agreement between self and others occurs across stimulus encounters.

The direct experience of sharing can also result even after agreements resulting in the We-feeling are schema encoded. This is most likely to happen when interpretation of a stimulus domain on which agreement exists between self and other (the We perspective) is challenged by another social entity (e.g., a new leader challenges the status quo in an organization). In this case, a mental dialogue between We and Other is required. I suggest that as a byproduct of crafting the arguments for We's point of view, awareness of sharing enters the individual's consciousness.

The experience of sharing can also be indirect and tacit. In social settings, the absence of sharing and the resultant social discord is likely to lead to discomfort and tension. Because resolving social conflicts over meanings requires conscious reflection, the effortlessness of unconscious sensemaking (made possible by previous social agreement or resolution) can be experienced as an absence of discord. In essence, tension is not experienced. Individuals can attribute this lack of tension to fitting in with the collective We.

Implications for the Experience of Subcultures

Closely related to the experience of sharing is the experience of subcultures. Many organizational scholars have argued for the importance of focusing on organizational subcultures rather than organization-wide cultures (e.g., Louis 1985b, Van Maanen and Barley 1985). The schema-based approach to the individual experience of cultural sharing helps clarify the demarcation of subcultures comprising a larger, more encompassing culture. An individual's ability to distill My Subgroup or They perspectives from their person-in-organization schemas provides evidence of the existence of subcultures. If individuals can articulate different arguments they would expect to be posed by different groups, evidence for subcultural differences between those groups is provided. For example, if a plant manager faced with a problem perceives that the corporate engineering function (They 1) and the corporate marketing function (They 2) would deal with a problem in fundamentally different ways, one can infer that from the perspective of the individual manager a clear and important subcultural difference exists between these two groups. The individual's schema-defined rules of inclusion for these subgroups define the subcultural boundaries that the individual experiences.

The ease with which one can mentally construct a group's perspective for use in intrapsychic dialogue is a gauge of the degree to which that group is a cultural entity. A more elaborate, detailed schema for a group makes taking their perspective easier and is suggestive of coherent culture. If an impression of a group is hard to form for a particular stimulus domain, that group cannot be considered to possess a cultural stance on that domain (at least from the perceiver's experience) and supplying a cogent, scripted dialogue will be difficult.

The Experience of Psychological Attachment

The literature on organizational commitment suggests that there are at least two basic dimensions along which an individual can be psychologically attached to an organization: normative (or attitudinal) and compliance (or calculative) (see Mathieu and Zajac, 1990, for a review of this literature). The schema-based perspective articulated in this chapter offers insight into the individual experience of psychological attachment along these two dimensions.

Normative commitment refers to attachment based upon an internalization of the values and beliefs characterizing the organization and valued affiliation with the organization (e.g., O'Reilly and Chatman 1986). From a schema-based mental dialogue perspective, this form of psychological attachment would be experienced as a result of agreement (We-feeling) between self and the generalized other of the organization (or organizational subgroup) during mental dialogues.

Compliance commitment refers to attachment based upon subordinating one's own preferences to the wishes of the group in expectation of extrinsic remuneration (e.g., pay and continued employment) (e.g., O'Reilly and Chatman 1986). Such commitment is reflected in resolutions of conflict aroused in the process of mental dialogue between I (or We in the case of a subcultural group) and Other in Other's favor. Individuals comply in the hopes of gaining valued outcomes and avoiding unpleasant outcomes under the control of the Other (Kelman 1958, Kiesler and Kiesler 1969). Organizational members whose commitment is primarily compliance-based would be expected to have few "We" experiences with the organization.

CONCLUSION

I have proposed and described a schema-based perspective on the individual-level dynamics of culturally influenced sensemaking in organizations. This perspective represents a step toward greater explicit consideration of the importance of studying organizational culture within the domain of individual sensemaking and offers a framework which can serve to stimulate and direct future organizational culture theory and research.

One benefit of the perspective I have proposed is stimulation of new approaches to the study of culture. First, it offers several propositions which require empirical examination. Second, the perspective suggests the appropriateness of adapting the diverse research designs employed by social psychologists studying schemas for the study of the schema manifestations of organizational culture. Third, it argues for the appropriateness of focusing on the individual experience of culture and as a result suggests that I, They, S/he, and We may serve as useful referents in both quantitative and qualitative data collection. Fourth, the perspective suggests that invoking a real or contrived Other may prove useful in surfacing individuals' I and We perspectives and making them more available for study. This phenomenon naturally occurs in newcomers rendering them excellent candidates for culture study (e.g., Louis 1980, Schall 1983).

The perspective advanced here also has implications for improving understanding of traditionally group-level topics in culture studies. For example, the dynamic quality of schemas makes the approach a potentially useful perspective from which to consider the maintenance and change of culture. In particular, the schema-based perspective would suggest the centrality of tension between I or We and They in surfacing culture and motivating its change. This is consistent with many writers on culture change who suggest that new leaders are in advantageous positions from which to instigate culture change (e.g., Lundberg 1985). From the schema perspective advanced here, such a new leader becomes an influential Other and stimulates the reconsideration of reality through the mental dialogue efforts of organizational members.

In conclusion, it is important to note that while the schema concept is widely embraced by social psychologists, it is not perfect (Markus and Zajonc 1985, Wilcox and Williams 1990). Schema theory applied to organizational culture is not a cure for all that currently ails culture theory and research. However, the perspective on culture offered by schema theory is significant because it highlights and challenges the neglect of the individual-level dynamics of organizational culture that exists in the literature and the conceptual truncation caused by that neglect. I hope that the perspective I have outlined can serve to facilitate building a more well-rounded understanding and appreciation of organizational culture in all of its multilevel complexity.

ACKNOWLEDGMENTS

I would like to thank Jim Meindl and four anonymous reviewers from *Organization Science* and Kevin Mossholder for their helpful comments on earlier versions of this manuscript. I would like to extend a special note of thanks to Doug Cowherd for his invaluable assistance in helping me think through the ideas contained herein. I would also like to thank Bob Kahn, Noel Tichy, Kim Cameron, and Rick Price for granting me the leeway to begin exploring these ideas in my dissertation. A much earlier version of this manuscript was awarded the 1989 Lou Pondy Award for the best paper based on a dissertation by the Organization and Management Theory Division of the Academy of Management.

REFERENCES

Ajzen, I. and M. Fishbein (1980), *Understanding Attitudes and Predicting Social Behavior,* Englewood Cliffs, NJ: Prentice Hall.

Barley, S. R. (1983), "Semiotics and the Study of Occupational and Organizational Cultures," *Administrative Science Quarterly,* 28, 393-413.

Bartunek, J. M. (1984), "Changing Interpretive Schemes and Organizational Restructuring: The Example of a Religious Order," *Administrative Science Quarterly,* 29, 355-372.

——— and M. K. Moch (1987), "First-Order, Second-Order, and Third-Order Change and Organizational Development Interventions: A Cognitive Approach," *Journal of Applied Behavioral Science*, 23, 483-500.

Berger, P. L. and T. Luckman (1966), *The Social Construction of Reality,* Garden City, NY: Doubleday.

Bransford, J. D. and M. K. Johnson (1972), "Contextual Prerequisites for Understanding: Some Investigations of Comprehension and Recall," *Journal of Verbal Learning and Verbal Behavior,* 11, 717-726.

Cantor, N., W. Mischel, and J. Schwartz (1982), "Social Knowledge: Structure, Content, Use, and Abuse," in A. Hastorf and A. Isen (Eds.), *Cognitive Social Psychology,* Hillsdale, NJ: Lawrence Erlbaum.

Denison, D. R. (1984), "Bringing Corporate Culture to the Bottom Line," *Organizational Dynamics,* Autumn, 4-22.

Dutton, J. E. and S. E. Jackson (1987), "Categorizing Strategic Issues: Links to Organizational Action," *Academy of Management Review,* 12, 76-90.

Fiske, S. T. and S. E. Taylor (1984), *Social Cognition,* Reading, MA: Addison-Wesley.

Gioia, D. A. and C. C. Manz (1985), "Linking Cognition and Behavior: A Script Processing Interpretation of Vicarious Learning," *Academy of Management Review,* 10, 527-539.

——— and P. P. Poole (1984), "Scripts in Organizational Behavior," *Academy of Management Review,* 9, 449-459.

Golden, K. A. (1992), "The Individual and Organizational Culture: Strategies for Action in Highly Ordered Contexts," *Journal of Management Studies,* 29, 1-21.

Gray, B., M. G. Bougon, and A. Donnellon (1985), "Organizations as Constructions and Destructions of Meaning," *Journal of Management,* 11, 83-98.

Harris, L. and V. E. Cronen (1979), "A Rules-Based Model for the Analysis and Evaluation of Organizational Communication," *Communication Quarterly,* Winter, 12-28.

Holyoak, K. J. and P. C. Gordon (1984), "Information Processing and Social Cognition," in R. S. Wyer and T. K. Srull (Eds.), *Handbook of Social Cognition* (Vol. 1), Hillsdale, NJ: Lawrence Erlbaum, 39-70.

Katz, D. and R. L. Kahn (1978), *The Social Psychology of Organizations* (2nd ed.), New York: John Wiley.

Kelman, H. C. (1958), "Compliance, Identification, and Internalization: Three Processes of Attitude Change," *Conflict Resolution,* 2, 51-60.

Kets de Vries, M. F. R. and D. Miller (1986), "Personality, Culture, and Organization," *Academy of Management Review,* 11, 266-279.

Kiesler, C. and S. Kiesler (1969), *Conformity,* Reading, MA: Addison-Wesley.

Kilmann, R. H., M. J. Saxton, and R. Serpa (1985), "Introduction: Five Key Issues in Understanding and Changing Culture," in R. H. Kilmann, M. J. Saxton, and R. Serpa (Eds.), *Gaining Control of the Corporate Culture,* San Francisco: Jossey-Bass, 1-16.

Krefting, L. A. and P. J. Frost (1985), "Untangling Webs, Surfing Waves, and Wildcatting: A Multiple-Metaphor Perspective on Managing Organizational Culture," in P. J. Frost, L. F. Moore, M. R. Louis, C. C. Lundberg, and J. Martin (Eds.), *Organizational Culture,* Beverly Hills, CA: Sage, 155-168.

Lofland, J. (1976), *Doing Social Life,* New York: John Wiley.

Lord, R. G. and R. J. Foti (1986), "Schema Theories, Information Processing, and Organizational Behavior," in H. P. Sims, Jr. and D. A. Gioia (Eds.), *The Thinking Organization: Dynamics of Organizational Social Cognition*, San Francisco: Jossey-Bass, 20-48.

——— and M. C. Kernan (1987), "Scripts as Determinants of Purposeful Behavior in Organizations," *Academy of Management Review*, 12, 265-277.

——— and K. J. Maher (1991), "Cognitive Theory in Industrial and Organizational Psychology," in M. D. Dunnette and L. M. Hough (Eds.), *Handbook of Industrial and Organizational Psychology* (Vol. 2), Palo Alto, CA: Consulting Psychologists Press, 1-62.

Lorsch, J. W. (1985), "Strategic Myopia: Culture as an Invisible Barrier to Change," in R. H. Kilmann, M. J. Saxton, and R. Serpa (Eds.), *Gaining Control of the Corporate Culture*, San Francisco: Jossey-Bass, 84-102.

Louis, M. R. (1980), "Surprise and Sense-Making: What Newcomers Experience in Entering Unfamiliar Organizational Settings," *Administrative Science Quarterly*, 25, 226-251.

——— (1983), "Organizations as Cultural-bearing Milieux," in L. R. Pondy, P. J. Frost, G. Morgan, and T. C. Dandridge (Eds.), *Organizational Symbolism*, Greenwich, CT: JAI, 39-54.

——— (1985a), "Introduction: Perspectives on Organizational Culture," in P. J. Frost, L. F. Moore, M. R. Louis, C. C. Lundberg, and J. Martin (Eds.), *Organizational Culture*, Beverly Hills, CA: Sage, 27-30.

——— (1985b), "An Investigator's Guide to Workplace Culture," in P. J. Frost, L. F. Moore, M. R. Louis, C. C. Lundberg, and J. Martin (Eds.), *Organizational Culture*, Beverly Hills, CA: Sage, 73-94.

——— and R. I. Sutton (1991), "Switching Cognitive Gears: From Habits of Mind to Active Thinking," *Human Relations*, 44, 55-76.

Lundberg, C. C. (1985), "On the Feasibility of Cultural Intervention in Organizations," in P. J. Frost, L. F. Moore, M. R. Louis, C. C. Lundberg, and J. Martin (Eds.), *Organizational Culture*, Beverly Hills, CA: Sage, 169-186.

Markus, H. (1977), "Self-schemata and Processing Information about the Self," *Journal of Personality and Social Psychology*, 35, 63-78.

——— and R. B. Zajonc (1985), "The Cognitive Perspective in Social Psychology," in G. Lindzey and E. Aronson (Eds.), *The Handbook of Social Psychology*, (3rd ed., Vol. 1), New York: Random House, 137-230.

Martin, J. (1982), "Stories and Scripts in Organizational Settings," in A. Hastorf and A. Isen (Eds.), *Cognitive Social Psychology*, New York: Elsevier-North Holland.

———, S. B. Sitkin, and M. Boehm (1985), "Founders and the Elusiveness of a Cultural Legacy," in P. J. Frost, L. F. Moore, M. R. Louis, C. C. Lundberg, and J. Martin (Eds.), *Organizational Culture*, Beverly Hills, CA: Sage, 99-124.

Mathieu, J. E. and D. M. Zajac (1990), "A Review and Meta-Analysis of the Antecedents, Correlates, and Consequences of Organizational Commitment," *Psychological Bulletin*, 108, 171-194.

Mead, G. H. (1934), *Mind, Self, and Society*, Chicago: University of Chicago Press.

Neisser, U. (1976), *Cognition and Reality*, San Francisco: Freeman.

O'Reilly, C. and J. Chatman (1986), "Organizational Commitment and Psychological Attachment: The Effects of Compliance, Identification, and Internalization on Prosocial Behavior," *Journal of Applied Psychology*, 71, 492-499.

Ott, J. S. (1989), *The Organizational Culture Perspective*, Chicago: Dorsey.

Ouchi, W. G. (1980), "Markets, Bureaucracies, and Clans," *Administrative Science Quarterly*, 25, 129-141.

Pfeffer, J. (1981), "Management as Symbolic Action: The Creation and Maintenance of Organizational Paradigms," in L. L. Cummings and B. M. Staw (Eds.), *Research in Organizational Behavior* (Vol. 3), Greenwich, CT: JAI, 1-52.

Pondy, L. R. (1983), "The Role of Metaphors and Myths in Organization and the Facilitation of Change," in L. R. Pondy, P. J. Frost, G. Morgan, and T. C. Dandridge (Eds.), *Organizational Symbolism,* Greenwich, CT: JAI, 157-166.

Prietula, M. J. and H. A. Simon (1989), "The Experts in Your Midst," *Harvard Business Review,* Jan.-Feb., 120-124.

Ray, C. A. (1986), "Corporate Culture: The Last Frontier of Control," *Journal of Management Studies,* 23, 287-297.

Rumelhart, D. E. (1984), "Schemas and the Cognitive System," in R. S. Wyer and T. K. Srull (Eds.), *Handbook of Social Cognition* (Vol. 1), Hillsdale, NJ: Lawrence Erlbaum, 161-188.

Saffold, G. S. (1988), "Culture Traits, Strengths and Organizational Performance: Moving Beyond 'Strong' Culture," *Academy of Management Review,* 13, 546-558.

Salancik, G. R. and J. Pfeffer (1978), "A Social Information Processing Approach to Job Attitudes and Task Design," *Administrative Science Quarterly,* 23, 224-253.

Sathe, V. (1985a), *Culture and Related Corporate Realities,* Homewood, IL: Irwin.

——— (1985b), "How to Decipher and Change Corporate Culture," in R. H. Kilmann, M. J. Saxton, and R. Serpa (Eds.), *Gaining Control of the Corporate Culture,* San Francisco: Jossey-Bass, 230-261.

Schall, M. S. (1983), "A Communication-Rules Approach to Organizational Culture," *Administrative Science Quarterly,* 28, 557-581.

Schein, E. H. (1985), *Organizational Culture and Leadership,* San Francisco, CA: Jossey-Bass.

Schneider, D. J. (1991), "Social Cognition," *Annual Review of Psychology,* 42, 527-561.

Schutz, A. (1964), *Collected Papers II: Studies in Social Theory,* The Hague, the Netherlands: Martinus Nijhoff.

Sutton, R. I. and R. L. Kahn (1987), "Prediction, Understanding, and Control as Antidotes to Organizational Stress," in J. W. Lorsch (Ed.), *Handbook of Organizational Behavior,* Englewood Cliffs, NJ: Prentice Hall, 272-285.

Taylor, S. E. and J. Crocker (1981), "Schematic Bases of Social Information Processing," in E. T. Higgins, C. A. Harman, and M. P. Zanna (Eds.), *Social Cognition: The Ontario Symposium on Personality and Social Psychology,* Hillsdale, NJ: Lawrence Erlbaum, 89-134.

Trice, H. M. and J. M. Beyer (1984), "Studying Organizational Cultures Through Rites and Ceremonials," *Academy of Management Review,* 9, 653-669.

Ulrich, W. L. (1984), "HRM and Culture: History, Ritual, and Myth," *Human Resource Management,* 23, 117-128.

Van Maanen, J. (1976), "Breaking-in: Socialization to Work," in R. Dubin (Ed.), *Handbook of Work, Organization, and Society,* Chicago: Rand McNally, 67-130.

——— and S. R. Barley (1985), "Cultural Organization: Fragments of a Theory," in P. J. Frost, L. F. Moore, M. R. Louis, C. C. Lundberg, and J. Martin (Eds.), *Organizational Culture,* Beverly Hills, CA: Sage, 31-54.

Weick, K. E. (1979a), "Cognitive Processes in Organizations," in B. M. Staw (Ed.), *Research in Organizational Behavior* (Vol. 1), Greenwich, CT: JAI, 41-74.

——— (1979b), *The Social Psychology of Organizing* (2nd ed.), Reading, MA: Addison-Wesley.

Wilcox, C. and L. Williams (1990), "Taking Stock of Schema Theory," *The Social Science Journal,* 27, 373-393.

10

Interpretive Barriers to Successful Product Innovation in Large Firms

DEBORAH DOUGHERTY

The development of commercially viable new products requires that technological and market possibilities are linked effectively in the product's design. Innovators in large firms have persistent problems with such linking, however. This research examines these problems by focusing on the shared interpretive schemes people use to make sense of product innovation. Two interpretive schemes are found to inhibit development of technology-market knowledge: departmental thought worlds and organizational product routines. The chapter describes in some depth differences among the thought worlds which keep innovators from synthesizing their expertise. The chapter also details how organizational routines exacerbate problems with learning, and how successful innovators overcome both interpretive barriers. The main implication of the study is that to improve innovation in large firms it is necessary to deal explicitly with the interpretive barriers described here. Suggestions for practice and research are offered.

(INNOVATION; NEW PRODUCTS; INTERDEPARTMENTAL COLLABORATION; INTERPRETATION)

Successful product innovation is vital to many firms. This chapter builds on three findings in the literature to explore the product innovation process in large firms. The first finding is that the commercial success of a new product

---

This chapter originally appeared in *Organization Science,* Vol. 3, No. 2, May 1992.

depends on how well the product's design meets customers' needs (Rothwell et al. 1974, Lilien and Yoon 1988). An effective design requires that technological possibilities for a product are linked with market possibilities, e.g., who are the users; what will they use the product for? The second finding is that collaboration among the technical, marketing, manufacturing, and sales departments contributes to a new product's success (Bonnet 1986, Dean and Susman 1989). The third finding is that product innovators often do not link technological and market issues, and often do not collaborate across departments (Cooper and Kleinschmidt 1986, Souder 1987).

This research seeks to explain why innovators failed to develop a comprehensive appreciation of their product in its market. Three implications are developed from the findings. First, collaboration is necessary to technology-market linking, which means that collaboration enhances the product's design along with improving the execution of the development process. Second, the styles in which people organize their thinking and action about innovation—their "interpretive schemes"—are major barriers to linking and collaboration. Like "culture," such schemes provide shared assumptions about reality, identify relevant issues, and help people make sense of those issues (Daft and Weick 1984, Bartunek 1984). In the case of product innovation, two interpretive schemes become interpretive barriers: (1) departments are like different "thought worlds," each focusing on different aspects of technology-market knowledge, and making different sense of the total; and (2) organizational routines separate rather than coordinate the thought worlds, further constraining joint learning. The third implication is that correcting the innovation problems caused by these interpretive barriers requires cultural solutions, not only structural ones.

OPCO—AN EXAMPLE

Before defining terms and then explaining how these implications arise, excerpts from a case in the research are presented to illustrate thought worlds and routines, and to introduce the research. The data management division of OPCO, a communications company, decided to develop and sell a software accounting system that would process credit card transactions over their data network. They purchased a start-up firm with a system under development to enter the business quickly, and, after several months additional work at OPCO, the service was introduced to the market. The system did not operate properly, however, and was canceled. As suggested by the quotes below, the innovation encountered many problems. The quotes also suggest that the participants interpret issues with unique departmental perspectives. The business manager sees no need to talk with customers since he considers the market opportunity to be obvious. He feels, however, that they failed to position the product properly against competitors:

> [Interviewer: Did you talk to customers?] No, because we knew that this was needed. We could see some competitors getting into the business. . . . We could see that this was logical for us to do, so we decided to go. . . . Had we done some market research and defined needs more carefully, and figured out the dozens of pieces we would need for a full system, we'd be positioned with a much better strategy.

The technical director sees no "market" problems at all with the effort. He describes design problems, however, that perhaps could have been resolved had a thorough analysis of users and how they operate been carried out:

> There were no market problems with this product. . . . Our mistake was we didn't understand the application in total. . . . We had a difficult time trying to figure out the relationships between us here at the operating level and the retail establishments, and the relationships between them and their banks and credit card clearing houses. . . . There were a lot of players involved, which is different from (our regular product), where we interface with one customer at a time. It looks very nice theoretically, but the more relationships there are, the more complex the recovery.

The sales support person downplays general positioning and technological design to blame instead their failure to specify which users in the market could best use the product:

> I have never seen a definition for this service. There are no criteria on what makes a good or bad customer for this product. . . . One person here had a pretty good understanding of what kind of customer would benefit from a system like this. More people here should have known. We needed a brain transplant.

The innovators also followed established routines at OPCO Data to develop and launch this new service. These routines included project teams and matrices, structures that are recommended for innovation (e.g., Tushman and Nadler 1986), but all participants note how they did not work. The routines did not synthesize components of the innovation itself nor relevant knowledge, and they squashed interaction:

> We were not successful in fully integrating the new business within the organization. A new product is unique—it has different distribution, different billing, a

> myriad of things have to work out well. It is difficult for a small organization [referring to the business unit] to handle all these issues, so things fall apart. We didn't see the pitfalls (business manager).
>
> At OPCO we tend to categorize people into roles, and give people only what they need to know. . . . There are little shadings of meaning that get lost in the requirements statement from marketing (technical director).
>
> They [from the small company] were a very tight group, and they all talked to one another all the time. But when we brought them here they were dispersed into our matrix . . . (sales support).

In hindsight at least, these innovators knew that they should link technological and market issues, but they did not. This case along with 17 others is analyzed to explain why.

CONCEPTUAL BACKGROUND

Components of Technology-Market Linking

To understand problems with technology-market linking, it is first necessary to understand what that linking comprises. Research suggests that technology-market linking has a process and a content component. On the process side, linking involves the construction of new knowledge about the product and the market. Henderson and Clark (1990) suggest that nonroutine innovations require new "architectures," in which innovators break out of existing procedures and know-how and reconfigure components of design and procedure into a new framework. Freeman (1982) describes product innovation as a "complex coupling" between market needs and technologies over time. Linking technological and market possibilities is challenging, because choices must be made among multiple design options, each with different outcomes. At the same time the market may be new so it is difficult to determine who the most likely customers are and what they actually need (Clark 1985). Developing innovative products is thus a process of double loop learning (Argyris and Schön 1978), in which new insights are incorporated and the premises themselves are reconsidered.

On the content side, linking means that a complex array of specific insights must be gathered and brought together. Dougherty (1990) finds that successful new product developers had more insight into users' applications, technological trends, distribution systems, and market segments. Urban and von Hippel (1988) suggest that developers determine key trends in both the technology and market areas, and then search for "lead users" who can identify viable design specifications. According to Bonnet (1986), integration of R&D and marketing facilitates both the assessment of commercial viability and the optimization of design characteristics. Requisite knowledge for new products is thus multi-faceted, multi-leveled, and detailed.

Organizational Barriers to Technology-Market Linking

To understand why people do not link technology and market issues effectively, it helps to understand what prevents them from frame-breaking learning, and from gathering and connecting diverse insights. Organization research contains numerous references to interpretive schemes at the department and organization levels which may intervene in these necessary innovation processes. Departments can develop different perspectives through which they might separate rather than combine information, including cognitive orientations such as goals, time frames, and formality (Lawrence and Lorsch 1967), languages (Tushman 1978), perceptions (Dearborn and Simon 1958), occupational cultures (Van Maanen and Barley 1984), or power (Riley 1983).

At the organizational level, firms create "programs" (March and Simon 1958) or "routines" (Nelson and Winter 1982) which can inhibit new product development. According to Nelson and Winter, routines are regular and predictable behavior patterns, which first comprise the organizational memory. When the firm is in a state of routine operation, each person knows his or her job, and there is no need to know others' jobs. Second, routines represent a truce for intra-organizational conflict, which, as Perrow (1986) notes, binds the firm in a network of practices that are difficult to alter. Third, routines are standards which managers try to keep from changing.

Few organization studies have connected departmental differences and organizational routines directly to new product development and technology-market linking, however. Lawrence and Lorsch's (1967) often cited insights concern ongoing businesses, not discrete new products. Several studies suggest that their cognitive differences do not differentiate departments for new product development (Harrison 1980, Gupta, Raj, and Wilemon 1986). And, while organization theorists may refer to knowledge development (Galbraith 1982, Kanter 1983), most concentrate on structures and cultures for innovativeness in general, not for product innovation in particular.

Toward a More Complete Model

Fleck (1979) was the first to apply differences in interpretive schemes to innovation (or at least to scientific discovery—Douglas 1987). His views suggest how to integrate the insights outlined above into a more complete understanding of the organizational and interpretive processes underlying product innovation and technology-market linking. Fleck emphasizes the social basis of cognition, and adds that innovations often are epistemologically unsolvable by any one person. They require insights from a variety of specialties, called "thought collectives" or "thought worlds" as Douglas (1987) proposes to retranslate the term. A thought world is a community of persons engaged in a certain domain of activity who have a shared understanding about that activity. Microbiologists, plumbers, opera buffs, and organizational departments all can be viewed as thought worlds.

Departmental Thought Worlds. Two aspects of thought worlds are relevant to product innovation: their "fund of knowledge"—what they know, and their "systems of meaning"—or how they know. According to Fleck what is already known influences the method and content of cognition. Thought worlds with different kinds of knowledge cannot easily share ideas, and may view one another's central issues as esoteric, if not meaningless. A thought world also evolves an internally shared system of meaning which provides a "readiness for directed perception" based on common procedures, judgments, and methods. These systems of meaning produce an "intrinsic harmony" for the thought world, so ideas that do not fit may be reconfigured or rejected outright.

For new product development, one could infer that departmental thought worlds would selectively filter information and insights. Because of specialization, a certain thought world is likely to best understand certain issues, but also to ignore information that may be equally essential to the total task. Their intrinsic harmony would also reduce the possibility for creative joint learning, since members of a department may think that they already know everything.

Organizational Routines. Fleck does not deal with organizations per se, but argues that the collective action necessary to innovation is motivated by pressure from the social context. "Collective work proper" (1979, p. 99) is different from additive work, as when people come together to lift a large rock. Rather, it refers to "the coming into existence of a special form, like a soccer match, conversation, or orchestra." This new social form alters the thought worlds' existing readiness for directed perception to allow new possibilities for discovery and new facts. Fleck studied the development of the Wassermann test for syphilis, and argues that the disease was undefined for 400 years in part because there were no means for collective action. Different groups such as astrologers, priests, pharmacists, and physicians operated with their own theories. If it were not for the "insistent clamor of public opinion for a blood test" (1979, p. 77), Wassermann would never have gathered the collective experiences necessary to develop a test. Wassermann began with the incorrect immunology perspective that syphilis is caused by a virus. But because of external pressure, his persistence coupled with developments from chemistry, medicine, and laboratory thought worlds to uncover the actual cause of the disease (a spirochete). A new social form among these diverse groups emerged, and they *collectively* produced a test for the disease.

Fleck's dynamics can be combined with Nelson and Winter's (1982) routines to suggest that the organizational context affects the thought world's capacity to collaborate, inhibits the development of new knowledge, and keeps innovators from creating a new social form.

Research Questions. This study will explore these dynamics by addressing the following questions: (1) What are the different funds of knowledge and systems of meaning for new products in the departmental thought worlds, and how do they affect product innovation? (2) What are the routines that inhibit product innovation, and how do they affect collective action among the thought worlds?

METHODS

Data regarding 18 new product efforts in five firms were collected by interviewing 80 people from different departments who worked on these products. Schall's (1983) multi-method analysis suggests that such interviews are a valid means to assess departmental interpretive differences. An embedded, multiple case design was used (Yin 1989) in order to consider the effects of organization and product success and failure on the findings (Bailyn 1977).

Organizations and Products

Two of the firms are in the computer/communications industries (OPCP and SALECO) and three are in the chemical materials industries (TECHCO, COMPCO, and PRODCO). All generate over $1 billion annually, employ over 20,000 people, and are over 35 years old. The criteria used to select products for the study are: (1) they incorporated new or unfamiliar technology for the firm and/or were marketed to new or unfamiliar users; (2) the products were almost or already introduced to the market, to eliminate variance due to development stage; and (3) some products were commercially successful, and some were failures. "Success" was defined as gener-

TABLE 10.1 Comparing Product Innovation Cases by Success Status

	Successful [a] *(4 cases)*	*Uncertain* [b] *(7 cases)*	*Failed* [c] *(6 cases)*
Comparisons			
Average Time in Development Before Introduction in Months[d]	31	26	23
Average Time After Introduction in Months	42	19	18
Unfamiliarity to Firm (percentage of cases)[e]			
Percentage of new technology	50	63	50
Percentage of new manufacture	75	88	83
Percentage of new market segments	50	75	50
Percentage of new applications	100	88	67
Percentage of new distribution	100	100	67

a. Successful = already introduced and meeting/exceeding expectations;
b. Uncertain = not meeting expectations but not cancelled (7 cases already introduced, 1 still in development);
c. Failed = already introduced and subsequently cancelled.
d. The starting time is when the particular product began to be developed, not when underlying technologies were invented.
e. If 2 of the participants said that the product was unfamiliar to the firm in this area, it was coded as unfamiliar.

ating at least as much profit as planned and "failure" as cancellation after introduction.

Data were collected in two stages. First, 11 cases were studied at TECHCO and OPCO. At TECHCO, a manager in each of the six product groups in its industrial division was asked to suggest a product from his group that met the criteria. One said he was too busy, so five products were selected. At OPCO, managers directed me to their voice venture (one product), and their data division, where five more cases were studied. Only one of these 11 cases was successful as defined above, however, and even though six were in the market their profitability was still uncertain. A second stage of data collection was undertaken to add more successful cases. SALECO, COMPCO, and PRODCO were asked to identify one success already introduced, and one failure that had been introduced but canceled. At COMPCO, people also described an uncertain product, and this was included.

Seventeen products were in the market, so all but one were in the post-introductory stage when people were interviewed. The products are described in Appendix A. In addition to success and failure, a new category labeled "uncertain" was made for the seven cases that were in the market but not generating profits as expected. Table 10.1 compares the successful, uncertain, and failed cases. The successful cases were in development longer on the average, but this difference is because of one case which took over five years. The uncertain cases, however, have been out on the market for less time than the successes. Post-introductory time may enhance success, since some of the uncertain cases will eventually become successful, while some will be canceled. The success or failure might depend on the case's unfamiliarity to the firm. To compare cases on unfamiliarity, if two people said that the product was unfamiliar in any of the five areas noted, it was coded as such. As can be seen in Table 10.1, there is no difference in unfamiliarity by success status.

The People and the Interviews

At least two people who worked on each product were interviewed, and most were still working on the product. All were operational and middle level managers, and only six had less than four years experience with the firm. All interviews followed the same protocol: describe the product; outline your role; tell the story of the product; and describe customers, technology, and working relationships with others. The interviews were structured around these general questions, but unstructured regarding what the person chose to emphasize. The interviews lasted from about one hour to over two hours. Notes were taken and filled in as soon as possible afterwards. Table 10.2 summarizes the people interviewed by product, department, and firm.

Retrospective interviews have two important sources of potential distortion: memory failure and attribution bias. To guard against memory failure, people were asked regularly for dates and names to keep them grounded in particulars, and one person was reinterviewed briefly to clarify any conflicts in reported events. In addition, archival data were reviewed for three of the products, and no conflicts with people's stories were found. To check for attribution bias, the uncertain cases were compared to the successes and failures. Many of these people presented their product as a success, yet the measures of their knowledge matched the failed people's more closely, suggesting that attribution bias does not seriously affect the measures (see Dougherty 1987, 1990, for details). Failed developers may have underreported the knowledge they had due to attribution bias. I conclude that memory failure and attribution bias do not dominate the data, but they may distort the findings somewhat.

Since labels vary by firm, people were categorized into departments (used in the same sense as "function") based on their responsibilities when they worked on the product. Four labels are used: (1) technical: those who worked in research or engineering; (2) field: those who worked in sales or customer relations; (3) manufacturing: plant and purchasing people, or manufacturing engineers; and (4) planners: those who handled market research or business analyses but were not in regular contact with customers.

TABLE 10.2 Number of People Interviewed by Department, Company, and Product Case

Company and Case:	*Technical*	*Field*	*Manufacturing*	*Planners*	*Total*
TECHCO (chemicals)					
F Battery	1			1	2
U CRT Device	3	1	1		5
U Video Device	2	1			3
U Medical System	2	1		1	4
S Film Cover		1	2		3
Others		1		2	3
OPCO (communications)					
F Accounting System	2	1		1	4
F Document System	2			2	4
U Software System	1			2	3
U Text System	4	1	1	2	8
U Voice System	1	5	1	1	8
U Transmit System	1			2	3
Others				3	3
SALECO (computers)					
F System II	2		3	2	7
F System I	1	1		2	4
Others				2	2
COMPCO (chemicals)					
F Hardpoly	2	2		1	5
U Stretchpoly	1			1	2
S Hotpoly	1	1		2	4
Others		2		1	3
PRODCO (chemicals)					
F Pit Liner	1			1	2
S Roof Liner	1	1			2
Others				1	1
TOTAL	28	19	8	30	85[a]

NOTE: F = failure; U = uncertain; S = successful.
a. Several people were interviewed twice, so figures add to more than 80.

DATA ANALYSIS AND FINDINGS

The findings and methods of analysis are interdependent, and are described together for each issue being studied.

Thought Worlds

Technology-Market Funds of Knowledge. The first research question asks what are the different funds of knowledge about technology-market issues in the different departmental thought worlds? It is assumed that the content of the thought worlds would be evident in the emphases in people's stories. To assess these emphases, a coding scheme to measure "technology" and "market" was developed with five categories: (1) product technology and design issues, (2) manufacturing (plant, suppliers, materials), (3) business issues including segments, competition, and size forecasts, (4) customer issues such as needs and problems, and (5) distribution or selling issues. The author coded each statement of each interview into one of these five areas. A research assistant coded a subset of interviews, and we had 80% agreement. Issues we disagreed over were redefined and all interviews were recoded by the author.

Measures were also developed for two of Lawrence and Lorsch's (1967) "cognitive orientations." Time orientation was measured by counting the number of statements that referred to events more than one year prior to the start of the product, or one year into the future beyond the date of the interview (divided by the number of pages to control for interview length). This assumes that people with a longer time orientation would discuss more long-term events. A task-versus-people orientation was measured by a ratio of statements that referred to working with people versus those that referred to a task in the development.

To make comparisons as similar as possible, only those people who worked directly on the product *prior* to introduction were included in the analysis. Table 10.3 summarizes the technology-market contents and cognitive orientations of each thought world using this subset of 71 interviews. One-way analyses of variance suggest differences on six measures, with long-short term orientation statistically significant at only $p = 0.11$. Planners dwell on business analyses in their stories and are the most long term, while technical people emphasize design issues. The field people discuss customer and distribution issues more often, and are the most people oriented.

If the departments are like thought worlds, however, one would also expect to see these differences regardless of company and success versus failure. Two-way analyses of variance between the thought world fund of knowledge measures and orientations were run by department and by company and success status to check on this expectation. See Appendix B for the results. The department has a main effect in five of the seven comparisons. There are also a few differences by company and success status, as discussed in the Appendix. Since the department main effect is found across the firms and success outcomes, however, these findings lend support to the idea that

TABLE 10.3 Technology-Market Content Analysis of Interviews and Cognitive Orientations by Department

Issues and Orientations	*Technology*	*Field*	*Manufacturing*	*Planners*	*Statistic*
Percentage of Interview					
Business Issues	23	24	17	42	$F = 16.1$ $p = 0.000$
Customer Issues	17	28	10	18	$F = 12.9$ $p = 0.000$
Selling Issues	4	22	3	10	$p = 0.000$[b]
Technical Issues	49	21	27	23	$F = 27$ $p = 0.000$
Manufacturing Issues	8	6	39	6	$F = 71$ $p = 0.000$
Orientations—Mean ranks[a]					
Long-Short Time	34	33	25	44	$p = 0.11$[b]
Task People	39	20	43	42	$p = 0.006$[b]

a. The four departments do not have homogeneous variances on these measures, per a Bartlett test. The original measures were ranked by case from 1 to 71 (71 of the original 85 interviews are used in this analysis because "others" and people who did not work on the product prior to its launch were deleted). A Kruskall-Wallis test that compares mean ranks was run. The mean percentage is reported for the Selling Issues to be consistent with the other content measures, but the statistic is a χ^2 used for the K-W test on the ranked scores. Two orientation measures are the mean ranks, with the higher rank reflecting more long-term or task orientation.
b. χ^2

departmental thought worlds differ systematically on technology-market issues regardless of the firm or product status.

Systems of Meaning. The Fleck model suggests that departments not only know different things, but also know things differently. That is, each would have a different system of meaning through which its members interpret technology-market issues. To understand these systems of meaning, dimensions to describe them were developed following Strauss's (1987) methods for qualitative analysis. First, people's descriptions of other departments and frustrations with them, how they thought about customers, and what they considered important to product development were written onto separate coding sheets. These were then compared across department, case, and firm to search for underlying patterns or themes which summarized the essence of the departmental differences. Preliminary themes were discussed with colleagues and with several of the people interviewed.

Three final themes seem to most distinguish how the four thought worlds interpret technology-market linking and new products: (1) what people see when they look into the future, including issues that are most uncertain; (2) what people consider to be the critical aspects of the product development process; and (3) how people understand the development task itself. By looking at technology-market issues through the unique combination of these themes, people in each thought world understood the product in qualitatively different ways. Each thought world had an "intrinsically harmonious" perspective on the product which did not overlap extensively with perspectives held by other departments. Table 10.4 summarizes the unique understandings about product innovation which arise from these different systems of meaning.

These themes are first outlined, and then the different views they engender are illustrated with case material. The first theme captures the future orientation inherent in new product development. It also highlights the fact that people understand the future by in effect sighting along different emerging trends—technological change versus customer shifts versus market evolution (see Table 10.4). They make different sense of the nebulous future by looking at disparate aspects of it. What they see seems uncertain, while what they do not see does not seem particularly uncertain or even noteworthy. These contrasts can be seen in the OPCO excerpts. The business planner worried about positioning against competition while the field person worried about identifying the right potential customers. They partitioned the product into separate sources of uncertainty, which may have kept them from developing a more comprehensive understanding of the market.

The second theme comprises people's understanding of the development process itself. Each department concentrates on different subsets of the overall process. People do not ignore the activities they do not deal with directly, and do not merely argue over relative priorities. Rather, they gloss over the concerns of others, and tend not to appreciate their complexities (Van Maanen 1979). Recall that OPCO's technical person saw no "market" problems for the product effort described. Had they identified a set of retailers who needed the service but who had simple transaction needs, however, perhaps they could have designed a workable system. As Table 10.4 suggests, each department seeks inputs from the others that differ from the others' primary focus. Technical people, for example, concentrate on solving design problems, and expect field people to tell them exactly what customers want in the design. Field people, however, cannot identify these "specs" because in their view users are uncertain. Rather, field people consider that product innovation is to meet *shifts* in customer needs, and expect technical people to produce alternate designs quickly.

The third category concerns how people understand the task itself. As Table 10.4 shows, all but the planners understand product development in

TABLE 10.4 Differences in the Thought World Systems of Meaning About Product Innovation

Themes That Differentiate Thought Worlds	*The Technical People*	*The Field People*	*The Manufacturing People*	*The Planning People*
What is seen when looking into future/ uncertainties	Future comprises emergence of the technologies underlying the new product: design problems and their solution, new technical possibilities to include, new trends which might change development. Uncertainties comprise finding out what the design parameters are.	Future comprises shifts or trends in the users' uses of and need for this and related products. Uncertainties comprise how to get to buyers, discern if they like product, and how to adjust product for user.	Future limited to capabilities in plant, need careful shifts in operations. Uncertainties concern if manufacture is possible, what are the volumes.	Future comprises emerging business opportunities, competitive changes, new niches. Uncertainties concern developing market forecasts and income projections.
Aspects of development considered most critical	Focus on devising the product, specifying what it should do. Want to know what users want in product specifications. Market is seen as what the product does, and as such is rather obvious.	Focus on matching products to users, adjusting the product quickly to meet their shifting needs, creating the sale. Want to know who makes buying decision, what problems customers want to solve. Market is seen as what the buyer wants, and as such is difficult to develop.	Focus on the product's durability, quality, how many types of prod-. uct Want to know how good is good enough in product quality. The market is seen in abstract terms as product's performance.	Focus on developing the business case and general marketing plans. Want to know the best segment to be in, how to position the product in this segment. Market is seen as a general business opportunity.
How development task is understood	Task is to build the product—a hands-on, tactile activity. Product is real, has a physical presence, and is "neat."	Task is to develop relationships with buyers, which occurs when products change to meet their needs. Sense of task is one of urgency. Also hands-on but product is not real—it is a possibility.	Task is to build the capacity to build the product. Also hands-on, tactile, product is well built.	Task is to analyze alternate possibilities, determine income potential—a conceptual, abstract activity. Product is a business.

concrete, hands-on terms, so all these departments have difficulty making sense of planners' reports. There are also significant differences within these three hands-on groups, however. The technical people think that the product has a specific reality, while field people think it is a possibility. These contrasting perspectives can seriously impede a dialogue over what the product is and how it should be developed. Excerpts from the interviews illustrate these thought worlds for product development.

The Technical People. The product's design dominates the technical people's understanding of product development. When they look into the future, they see ever emerging design possibilities and numerous technological trade-offs. For example, an engineer with SALECO's System II discussed the decision over the disk drive at some length:

> The diskette started as a single side, but we had technical problems with that. . . . Also when we started there was no question that we'd do half size. That was a new technology so it had to be single sided. But a guy in the group said in a few months we could fix the problems, so let's take a risk and forget single sided and do double sided. That helped push the technology . . . (SALECO).

Consistent with this view of the future, technical people emphasize establishing the product's performance specifications rather than what the customer does with the product. This is a complex and often frustrating process, as this engineer's comments about a communication system illustrate:

> There were a lot of specs, but these were only detailed conceptually. They wanted "something like this." What ended up as a result is that the specs get interpreted more widely. You end up delivering something they didn't ask for. . . . I was working with one or two people (at the customer organization). Then they show it to fourteen others who say: "Oh My God!! We didn't want that!!" (OPCO)

Technical people define the market in terms of what the product does, and may overlook business aspects such as how many people will pay how much for the product. For example, the market for the battery was defined as "battery users," not particular sets of industrial customers who might need a more permanent energy source. Most technical people view the development task as a tactile activity that results in something objectively real. By concentrating on technological possibilities, however, they may assume the market is obvious and that customer needs are straightforward.

The Field People. As field people look into the future, they see constantly emerging customer applications rather than changing technological possibilities. Such changes are more immediate, often shifting with the user's model changes or competitor's product or price changes, giving them a short-term, action orientation. Field people also seem to take a customer-by-customer view of the market. Consider:

> You need to listen to what the customers want; what is he ready to buy; what is he looking for? . . . You have to be specific, applications oriented. I want the least amount possible in the shortest time, but [engineering] may take three years. . . . The more (engineering and operations) are buffered from customers, the more they tend not to understand the urgency. (OPCO)

Field people emphasize creating or crafting the sale, not the product, and describe this activity as vividly as the engineers discuss disc drives or communication networks. Explains a voice service field person:

> It's a blast to let it go. I never go on a one on one meeting. I always try to have a minimum of three people (from the prospective customer's organization) and I throw out functions until I find a use. . . . It's the most amazing thing in the world. Usually there's at least one guy who's determined not to like the product. He sits pulled away from you like he won't let you penetrate his shield. But then after ten minutes he pops up in his chair and starts coming up with ideas . . . (OPCO)

To field people, the task is real but not tactile. Developing a new product means establishing new relationships and buying-selling arrangements. The relational nature of their work is evident in this quote:

> We know what they need. The market is obvious. But the selling process is complex. Who are they and what do they want is clear. But there are six or eight decision makers. No one says yes but anyone can say no. . . . The production guy wants to know if his yield will be better. . . . The quality control guy says "will I have to change my tests?" The sales manager says "will my customers like the finished product as well?" The purchasing guy says "what will you do for me?" . . . You need to work with all these guys and their bosses. (COMPCO)

Note also that the speaker downplays the complexities of doing a market analysis by focusing on his own tasks. Field people concentrate on what the user wants to do with the product, but also assume that customer needs are unique or constantly changing.

The Manufacturing People. Manufacturing people worry about the plant or operations, and are concerned that the others do not appreciate their special inflexibilities. A person at COMPCO explained that manufacturing is very concerned that marketing will take orders for products they cannot produce ". . . I don't like (them) taking risks (they) don't know (they) are taking." It seemed that these inflexibilities push manufacturing people to live in the ever present now. The director of operations for the voice service explained his problems with the others as follows:

> Sales and marketing live in the future and my needs are today. They are forever saying "why don't we do this?" or "isn't that easy to do?" But based on limited capacity now I can't do that. It's the same with networking. Sales and engineering wanted to bring up all the nodes at once! We said no, let's test it and do it one at a time. . . . They know, they hear, but they aren't involved (as closely). And they don't get the 5,000 calls from customers (when the system fails). . . . There needs to be more interface between those who design the future and those who live in the real world. (OPCO)

Note that, like the others quoted above, the person is aware of the others' concerns and issues, but emphasizes his problems over theirs.

Manufacturing people concentrate on reliability and quality, evaluating and defining the product in these terms. For example, a manufacturing engineer picked up a keyboard for the failed System II and threw it into a corner of the room to show how well built it was. "Look at that!" he said. "That's a damn fine keyboard!" (SALECO). It turns out that the system was a commercial failure (in part) because the keyboard was difficult to use. How often it could be thrown around was not a factor.

The Planning People. The future that planners see consists of emerging business possibilities such as the size of the market and total revenue potential. For planners, both the technological trends and specific customer applications pale into abstraction. As a planner at TECHCO put it: "We locate markets and make recommendations if it's worthwhile to enter them. And that depends on the margins, or the amount of money you will make." Analyzing "the business" also can be very frustrating and uncertain, as one explained:

> The environmental scan is the most difficult part. There isn't enough information available. We looked at traditional sources (of information) including market research firms. But the problem is they are guessing too, they develop scenarios. An awful lot of projecting from just a few numbers goes on in this business. (OPCO)

The information the planners need for their reports is difficult to gather, so they resort to modeling. For example, several people at OPCO spent three months developing a model to predict the size of an electronic data transfer market, and then they developed their business proposal around the estimate. To do such extensive analyses with such ambiguous data, planners cannot treat design and applications as constantly emerging. Instead they abstract these issues into more general scenarios. The nature of the planners' work is conceptual, not concrete, which means that their concrete-thinking colleagues will have trouble with their plans. For example, a technical person said: "It's hard to know what to do with reports we get from marketing." A field person said: "I'll take luck to market research any day."

Thought Worlds and Product Innovation. Interpretive differences between departmental thought worlds play a strong role in problems with collaboration over technology-market linking. From the outside looking in, one can see the conventional stereotypes for each department in the sketches above: Technical people never settle on a design, field people are short term, manufacturing people always say no, and planning people are conceptual. But from the inside looking out, each thought world is truly concerned with the successful development of the product. And as can be seen, each has an important insight into the product or market that is essential to a new product's development. Each emphasizes different aspects of development, however, and conceives of the whole in a different way.

When seen from the perspective of thought worlds, the collaboration problem runs deeper than conflicts over personality types or goals. Indeed, to attempt to resolve the problem through negotiation over goals may only begin to touch on the divergent understandings which lay at the heart of the problem. Nor is the problem like the proverbial set of blind men touching a different part of an elephant. It is more like the tales of eye witnesses at an accident, or of individuals in a troubled relationship—each tells a "complete" story, but tells a different one. Despite their potential benefits, departmental thought worlds separate the market-technology issues, limiting the possibility of a comprehensive understanding. The thought worlds also focus inward, reducing the possibility of learning. These data suggest that, to overcome the thought worlds' "inherent tenacity" (Fleck 1979) to focus on their own perspectives, managers may need to proactively foster collective action.

Organizational Routines

It became clear from the research that the thought worlds did not operate independently from the organizational context, however. Next, the analysis seeks to identify the organizational routines that affect product innovation, and how they affect collective action among the thought worlds. Most people described how products are usually developed in their firm, so the data provide some insight into routines. Descriptions of usual practice for product development (including evaluating the product, making decisions, and determining market needs) were transcribed onto coding sheets. The same kinds of practices used for the new product were also extracted, and compared with the usual practices by success status.

The analysis suggested three important patterns. First, three routines encourage thought world separation and inhibit learning. These routines were systematically violated in the successful cases, followed in the failed cases, and followed partly in uncertain cases. Second, the successful innovators did create a new social order for innovation. Third, the routines in these firms were very strong. Breaking out of them to establish an innovative social order seemed to be an unusual and often temporary event.

Organizational Routines, New Products, and Thought Worlds. The three routines found to affect product innovation concerned interdepartmental relations, market definition, and product standards. The first routine governed thought world relations by prescribing narrow roles and limited relationships. People would routinely do their own work and expect the same of others. Even when interactive structures such as task forces were used routinely, relationships were constrained, so the possibility of creating a new collective order which produced cross-fertilization and mutual learning was limited. The second routine imposed a predetermined definition of technology-market issues on product efforts. This reduced people's search for new information as well as the likelihood of frame-breaking learning. The third routine imposed standards which did not fit these new products. The standards varied by firm, and included set pay-back periods, profit margins, quality, and use of inhouse facilities. Following them forced developers to redefine the new product as an established business, further reducing new learning.

Successful developers violated all three routines, and created a new social order for their collaborative efforts. They developed mutually adaptive interactions in which knowledge of the work was developed as the work unfolded, as Mintzberg (1979) describes. They also created an alternate definition of the product in its market that was grounded in actual use, and developed appropriate standards to evaluate their efforts. The outcome was collective action as Fleck (1979) describes it: Each thought world rechanneled its readiness for directed perception from an inward to an outward focus so that their knowledge could join to produce new insights and new facts.

An Example of Routines at SALECO: System I Vs. System II. To illustrate the routines and how successful developers stepped out of them to create a new social order, SALECO's successful System I is contrasted with its failed System II. Both products used similar technology and some of the same people, and the failure followed the success, so the comparison holds constant some of the effects of individuals, technology, and experience. Appendix A summarizes how the other cases related to their organization's routines.

SALECO is a computer and communications manufacturer which has dominated several niches in these markets. The director of market research explained that, until five or ten years previously, SALECO's products were self-contained "turnkey" operations. SALECO maintained close relations with their dependent, installed base of business users through an extensive sales force. These customers' changing needs were easily monitored with in-depth customer profiles; product development became a sequential and highly organized process which abstracted customers' needs into financial indicators. A planner explained that they would look at a price-performance curve, and come up with a new product that sits further down the curve. "We would know what the market requirement is, and would invent nuances on the technology to do it." Predetermined goals and specifications were used to coordinate complex interdepartmental relationships, managed in a matrix structure. "The market" was given, so little energy would routinely go into ferreting out user needs. And, befitting a company with market dominance, product norms included high profit margins, high-quality production, and complete control of the product by handling all aspects inhouse.

The successful System I violated these carefully orchestrated, big business-oriented, financials-focused product routines, while the failed System II followed them. One person explained the overall routine violation as follows:

> The unique thing was they cut off (the System I group) from the culture. Basically a few top executives decided to play Daddy Warbucks. They disconnected (the team leader) from the normal process of building business cases.

The System I team's interdepartmental relationships encouraged ideas to be heard and built on and enhanced appreciation of one another's contributions. They interacted extensively, and, according to a field person, all participated in all the aspects of the product. Thus, rather than separating various concerns into pre-established role behavior, all problems and ambiguities were addressed from all angles, producing a more comprehensive design. Rather than coordinate by the usual formal but abstract plans, one member said ". . . we had no formal business plan, but everybody knew what it was." They did not create a single group mind, however. One explained that each department considered itself to be the one most important to the project, but that the leader fostered a sense of appreciation:

> . . . (the team leader) always listened to everyone when it came to making a decision, so even if his decision differed from your recommendation, you knew your information was as important as the others.

Along with redefining relationships, they redefined the task, and perhaps stepped out of the usual political truce that Nelson and Winter (1982) describe. The group created a vivid view of the product in its market which was more simple yet more realistic than SALECO's usual abstractions of price-performance ratios, market penetration estimates, and volume projections. The team used these general data, but combined them with first-order, direct experience with customers. An engineer describes their technology-market linking in what is almost a field person's perspective, as follows:

> The first thing was to define what the product was, who would buy it, and what they would use it for. . . . You have to get into the hearts and minds of users. . . . If you can't explain the product in 30 seconds, you're dead.

People's descriptions of their development process were full of instances in which they broke out of usual perspectives. For example, they broke out of SALECO's notion of customers as business people, and came to appreciate the new users for themselves. According to a planner:

> I remember our first focus group. It was a riot. There was this guy out there in a green T-shirt, long sideburns and a flattop, jeans, a belt with a big silver buckle, and cowboy boots. He happened to be the president of the local microcomputer club. It's frightening when you realize that on the other side of the one-way mirror there was a room full of men in [conservative business attire]. We had to understand that that guy was our new customer. It took a leap of faith.

Third, they broke most of SALECO's product norms and created new standards appropriate to the System I market. Instead of the usual inhouse manufacture which "made equipment you can drop off ten-story buildings," according to one, the machine was assembled from off-the-shelf parts purchased externally. This more effectively met the needs of low price in a market where "industrial strength" durability was not critical. Instead of total control by SALECO, they designed an open architecture to allow others to write software for sale. The group even published a book explaining how outsiders could build on the machine with their own products. Instead of careful quality control, some of the external software had bugs in it—the number of applications was more important to this market than perfect operation.

Less than a year later, this business unit began work on a follow-on product aimed at both professionals and home use. A number of new people were involved, but so were many of the System I group, including the leader and the senior people who played "Daddy Warbucks." More like SALECO's usual product development, however, the plan was simply to continue the momentum begun by System I. Interdepartmental relationships seemed to have also reverted to routine, and the inwardness of thought worlds dominated the people's work. When asked to describe the System II organization, an engineer went to his board and drew a circle to show the System I team. Then he drew an arrow over to a matrix to represent the System II organization, with columns for departments, and rows for various products under development—SALECO's routine matrix form. A planner explained that some people from the first effort were not fully focused on this product, that several key people left, and that the group had lost what he called its "group think."

For the technology-market definition, System II developers relied on assumed applications and users, as usual. A market had been "analyzed" with the routine calculus of price-performance trade-offs and buyer potential, and not questioned again. The design had unique features but these were not tested with users. As it turns out, few users liked the product. An engineer explained:

> We didn't get the system into real scenarios to test out our premises. We were overconfident. . . . We all thought we were very smart. . . . We made a lot of decisions daily to change the product based on what we thought we understood about the marketplace.

A market researcher noted that perhaps some focus groups would have picked up the problem they found after introduction with certain features. But he said that the design and manufacturing process had generated such a momentum, that:

> We would have been disappointed with the negative feedback, but we would have gone on with (the design) anyway.

Third, the System II team followed some of SALECO's usual product standards that were appropriate to its large systems, but not, perhaps, for System II. Inhouse manufacturing rather than assembly was used, and reliability and durability were emphasized. According to a manufacturing person:

> The product was fantastic. But it was high priced. You can't cut price or quality. There is no way SALECO would sell a lower-quality product. But then people would say why should I pay so much for this computer, instead of paying attention to all the enhancements we put on it. . . . It has half-size disk drives. . . . Our fundamental error was in the design of [a certain part]. It didn't have user flexibility. That got us a lot of negative press. But the function was great. It should have sold like hotcakes.

By following the usual product development routines, the System II team produced a high quality, rather expensive but durable machine—just what SALECO's routines are designed to produce. Unfortunately the team did not begin with an established market, which the routines also presume, so the system did not fit any real needs. Sales were not high enough to cover the manufacturing costs, so the company shut down the plant, laid off the factory workers, and canceled the product.

DISCUSSION

An extensive literature tells managers how they ought to develop new products, and how they ought to design their organizations for innovation. This study has examined product innovation in practice in order to understand why these prescriptions are not often achieved. The research is limited by its exploratory nature, and the fact that commitment, leadership, politics, and other possible factors have not been included. However, it describes how two interpretive schemes can become barriers to effective technology-market linking. Departmental thought worlds partition the information and insights. Each also has a distinct system of meaning which colors its interpretation of the same information, selectively filters technology-market issues, and produces a qualitatively different understanding of product innovation. Organizational product routines reinforce thought world separation by providing for only limited interaction, and further inhibit the kind of collective action that is necessary to innovation.

Implications for Theory and Practice

This research suggests two important implications for the study and practice of innovation. The first is that theorists and practitioners need to pay attention to the effects of thought worlds and organizational routines. Innovation is an interpretive process, so the management of innovation must involve the management of the interpretive schemes that shape and frame how people make sense of their work. Innovation requires *collective action,* or efforts to create shared understandings from disparate perspectives. The advocation of rational tools and processes, the infusion of market research information, and the redesign of structures, while important, are not enough.

The second implication is that the potential barriers these interpretive schemes may become need to be dealt with specifically and in depth. This study suggests three intermediary processes which together can help overcome the barriers. Innovators must: (1) use and build on the unique insights of each thought world, (2) develop collaborative mechanisms that deal directly with the interpretive as well as structural barriers to collective action, and (3) develop an organizational context for collective action that enables both. The work suggests that, unless all three processes occur together, the thought world boundaries and routines may dominate. If so, pitfalls will be overlooked, meanings lost, and communication curtailed, as was the experience of OPCO's accounting system developers.

Building on the Thought Worlds. Each thought world knows about aspects of technology-market knowledge that others may gloss over. All must actively contribute to the product design, and actively challenge each other, or the final design will be awry. This means that reservations or skunkworks comprised solely of R&D people, as some theorists suggest (e.g., Galbraith 1982), would not be effective. The management of innovation is not merely the management of the R&D group or the coordination of activities, it comprises the *collective* creation of the product in its market.

This analysis has gone beyond the general differences in orientations usually cited to identify specific interpretive differences that must be confronted and overcome for new products. As argued here, innovators from different departments may *not* conflict over general goals or even over such intermediate goals as being "market oriented." They do, however, have unique interpretations of these goals, along the themes described in Table 10.4. Technical and field people focus on customers and have a concrete view of development. This means that reports from the conceptual market researchers may not make any sense to them, and may be ignored. Field people's close view of customers could contribute important insights to design, but it may also keep them from summarizing specifications that technical people need. Technical people's search for a general design makes them seem unresponsive to field people's requests for specific changes. Manufacturing people worry that others do not understand the limits of the plant, and so may dig in their heels unless their concerns are handled openly. These differences can preclude the development of an optimal design by producing severe frustrations and perhaps withdrawals into separate thought worlds. They must be deliberately and directly addressed as they come up.

Developing Collaboration Mechanisms. Collaboration mechanisms need to take into account the interpretive dynamics that separate the thought worlds. Their "intrinsic harmony" prompts people to focus inward on their own tasks, and to fill in unknowns from their thought world. Thought worlds most likely always exist where tasks are specialized, so efforts to surmount them always have to be made. Participants in interdisciplinary teams may feel "drawn inward" into their thought world over time, especially if they have other assignments, as is often the case. The analysis suggests one important way to overcome the inward dynamic. As in the SALECO System I case, thought worlds can come to a similar understanding of the product in the user's hands, and innovators can perhaps build a comprehensive appreciation from this common view. Interdisciplinary responsibility for focus groups, market research plans, technology audits, and visits with users should enhance collaboration. Structures alone such as liaison and boundary spanner roles or project groups do not assure that these dynamics of separation will be overcome. A realistic customer focus may.

Developing the Context for Collective Action. This research also suggests that thought world barriers cannot be overcome unless aspects of the organizational context which foster separation are also overcome. The capacity for collective action depends in part on organization level interpretive dynamics. It is inferred that an innovative social order must be designed specifically for new products so that: (1) interactions between thought worlds are based on appreciation and joint development, (2) product definitions are based on collective, first-order customer knowledge, and (3) product norms are based on the specific market. It is inferred further that general organizational attributes such as a risk-taking climate, visionary leadership, and/or an integrative culture may not address these day-to-day practices, although perhaps they increase innovative activity. Moreover, routines, like thought worlds, are probably inertial, and thus always have to be overcome. No matter what the general organizational design, managers must foster ongoing processes of knowledge development, joint learning, and customer interactions.

Future Research

Research is necessary to clarify and test all these implications. This study has not considered the structural aspects of thought worlds that might affect their collective action. Fleck (1979), for example, theorizes that stability of membership, the strength of the established beliefs, the clarity of boundaries, and power relationships within the thought world can all have an effect. For departments, one could speculate that people's training, experience, and professionalization would affect thought world separation or integration.

Studies might explore whether and how job rotation, team experience, and bringing the tacit thought world differences to conscious awareness improve the propensity for collective action. Research on the R&D-manufacturing relationship is perhaps the most advanced (Adler 1990, Dean and Susman 1989), and these insights can be elaborated to include all four departments. Other approaches for mapping frames of reference (Dunn and Ginsberg 1986) should expand our understanding of departmental differences.

The implications for organizational routines are the most potentially confounded by attribution bias and the limited number and types of firms in the study. Additional research is essential to define the routines that inhibit innovation and articulate more clearly how they work. Research should also identify the routines, if any, which can foster innovation. The literature contains numerous discussions of *general* organizational attributes and phenomena that presumably engender innovation (e.g., Kanter 1983, Galbraith 1982). An important next step is to understand the relationships between such general contexts and the specific tasks of innovation, including technology-market knowledge development and thought world collective action. Focused research which examines these dynamics directly, and longitudinal research which sorts out the causal relationships between interpretive barriers and other factors are necessary.

In conclusion, this work indicates that improvements in the new product success rate are possible if innovators combine the prescriptive models with attention to these interpretive barriers, and the *ongoing processes* necessary to overcome them. Rather than test theory, this study has applied theory to the problem of new product development. The insights are more practical than theoretical, but the findings support the growing literature that understanding the interpretive dynamics of innovation and change is crucial (Bartunek 1984, Schein 1985, Barley 1986). The results show that such dynamics apply to product innovation, and can be studied systematically. Continued research into these interpretive dynamics, along with continued efforts to join organization theory with insights from marketing and technology, should advance our understanding of the complex problem of product innovation in large firms.

ACKNOWLEDGMENTS

The data on which this chapter are based come from a study sponsored by the Marketing Science Institute and a pre-doctoral fellowship from the American Association of University Women. A grant from the Reginald Jones Center and a Doris and Michael Goldberg Fellowship from the Snider Center for Entrepreneurial Studies, both of the Wharton School, supported this analysis. I would like to thank Ed

Schein, John Van Maanen, David Thomas, Larry Hirschhorn, Stew Friedman, and Marsha Wilkof for insightful critiques. This chapter has also benefited significantly from critiques by editor Richard Daft and three anonymous reviewers for *Organization Science.*

Appendix A

Summary of Cases and Their Relationships with Routines

This appendix provides a thumbnail sketch of products in this study. See Dougherty (1987) for a complete description of each case, and Dougherty (1990) for an analysis of development processes. Since the relationships with organizational routines are important, so the cases are reported by company rather than success status. All firms and products are disguised.

TECHCO: Producer of chemical based products. Routines for product development stress technological innovativeness, and market analyses routinely not done. High quality was also a standard. Product development usually begins in R&D; procedure was to include others in sequence as the product was ready for a business analysis and marketing plan. People interviewed in Fall 1985.

1. *Failed Battery.* A technologically unique no-leak battery; originally invented for a product line, but because of excess production capacity, TECHCO decided to sell battery to others. Toy manufacturers were selected as market since toys were a big user of batteries; no analyses of needs, problems, etc. Introduced in late 1981. Product required redesign of toys, and was not widely available so toy companies were not interested. Canceled after 3 years. *Routines.* A technology dominant task force used for development, sponsored by senior VP; market definition based on what the battery could do, not what users needed; standards of uniqueness and high quality met.

2. *Uncertain CRT Device.* Electronically transfers computer images to produce a hardcopy. Began in R&D. Introduced in Fall 1983. Sales very slow; an interdisciplinary team was set up after introduction, and they were redesigning the product and changing the distribution system. *Routines.* Technology driven, limited interdepartmental interaction; marketing research advised against the product but were ignored. Market defined as white collar office workers; development delayed until quality standards could be met.

3. *Uncertain Video Device.* Similar to CRT device, but captures television signals. Also began in R&D, developed for home use. Commercial division took it, so product redesigned for commercial use. Were design, manufacturing, and quality problems. Concerns over quality and technical design persist. *Routines.* Partially broke routines by doing a market test jointly with R&D and marketing people; interaction seemed good; hung up on established product standards based on chemicals (this was electronic).

4. *Uncertain Medical Hardcopy System.* A chemical and mechanical technology that produces hardcopy from medical diagnostics machines. Requires redesign by diagnostics manufacturers. Delayed for over a year because of manufacturing problems; in the interim a competitor came out with similar product at much less cost. Now looking for alternate markets and uses. *Routines.* Set up an interdisciplinary task force; good interaction except with manufacturing; market plans good but limited to existing markets, contrary to original plan. Hung up on usual markets and standards.

5. *Successful Film Cover.* Adapts a light-proof paper wrap TECHCO makes for other products to contain professional grade photography film purchased from others. Very "low-tech" but intended for new markets and applications. Test market sales exceeded projections, so introduction advanced by 6 months. *Routines.* Began in business unit; product champion incorporated manufacturing and purchasing people on informal or "bootleg" team; all visited users together; considerable market data gathered; design adjusted to meet particular problems. Violated product approval and quality procedures.

OPCO: An operating phone company whose routines stressed low risk ventures, short-term planning, and quarterly operations reviews of all businesses and senior managers. Corporate requires extensive analyses of all new business plans. OPCO's Data Division evolved a "fast-out" product routine to avoid the "corporate gauntlet." They sneaked their first product, the Text System, into the market. Interviews from February to April 1986.

1. *Uncertain Voice System.* (Not associated with OPCO Data) Electronically transfers voice to digitalized packets transmitted over network. One of the first uses of this technology, introduced in 1983; still losing money. *Routines.* Began by a planner; general plans with no applications analyses (files reviewed by author). No interdisciplinary work. During test market product redesigned for discovered market of interoffice uses; multiple market definitions still operate. A venture group formed 2 years after test market.

2. *Uncertain Text System.* Similar technology to voice but transfers text. Introduced in the early 1980s; sales growth high but competition is strong and earnings uncertain. *Routines.* Developed by a technical skunkworks, and introduced as a technology. Market plan based on the number of salespeople, not users or needs. Violated OPCO corporate's analysis, but followed technology driven, fast-out routines in division. No interdisciplinary group or comprehensive market definition; these now being developed.

3. *Failed Document System.* Allows text system users to produce a hardcopy delivered overnight to people not on the network. System failed since some mail took 2 weeks; removed from the market. *Routines.* Business planning and technical development done separately. Technical and operational plan poor but chosen because it could be done by the end of the quarter. Original market defined in vague terms.

4. *Failed Accounting System.* Transacts credit card purchases for retailers over a network. System double-debited and double-credited, and then crashed. Removed from market. *Routines.* Followed usual planning process with little connection between technology and marketing; business plan was complete, but particular applications not examined for design. Followed fast-out standard.

5. *Uncertain Transmit System.* Product still in development. It will transmit data between manufacturers and suppliers. Plan created by an interdisciplinary team. The plan violates OPCO's standards for a 2-year payback, so developers were unsure if it would be approved.

6. *Uncertain Software System.* Product transfers software over the network from terminal to terminal or downloading from a central file. Just introduced, and is being given 90 days to "make" it. Market very uncertain. *Routines.* Developed by a planner, with some interaction from technical people. Targeted market has changed because software firms initially agreed to cooperate but then refused. Market definition very general—now the "Fortune 1000." Followed standards of general business analyses.

SALECO: see text. Interviews Summer 1986.

COMPCO: Chemical materials producer. Has a dominant market position with a certain grade of plastic. Product development usually begins with requests from customers processed through field, and these requests are responded to quickly. Market need is always known, so little analysis is routinely done. COMPCO has 102 variations of basic plastic. Interviews Fall 1986.

1. *Failed Hardpoly.* Combines a harder polymer with its basic one, giving the plastic more strength yet a lower cost than the stronger polymer alone. Previous efforts to combine these polymers could not overcome certain problems. The material was introduced into an application but failed the heat test and was withdrawn. *Routines.* The material began in technical, not field, but was then treated as a typical user request. An interdisciplinary task force was appointed, as is the routine, but there was little interaction between departments, and field assumed that it would perform as they expected.

2. *Uncertain Stretchpoly.* Combines a flexible polymer with COMPCO's basic material, for added flexibility and water resistance. The material was introduced 2 years ago into automotive, but does not meet those needs, and new niches are being explored. *Routines.* Like hardpoly, the material began in research, contrary to routines, so it had no clear market demand. Some market research was not used, and they assumed it would fit into their major market, the automotive business. An interdisciplinary project team has since been set up, and they are actively monitoring the product.

3. *Successful Hotpoly.* This is a new kind of polymer for COMPCO, with much greater heat resistance, and it opens up new market areas for the firm. The material was introduced in later 1982; only 1 other firm made it. Initial sales slow; field was not selling the product, and they overestimated users' willingness to adopt a new product. With changes in sales-rewards and market analyses hotpoly has become successful, and COMPCO is building a multi-million dollar plant. *Routines.* A new task force was set up from the beginning with everyone but field involved; senior management gave strong support; new business and market plans were made.

PRODCO: A chemical materials producer. The five interviews were not adequate to develop a general appreciation of PRODCO routines. Interviews Fall 1986.

1. *Failed Pit Liner.* The product is a membrane-like material that lines industrial waste pits, creating large containment areas. Previous materials had to be buried a foot underground to avoid exposure to the sun. A supplier created a new material that resisted the sun, or so they thought. PRODCO entered the pit business with the new material in the early 1970's. After 3 years, material decayed. All pits had to be replaced. It seems that usual routines were followed, but in this case failure was an "act of God."

2. *Successful Roof Liner.* The product is a membrane-like material (but does not decay in the sun) used for industrial roofs. It was introduced in 1981 and has become a multi-million dollar business. *Routines.* A separate business unit was created with people from all departments in it. They worked together extensively, and the product was designed based on first-order data from users. They violated PRODCO's usual distribution process, planning process, and reporting structure. The team continues to run the business.

Appendix B

Thought Worlds Controlling for Company and Success or Failure of Product

The market-technology knowledge and cognitive orientations were analyzed with a two-way ANOVA by department and company to see if the thought world differences held across company. Manufacturing people and the 4 PRODCO people were deleted from the analysis since there are so few of them, so the results are for 4 firms and 3 departments. The figures in Table B.1 are the means by company, weighted by thought world—the mean for planners, technical and field was added and divided by 3 to adjust for the different proportions of thought worlds in each firm. There is one interaction effect, and subsequent analysis shows that OPCO's field people are below average on business issues. There is also one company effect; analysis indicates that SALECO is below average on customer issues. The results, overall, however, suggest that the differences by department reported in Table 10.3 hold regardless of company. These analyses are exploratory only since there are problems with the variances.

Table B.2 summarizes the means by success status (again, weighted so each thought world has an equal effect) on the 7 thought world measures. Analyses were also run without the manufacturing people to check for problems with the small cell sizes, and the results are similar. The department effect is found for all 7 measures. Successful developers also emphasize customer issues more and technology and manufacturing issues less. In addition, the successful developers are long term and people oriented, consistent with the qualitative result that they have a more comprehensive technology-market knowledge and more collaborative relationships. Since the successful cases have been out longer, the results may be biased by time. To check for this, uncertain and failed cases which have been out for less than 2 years were deleted and the analysis rerun. The results were similar, which suggests no time bias.

TABLE B.1 Thought World Measures by Company

	Weighted Mean Score					ANOVA results Dept. effect Company effect Interaction effect (prodco, manuf not included)
Thought World Measures	*SALECO*	*OPCO*	*COMPCO*	*TECHCO*		
Percentage of Interview						
Business Issues	32	27	29	33		D F = 12.7*
						C 0.9
						I 1.96**
Customer Issues	16	23	23	19		D F = 6.6*
						C 2.5**
						I 1.2
Selling Issues	12	12	17	9		D F = 12.5*
						C 1.6
						I 1.6
Technical Issues	32	32	25	29		D F = 31.3*
						C 1.5
						I 0.4
Manufacturing	7	5	6	8		D F = 0.5
						C 1.8
						I 0.3
Orientations—Mean Ranks						
Long-Short Time	37	32	37	38		D F = 0.3
						C 0.7
						I 1.8
Task-People	38	29	32	38	33	D F = 2.6**
						C 1.0
						I 1.4

*$p < 0.05$.
**$p < 0.1$; Department $df = 2, 48$; Company $df = 3, 48$; Interaction $df = 6, 48$.

TABLE B.2 Thought World Measures by Success Status

Thought World Measures	*Weighted Mean Score* Successful	Uncertain	Failed	*ANOVA results: Dept. Effect Success Effect Interaction Effect*	
Percentage of Interview					
Business Issues	32	25	24	D F =	13.2*
				S	2.0
				I	1.38
Customer Issues	20	21	15	D F =	4.12*
				S	8.1*
				I	0.99
Selling Issues	13	10	8	D F =	9.7*
				S	1.3
				I	1.3
Technical Issues	23	29	30	D F =	20.7*
				S	4.8*
				I	1.3
Manufacturing	14	14	17	D F =	71.3*
				S	2.5**
				I	2.3
Orientations—Mean Ranks					
Long-Short time	46	32	30	D F =	3.08*
				S	2.5**
				I	0.72
Task-People	25	40	44	D F =	3.6*
				C	3.4*
				1	0.60

*$p < 0.05$.
**$p < 0.1$; Department $df = 3, 59$; Success $df = 2, 59$; Interaction $df = 6, 59$.

REFERENCES

Adler, P. (1990), "Shared Learning," *Management Science*, 36, 938-957.

Argyris, C. and D. Schön (1978), *Organizational Learning: A Theory of Action Approach*, Reading, MA: Addison Wesley.

Bailyn, L. (1977), "Research as a Cognitive Process: Implications for Data Analysis," *Quality and Quantity*, 11, 97-117.

Barley, S. R. (1986), "Technology as an Occasion for Structuring: Evidence from Observations of CT Scanners and the Social Order of Radiology Departments," *Administrative Science Quarterly*, 31, 78-108.

Bartunek, J. M. (1984), "Changing Interpretive Schemes and Organizational Restructuring: The Example of a Religious Order," *Administrative Science Quarterly*, 29, 355-372.

Bonnet, D. (1986), "Nature of the R&D/Marketing Co-operation in the Design of Technologically Advanced New Industrial Products," *R&D Management*, 16, 117-126.

Clark, K. (1985), "The Interaction of Design Hierarchies and Market Concepts in Technological Evolution," *Research Policy*, 14, 235-251.

Cooper and E. Kleinschmidt (1986), "An Investigation into the New Product Process: Steps, Deficiencies, and Impact," *Journal of Product Innovation Management*, 3, 71-85.

Daft, R. and K. Weick (1984), "Toward a Model of Organizations as Interpretive Systems," *Academy of Management Review*, 9, 43-66.

Dean, J. and G. Susman (1989), "Organizing for Manufacturable Design," *Harvard Business Review*, (January-February), 28-37.

Dearborn, D. and H. Simon (1958), "Selective Perception: A Note on the Departmental Identification of Executives," *Sociometry*, 140-144.

Dougherty, D. (1987), "New Products in Old Organizations: The Myth of the Better Mousetrap in Search of the Beaten Path," unpublished Doctoral Dissertation, MIT, Sloan School of Management.

——— (1990), "Understanding New Markets for New Products," *Strategic Management Journal*, 11, 59-78.

Douglas, M. (1987), *How Institutions Think*, London: Routledge & Kegan Paul.

Dunn, W. and A. Ginsberg (1986), "A Sociocognitive Network Approach to Organization Analysis," *Human Relations*, 40, 955-976.

Fleck, L. (1979), *Genesis and Development of a Scientific Fact*, T. Trenn and R. K. Merton (Eds.), translated by F. Bradley and T. Trenn; originally published 1935; Chicago: University of Chicago Press.

Freeman, C. (1982), *The Economics of Industrial Innovation*, Cambridge: MIT Press.

Galbraith, J. (1982), "Designing the Innovative Organization," *Organization Dynamics*, (Winter), 5-25.

Gupta, A., S. Raj, and D. Wilemon (1986), "R&D and Marketing Managers in High-Tech Companies: Are They Different?" *IEEE Transactions on Engineering Management*, 33, 25-32.

Harrison, F. (1980), "Goal orientations of Managers and Scientists: An Illusory Dichotomy," *IEEE Transactions on Engineering Management*, 27, 74-78.

Henderson, R. and K. Clark, (1990), "Architectures for Innovation: The Reconfiguration of Existing Product Technology and the Failure of Existing Firms," *Administrative Science Quarterly*, (March).

Kanter, R. M. (1983), *The Change Masters*, New York: Simon & Schuster.

Lawrence, P. and J. Lorsch (1967), *Organization and Environment*, Boston: Harvard School of Business Administration Press.

Lilien, G. and E. Yoon (1988), "Determinants of New Industrial Product Performance: A Strategic Re-Examination of Empirical Literature," *IEEE Transactions on Engineering Management,* 36, 3-10.

March, J. and H. Simon (1958), *Organizations,* New York: John Wiley.

Mintzberg, H. (1979), *The Structuring of Organizations,* Englewood Cliffs, NJ: Prentice Hall.

Nelson, R. R. and S. G. Winter (1982), *An Evolutionary Theory of Economic Change,* Boston: Belknap.

Perrow, C. (1986), *Complex Organizations: A Critical Essay* (3rd ed.), New York: Random House.

Riley, P. (1983), "A Structurationist Account of Political Culture," *Administrative Science Quarterly,* 28, 414-437.

Rothwell, R., C. Freeman, A. Horsley, V. Jervis, A. Robertson, and J. Crawford (1974), "SAPPHO Updated. Project SAPPHO Phase II," *Research Policy,* 32, 58-291.

Schall, M. (1983), "A Communication Rules Approach to Organizational Culture," *Administrative Science Quarterly,* 28, 557-581.

Schein, E. (1985), *Organizational Culture and Leadership,* San Francisco: Jossey-Bass.

Souder, W. (1987), *Managing New Product Innovations,* Lexington, MA: Lexington Books.

Strauss, A. (1987), *Qualitative Analysis for Social Scientists,* Cambridge, UK: Cambridge University Press.

Tushman, M. (1978), "Technical Communication in R&D Laboratories: The Impact of Project Work Characteristics," *Academy of Management Journal,* 21, 624-645.

——— and D. Nadler (1986), "Organizing for Innovation," *California Management Review,* 28, 74-92.

Urban, G. and E. von Hippel (1988), "Lead User Analyses for the Development of New Industrial Products," *Management Science,* 34, 569-582.

Van Maanen, J. (1979), "On the Understanding of Interpersonal Relations," in W. Bennis, J. Van Maanen, E. Schein, and F. I. Steele (Eds.), *Essays in Interpersonal Communication,* Homewood, IL: Dorsey, 13-42.

——— and S. R. Barley (1984), "Occupational Communities: Culture and Control in Organizations," *Research in Organizational Behavior,* 6, Greenwich, CT: JAI, 287-365.

Yin, R. (1989), *Case Study Research: Design and Methods,* Newbury Park, CA: Sage.

11

Organizational Routines Are Stored as Procedural Memory

Evidence from a Laboratory Study

MICHAEL D. COHEN
PAUL BACDAYAN

This original, well-crafted chapter makes a significant contribution to the understanding of organizational routines and extends, in a rather novel way, the treatment and properties of procedural memory. The chapter also exemplifies how individual/group laboratory work can be creatively extended to organizational phenomena.

—Arie Y. Lewin

Organizational routines—multi-actor, interlocking, reciprocally triggered sequences of actions—are a major source of the reliability and speed of organizational performance. Without routines, organizations would lose efficiency as structures for collective action. But these frequently repeated action sequences can also occasionally give rise to serious suboptimality, hampering performance when they are automatically transferred onto inappropriate situations.

While the knowledgeable design and redesign of routines presents a likely lever for those wishing to enhance organizational performance, the lever remains difficult to grasp because routines are hard to observe, analyze, and describe. This

This chapter originally appeared in *Organization Science*, Vol. 5, No. 4, November 1994.

chapter argues that new work in psychology on "procedural" memory may help explain how routines arise, stabilize, and change. Procedural memory has close links to notions of individual skill and habit. It is memory for how things are done that is relatively automatic and inarticulate, and it encompasses both cognitive and motor activities.

We report an experiment in which paired subjects developed interlocked task performance patterns that display the chief characteristics of organizational routines. We show evidence from their behavior supporting the claim that individuals store their components of organizational routines in procedural memory. If routines are stored as distributed procedural memories, this may be the source of distinctive properties reported by observers of organizational routines. The chapter concludes with implications for both research and practice.

(ROUTINES; ORGANIZATIONAL LEARNING;
STANDARD OPERATING PROCEDURES;
PROCEDURAL MEMORY;
ORGANIZATIONAL MEMORY SKILLS)

Recent work in psychology on "procedural" human memory may help organization theorists explain key properties of organizational routines, including the dynamics of how they arise, stabilize, and change. We view organizational routines as interlocking, reciprocally triggered sequences of skilled actions. Striking characteristics of collective routines, such as the tendency to occasionally "misfire" in inappropriate circumstances, may be grounded in the properties psychology has demonstrated for the procedural memories of individual participants.

Procedural memory has close links to notions of individual skill and habit. It is memory for how things are done that is relatively automatic and inarticulate, and it encompasses cognitive as well as motor activities. While others (notably, Nelson and Winter 1982) have pointed eloquently to the similarity of individual skill and organizational routine, we extend the idea by asserting that the similarity is founded on specific characteristics of the memories of organizational members, and we present evidence for the claim from experimentally induced group routines.

Our argument proceeds as follows. First, we identify the need for improved understanding of organizational routines and the barriers to understanding that must be overcome. Second, we argue for the theoretical fruitfulness of incorporating the concept of procedural memory into our thinking about routines: We also argue that laboratory experimentation provides an especially useful kind of evidence for investigations of organizational routine. Third, we describe our experimental method of establishing routines in laboratory dyads. Fourth, we report two major results: that the behaviors of our subject pairs have the distinctive features of *organizational* routines, and that individual memories of parts in those routines have the characteristics of the procedural mode. Fifth, we close by exploring the implications of our results both for managers and for organization theorists, paying particular attention to organizational learning and bounded rationality.

We aim to begin unlocking the *dynamics* of organizational routines, the ways they arise and change, by demonstrating that they can be induced in the laboratory and by showing that organizational routines emerge from the interaction of procedurally remembering individuals.

THE IMPORTANCE OF ROUTINES AND THE DIFFICULTIES OF UNDERSTANDING THEM

Routines appear prominently and persistently in descriptions of organizational action (March and Simon 1958, Cyert and March 1963, Allison 1971, Nelson and Winter 1982, Levitt and March 1988, Gersick and Hackman 1990). Their properties clearly merit deeper explanation since, for both good and ill, routines structure so much organizational behavior. On the good side, routines are a major source of organizational competence. Routines arise in repetitive situations where the recurring cost of careful deliberation can become a heavy burden; they store organizational experience in a form that allows the organization to rapidly transfer that experience to new situations.

When the experience is transferred to appropriate situations, routines benefit the organization. They not only provide a major determinant of the nature of short-run organizational responses to familiar and unfamiliar environmental stimuli, but they do so efficiently by decreasing the effort spent on decision making and implementation. Without routines, organizations would not be efficient structures for collective action (Stinchcombe 1990, March and Simon 1958).

When, however, the organization's experience is automatically transferred to inappropriate situations, routines can be bad. Consider, for example, control room operators or pilots whose vigilance erodes when they become so accustomed to answering each safety check "okay" that they don't see trouble when it actually is present (Gersick and Hackman 1990). Or again, consider the case of civilian-clothed Soviet troops arriving secretly in Cuba who nonetheless formed into ranks on the dock and marched conspicuously away (Allison 1971, p. 109). Thus routines are like a two-edged sword. They allow efficient coordinated action, but also introduce the risk of highly inappropriate responses.

By "organizational routines," we mean patterned sequences of learned behavior involving multiple actors who are linked by relations of communication and/or authority. Though they are organized by such relations, the actors may have heterogeneous objectives, information, capabilities, or world models. We use "routine" to designate established patterns of organizational action and we distinguish routines from "standard operating procedures" which are more explicitly formulated and have normative standing. Thus the working routines of an organization may or may not be equivalent to its official standard operating procedures. The value of the distinction becomes clear when one observes that "working-to-rule" can be a profoundly disruptive tactic of labor protest. We also reserve "routine" exclusively for organizational actions and use "skill" or "habit" at the individual level.

Given the important role of routines in patterning the behavior of organizations, it follows that in our efforts to create change we often want to design or redesign routines, and for this we need to better understand the forces that create and maintain them. Information technology, for example, is often introduced with the aim of augmenting or replacing existing routines. But research on information technology (Zuboff 1988), and on other innovations in manufacturing (Womack et al. 1990), shows us that even the most advanced new systems can end up gathering dust, and that major reorganizations and technical investments can dramatically fail to increase productivity if the technology is founded on a misunderstanding of the underlying system of routines. Such observations make painfully clear both the pressing need for intelligent (re)design of routines and the poverty of our understanding.

The understanding of organizational routines is hampered, however, by three basic characteristics. First, routines are multi-actor, and thus harder to observe and grasp than single-actor phenomena. (Indeed, the multi-actor character of routines is a major way in which organization is constituted out of member individuals.) The distributed character of the action complicates the work of both managers and field researchers. Landing a commercial airline flight is highly routinized, but we cannot understand it only by examining the pilot's part.

A second characteristic of organizational routines that hinders both understanding and design is their emergent quality. Organizations provide fertile conditions for the evolution of behavior patterns by experiential learning rather than explicit decision making. Documentation is typically sparse and turnover eliminates individuals who recall the intended functions of particular acts. Moreover, there is frequently no one with the intellectual grasp or authority to self-consciously analyze or design a major routine in its entirety. Thus organizational routines often emerge through gradual multi-actor learning, and exhibit tangled histories that may frustrate both understanding and reform.

Experiential learning is often accretionary—hence over time routines can become "contaminated" with extraneous, historically specific and arbitrary components. Most real-world routines will contain, in addition to valuable elements (e.g., those which might maintain dignity of participants, enhance communication of unstructured information, or overcome individual cognitive limitations), less valuable components. Routines may preserve artifacts of old technology (e.g., continuing to do something in an inconvenient way that originally avoided a technological obstacle that no longer exists). Thus a time-and-motion expert studying motorized British artillery crews around the time of World War II was puzzled by a recurring three-second pause just before firing. Finally, an old timer watching slow-motion films said, "Ah, I have it. They are holding the horses" (Morison 1966). Or, as another example, routines may simply sustain accidents of history. So an experimental group's pace and style in working on a second, comparable task resembles that of their first session even though the experimenter has doubled or halved the time available (Kelly and McGrath 1985). These emergent, historical qualities imply that sorting out the real functions of the different components of a routine can become a very challenging task.

A third, and pivotal, characteristic of routines which hinders redesign is that the underlying knowledge of the parts of routines held by individual actors is often partially inarticulate. Although it may seem that a manager or researcher ought to be able to understand a routine by interviewing the participants, it frequently turns out that they simply cannot put into words what they do and why. For example, the artillery crews mentioned above could not tell the researcher why they paused. This is most striking for nonverbal tasks such as operating machinery (Nelson and Winter 1982, Zuboff 1988), but the problem is encountered even when tasks have significant verbal components, such as forms processing or filing (Sheil 1981, Suchman 1983).

Organizational actors who cannot give meaningful responses to typical interview questions are like subjects in some experiments who prove unable to give accurate reports of the causes of their own actions (Nisbett and Wilson 1977), or experts who have difficulty providing clear accounts of the skills to be coded into expert systems programs (Gaines and Boose 1988) The problem is to surface hard-to-verbalize knowledge and skill. Thus routines reside partially in an "organizational unconscious," which greatly compounds the observational and analytical problems associated with their multi-actor and learned character.

To summarize, routines offer a powerful concept that accounts for much of what happens—both good and bad—in organizations, and the knowledgeable design of routines presents a potential lever to those interested in enhancing organizational performance. This lever remains hard to grasp, however, because the characteristics described earlier block observation, analysis, and description of specific routines. As we will suggest in the following sections, these properties may be due to the storage of the individual actors' parts in organizational routines as procedural memories.

REQUIREMENTS FOR THEORETICAL PROGRESS

If organizational routines are learned behaviors involving multiple actors, it follows that if we want to control, design, or modify them with increased precision, we need to understand how organizational members learn their parts in routines. And to do this we need advances both in theory and in observation. It may seem strange to call for theory development when routine and standard operating procedure have been cornerstone concepts of behavioral organization theory since Cyert and March (1963). But, in fact, there has been very little advance of basic theory since their pathbreaking work. There have been many applications of the theory to interpretation of field observations of routine. Thus the *Social Science Citation Index* shows 71 citations of Cyert and March in a recent five-year period, but none of the citing articles attempts to further develop their theory of routines and standard operating procedures. For the most part, the concept of routine has been applied to mop up the "residuals" of rationality, i.e., as *post hoc* explanation of apparently nonrational behavior. The many studies do not seem to have yielded a better theoretical understanding of routines themselves—where they come from or how they change.

Both theory and observation need new impetus. Our approach on the theoretical side is to point out the potential of developments in recent psychological research that, we feel, give hope of improving our grasp of the dynamics of routines (Cohen 1991). On the observational side, we show here the value of supplementing field work with laboratory studies, where increased control makes it easier to assess the promise of new theory and to arrange observations that have the chance of generalizing to multiple settings.

Procedural Memory

Psychological work over the last decade has accumulated substantial evidence for several partially independent modes of memory (Squire 1987,

Tulving and Schacter 1990). "Procedural" memory appears to be the form that stores the components of individual skilled actions—for both motor *and cognitive* skills. It is distinguished from "declarative" memory, which provides the storage of facts, propositions, and events.[1]

One of the most striking illustrations comes from work with patients suffering certain forms of amnesia. They may be unable to remember daily exposures to therapists, apparatus, and training, but nonetheless show improvement on tasks as complex as the game of checkers or the difficult puzzle known as "The Tower of Hanoi" (Cohen 1984). With only procedural memory available, they learn and exhibit improved performance, but are unaware of what (or even that) they have learned. A crucial observation is that they also perform well in priming experiments, producing appropriate responses when cued in context at the same rates as normal subjects. although their ability to recall items from learned lists is severely impaired (Graf et al. 1984).

Though normal individuals have both procedural and declarative memory, studies have shown that each mode has distinctive properties. Among the differences of interest to students of organizational routine, we focus on three. Procedural knowledge is less subject to decay, less explicitly accessible, and less easy to transfer to novel circumstances.

The low decay rate of procedural memory corresponds to long-standing casual observations about the durability of skills (e.g., the commonplace claim that "you never forget how to ride a bicycle"). People may forget the grammatical rules of a language studied long before, but still be able to distinguish grammatical sentences in that language after years of nonuse (Bahrick 1984). Studies of people solving puzzles in sessions separated by intervals of up to three months show that memory for specific puzzles solved earlier decays rapidly, but memory for how to solve puzzles of that type does not (Bunch 1936). Such disjunctions indicate that procedural knowledge has decayed far less than its declarative counterpart.

The lowered accessibility of procedural memory has been revealed in studies (Graf et al. 1985) in which a response acquired in written mode is not available when cued verbally but is available when cued visually. Declarative memories, in contrast, are more equally available across communication modes. This property appears to lie behind the common experience of a telephone number or lock combination which cannot be stated, but becomes available once a phone or lock is under the hand.

The restricted range of transfer of procedurally encoded skills has been a particular focus of work by Singley and Anderson (1989) who have demonstrated such phenomena in activities such as LISP programming and problem solving in calculus and geometry. Their findings concur with those of others who have shown that physics students fail to apply well-learned methods to the interpretation of nonclassroom physical events (McCloskey 1983) and

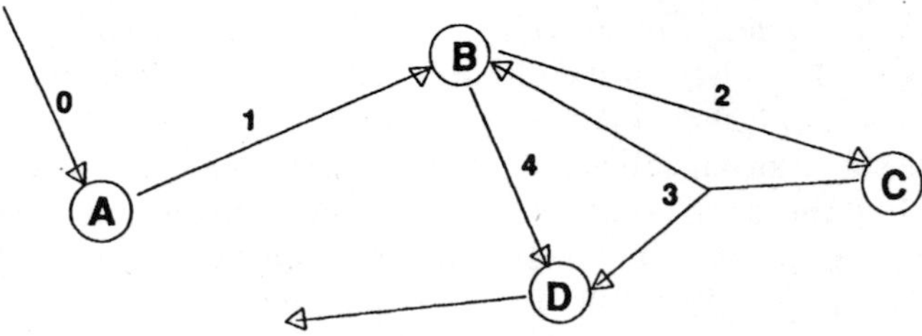

Figure 11.1. A Routine Among Four Actors Shown as Mutual Priming of Procedurally Stored Actions

that Brazilian school children, who could correctly determine on the street the total cost of a purchase such as five lemons at 35 cruzeiros apiece, could not compute the answer to the matching arithmetic problem $5 \times 35 = ?$ (Carraher et al. 1985).

We take it as a significant similarity that the characteristic costs and benefits of routines discussed above resemble observations by psychologists on transfer of learning. The development of routines in organizations is good for reasons parallel to the psychologists' positive transfer effects. Groups of people get better at doing "the same" thing. That generates rising learning curves, in which the world business community is today intensely interested: Senge (1990) is illustrative. On the other hand, the development of routines in organizations can be bad because of an effect at the individual level similar to negative transfer. Groups do things in "the same" way when the situation (as others see it) is not really "the same."

We argue that this similarity of transfer of learning at the individual and organizational levels is far from coincidental. The properties of organizational routines arise from the way individuals store and enact their parts in those routines. As individuals become skilled in their portions of a routine the actions become stored as procedural memories and can later be triggered as substantial chunks of behavior. The routine of a group can be viewed as the concatenation of such procedurally stored actions, each primed by and priming the actions of others (Tulving and Schacter 1990).

Figure 11.1 gives a schematic example. An action or situation (labeled 0) triggers action 1 by actor A. This alters the situation so that action 2 is triggered for actor B. C is then primed to take action 3, which alters the situation for both B and D. B now takes action 4. D then responds to 3 and 4 with a further step, and the chain may continue.

This model is certainly not entirely new. It is closely connected to Weick's account of the "double-interact," which itself has a long history (Allport

1924, Weick 1979). And, as we mentioned at the outset, the simile of organizational routine and individual habit has been noted by many others (e.g., Dewey 1922, Stene 1940, Nelson and Winter 1982). But we take an additional step in suggesting a specific psychological mechanism that may generate the phenomenon, and we provide evidence from experimentally induced routines that supports our claim. Establishing tighter links to relevant individual psychology and adding to our observational repertoire both should help us to unlock the *dynamics* of organizational routines. This will shed new light on their interactions with organizational learning and structure (Levitt and March 1988, Drazin and Sandelands 1992).

Experimental Observation

The vast majority of what organization theorists know of routine comes from field observation. But laboratory studies provide a very useful auxiliary approach, especially when the question is a possible linkage to individual psychological phenomena that have also been uncovered with laboratory methods. The enhanced control of the laboratory offers the possibility of carefully testing ideas that claim to explain the rich observations of the field.

Laboratory study of organizational routines is not new, of course. Cyert and March included such studies in *A Behavioral Theory of the Firm.* And many classic experiments in which small groups repeatedly solve variants of a given type of problem can be regarded as inducing a set of differentiated and interlocked behavior patterns that we would classify as routines (e.g., Shaw 1954, Weick and Gilfillan 1971, Laughlin and Shippy 1983). The early literature is reviewed with great conceptual clarity in Weick (1965).[2]

In the present study we want to be more explicit than has commonly been the case in showing that the behavior patterns of our subject groups have the characteristics commonly reported in field studies of organizational routine. Then we can go on to show that the same experiments provide evidence that elements of the routines are stored by individuals as procedural memory. The experimental instrument we will describe below has been carefully designed not only for the present purpose of demonstrating the linkage of organizational and individual levels, but also to support later studies exploring the impacts on routines of organizational variables such as authority relations, incentive structures, size, and communications channels.

As the first step, then, we want to establish that our procedures generate patterns of behavior in the laboratory with four features characteristic of field-observed routines:

1. *Reliability.* Students of organizational routine have always stressed that a key advantage of routinization is the increased ability of the organiza-

tion to produce an acceptable result (Cyert and March 1963, Allison 1971, Inbar 1979). Thus we want to show that the patterns of behavior that form in our experiments deliver this same advantage.

2. *Speed.* Along with reliability routinized behavior is expected to be faster than behavior being generated as deliberate decision making in unfamiliar circumstances.

3. *Repeated Action Sequences.* A characteristic feature of routines is that the actions that compose them are substantially the same over time, so that multiple occurrences can be identified as instances of the same routine. This is a key feature in the definition of group routine offered by Gersick and Hackman (1990).

4. *Occasional Suboptimality.* One of the reasons attention has been drawn to routines is the observed tendency for them to "fire off" in circumstances where, to an observer, some other action would have been more appropriate. This is the "blind-spot" property that makes so striking a story like Allison's report of soldiers in Cuba failing to achieve disguise. More generally, it is the property usually regarded as a chief cost of routine that must be traded off against benefits such as those mentioned above, and it is evidence that action is occurring without full deliberation, another marker cited by Gersick and Hackman (1990).

EXPERIMENT

After we describe the experimental task, we will show that our subjects' behavior has these four features and thus that our dyads can be seen as miniature organizations with behavior patterns that are organizational routines. Then we will turn to evidence that our individual subjects are encoding their elements of those routines as procedural memories.

Experimental Task

The task we employ in this study is a card game. This is an ideal environment for our purposes, as each hand requires precise rational problem solving, but in the play of many hands there is opportunity for routines to form. The game is played by two players using six cards: the 2, 3 and 4 of a red suit and the 2, 3, and 4 of a black suit. It is played on a board resembling Figure 11.2. Because there are six hundred legal ways to deal the cards in the game, it creates a task setting with a key realistic property: routines can

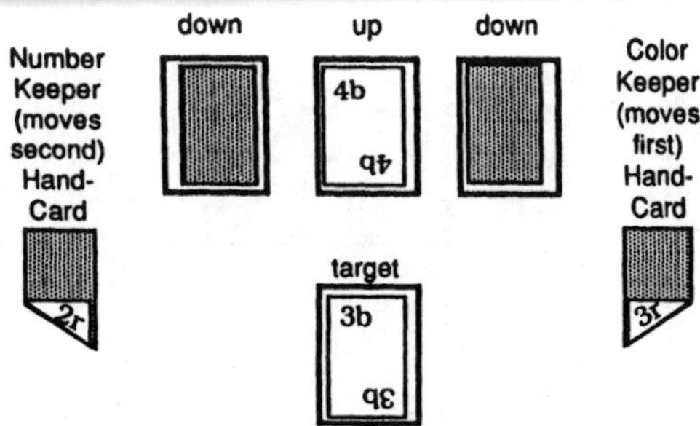

Figure 11.2. Playing Board as It Appeared to Subjects After Deal of Training Hand

form because jobs (deals of the cards) are similar, but each particular job is usually novel in some aspect. When the cards are dealt by the experimenter, each player has a card in hand that cannot be seen by the other player. (The figures indicate this one-sided visibility with a turned-up corner) On the board, in the marked rectangles, are two face-down cards that neither player can see, and two face-up that both can observe.

In each hand that is played the ultimate object is to maneuver the red 2 (2r in the figure) into the area marked "target." A move in the game is an exchange of the card in a player's hand with one of the cards on the board (or a "pass," making it the other player's turn). Each player is subject to a restriction on moves. The player on the right, called "Color Keeper," may make exchanges with the target area card only if the *color* in the target is preserved. The player on the left, "Number Keeper," may exchange with the target only if the action preserves the *number* in the target area. Exchanges with board areas other than the target are not restricted.

The successive situations in Figures 11.3 through 11.5 illustrate the play of the example hand in Figure 11.2. This is the sequence that was demonstrated to the subjects during training. In Figure 11.3, the Color Keeper has exchanged her card for the down card at the upper left of the figure. (We will use the convention of referring to Color Keeper as "she" and Number Keeper as "he.") The rectangle background is highlighted to show where the most recent action occurred. Her hand now contains the black 2 (2b). The red 3 (3r) has been placed face down on the upper left rectangle of the board without being seen by her partner.

It is now the Number Keeper's turn and he would like to put the 2r in his hand into the target, but the restriction prohibits that. Four other possibilities are available: exchange with the up card; exchange with one of the two down cards; or pass. In the training hand we instructed the subjects to pass. Since the board is unchanged, no separate panel appears in the figures.

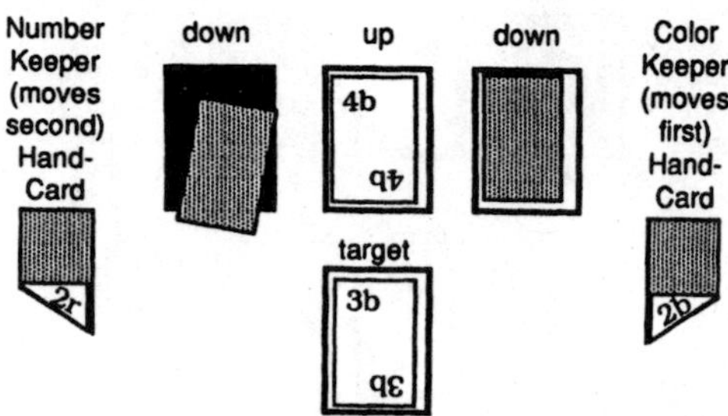

Figure 11.3. Board After Color Keeper Exchanges with Left Down Card

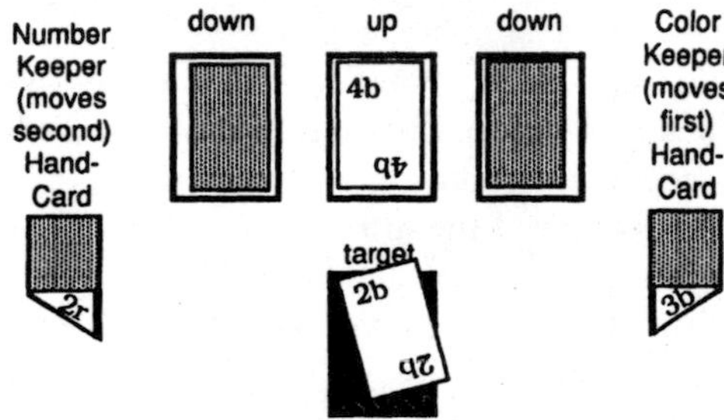

Figure 11.4. Board After Number Keeper Passes and Color Keeper Exchanges with Target Card

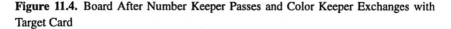

It is the Color Keeper's turn again. This time it is legal for her to exchange her hand with the target, since the action will leave a black card in the target. We instructed the subjects to make this move, and the result is shown as Figure 11.4.

The Number Keeper can now legally exchange his card with the target, which produces the situation shown in Figure 11.5. The hand is finished. Four moves were used to complete it.

The incentive system in the experiment reported here was that subjects had 40 minutes to play up to 40 hands of the game. Each hand they successfully completed earned their partnership one dollar. Each move they made (including passes) cost their partnership a dime. In the example hand they would have netted 60 cents. At the conclusion of a 40-minute session, they split their winnings equally. This arrangement placed the subjects in a

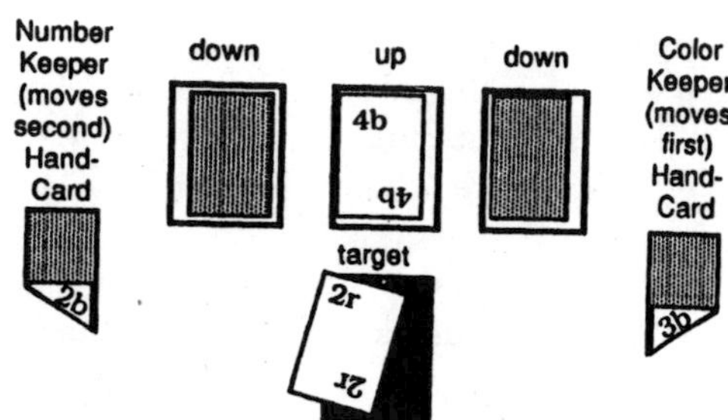

Figure 11.5. Board After Number Keeper Exchanges with Target Card, Finishing Hand

fully cooperative relationship with each other, but created a tension between the two performance measures. The team needed to play *quickly* in order to increase the number of hands completed, but they needed to play *carefully* in order to avoid unnecessary moves in completing each hand. The incentives were deliberately quite substantial. Including base pay and variable winnings, a typical subject in the study took home about 35 dollars from two sessions of play.

By design, the experiment incorporates a number of fundamental features characteristic of organizational life. The color and number restrictions create asymmetry of capabilities and thus the potential for division of labor and distinctive roles. On average there are substantial returns to coordination of the multiple actors, but when coordination fails performance can actually be worse than what a single actor could achieve. There is uncertainty and asymmetry of information as a result of the face-down cards and hand cards. As each pair develops its method for effectively playing successive hands, it implicitly constructs an interlocked system of roles for the individual members that addresses these classical organizational issues. Their learning creates an organization, albeit one small and short-lived.

Our subjects were graduate and upper-level undergraduate students in business, public policy, and the social sciences grouped into 32 pairs at random. They were both male and female. All-male, all-female, and mixed-gender pairs were allocated as evenly as possible into the four experimental conditions. Assignment to partners, game roles, and conditions was otherwise random.

After training, which consisted of reading printed rules and being led through the example hand shown above, each pair played two sessions of 40 minutes separated by a delay. In one experimental condition this delay was a break over dinner time that took two to four hours. In the other condition, the delay was one to two weeks. A second manipulation involved novelty of the second session task. Half the subjects played in a same-task condition. They had identical rules and occupied the same roles at the table as in their first session. The other half were in a novel condition. On their return for the second session, these subjects were asked, without prior warning, to reverse roles. They sat on opposite sides of the playing board from their prior experience and were therefore subject to the reversed form of the restriction on target exchanges. They were also told that their object was now to work the *black* 2 into the target.

The hands played by the pairs were pre-dealt. All pairs got the same sequence of 80 hands, involving 60 distinct deals of the cards. Some deals were repeated to permit comparisons of play early and late in the first session and between sessions one and two. In the experimental context where they were repeatedly rearranging the same six cards, subjects appeared to have little sense that they might have seen any particular deal previously. For the subjects in the novel condition, the second session deals were transformed so that black cards were in the positions occupied by red cards in the deals going to subjects without novel rules. From a logical point of view this means that hands in the novel and same rules conditions were of identical difficulty.

Subjects were strongly urged not to discuss the experiment between sessions and no talking was allowed during play. A factorial design crossing these two manipulations, short versus long delay between sessions and same or novel rules in the second session, yielded four experimental groups. Each contained eight pairs. This design allowed us to test for procedural memory by examining how delay and novelty affected play. The logic of this test is described below.

The experimental sessions were videotaped. The resulting recordings were converted to machine readable records of every move made, and the time period preceding every move. The method was to watch each hand, recording the moves made, then watch each hand again, making a computer keystroke at the moment each card was released onto the playing board. These data are the basis of the analyses below.

RESULTS

We turn now to reporting analyses of the experimental data. These show that routines actually do form as pairs play many hands of the card game and that memory for the actions involved is procedural.

TABLE 11.1 Repeated Measures Analysis of Variance of Average Move Time per Hand for Five Recurring Deals

Source	*SS*	*DF*	*MS*	*F*	p
Hypothesis	217.894	1	217.894	88.998	< 0.0005
Error	389.281	159	2.448		

Evidence That the Actions Are Routines

We want to assess whether the behavior of our subject pairs displays the four indicators of organizational routinization described above: increasing reliability, increasing speed, the development of repeated action sequences, and occasional suboptimality.

Reliability. We can assess reliability by examining the variation across pairs in the number of moves required to complete play of a hand. The three quartile range reflects this variation well. As fewer pairs encounter serious difficulties in playing a hand, this range should decrease. Over the course of the 40 hands in the first session, the moves-per-hand required by the best pair and by the twenty-fifth best pair do grow increasingly similar. The regression of hand number on the three quartile range of moves per hand shows a decrease of about 0.06 per hand ($t = -2.70$; $p < 0.01$, two tail; $r^2 = 0.161$). Because the individual hands vary in difficulty it is at least conceivable that this reflects a trend in the arrangement of the deals. But we can control for difficulty variation by comparing the three quartile range of moves used to complete a hand early in the first session with that of an identical deal later in the session. There are five replicated deals available for this purpose. Each one occurs early and is repeated 25 hands later. The mean of the range is 3.7 moves for the early set, but only 1.8 moves when the set reoccurs. Thus we can say that the performance of the pairs is becoming more reliable.

Speed. The second indicator of routinization was speed. Here we can examine the time used in making a move in any hand of the experiment. This is quite distinct from the number of moves made in that hand. Players could go fast and not necessarily be selecting moves that led to solutions in few steps. In fact, the correlation of moves per hand and average move time in that hand over both sessions is 0.302 ($N = 2560$; $p\ [r = 0] < 0.0005$). As in the previous discussion, it is consistent with the formation of routines that speed increases over time. The regression of hand number on the average move time per hand indicates that each added hand of experience improves performance by about –0.016 seconds per hand ($t = -6.46$; $p < 0.0005$; $r^2 = 0.116$). And we can control for difficulty of hands by the same repeated measures strategy used earlier. Table 11.1 shows that move time was significantly faster on the second occurrence of each of the repeated five hands. The pairs are taking the steps in their work at increasing speeds.

Repeated Action Sequences. Our third indicator of the formation of routines is the development of repeated action sequences. Steps in playing the card game that occur in the early going while the subjects are proceeding "one move at a time" develop into "chunks" that are run off as units. Our observation is that a number of these chunks form within experimental pairs over the course of a session. Different pairs actually form different stable action patterns. We demonstrate the phenomenon here by reporting on one such sequence, which we refer to as "up-up-anything-target" and abbreviate UU*T. As the name suggests, this is a sequence that begins with either player making an exchange with the nontarget face-up area on the board. The other player then makes an exchange with that same area. The third element of the sequence can be any move. The fourth step is an exchange with the target area.

Figure 11.6 gives an example. Here, as is generally true, the sequence solves the problem faced by a player (Number Keeper here) who has a card in hand (the 2r in this case, but it could be the 2b or something else) that should go into the target. The basic restriction on number (or color) prevents this. Instead the player puts it in the up area, making it known and available. The other player picks it up. The initiating player does something else (frequently a pass). And the partner puts it into the target. A functional interpretation of this sequence is "moving a card you cannot play into the hand of your partner, who can." It nicely exemplifies the teamwork required of a pair to solve the problems they confront and the way the UU*T routine is a property of the group rather than of either of its members.

This sequence occurs 817 times across the 2,560 hands of the two sessions, where the chance expectation would be less than 25 occurrences. The median pair uses the sequence 26.5 times, but some pairs rely on it much more heavily than others ($SD = 5.143$). The time the sequence takes to run off is instructive. In early play subjects take about the same amount of time to make a move that is part of the sequence as they do to make any other move. In the first two hands the time per move of each type is not significantly different ($t = 1.476$; $df = 25$). But as practice accumulates, and the sequence becomes more of a "chunk," a move in the sequence is

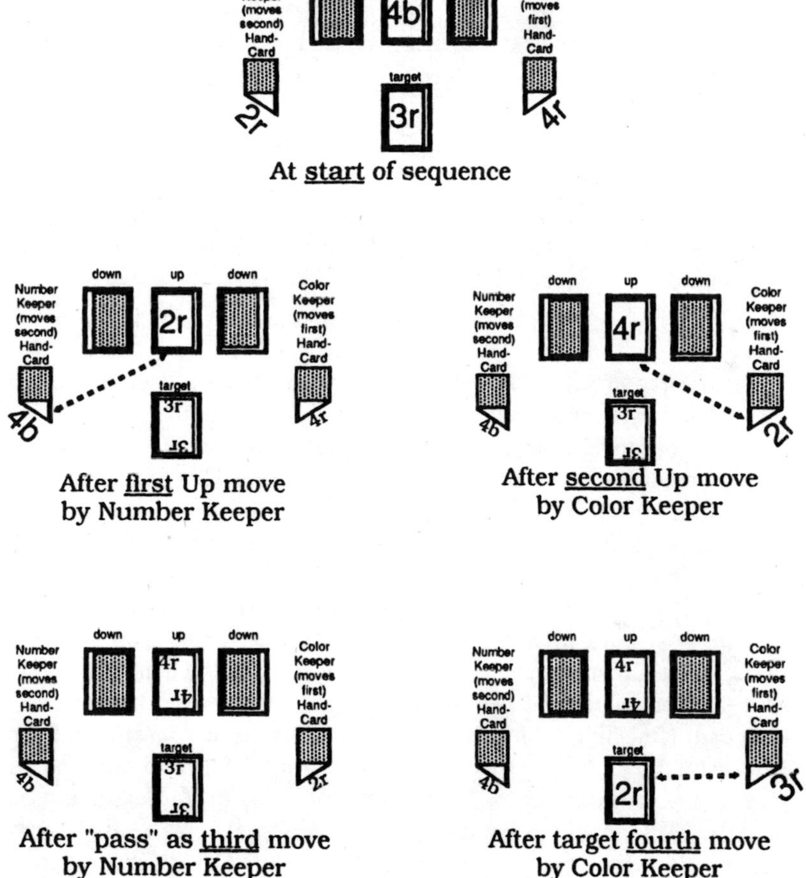

Figure 11.6. Illustration of UU*T Repeated Sequence

much faster than a normal move at the same experience level by the same players ($t = 3.442$; $df = 48$; $p < 0.001$). The fastest instances we see by the second session make four moves in less than four seconds. They have virtually overlapping movements by the actors. Each knows what the other is about to do. Watching these cases in the lab, one is reminded of the way a skilled touch typist rapidly generates a familiar word with overlapping keystrokes—except that here the two hands are on different bodies.

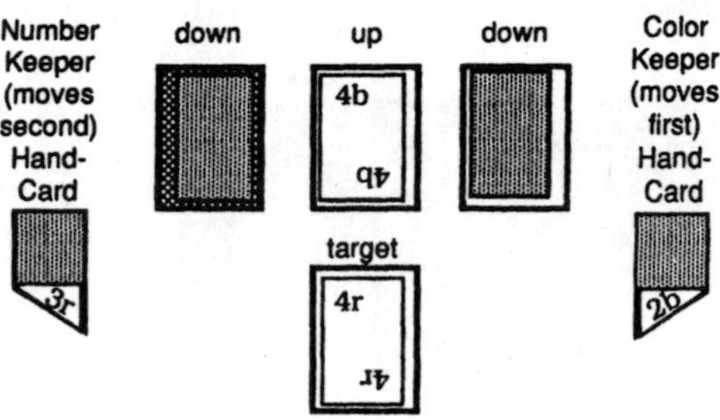

Figure 11.7. Cards Dealt in Thirty-Eighth Hand, Which Has Possible Solution in Three (or Five) Moves

Occasional Suboptimality. A final remark about these sequences such as UU*T is that they contribute to suboptimality, our fourth indicator of routinization. Across the 32 subject pairs, the number of uses of UU*T is positively correlated with the average number of moves used in resolving the 80 hands ($r = 0.146$; p [$r = 0$] < 0.0005).

However, there is more striking evidence than this of suboptimality. The thirty-eighth hand in our first session was dealt as shown in Figure 11.7. This is a hand in which it is easy to show that the best play would be for Number Keeper to "stay out of it." The 4r is already in the target. The remaining problem is for Color Keeper get the 2r into her hand. If Number Keeper doesn't interfere, Color Keeper will find the 2r either on her first search of a down card (finishing in three moves), or on her second search (finishing in five). Any moves by Number Keeper that bring the 2r into his hand will only require passing it over to Color Keeper at a cost of four extra moves.

In only 7 of our 32 pairs did both players make two initial moves consistent with Number Keeper staying out of it while Color Keeper searches and finishes. Most of the remaining 25 pairs used one of two suboptimal approaches. In 10 of the remaining cases, Color Keeper's opening move was to exchange with the up pile. This repeats a frequent strategy of making the 2b, or other cards which may be useful, visible to her partner. In 12 additional cases Color Keeper opened by searching and then Number Keeper searched as well. Here Number Keeper seems to be adhering to the common approach in which both players look for the red 2 during the early stages of play. Unfortunately, Number Keeper actually drew the 2r in nine of these cases. The unlucky pairs then spent many extra moves undoing the ill effects of Number Keeper's "success." Thus we have a case where an approach to the problem that left all the action to one individual would actually be better than the more organizationally balanced one, but the groups use the approach they have learned.

We have isolated other deals with similar features. In effect, our pairs are like individuals who have been practicing left turns so long that they will pass by a right turn to make three lefts instead. Action is occurring without full deliberation.

Summarizing, there are four kinds of evidence for the formation of organizational routines in the performance of this task: increasing reliability (decrease in moves required), increasing speed (decrease in time per move), repeated action sequences (recurring dyad-specific sequences of joint behavior), and suboptimality (pairs failing to see solutions superior to their routine methods).

Evidence That Memory for Routines Is Procedural

Having shown that routines emerge in our laboratory task, we turn now to findings on our second question: May these characteristic features of organizational routine that have often been likened to habits and skills derive from the fact that actors store elements of a routine in procedural memory, the same form of memory that psychologists are now arguing is the storage form of individual habits and skills? We proceed by examining the effects of two kinds of experimental manipulations.

First, recall that we earlier characterized declarative memory (for facts, propositions, and events) as being slower than procedural memory. It has been shown by Singley and Anderson (1989) that individuals engaged in skilled activities such as solving calculus or computer programming problems can apply well-learned methods very rapidly to new problems of the familiar type, but are dramatically slowed when novelties are introduced (e.g., differentiating a new form of expression or programming a new type of control structure). They argue that confronting novelties requires switching from skills that are stored in procedural memory to propositional knowledge about possible actions that is stored in declarative memory. The latter is dramatically slower. The novelty of our experimental manipulation after the first session was modest, asking half the subjects to sit on the opposite sides of the table and work with the black two instead of the red two. But if that requires them to revert to declarative processing, then we should expect that *our subjects would be noticeably slowed by the introduction of novelty into the rules of their routinized game.*

Second, Singley and Anderson (1989) also report, and many others have found, that memory for skills (which they view as procedural) decays far less than memory for propositions (which they view as declarative). Thus we

TABLE 11.2 Repeated Measures Analyses of Variance of Time per Move in Two Hands from First Session Compared to First Hand of Second Session

Source	Error				Hypothesis			
	SS	*DF*	*MS*	*SS*	*DF*	*MS*	*F*	p
Hand 23 vs. Hand 41								
Between Subjects								
Delay (D)	135.760	28	4.849	6.504	1	6.504	1.341	0.257
Novelty (N)	135.760	28	4.849	30.159	1	30.159	6.220	0.019
D × N	135.760	28	4.849	5.154	1	5.154	1.063	0.311
Within Subjects								
Constant	83.601	28	2.986	29.478	1	29.478	9.873	0.004
Delay	83.601	28	2.986	1.667	1	1.667	0.558	0.461
Novelty	83.601	28	2.986	36.844	1	36.844	12.34	0.002
D × N	83.601	28	2.986	0.360	1	0.369	0.123	0.728
Hand 40 vs. Hand 41								
Between Subjects								
Delay	122.89	28	4.389	1.000	1	1.000	0.228	0.637
Novelty	122.89	28	4.389	22.975	1	22.975	5.235	0.030
D × N	122.89	28	4.389	5.106	1	5.106	1.163	0.290
Within Subjects								
Constant	109.87	28	3.924	48.536	1	48.536	12.370	0.002
Delay	109.87	28	3.924	8.072	1	8.072	2.057	0.163
Novelty	109.87	28	3.924	45.812	1	45.812	11.675	0.002
D × N	109.87	28	3.924	0.382	1	0.382	0.097	0.757

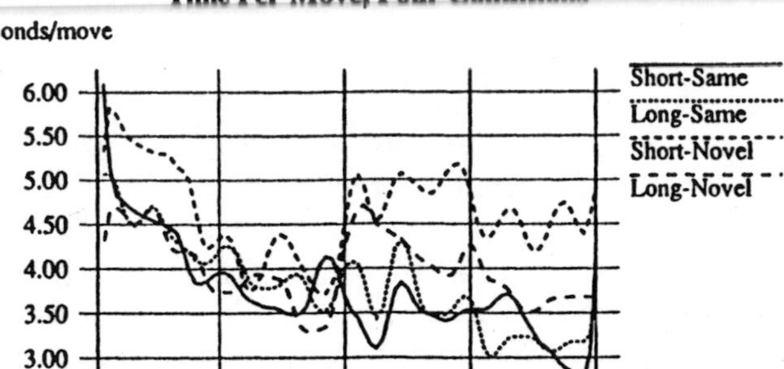

Figure 11.8. Time Series of Time per Move for Four Experimental Conditions
NOTE: First session is hands 1–40, Second session is hands 41–80.

should expect that *our subjects, if playing under the same rules for which their routines were built, would not be much affected by the addition of a substantial time interval between sessions of play.*

If we turn to our results, we find these two central expectations are borne out by the repeated measures analysis of variance in Table 11.2. It shows two different comparisons: hand 23 to hand 41; and hand 40 to hand 41. Hand 41 is the first hand of the second session. Hands 23 and 40 are the two hands from the first session with the logical structure most similar, though not identical, to hand 41. Across both comparisons, novelty proves consistently to have significant effects, both within and between subjects. Delay does not.

The nature of the effect can be seen in Figure 11.8, a time series plot of the average time per move for each of the eighty hands for each of the four conditions. The data have been smoothed with the 4253H robust filter of Tukey (Velleman and Hoaglin 1981). For the two conditions where rules were "Same," the transition from hand 40 to hand 41 makes little difference and, in particular, the long delay group plays quickly despite a break of one to two weeks. For these two groups, the long term steady decrease of time at a decreasing rate suggests typical data for the "power law of practice" that is seen in tasks such as typing (Newell 1990).

On the other hand, the two "Novel" rule groups have great difficulty for a few hands. One gradually returns to speeds comparable to the "Same" groups. The other, the one with short delay between sessions, seems to have greater trouble in recovering. (We speculate that the short delay may be related to this, perhaps through a mechanism of interference by the still-fresh prior experience. However, from a statistical point of view the apparent effect is not very reliable.)

SUMMARY, INTERPRETATION, AND IMPLICATIONS

Our experiment induces, in the laboratory, behavior patterns that exhibit major characteristics of organizational routines, and the effects of novelty and delay manipulations are consistent with what would be expected if individual memory for elements of routinized performance is procedural. The speed of task performance, itself a principal indicator of routinization, seems to be little affected by delay, but substantially impaired by the introduction of novelty into the task. This is what we should find if elements of those routines were stored as procedural memory, which shows little decay, while subjects reasoning about response to rule changes required slower declarative memory processing.

The marked suboptimality of our groups on hand 38 can be interpreted as a group *Einstellung* (or set) effect (Luchins 1942). Seen this way, the subjects in our laboratory are exhibiting *at a group level* what Singley and Anderson observe to be the characteristic form of negative transfer of learning for procedurally stored individual skills (Singley and Anderson 1989). Since other group members serve as powerful contextual cues, we might expect them to "prime" responses from each other and thus to trigger inappropriate sequences of action at the organizational level. Thus organizational negative transfer operates by a mechanism akin to that seen in isolated individuals. However, what the behavior of an actor triggers is not further action by the same person, but rather action by another. In short, we believe that, to a significant degree, organizational routines are stored as distributed procedural memories and derive many of their important properties from this fact.

If further work establishes a psychologically informed theory of routines along the lines we propose, it will have significant consequences for research. It can provide a theoretically grounded basis for explaining observed deviations from rationality. This is an important step beyond criticizing rational models and toward an alternative positive theory. In one sense, it offers a return to the original objectives of the bounded rationality research tradition (Simon 1957). We can transcend the simple cataloging of departures from rationality and begin to explain them in terms of the actual processing capabilities of the individuals and of the system of relations that organizes the actors. But, in another sense, this approach departs somewhat from the typical emphases in the bounded rationality tradition on decision making by individual actors seen as relatively self-conscious, static, emotionally neutral problem solvers. In contrast, our stress is on learning that is dynamic, deeply embedded in a group context, and gives rise to partially unconscious skilled performances. Among the most fascinating opportunities we see are possible connections of our approach to experimental work showing that priming phenomena, which play an important role in procedural memory, are also significant in processes of individual emotional reactions to situations. For example, work by Robert Zajonc and his collaborators have shown that simple prior exposure to a stimulus can increase the chance that it will later be preferred, even when the exposure is so brief that it has no effect on the chance the stimulus will later be recognized (Kunst-Wilson and Zajonc 1980).

We also see an opportunity to connect our rich experimental data to emerging achievements in the machine-learning field. We hope to compare our subjects' behavior to the way multi-actor versions of learning systems such as Soar (Laird et al. 1987) and Holland Classifiers (Holland et al. 1986, Riolo 1991) acquire the ability to play the card game. Both systems have good prospects as models of the human acquisition of procedural knowledge. Further, there are many possible experiments that can build upon the demonstration here that routines can be induced in the laboratory. Subjects who have developed routines in one group can be reassigned to other groups to study a laboratory analog of a "clash of cultures." Variations in the card game can accommodate larger numbers of actors and can create conditions that mimic common problems of real organizations, such as conflicting incentives or restrictions on communication due to role asymmetries or physical separation. Then we can observe their effects on the development of routines.

Since routines pattern so much of organizational life—both its possibilities and its limitations—the unfolding of this line of research may hold many significant implications for managers. For example, by drawing on research on the low verbal accessibility of procedurally encoded skills, practitioners may better understand the difficulty that a routine's participants have in articulating their activities to managers or computer systems designers. The findings encourage us to recognize and explore the possibility of an "organizational unconscious," a body of largely inarticulate know-how that underpins so much of an organization's capabilities and which must be accommodated if there is to be effective redesign of organizational processes.

A major contribution to practice could come if improved understanding enables us to reduce the chances of the kind of inappropriate "firing" of routines that we saw from our pairs as they dealt with hand 38. We can probably never eliminate tragic "misfirings" such as the experienced surgical team that worked from a reversed X ray and efficiently removed a patient's one healthy kidney (*L.A. Times* 1985). But we may find ways to make such cases less likely. There is promise in devices as homely as deliberately varying which team member has responsibility for reading off the items of a safety checklist.

Managers will also benefit from better appreciating the difficulty of transferring procedural knowledge across modes, such as from written to verbal form. This may cast light on some perennial problems. Written rules frequently fail to inform actual practice. Improved practices discovered in one part of an organization often cannot be propagated with written descriptions. These are fundamental limits on the speed and quality of organizational learning (Brown and Duguid 1991). They may help to explain findings about organizational learning such as the observation that General Motors learned less from circulating careful research reports on its NUMMI joint venture than Toyota did by rotating managers through work in the plant (Krafcik 1989).

The idea of organizational learning has already contributed significantly to the understanding of "resistance to change" (Argyris and Schön 1978, Nystrom and Starbuck 1984). Our conclusion that routines reside in hard-to-access procedural memory offers a different view of the problem, one that provides more precise foundations for the observations in earlier work. In particular, it suggests one detailed mechanism that may give rise to the divergence Argyris and Schön (1978) describe between theory-in-use and theory-in-practice. Among other things, it suggests that methods of making actors more conscious of their current practices may facilitate change. Experimental work has explored the use of such methods in the context of improving eyewitness legal testimony (Kassin 1985). And several of the standard techniques in contemporary systems of "quality management" appear to exploit this principle. Deming, for example, argues that we must abandon slogans in favor of detailed and participative examination of production processes (Deming 1982).

With the aid of the distinction between procedural and declarative memory, we may be better able to understand important features of organizational memory (Walsh and Ungson 1991). We can see how the procedural character of information-handling routines (Cyert and March 1963) limits the ability of an organization to "remember," as when the seemingly simple task of recovering a misfiled document proves extraordinarily difficult. We may better appreciate how an organization could lose its memory of the reasons for an action (as in our earlier example of artillery teams).

Our argument is not to be taken as "routines are simply procedural memory and only that." It hardly seems likely that normal human action does not intertwine procedural and other forms of memory in intricate relationships. And we fully expect that the psychological literature on procedural memory will continue to develop in complex ways. Nonetheless, the distinctive properties of individual memory for skills that have now been documented are not going to disappear, and our experiments will therefore continue to imply that organization theorists must pay scrupulous attention to the profound ways in which individual memories interact to shape the character of organizational routine.

ACKNOWLEDGMENTS

The authors acknowledge with gratitude the support of the National Science Foundation Program on Decision, Risk and Management Science under grant SES 9008853. We thank Jessica Francis for her assistance in coding, Pauline Kelvin and Dr. Richard Kelvin for research assistance, and Mary Tschirhart, Melissa Succi, and LaMont McKim for their help in collecting the experimental data.

NOTES

1. Here we follow Squire (1987) and Singley and Anderson (1989) in using the term "procedural." But see Squire (1987) for a listing of contending taxonomies with more than a dozen variant labels including "implicit/explicit," "skill memory/fact memory" and "semantic/episodic." Most of these distinctions separate the properties we group under "procedural" from those we group under "declarative." It is conceivable that the procedural/declarative label-pair itself may be superseded. But we are convinced that future results in psychology will continue to support the central ideas used here, that memory is not one homogeneous capacity (Baddeley 1990), and that memory for skilled actions has properties, especially properties related to "priming" phenomena (Tulving and Schacter 1990), that distinguish it from other kinds.

2. While the general methods are not new, we observe that the growth of information technology is presenting many fresh laboratory observational possibilities. These include captured keystrokes and messages, and videotape for experimenter analysis and for retrospective reconstruction—a method that collects thinking-aloud protocols while avoiding social contamination from subjects verbalizing in real time (Kassin 1985).

REFERENCES

Allison, G. (1971), *Essence of Decision: Explaining the Cuban Missile Crisis,* New York: Little, Brown.

Allport, F. H. (1924), *Social Psychology,* Cambridge, MA: Houghton Mifflin.

Argyris, C. and D. Schön (1978), *Organizational Learning,* Reading, MA: Addison-Wesley.

Baddeley, A. (1990), *Human Memory,* Boston: Allyn & Bacon.

Bahrick, H. P. (1984), "Semantic Memory Content in Permastore: 50 Years of Memory for Spanish Learned in School," *Journal of Experimental Psychology: General,* 113, 1-29.

Brown, J. S. and P. Duguid (1991), "Innovation in the Workplace: A Perspective on Organizational Learning," *Organization Science,* 2, 1, 40-57.

Bunch, M. (1936), "Amount of Transfer in Rational Learning as a Function of Time," *Journal of Comparative Psychology,* 22, 325-337.

Carraher, T. N., D. W. Carraher, and A. D. Schliemann (1985), "Mathematics in the Streets and in the Schools," *British Journal of Development Psychology,* 3, 21-29.

Cohen, M. D. (1991), "Individual Learning and Organizational Routine: Emerging Connections," *Organization Science,* 2, 1, 135-139.

Cohen, N J. (1984), "Preserved Learning Capacity in Amnesia: Evidence for Multiple Memory Systems," in L. Squire and N. Butters (Eds.), *Neuropsychology of Memory,* New York: Guilford, 88-103.

Cyert, R. M. and J. G. March (1963), *A Behavioral Theory of the Firm,* Englewood Cliffs, NJ: Prentice Hall.

Deming, W. E. (1982), *Quality, Productivity, and Competitive Position,* Cambridge: MIT, Center for Advanced Engineering Study.

Dewey, J. (1922), *Human Nature and Conduct: An Introduction to Social Psychology,* New York: Henry Holt.

Drazin, R. and L. Sandelands (1992), "Autogenesis: A Perspective on the Process of Organizing," *Organization Science,* 3, 2, 230-249.

Gaines, B. and J. Boose (1988), *Knowledge Acquisition Tools* (Vols. 1 and 2), New York: Academic Press.

Gersick, C. J. G. and J. R. Hackman (1990), "Habitual Routines in Task-Performing Groups," *Organizational Behavior and Human Decision Processes,* 47, 65-97.

Graf, P., A. P. Shimamura, and L. R. Squire (1985), "Priming across Modalities and across Category Levels: Extending the Domain of Preserved Function in Amnesia," *Journal of Experimental Psychology: Learning, Memory, Cognition,* 11, 386-396.

———, L. R. Squire, and G. Mandler (1984), "The Information That Amnesic Patients Do Not Forget," *Journal of Experimental Psychology: Learning, Memory, Cognition,* 10, 164-178.

Holland. J., K. Holyoak, R. Nisbett, and P. Thagard (1986), *Induction: Processes of Inference, Learning and Discovery,* Cambridge: MIT Press.

Inbar, M. (1979), *Routine Decision Making: The Future of Bureaucracy,* Beverly Hills, CA: Sage.

Kassin, S. M. (1985), "Eyewitness Identification: Retrospective Self-Awareness and the Accuracy-Confidence Correlation," *Journal of Personality and Social Psychology,* 49, 878-893.

Kelly, J. R. and J. E. McGrath (1985), "Effects of Time Limits and Task Types on Task Performance and Interaction of Four-Person Groups," *Journal of Personality and Social Psychology,* 49, 395-407.

Krafcik, J. (1989), "A New Diet for U.S. Manufacturing," *Technology Review,* 92, 1, 28-34.

Kunst-Wilson, W. R., and R. B. Zajonc (1980), "Affective Discrimination of Stimuli That Cannot Be Recognized," *Science,* 207, 4430, 557-558.

L.A. Times (1985), "Jury Gives Victim $5.2 Million After Bungled Surgery," in *Los Angeles Times* (pp. 1 and 6, Part II), Times Mirror.

Laird, J., P. Rosenbloom, and A. Newell (1987), "Soar: An Architecture for General Intelligence," *Artificial Intelligence,* 33, 1-64.

Laughlin, P. R. and T. A. Shippy (1983), "Collective Induction," *Journal of Personality and Social Psychology,* 45, 94-100.

Levitt, B. and J. G. March (1988), "Organizational Learning," *Annual Review of Sociology,* 14, 319-340.

Luchins, A. S. (1942), "Mechanization in Problem Solving," *Psychological Monographs,* 54.

March, J. G. and H. A. Simon (1958), *Organizations,* New York: John Wiley.

McCloskey, M. (1983), "Naive Theories of Motion," in D. Gentner and A. L. Stevens (Eds.), *Mental Models,* Hillsdale, NJ: Erlbaum Associates.

Morison, E. E. (1966), *Men, Machines, and Modern Times,* Cambridge: MIT Press.

Nelson. R, and S. Winter (1982), *An Evolutionary Theory of Economic Change,* Cambridge MA: Belknap.

Newell, A. (1990), *Unified Theories of Cognition,* Cambridge, MA: Harvard University Press.

Nisbett, R. and T. D. Wilson (1977), "Telling More than We Can Know: Verbal Reports on Mental Processes," *Psychological Review,* 84, 231-259.

Nystrom, P. and W. Starbuck (1984), "To Avoid Organizational Crisis, Unlearn," *Organizational Dynamics*, 12 (Spring), 53-65.

Riolo, R. L. (1991), "Modelling Simple Human Category Learning with a Classifier System," in R. K. Belew and L. B. Booker (Eds.), *Proceedings of the Fourth International Conference on Genetic Algorithms*, San Mateo, CA: Morgan Kaufmann, 324-333.

Senge, P. M. (1990), *The Fifth Discipline*, New York: Doubleday/Currency.

Shaw, M. (1954), "Some Effects of Unequal Distribution of Information upon Group Performance in Different Communication Nets," *Journal of Abnormal and Social Psychology*, 49, 547-553.

Sheil, B. (1981), "Coping with Complexity," Working Paper, Xerox Palo Alto Research Center, Laboratory for Artificial Intelligence.

Simon, H. A. (1957), *Models of Man*, New York: John Wiley.

Singley, M. K. and J. R. Anderson (1989), *The Transfer of Cognitive Skill*, Cambridge, MA: Harvard University Press.

Squire, L. R. (1987), *Memory and Brain*, New York: Oxford University Press.

Stene, E. O. (1940), "An Approach to the Science of Administration," *American Political Science Review*, 34, 6, 1124-1137.

Stinchcombe, A. (1990), *Information and Organizations*, Berkeley: University of California Press.

Suchman, L. (1983), "Office Procedure as Practical Action: Models of Work and System Design," *ACM Transactions on Office Information Systems*, 1, 320-328.

Tulving, E. and D. L. Schacter (1990), "Priming and Human Memory Systems," *Science*, 247, 301-306.

Velleman, P. F. and D. C. Hoaglin (1981), *Applications, Basics, and Computing of Exploratory Data Analysis*, Belmont, CA: Duxbury.

Walsh, J. P. and G. R. Ungson (1991), "Organizational Memory," *Academy of Management Review*, 16, 57-91.

Weick, K. E. (1965), "Laboratory Experimentation with Organizations," in J. G. March (Ed.), *Handbook of Organizations*, Chicago: Rand McNally, 194-206.

Weick, K. E. (1979), *The Social Psychology of Organizing* (2nd ed.), Reading, MA: Addison-Wesley.

——— and D. P. Gilfillan (1971), "Fate of Arbitrary Traditions in a Laboratory Microculture," *Journal of Personality and Social Psychology*, 17, 179-191.

Womack, J. P., D. T. Jones, and D. Roos (1990), *The Machine That Changed the World: The Story of Lean Production*, New York: Macmillan.

Zuboff, S. (1988), *In the Age of the Smart Machine: The Future of Work and Power*, New York: Basic Books.

12

Organizing Work by Adaptation

EDWIN HUTCHINS

Common sense suggests that work is organized in accordance with plans that are created by designers who reflect on the work setting and manipulate representations of the work process in order to determine new and efficient organizational structures. Or, even if "outside" designers are not involved, the reorganization of work is normally attributed to the conscious reflection by members of the work group itself. A detailed examination of the response of a real-world group to a sudden and unexpected change in its informational environment shows that these common sense assumptions may be quite misleading.

While entering a harbor, a large ship suffered an engineering breakdown that disabled an important piece of navigational equipment. This chapter considers the response of the ship's navigation team to the changed task demands imposed by the loss of this equipment. Following a rather chaotic search of the space of computational and social organizational alternatives, the team arrived at a new stable work configuration.

In retrospect, this solution appears to be just the sort of solution we would hope designers could produce. However, while some aspects of the response appear to be the products of conscious reflection, others, particularly those concerning the division of cognitive labor, are shown to arise without reflection from adaptations by individuals to what appear to them as local task demands. It is argued that while the participants may have represented and thus learned the solution after it came into being, the solution was clearly discovered by the organization itself before it was discovered by any of the participants.

(NAVIGATION; ORGANIZATIONAL DESIGN;
SOCIAL INTERACTION; MENTAL ARITHMETIC)

This chapter originally appeared in *Organization Science*, Vol. 2, No. 1, February 1991.

INTRODUCTION

This chapter attempts to raise some questions about the processes by which the organization of work arises. Common sense suggests that work is organized in accordance with plans that are created by designers who reflect on the work setting and manipulate representations of the work process in order to determine new and efficient organizational structures. Or, even if "outside" designers are not involved, the reorganization of work is attributed to the conscious reflection by members of the work group itself. Here I examine the response of a work group to a change in its informational environment. I will argue that several important aspects of a new organization are achieved not by conscious reflection but by local adaptations. The solution reached is one that we recognize in retrospect as being just the sort of solution we would hope designers could produce, yet it is a product of adaptation rather than of design.

The setting is the pilothouse or navigation of a large navy ship. The bridge is the "brain" of the ship. It is where the captain sits, where the helmsman stands and steers, and where the navigation team works to ensure that the ship knows where it is located and where it is going at all times. Several years ago, while I was recording both video and audio data of the performance of an actual navigation team bringing a real ship into a narrow harbor, the ship's propulsion system failed unexpectedly. This was a bit of bad luck for the ship, simultaneously robbing it of its ability to maneuver and interrupting all electrical production. The loss of electrical power caused a cascade of failures of electrical devices including one that is literally and figuratively instrumental to navigation. This incident provided an opportunity to witness and record the response of a complex organizational system to a very real crisis situation. In this chapter I will describe the way a navigation team adapted to the loss of an important piece of navigational equipment while the ship was entering a harbor. Before doing so, it is necessary to provide some background on the nature of navigation work and the navigation team.

NAVIGATING LARGE SHIPS

Guiding a large ship into or out of a harbor is a difficult task. Ships are massive objects: their inertia makes them slow to respond to changes in propeller speed or rudder position. Because of this response lag, changes in direction or speed must be anticipated and planned well in advance. Depending on the characteristics of the ship and its velocity, the actions that will bring it to a stop or turn it around, for example, may need to be taken tens of seconds, or even minutes, before the ship arrives at the desired turning or stopping point. Aboard naval vessels, a continuous plot of the position of the ship is maintained to support decisions concerning its motion.[1] The *conning officer* is nominally responsible for the decisions about the motion of the ship, but usually, such decisions are actually made by the navigation team and passed to the conning officer as recommendations, such as, "Recommend coming right to zero one seven at this time." The conning officer considers the recommendation in the light of the ship's overall situation, and if the recommendation is appropriate, he acts upon it by giving orders to the *helmsman,* who steers the ship, or to the *leehelmsman,* who controls the ship's engines.

The navigation activity is event-driven in the sense that the navigation team must keep pace with the movements of the ship. Unlike many decision-making settings, when something goes wrong aboard ship, quitting the task or starting over from scratch are not available options. The work must go on. In fact, the conditions under which the task is most difficult are usually the conditions under which its correct and timely performance is most important.

Position Fixing by Visual Bearings

In order to plan the motions of the ship, the navigation team must establish the position of the ship and compute its future positions. The most important piece of technology in this task is the navigation chart, a specially constructed model of a real geographical space. The ship is somewhere in space, and to determine or "fix" the position of the ship is to find the location on the appropriate chart that corresponds to the position of the ship in the world.

The simplest form of position fixing, and the one that concerns us here, is position fixing by visual bearings. For this, one needs a chart of the region around the ship, and a way to measure the direction, conventionally with respect to north, of the line of sight connecting the ship and some landmark on the shore. The direction of a landmark from the ship is called the landmark's *bearing.* A line drawn on the chart starting at the location of the symbol for the landmark and extending past the assumed location of the ship is called a *line of position.* The ship must have been somewhere on that line when the bearing was observed. If we have another line of position, constructed on the basis of the direction of the line of sight to another known landmark, then we know that the ship is also on that line. If the ship was on both of these lines at the same time, the only place it can have been is where the lines intersect. In practice, a third line of position with respect to another landmark is constructed. The three lines of position form a triangle, and the size of the triangle formed is an indication of the quality of the position fix. It is sometimes said that the anxiety of the navigator is proportional to the size of the fix triangle.

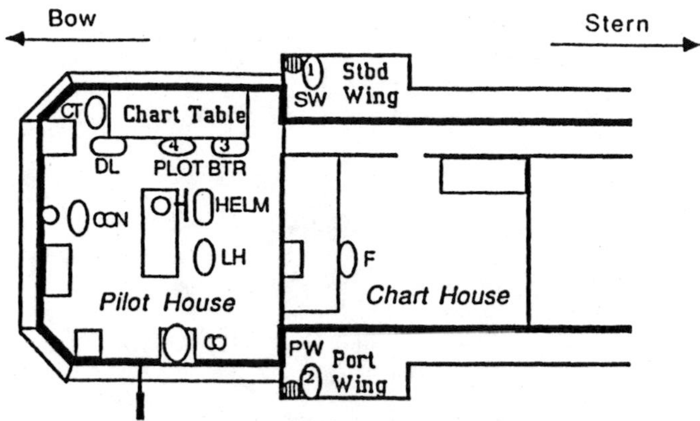

Figure 12.1. Plan View of the Navigation Bridge Showing the Location of the Chart Table and the Main Navigation Duty Stations. Position 1, starboard wing bearing taker; Position 2, port wing bearing taker; Position 3, bearing timer; Position 4, plotter.

The Fix

The necessity for continuously plotting the ship's position, projecting the future track, and preparing to plot the next position is satisfied by a cycle of activity called the fix cycle. When the ship is operating near land, the work of the fix cycle is distributed across a team of six people.[2] The duty stations of the members of the team in the configuration called Sea and Anchor Detail are shown in Figure 12.1 as elliptical shapes. We can follow the fix cycle by following the trajectory of information through the system.

New information about the location of the ship comes from the bearing takers on the wings of the ship (Position 1 and 2 in Figure 12.1). They find landmarks on the shore in the vicinity of the ship and measure the bearings of the landmarks (direction with respect to north) with a special telescopic sighting device called an *alidade*. The true north directional reference is provided by a gyrocompass repeater that is mounted under the alidade. A prism in the alidade permits the image of the gyrocompass scale to be superimposed on the view of the landmark. (An illustration depicting the view through such a sight is shown in Figure 12.2.) The bearing takers read the measured bearings and then report them over a telephone circuit to the bearing timer.

The bearing timer (Position 3 in Figure 12.1) stands at the chart table inside the pilothouse. He talks to the bearing takers out on the wings and writes the reported bearings in a book called the bearing log which he keeps on the chart table in front of him.

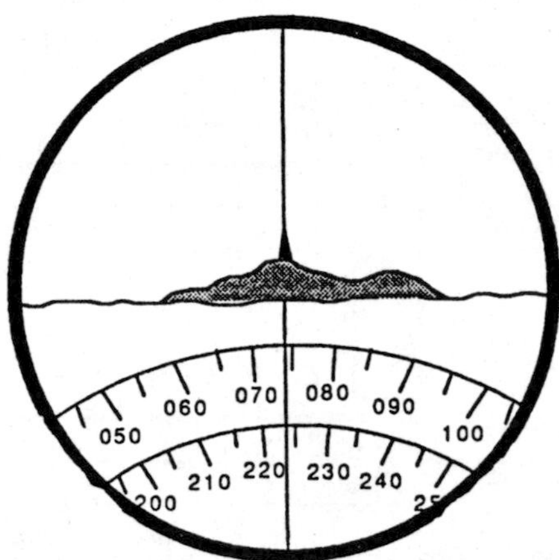

Figure 12.2. The View through the Alidade. The upper scale shows bearings relative to the ship's head, the lower scale swings with the gyrocompass and shows true bearings.

The plotter (Position 4 in Figure 12.1) plots the reported bearings. He normally has no direct communication with the bearing takers, but either is told the bearings by the bearing timer, or reads them out of the bearing log. From the perspective of the plotter, the bearing timer is an information buffer. In order to make a high-quality fix, the bearings should be observed as quickly and as nearly simultaneously as possible. Since it takes much longer to plot a line of position than it does to make the observation of the bearing, the activities of the plotter and the bearing takers have different distributions in time. The activities of the bearing timer not only provide a permanent record of the observations made, but also permit the bearing takers and the plotter to work, each at his most productive rate, without having to coordinate their activities in time.

Once he has plotted the ship's position, the plotter also projects where the ship will be at the time of the next few fix observations. To do this he needs to know the heading and speed of the ship. The plotter normally reads these from the deck log, which lies on the chart table near his left hand.

When the projected position of the ship has been plotted, the bearing timer consults with the plotter to decide which landmarks will be appropriately situated for the next position fix, and assigns the chosen landmarks to the bearing takers by talking to them on the phone circuit. The bearing timer times the fix intervals, and about 10 seconds before the next fix time, he says "Stand by to mark." This alerts the bearing takers that they should find their landmarks and aim their telescopic sights at them.

At the time chosen for the fix observations, the bearing timer says "Mark," and the bearing takers observe and report the bearings of the landmarks they have been assigned. Thus the cycle begins again.

THE CASUALTY

Crisis

After several days at sea, the USS Palau[3] was returning to port, making approximately 10 knots in the narrow channel between Ballast Point and North Island at the entrance to San Diego harbor. A junior officer had the con under the supervision of the navigator and the captain was on the bridge. Morale in the pilothouse had sagged during two frustrating hours of engineering drills conducted just outside the mouth of the harbor, but was on the rise now that the ship was headed toward the pier. Some of the crew talked about where they should go for dinner ashore and joked about going all the way to the pier at 15 knots, so they could get off the ship before nightfall.

The bearing timer had just given the command, "Standby to mark time three eight"[4] and the fathometer operator was reporting the depth of water under the ship, when the intercom erupted with the voice of the engineer of the watch, "Bridge, Main Control, I am losing steam drum pressure. No apparent cause. I'm shutting my throttles." Moving quickly to the intercom, the conning officer acknowledged, "Shutting throttles, aye." The navigator moved to the captain's chair repeating, "Captain, the engineer is losing, ah, steam on the boiler for no apparent cause." Possibly because he realized that the loss of steam might affect the steering of the ship, the conning officer ordered the rudder amidships. As the helmsman spun the wheel to bring the rudder angle indicator to the centerline, he answered the conning officer, "Rudder amidships, aye sir." The captain began to speak, saying, "Notify . . . ," but the engineer was back on the intercom, alarm in his voice this time, speaking rapidly, almost shouting, "Bridge, Main Control, I'm going to secure number two boiler at this time. Recommend you drop the anchor!" The captain had been stopped in mid-sentence by the blaring intercom, but before the engineer could finish speaking, the captain restarted in a loud, but cool, voice, "Notify the bosun." It is standard procedure on large ships to have an anchor prepared to drop in case the ship loses its ability to maneuver while in restricted waters. With the propulsion plant out, the bosun, who was standing by with a crew forward, ready to drop the anchor, was notified that he might be called into action. The falling intonation of the Captain's command gave it a cast of resignation, or perhaps boredom, and made it sound entirely routine.

In fact, the situation was anything but routine. The occasional cracking voice, a muttered curse, the removal of a jacket that revealed a perspiration-soaked shirt on this cool spring afternoon, told the real story: the Palau was not fully under control, and careers, and possibly lives, were in jeopardy.

The heart of the propulsion plant had stopped. The immediate consequences of this event were potentially grave. Despite the crew's correct responses, the loss of main steam put the ship in danger. Without steam, it could not reverse its propeller, which is the only way to slow a large ship efficiently. The friction of the water on the ship's hull will eventually reduce its speed, but the Palau would coast for several miles before coming to a stop. The engineering officer's recommendation that the anchor be dropped was not appropriate. Since the ship was still traveling at a high rate of speed, the only viable option was to attempt to keep the ship in the deep water of the channel and coast until it had lost enough speed to safely drop an anchor.

Within 40 seconds of the report of loss of steam pressure, the steam drum was exhausted and all steam turbine operated machinery came to a halt. This machinery includes the turbine generators which generate the ship's electrical power. All electrical power was lost throughout the ship and all electrical devices without emergency power backup ceased to operate. In the pilothouse a high pitched alarm sounded for a few seconds, signaling an under-voltage condition for one of the pieces of equipment. Then the pilothouse fell eerily silent as the electric motors in the radars and other devices spun down and stopped. The port wing bearing taker called in to the bearing timer, "John, this gyro just went nuts."

"Yah, I know, I know, we're havin' a casualty."

Because the main steering gear is operated with electric motors, the ship now not only had no way to arrest its still considerable forward motion, it also had no way to quickly change the angle of its rudder. The helm does have a manual backup system located in a compartment called *after-steering* in the stern of the ship, a worm gear mechanism powered by two men. However, even strong men working hard with this mechanism can change the angle of the massive rudder only very slowly.

Shortly after the loss of power, the captain said to the navigator, who is the most experienced conning officer on board, "O.K., ah, Gator, I'd like you to take the con." The navigator answered "Aye, Sir," and turning away from the captain announced to the pilothouse, "Attention in the pilothouse. This is the navigator. I have the con." As required, the quartermaster of the watch acknowledged, "Quartermaster, aye," and the helmsman reported, "Sir, my rudder is amidships." The navigator had been looking over the bow of the ship trying to detect any turning motion. He answered the helmsman, "Very well. Right five degrees rudder." Before the helmsman could reply, the navigator increased the ordered angle, "Increase your rudder right ten degrees." The rudder angle indicator on the helm station has two parts; one shows the rudder angle that is ordered, and the other the actual angle of the rudder. The helmsman spun the wheel causing the desired rudder angle indicator to move to right ten degrees, but the actual rudder angle indicator seemed not to move at all. "Sir, I have no helm sir!" he reported.

Meanwhile, the men on the worm gear were straining to move the rudder to the desired angle. Without direct helm control, the conning officer acknowledged the helmsman's report and sought to make contact with after-steering by way of one of the bridge phone talkers. "Very well. After-steering, Bridge." The navigator then turned to the helmsman. "Let me know if you get it back." And before he could finish his sentence, the helmsman responded, "I have it back, sir." When the navigator acknowledged the report, the ship was on the right side of the channel, but heading far to the left of track. "Very well, increase your rudder to right fifteen." "Aye, sir. My rudder is right fifteen degrees. No new course given." The navigator acknowledged, "Very well," and then, looking out over the bow of the ship itself, whispered, "Come on, damn it, swing!" Just then, the starboard wing bearing taker spoke on the phone circuit, "John, it looks like we're gonna hit this buoy over here." The bearing timer had been concentrating on the chart and hadn't heard. "Say again," he said. The starboard wing bearing taker leaned over the railing of his platform to watch the buoy pass beneath him. It moved quickly down the side of the ship, staying just a few feet from the hull. When it appeared that it would not hit the ship, he said, "Nuthin," and that ended the conversation. Inside, they never knew how close they had come. Several subsequent helm commands were answered, "Sir, I have no helm." When asked by the captain how he was doing, the navigator, referring to their common background as helicopter pilots, quipped, "First time I ever dead-sticked[5] a ship, captain." Steering a ship requires fine judgments about the angular velocity of the ship. Even if helm response were instantaneous, there would still be a considerable lag between the time a helm command was given and the time the ship's response to the changed rudder angle was first detectable as the movement of the bow with respect to objects in the distance. Operating with this manual system, the conning officer did not always know what the actual rudder angle was, and could not know how long to expect to wait to see if the ordered command was having the desired effect. Because of the slowed response time of the rudder, the conning officer ordered more extreme rudder angles than usual, causing the Palau to weave erratically from one side of the channel to the other.

Within three minutes, the emergency diesel electric generators were brought on the line and electrical power was restored to vital systems throughout the ship. Control of the rudder was partially restored, but remained intermittent for an additional four minutes. Although the ship still could not control its speed, it could at least now keep itself in the dredged portion of the narrow channel. Based on the slowing down over the first fifteen minutes following the casualty, it became possible to estimate when and where the ship would be moving slowly enough to drop the anchor. The navigator conned the ship toward the chosen spot.

About five hundred yards short of the intended anchorage, a sailboat took a course that would lead it to cross in front of the Palau. The Palau's enormous horn is steam driven and could not sound. The keeper of the deck log was ordered outside with a small manually pumped horn. Men on the flight deck ran to the bow to watch the impending collision. Five feeble blasts were sounded from the middle of the flight deck, two stories below. There is no way to know whether or not the signal was heard by the sailboat—by then it was directly ahead of the ship, and so close that only the tip of its mast was visible from the pilothouse. A few seconds later, the sailboat emerged, still sailing, from under the starboard bow and the keeper of the deck log continued to the bow to take up a position there in case other horn blasts were required.

The Consequences for the Navigation Team

The immediate response of the navigation team to the loss of steam and electrical power was simply to continue with the fix they were in the midst of taking. However, one of the pieces of electrical equipment that was subjected to loss of power was the Mark-19 gyrocompass. There are two layers of redundant protection for the gyrocompass function—independent emergency electrical power and a backup gyrocompass. Unfortunately, the emergency power supply for the gyrocompass failed, and the backup gyrocompass had been taken out of service earlier due to a maintenance problem. So when the power failed, the Mark-19 lost power. The gyrocompass did not fail completely when the lights went out, but it did appear to be mortally wounded. Sixteen minutes after the loss of power, the Palau's speed had dropped to less than 4 knots and the ship was less than half a mile from its intended temporary anchorage, when word was passed to the bridge from the forward IC room that the gyrocompass had ceased operation. This was an especially critical period for the navigation team. The chosen anchorage location was out of the navigation channel, and near an area where the water shoaled rapidly. Dropping the anchor too soon would leave the ship obstructing traffic in the channel, while dropping too late would risk the ship swinging over and grounding upon a shoal. Simply restoring the power to a gyrocompass is not sufficient to bring it to a usable state; several hours are usually required for the gyro to "settle-in" and provide reliable readings.

As we saw in the description of the normal activities of the navigation team provided earlier, the gyrocompass provides input to the determination of true bearings of landmarks for position fixing. For the navigation team, then, the primary consequence of the power outage was the loss of the only remaining functioning gyrocompass on the ship.

Computational Structure of the Task

Figure 12.3 shows the relationships among the various terms of the computation. With the gyrocompass working, the alidade (telescopic sight) mounted on the pelorus permits the direct measurement of the direction of the bearing of the landmark with respect to true north (TB in Figure 12.3). When the gyrocompass failed, all that could be measured by the bearing takers with the pelorus was the direction of the landmark with respect to the ship's head (RB in Figure 12.3). In order to compute the true bearing of the landmark, once the relative bearing has been determined, it is necessary to determine the direction of the ship's head with respect to true north. The compass measures the direction of the ship's head with respect to magnetic north (C in Figure 12.3). But the compass reading must first be corrected for errors, called deviation, that are specific to the compass and dependent upon heading (D in Figure 12.3). Cartographers measure the difference between true north and magnetic north for all mapped regions of the world. This is called the variation (V in Figure 12.3). The sum of these terms is the true bearing of the landmark, that which was directly measured when the gyrocompass was working.

There is a mnemonic in the culture of navigation that summarizes the relations among the terms that make up the ship's true head. It is "Can Dead Men Vote Twice?" and it stands for the expression "C + D = M, M + V = T" or "compass heading plus deviation equals magnetic heading, magnetic heading plus variation equals true heading." This specifies a meaningful order for the addition of the terms in which every sum is a culturally meaningful object in the world of navigation. Every competent navigation practitioner can recite this mnemonic, and most can give an accurate account of what it means. The knowledge that is embodied in this formula will be an important component of the solution discovered by the navigation team. Notice, however, that this mnemonic says nothing about relative bearings.

The computational structure of the task is well-known. As described above, computing true bearings for landmarks from relative bearings involves adding together the ship's compass heading, the compass deviation for that heading, the magnetic variation appropriate for the geographic location, and the bearing of the landmark relative to the ship's head. The procedure for a single line of position, therefore, requires three addition

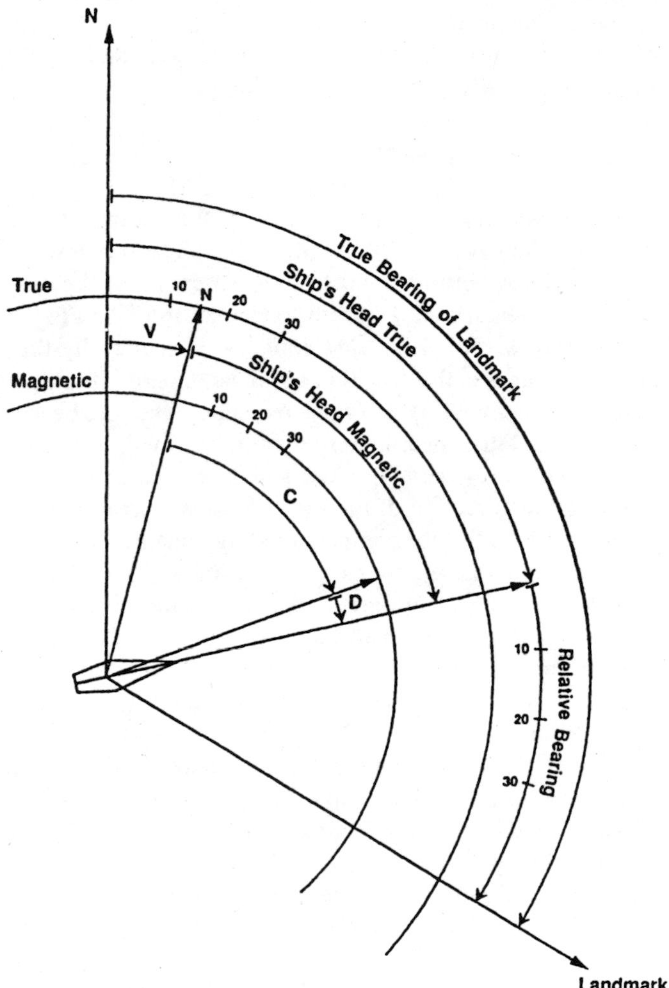

Figure 12.3. The Relationships Among the Terms of the Bearing Correction Computation. True bearings of landmark from ship equals compass heading (C), plus deviation (D), plus magnetic variation (V), plus relative bearing (RB).

operations. If one used this procedure for each line of position, the set of three lines of position that make up a position fix would require nine addition operations. There is a substantial savings of computational effort to be had, however, by modularizing the computation in a particular way. Since all three lines of position in any given fix are observed as nearly simultaneously as is possible, the ship's head for all of them must be the same. Thus, one can compute the ship's true heading (sum of compass heading, deviation and variation) just once, and then add each of the three relative bearings to that intermediate sum. This procedure requires only five addition operations for the entire fix, two for the ship's true head and one for each of the relative bearings, while nine addition operations are required by the nonmodularized procedure. As we shall see when we consider the details of the actual performance of the team, even a small savings of computational effort can be very helpful in this high workload environment.

THE PROBLEM OF ORGANIZATION

A search of ship's operations and training materials revealed many documents that describe in detail the nominal division of labor among the members of the navigation team in the normal crew configurations, and many that describe the computational requirements for deriving a single line of position from compass heading, deviation, variation, and relative bearing. There was, however, no evidence of a procedure that describes how the computational work involved in doing position fixing by visual observations of relative bearings should be distributed among the members of the navigation team when the gyrocompass has failed. The absence of such a procedure is not surprising. After all, if the ship had a procedure for this situation, it should have one for hundreds of other situations that are more likely to occur, and it is simply impossible to train a large number of procedures in an organization characterized by high rates of personnel turnover.

Even though no such procedure exists, since this event did occur, we may ask what a procedure for dealing with it should be like. Clearly, the design of a procedure for this situation should take advantage of the benefits of modularizing the computation. Perhaps one would design a procedure that calls for the initial computation of ship's true head followed by the computation of each of the true bearings in turn. That much seems straightforward, but how should one organize the activities of the separate team members so that they can each do what is necessary and also get the new job done in an efficient way? This is a non-trivial problem because there are so many possibilities for permutations and combinations of distributions of human effort across the many components of the computational task. The design should spread the workload across the members of the team to avoid overloading any individual. It should incorporate sequence control measures of some kind to avoid dissonance-coordinations, in which crew members undo each other's work; collisions, in which two or more team members attempt to use a single resource at the same time; and conflicts in which members of the team are working at cross purposes. It should exploit the potential of temporally parallel activity among the members of the team and, where possible, avoid bottlenecks in the computation.

As specified, it is quite a complicated design problem, and it looks even more difficult when we examine the relationships between the members of the navigation team and their computational environment. Given the nature of the task they were performing, the navigation team did not have the luxury of engaging in such design activities. They had to keep doing their jobs, and in the minutes between the loss of the gyrocompass and the arrival of the ship at anchor, the requirements of the job itself far exceeded the available resources.

THE ADAPTIVE RESPONSE

Viewing the navigation team as the cognitive system leads us to ask where in the navigation team this additional computational load was taken up and how the new tasks were accomplished. To summarize before examining the performance of the team in detail, the additional computation originally fell to the quartermaster chief who was acting as plotter. To correct the relative bearings passed to him, he attempted to do the added computations using mental arithmetic, but it was more than he could do within the severe time constraints imposed by the need for fixes on one-minute intervals. By trading some accuracy for computational speed, he was able to determine when the ship had arrived at its intended anchorage. After the Palau came to anchor, the plotter introduced a hand-held calculator to relieve the burden of mental arithmetic under stress, and recruited the assistance of the bearing timer in the performance of the computation. There was no explicit plan for the division of the labor involved in this added task between the plotter and bearing timer. Each had other duties that were related to this problem that had to be attended to as well.

Since this correction computation has well-defined sub-parts, we may ask how the sub-parts of the task were distributed among the participants. But here we find that at the outset there was no consistent pattern. The order in which the various correction terms were added, and who did the adding, varied from one line of position to the next, and even the number of correction terms applied changed over the course of the 66 LOP's that were shot, corrected, and plotted between the loss of the gyrocompasses and the arrival of the Palau at its berth. Gradually, an organized structure emerged out of the initial chaos. The sequence of computational and social organizational configurations through which the team passed is shown in Figure 12.4. After

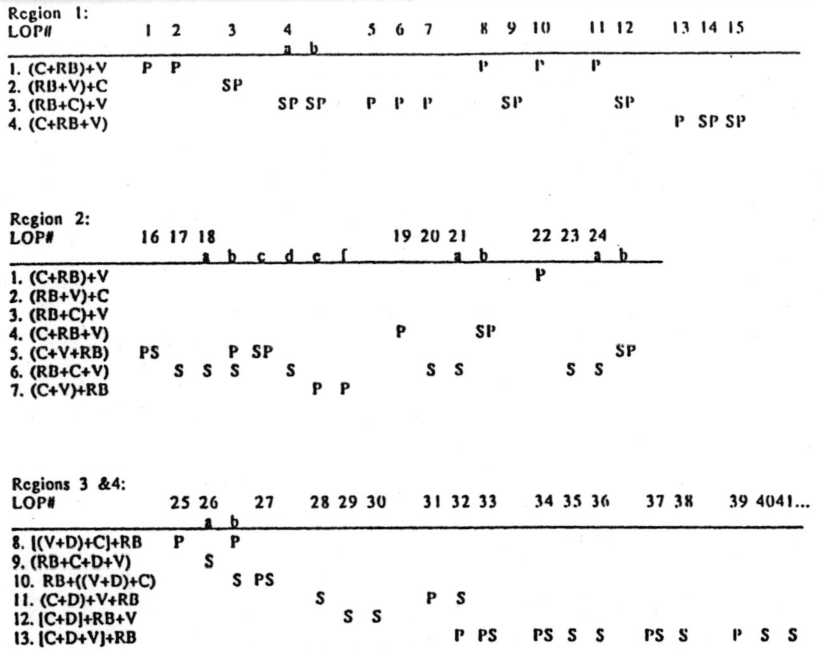

Region 1:

LOP#	1	2	3	4 a	4 b	5	6	7	8	9	10	11	12	13	14	15
1. (C+RB)+V	P	P							P		P	P				
2. (RB+V)+C			SP													
3. (RB+C)+V				SP	SP	P	P	P		SP			SP			
4. (C+RB+V)														P	SP	SP

Region 2:

LOP#	16	17	18 a	18 b	18 c	18 d	18 e	18 f	19	20	21 a	21 b	22	23	24 a	24 b
1. (C+RB)+V													P			
2. (RB+V)+C																
3. (RB+C)+V																
4. (C+RB+V)									P			SP				
5. (C+V+RB)	PS			P	SP											SP
6. (RB+C+V)		S	S	S		S				S	S			S	S	
7. (C+V)+RB							P	P								

Regions 3 &4:

LOP#	25	26 a	26 b	27	28	29	30	31	32	33	34	35	36	37	38	39	40	41...
8. [(V+D)+C]+RB	P		P															
9. (RB+C+D+V)		S																
10. RB+((V+D)+C)			S	PS														
11. (C+D)+V+RB					S			P	S									
12. [C+D]+RB+V						S	S											
13. [C+D+V]+RB									P	PS	PS	S	S	PS	S	P	S	S

Figure 12.4. Line of Position Computations. The structure of the computation performed is given in the left hand column. Lines of position are numbered across the top of each section of the table. "P" indicates an LOP computation performed entirely by the plotter. "S" indicates an LOP computation performed entirely by S. "SP" indicates an LOP computation begun by or structured by S and completed by P. "PS" indicates a computation begun by or structured by P and completed by S.

correcting and plotting about 30 LOP's, a consistent pattern of action appeared in which the order of application of the correction terms and the division of labor between plotter and bearing timer stabilized. While the computational structure of this stable configuration seems to have been, at least in part, intended by the plotter, the social structure (division of labor) seems to have emerged from the interactions among the participants without any explicit planning.

Analysis

The bearing takers out on the wings of the ship were only slightly affected by the loss of the gyrocompass. For them, it meant only that they had to remember to shoot the bearings relative to the ship's head, the outer rather than the inner of the two azimuth circles in the alluded view-finder (see Figure 12.2). The analysis will therefore focus on the activities of the plotter, a quartermaster chief (designated "P" in the analysis), and the bearing timer, a quartermaster second class (designated "S" in the analysis).

We can consider the behavior of the plotter and the bearing timer to be a search in a very complex space for a computational structure and a social structure that fit each other and that get the job done. As Figure 12.4 shows, on their way to a stable configuration, these two explored 13 different computational structures and many social configurations.

How can we account for this seemingly bizarre search of computational and social space? I will claim that there are four main principles of the organization of computation involved. They are:

1. computational structure driven by the availability of data
2. the use of a normative description to organize computation
3. the computational advantages of modularizing the addition task
4. the fit between computational and social organization.

The events between the failure of the gyrocompass and the end of the task can be partitioned into four regions based on these principles. In the first region, Lines of Position (LOP's) 1-15, P does all the computation himself and the computational structure is driven primarily by the availability of data. The end of this region is marked by the introduction of an electronic calculator. In the second region, LOP's 16-24, P begins to push some of the computational load onto the bearing timer, S, and while providing the bearing timer instruction on how to do the computation, begins to use a normative description to organize the computation. In the third region, LOP's 25-33, the modularity of the computation becomes a shared resource for the two workers through their joint performance of the modular procedure. In the fourth and final region, LOP's 34-66, they discover a division of labor that fits the computation, and they coin a lexical term for the modular sum, thus crystallizing the conceptual discovery in a shared artifact. Let's look now at the details of the work at the chart table, considering the lines of position plotted from the time the gyrocompass failed until the system had settled into its new stable configuration (refer to Figure 12.4).

Region 1: Computational Structure Driven by Data Availability

The first 12 lines of position are computed by P, using what would normally be called mental arithmetic. In some cases, this arithmetic is aided by artifacts in the environment. In the very first LOP, for example, he uses the scale of the hoey (chart plotting tool) as a medium for addition, lining up the scale index with 29 (the compass course), sliding it 52 gradations upward (the relative bearing), etc., and in LOP 2 he uses the bearing log itself as a memory during the computation, tracing out the addition columns with his fingers. LOP's 8 and 9 were computed using paper and pencil in the margins of the chart. P had a good deal of trouble keeping up with the demands of the task, as shown by the fact that the first fix has only two LOP's in it, the second fix has but one LOP and the third fix has two LOP's. The anchor was dropped at 17:06 in the afternoon just before the fifth line of position was plotted. Once the anchor was down, the team went from one-minute-fix intervals to six-minute-fix intervals, but P was still having trouble keeping up while doing mental arithmetic.

P's behavior in this region can be described as opportunistic. He used three different computational orderings and several different media in computing the first twelve lines of position. While at first glance this behavior looks unsystematic, there is a simple but powerful regularity in it. The order in which P took the terms for addition depends upon where the terms were in his environment, and on when and with how much effort he could get access to them. For example, in LOP 8, P returned to the chart table verbally rehearsing the ship's magnetic heading. He began his computation with that term. In LOP 9, where P had to consult S in order to establish the identity of the next relative bearing to add, he began his computation with relative bearing. In LOP 10, P was again doing the calculation on his own and again he began with ship's magnetic head. These patterns are hints to a more general organizing principle that we will see throughout this event. An examination of Figure 12.4 shows that in the first two regions, twelve out of fifteen LOP's for which the computation is initiated by P begin with the ship's magnetic head, and thirteen out of eighteen computations initiated by S begin with the relative bearing of the landmark.

This regularity appears to be a consequence of local strategies for individual cognitive economy. From the perspective of a person trying to do the addition, if one of the terms is already in working memory when it is time to begin the computation, then it is most efficient to start with that term.

Consider the situation of the bearing timer. When the computations are done on-line, the bearing timer is an interaction with the bearing takers. He has listened to, written down, and verbally acknowledged relative bearings. These activities, although not part of the addition procedure itself, influence the course of the addition procedure because they put the RB term into the working memory of the bearing taker. With RB already in working memory, in order to do the computation in the order that supports modularization,

(C + V + RB), S must either somehow keep RB active in working memory, or he must overwrite RB in working memory and read it again later when it is needed. If he chooses to maintain RB in working memory, then it must remain unaltered (and must not alter the other number representations present) during the reading of C, the recall of V and the addition of C and V. This may require him to maintain up to 11 digits in working memory (eight for the addition of V + C, plus up to three for RB.) If the memory load of that task is too great, S may choose to let RB be overwritten in working memory and read it in again later. Of course, doing that involves wasted effort overwriting and rereading RB.

In contrast to the costs of this "preferred" order, taking the terms in the order (RB + C + V) or (RB + V + C) involves lighter loads on working memory and no wasted effort. Thus, from the bearing taker's local perspective, it was simply easier and more efficient to begin each computation with the relative bearing.

P was in a different position. In most cases, he went to the helm station to get the ship's compass head while the relative bearings were being reported. This puts the C term into P's working memory at the beginning of the fix. Notice in Figure 12.4 that except for LOP's 5-7, every LOP initiated by P himself begins with C as the first term. But interaction with S or with other representational systems can change P's position in the computation. In each case where P began by asking S for a term to add, that term was the relative bearing and the relative bearing was taken as the first item in the addition. On closer inspection, the apparent exceptions to the rule in LOP's 5-7 are not exceptions at all. These computations were not done while the data were coming in. The observations of the three relative bearings were made while P worked to determine the location of the anchor. Then he set out to compute the LOP's with all of the data in the book in front of him —relative bearings in the left hand columns of the bearing book page and the ship's magnetic head in the rightmost column. This interaction with the bearing book changed the temporal pattern of availability of data, which in turn changed the organization of the most efficient ordering of terms for the performance of mental arithmetic.

It is unlikely that either man was ever aware of having made a decision concerning the order in which to add the terms. Rather, each was simply trying to do the additions as correctly and as efficiently as possible. Since the two participants at the chart table experienced different patterns of availability of data, this principle produced characteristically different results for each of them.

The principle at work so far can be summarized as follows: Individual actors can locally minimize their work load by allowing the sequence of terms in the sum to be driven by the availability of data in the environment.

But, since data become available primarily via social interactions, the computational structure is largely an unplanned side effect of this interactional structure. The interactional structure itself is chaotic because it is shaped by interference from other tasks and social interactions with other members of the navigation team and members of other work teams on the bridge.

After LOP 12, S initiated a round of bearings on a two-minute interval. P instructed him to take the fix on six-minute intervals, and complained about trying to keep up doing mental arithmetic. When asked if he had been able to keep up with the work he said,

P: No, I was running it through my head and it wouldn't add. It wouldn't make numbers, so I was making right angles in my head to see where the hell it was at.

S: You take the variation out of it.

P: Yes, you add the, you add the magnetic head, then you add the variation.

This conversation is the first evidence of reflection on the structure of the computation. P explicitly names the variables, saying, ". . . you add the magnetic head, then you add the variation." After this, P remarked that the only way to keep up with the work would be to use a calculator. Shortly after this conversation, P went to the chart house and returned with a navigation calculator.[6]

The use of the calculator eliminated the need for the intermediate sums that P computed when doing mental arithmetic. In LOP's 13-15, P keyed in the data. He started each LOP computation by keying in C +, then he looked for RB in the bearing book, keyed RB +, then keyed V =. Here the calculator was not only a computational device; P also used it as a temporary external memory for the C term while he looked for the RB term. The immediate consequences of the introduction of the calculator were that it eliminated that production of intermediate sums (this will be important in the development of the modular solution below), and it changed the memory requirements for P by serving as an external memory. It did not change the fact that the order in which the terms were added was dependent on the pattern of availability of data in the task environment.

The dependence of the computational sequence on the availability of data is the main characteristic of events in the first region. It will survive into later regions in the behavior of the bearing timer, but the introduction of the calculator marks the beginning of the end of this sort of data-driven task organization for P. Up until and including the first calculator round, S has sometimes fed values of RB to P, but has done no arithmetic, mental or otherwise. That is about to change.

Region 2: The Emergence of Mediating Structure

The most important consequence of the introduction of the calculator was that it created a new context of interaction between P and S, in which P gave S instruction in the procedure. For example, in LOP 16, P returned from the helm station where he had read the compass heading and keyed in the value of C.

LOP 16: **(C + V + RB)**
P returns from helm.
P: 2 3 1. What have we got? {231 + }
(Then slides the calculator to S.)
P: Here, add these things.
P: You want . . . You want the head. You want the head | which is 2 3 1.
S: | and add variation.
P: Plus variation.
S: Oh, 231 is the head?
P: 2 3 1. Here {Clear **2 3 1**}
S: I got it. *(puts his hands on the keys.)* {clear, 2 3 1}
P: Plus 14.
S: {+ 14} Okay.
P: Okay. *(intermediate sum not computed)*
S: {+ **0 0 7** –} is 252 on Silvergate.
P: 2 5 2 Silvergate.

P controlled the order of the arguments in this LOP. S seemed surprised that he started with the ship's head.

In LOP's 17 and 18a, P was busy plotting a previous bearing. S initiated the computation himself by reading the RB from the book and beginning with it. In LOP 18a, the result was in error because the bearing that was reported was misread by the bearing taker. But the context of the error provided an opportunity to restructure the work. S slid the calculator over in front of P and began to dictate values starting with what was, for him, the most salient term, RB. P, however, ignored S and began keying in the data in the sequence C + V. P made an error and cleared the calculator. S, having seen the sequence in which P wanted to add the terms, dictated the terms in the order C + V + RB as seen in LOP 18c.

LOP 18c: **(C + V + RB)**
S: 2 3 1, Chief, plus 14 plus |
P: {2 3 1 + 1 4 + } |Okay, what was ah,
S: The bearing was 1 5 7 (3 sec) | Okay

P: {1 5 7 =} | 4 0 2

S: Minus 3 60 | is

P: { –| 3 60 = } is 0 4 2. No it ain't. I isn't no 0 4 2. It's just not working. Look where 0 4 2 goes. (*P points to the chart.*) If it's 0 4 2, we're sitting over on Shelter Island!

There were three more attempts to compute this LOP. In LOP 18d, S made a data entry error and passed the calculator to P in frustration. In LOP 18e, P made a data entry error, cleared the calculator and began again.

We might have thought that the importance of the introduction of the calculator would be its power as a computational device. In fact we see that using the calculator, the team was neither faster nor more accurate than they were without it! The important contribution of the calculator was that it changed the relation of the workers to the task. When P pushed the calculator over to S and told him to add the terms, he engaged in a new task, that of instructing S in the computation, and he organized his instructional efforts in terms of the normative computational structure, "C + D = M + V + T." This was evident in LOP 16 where P named the variables, "You want the head, which is 2 3 1 . . . plus variation." Note that S did not seem to learn from the explicit statements of P. He returned to taking the RB first in LOP's 17, 18a and b. However, once P had articulated this structure, it became a resource he could use to organize his own performance of the task. In LOP 18b, in spite of S having dictated the RB to him first, he keyed in C + V. There, S verbally shadowed P's keystrokes. This joint performance was the first time S had taken ship's head as the first term. Once P began behaving this way, S was able to internalize that which appeared in interpersonal work and under certain social conditions, could use it to organize his own behavior. Thus, in LOP 18c where S took the role of dictating the values to P who was keying them in, S said, "2 3 1, Chief, plus 14, plus . . ." But the structure was not yet well-established for S. In the next attempt, LOP 18d, a new RB was observed and, driven by the data, S began the computation with it.

The introduction of the calculator and the errors that were committed with it provided a context for instruction in which the sequence of terms could be explicitly discussed. The errors they were responding to were not sequence errors, but simple key-pressing errors, yet they still served as contexts for sequence specification. P appeared to learn from his own instructional statements (intended for S) and changed his own behavior. Until he tried to instruct S on what to do, he took the terms in the order in which they were presented by the environment. S appeared to change his own behavior to fit with what P *did,* not what he *said.* This newly emergent normative structure dominated P's instructional efforts and came to dominate the organization of his task performance as well.

In LOP 21a, S made a key pressing error while adding the terms in the order (RB + C + V). The error drew P's attention and he turned to watch S.

LOP 21b: **(C + RB + V) & ((C + V) + RB) = ((C + V) + RB + V)**

S: {clear **2 2 1** | + **14**}

P: | plus 14 is 2 3 5, *(C + V, P does it in his head.)*

S: 2 3 5?

P: Yah, it's 2 3 5 plus 1 1 8. **((C + V) + RB)**

S: Oh. {clear} *(S doesn't realize that hitting = would have produced 235.)*

P: 2 3 5 is | 3 3 5, 3 4 5, how about 3 5 3. Right?

S: { 235 | + **1 1 8** + 14 = } How about 0 0 7. **((C + V) + RB + V)**

P: 0 0 7.

S: Chief, the computer just beat you. *(Chief glares at S)*

P: Just kidding. *(all laugh 4 sec)* The modern technology.

S: I'll modern technology you.

Here, in LOP 21b, two important things happened. First, S demonstrated that he could produce the normative sequence when trying to show P he could do the addition correctly. Second, this was the first time P had organized a properly modular computation. Unfortunately, it is also clear that S did not yet understand the meaning of the intermediate sum (C + V), which is the key to the modularization. He mistook it for C alone, and added in RB and V, generating an error. P seemed intimidated by the calculator and did not challenge the result. It led to a poor fix, but he had been getting really poor fixes all along. Fortunately, the anchor was holding and they were in no danger, but at this point if they had had to rely on the quality of the fixes, they would have been in trouble.

P performed LOP 23 with the non-standard sequence (C + RB + V). However, this is not a violation of the principles described above. P did not get C from the helm at the beginning of the fix as he usually did. Instead, he was busy asking whether the anchor was being hoisted at this time. S announced C when P returned to the table. P looked in the bearing book for C. He read it aloud, and while still leaning over the book he added in the RB nearest him in the book, pointing to the place digits in it with the butt of his pencil as he added the numbers. Once again, the availability of data in the environment drove the organization of the computation.

LOP 24a: **(RB + C + V)**

S: 1 1 2 plus 2 2 6 plus 14, 3 5 2 on ship's head. *(means Hamm's light)*

P: Which tower is he shooting for North Island Tower? *(P leaves table for wing)*

P: Hey, which tower are you shooting for North Island Tower? *(PW points to tower)* You are? Okay.

PW: Is that the right one?
P: Yep.
(P returns to table)

LOP 24b: **(C + V + RB)**
S: Which tower | wa—
P: | And ah, what was Hamm's?
S: And Hamm's was **{2 2 6 + 1 4 + 1 1 2 =}** 3 5 2. (5 sec) Time 56 Chief.

In LOP 24a, S, working on his own, took the terms in the order (RB + C + V). A few moments later when P asked S what the bearing was to Hamm's, instead of remembering it, S re-computed it. This time, LOP 24b, he did it in the prescribed order, (C + V + RB). This is evidence that he knew the sequence preferred by P, but he seemed to produce it only in interactions with P.

This is the end of the second region. In this region we have seen that a mediating structure is being remembered by P, but S's organization of the computation is still driven largely by the pattern of availability of data. The clear boundary between this region and the first one is not marked by the introduction of the calculator, but by P's order "Here, add these things." The change in computational structure follows from a social innovation that was made possible by a technological change rather than from the technological innovation itself.

Region 3: Partial Modularization

In the description of the computational structure of the task given above, we noted that the true bearing is the sum of four terms: ship's magnetic head, C; deviation, D; variation, V; and relative bearing, RB. By now the team had computed and plotted 24 lines of position and the deviation term was not included in any of them. This seems surprising, since we have ample evidence that both of them knew well what deviation is and how to use it. One can only surmise that they were so busy trying to do the job that they forgot this term. The absence of the deviation term had no effect on the quality of the fixes plotted until LOP 22, because until then the ship was on a heading for which the deviation was near zero. Just before LOP 22, however, the ship's head swung southwest, and on that heading there was a three-degree deviation. The fix triangles started opening up, and it became clear to P that something was wrong. He lay the hoey on the chart from various landmarks and moved it slightly, seeing what sort of different bearings would make the triangle smaller. LOP's 25-27 are a re-working of LOP's 22-24, this time taking deviation into account.

1\. P: I keep getting these monstrous goddamn, these monstrous frigging goddamn triangles. I'm trying to figure out which one is fucking off.

2. S: You need another round?
3. P: No, no no, uhuh. 1 2 0 I know what he's doing. Let me try, let me try, *(turns and moves to helm station)* let me try, with my new ones, say three. *(reads deviation card posted on compass stand).* Say three, add three to everything.
4. S: Add three?
5. P: Yah.
6. S: 'Cause he's using magnetic? *(S does not get it yet.)*

LOP 25: **([(V + D) + C] + RB)**

7. P: On a southwest heading add three. So it's (14 + 3 =)17 plus 2 2, 17 plus 2 2 6 is ah, 2 3 ah
8. S: Plus 2 2 6 is 3 4 is 2 4 3 *(S working on paper with pencil)* ((V + D) + C)
9. P: Okay, 2 4 3 and 0 1 3 is 2 5 6, 2 | 5 6
([(V + D) + C] + RB)
10. S: | 2 5 9 *(this is an error)*
11. P: 2 5 nuhuh?
12. S: 2 5 9, plus 0 1 3? It's 2 5 9.
13. P: 2 5 9 that's right. Okay. And plus 1 1 2 was what?

LOP 26a

14. S: 1 1 2 plus 2 2 6. *(Here is clear evidence that S doesn't understand the attempt to modularize.)* **(RB + C)**

LOP 26b: **([(V + D) + C] + RB) & (RB + [(V + D) + C])**

15. P: Plus 2 4 3, 2 4 3 plus 1 1 2.
([(V + D) + C] + RB)
16. S: 1 1 2 plus 2 4 3 is 5 5, 3 5 5, *(still working on paper)*
(RB + [(V + D) + C])

In P's moment of discovery, line 3, where he said "I know what he's doing," he noticed that the geometry of the triangle was such that a small clockwise rotation of each of the lines of the previous fix would make the triangle smaller. Any small error that belongs to all the LOP's suggests deviation. He went to the helm station and consulted the deviation card to determine the deviation for this heading. Although he describes the results as "much better," with deviation included, the two errors introduced by S still result in a poor fix.

The computation of 243 as the ship's true head, and its use in LOP 26b is the very first full modularization of the computation. P has control of the computations in all three LOP's, although in LOP 26b he has to fight S's strong propensity to put the RB first. S clearly does not yet understand either the benefits of modularization or the necessity to add the RB last in the modular form. The structure of LOP 27 was modular too, but the value of ship's true head, while properly computed, was not correctly remembered.

P seems to have taken the discovery of deviation and the recomputation of the bearings as an opportunity to think about the structure of the computation itself. The reflection that came in the wake of the introduction of the calculator led him to organize the computation in accordance with the normative form. The reflection that came with the addition of the deviation term led him to the modular structure. He never explicitly mentioned the advantages of modularization, but if he was not aware of the advantages when he organized the computation, he must certainly have been aware of them once the computation had been performed.

S computed LOP 28 while P explained to the keeper of the deck log why the gyrocompass could not be restarted in time to help, and why they would therefore make the remainder of the trip using magnetic bearings. P's conversation was interrupted by S, who checked on the procedure for using the deviation table.

LOP 28: **([(C + D] + V + RB)**
S: Charles? (2 sec) Head?
H: 2 2 6.
S: 2 2 6.
S: So it's 2 2 6. You wanna add 3, right? On a southerly course? (3 sec) Chief?
P: Say again.
S: You wanna add 3 to that / ? / southerly course? *(pointing at the entry on the deviation table.)* (2 sec) It's 2 2 6. The magnetic head is 2 2 6.
P: Yah.
S: 2 2 6 plus | 3, okay, so that makes 2 2 9, **{2 2 9 + 14}**
P: | right.
S: **{ + 1 1 5 =}** (3 sec) 3 5 8 on Hamm's light.
([(C + D] + V + RB)

Thus, S took the arguments in the right order in LOP 28, but did only a partial modularization. He computed (C + D) = 229 as a modular sum. Then he added V and added RB without producing ship's true head as an intermediate sum. In LOP's 29 and 30, S started with the partially modular sum, and added the terms in the order [C + D] + RB + V. Even this partial modularization is an important step forward for S. It appears to be due to two factors. First, including deviation in the computation may have made the C term more salient. Second, S's location in the computation had changed. He recorded the relative bearings as usual, but he had to go to the helm station himself to get the compass heading because P was otherwise occupied. At that point he had the C term in working memory and it was time to begin the computation. This change in position meant that what was best for the computation was also easiest for S. This is not the best division of labor, but it is one for which there is a momentary local fit between social and computational structure. The pattern of availability of data was not running counter to the computational structure. Paradoxically, then, the extra work that took P away from the chart table (a burden on the system) may have been a factor that permitted the system to improve.

Weighed Anchor

LOP's 32-33 are a turning point in the procedure. In LOP 32 there is a clear conflict of understanding between P and S. In LOP 33 they perform what will be the stable configuration for the first time.

LOP 32: **([(C + D) + V] + RB)**

1. S: You want the aero beacon?
2. P: Yah, I want the aero beacon now, yah. It's just . . . 1 8 7, 8 8, 8 7, 8 8.
3. S: 0 2 0, what's the ship's head?
4. P: Huh? 0 8 7, 8 7, It's | I west
5. S: | 0 87 it's 1 west, 7
6. P: it's 8 6 **(C + D)**
7. S: **{8 6.}**
8. P: And 14 | is 1 0 0 **((C + D) + V)**
9. S: | **{ + 14}**
10. S: **{ + 1 0 0}**, hold it
11. P: No, it's 1 0 0 plus whatever. **([(C + D) + V] + RB)**
12. S: 1 0, where are you getting? . . .
13. P: 1 0 0 is the heading, the whole thing, | plus relative.
14. S: | Oh, the whole thing, plus relative, **{ + 20 =}**.
1 20.
15. P: Okay
16. S: 1 20 |is for North Island Tower.

LOP 33: **([(C + D) + V] + RB)**

17. P: | and Hamm's? (2 sec) 1 0 | 0 plus whatever for Hamm's.
18. S: | Hamm's
19. Okay, {100 + **2 2 4** =}. 3 2 4 on|Hamm's
20. P: | 3 2 4. That's all three of 'em. I got 'em all.
21. S: Okay.
22. P: Looks good. Right on. Perfect. Pinpoint fix.
23. S: Alright!

In LOP 32, P works with S to recompute the ship's true heading. This joint work in lines 4-16 provides the opportunity for S to understand that the "whole thing" is the modular sum to which the RB can be added. The order in which S added the terms still followed the pattern of data availability, but

P actively constructed the pattern of data availability such that the sequence produced by S was the desired one. That is, P acted as a mediator between the pattern of data availability in the task environment and the addition activities of S.

The most salient features of this region were the emergence of the partial modularization of the computation and the conflicts between P's newly solidified conceptual schema, and S's practices. In this region, P began to provide mediating structure that changed the pattern of data availability experienced by S. In LOP 33, S showed signs of using this mediating structure himself. For S, the addition activity was no longer on the surface being applied opportunistically. It now lay behind a conceptual and social organization that fed it the terms of the expression in a particular order.

Region 4: The New, Stable Solution

In the previous section, we saw how the behavior of one individual can act as a mediating device that controls the pattern of availability of data for the other. In this, the last region, the team discovered a division of labor in which each of them could use a computational sequence that followed the availability of data in the task environment (thus minimizing memory load and wasted effort) while each simultaneously produced for the other patterns of data availability that supported the modular form of the computation. In this region the computational structure was still driven primarily by the pattern of availability of data, but the availability of data itself was determined by the social organization of the actions of the members of the team. Thus, the issue here is the fit between the constraints of cognitive processing (memory limitations, e.g.) and the social organization of work (distribution of cognitive labor), as mediated by the structure of the computational task (modularity of addition).

In LOP's 34-36 they tuned their division of labor, jointly computing the modular sum in LOP 34, and S remembering it in LOP's 35 and 36.

LOP 34: **(|(C + D) + V| + RB)**
P: Okay, what's he on? (to helm) What are ya on right now? 8, 8 5, 8 5,
0 8 5, 0 8 | 4 plus 14 0 9 8. **((C + D) + V)**
S: | 0 8 5 is / 0 8 4 plus 14, {8 4 + 14 =} that's
P: Okay
S: 98
P: 9 8 and 2 6
S: 9 8 { + 2 6 = } 1 2 4, **(| (C + D) + V | + RB)**
P: | 1 2 4
S: | 1 2 4 North Island Tower
P: Okay

LOP 35:

S: {9 6 + 2 1 2 = } 3 0 8 on Hamm's light. **(/(C + D) + V/ + RB)**

(S has mis-remembered the true head. Should be 98, not 96)

P: Okay

LOP 36:

S: {98 + 3 5 7}

P: Damn near reciprocals.

S: {–3 6 0 = }

P: 3 60 is I 0 9 5

S: ah I 0 9 5 **(I(C + D) + VI + RB)**

This is essentially the pattern of work they would maintain all the way to the dock. By LOP 38 the final pattern was achieved. In this, P computed the modular sum alone, finding C and D at the helm station and recalling V from long-term memory. Meanwhile, S recorded the relative bearings. P then added the first relative bearing to the modular sum, usually while S was recording the last of the relative bearings. P announced the modular sum to S, and S then added each of the other relative bearings to the modular sum. The only important event not included in these first 38 LOP's was the advent of a linguistic label for the ship's true head. They called it "total" in LOP 42 at 18:42. Once they had a name for it, they could pass it around among themselves more easily. The "publication" of the modular sum is essential to the final solution, since it acts as the bridge between the portion of the computation done by P and that done by S.

DISCUSSION

It appears that four forces control the navigation team's bizarre search of the space of computational and social structures. They are (1) the advantages of operating first on the contents of working memory which leads computational sequence to be entrained by the pattern of availability of data, (2) the use of normative computational structure, which permitted the discovery of (3) the advantages of modularization of computation, and (4) the fit of social to computational structure. Each region of the adaptation process is dominated by one of these forces. In fact, all of them, except the advantages of modularization, are present to some extent in all regions of the adaptation history.

Memory Limitations and the Availability of Data

In the beginning, the structure of the computation seems to be driven exclusively by an interaction of limitations of the human cognitive system, specifically memory limitations, and the availability of data in the environment (Newell and Simon 1972, Anderson 1983). Memory limitations make it advantageous to add the terms of the correction in the order they become available. The availability of data depends on the pattern of social interactions. This seems to characterize P's behavior until he assumes a different relation to the computation at LOP 16. It describes S's behavior at least until LOP 32, and possibly to the end of the task.

At LOP 16, the introduction of the calculator gave rise to a new social arrangement (S punching keys while P told him which keys to press) that gave P a new relation to the computational task, that led, in turn, to the introduction of the normative computational structure. What P remembered was acted out in interaction with S. When S took dictation from P while keying in values, P was mediating the task for him. P was changing S's relation to the task such that what was convenient for S was also what was effective for the computation.

The Normative Computational Sequence, **C + D = M, M + V = T, T + RB = TB**

There is no doubt that P's computations were shaped by variants of the normative structure from LOP 16 on. There was only one exception to this (LOP 19), and in that case the RB had a value that was particularly easy to handle: 0 0 7. P maintained this structure even when it ran counter to the pattern of availability of data as in LOP 18b.

S appeared to be capable of producing the normative sequence when in interaction with P (LOP's 24b, 27); but when on his own, he seemed clearly driven by the availability of data. Thus, when computing the true bearings on-line as he recorded the values of relative bearings, he always took the RB as the first term. Before the discovery of the deviation term he used the sequence (RB + C + V) and after the inclusion of deviation (RB + C + D + V). In one instance, however, P was removed from the table by another task, and S computed the true bearings alone. After having recorded the relative bearings and having obtained the ship's magnetic head from the helmsman (C term in working memory), he began with the C term.

The computational importance of the normative sequence is that it makes the modularization possible. Since addition is a commutative operation, there is no difference in the sum achieved by adding the terms in any of the 24 possible sequences. But if the addition is to take advantage of the modularity of ship's true head, the terms C, D and V will have to be added together before any of them is added to a relative bearing. The normative structure provides a rationale for doing this, and it provides culturally meaningful interpretations of the intermediate sums that are lacking from such non-normative additions as (RB + V) or (V + D) (see Figure 12.3).

The Modular Computation

The modular organization of the computation emerges haltingly from P's attempts to apply the normative form, but it seems unlikely that P took up the normative form for its links to modularized form of the computation. It is more likely that it gave him a better understanding of what was going on by providing intermediate sums that have meaningful interpretations in the world of the ship. For an experienced navigator, a bearing is not simply a number, it is a body-centered feeling about a direction in space. Taking the terms in non-normative sequence results in intermediate sums that are just numbers. Taking them in measurement sequence results in intermediate sums that are meaningful directions in the world of the navigator. In this form they become directions that make sense (or don't), and this gives the navigator another opportunity to detect error or to sense that the computation is going well or badly even before it is completed.

There was a hint of modularity in LOP's 18e and f where P computed C + V and then asked for the RB. Similarly in LOP 21b he said, "... it's 2 3 5 (C + V) plus 1 1 8 (RB)." In each of these cases, there was only one LOP involved, so it was not possible to exploit the advantages of modularization. The first unambiguous case of modular computation was in the LOP's 25-27, that introduced the deviation term. These were performed in the non-standard sequence ([(V + D) + C] + RB). It is probably significant that P chose to perform these calculations with paper and pencil rather than with the calculator. The paper and pencil computation produced, as a natural side effect, a written record of the sum [(V + D) + C] which was then easily at hand for addition to each of the relative bearings. The written record of the modular sum in this instance was functionally similar to the verbal "publishing" of the labeled modular sum in the later fixes.

The Fit of Social and Computational

The modular form of the computation only became stable when a new division of cognitive labor was established in LOP 32 and 33. The pattern of availability of data produced by the division of labor in this stable configuration fit the computational structure of the problem. P obtained C from the helmsman and D from the deviation table, added them and then added the variation (easily availble in memory). At the same time, S recorded the relative bearings of the landmarks. P told S the modular sum, which S recorded, and S provided P with the first relative bearing. P added this relative bearing to the remembered modular sum. While P plotted the first LOP, S then added each of the other recorded relative bearings to the modular sum. Thus, the team arrived at a division of cognitive labor in which the behavior of each of the participants provided the necessary elements of the information environment of the other, just when they were needed. Each could behave as though driven by the availability of data in the world; and at the same time, as a team, they performed the additions in the sequence that provided the benefits of modularization.

Adaptation by Design?

Since the work of Cyert and March (1963), organization theory has viewed routines as fundamental building blocks. Thus the processes that change routines are very important to study. The description of the behavior of the four factors shows how a variety of solutions may be explored, but it does not in itself answer the question of how better solutions may become the routine operations of the system.

A classical view of organizational change (a folk view?) is that an analyst looks at the behavior of the system, represents it explicitly, and plans a better solution (e.g., Chandler's (1966) well-known account of the reorganization of Dupont). The better solution is expressed as an explicit description of system operation that is subsequently implemented in the real system by somehow altering the behavior of the participants to bring it into line with the designed solution. We often think of the organization of a system as a consequence of this sort of planning or design. We imagine an "outside" observer who observes the system's performance, represents it, operates on the representation to determine how to change the system, and then uses a channel of communication from outside the system to effect the changes (see Figure 12.5).

In her work on energy policy analysts, Feldman (1989, p. 136) adds some complexity. She describes organizational routines as "complex sets of interlocking behaviors held in place through common agreement on the relevant roles and expectations." She says, "Any particular set of agreements about rules and roles is a sort of equilibrium satisfying the demands of many different parties" (p. 136). A similar view is expressed by Nelson and Winter (1982) when they characterize routines as memory, truce, and target. This is a more subtle and interactive sense of the nature of the solutions to the problem of organization. An organization has many parts, and the operation

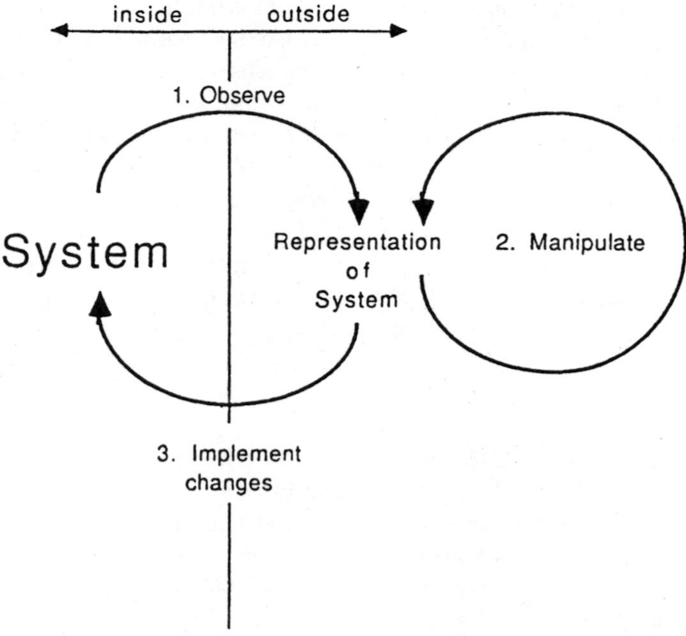

Figure 12.5. The Basic Design Process. A representation that is "about" the entire system is created from observations of the system. This representation is manipulated in order to plan an intervention in the system.

of the whole emerges from the interactions of those parts. Each part may simultaneously provide constraints on the behavior of other parts and be constrained by the behavior of other parts. Elsewhere (Hutchins, in press), I have referred to this sort of system of mutually adaptive computational sub-parts as a "cognitive ecology." This describes the sort of solution discovered by the navigation team. The parties to the computation are the plotter and the bearing recorder, and the demands on them are constructed in the interactions among their cognitive processing capabilities, the structure of the computation, the availability of data, and the fit between computational and social organization. They settled into a solution that simultaneously satisfied all these constraints. Feldman continues in the same vein:

> Many organizations or parts of organizations must coordinate their behavior in such a way that each can cope adequately with the pressures and constraints it has to satisfy. While there may be many possible solutions to such a problem, they are not necessarily easy to find. (1989, p. 136)

The question is now posed. Given that organizations are the kinds of systems that consist of many interlocking, interacting, and mutually dependent parts, how can solutions to the organization problem be discovered? Feldman provides one answer as follows:

> Even if one of the participants finds a new solution that will satisfy the constraints of all parties, the problems of persuading everyone else that this would be a beneficial change may still be considerable. (1989, pp. 136-137)

Clearly the process described in this passage must happen frequently. Parts of the behavior of the navigation team fit this description nicely. P's use of the normative computation scheme and his attempts to make that scheme explicit for S are examples. But this answer is a retreat to the classical view. It posits a designer, albeit "one of the participants" who "finds a new solution," and then must "persuade everyone else" that it is a good solution. And there remain aspects of the adaptive responses of the members of the navigation team, particularly those involving the changing division of labor, that are simply not captured by *any* description which relies on explicit representation of the shape of the solution.

ADAPTATION AND LOCAL DESIGN

In the analysis presented above, there are no instances of anyone reflecting on the whole process. P seems occasionally to represent the entire computation, but there is no evidence he ever imagined the structure of the division of labor. The adaptation process seemed to take place by way of local interactions, mostly of two types. First, team members put constraints on each other by presenting each other with partial computational products. When there is no previously worked out division of labor and assignments of responsibility for various parts of the computation, team members negotiate the division of labor by doing some (what they can, or what is convenient) and hoping that others can do whatever else is required. These are changes that result from the interactions among the behaviors of the subparts of the system as they adapt to the information environment and to each other's behaviors. There is no need to invoke any representation of the behavior of any part of the system to account for these adaptations. The way the computation was driven by the availability of data is an example of this kind of unreflective adaptation process. Even though they are not planned, these changes are not necessarily chaotic. If one part of the system behaves in a systematic way, another part may come to behave in a systematic way by adapting to the behavior of the first. In the interaction between P and S we saw that the behavior of one subsystem can be entrained by that of another.

A second adaptive process involves local design. When implicit negotiations of the division of labor fail, an actor may become aware of his own inability to keep up with the computation and attempt to recruit others to take on parts of it. Thus, the most striking thing P said during the search for a new configuration was something he said to S while falling behind in his attempts to compute bearing corrections with a pocket calculator. He pushed the calculator at the timer and said, "Here, add these things." There is no need to attribute a global awareness of the process to P to account for this. He doesn't have enough time to do his own work, much less reflect on the overall division of labor. He is just acutely aware that he is falling behind and that he needs help to catch up. This is a case of local design. As shown in Figure 12.6, design processes may be local to subsystems. Figure 12.6 depicts an overall system that can change in three modes:

1. Without any design activity at all, through the adaptive interactions among the subsystems.
2. Through local design activities in which manipulations are performed on representations of local subsystems in order to discover more adaptive relationships with the sub-system's environment. These changes may, in turn, lead to adaptive changes, either designed or not, by the other subsystems.
3. Through classical global activities in which the representation is of the entire system of interest.

The response of the system to the change in its environment was eventually successful, but it was the consequence of a large number of local interactions and adjustments, some of which led the system away from the eventual solution. Many of these adjustments appear to have been local design decisions by the participants. Prior to its discovery by the system as a whole, however, the final configuration appears not to have been represented or understood by any of the participants. To the extent that the acquisition of a useful adaptation to a changing environment counts as learning, we must say that this is a case of organizational learning.

Evolution and Design

It seems to me that there is an important difference between the process of change by supervisory reflection and intervention imagined in the classical view, and the process of change by local adjustment described above. It strongly resembles the difference between design and evolution (Alexander 1964).

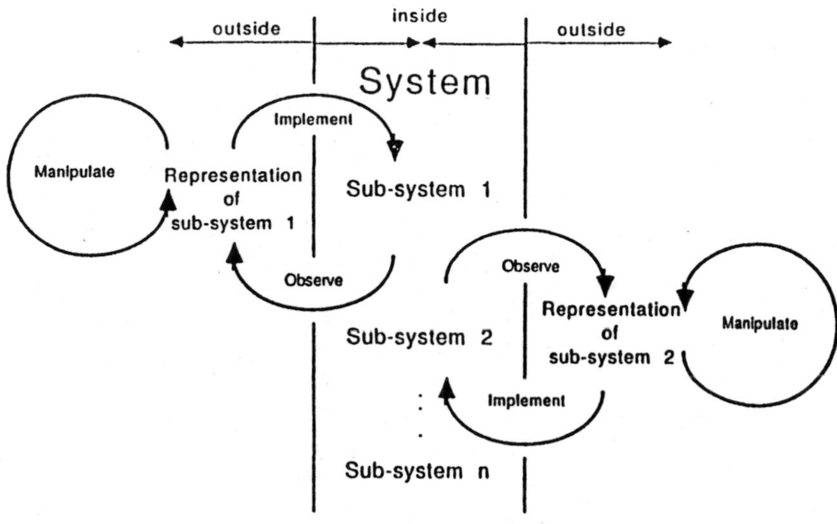

Figure 12.6. Local Design Activity. Subsystems interact with each other and adapt to each other's behaviors. Representations of local subsystem behavior are created and manipulated in order to plan changes to subsystem operation. These changes may trigger adaptive responses in other subsystems.

Both evolution and design can be characterized as searches. The evolutionary search is conducted by the system itself in terms of itself, while the design search is conducted by an "outsider" on representations of the system. The evolutionary search *is* the process of adaptation (cf. Weick's view of enactment, 1979), while the design search precedes and guides an implementation of the, hopefully adaptive, design. Pure evolution is, in fact, a process without design (cf. Dawkins 1986). What we see in the case of the adaptation by the navigation team is an organizational change that is produced in part by an evolutionary process (adaptive search without representation of the search space), and in part by a process that is something that lies between evolution and classical global-perspective design.

From this perspective, human institutions can be quite complex because they are composed of sub-systems (people) that are "aware" in the sense of having representations of themselves and their relationships with their surroundings. Whether we consider a particular change at the upper system level to be the result of evolution or the result of design depends on what we believe about the scope of the awareness of the subsystems. If we think that some of the subsystems have global awareness, and can represent and anticipate the consequences of possible changes, then we may view an organizational change as a result of design. If we believe that the subsystems do not form and manipulate representations of system operation, then we must view organizational change as evolutionary. What do we say when the individual sub-systems only engage in local design activity—say, crying out for help when one is overworked? In that case, design is clearly involved, and the change in the local environment of the individual that adapts this way is a *designed* change. Now, that local designed change may have undesigned and unanticipated consequences for other parts of the system. It may thus provoke local adaptations by other parts of the system as all of the parts seek (either by design or not) to satisfy the new environment of constraints produced by the changes in the behaviors of other parts. Ultimately, this process may produce a change in the behavior of the system as a whole. Even when many local design decisions are involved, such an adaptation that occurs at the system level appears to be evolutionary in the sense that the system level change that resulted was never represented. I believe most of the phenomena labeled as social or organizational "evolution" are instances of this kind of change.

Is the navigation task setting primarily the product of evolution or of design? When we consider human systems, we have to acknowledge that every participant in the system can be both inside and outside some systems in this sense. The changes in the organization of the navigation team were brought about by changes in the thinking of the participants of the system, that is, the agreements about rules and roles that constitute the organizational routine. To this extent, the structure of the setting is a product of design. But, since the observed reorganization was never fully represented by any of the participants in the system, the actor's designs alone cannot account for the solution that was achieved. Thus, the organization of the navigation task is also a product of evolution. Finally, while the participants may have represented and thus learned the solution after it came into being, the solution was clearly discovered by the organization itself before it was discovered by any of the participants.

ACKNOWLEDGMENTS

A preliminary version of this manuscript was prepared for the conference on Organizational Learning, May 18-20, 1989, at Carnegie Mellon University, June 1990. Editorial revisions were made by Michael Cohen and Lee Sproull.

Appendix

Transcription Conventions

Speakers

P: Quartermaster Chief, acting as plotter. The Chief is the ranking enlisted man in the navigation department. Also has the title Assistant to the Navigator.

S: Quartermaster Second Class, acting as bearing timer-recorder. Sometimes referred to by his first name, John.

H: The helmsman who is steering the ship. First name, Charles.

PW: Port Wing bearing taker.

Conventions for Transcription

( ) Words enclosed in parentheses are comments or annotations of the actions observed in the video record. Never verbatim transcription. Vertical bars

| are used in adjacent lines of transcription to indicate simultaneity of occurrence.

/?/ Unintelligible portion of utterance.

{ } Numbers and actions enclosed in curly brackets denote key presses on the calculator.

{3 + } Numbers and actions in bold font enclosed in curly brackets are key presses on the calculator that are verbally shadowed. This would mean a person pressed the 3 and the + key while saying "Three plus." In addition to numbers, the most frequent key presses are +, –, =, and clear.

1 20 Spoken numbers have been transcribed mostly as numerals for convenience. If they are separated by spaces, each numeral was pronounced separately. If they are not separated by space, then they are read as conventional numbers. This example could also have been transcribed, "One twenty."

Formulas for the Computation

C The compass heading of the ship with no corrections.

D Compass deviation. A function of heading.

V Magnetic variation. Approximately 14 degrees East in San Diego harbor.

RB The relative bearing of a landmark. This is the bearing of the landmark with respect to ship's head.

TB True bearing (T + RB).

M Ship's magnetic heading (C + V).

T Ship's true head (M + V).

( ) Terms enclosed in parenthesis were entered into the calculator with only plus or minus operators among them. The = operator closes the parenthesis. Thus (C + V + RB) means the three terms were added together as a group, whereas ((C + V) + RB) means that the = operator was applied to (C + V) which was then added to RB.

[ ] Sums in square brackets were spoken as intermediate sums. Thus, +RB denotes the following actions: key V, key +, key D, key =, key +, key C, key =, read the displayed value aloud, key +, key RB, key =.

NOTES

1. Such complete records are not always kept aboard merchant vessels and are not absolutely essential to the task of navigating the ship in restricted waters. It is possible for an experienced pilot to "eyeball" the passage and make judgments concerning control of the ship without the support of the computations that are carried out on the chart. Aboard naval vessels, however, such records are always kept for reasons of safety primarily, but also for purposes of accountability so that, should there be a problem, the ship will be able to show exactly what it was doing and where it was at the time of the mishap.

2. On other ships, and on this ship in different circumstances, the team may be somewhat larger or smaller depending on the availability of qualified personnel.

3. All of the names appearing in this document are pseudonyms, including that of the ship itself.

4. All of the discourse reported in this passage is direct transcription from the audio record of actual events. Rather than presenting the transcript itself with annotation, I have combined the transcript and annotation into a single narrative structure. The purpose of this passage is to convey a sense of the drama of the situation and to set the scene for subsequent events that will be analyzed in detail.

5. To "dead stick" an aircraft is to fly it after the engine has died.

6. The calculator was capable of computing a number of specialized navigation functions, but only addition and subtraction were used in what follows.

REFERENCES

Alexander, C. (1964), *Notes on the Synthesis of Form,* Cambridge, MA: Harvard University Press.

Anderson, J. (1983), *Architecture of Cognition,* Cambridge, MA: Harvard University Press.

Chandler, A. (1966), *Strategy and Structure,* Cambridge, MA: Harvard University Press.

Cyert, R. M. and J. G. March (1963), *A Behavioral Theory of the Firm,* Englewood Cliffs, NJ: Prentice Hall.

Dawkins, R. (1986), *The Blind Watchmaker,* New York: Norton.

Feldman, M. S. (1989), *Order without Design,* Berkeley: University of California Press.

Hutchins, E. (in press), "The Social Organization of Distributed Cognition," in L. Resnick and J. Levine (Eds.), *Perspectives on Socially Shared Cognition,* Washington, DC: APA Press.

Nelson, R. and S. Winter (1982), *An Evolutionary Theory of Economic Change,* Cambridge, MA: Harvard University Press.

Newell, A. and H. Simon (1972), *Human Problem Solving,* Englewood Cliffs, NJ: Prentice Hall.

Weick, K. E. (1979), *Social Psychology of Organizing,* Reading, MA: Addison-Wesley.

13

Intraorganizational Ecology of Strategy Making and Organizational Adaptation

Theory and Field Research

ROBERT A. BURGELMAN

This chapter presents an intraorganizational ecological perspective on strategy making and examines how internal selection may combine with external selection to explain organizational change and survival. The perspective serves to illuminate data from a field study of the evolution of Intel Corporation's corporate strategy. The data, in turn, are used to refine and deepen the conceptual framework. Relationships between induced and autonomous strategic processes and four modes of organizational adaptation are discussed. Apparent paradoxes associated with structural inertia and strategic reorientation arguments are elucidated and several new propositions derived. The chapter proposes that consistently successful organizations are characterized by top managements who spend efforts on building the induced and autonomous strategic processes, as well as concerning themselves with the content of strategy; that such organizations simultaneously exercise induced and autonomous processes; and that successful reorientations in organizations are likely to have been preceded by internal experimentation and selection processes effected through the autonomous process.

(ORGANIZATIONAL ECOLOGY;
CORPORATE STRATEGY;
SELECTION AND ADAPTATION;
EVOLUTIONARY MANAGEMENT)

This chapter originally appeared in *Organization Science*, Vol. 2, No. 3, August 1991.

The emergence of an ecological perspective, producing new insights in organizational change and adaptation (e.g., Carroll 1988, Hannan and Freeman 1989), has triggered several debates in organizational science that are important for the field of strategic management. One debate centers around the issue of environmental determinism versus strategic choice (Child 1972, Aldrich 1979, Astley and Van de Ven 1983, Bourgeois, 1984, Hrebiniak and Joyce 1985). Another debate concerns the relative importance of selection and adaptation in explaining organizational change and survival (Miles and Cameron 1982, Hannan and Freeman 1984, Singh et al. 1986). These sorts of debates have sometimes been interpreted as reflecting a fundamental opposition between the ideas of ecology and strategy.

The present chapter is based on the premise that there need not be a fundamental opposition of ecological and strategic perspectives, and that a fruitful integration of these ideas is possible in some ways. To do so, the chapter uses the variation-selection-retention framework of cultural evolutionary theory (Campbell 1969, Aldrich 1979, Weick 1979) which has previously been applied to strategy making by western (Burgelman 1983a) as well as Japanese (Kagono et al. 1985) scholars. The chapter extends earlier work by addressing research questions motivated by the evolutionary perspective. Some of these concern strategy content and process: How does the content of an organization's strategy come about and how does it evolve? How do strategy-making processes take shape over time? Of particular interest for this chapter are questions concerning some of the connections between strategy-making processes and different forms of organizational change and adaptation: What, if any, is the link between strategy making and inertia? Which sorts of strategy-making processes lead to major strategic change that is survival-enhancing? The chapter uses field research at Intel Corporation, a leading semiconductor company, to explore these questions.

The purposes of the chapter are twofold. First, the chapter proposes the usefulness of an *intraorganizational* ecological perspective on strategy making. An organization is viewed as an ecology of strategic initiatives which emerge in patterned ways, and compete for limited organizational resources so as to increase their relative importance within the organization. Strategy results, in part, from selection and retention operating on internal variation associated with strategic initiatives. Variation in strategic initiatives comes about, in part, as the result of individual strategists seeking expression of their special skills and career advancement through the pursuit of different types of strategic initiatives. Selection works through administrative and cultural mechanisms regulating the allocation of attention and resources to different areas of strategic initiative. Retention takes the form of organizational-level learning and distinctive competence, embodied in various ways—organizational goal definition, domain delineation, and shared views of organizational character. In this perspective, strategic initiatives rather than individuals are the unit of analysis (Cohen and Machalek 1988).

Second, the chapter proposes patterned links between the intraorganizational ecological processes and different forms of adaptation that have previously been identified in the literature. More specifically, the chapter suggests how opposing ideas concerning expected consequences of major strategic change (Hannan and Freeman 1984, Tushman and Romanelli 1985) can possibly be reconciled. This, in turn, suggests directions for further research.

The next section of the chapter discusses a field study carried out at Intel Corporation. The following two sections examine, first, strategic content and process from an evolutionary perspective and, second, relationships between strategy-making processes and modes of organizational adaptation. Throughout these sections, references to and vignettes from the Intel study are provided. The discussion section presents conclusions from the research and several propositions derived from it. The final section presents implications for theory and further research.

A FIELD STUDY OF INTEL CORPORATION

To explore the research questions motivated by the evolutionary perspective, a field study of the evolution of Intel Corporation's corporate strategy was carried out. Intel is a leading semiconductor company which has survived for more than 20 years as an independent company in an extremely dynamic industry. The firm grew from one million dollars of sales in 1968 to almost three billion in 1989. Profits rose from a loss of two million dollars in 1969 to $453 million in 1988.

After initial interviews with CEO Andrew S. Grove and his assistant, Dennis Carter, it was decided to focus the first stage of the research on Intel's decision, in 1985, to exit from the Dynamic Random Access Memory (DRAM) business. The second stage of the research focused on the period since 1985 and on Intel's current strategy. The study, encompassing archival data collection as well as interviews, was carried out during the period August 1988-October 1989. Company documents describing Intel's history, industry publications, and other written materials were analyzed. Some 20 key Intel managers were interviewed, many of them repeatedly. Some top managers who had previously left the company were included as well. The research is embodied in two case studies (Cogan and Burgelman 1989a, 1989b).

The research began with a broad examination of how Intel's strategy as a "memory company" had taken shape in the early years and then focused on

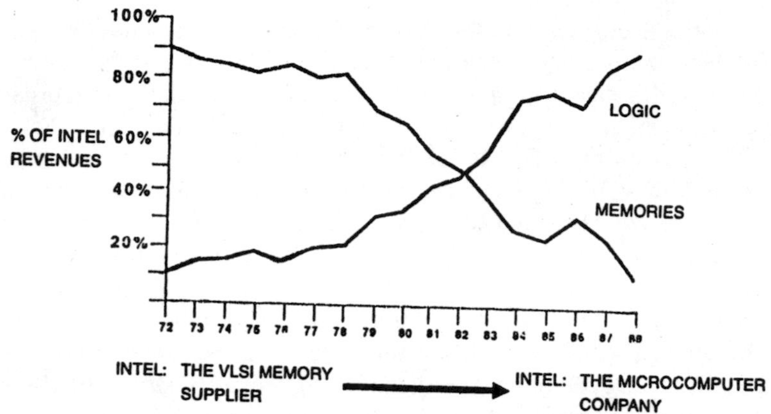

Figure 13.1. Intel's Evolution from Memory Company to Microcomputer Company
SOURCE: Intel Corporation.

the decision to exit DRAM's. In 1985, Intel was faced with a large cyclical downturn in the semiconductor industry, and fierce Japanese price competition in DRAM's. The firm expected a loss of more than 100 million dollars in 1986, yet needed to invest several hundred million dollars in new plant and equipment if it wanted to be competitive for the next generation of DRAM's. Top management decided that to exit from DRAM's was the best alternative for Intel. Managers from different levels and different functional and business groups who had been involved in and/or affected by the decision were asked to discuss the causes of Intel's exit and the aftermath of the decision. Looking at numerical archival data, it was a surprise to find that DRAM's had been a relatively small part of Intel's business for several years before the decision to exit was actually made.

Intel's market share in DRAM's was only 3.4%, ranking ninth in the industry, in 1985. Yet, there was a pervasive feeling among the interviewees that getting out of DRAM's had been perhaps the most momentous decision in Intel's history. The research then sought to understand Intel's evolution from a "memory" company in 1968 to a "microcomputer" company in 1985. This evolution is illustrated in Figure 13.1.

The second stage of the research focused on events since 1985, covering several key strategic areas, including the development of Intel's major Complex Instruction Set Computing (CISC) microprocessor business (the x86 product family); the evolution of the strategic importance of the Erasable Programmable Read Only Memory (EPROM) business; Intel's experience with the Application Specific Integrated Circuits (ASICS) business; the emergence and spinoff of the Electrically Erasable Programmable Read Only

Memory (EEPROM) venture; the growing importance of the Systems business; the emergence of Reduced Instruction Set Computing (RISC) processors as part of Intel's strategy; and questions regarding the potential strategic importance of a new form of memory called "FLASH." While most of the research was retrospective, the research period was long enough to observe some strategic decisions in real time, especially the decision to adopt RISC as part of Intel's corporate strategy, and the current uncertainty about FLASH memories.

The field study was guided by an evolutionary framework, derived from earlier research (Burgelman 1983a), which posits the existence of induced and autonomous processes in strategy making. The induced process concerns initiatives that are within the scope of the organization's current strategy and build on existing organizational learning; the autonomous process concerns initiatives that emerge outside of it and provide the potential for new organizational learning. These processes are considered important determinants of the evolution of the organization's strategy. The field data serve to test, to some extent, the validity of this framework. Campbell (1975) discusses several conditions for making a single case study useful as a probe for theory, two of which can be addressed in relation to the Intel study: (1) keeping track of confirming and disconfirming observations, (2) choosing the theory without knowledge of the confirmatory value of the case study. First, while initially not intended to serve as a test of an evolutionary theory of strategy making, the study does offer confirmatory support for the existence of the strategic processes proposed in the framework. Disconfirming observations were not systematically sought out, but some unexpected findings are presented that suggest the need for some amendment of the theory. Second, the availability of Intel as a research site was a fortuitous event and the researchers did not know whether the Intel case study would show support for the evolutionary framework or not. They were not familiar with the strategic management approaches of Intel. Also, many of the open-ended interviews were done by the research assistant, who was not involved in developing the conceptual framework. This limited somewhat the potential for confirmatory bias in the data collection. The research assistant wrote up detailed interview transcriptions which were analyzed together with data collected by the author.

While offering support for the existence of the proposed strategy-making processes, the research also offers the opportunity to refine and deepen some of the ideas underlying the initial conceptual framework. The chapter reflects iterations between theory and data, using the data to identify some new aspects of an evolutionary perspective on strategy-making processes. In the context of grounded theorizing (Glaser and Strauss 1967), the chapter intends to move from theory building based on research in substantive areas, such as internal corporate venturing (Burgelman 1983b), to a more general theory of strategy-making processes in organizations. The theory concerns corporate strategy rather than business strategy, and substantive strategy making rather than corporate restructuring (Snow and Hambrick 1980).

The research has several limitations. It concerns a single high-tech organization still run by some of its founders. The firm has grown up in a cyclical but very expansive industry. And it is a successful organization. Clearly it would be useful to study a larger sample also including failing organizations. On the other hand, by concentrating on one organization with 20 years of continuity in leadership, the research could access sources with intimate knowledge of the details of the firm's evolution and could examine in depth how the organization had dealt with partial failure—and the threat of complete failure—at a critical point in its history. Also, the semiconductor industry has previously been studied by organizational ecologists (e.g., Brittain and Freeman 1980, Boeker 1989), but no in-depth study of the strategy making of semiconductor firms is currently available.

INTRAORGANIZATIONAL ECOLOGY OF STRATEGY MAKING

Research on strategy-making processes can be classified in terms of two primary foci (Snow and Hambrick 1980). Some scholars, focusing on strategic change, have documented major epochs (Mintzberg 1978, Mintzberg and Waters 1982), periods of quantum change (Miller and Friesen 1984), and reorientations (Tushman and Romanelli 1985) in strategy making. Others have documented the *ongoing* process of strategy making in organizations (e.g., Quinn 1982). The evolutionary framework encompassing induced and autonomous strategic processes builds on both streams of work. This section discusses the induced and autonomous processes in terms of variation-selection-retention mechanisms, and uses them to elucidate strategy making at Intel.

Induced Strategic Process

Retention. Consider a newly founded and successful organization like Intel in the late sixties. Whether initial success is the result of competence or luck, top management's role is to articulate an organizational strategy that will help secure continued survival. Such a strategy is likely to be based, at least in part, on retrospective sense making and attempts to capture top management's learning about the basis for the organization's success. The strategy is embodied in the managers who rose to (or stayed at) the top while pursuing a particular set of strategic initiatives. It is also embodied in oral and written statements regarding the technical/economic as well as cultural factors—such as key values and company traditions—perceived to be associated with past success (Pettigrew 1979, Beyer 1981, Haggerty 1981, Donaldson and Lorsch 1983, March 1981b, Pfeffer 1981, Weick 1987). Organizational strategy, conceived in this fashion, identifies the distinctive competences of the organization, defines its goals, delineates its action domain, and defines its character (Selznick 1957, Andrews 1971, McKelvey and Aldrich 1983). The organizational strategy may be expressed in substantive rules and prescriptions, referring to the technical/economic and cultural factors (March 1981a, Nelson and Winter 1982) which guide organizational-level strategic action and induce strategic initiatives in line with it at lower levels. Through the application of these rules and prescriptions, strategic decisions are joined over time (Freeman and Boeker 1984), distinct patterns of organizational-level strategy are realized (Miles and Snow 1978, Mintzberg 1978, Miller and Friesen 1984), and the organization's character is maintained (Selznick 1957).

The Intel study illustrates this evolutionary perspective on organizational strategy. Les Vadasz, a top-level manager, described how Intel's strategy making had evolved:

> Intel was a successful start-up in the late '60s, and one of the first things I did (when asked to think about strategic planning) was to try to understand what led to Intel's success. The reasons for success were embedded in the combined talents of the group that was in charge. We had a "sense" about the technology and the business which led to a series of correct decisions.

Having a "sense" about the technology meant that Intel's top management understood that silicon rather than metal was the key material for memories and that process technology was the driver of the memory business. In fact, it was manufacturing prowess that made it possible for Intel to succeed with DRAM's where other memory start-ups (such as Advanced Memory Systems) had previously failed. Andy Grove, in charge of engineering and manufacturing in the early days, and other team members solved the technical problems with silicon-based memories, and were able to get Intel's production yields to surpass the threshold for viability in the market against core memories. Once the fundamental manufacturing problems had been solved, Intel's technological efforts focused on how to get more transistors on the same amount of silicon real estate. The ability to make smaller and denser devices was the result of Intel's research and was kept proprietary.

Top management also believed that initial success was associated with using small business teams, which affected the way Intel tried to implement its strategy as it grew larger. While Intel's success with silicon-based memories set the stage for a fundamental transformation of the computer industry, such transformation was not the founders' purpose: they simply saw the entrepreneurial opportunity of offering replacement parts for mainframe computer memories (Gilder 1989).

Of course, an organizational strategy largely based on retrospective rationality does not preclude prospectively rational efforts on the part of top management. One upper-level manager at Intel expressed this as follows: "Grove has been preaching: 'Make the tough decisions! Don't do something tomorrow because you did it today.' " However, as will be seen later on, Grove himself experienced how difficult it was to actually do this.

Selection. Research suggests that the awareness of a firm's strategy is likely to be concentrated at the top level of the organization (Hambrick 1981), and that there may be less than full agreement on what the firm's distinctive competences are (Stevenson 1976, Snow and Hrebiniak 1980). Also, as an organization grows, strategy making becomes increasingly differentiated over multiple levels of management (Williamson 1970) and the strategy can no longer be directly communicated in substantive detail to all levels of management. Participants differentially situated in the organization are likely to perceive different strategies as having the best potential for their own and the organization's advancement. This provides an important source of internal variation, as individuals who possess data, ideas, motivation, and resources all strive to undertake specialized initiatives. But unless an organization is able to establish internal selection mechanisms to maintain a level of coherence, it seems likely that the strategy eventually will become unrealized (Mintzberg 1978). Top management is expected, therefore, to establish a structural context encompassing administrative (Bower 1970) and cultural (Ouchi 1980) mechanisms. Administrative mechanisms include, among others, strategic planning and control systems, approaches to measuring and rewarding managers, and rules governing resource allocation. Cultural mechanisms include, among others, socialization rituals and behavioral norms (do's and don'ts). Different forms of structural context provide more or less tight coupling between the organizational strategy and strategic initiatives of managers at various levels (e.g., Chandler 1962, Mintzberg, 1979, Rumelt 1974, Williamson 1970, Haspeslagh 1983).

The Intel data support the importance of having the induced process driven by top management strategic intent, and also offer insight in the consequences of losing the coupling between strategic initiatives of middle managers and strategic intent. Commenting on the evolution of Intel's Strategic

Long Range Planning (SLRP) process, Les Vadasz described the efforts to establish an induced process:

> As the company grew, we tried to replicate the environment that had led to making "correct" decisions by forming relatively small business units and creating a bottoms-up strategic planning system. However, that became very unwieldy. The notion of pushing decisions down may have been a good one, but the task-relevant maturity was not great enough. Managers started gaming with the system. One key symptom was that new ideas were often co-opted by groups and molded to fit immediate needs rather than developed as originally intended. The system is now more top down. A high-level group sets the corporate strategy, and business units operate within that locus. Business units must focus on a few things and do them right. Neither the old nor the new system is perfect . . . Some managers complain that their "sandbox" is too well-defined.

CEO Grove elaborated on the problems of letting middle-level managers drive the induced process in the face of unclear top management strategic intent:

> The SLRP process turned into an embarrassment. Top management didn't really have the guts to call the shots, so we were trying to get middle management to come up with strategies and then taking pot shots at them. It wasn't clear whether middle management had either positional *or* informational power.
>
> In addition to being unpleasant, the system resulted in unrealistically high projections. One year, someone had the idea to put all the previous SLRP forecasts for unit sales on one chart along with the actual growth for the same period. The result was a series of "hockey sticks" which demonstrated the ineffectiveness of the process.

The data also confirm that rules concerning resource allocation are a potent part of structural context (Bower 1970). Intel was the first company able to manufacture and market DRAM's successfully and viewed itself as the "memory company." As one manager put it, "In a way, DRAM's created Intel." However, as new business opportunities in EPROM's and microprocessors were pursued, and competed for resources, DRAM's began to lose out. As a result of adopting a resource allocation rule that shifted resources systematically to products that maximized margin-per-manufacturing activity, DRAM's found it very difficult to continue to obtain capital investment in competition with other products. In fact, the VP of Finance at Intel insisted, at one point, that the DRAM manager sign a symbolic check equal to the margin foregone when high-margin products were bumped by DRAM's. So even though most managers at Intel continued to believe the mythology (the "self-evident truth" as CEO Andrew Grove put it) of Intel as a memory company, the effect of these capital investment decisions was that Intel became a microprocessor company during the early 80's. The mythology was kept alive, in part, because important amounts of resources continued to flow to DRAM R&D (estimated at one third of the total of about $195 million in 1985).

The data suggest that Intel's internal selection processes were consistent with the selection pressures in the external environment. Resources were allocated to the more profitable businesses rather than to DRAM's, even though a major change in organizational-level strategy had not yet been explicitly made. Given the relative size of the capital investments involved (hundreds of millions of dollars), this was extremely important. Eventually, of course, the discrepancy between internal selection and organizational strategy needed to be resolved.

The finding of a significant discrepancy between the internal selection mechanisms and the organizational strategy suggests that the induced strategic process may be driven more by the structural context than by the strategy (Bower 1970): Managers may respond more to incentives than to directions. In addition, this finding suggests that the induced process can continue to be effective if the internal selection mechanisms reflect the selective pressures of the environment, even while becoming decoupled from the espoused organizational strategy. In this situation, positive performance provides a time cushion for bringing organizational strategy in line with structural context. One expects that the opposite would not hold. That is, internal selection mechanisms coupled strongly to the organizational strategy but not reflecting the selective pressures of the environment are not likely to be associated with effectiveness of the induced process. The importance of internal selection being linked directly to environmental pressures as well as to organizational strategy provides a refinement of earlier theory concerning strategy and structure.

Variation. The induced strategic process is intended to preserve the coupling of strategic initiatives at operational levels with the organization's strategy through shaping managers' perceptions about which types of initiatives are likely to be supported by the organization. As a consequence, the induced process may have a variation-reduction effect on the set of strategic initiatives that it spawns. In the Intel case, Chairman Gordon Moore addressed this issue in relation to Intel's strategy in 1989:

> We can do variations on present businesses very well, but doing something new is more difficult. Today, the likelihood of someone killing an effort like the one of Dov Frohman (inventor of the EPROM) is very high, because you need a well-

> defined application to a market from the outset. This is especially so because we are not looking for additional opportunities. There is still a lot of evolution left in the current technology. If you consider the possibilities with reducing line-width, you can see another twelve years of evolution along the same curve.

Gordon Moore's observations also seem to imply that the induced process depends on the growth opportunities remaining in the current domain. To the extent that these growth opportunities are perceived to be high, it is expected that top management will favor initiatives that fit with the current strategy.

Of course, this does not imply that there is no planned variation in the induced process. Clearly, there is room for core technology advances, new product development for existing product families, new approaches to marketing and manufacturing, and so on. Hundreds of examples of such planned variations could be documented at Intel. And these variations are not always small, since new equipment, for instance, may require very large investments. Later in this chapter, the adaptive implications of the variation reduction tendency of the induced process will be further examined.

Autonomous Strategic Process

Variation. Studies of public organizations (e.g., Daft and Becker 1978, Lewis 1980) and private organizations (e.g., Shepard 1967, Kidder 1981, Kanter 1982, Burgelman 1983b, Mintzberg and McHugh 1985) suggest that, at any given time, some individuals or small groups are likely to try to get their organization to engage in activities that are outside of the scope of its current strategy. As the Intel examples provided below may illustrate, such autonomous initiatives are often significantly different from induced ones in terms of technology employed, customer functions served, and/or customer groups targeted. They often derive from new combinations of individual and organizational skills and capabilities (Penrose 1968, Teece 1982) that are not currently recognized as distinctive or centrally important to the firm. While autonomous initiatives are probably quite often triggered by ideas or events external to the organization, they involve more than imitation in order to be of evolutionary importance for the organization's strategy. Imitation usually does not lead to sustainable competitive advantage. Autonomous initiatives are important for the firm's evolution to the extent that they involve the creation of new competences that may combine in unique ways with the resources and competences already available to the organization. While autonomous initiatives often emerge fortuitously and are difficult to predict, they are usually not random because they are rooted in and constrained by the evolving competence set of the organization (McKelvey and Aldrich 1983).

Autonomous initiatives can originate at all levels of management. But they are most likely to emerge at a level where managers are directly in contact with new technological developments and changes in market conditions, and have some budgetary discretion. As the organization grows, they are increasingly likely to emerge at levels below top management, even in the case of a company like Intel where senior executives have strong technical backgrounds.

The Intel study shows that, in spite of Gordon Moore's concerns, the autonomous strategic process is not easily suppressed. This is illustrated by a recent example of how Intel got into the RISC processor business with its i860 processor.[1]

The i860 Story. The story of Intel's entrance into the RISC (Reduced Instruction Set Computing) processor business details the emergence of a new product family which may ultimately challenge Intel's core microprocessor strategy. It illustrates the ability of an astute technologist, Les Kohn, to test the boundaries of the currently articulated corporate strategy and to modify them. Intel's deliberate corporate strategy was *not* to enter the RISC business, but rather to focus on the extremely successful x86 architecture. Kohn had been attempting to get Intel into the RISC processor business since he joined the company in 1982. As he puts it: "RISC was not an existing business and people were not convinced a market was there." In fact, the strength of the organization's aversion to RISC architectures was demonstrated by the corporate argot, YARP, for "Yet Another RISC Processor." While talking in understated terms about his approach, it seemed clear that Kohn had a deliberate strategy which could be viewed as surreptitious from the perspective of corporate strategy. He mentioned that there was some realization at levels below top management that "Intel needed to broaden beyond the 386[2] market, but there was no agreement on what to do and how to do it." He also intimated that "there were various contenders at different points." From a technical point of view, Kohn believed that RISC architecture had intrinsic advantages over CISC architecture. However, he had learned from several more straightforward attempts at the product approval process that an approach which supported rather than challenged the status quo would be more likely successful. Also, the investment needed was too large to do the development "under the table." His solution was to disguise his product. Andrew Grove, Intel's CEO, mentioned that Kohn sold the design to top management as a co-processor, rather than a stand-alone processor. Kohn confirmed that "We designed it as a stand-alone processor, but made it very useful as an accessory to the i486.[3]" By the time top management realized what their "co-processor" was, Kohn, with the help of two other champions, had already lined up a customer base for the stand-alone processor, a base he suggested was different than the companies who purchase the 486 chips: in Kohn's own words, "a lot of customers who before did not even talk to Intel."

> Thus Kohn could argue that he was broadening Intel's business rather than cannibalizing it. During 1989 Intel's top management decided to amend the corporate strategy to incorporate the RISC chip business.

Another example, still in a much earlier stage, concerns a new type of memory, called "FLASH." A middle-level manager who is currently championing FLASH memories at Intel emphasized that FLASH might ultimately provide a replacement for the microprocessor business. Asked to describe life as a champion at Intel, this manager said:

> You have to be naive, but mature enough to realize that the process takes a long time. You have to be sensitive to political toes. You have to be a religious zealot, but not too religious because then you lose your credibility. Finally, you have to succeed. . . . It is most difficult to champion a product that threatens the company's [current] business.

Selection. At the time it emerges, the importance of an autonomous strategic initiative in relation to the firm's current strategy remains more or less indeterminate. To resolve the indeterminacy, the strategic context for the new initiative must become clear to, and accepted by, top management. Strategic context determination processes (Burgelman 1983b, Haspeslagh 1983) allow autonomous initiatives to be internally evaluated and selected outside the regular structural context, usually through the interactions of various types of "champions" and top management, and may lead to a change in the organization's strategy. Such amendments, in turn, integrate the new business activities with the induced strategic process.

Strategic context determination processes may be among the more elusive, volatile, and precarious decision processes in organizations. They deal with highly equivocal inputs and are therefore expected to involve relatively few rules but many interlocked cycles for their assembly (Daft and Weick 1984, Weick 1979). That is, they require much iterative, substantive interaction between managers from different levels in the organization. In contrast to the structural context, which selects initiatives that are consistent with an ex ante vision, strategic context determination processes select initiatives for which the vision becomes articulated ex post (Burgelman 1983c). They require that viability be established, in both the internal and external environments, at each intermediate stage of their development. As the process unfolds, and more information becomes available, top management is able to evaluate the adaptive potential of the new activities for the organization. From an evolutionary point of view, only after it has become reasonably certain that an autonomous initiative is viable can it legitimately become part of the organizational strategy. In a study of the autonomous strategic process in the area of marketing strategy, Hutt, Reingen, and Ronchetto (1988) operationalize the process in terms of network analysis, communication patterns, and coalition building. They conclude: "If the efforts of the product and organizational champions are successful, the autonomous strategic initiative blends into the firm's formal planning routine and concept of strategy" (1988, p. 16).

Commenting on how the strategic context for a potential new business gets defined at Intel, Les Vadasz, who had been responsible for Intel's internal corporate venturing efforts, mentioned that these efforts require alternative avenues for obtaining resources so that the new business has a chance to demonstrate its viability. This is illustrated with Intel's add-on boards venture.

> *The Add-On Boards Story.* Some middle-level managers had the idea to develop add-on boards for personal computers. The strategic planning process initially rejected the idea since channels of distribution were too different. The idea, however, was able to get support through Intel's internal corporate venturing program and became a separate business. After success of the business became evident, the venture was folded back into Intel's Systems business.

In a similar vein, the general manager of the components development group said he keeps the process fluid by "carving out a certain amount of resources for unplanned things. Usually you need no more than a million dollars to get something going." These examples suggest that the availability of "unabsorbed slack" (e.g., Singh 1986) may be an important factor affecting the rate at which autonomous strategic behavior can be supported within the organization.

Retention. Both EPROM's and microprocessors were the result of unplanned initiatives that were outside of the scope of the strategy of the early 70's. These initiatives had been able to obtain resources because top management recognized *some* of their potential *after* they had come into existence. Obtaining resources allowed the new initiatives to demonstrate their viability in the environment. The evolutionary success of microprocessors and the accompanying shift in relative importance in Intel's action domain from memory (low design content) to microprocessor (high design content) had important consequences for the evolution of Intel's distinctive competences. As differences in process technology leveled among competitors in the industry, distinctive competence in circuit design increasingly became the new basis for Intel's competitive advantage. And, as customers had to be taught what the powerful microprocessors could do for them, it also led Intel to develop new distinctive marketing capabilities (Davidow 1986).

The RISC story, presented earlier, is important because it shows how the autonomous strategic process allows the organization to become more clearly aware of, and prepare itself to cope with, environmental variations that have already come into play and might potentially threaten its competitive position. RISC had been invented at IBM but had remained dormant until it found a major application in work stations. Craig Barrett, a top-level manager, pointed out that RISC is still viewed as relatively less important than CISC in Intel's strategy, but that its availability makes it possible for Intel to be a strong competitor in what may become an important new market:

> Intel's bread and butter is in the x86 product family. There is a 586[4] on the drawing board and a 686 planned to follow that. If there was ever any question of which comes first, it could be answered quickly. But if there are enough people out there who want to buy YARP's, then we call the i860 a YARP killer. It is the highest performance RISC processor on the market.

Kohn's autonomous efforts now make it possible for Intel to be prepared in case RISC would ever pose a threat to CISC.

Autonomous initiatives provide the organization with an internal window on future, potentially major environmental variations in markets and technologies, and with strategic options. This may perhaps be the case with FLASH memories. While the implications of FLASH may eventually be less revolutionary than its champion predicts, and the strategic context for FLASH so far remains unclear at Intel, this champion's efforts offer Intel top management the opportunity to anticipate and evaluate a potential environmental variation.

Sometimes, the strategic context for a new business cannot be successfully defined, and the business dies out or spins off. The Intel data reveal that, in some instances, a failed attempt to define the strategic context for an initiative outside the scope of the current strategy may nevertheless lead to a sharper articulation of the firm's strategy. An example (in this case resulting from imitation) is provided with the Application Specific Integrated Circuit (ASIC) venture. Intel had been late moving into ASIC's. Tens of millions of dollars were invested for a fast ramp up, and a separate division was established. However, top management soon realized that ASIC was simply a delivery vehicle for circuit designs. As one middle level manager observed, "In ASIC the customer added all the value. So we realized that we should add the value ourselves." The separate division was eventually folded back into Intel's mainstream as the corporate focus on design as a competitive advantage was adopted by the entire organization. Later on, Intel disengaged from ASIC's in fact because its core design skills were different.

Managing the autonomous strategic process seems difficult. The history of areas such as Silicon Valley indicates that autonomous strategic initiatives in established firms often result in the creation of new firms, rather than in new businesses for the firms where they originated. Many internal entrepreneurs seem to have left reluctantly because of lack of organizational support. In the Intel case, one example, among others, concerns a group involved in EEPROM's, who left after a majority of top management determined that EEPROM's were too small and specialized. The group formed a venture called Xicor. On the other hand, autonomous initiatives can have a dissipating effect on the spawning organization's research and/or distinctive competence. Resources can be spread thin if too many autonomous initiatives are supported, perhaps at the expense of the mainstream businesses. Distinctive competences can be diluted or lost if an autonomous initiative is not internally supported and important talent decides to leave the firm, with or without the help of venture capital. (It is interesting to note that Intel significantly increased its legal staff during the 80's in order to better be able to protect its intellectual property.) Yet sometimes it seems quite clear, in retrospect, that an established company lost out severely because it failed to capitalize on autonomous initiatives (this is well-illustrated, for instance, in the case of Bendix Corporation and electronic fuel injection; Porter 1981). Later in this chapter, the adaptive implications of the variation-increasing tendency of the autonomous strategic process will be further discussed.

Rationality of Strategy Making as Internal Selection

From the perspective of the organization, the rationality of the induced strategic process seems clear. In this process, intentional strategy may serve the organization to leverage—do as much as possible with—its currently available learning, to fully exploit the opportunities associated with the current action domain. From the perspective of individual managers, operating in the induced process would seem attractive. This is so because the organizational learning, guiding participants operating in the induced process, is likely to have been achieved at significant organizational and individual costs (Langton 1984). For instance, top managers may remember former colleagues who tried to do different things and suffered high costs in terms of their career progress, or they may recall instances where the organization tried something different, say an unrelated diversification move, and it ended up being very costly. Participants at lower levels can be expected to be aware of this and therefore motivated to pursue initiatives in line with the current strategy. Induced initiatives allow managers to propose projects that take advantage of the available organizational learning, rather than to incur the potentially high costs of new individually driven learning associated with pursuing projects through the autonomous process. The induced process is part of the organization's regular opportunity structures for career advancement.

But why then are some managers willing to engage in autonomous strategic behavior? March (1988) observes that their motivation may be rooted in (a) an "obligatory logic" or (b) a "consequential logic." Managers operating within an obligatory logic engage in autonomous initiatives because it is congruent with their self-image. Managers operating within a consequential logic may feel that they have capabilities and skills that make autonomous initiatives no riskier than induced ones, or because they want to emulate colleagues who have received unusually high internal rewards for successfully pursuing a highly risky autonomous initiative, or they pursue it because they expect to receive venture capital support if no internal support is forthcoming. From the viewpoint of consequential logic, managers may see the autonomous process as an alternative opportunity structure for career progress if they consider that their access to the opportunity structure as defined by the induced process is limited, e.g., because of previous "bad luck" with performance outcomes, poor prospects of available opportunities in the induced process, or because other strategists have already preempted access to the induced process.

The organization may, within resource constraints, rationally tolerate autonomous strategic initiatives because it offers, as the Intel data suggest, opportunities to explore and extend the boundaries of its capabilities set, to engage new environmental niches in which environmental forces such as competition or institutional pressures (e.g., DiMaggio and Powell 1983) are as yet not as strong (Astley 1985, Burgelman 1983c, Itami 1983), to help the organization enter new niches that have already been opened up by others and that might eventually pose a threat to the current strategy, or to learn about future potential variations in markets and technologies. In the autonomous strategic process, myopically purposeful (McKelvey 1982) initiatives by individuals may help the organization find out what its intentions could be. The possibilities for participants to engage in opportunistic behavior (Bower 1970, Williamson 1970, Rumelt 1987, Cohen and Machalek 1988), however, underscore the importance of the structural and strategic contexts.

Structural and strategic contexts, together, constitute internal selection processes operating on strategic initiatives. The effectiveness of internal selection processes may depend on how closely they correspond to the selection pressures exerted by the current external environment, while simultaneously allowing new environments to be sought out. As seen earlier, at Intel there seemed to exist a close correspondence between key parts of the structural context and the current external environment: Resource allocation in the induced process favored business activities that were able to get high returns in the current external environment. At the same time, Intel kept open the possibility to activate processes of strategic context determination through which new, unplanned business activities got a chance to obtain resources to demonstrate their viability.

STRATEGY MAKING AND ORGANIZATIONAL ADAPTATION

The view of strategy making as an intraorganizational ecological process yields a new theoretical question: How important are internal selection processes for explaining continued organizational survival? This question can be addressed by linking the induced and autonomous processes to different forms of adaptation identified previously in the literature: (1) relative inertia (Hannan and Freeman 1984), (2) adjustment (Snow and Hambrick 1980), (3) reorientation (Tushman and Romanelli 1985), and a new form proposed here: (4) strategic renewal.

The Adaptation Paradox Revisited

Relative Inertia. Overcoming the liabilities of newness (Stinchcombe 1965) requires organizations to develop a capacity for reliability and accountability in their transactions with the environment (Hannan and Freeman 1984) and to structure themselves so as to be considered legitimate (e.g., DiMaggio and Powell 1983). But doing so may create structural inertia (Hannan and Freeman 1984). Paradoxically, adaptation to existing environmental demands may reduce the organization's capacity to adapt to future changes in the environment or to seek out new environments.

The existence of an induced strategic process seems to be consistent with *relative inertia* arguments. Relative inertia means that the rate of strategic change that the organization can implement will, in the long run, be lower than the rate of change in the environment (Hannan and Freeman 1984). Some ecological research has shown that the inertial consequences of environmental selection are likely to affect the core features of an organization (Scott 1981, Hannan and Freeman 1984, Singh et al. 1986). While the difference between core and peripheral features of organizations has not been definitively established, it seems reasonable to view a firm's strategy as a core feature. Because the strategy is rooted in organizational experience and learning, top managers are likely to be reluctant to make frequent changes in it. As noted earlier, research (e.g., Mintzberg and Waters 1982, Miller and Friesen 1984, Tushman and Romanelli 1985) suggests that an organization's strategy tends to remain in place for extended periods of time. So it seems plausible in many instances to expect the evolution of the strategy to be inert relative to the accumulation of changes in the environment (Snow and Hambrick 1980).

The Intel case provides further insight in this. The articulation of corporate strategy in terms of microprocessor leadership versus memory leadership came almost five years after the company had stopped being a major player in DRAM's. Reflecting on how difficult it had been to get top management to come to grips with this change, Andrew Grove observed:

> Don't ask managers, "What is your strategy?" Look at what they do! Because people will pretend. . . . The fact is that we had become a non-factor in DRAM's, with 2-3% market share. The DRAM business just passed us by! Yet, in 1985, many people were still holding to the "self-evident truth" that Intel was a memory company. One of the toughest challenges is to make people see that these self-evident truths are no longer true.

Intel's top management took a long time to finalize a decision that had been in the making since the early 80's. Several managers pointed out in the interviews that the decision could and should have been made sooner. The delay was, in part, caused by the fact that some managers sensed that the existing organizational strategy was no longer adequate and that there were competing views about what the new organizational strategy should be. There was still an important group of managers who believed that DRAM's were critically important to Intel. Some of the top technologists saw DRAM's as the technology driver of the corporation. This group was convinced that DRAM's, being the largest volume product, were key to Intel's learning curve. Some of the top sales people also saw the need for offering a complete product line to the customer. Top management as a group, it seems, was watching how the organization sorted out the conflicting views. CEO Grove observed:

> By mid '84, some middle-level managers had made the decision to adopt a new process technology which inherently favored logic (microprocessor) rather than the memory advances, thereby limiting the decision space within which top management could operate. The faction representing the x86 microprocessor business won the debate even though the 386 had not yet become the big revenue generator that it eventually would become.

While clearly demonstrating a degree of relative inertia, Intel's exit decision was not too late. Intel lost a lot of money in DRAM's, but the hemorrhaging was stopped before its viability became threatened. In fact, Intel lost less money than its competitors, including the Japanese. So, why was Intel's relative inertia as low as it was? The data suggest that this was not due, in the first instance, to a prescient or exceptionally agile top management, but to the way in which the internal selection processes were allowed to work themselves out.

An atmosphere in which strategic ideas can be freely championed and fully contested by anyone with relevant information or insight may be a key factor in developing internal selection processes that maximize the probability of generating viable organizational strategies. Such processes generate strategic change that is neither too slow nor too fast (Hambrick and D'Aveni 1988, Levitt and March 1988). They take time to develop and have a large tacit component. That is, it is difficult to provide a full explanation of how they actually work. The role of founders, such as Bob Noyce, Gordon Moore, and Andy Grove at Intel, seems important in setting the initial tone and maintaining continuity. The data suggest that the influence of top management in strategy making at Intel was undeniably very strong, but that there was also a perception on the part of most managers that, most of the time, knowledge and facts tend to win over positional power at Intel. The possibility for a young engineer like Les Kohn to directly interact with the CEO on substantive technical issues and to be able to prevail on the merits of the argument is a vivid illustration of that. It is also illustrated in CEO Grove's view on his role in decisions to continue to support or not a business activity:

> You need to be able to be ambiguous in some circumstances. You dance around it a bit, until a wider and wider group in the company becomes clear about it. That's why continued argument is important. Intel is a very open system. No one is ever told to shut up, but you are asked to come up with better arguments. People are allowed to be persistent.

Once the decision to exit DRAM's was made, top management showed strong intent to implement it. In the face of some lingering opposition, Grove himself took charge and made several organizational and personnel changes. Perhaps most important, from a symbolic point of view, he visited several groups affected by the decision and addressed them with the phrase, "Welcome to the Mainstream Intel," that is, Intel the microprocessor company, thereby ratifying the results of the internal selection processes that had been going on for several years. Top management also reassigned the highly regarded memory R&D group to microprocessors, thereby protecting the firm's distinctive technical competences.

Adjustment. Inherent tendencies toward relative inertia in organizational strategy do not preclude adjustments (Snow and Hambrick 1980) in the strategy. Such adjustments leave the overall strategy in place and operate on more peripheral features. Recent ecological research suggests that some types of peripheral changes may enhance an organization's life chances (Singh et al. 1986). Adjustments are to a large extent deliberate, reflecting strategic choice and managerial discretion (Hambrick and Finkelstein 1987), and are instances of nonrandom adaptation.

The Intel study offers several examples of deliberate adjustments that were made to try to stay viable in the DRAM business. Some of these involved efforts to differentiate Intel's DRAM offering from the commodity business; others involved efforts to reduce cost and design time. One move involved the introduction of the first 5-volt 16K DRAM in 1980 (differentiation). Another move involved introducing "redundancy" in the 64K DRAM design in order to increase yields (cost reduction). Still another move was to "go CMOS" for the 64K and 256K (differentiation). A final move involved focusing on "thin dielectrics" for the 1 Meg DRAM in order to reduce the minimum feature size to one micron instead of changing the entire cell design (cost reduction). None of these moves, however, was sufficient to make DRAM's viable again as a business for Intel. Eventually, as was noted earlier, the decision to exit became unavoidable.

Relative inertia and adjustment both seem possible outcomes of the induced strategic process. Relative inertia does not preclude adjustment and adjustments may temporarily result in improved performance. In the long run, however, cumulative environmental selection pressures are expected to overwhelm adjustments effected through the induced strategic process, and it seems likely that the strategy itself will eventually have to change in major ways.

Theory (Hannan and Freeman 1984) and empirical evidence (Singh et al. 1986) suggest that major strategic changes are governed by environmental selection processes. That is, such changes subject the organization to powerful environmental pressures and are likely thereby to reduce the chances of survival. On the other hand, Tushman and Romanelli (1985) suggest that strategic reorientations, which imply major changes in the concept of strategy, are an integral part of a punctuated equilibrium model of firm evolution. Firms that do not reorient when major changes are necessary, or reorient when the need for such changes is not compelling, they argue, will see their life chances reduced. The seeming contradiction between these two positions can be resolved in terms of the role of the autonomous strategic process, as explained below.

Reorientation. Major changes in the strategy seem likely to upset the induced strategic process in fundamental ways. The necessity for a major strategic change suggests that selective pressures from environmental variations have made the organization's capacity for relatively modest adjustments largely irrelevant. At first, threat-rigidity (Staw, Sandelands, and Dutton 1981) may lead top management to reaffirm familiar approaches. For instance, Cooper, and Schendel (1976) found that established firms, confronted with the threat of radically new technologies, were likely to increase their efforts to improve the existing technology rather than switch to the new technology, even after the latter had passed the threshold of viability. Eventually, however, confronted with chronic low performance, top management is more likely to take major risks (March 1981b, Singh 1986) by making extreme and vacillating changes in the strategy, potentially involving a complete change of domain (Hambrick and D'Aveni 1988). When an organization finds itself in a precarious situation, reorientation may be perceived by top management as necessary to maintain or regain viability (Miles and Cameron 1982) and may be better than doing nothing. However, as March (1981b) has observed, organizations facing bad times, and therefore following riskier and riskier strategies, may simultaneously increase their chances of survival through the present crisis, but also reduce their life expectancy: "For those organizations that do not survive, efforts to survive will have speeded the process of failure" (1981b, p. 567).

Strategic Renewal. Major changes in the strategy effected through the autonomous strategic process, however, need not be completely governed by external selection processes. Autonomous strategic initiatives, as seen in the Intel case, offer opportunities to open new niches or provide early warning of impending radical, external changes. To the extent that strategic context determination processes are effectively activated, the organization may learn new capabilities and skills in anticipation of making major changes in its strategy, but without knowing in advance how it should be changed. Changes of this sort form the basis for "strategic renewal"—major strategic change preceded by internal experimentation and selection. In the Intel case, EPROM's and microprocessors, like the recent i860 (RISC) chip, were unplanned developments, but Intel management was capable of recognizing the importance of these developments after they had occurred, and keeping them inside the firm through shifts in resource allocation.

Reorientations are *not* expected outcomes of the autonomous strategic process. Consistent with the view of organizational ecology (Hannan and Freeman 1984), environmental selection is expected to govern reorientations, because reorientations seem fundamentally incompatible with strategy making as an organizational learning process based on internal experimentation and selection. Reorientations inherently seem to involve "betting the organization" because they eliminate a good deal of its cumulative learning. On the other hand, strategic renewal—major strategic change preceded by internal experimentation and selection—is the critical outcome of the autonomous process through which an organization can indefinitely remain adaptive.

Table 13.1 summarizes the analysis of the induced and autonomous strategic processes and their proposed ties to modes of organizational adaptation.

DISCUSSION

Organizations are both creators and prisoners of their environments (Miles and Cameron 1982). Organizational survival depends to a significant extent on the adjustment and renewal capacities of strategy-making processes. Such processes are an emergent property of organizations and may be differentially distributed within a population of organizations. Firms overcome the liabilities of newness by accumulating and leveraging organizational learning, and by deliberately combining distinctive competences in the induced process. Adjustments effected through the induced strategic process serve the organization in its attempts to remain adaptive over some range of environmental variation and over a certain time horizon (Chakravarthy 1982, Burgelman 1983c). The autonomous strategic process, on the other hand, helps organizations develop, appropriate, and retain new learning. Strategic renewal through internal experimentation and selection offers an organization the possibility to remain adaptive over a wider range of environmental variation and a longer time horizon (Chakravarthy 1982, Burgelman 1983c).

Selection and adaptation have sometimes been viewed as alternative explanations in organizational research (e.g., Singh et al. 1986). The analysis presented in this chapter suggests that they may be viewed, to some extent, as complementary: selection processes at the intraorganizational level, working themselves out through the strategy-making processes, may generate strategies that are adaptive at the organizational level.

Structural and strategic contexts thus emerge as critical process design parameters from this analysis. In the induced strategic process, top management's role is to ensure the pursuit of an intended strategy through administrative and cultural mechanisms that couple operational-level strategic initiatives with the intended strategy. Doing so makes it possible for the organization to build on past success and to exploit the opportunities associated with the current domain. However, the Intel study also suggests that it is important that the structural context reflect the selective pressures of the

TABLE 13.1 Intraorganizational Ecological Processes

Strategic Processes	*Variation*	*Selection*	*Retention*	*Ties to Adaptation*
Induced	Strategic initiatives seeking resources for projects that correspond to internal selection pressures of structural context, fit with the current organizational strategy, and offer access to regular opportunity structure for career advancement. Originate at operational-level but intended to be driven by top management's ex ante vision. Enhanced by availability of growth opportunities remaining in current action domain.	Initiatives selected through administrative mechanisms (e.g., strategic planning) and/or cultural influencing (e.g., reference to key values). Differential allocation of resources to different areas of strategic initiative. Key is that internal selection reflects current external selection pressures.	1. Organizational learning about bases for past/current survival (variously embodied). 2. Distinctive competences (variously embodied). 3. Organizational goals. 4. Organizational action domain. 5. Organizational character. All of these elements integrated in ex ante vision.	1. *Relative inertia.* Organizational survival is due to a good fit of internal selection processes with the environment. Survival motivates conservatism on the part of top management and desire to leverage existing organizational learning through induced process. Reluctance to change organizational strategy. 2. *Adjustment.* Relatively minor changes in strategy to accommodate environmental change.
	Radically new induced initiatives initiated by top management.	Major changes in structural context	Major changes in the dimensions of organizational strategy.	3. *Reorientation.* Major changes in strategy in response to major environmental change.
Autonomous	Strategic initiatives outside scope of current strategy. Driven by operational-level managers seeking to use their skills in new combinations with organization's distinctive competences and, in some cases, seeking career advancement through alternative opportunity structure. Enhanced by availability of unabsorbed slack	Defining strategic context for new initiatives through: • finding resources outside regular resource allocation process; • demonstrating viability in external environment through entrepreneurial activity; • mobilizing internal support on the part of upper level managers; • developing new competences/ skills; • setting stage for an amendment in the organizational strategy.	Changes in organizational learning, distinctive competence, and relative importance of new activities in total domain activity, which, cumulatively, lead top management to recognize that a major change in strategy is necessary and feasible. Lead to new, ex post vision. Once formally ratified, new vision becomes part of the basis for the induced process.	4. *Strategic renewal.* Major change in organizational strategy preceded by internal experimentation and selection offers organization possibilities for anticipatory adaptation to new environmental demands and/or to enter new niches.

environment. This provides a reality test for the organizational strategy. In the autonomous strategic process, top management's role is strategic recognition rather than planning (Burgelman 1983c, Van de Ven 1986). Top management needs to facilitate the activation of strategic context determination processes to find out which of the autonomous initiatives have adaptive value for the organization and deserve to become part of the organization's strategy. The proposed importance of a continued concern with managing strategic processes, as well as with strategy content (or "strategic choice") at an given time, is consistent with a wide range of research findings (e.g., Hedberg, Nystrom and Starbuck 1976, Bower and Doz 1979, Padgett 1980). More formally,

PROPOSITION 1. *Firms that are relatively successful over long periods of time, say, ten years or more, will be characterized by top managements that are concerned with building the quality of the organization's induced and autonomous strategic processes as well as with the content of the strategy itself.*

Combining induced and autonomous processes in their strategy making would seem to give organizations a chance to outsmart or outrun the selective pressures associated with environmental variations. The analysis suggests that organizations may have to keep both processes in play at all times, even though this means that the organization never completely maximizes its efforts in the current domain. This implies that strategic intent and internal entrepreneurship, separately, are not sufficient for organizational survival (e.g., Hamel and Prahalad 1989). Both are needed *simultaneously.* The ability to maintain these different concerns simultaneously seemed to be missing in the failing corporations studied by Hambrick and D'Aveni (1988), who found that failing firms tended to operate either in an inactive (no strategic change) or hyperactive (excessive and vacillating change) mode. This also implies that a sequential approach involving, for instance, sequences of reorientation and convergence (Tushman and Romanelli 1985) may not be optimal in the long run. More formally,

PROPOSITION 2. *Firms that are relatively successful over long periods of time, say, ten years or more, will be characterized by maintaining top driven strategic intent while simultaneously maintaining bottom-up driven internal experimentation and selection processes.*

The analysis also suggests that successful reorientations, as defined by Tushman and Romanelli (1985), are likely to be *preceded* by internal experimentation and selection processes effected through the autonomous strategic process. More formally,

PROPOSITION 3. *The population of firms with successful strategic reorientations will contain a significantly higher proportion of firms whose strategic reorientations were preceded by internal experimentation and selection processes than the population of firms with failing strategic reorientations.*

Of course, these propositions do not imply that there is only one way to organize the strategic processes or that managers should get overly absorbed in the details of these processes. Also, there does not seem to be a fixed optimal ratio in terms of emphasis on induced versus autonomous processes. At different times in an organization's development, different emphases on the induced and autonomous strategic processes may be warranted, and there may not be a fixed series of stages in firm evolution as some researchers seem to suggest (e.g., Kimberly and Miles 1980, Miller and Friesen 1984). Old firms may continue to be able to act like young ones, even though young ones may not be equally able to act like old ones. The renewal capacity associated with the autonomous strategic process may enable organizations to negate the inevitability of aging and decline. By the same token, it may expose them again, to some extent, to the liabilities of newness (Hannan and Freeman 1984).

The intraorganizational ecological perspective has offered useful insights into Intel's strategic evolution. Intel may have survived as an independent company in part because it was able to recognize important internal variations that were externally viable and to allocate resources to these through the internal selection mechanisms, almost in spite of the pervasive desire to continue to be a "memory company." The procrastination in finalizing the DRAM-exit decision and Gordon Moore's current concerns about the inexorable tendency toward narrowing down the technology base of the firm suggest some inertial tendencies in Intel's strategic process. But events like the emergence of the i860 (RISC) chip also suggest that the autonomous strategic process is still alive and well. Although Intel went through a major strategic change—from "memory company" to "microcomputer company" —it did not do so through a dramatic and sudden reorientation. Instead, unplanned, autonomous processes were allowed to run their courses, with many losers and some winners. And as these processes unfolded, the company developed new learning that made the ratification of the strategic change a reasonably safe bet for top management.

IMPLICATIONS AND CONCLUSIONS

This chapter has offered an intraorganizational ecological perspective on strategy making and organizational adaptation. The framework proposes balancing of variation-reduction and variation-increasing mechanisms. It suggests that one process leads to relative inertia and incremental adjustments, while the other expands the firm's domain and renews the organization's distinctive competence base, countering inertia and serving some of the functions of a reorientation. The research reported here provides some confirmation of the existence of these two processes, suggests some amendments to the initial conceptual framework, and offers additional insights into the working of the processes.

The research is part of emergent efforts to integrate evolutionary views of strategy making and organization. These efforts recognize the importance of some forms of rationality and learning and the need to go beyond biological evolutionary arguments (e.g., Langton 1984, Boyd and Richerson 1985, Gould 1987). They reflect a belief that evolutionary theory may be useful for integrating insights from organizational ecology, rational adaptation, and random transformation perspectives (Hannan and Freeman 1984). Other seeds for such a synthesis already exist. Economic evolutionists (Nelson and Winter 1982, Winter 1990) provide a detailed theoretical picture of some of the mechanisms of inheritance, selection, and survival. Organizational evolutionists have shown that some forms of organizational change are adaptive while others reduce an organization's life chances (e.g., Singh et al. 1986), and that the "imprinting" effects of founding characteristics of organizations affect subsequent rates of organizational change (Tucker et al. 1990, Boeker 1989). This chapter sketches the outlines of an intraorganizational perspective on strategy making and proposes this as a fourth level in the hierarchy of ecological systems which currently comprises only organization, population, and community levels (Carroll 1984, Astley 1985, Aldrich and Auster 1986). Incorporating this additional level may facilitate the rapprochement between ideas of ecology and strategy, and enhance the prospects of an evolutionary theory of organizations (Burgelman and Singh 1987).

The intraorganizational perspective on strategy making also extends frameworks presented by Mintzberg (1978) and Quinn (1982) in the strategic management literature. It does so by documenting more explicitly some of the sources of emergent strategy, by further elucidating the organizational decision processes through which emergent strategies become part of realized strategies (strategic context determination), by identifying feedback mechanisms between realized and intended strategy, and by providing some evidence that logical incrementalism is likely to be variation reducing and may need to be augmented with an autonomous strategic process to enhance long-term organizational survival. The perspective presented in the chapter adds some additional dynamism to these earlier frameworks and draws more explicit attention to the simultaneity of multiple strategy-making processes in organizations.

Implications for Theory and Future Research

Several specific avenues for further research derive from the propositions discussed earlier. For instance, future research could examine whether consistently successful firms are characterized by top managements' spending efforts on building each organization's strategy-making processes; whether such firms simultaneously exercise induced and autonomous strategic processes; and whether successful reorientations are more likely to be preceded by internal experimentation and selection processes effected through the autonomous strategic process than are the unsuccessful ones.

Effective internal selection seems to depend on top management's capacities to adjust the structural and strategic contexts in the organization. Discovering the determinants of such capacities and how the latter relate to rates of adjustment and strategic renewal remains an important agenda for further research (March 1981b, Hannan and Freeman 1984). Future research could also examine the possibilities that there may be an optimal level of ambiguity in the concept of strategy (March 1978) and an optimal degree of coupling in the structural context (Weick 1976). This would require studying the working of strategy-making processes in different types of organizations, such as generalists versus specialists (Freeman and Hannan 1983) or defenders, prospectors, analyzers, and reactors (Miles and Snow 1978), and under different types of environmental conditions (e.g., Freeman and Hannan 1983, Eisenhardt 1989). This, in turn, may raise further questions about the relationships between strategy making and organization form, provide deeper insight into the distinction between core and peripheral features, and elucidate the mechanisms that determine structural features and their transformation—that is, organizational morphology.

For internal selection mechanisms to be useful, organizations must generate internal variation. That is, they must motivate strategic initiatives on the part of their participants. As a result of internal selection, some participants may win big and others may lose big. But the genius of surviving organizations lies in their ability to benefit from both winning and losing individual strategic initiatives through their capacity for learning. This suggests an organizational-level analogy to societal-level processes described by Rosenberg and Birdzell (1986). Rosenberg and Birdzell provide some evidence for how western capitalism has used decentralized entrepreneurism: It has allowed innovators to bear the losses of failed experiments and to gain the profits of successful ones, and it has benefited from both in terms of growth. This analogy also suggests a link between strategy making and "foolishness" (March 1981b). Organizations may use individual-level "foolishness" to enhance organizational-level survival in somewhat the same way that organizational-level foolishness may enhance the survival chances of a system of organizations. March views organizational foolishness as a form of altruism, but it might be possible to link such individual-level behavior to the idea that strategy making may be viewed as part of the organization's opportunity structures for career advancement.

This, in turn, motivates interest in further examining how the Barnard-March-Simon theory of inducements and contributions may be realized. It raises, for instance, the issue of how the balance between inducements and contributions may be different in the induced and autonomous strategic processes and how shifting balances may affect organizational adaptation. It also directs attention to the effects that external resource constraints (e.g., remaining growth opportunities in an organization's current action domain) and internal resource constraints (e.g., "sustainable growth" (Donaldson and Lorsch 1983) and "unabsorbed slack" (e.g., Singh 1986)) may have on the degree to which induced and autonomous strategic initiatives are supported during any given period in the firm's history. These links open new directions for research.

In conclusion, the theory and field research presented in this chapter suggest that the opposite views of blind natural selection or prescient and comprehensive strategic planning as the basis for understanding organizational adaptation both are too narrow. The pure environmental-selection view misses the additional insights that can be obtained from considering internal selection. The pure strategic-planning view misses the ecological components altogether. Rich behavioral phenomena are currently being documented in a variety of studies and will have to be accounted for by equally rich theories of organizations. An intraorganizational ecological perspective on strategy making seems likely to provide a useful input to organization theory. It also suggests the need to reconsider important precepts of received strategic management theory.

ACKNOWLEDGMENTS

Support from the Strategic Management Program and from the BP American Faculty Fellowship of Stanford University's Graduate School of Business is gratefully acknowledged. Glenn Carroll, Don Hambrick, Arie Lewin, Jim March, Ann Miner, Brian Mittman, Jeffrey Pfeffer, Dick Scott, Jitendra Singh, and anonymous *Organization Science* reviewers have provided helpful and encouraging comments along the way, shaping the arguments presented in this chapter. The outstanding research assistance of George W. Cogan and the generous collaboration of Intel

Corporation are much appreciated. The conclusions reached in this chapter are my own. Thanks also to Jiranee Kovattana for excellent administrative assistance.

NOTES

1. i860 is a trademark of the Intel Corporation.
2. 386 is a trademark of the Intel Corporation.
3. i486 is a trademark of the Intel Corporation.
4. 586 and 686 are trademarks of the Intel Corporation.

REFERENCES

Aldrich, H. E. (1979), *Organizations and Environments,* Englewood Cliffs, NJ: Prentice Hall.

———and E. R. Auster (1986), "Even Dwarfs Started Small: Liabilities of Age and Size and Their Strategic Implications," in L. L. Cummings and B. Staw (Eds.), *Research in Organizational Behavior,* Greenwich, CT: JAI, 8, 165-198.

Andrews, K. (1971), *A Concept of Corporate Strategy,* Homewood, IL: Irwin.

Astley, W. G. (1985), "The Two Ecologies: Population and Community Perspectives on Organizational Evolution," *Administrative Science Quarterly,* 30, 224-241.

——— and A. H. Van de Ven (1983), "Central Perspectives and Debates in Organization Theory," *Administrative Science Quarterly,* 29, 245-273.

Beyer, J. M. (1981), "Ideologies, Values and Decision Making in Organizations," in P. E. Nystrom and W. H. Starbuck (Eds.), *Handbook of Organization Design,* New York: Oxford University Press, 2, 166-202.

Boeker, W. (1989), "Strategic Change: The Effects of Founding and History," *Academy of Management Journal,* 32, 489-515.

Bourgeois, L. J., III (1984), "Strategic Management and Determinism," *Academy of Management Review,* 9, 586-596.

Bower, J. L. (1970), *Managing the Resource Allocation Process,* Boston: Harvard University, Graduate School of Business Administration.

——— and Y. Doz (1979), "Strategy Formulation: A Social and Political Process," in D. E. Schendel and C. W. Hofer (Eds.), *Strategic Management,* Boston: Little, Brown, 152-166.

Boyd, R. and P. J. Richerson (1985), *Culture and the Evolutionary Process,* Chicago: University of Chicago Press.

Brittain, J. W. and J. Freeman (1980), "Organizational Proliferation and Density Depen-dent Selection: Organizational Evolution in the Semiconductor Industry," in J. R. Kimberly and R. H. Miles (Eds.), *The Organizational Life Cycle,* San Francisco: Jossey-Bass.

Burgelman, R. A. (1983a), "A Model of the Interaction of Strategic Behavior, Corporate Context, and the Concept of Strategy," *Academy of Management Review,* 8, 1, 61-70.

——— (1983b), "A Process Model of Internal Corporate Venturing in the Diversified Major Firm," *Administrative Science Quarterly,* 28, 223-244.

——— (1983c), "Corporate Entrepreneurship and Strategic Management: Insights from a Process Study," *Management Science,* 29, 1349-1364.

——— and J. V. Singh (1987), "Strategy and Organization: An Evolutionary Approach," Paper presented at the Annual Meetings of the Academy of Management, New Orleans, August.

Campbell, D. T. (1969), "Variation and Selective Retention in Sociocultural Evolution," *General Systems,* 14, 69-85.

——— (1975), "Degrees of Freedom and the Case Study," *Comparative Political Studies,* 8, 178-193.

Carroll, G. R. (1984), "Organizational Ecology," *Annual Review of Sociology,* 10, 71-93.

——— (1988), *Ecological Models of Organizations,* Cambridge, MA: Ballinger.

Chakravarthy, B. S. (1982), "Adaptation: A Promising Metaphor for Strategic Management," *Academy of Management Review,* 7, 1, 35-44.

Chandler, A. D. (1962), *Strategy and Structure,* Cambridge: MIT Press.

Child, J. (1972), "Organization Structure, Environment, and Performance: The Role of Strategic Choice," *Sociology,* 6, 1-22.

Cogan, G. W. and R. A. Burgelman (1989a), "Intel Corporation (A): The DRAM Decision," *Stanford Business School Case PS-BP-256.*

——— and ——— (1989b), "Intel Corporation (B): Strategy for the 1990's," *Stanford Business School Case.*

Cohen, L. E. and R. Machalek (1988), "A General Theory of Expropriative Crime: An Evolutionary Ecological Model," *American Journal of Sociology,* 94, 465-501.

Cooper, A. C. and D. E. Schendel (1976), "Strategic Responses to Technological Threats," *Business Horizons,* (February), 61-63.

Daft, R. L. and S. W. Becker (1978), *The Innovative Organization,* New York: Elsevier.

——— and K. E. Weick (1984), "Toward a Model of Organizations as Interpretation Systems," *Academy of Management Review,* 9, 284-295.

Davidow, W. H. (1986), *Marketing High Technology: An Insider's View,* New York: Free Press.

DiMaggio, P. J. and W. W. Powell (1983), "The Iron Cage Revisited: Institutional Isomorphism and Collective Rationality in Organizational Fields," *American Sociological Review,* 48, 147-160.

Donaldson, G. and J. W. Lorsch (1983), *Decision Making at the Top,* New York: Basic Books.

Eisenhardt, K. M. (1989), "Making Fast Strategic Decisions in High Velocity Environments," *Academy of Management Journal,* 32, 543-576.

Freeman, J. and M. T. Hannan (1983), "Niche Width and the Dynamics of Organizational Populations," *American Journal of Sociology,* 88, 1116-1145.

——— and W. Boeker (1984), "The Ecological Analysis of Business Strategy," *California Management Review,* 26, Spring, 73-86.

Gilder, G. (1989), *Microcosm,* New York: Simon & Schuster.

Glaser, B. G. and A. L. Strauss (1967), *The Discovery of Grounded Theory,* Chicago: Aldine.

Gould, S. J. (1987), "The Panda's Thumb of Technology," *Natural History,* (January), 14-23.

Haggerty, P. E. (1981), "The Corporation and Innovation," *Strategic Management Journal,* 2, 97-118.

Hambrick, D. C. (1981), "Strategic Awareness Within Top Management Teams," *Strategic Management Journal,* 2, 263-279.

——— and S. Finkelstein (1987), "Managerial Discretion: A Bridge Between Polar Views of Organizational Outcomes," in L. L. Cummings and B. Staw (Eds.), *Research in Organizational Behavior,* Greenwich, CT: JAI, 4, 369-406.

——— and R. A. D'Aveni (1988), "Large Corporate Failures as Downward Spirals," *Administrative Science Quarterly,* 33, 1-23.

Hamel, G. and C. K. Prahalad (1989), "Strategic Intent," *Harvard Business Review,* 67 (May-June), 63-76.

Hannan, M. T. and J. H. Freeman (1984), "Structural Inertia and Organizational Change," *American Sociological Review,* 49, 149-164.

——— and ——— (1989), *Organizational Ecology,* Cambridge, MA: Harvard University Press.
Haspeslagh, P. (1983), "Portfolio Planning Approaches and the Strategic Management Process in Diversified Industrial Companies," doctoral dissertation, Harvard Business School.
Hedberg, Bo L. T., Paul C. Nystrom, and William H. Starbuck (1976), "Camping on Seesaws: Prescriptions for a Self-Designing Organization," *Administrative Science Quarterly,* 21, 41-65.
Hrebiniak, L. G. and W. J. Joyce (1985), "Organizational Adaptation: Strategic Choice and Environmental Determinism," *Administrative Science Quarterly,* 30, 336-349.
Hutt, M. D., P. H. Reingen, and J. J. Ronchetto, Jr. (1988), "Tracing Emergent Processes in Marketing Strategy Formation," *Journal of Marketing,* 52, 4-19.
Itami, H. (1983), "The Case for Unbalanced Growth of the Firm," Research Paper Series #681, Graduate School of Business, Stanford University.
Kagono, T., I. Nonaka, K. Sakakibara, and A. Okumura (1985), *Strategic Versus Evolutionary Management,* New York: North-Holland.
Kanter, R. M. (1982), "Middle Managers as Innovators," *Harvard Business Review,* 60, (July-August), 95-105.
Kidder, T. (1981), *The Soul of a New Machine,* Boston: Little Brown.
Kimberly, J. R. and R. H. Miles (1980), *The Organizational Life Cycle,* San Francisco: Jossey-Bass.
Langton, J. (1984), "The Ecological Theory of Bureaucracy: The Case of Josiah Wedgewood and the British Pottery Industry," *Administrative Science Quarterly,* 29, 330-354.
Levitt, B. and J. G. March (1988), "Organizational Learning," *Annual Review of Sociology,* 14, 319-340.
Lewis, E. (1980), *Public Entrepreneurship,* Bloomington: Indiana University Press.
March, J. G. (1978), "Bounded Rationality, Ambiguity, and the Engineering of Choice," *Bell Journal of Economics and Management Science,* 9, 435-457.
——— (1981a), "Decisions in Organizations and Theories of Choice," in A. H. Van de Ven and W. F. Joyce (Eds.), *Perspectives on Organization Design and Behavior,* New York: John Wiley.
——— (1981b), "Footnotes to Organizational Change," *Administrative Science Quarterly,* 26, 563-577.
——— (1988), "Wild Ideas: The Catechism of Heresy," *Stanford Magazine* (Spring).
McKelvey, B. (1982), *Organizational Systematics: Taxonomy, Evolution, Classification,* Berkeley and Los Angeles: University of California Press.
——— and H. E. Aldrich (1983), "Populations, Organizations and Applied Organizational Science," *Administrative Science Quarterly,* 28, 101-128.
Miles, R. E. and C. C. Snow (1978), *Organizational Strategy, Structure, and Pro-cess,* New York: McGraw-Hill.
Miles, R. H. and K. Cameron (1982), *Coffin Nails and Corporate Strategies,* Englewood Cliffs, NJ: Prentice Hall.
Miller, D. and P. H. Friesen with the collaboration of H. Mintzberg (1984), *Organizations: A Quantum View,* Englewood Cliffs, NJ: Prentice Hall.
Mintzberg, H. (1978), "Patterns in Strategy Formation," *Management Science,* 24, 934-948.
——— (1979), *The Structuring of Organizations,* Englewood Cliffs, NJ: Prentice Hall.
——— and J. A. Waters (1982), "Tracking Strategy in an Entrepreneurial Firm," *Academy of Management Journal,* 25, 465-499.
——— and A. McHugh (1985), "Strategy Formation in an Adhocracy," *Administrative Science Quarterly,* 30, 160-197.
Nelson, Richard R. and Sidney G. Winter (1982), *An Evolutionary Theory of Economic Change,* Cambridge, MA: Harvard University Press.

Ouchi, W. (1980), "Markets, Bureaucracies, and Clans," *Administrative Science Quarterly,* 25, 129-141.

Padgett, J. F. (1980), "Managing Garbage Can Hierarchies," *Administrative Science Quarterly,* 25, 583-604.

Penrose, E. T. (1968), *The Theory of the Growth of the Firm,* Oxford: Basil Blackwell.

Pettigrew, A. (1979), "On Studying Organization Cultures," *Administrative Science Quarterly,* 24, 570-581.

Pfeffer, J. (1981), "Management as Symbolic Action: The Creation and Maintenance of Organizational Paradigms," in Barry Staw (Ed.), *Research in Organizational Behavior,* Greenwich, CT: JAI, 3, 1-52.

Porter, M. E. (1981), Bendix Corporation (A)-(9-378-257-rev. '81), HBS Case Services, Harvard Business School.

Quinn, J. B. (1982), *Strategies for Change,* Homewood, IL: Irwin.

Rosenberg, N. and L. E. Birdzell, Jr. (1986), *How the West Grew Rich,* New York: Basic Books.

Rumelt, R. P. (1974), *Strategy, Structure and Economic Performance,* Boston: Harvard University, Graduate School of Business Administration.

——— (1987), "Theory, Strategy, and Entrepreneurship," in David J. Teece (Ed.), *The Competitive Challenge,* Cambridge, MA: Ballinger, 137-158.

Scott, W. R. (1981), *Organizations: Rational, Natural, and Open Systems,* Englewood Cliffs, NJ: Prentice Hall.

Selznick, P. (1957), *Leadership in Administration,* New York: Harper & Row.

Shepard, H. A. (1967), "Innovation-Resisting and Innovation-Producing Organizations," *Journal of Business,* 40, 470-477.

Singh, J. V. (1986), "Performance, Slack, and Risk-Taking in Organizational Decision Making," *Academy of Management Journal,* 29, 562-585.

———, R. J. House, and D. J. Tucker (1986), "Organizational Change and Organizational Mortality," *Administrative Science Quarterly,* 31, 587-611.

Snow, C. C. and L. G. Hrebiniak (1980), "Strategy, Distinctive Competence, and Organizational Performance," *Administrative Science Quarterly,* 25, 317-336.

——— and D. C. Hambrick (1980), "Measuring Organizational Strategies: Some Theoretical and Methodological Problems," *Academy of Management Review,* 26, 147-160.

Staw, B., L. E. Sandelands, and J. E. Dutton (1981), "Thrust-Rigidity Effects in Organizational Behavior: A Multilevel Analysis," *Administrative Science Quarterly,* 26, 147-160.

Stevenson, H. E. (1976), "Defining Corporate Strengths and Weaknesses," *Sloan Management Review,* 17, 51-58.

Stinchcombe, A. L. (1965), "Social Structure and Organizations," in March, J. G. (Ed.), *Handbook of Organizations,* Chicago: Rand McNally.

Teece, D. J. (1982), "Towards an Economic Theory of the Multi-product Firm," *Journal of Economic Behavior Organization,* 3, 39-63.

Tucker, D. J., J. V. Singh, and A. G. Meinhard (1990), "Founding Characteristics, Imprinting and Organizational Change," in J. V. Singh (Ed.), *Organizational Evolution: New Directions,* Newbury Park, CA: Sage, 182-200.

Tushman, M. L. and E. Romanelli (1985), "Organizational Evolution: A Metamorphosis Model of Convergence and Reorientation," in L. L. Cummings and B. Staw (Eds.), *Research in Organizational Behavior,* Greenwich, CT: JAI, 7, 71-222.

Van de Ven, A. H. (1986), "Central Problems in the Management of Innovation," *Management Science,* 32, 4, 590-607.

Weick, K. E. (1976), "Educational Organizations of Loosely Coupled Systems," *Administrative Science Quarterly,* 21, 1-19.

——— (1979), *The Social Psychology of Organizing,* Reading, MA: Addison-Wesley.

——— (1987), "Substitutes for Corporate Strategy," in D. J. Teece (Ed.), *The Competitive Challenge,* Boston: Ballinger.

Williamson, O. E. (1970), *Corporate Control and Business Behavior,* Englewood Cliffs, NJ: Prentice Hall.

Winter, S. G. (1990), "Survival, Selection, and Inheritance in Evolutionary Theories of Organization," in J. V. Singh (Ed.), *Organizational Evolution: New Directions,* Newbury Park, CA: Sage, 269-297.

Part IV

COGNITION BETWEEN ORGANIZATIONS

14

A Socio-Cognitive Model of Technology Evolution

The Case of Cochlear Implants

RAGHU GARUD
MICHAEL A. RAPPA

This chapter examines the social and cognitive processes that unfold over time as a technology develops. Our model focuses on the relationships between the beliefs researchers hold about what is and is not technically feasible, the technological artifacts they create, and the routines they use for evaluating how well their artifacts meet their prior expectations.

The historical development of cochlear implants serves as an illustration of the model. The evidence suggests that there is a reciprocal interaction between beliefs, artifacts, and routines that gives rise to two cyclical processes. One is a process of inversion at the micro level of individual cognition wherein evaluation routines designed to judge specific artifacts begin reinforcing researchers' beliefs. Once evaluation routines become the basis for constructing individual reality, technological claims are perceived as relevant only to those who employ the same routines while appearing as noise to those who employ different routines.

The other is a process of institutionalization at the macro level of shared cognition. By institutionalization we mean the development of a common set of evaluation routines that can be applied to all technological paths. Commonly accepted evaluation routines represent a shared reality that strongly shapes the direction of future technological change.

The micro- and macro-level processes that shape individual and shared realities place paradoxical demands on researchers in their efforts to develop a new

This chapter originally appeared in *Organization Science,* Vol. 5, No. 3, August 1994.

technology. On the one hand, researchers must create and believe in their own realities in order to make progress in their chosen paths and convince others. On the other hand, researchers must also be ready to disbelieve their realities and be willing to embrace the emerging shared reality even if it does not match theirs. How well this paradox is managed can profoundly influence who emerges as the victor or the vanquished during the genesis of a technology.

(TECHNOLOGY EVOLUTION;
COGNITION, SOCIAL CONSTRUCTION;
PATH CREATION; INSTITUTIONALIZATION)

Among organization scholars there is a growing interest in the technological wellspring, and with good reason. Technological change can permeate all spheres of human activity, but nowhere are the effects of such change more discernible than with industry. New technologies can dramatically alter the competitive landscape, and by doing so, shake the foundation of the largest and most formidable firm, while bolstering the entrepreneurial dream of an individual who possesses little more than the power of an idea. It is precisely this creative and destructive duality first noted by Schumpeter (1975) that gives technology its allure.

Previous attempts to understand technological change show how even the simplest of questions can become elusive: For example, *how do new technologies emerge?* While cursory observations into this question may suggest a linear progression from the conception of an idea to its commercial application, a more probing examination exposes a complex web of interactions between those who develop the technology, the physical artifacts they create, and the institutional environments they foster. By scrutinizing one or more of these interactions, several different perspectives on technological change have been proposed.

One perspective examines the macro-level processes that can only be appreciated through the careful examination of the long-term struggle for survival among organizations. It is suggested that a new technology's emergence can be explained in terms of its capacity to diminish or enhance the value of a firm's existing human and capital investment (Abernathy and Clark 1985, Tushman and Anderson 1986). Technologies that diminish existing competencies are more likely to be introduced by newly created firms, while technologies that enhance existing competencies are more likely to be introduced by established firms. Thus, understanding the characteristics of a technology can help explain whether a firm will embrace it or avoid it, and consequently, the likelihood that its emergence will cause a major disruption within an industry.

Another approach is to examine the micro-level dynamics of technological emergence. Historians have examined how a combination of individuals and events lead to the creation of alternative technological paths (Rosenberg 1982, David 1985, Arthur 1988). In a similar vein, other scholars have examined how individuals create an institutional environment that shapes a technology's emergence (Barley 1986, Weick 1990). The "institutional" perspective has given rise to the notion that technological development is a co-evolutionary phenomenon, wherein there is a continual and reciprocal interaction between a technology and its environment (Rosenkopf and Tushman 1993, Van de Ven and Garud 1993). When studied over time, the co-evolutionary perspective provides an appreciation of the view that technological environments are both medium and outcome of the reproduction of technological practices (Giddens 1979). These environments both constrain and enable the development of new technologies even as both are created in a co-evolutionary fashion.

The co-evolutionary perspective underscores that technological development must be studied contemporaneously. We cannot fully understand the emergence of technology by means of assessments after the fact (Bijker et al. 1987, Latour 1987). Indeed, when we observe technology-in-the-making, there is very little about the process of technological change that is obvious: It involves the "constant negotiation and renegotiation among and between groups shaping the technology" (Bijker et al. 1987, p. 13). Therefore, as social constructivists claim, it is important to closely follow researchers in order to understand how their negotiations influence what form technology will or will not take (Latour 1987).

The view that technology is socially constructed stops short of asking how it is that individuals create a new technology with nothing else but the sheer strength of their ideas and beliefs. However, as Usher (1954) suggests, it may be important to scrutinize the cognitive roots of a technology to understand its subsequent development. Thus, while previous investigations have pointed to how the socially negotiated order of institutional environments directs technological change, we suggest that it may also be useful to examine the negotiated order of beliefs themselves. Beliefs are the generative forces that set in motion *path-creation processes;* that is, the initial conception and enactment of technological artifacts and evaluation routines when nothing else exists but beliefs about what is or is not feasible.

Much can be learned from the literature on social and organizational cognition (e.g., Bateson 1972, Berger and Luckmann 1967, Neisser 1976, Weick 1979). From the point of view of cognitive theory, reality is selectively perceived, cognitively rearranged, and interpersonally negotiated. At the extreme, social order has no existence independent of its members. Technology in the abstract resides in the minds of individuals, and therefore, can be understood more clearly through cognitive variables and decision premises than through behavior (Weick 1990).

In this chapter we seek to bridge the gap between the social and the cognitive processes that eventually become manifest in the form of technological artifacts. We propose a socio-cognitive model of technology evolution, which we illustrate with data on the development of cochlear implants: a surgically implanted electronic device that provides the profoundly deaf with a sensation of sound. While previous studies of cochlear implants (Garud and Van de Ven 1987, Van de Ven and Garud 1993) have examined the social creation of the institutional environment, in the present study, we show how the interaction between beliefs, artifacts, and evaluation routines leads to the creation of alternative technological paths. In contrast to conventional methods used to study intraorganizational cognitive structures, we use interpretive methods to present evidence on the interorganizational belief system; that is, the socio-cognitive structure of a technological field.

SOCIO-COGNITIVE MODEL OF TECHNOLOGY

The foundation of the socio-cognitive model we propose rests on three basic definitions of technology: technology as beliefs, artifacts, and evaluation routines. The first definition of technology is based on its representation as knowledge (Rosenberg 1982, Laudan 1984, Layton 1984). Technology as knowledge provides the critical connection with the cognitive theory literature, where cognition is defined as "the activity of knowing: the acquisition, organization, and use of knowledge" (Neisser 1976, p. 1). Defining technology as knowledge has important implications for how we comprehend technology in the making because it conceivably includes not only what exists, but what individuals believe is possible. These beliefs may include the "rules of thumb" (Sahal 1981) or "search heuristics" (Nelson and Winter 1982) that researchers employ to address technological problems. At a deeper level, beliefs may include a mosaic of cause-and-effect relationships between different facets that might influence technological outcomes (Huff 1990). To understand the evolution of technology from this perspective requires an appreciation of how beliefs form over time.

The second definition, physical artifacts, highlights the form and functional characteristics of a technology (Sahal 1981, Constant 1987). Constituents of a technology's form may vary, but it usually implies attributes such as its dimensional shape and material of construction. Functional characteristics refer to how the technology is used. To understand the evolution of technology from this perspective requires an appreciation of not only how the form evolves, but also what functions the technology serves over time.

Technology can also be defined in terms of a set of evaluation routines. For example, Jagtenberg (1983) suggests that technology manifests itself in certain practices that become institutionalized within a community of researchers. Such practices consist of testing routines and normative values that sustain and define the technology; what Constant (1987) calls "traditions of testability." The traditions of testability are inextricably linked to the instruments employed to generate the facts that are required to evaluate the technology (Latour and Woolgar 1979). To understand the evolution of technology from this perspective requires an appreciation of how these evaluation routines emerge over time.

Each definition in our model highlights a unique, and therefore necessary, aspect of the process of technological development. In our approach, we draw on Neisser's (1976) cognitive theory of perceptual cycles, which consists of interactions between schemas, perceptions, and objects. Neisser defines a schema as an organization of experience that serves as an initial frame of reference for action and perception (Neisser 1976, p. 54). Schemas direct an individual's perceptual explorations, which in turn lead to a selective sampling of objects, which in turn results in a modification of schemas. In this manner, the perceptual cycle revolves between schemas, perceptual exploration and objects.

Parallel with Neisser's model, we propose a "technology cycle" linking researchers' beliefs, the artifacts they create, and the evaluation routines they foster (see Figure 14.1). However, in contrast to Neisser's one-way interaction, we posit a reciprocal interaction between the three constituent constructs of our model. The genesis of a technology, we suggest, begins with the co-evolution of beliefs, artifacts, and evaluation routines over time.

Reciprocal Interactions Between Beliefs and Artifacts

Weick (1979, 1990) suggests that technologies reside in two intersecting arenas: the mental and the physical (see also Kelly 1963). The intersection of these two arenas captures the notion of enactment whereby people "actively put things out there" (Weick 1979, p. 165) in the form of physical artifacts. Physical artifacts set sense making in motion as individuals interpret artifacts only in an abstract way in order to cope with the complexity involved (Weick 1990). Artifacts are cognitively worked upon by categorizing them with reference to existing beliefs. At the same time, individuals

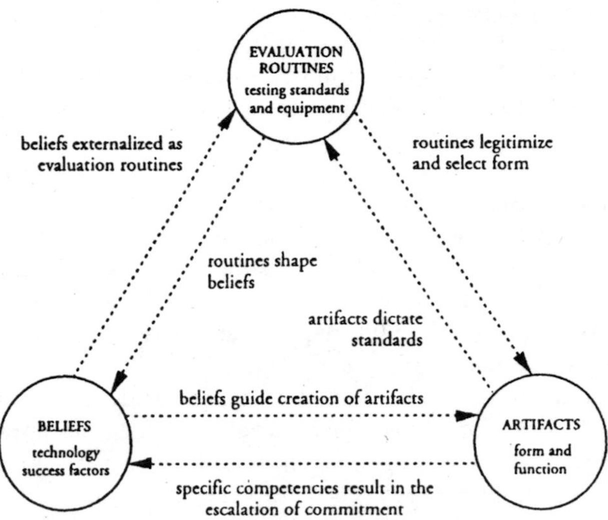

Figure 14.1. Socio-Cognitive Model of Technology Evolution

interact with and constitute these artifacts, thereby shaping their evolution in particular directions.

Thus, there is a reciprocal linkage between beliefs and artifacts. This reciprocal linkage is discussed by Dosi (1982) in terms of technological trajectories. Trajectories represent specific paths of technological change based on researchers' beliefs. Early on during the development of a technology, researchers may hold divergent beliefs about "what is feasible or at least worth attempting" which leads them to pursue different paths (Nelson and Winter 1982, pp. 258-259). Because of the high degree of uncertainty involved (Anderson and Tushman 1990), it is not possible to ex ante determine the success or failure of any particular technological path. Different researchers therefore "place their bets" on different paths.

Researchers develop specific technological competencies over time. These competencies accumulate in a path-dependent manner as earlier technological choices direct future options and solutions (Cohen and Levinthal 1990, Arthur 1988, David 1985). As competencies become specialized, researchers find it increasingly difficult to redirect themselves to other paths. As a consequence, there are powerful incentives for a researcher to persist along a chosen path. In this way, beliefs are externalized as artifacts, which in turn shape the beliefs of the researchers associated with the development of these artifacts.

Reciprocal Interactions Between Beliefs and Evaluation Routines

Geertz (1973, p. 5) describes man "as an animal suspended in webs of significance he himself has spun" through the process of enactment and interpersonal negotiation (Weick 1979). Similarly, Kelly (1963) suggests that individuals create templates which they attempt to fit over the realities of which the world is composed. These templates consist of constructs that enable individuals to validate knowledge and evaluate phenomena. Employing insights from gestalt psychology, Bateson (1972) argues that "individual validation" is required because we operate more easily in a universe in which our own psychological characteristics are externalized.

From this perspective, evaluation routines are an external manifestation of our beliefs and serve as second-order frames (Bateson 1972, p. 187). Data inconsistent with an individual's evaluation routines are either ignored or appear as noise. Data consistent with evaluation routines are perceived as information and cognitively rearranged in a manner that reinforces an individual's beliefs. Given bounds to rationality, this bracketing of perception occurs because individuals may be more interested in confirming their beliefs than in actively trying to disprove them (Weick 1979).

In this manner, an individual's beliefs are externalized, then objectified, and finally internalized (Berger and Luckmann 1967). When this process occurs in groups, it may lead to multiple environments, with each subgroup enacting its own environment and finding itself constrained by it. However, through a process of negotiation and shared interpersonal experiences, a "consensual validation" (Munroe 1955) occurs about facets of reality that groups can agree upon.

Weick (1990) suggests that these insights from cognitive psychology are particularly useful in exploring the development of new technologies for several reasons. First, new technologies are complex and therefore reside as abstract notions in the minds of their users and developers. Second, there is often little agreement about a technology's ultimate form or function. Third, the amount of raw data concerning new technologies places tremendous demands on the information processing capabilities of individuals. Given these challenges, individual and consensual validation become important processes whereby institutional environments are created.

Several facets of cognition are reflected in the social construction literature, albeit with a different language. Researchers externalize their technological beliefs by creating routines (Constant 1987) that are then employed to evaluate the technology. The evaluation routines, in turn, filter data in a way that influences whether or not researchers perceive information as useful. Researchers with different beliefs attempt to sway each other with respect to the routines utilized to judge the technology. It is in this sense that technological systems are negotiated. Therefore, competition between different paths occurs not only in the market, but also in the institutional environment (Meyer and Rowan 1977, Constant 1987). Eventually, certain evaluation routines are institutionalized, reinforcing some technological paths in place of others, thereby enabling their dominance.

Reciprocal Interactions Between Evaluation Routines and Artifacts

An appreciation of the reciprocal linkage between evaluation routines and artifacts is required to understand why routines are required to legitimize a new technology, why they may result in the escalation of commitment and conflict, and how they develop the power to select out specific paths. Kuhn's (1970) theory of scientific revolutions is suggestive in this regard. By introducing the idea of scientific paradigms, which embody accepted examples of scientific practice as they relate to laws, theory, application, and instrumentation, Kuhn points out that researchers whose activities are based on shared paradigms are committed to the same rules and routines for scientific evaluation. While routines are particularly well-suited to study phenomena from within the perspective of a paradigm, they are ill-suited to study the phenomena from a contrasting paradigm. Therefore, evaluation routines have a tendency to reinforce an established paradigm and preclude the emergence of others.

More recently, Dosi (1982) has utilized the notion of paradigms in the study of technological development. Dosi points out that technological paradigms have a powerful "exclusionary effect" rendering researchers blind to alternative technological possibilities. That is because researchers are unable to evaluate (or perceive as noise) data about new technological paradigms when they employ their traditional evaluation routines. Consequently, the application of existing evaluation routines to the assessment of artifacts created within a new technological paradigm may prematurely terminate its growth.

It is for this reason that van den Belt and Rip (1987) suggest that new artifacts be protected from the myopic selection pressures of existing evaluation routines. This can be accomplished by creating routines appropriate to evaluate the form and function of new artifacts (Constant 1987). Akin to the formation of a new vocabulary and a grammar, evaluation routines help researchers communicate with one another and legitimize artifacts that represent a new technology. Initially, several evaluation routines may exist, each tautological with the specific paths that different researchers pursue. Each evaluation routine can therefore create different individual realities. As a result, researchers' claims make sense to those who employ similar evaluation routines while appearing erroneous to those who employ different routines. Faced with this ambiguity, researchers continue to commit themselves to their paths in order to demonstrate the validity of their claims.

Evaluation routines develop the power to select out particular paths only when they become widely accepted and commonly applied through a highly negotiated political process. The application of commonly accepted evaluation routines results in the emergence of a dominant design (Utterback and Abernathy 1975, Anderson and Tushman 1990). Subsequent technological activities elaborate selected artifacts.

In summary, we propose a socio-cognitive model of technology evolution based on an understanding of the interaction between researchers' beliefs, the artifacts they create, and the evaluation routines they foster. We will now examine the development of cochlear implant technology in order to illustrate this model.

RESEARCH SITE AND METHODS

The evidence presented in this chapter comes from a longitudinal study of the development of cochlear implant technology. Cochlear implants are electronic biomedical devices that provide the profoundly deaf a sensation of sound. These devices have been described as unique "sociopsychological" products because several different interpretations of their safety and effectiveness have been possible. Consequently, the emergence of cochlear implants provides an ideal setting for the socio-cognitive model developed in this chapter.

A longitudinal approach is required to examine technology evolution for several reasons. Foremost, it is important to identify and track the beliefs, artifacts, and evaluation routines before they become impervious to scrutiny. The uncertainty and ambiguity that pervades the development of a new technology renders post-hoc efficiency and functional explanations inadequate. To avoid this retrospective rationality trap, it is important to provide a symmetric account of different paths irrespective of whether or not they were eventually successful (Bijker et al. 1987).

Uncovering the different facets of technology requires a comprehensive data collection effort using multiple sources and multiple methods. The study began with interviews and archival data collection to establish a baseline for the history of cochlear implants prior to 1983 (see Garud and Van de Ven 1987). Real-time collection of data was initiated in 1983 using instruments developed by the Minnesota Innovation Research Program (Van de Ven and Poole 1990). The instruments consisted of schedules for on-site observations, interviews, questionnaires, and archival records. Periodic meetings were held with several cochlear implant participants so that information could be collected consistently over time.

Starting in 1985, observations were made during one firm's cochlear implant steering committee meetings, initially held twice a month and then once a month. Meeting notes were transcribed and shared with other members of the research team. This led to an intimacy with the technology, the key researchers involved, and the complex decisions they faced. It also alerted us to other activities that were taking place in the cochlear implant industry.

Several actions were initiated to gain a wider appreciation of events unfolding in the industry. First, we attended cochlear implant conferences, which enabled us to conduct interviews with researchers and to collect product and technical information. Second, we initiated a systematic effort in 1985 to access publicly available information from organizations involved in the development of cochlear implants. This effort yielded many sources of data, including: Food and Drug Administration (FDA) status reports, National Institutes of Health (NIH) contract and grant information, insurance agency policies covering cochlear implants, activities of cochlear implant institutional bodies, various trade brochures distributed by cochlear implant manufacturers, and scientific activities conducted by researchers.

A search was conducted using bibliographies and electronic databases to collect scientific and technical papers on cochlear implants. A bibliographic database was created, consisting of 1,329 articles written over a period of two decades (see Rappa and Garud 1992). A chronological analysis was conducted to understand the technical debates and key developments in the field. Crucial articles, as identified by researchers in the cochlear implant field, were content analyzed in order to develop the important points and themes underlying the main technological issues.

In addition to the aforementioned sources, we collected data from the files and notes that several researchers from one organization had accumulated over a nine-year period. The data provided a richness that was not possible by direct observation alone; but more importantly, allowed us to uncover the retrospective bias introduced by respondents due to rationalizations or memory lapses when clarification was sought from them postscriptively.

Following procedures discussed by Van de Ven and Poole (1990), a chronological list of events in the development of cochlear implants was created. Events were defined as critical incidents occurring in major functions related to the development of the technology. A qualitative database was used to record the date, the actor, the action, the outcome (if evident), and the data source of each event (see Appendix for an illustration of events). A total of 1,009 events were recorded in the database over a period of seven years, including the historical baseline data. The consensus of two researchers was required to identify events to be entered into the data file. The events were also reviewed for content and accuracy by informants engaged in cochlear implant development. It is from this database that events pertaining to beliefs, artifacts, and evaluation routines were selected as the basis of the data used in this study.

THE DEVELOPMENT OF COCHLEAR IMPLANTS

At a cochlear implant consensus development conference organized jointly by the NIH and the FDA in May 1988, NIH director Ralf Naunton quoted Winston Churchill to signify the remarkable legitimacy that the cochlear implant had achieved: "This is not the end. This is not even the beginning of the end. This is only the end of a beginning."

Addressing a crowd of over 400 researchers, Naunton remarked that several years ago, any researcher who became involved with cochlear implant research did so at his or her own professional risk. Indeed, NIH had earlier condemned human implantation as being morally and scientifically unacceptable. It was remarkable, Naunton stated, that cochlear implants had become an acceptable clinical practice in such a short time.

One objective of the NIH/FDA consensus development conference was to help resolve a debate between single- and multi-channel cochlear implants. In a statement released at the conclusion of the three-day conference, researchers came out strongly supporting the superiority of multi-channel devices over single-channel devices (National Institutes of Health 1988). This conclusion was based on several years of accumulated evidence that multi-channel devices were superior to single-channel devices. Reading the consensus statement, it is difficult to understand why any resources at all were deployed to develop the single-channel cochlear implant. However, there was a period during the early 1980s in which the use of single-channel cochlear implants far outstripped that of multi-channel devices (Figure 14.2). Indeed, some researchers were dedicated to the development of single-channel technology and remained strongly in its favor even after it became apparent that multi-channel technology might predominate in the future.

Both single- and multi-channel cochlear implants consist of several parts: a microphone, signal processor, transmission device, and an electrode device that is surgically implanted into the cochlea (see Figure 14.3). Sound impulses detected by the microphone are converted into electrical impulses by the signal processor which are then transmitted through a receiver to the electrodes in the cochlea. The electrical impulses are interpreted as sound by the patient.

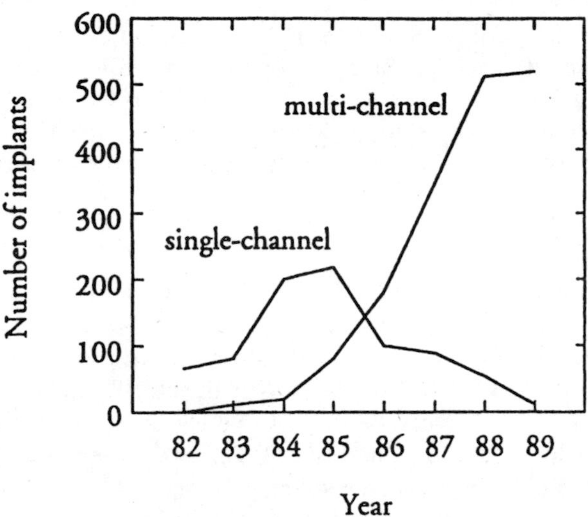

Figure 14.2. Annual Number of Single- and Multi-channel Cochlear Implants, 1982-1989
SOURCE: Cochlear Corporation, 1990

As with any biomedical device, cochlear implants would be judged suitable for human use if found to be safe and effective. In the U.S., the government plays a major role in sanctioning the safety and efficacy of medical devices through a regulatory approval process. Applications to the FDA must contain specific and thorough information relating to safety and efficacy (Yin and Segerson 1986). Consequently, the need to establish safety and efficacy are the two most salient technology constructs that constitute researchers' beliefs.

Cochlear implant researchers understood the importance of safety and efficacy, but they differed in how they operationalized these two criteria in the course of their research. This is where the negotiated order of cochlear implant technology came into play. For some researchers, safety implied reducing the immediate potential for neuro-physiological damage to patients from the implanted electrodes. William House, the founder of the House Ear Institute (HEI) and a pioneer in the development of cochlear implants, is perhaps most notable for embracing this philosophy (House et al. 1979, p. 183). Given the limited state of knowledge regarding hearing, House reasoned that researchers should begin with a simple device, as it would present the least potential for neuro-physiological harm to patients while providing researchers valuable knowledge required for future improvements. This led House to develop single-channel technology, which uses a single electrode implanted at a relatively shallow depth into the cochlea (see Figure 14.4).

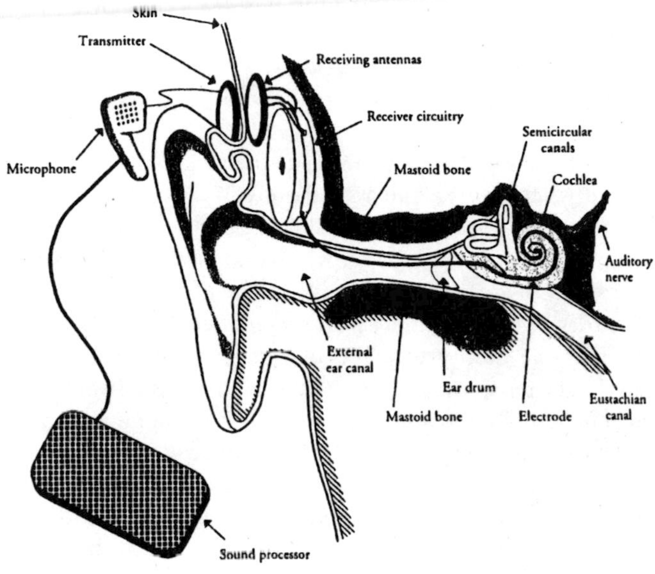

Figure 14.3. Cochlear Implant Device Adapted from Loeb, 1985

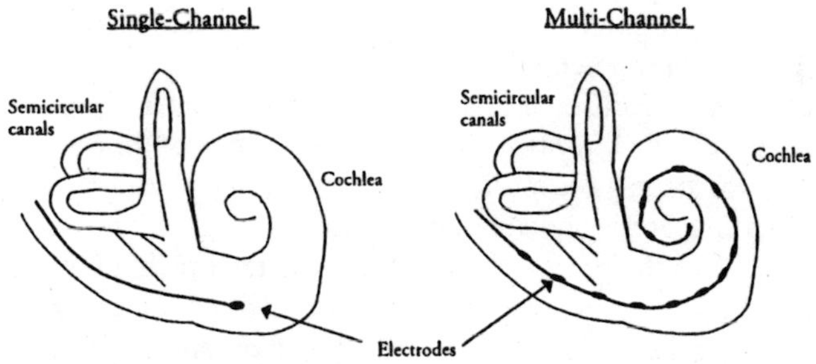

Figure 14.4. Comparison of Single- and Multi-Channel Cochlear Implants

By restricting the length of the electrode's insertion, House believed that the likelihood of neuro-physiological damage would be minimized.

House's preference for the shallow insertion of electrodes conformed with his expectation of how the implant should perform. The single-channel device had been designed to provide profoundly deaf individuals a perception of environmental cues rather than an ability to discriminate between spoken words. To accomplish this objective the device transmitted all the sound impulses picked up from the environment into the cochlea. It was believed that this would allow patients to perceive environmental sounds based on the rate at which electrical impulses were transmitted into the cochlea.

House and others who chose to pursue the single-channel route believed that profoundly deaf individuals would prefer and benefit from a device that could provide them with environmental cues rather than an ability to discriminate spoken words. This belief was based on their understanding of the needs of profoundly deaf individuals. House and his colleagues thought that the ability to discriminate spoken words would require considerable time and effort, whereas the ability to perceive environmental sounds would yield immediate benefits. Consequently, those who pursued the single-channel approach believed that the ability to perceive environmental cues should be the appropriate measure of cochlear implant efficacy.

Other researchers held contrasting assumptions about cochlear implant safety and efficacy. They believed that normal hearing could only be replicated with multiple electrodes, each inserted deep into the cochlea so that different frequency signals could be delivered at different spots in the cochlea (see Figure 14.4). The deeper insertion of multiple electrodes might eventually provide profoundly deaf patients the ability to understand speech.

Graem Clark, a researcher at the University of Melbourne, embraced the multi-channel philosophy (Clark et al. 1977). For him and his colleagues, the ability to recognize speech, as opposed to environmental cues, was the primary function of cochlear implants, and therefore, the appropriate measure of efficacy. Indeed, in order to enhance speech recognition, multi-channel researchers designed implants that reduced the perception of environmental sounds by extracting certain frequencies from the sound signals and delivering them to specific spots in the cochlea.

In contrast to the proponents of single-channel technology, advocates of the multi-channel approach perceived the risk to patients differently. Multi-channel researchers rejected the likelihood of cochlear damage, largely because of the lack of scientific evidence that deep electrode insertion would cause neurophysiological trauma in humans. Instead, multi-channel researchers saw more harm in what they considered to be an inferior single-channel technology. What was of greater concern to them was the potential future damage when single-channel patients sought to replace their implants with multi-channel devices (Health Technology Assessment Reports 1986).

Besides House and Clark, other pioneering researchers include Blair Simmons and Robert White of Stanford University, Robin Michelson of University of California—San Francisco (UCSF), Ingeborg and Ervin Hochmairs of the University of Innsbruck, and Donald Eddington of the University of

Utah. Although these researchers played an important role in the development of cochlear implants, we will limit our discussion to the beliefs, artifacts, and routines of House's group (in cooperation with 3M Corporation), and Clark's group (in cooperation with Nucleus Corporation) as the House and Clark cochlear implant designs account for over 90% of the patients who received implants in the decade since commercialization began in 1978. By focusing on researchers associated with Nucleus/Melbourne and 3M/House, we seek to highlight the key dynamics during the development of cochlear implants without necessarily capturing all of the variations within the research community. These dynamics are summarized in Table 14.1 and described in greater detail employing our socio-cognitive model of technology evolution.

In our description, we also discuss the perspectives of investigators associated with independent evaluation centers who mediated the debate between single- and multi-channel advocates. We single out the University of Iowa for examination because it became one of the most influential centers in the United States. Beyond mediating the debate between principle investigators, independent research centers also served as a conduit of information to institutional bodies such as the NIH and the FDA.

Beliefs and Artifacts in Cochlear Implants

In 1978, House entered into a licensing agreement with 3M. House's single-channel device embodied safety and efficacy features that allowed 3M's cochlear implant team to pursue their business plan for the commercial introduction of cochlear implants. The plan was to seek early regulatory approval for a safe and simple device in order to create a "window of business opportunity." The early introduction of the House technology would enable 3M to establish itself as a leader in cochlear implants. Meanwhile 3M researchers would have the time to develop a more complex multi-channel device for introduction in the near future.

3M had recognized the importance of demonstrating device safety during their interactions with the FDA. The FDA's interest in device safety heightened after reports about neurophysiological damage in animals were published (Berliner and House 1981). Sensitized to FDA concerns, the issue of device safety dominated the 3M research agenda. Researchers concentrated their efforts on reducing the electrode insertion length of the House design further from 15 mm to 6 mm, while freezing core design changes that might enhance the efficacy of their device.

Researchers at Nucleus were among those who believed that 3M's efforts were misguided. In 1979, Nucleus had entered into a licensing agreement with Clark and his colleagues from Melbourne (after 3M had decided not to

TABLE 14.1 Elements of the Socio-Cognitive Model for Cochlear Implants

Research Group	*Beliefs*	*Socio-Cognitive Elements Artifacts*	*Evaluation Routines*
3M/House	Safety: reduce neuro-physiological trauma during use	Form: simple single-channel device with shallow electrode	Routines evaluate the ability to perceive environmental sounds and ability to lip read
	Efficacy: environmental sounds environmental sounds	Function: improve ability to provide environmental sounds	
Nucleus/Melbourne	Safety: reduce trauma of upgrading from single-to multiple-channel	Form: complex multi-channel device with deep electrodes	Routines evaluate the ability to discriminate between open-set-speech
	Efficacy: speech recognition	Function: improve ability to recognize speech	
Food and Drug Administration (FDA)	Before 1984, neuro-physiological safety is more of a concern than efficacy	In 1984, granted regulatory approvals for 3M/House single-channel device for adults because it is considered simplest and safest	Before 1984, relies on investigators to develop pre-market approval evaluation routines
	After 1984, focus shifts to upgradability and speech recognition efficacy	In 1987, rejects application for single-channel devices for children	After 1984, begins to employ routines that demand increasing evidence of safety and efficacy
National Institutes of Health (NIH)	Before 1973, condemns cochlear implants on moral and scientific grounds	Before 1973, refuses to support any group working on cochlear implants	Sponsors Bilger to compare cochlear implants in 1975 and Iowa to develop comparative evaluation routines in 1983
	After 1973, believes it is important to demonstrate safety and speech recognition efficacy	After 1973, extends grants and contracts to multi-channel development and safety-related research	
University of Iowa	Neutral position about safety and efficacy	Before 1987, finds that multi-channel technology is superior with respect to speech recognition ability	Develops evaluation routines that subsequently gain widespread acceptance
		After 1987, finds that single channel technology can provide speech recognition for children	

pursue a similar arrangement). The Nucleus/Melbourne group felt that providing patients with the ability to understand speech was of central importance. Consequently, while 3M/House researchers reduced the electrode length, Nucleus/Melbourne researchers moved in the opposite direction, toward increasing electrode insertion to 25 mm into the cochlea. Moreover, while 3M sought to establish the safety of their device, Nucleus/Melbourne sought to develop the capability to upgrade their device so that patients could easily benefit from future technological advances.

The Melbourne group was supported by NIH grants totaling $1.7 million between 1985 and 1989 (Hambrecht 1991). NIH chose not to support the development of single-channel technology monetarily. By doing so, the NIH did more than underwrite multi-channel researchers; it legitimated Nucleus's multi-channel technology at the expense of the 3M/House single-channel technology.

3M moved quickly to prepare the clinical documentation necessary to submit a pre-marketing approval application (PMAA) to the FDA. Fearing early approval of single-channel technology, multi-channel researchers attempted to dissuade the FDA from making a decision, claiming that the 3M/House technology was "archaic." 3M countered by claiming that existing multi-channel technology did not provide a clear enough benefit in speech discrimination to justify the increased possibility of cochlear damage and decreased reliability. Fortunately for 3M, the FDA's ear, nose, and throat committee ruled that single-channel devices could not be considered inferior until a superior device was actually available. The FDA committee believed it would be wrong to wait for improved cochlear implant technology when an existing technology could offer immediate benefits to patients.

Based on an application submitted on October 1983, the FDA advisory panel granted approval for the commercial sale of the 3M/House device in June 1984. Noting the historic nature of this approval (actually granted in November 1984), the FDA stated in its press conference: "This is the first time that one of the five human senses has been replaced by an electronic device."

However, the FDA sent a mixed signal to researchers and potential patients alike by approving the single-channel device while at the same time circulating a report that suggested the possible superiority of multi-channel technology. The FDA report stated:

> The single-channel implant involves the placement of a single electrode within the cochlea. This type of device provides rhythm and intensity information to the patient but it does not provide any perception of pitch and is not effective in speech comprehension. Multi-channel implants have an array of several electrodes placed within the cochlea. Preliminary results indicate that by stimulating

the proper electrodes in the array in multi electrode devices, the patient can perceive pitch and may be able to comprehend speech more effectively than with a single-channel implant. (*Current Status of Cochlear Implants, Update* 1984)

Thus, while 3M's efforts to appeal to FDA safety concerns were successful in obtaining early regulatory approval, the FDA effectively undermined single-channel technology by raising reasonable doubts in the minds of potential implant patients. Soon after the FDA's announcement, testimonials appeared in the mass media promoting the superiority of multi-channel devices. Daniel Ling, dean of the School of Applied Health Sciences at the University of Western Ontario and a consultant to Nucleus, stated: "Single-channel implants are better than nothing. But that is all they are—better than nothing. Why implant a single-channel today when you know a 22-channel is right around the corner?" (*Wall Street Journal* 1984).

The scientific debate between single- and multi-channel proponents quickly became embedded in the mass media. Surgeons pursuing the single-channel route claimed that there was no evidence to suggest that multi-channel devices were superior. In a 1984 newspaper article entitled "Local surgeons involved in ear war over implants," a Yale University researcher stated:

There is no scientifically controlled evidence to indicate which type of implant is superior to others for most implanted patients. Those who claim the superiority of the multi-channel device over the single-channel device do so to mislead the public either intentionally or out of profound ignorance. (Newspaper article, source unknown)

Such protests notwithstanding, by March 1985, Nucleus's multi-channel device had, in effect, achieved "FDA-approved" status even though the FDA had yet to make a ruling on the technology. Meanwhile, the usefulness of the FDA-approved 3M/House device continued to be challenged on grounds that the ability to upgrade might be limited, thereby locking early users of single-channel implants into that technology. For instance, one surgeon claimed:

If it is true that more sophisticated devices will be developed in the future, then it would be wise to postpone the implantation of single-channel units since this will probably cause enough damage of the inner ear so that it cannot later be replaced by me.

3M fully recognized that cochlear implant technology would evolve into more complex devices, but it hoped to exploit the single-channel to establish itself as the leading producer of cochlear implants. This put 3M in the difficult position of having to convince practitioners and users (who would be required to undergo delicate surgery) that its cochlear implant would provide immediate benefits while still allowing users to take advantage of potential technological innovations in the future. In a widely read issue of *Hearing Instruments,* 3M outlined its position in the following manner:

> 3M has designed its cochlear implants to provide the many benefits of today's devices without compromising the patient's ability to benefit from future improvements in technology by preserving the delicate membranes of the cochlea. At this point in the cochlear implant's short history, not enough is known about the long-term effects of implanting an electrode into the cochlea. For this reason, 3M has taken a "prudent" approach to minimizing risk to the cochlea and to preserve remaining functions for the future products and technologies. Several studies have shown that serious, irreversible damage may result from inserting a multi-electrode cluster into the cochlea. This damage may be due to presence of multiple electrodes (up to 22 in one device) as well as the lengths of the electrodes (up to 25 mm long). Based on today's evidence of the neural degeneration from mechanical damage, 3M feels it is irresponsible to take such a risk. Patients who might be able to benefit from deep-penetrating electrodes today may find that in five or ten years the damage to their cochlea may prevent them from using any cochlear implant. (*Hearing Instruments* 1985, p. 14)

Despite 3M's cautions, FDA granted regulatory approval for Nucleus's 22-channel cochlear implant device in October, 1985 while not approving the 3M/House single-channel device for implantation in children. Implantation of multi-channel devices subsequently increased, while single-channel devices declined. Reflecting on this outcome, 3M's top management challenged its researchers to demonstrate the commercial viability of the 3M/House device. Unable to show management the commercial viability of the 3M/House implant, 3M researchers discontinued their effort and instead initiated the development of a next-generation device. Despite the overwhelming support that was building for multi-channel technology, 3M researchers decided to pursue another single-channel technology, a variation developed by Austria's Ingeborg and Ervin Hochmairs. The "Vienna" device was considered even safer than the 3M/House technology because of its extracochlear orientation, wherein the electrode did not penetrate the cochlea.

3M researchers reasoned that the added measure of safety would enable them to market the device to a much larger pool of potential patients (those with some residual hearing). For these patients, the extracochlear orientation reduced the potential of neurophysiological cochlear damage while providing them with the benefits of enhanced hearing. 3M's earlier decision against a multi-channel device also may have influenced their decision: switching from single- to multi-channel technology now would require a major reorientation achievable only via a long-term R&D project. By embracing the Vienna device, 3M researchers would be able to sustain their cochlear implant effort and emphasize the issue of safety in order to enlarge the potential market. In this manner, the artifacts that 3M researchers developed reinforced their beliefs about safety and efficacy, which in turn influenced their future direction of technological development.

Beliefs and Evaluation Routines in Cochlear Implants

It is important to recognize the differences in how cochlear implant researchers operationalized safety and efficacy. Not only are safety and efficacy largely subjective in nature, but any consensus among researchers requires a degree of coordination and agreement about what should be measured and how it should be measured which did not exist during the early years of cochlear implant development. Even as late as 1973, researchers at an international conference at UCSF decried the absence of systematic routines to evaluate the efficacy and safety of cochlear implants. Several pleas were made to standardize evaluation routines so that research on cochlear implants, as well as other hearing aid devices, could be coordinated and systematic comparisons could be made (Merzenich and Sooy 1974).

In an attempt to remedy this situation, NIH issued a request for a proposal asking researchers to describe how they would evaluate patients fitted with cochlear implants. The contract was won by Robert Bilger, who, with his colleagues at the University of Pittsburgh, set out to study thirteen patients in 1975. What Bilger found was that any comparative assessment of cochlear implants was severely limited by the lack of systematically collected performance data (Bilger 1977). Indeed, Bilger characterized the evidence regarding House's implant technology as anecdotal, dealing mainly with reports of patients' experiences and reactions. Nonetheless, Bilger found there were discernible benefits from cochlear implants. While these benefits fell short of what had been claimed in the press, the "Bilger Report" had, in effect, legitimized cochlear implants. Subsequently, a number of researchers were convinced enough to initiate work on the technology.

The need for straightforward measures of safety and efficacy was further reinforced by the regulatory process. To gain FDA approval, cochlear implant manufacturers had to demonstrate the safety and efficacy of their device through controlled clinical trials. The results of the clinical trials were submitted to the FDA in the manufacturer's pre-market approval application, or PMAA (Yin and Segerson 1986). But no matter how formalized, the FDA process cannot mask the fact that what is measured and how it is measured is subject to interpretation. When 3M first approached the FDA to set the groundwork for PMAA approval, they found that the FDA did not possess the prerequisite knowledge about cochlear implant technology needed to determine an acceptable evaluation scheme. Moreover, the resolution of acceptable measures of efficacy and safety depended on the congruence of beliefs among 3M researchers and FDA administrators. Reflecting on a meeting with the FDA in August 1982, the manager of the 3M Bio-sciences Laboratory explained his frustration with the situation this way:

> [A] considerable amount of teaching was required. There was little discussion about efficacy. They were not familiar with the various audiological tests. Generally, the FDA had to be reminded again and again that our device is the simplest one with the least amount of complexity. But it still provides a clearly demonstrated benefit.

The difference between single- versus multi-channel devices also manifested itself in the kind of tests employed to record implant performance. 3M/House researchers measured a patient's ability to understand environmental sounds—the Monosyllable Tronchee Spondee test—and the resultant improvement in quality of life. Although these tests evaluated a patient's ability to discriminate between some speech elements, they fell short of measuring a patient's ability to discriminate the kind of speech that occurs in normal conversation. 3M explained that these tests were appropriate because current and near future advances lay "not in solving deafness but in providing useful, conservative devices to improve lip-reading skills to allow for mainstreaming." In contrast, researchers at Nucleus/Melbourne employed tests that measured a patient's ability to perceive speech and tracked improvements in speech recognition over time.

Consequently, each technology led to the development and usage of its own unique evaluation routines, which selectively reinforced the advantages (or ignored the limitations) of the respective devices. A researcher's determination of safety and efficacy ultimately depended upon the evaluation routines believed to be most appropriate. However, the evaluation routines developed by researchers were influenced by individual perceptions of what safety and efficacy meant. The resulting proliferation of evaluation routines made it difficult, if not impossible, to objectively compare test results, leading Gantz to exclaim:

> A major obstacle preventing accumulation of comparative data is that each center has reported results based on different measures, and in some instances investigators have developed tests tailored to their implants. (Gantz et al. 1985, p. 444)

Like Bilger, Gantz and his colleagues, with a contract from the NIH, had positioned the University of Iowa as an independent evaluation center. Initially, 3M researchers interacted with the Iowa researchers, as did other cochlear implant research groups. However, 3M began distancing itself from the Iowa group when their test results began to favor the multi-channel technology. While Nucleus supported Iowa in their efforts to develop their evaluation routines, 3M fostered alternative evaluation routines under the auspices of the American Association of Otolaryngology (AAO). Although 3M was successful in helping create several guidelines issued by the AAO, the standards had little tangible effect on the development of cochlear implant technology outside 3M. A member of the AAO committee on the comparison, testing, and reporting of cochlear implants suggested this was due, in part, to the group being headed by a researcher associated with HEI.

The negotiated order of cochlear implant development can be further exemplified by researchers' efforts to influence emerging regulatory guidelines. For example, when the FDA sought input for crafting PMAA guidelines, 3M recommended that a minimum of 100 patients be required for establishing efficacy. This number was based on clinical experience with the 3M/House single-channel device. To build support for their position, 3M organized a technical seminar on safety issues for FDA researchers in January 1985. In subsequent meetings, 3M researchers also presented arguments to dispel any "misconceptions about the apparent sophistication and superior performance of multi-electrode devices."

Nucleus also made recommendations to the FDA for PMAA guidelines. The number of patients required to support efficacy claims was important to Nucleus since it had clinical data on only 43 patients when it submitted its PMAA in 1984. If the FDA accepted 3M's proposal and imposed a minimum requirement of 100 patients, the Nucleus PMAA would be significantly delayed. To prevent this eventuality, Nucleus audiologists visited the FDA and argued that the sample size required to demonstrate safety and efficacy should be a function of the actual performance of each device, the claims each manufacturer wanted to make about its device, and the statistical approach adopted to support such claims. The FDA eventually agreed with Nucleus. Draft guidelines circulated in June 1985 stated that the FDA would not specify the number of patients required for a PMAA. Instead, the FDA would leave the minimum sample size flexible so that clinical investigators could tailor their studies to collect sufficient data to achieve statistically valid results (*MDDI Reports* 1985, p. 11).

While evaluation routines were congruent with the beliefs held by researchers, routines in turn reinforced the beliefs of some researchers. This can be understood by considering the charges of exaggeration researchers leveled against each others' claims. From the vantage point of 3M, researchers felt that proponents of multi-channel technology had overstated the benefits and minimized the risks. Responding to a survey made by the American Speech Hearing Association (ASHA) in May 1985, a 3M spokesman stated:

> One of 3M's biggest concerns is the issue of realistic expectations. To be sure, the cochlear implant is an exciting medical advance; it is the first device that can substitute for one of the body's five senses. 3M believes that it is the responsibility of everyone in the cochlear implant field to present a balanced picture of this new technology. We are particularly concerned about the accuracy of some of the stories that have appeared recently in the mass media. We urge hearing health professionals to take an active role in providing accurate, responsible information to their communities. (ASHA, 1985)

In their counterattacks, multi-channel proponents alleged that 3M exaggerated the performance of their single-channel device. During the Thirteenth International Conference on Cochlear Implants held in 1985, 3M researchers used clinical results obtained in Europe to promote the efficacy of their Vienna device. However, researchers associated with Nucleus and Symbion questioned the validity of 3M's claims on device performance, arguing that 3M should first replicate the European findings in the U.S.

Although researchers accused each other of making claims that were based on faulty assumptions or lacked scientific rigor, given the divergence of technological paths, it was not clear who, if anyone, was exaggerating most. The claims simply reflected the beliefs and evaluation routines that each researcher had adopted. Indeed, if anything, the escalation of claims in the face of opposition illustrates the tendency for researchers to become even more committed to their artifacts and routines in order to validate their claims. Rather than being persuaded by "objective" evaluations, controversy was more likely to lead researchers to become even more entrenched in their own positions.

It is here that one can observe the tremendous influence researchers' beliefs had on how they perceived what was or was not technologically possible. House and Berliner (1990, p. 16) note that Bilger's study was inadvertently swayed by the prevailing view that single-channel devices could not aid a patient in speech recognition. Since, as Bilger (1977, p. 4) stated, "it is well accepted that subjects using auditory prosthesis cannot understand speech with them," they did not even attempt to evaluate patients for speech discrimination. House and Berliner (1990) suggest that this omission had a profound impact on researchers' beliefs in the efficacy of single-channel implants. They claim that the Bilger report:

> . . . Continued to fuel the then existing assumption that no speech understanding was possible with a single-channel device. The belief that single-channel cochlear implants could not provide speech discrimination persisted throughout the 1970's and had lasting effects on device development. It greatly narrowed the perspective of workers in this field and excluded from pursuit many possible approaches to signal processing. (House and Berliner 1990, p. 17)

The struggle to define safety and efficacy, and then measure it, illustrates how researchers projected their own beliefs onto cochlear implants and attempted to influence each other, including regulators. The evaluation routines adopted by researchers were congruent with their beliefs about cochlear implants. These routines, in turn, further reinforced researchers' beliefs.

Evaluation Routines and Artifacts in Cochlear Implants

The lack of agreement on evaluation routines during the early years of cochlear implants fostered a situation in which media reports inevitably exaggerated scientific evidence. Simmons likened one particularly extravagant news story on cochlear implants to the headline: "Mom gives birth to a 2-year-old baby" (Simmons 1988). Unfortunately, media hyperbole had the effect of discouraging researchers from working in the field, thereby leaving it more or less dormant for a considerable number of years (House and Berliner 1990, p. 6, Simmons 1985, p. 4).

The leeway in designing evaluation routines led researchers to formulate tests that tended to highlight the benefits of their devices and thus validate the claims they were making. Calvert, the program manager of one of the business firms, stated:

> The clinical trials allow the claims of each manufacturer to be proven. It is important that the tests be standardized. That should include both the method used to administer the tests and the type of tests used. (*The Hearing Journal* 1986, p. 9)

With time, some tests did become standardized among researchers. However, initially, these tests did little to help in the comparison of devices, since different clinics employed variants of the same test. One example was the Minimum Auditory Capability (MAC) test. Developed by Elmer Owens of UCSF in the early 1980s, MAC is a diagnostic tool used to measure the auditory capability of patients prior to implantation by having them listen and respond to taped cues. According to Owens, the original MAC tapes were poorly recorded, prompting centers to retape the cues with the help of an articulate speaker. In some cases male voices were used, while in others, female voices were used. As Owens explained, even though these modifications undoubtedly improved the reliability of the MAC test, they also reduced its validity: Patients were tested against a voice pattern that they would not actually encounter in real life. Moreover, the proliferation of different MAC versions made it difficult to compare test results from center to center.

Nonetheless, comparative tests conducted by Iowa researchers (with their own version of the MAC test) were influential because Iowa was seen as an independent evaluation center. The Iowa results, which appeared in clinical journals in 1985, showed that multi-channel devices were superior to single-channel devices. To the dismay of single-channel proponents, the results had an enduring impact on perceptions. A manager from 3M stated:

> People think that if an article is published, it will be forgotten after a couple of months. But, actually, other people keep on referencing [it] and [it] never really dies away.

One organization influenced by the Iowa findings was the Office of Health Technology Assessment (OHTA). The OHTA conducted an extensive review of the growing literature to evaluate the suitability of cochlear implants for Medicare coverage. In its report, the OHTA joined with the Iowa researchers to suggest that multi-channel devices might be superior to single-channel devices. Ernest Feigenbaum, a health science analyst with OHTA, explained the difficulties involved in reaching their conclusion. Referring to implants as a unique "psycho-social" therapy, he stated:

> One fascinating issue in this area is the fact that different aspects of the technology require different types of underlying methodologies to evaluate. For instance, there are speech pathologists, social scientists, audiologists, and others involved. Consequently, it is very difficult to pinpoint what an "objective scientific" method should be to evaluate the performance of a device such as the cochlear implant.

The influence of the Iowa study was widespread. In addition to the FDA status report, a study published by ASHA also sided with multi-channel devices (ASHA 1986). The fact that Iowa researchers were instrumental in many of these forums led one 3M researcher to exclaim that "the University of Iowa is controlling our destiny."

In 1987, however, comparative evidence emerged, which was inconsistent with the theory that single-channel devices were too simplistic to provide speech recognition (Berliner et al. 1989). Notably, Richard Tyler of the

University of Iowa found that ten of the Hochmairs' best single-channel patients could discriminate aspects of speech. Similarly, Jean Moogs from the Central Institute for the Deaf, evaluated patients with 3M/House implants and found encouraging performance among children. Previously a staunch critic of single-channel technology, Moogs conceded that she had to re-examine her assumptions.

In light of the new results, HEI's Berliner and Eisenberg (1987) called on fellow cochlear implant researchers to re-evaluate single-channel technology: "We should be more open to possibilities and less tied to theory, at least until we have an objective basis for defining our expectations." They admitted that the initial expectations of HEI's own clinicians' about the performance limits of the single-channel device had led them to commit a "serious error" in not exploring the full potential of the technology:

> Unfortunately, because of our past assumption, we never routinely tested for [a patient's ability to understand speech]. Worse yet, we dismissed some of our own patients' reports of this as their lack of understanding of other cues they might have been using. (Berliner and Eisenberg 1987)

The call for a renewed investigation of single-channel devices came too late. The NIH/FDA consensus development conference in 1988 set forth funding and regulatory guidelines that favored multi-channel technology. Although House raised objections based on the results documented by Moogs and Tyler, few at the conference were persuaded. From the conference a consensus emerged that multi-channel devices were superior to single-channel devices, at least in adults (National Institutes of Health 1988). 3M's Group Vice President lamented that although theory had initially driven research, incongruities between theory and clinical results did not lead to a reexamination of strongly held theoretical biases but rather a reinterpretation of the clinical results. Berliner viewed the consensus statement as an attempt by otologists to "converge onto the multi-channel device in order to reduce cognitive dissonance on the choice of the most appropriate device that they should implant." While conceding that multi-channel devices had become the dominant design. 3M's lab manager stated that other design aspects had yet to be resolved. He spoke of a hierarchy of designs and the battle now shifting to processing schemes and other aspects of the cochlear implant.

DISCUSSION AND CONCLUSION

We began with the premise that technology should be viewed as beliefs, as artifacts, and as evaluation routines. While each perspective is useful in and of itself, together they form the basis for unraveling the path-creation processes that unfold during the genesis of a technology. Pioneering researchers build artifacts that bare the imprint of what they believe can and should be done. In turn, the form and function of an artifact affects the kind of routines that are created to evaluate how well expectations are met. The discrepancies that arise between reality and expectations subsequently influence the beliefs that researchers hold, thereby giving further impetus to the cyclical dynamic of path-creation.

What is equally important to recognize is that the pattern of influence runs in both directions. It is difficult to create evaluation routines when artifacts do not exist or are not fully developed. Without evaluation routines, a technology cannot gain legitimacy in the eyes of researchers who have no other choice but to apply their existing routines to evaluate an incommensurate technological artifact. Moreover, without legitimacy, it is difficult to attract others to participate in developing the technology to a more advanced state. Thus a new technology is in a precarious state during its early stages of conception.

The historical development of cochlear implants illustrates how each facet of a technology mutually shapes the other. In order to maintain interest in cochlear implants, for example, pioneering researchers created their technological paths by externalizing beliefs as artifacts. They also had to develop evaluation routines to make sense of their path and establish its legitimacy. But at the same time, the evaluation routines used by researchers prescribed their boundaries of exploration. In the case of 3M/House, researchers reinforced their own beliefs about single-channel technology on the basis of "avoided tests" (Weick 1979, pp. 149-152) rather than on the basis of tests that could have proven that speech recognition was possible. Thus, once created, the evaluation routines became the basis for the construction of reality.

Such a situation can be viewed as a process of "inversion" (Latour and Woolgar 1979, p. 240) wherein routines designed to evaluate specific artifacts begin reinforcing researchers' beliefs, which we represent by the counter-clockwise arrows connecting beliefs, artifacts, and evaluation routines in Figure 14.1. Once evaluation routines become the basis for constructing reality, technological claims are seen as relevant only to those who employ the same routines, and appear as noise to those who employ different routines.

The existence of divergent evaluation routines leads researchers to be suspicious of each other's claims. However, given the lack of commonly accepted testing and reporting standards, it is not clear who, if anyone, is at fault. Indeed, the apparent extravagance of various claims may simply reflect the diversity of researchers' paths. The ambiguities facing researchers lead them to simply enact a solution (Daft and Lengel 1986, Weick 1979). Cochlear implant researchers could do little else but embellish their routines while persisting in their efforts to develop specific artifacts in order to demonstrate to their colleagues that their claims were indeed "true." When multiple routines surfaced, each with the power to select data that shape beliefs without the power to select specific artifacts themselves, the result was an escalation of commitment and conflict.

Only when evaluation routines become widely accepted, do they have the power to select out certain artifacts while reinforcing others. Thus, the critical question is: How do certain evaluation routines become commonly accepted? Economists have traditionally looked to markets for an answer. But only "efficient" markets have the power to select out paths. When it comes to complex technologies that are difficult to evaluate, such as cochlear implants, markets are often inefficient. Patients are ill-equipped to evaluate the safety and efficacy of different cochlear devices, and therefore cannot be expected to choose between alternatives. Consequently, patients have to rely on audiologists and otologists to act on their behalf. However, audiologists and otologists themselves must rely on information made available by researchers directly engaged in the development of the technology, and as we illustrated, the information that researchers make available represents only one facet of technological reality.

Therefore, it is unlikely that markets are able to select out complex technologies that are difficult to evaluate. At the macro-level of shared beliefs, institutional closure is required for such technologies (van den Belt and Rip 1987). It is for this reason that independent testing and regulatory institutions, such as the NIH and the FDA, exist. Nonetheless, the timing of closure is open to question. If undertaken prematurely, institutional closure may preclude promising avenues of inquiry; if undertaken too late, an escalation of commitment and a waste of resources may result.

When institutions sanction comparative tests, evaluation routines develop the power to select out certain paths and reinforce others. This happened when researchers at the University of Iowa, with the support of NIH, initiated comparative testing. Iowa's efforts represent the beginning of a period of "institutionalization." By this, we mean the development of a common set of evaluation routines that can be applied to all technological paths. During the process of institutionalization, which we represent by the clockwise arrows connecting beliefs, artifacts, and evaluation routines in Figure 14.1, researchers attempt to shape the activities of independent testing centers in their own favor. As the process solidifies, a transition occurs from normative control (DiMaggio and Powell 1983), wherein researchers shape emerging evaluation routines, to coercive control, wherein institutional organizations such as the FDA begin regulating the form and function of the artifacts that researchers create. It is interesting to see that despite coercive controls, 3M/House researchers continued advocating the single-channel path.

Thus, there are two processes that unfold simultaneously during the evolution of a technology. One is a process of inversion at the micro-level of individual cognition. The second is a process of institutionalization at the macro-level of shared cognition. It is at the nexus of these two processes that the form and function of artifacts are manifest over time. Researchers attempt to manage this nexus. At one level, they externalize their beliefs as evaluation routines that then create their personal reality. At another level, they attempt to shape the realities of other researchers who evaluate their technology.

The micro- and macro-level processes that shape individual and shared realities place paradoxical requirements on researchers. On the one hand, researchers must create and believe in their own realities to make progress in their chosen paths and convince others. On the other, researchers must also be ready to disbelieve their realities and be willing to embrace the emerging shared reality even if it does not match theirs (Weick 1979, p. 218). It has been suggested that technological development is not about nature, but rather, a "fierce fight to construct reality" (Latour and Woolgar 1979, p. 243), where reality is the consequence of the settlement of a dispute rather than its cause (Latour 1987). The victors of this dispute emerge as the champions that history will remember. Others, we say, were caught in webs of significance of their own making.

ACKNOWLEDGMENTS

We thank Andrew H. Van de Ven, Joseph Porac, Hayagreeva Rao, Bhatt Vadlamani, and two anonymous reviewers for their comments on an earlier draft of this chapter. We are indebted to several cochlear implant industry participants for providing the information contained in this chapter.

APPENDIX Illustrative Events in the Development of Cochlear Implants

Date	*Event*	*Description*	*Source*
01/01/73	First International conference on the electrical stimulation of the acoustic nerve at UCSF	Otologic community recommends development of routines to increase objective evaluation of subjects fitted with cochlear implants.	Report on workshop on Cochlear Implants, 1973.
12/21/81	Eddington of MIT advises 3M on evaluation routines	Eddington states that there are an infinite number of psycho-acoustic tests that could be performed on subjects and that without a very specific goal, it would be difficult to decide which of these tests should be implemented.	Letter from Eddington to 3M researcher dated 12/21/81.
02/17/84	Pre-market application approval meeting at the FDA	3M researchers explain that they have used the MTS and environmental sound tests as these best measure the performance capability of the 3M/House device in helping patients distinguish between environmental sounds.	Notes from PMAA presentation dated 02/17/84.
02/01/85	Nucleus researchers provide an overview of their cochlear implant program.	Nucleus researchers report that they have been using three tests including the MAC battery, live-voice presentation and a speech-tracking test	*Seminars in Hearing,* Vol. 6, No. 1, pp. 41-51.

04/01/85	University of Iowa article appears in *Laryngoscope* assessing the development of cochlear implants	Gantz of University of Iowa states that comparative uniform evaluation of cochlear implants is vital to the future development. A major obstacle preventing accumulation of data is that each center has reported results based on different measures and in some instance investigators have developed tests tailored to their implants.	Gantz et al. 1985, pp. 443-449.
07/22/85	FDA pre-market-approval guidelines	Guidelines leaves patient sample size requirement flexible so that a clinical trial sponsor can tailor its study to collect sufficient data to achieve statistically valid results while keeping to a minimum the number of patients at risk.	MDDI reports dated 07/22/1985, p. 11.
08/01/86	Review article on cochlear implant status published in *The Hearing Journal*	Calvert of Storz states that it is important for tests to be standardized including both the method used to administer the tests and the type of tests used.	*The Hearing Journal*, 1986, 39:9.
05/02/88	NIH/FDA consensus development conference	NIH/FDA cochlear implant consensus development conference. Consensus that emerges is that multi-channel stimulation produces superior speech recognition performance in adults compared with single channel stimulation. However, interpretation of present data is complicated by a lack of common body of standardized tests. It is not possible to determine which type of device is superior for children based on available evidence.	National Institutes of Health, 1988, Consensus Develop. Conf. Statement.

REFERENCES

Abernathy, W. J. and K. B. Clark (1985), "Innovation: Mapping the Winds of Creative Destruction," *Research Policy,* 14, 3-22.

Anderson, P. and M. L. Tushman (1990), "Technological Discontinuities and Dominant Designs," *Administrative Science Quarterly,* 35, 604-633.

Arthur, B. (1988), "Self-Reinforcing Mechanisms in Economics," in P. Anderson et al. (Eds.), *The Economy as an Evolving Complex System,* Reading, MA: Addison-Wesley.

ASHA (1985), *Cochlear Implant: Five Companies Respond to ASHA Survey,* American Speech Hearing Association.

——— (1986), *Report of the Ad-Hoc Committee on Cochlear Implants,* American Speech Hearing Association.

Barley, S. (1986), "Technology as an Occasion for Structuring," *Administrative Science Quarterly,* 31, 78-108.

Bateson, G. (1972), *Steps to an Ecology of the Mind,* San Francisco: Chandler.

Berger, P. and T. Luckmann (1967), *The Social Construction of Reality,* London: Penguin.

Berliner, K. I. and L. S. Eisenberg (1987), "Our Expectations with Cochlear Implants: Have We Erred in Our Expectations?" *American Journal of Otology,* 8, 222-229.

——— and W. F. House (1981), "Cochlear Implants: An Overview and Bibliography," *American Journal of Otology,* 2, 277-282.

———, L. L. Tonokawa, L. M. Dye, and W. F. House (1989), "Open Set Speech Recognition in Children with a Single-Channel Cochlear Implant," *Ear and Hearing,* 10, 237-242.

Bijker, W. E., T. P. Hughes, and T. J. Pinch (1987), *The Social Construction of Technological Systems,* Cambridge: MIT Press.

Bilger, R. C. (1977), "Evaluation of Subjects Presently Fitted with Implanted Auditory Prosthesis," *Annals of Otology, Rhinology, and Laryngology,* 86, 3, 2, Suppl., 38, 3-10.

Clark, G. M, Y. C. Tong, R. Black, et al. (1977), "A Multiple Electrode Cochlear Implant," *Journal Laryngology Otology,* 91, 935-945.

Cohen, W. M. and D. A. Levinthal (1990), "Absorptive Capacity: A New Perspective on Learning and Innovation," *Administrative Science Quarterly,* 35, 128-152.

Constant, E. W. (1987), *The Origins of the Turbojet Revolution,* Baltimore, MD: Johns Hopkins University Press.

——— (1987), "The Social Locus of Technological Practice?" in W. E. Bijker et al. (Eds.), *The Social Construction of Technological Systems,* Cambridge: MIT Press.

Current Status of Cochlear Implants, Update (1984), Division of OB/GYN, ENT, and Dental Devices, Office of Device Evaluation, Center for Devices and Radiological Health.

Daft, R. L. and R. Lengel (1986), "Organizational Information Requirements, Media Richness, and Structural Design," *Management Science,* 32, 554-571.

David, P. (1985), "Clio and the Economics of QWERTY," *Economic History,* 75, 227-332.

DiMaggio, P. J. and W. W. Powell (1983), "The Iron Cage Revisited: Institutional Isomorphism and Collective Rationality in Organizational Fields," *American Sociological Review,* 48, 147-160.

Dosi, G. (1982), "Technological Paradigms and Technological Trajectories," *Research Policy,* 11, 147-62.

Gantz. B. J., R. S. Tyler, B. F. McCabe, et al. (1985), "Iowa Cochlear Implant Clinical Project," *Laryngoscope,* 95, 443-449.

Garud, R. and A. H. Van de Ven (1987), "Innovation and the Emergence of Industries," *Best Paper Proceedings, Academy of Management Annual Meeting,* New Orleans, LA.

Geertz C. (1973), *The Interpretation of Cultures,* New York: Basic Books.

Giddens, A. (1979), *Central Problems in Social Theory,* Los Angeles: University of California Press.
Hambrecht, T. (1991), "Details of Contracts NIH Entered into with Principle Investigators."
Health Technology Assessment Reports (1986), *Cochlear Implant Devices for the Profoundly Hearing Impaired,* Office of Health Care Technology Assessment.
Hearing Instruments (1985), "Why Combine Multi-Channel Processing with a Single Electrode?" 36, 14-16.
The Hearing Journal (1986), "Update Cochlear Implants: Beyond the First Generation," 39, 8, 9.
House, W. F. and K. I. Berliner (1990), "Cochlear Implants: From Idea to Clinical Practice," in H. Cooper (Ed.), *Practical Aspects of Cochlear Implants,* London: Taylor & Francis.
———, ———, and L. S. Eisenberg (1979), "Present Status and Future Directions of the Ear Research Institute Cochlear Implant Program," *Acta Otolaryngology,* 87, 176-184.
Huff, A. (1990), "Mapping Strategic Thought," in A. Huff (Ed.), *Mapping the Mind of the Strategist,* New York: John Wiley.
Jagtenberg, T. (1983), *The Social Construction of Science,* Boston: Reidel.
Kelly G. A. (1963), *A Theory of Personality,* New York: Norton.
Kuhn T. S. (1970), *The Structure of Scientific Revolutions,* Chicago: University of Chicago Press.
Latour, B. (1987), *Science in Action,* Cambridge, MA: Harvard University Press.
——— and S. Woolgar (1979), *Laboratory Life,* Beverly Hills, CA: Sage.
Laudan R. (1984), *The Nature of Technological Knowledge,* Dordrecht, The Netherlands: Reidel.
Layton, E. (1984), "Technology as Knowledge," *Technology and Culture,* 15, 31-41.
Loeb, G. E. (1985), "The Functional Replacement of the Ear," *Scientific American,* 252, 104-111.
MDDI Reports (1985), July 22, p. 11.
Merzenich, M. M. and F. A. Sooy (1974), *Report on a Workshop on Cochlear Implants,* held at the University of California at San Francisco.
Meyer, J. and B. Rowan (1977), "Institutionalized Organizations: Formal Structure as Myth and Ceremony," *American Journal of Sociology,* 83, 340-363.
Munroe, R. L. (1955), *Schools of Psychoanalytic Thought,* New York: Henry Holt.
National Institutes of Health (1988), *Consensus Development Conference Statement: Cochlear Implants,* 7, 2.
Neisser, U. (1976), *Cognition and Reality,* San Francisco: W. H. Freeman.
Nelson, R. R. and S. G. Winter (1982), *An Evolutionary Theory of Economic Change,* Cambridge, MA: Harvard University Press.
Powell, W. W. (1988), "Review Essay: Explaining Technological Change," *American Journal of Sociology,* 83, 185-191.
Rappa, M. A. and R. Garud (1992), "Modeling Contribution Spans of Scientists in a Field: The Case of Cochlear Implants," *R&D Management,* 22, 4, 209-220.
Rosenberg, N. (1982), *Inside the Black Box,* Cambridge, UK: Cambridge University Press.
Rosenkopf, L. and M. L. Tushman (1993), "On the Co-Evolution of Organization and Technology," in J. Baum, and J. Singh (Eds.), *Evolutionary Dynamics of Organizations,* New York: Oxford University Press.
Sahal, D. (1981), *Patterns of Technological Innovation,* Reading, MA: Addison-Wesley.
Schumpeter, J. A. (1975), *Capitalism, Socialism, and Democracy,* Reading, MA: Addison-Wesley.
Simmons, B. F. (1985), "History of Cochlear Implants in the United States: A Personal Perspective," in R. A. Schindler and M. M. Merzenich (Eds.), *Cochlear Implants,* New York: Raven Press.
——— (1988), Presentation, NIH/FDA Consensus Development Program, May 2-5.

Tushman, M. L. and P. Anderson (1986), "Technological Discontinuities and Organizational Environments," *Administrative Science Quarterly,* 31, 439-465.

Usher, A. P. (1954), *A History of Mechanical Inventions,* Cambridge, MA: Harvard University Press.

Utterback, J. M. and W. J. Abernathy (1975), "A Dynamic Model of Process and Product Innovations," *Omega,* 3, 639-656.

Van de Ven, A. H. and R. Garud (1993), "The Co-Evolution of Technical and Institutional Events in the Development of an Innovation," in J. Baum and J. Singh (Eds.), *Evolutionary Dynamics of Organizations,* New York: Oxford University Press.

——— and M. S. Poole (1990), "Methods for Studying Innovation Development in the Minnesota Innovation Research Program," *Organizational Science,* 1, 3, 313-334.

van den Belt, H. and A. Rip (1987), "The Nelson-Winter-Dosi Model and Synthetic Dye Chemistry," in W. E. Bijker et al. (Eds.), *The Social Construction of Technological Systems,* Cambridge: MIT Press.

Wall Street Journal (1984), November 30.

Weick, K. (1979), *The Social Psychology of Organizing,* New York: Random House.

——— (1990), "Technology as Equivoque," in P. Goodman and L. Sproull (Eds.), *Technology and Organizations,* San Francisco: Jossey-Bass.

Yin, L. and P. E. Segerson (1986), "Cochlear Implants: Overview of Safety and Effectiveness: The FDA Evaluation," *Otolaryngologic Clinics of North America,* 19, 2.

15

Industry Mindsets

Exploring the Cultures of Two Macro-Organizational Settings

MARGARET E. PHILLIPS

Cultures are dynamic, shared mindsets that, in organizational settings, are usually believed to be nationally or organizationally based. In this chapter, the existence of *industry* cultures is explored. Previous studies of industry-based cognitive constructs have narrowly focused on top managers' mental models for strategic decision making. Here, broad-based assumption sets comprising the cultural knowledge widely shared among organizational participants within two industries (fine arts museums and California wineries) are surfaced and compared. A cognitive definition of culture and a modified ethnographic methodology frame the inquiry. The research process balances the requirements of the inductive method with the logistics of doing research in settings as broad in scope as "industry" and into issues as amorphous as "culture in modern organizations." This process involves the selection and in-depth interviewing of 96 informants in 12 organizations, representing a cross-section of members of these two industries. The distinct assumption sets that surface for each industry demonstrate, among other things, substantial differences in conceptualizations of membership, competition, the origins of "truth," the purpose of work, and the nature of work relationships. The findings suggest that the current narrow focus in research on industry-based cognitive constructs can be productively broadened to include a fuller range of cultural elements and a wider set of industry participants. The surfacing of distinct industry mindsets reinforces the emerging belief that a multiplicity of dynamic, shared mindsets exist within an organization's environment. A new cognitive lens—that of *industry*—is offered, through which scholars and managers alike can view behavior in organizational settings.

(ORGANIZATIONAL CULTURE; INDUSTRY CULTURES; QUALITATIVE RESEARCH METHODS; MUSEUMS; WINE INDUSTRY; MANAGERIAL COGNITION; ORGANIZATIONAL FIELDS)

This chapter originally appeared in *Organization Science,* Vol. 5, No. 3, August 1994.

INTRODUCTION

It has long been recognized that the *culture* of an organization's members provides the context for cognition, frames local sense making, and serves as the socially constructed lens through which organization members perceive, process, and structure information. These conceptions flow from the cognitive stream of anthropological and sociological theory (e.g., Goodenough 1957, Kroeber and Parsons 1958, Spradley 1972) in which culture is viewed as "ideas, beliefs, and knowledge" (Spradley 1972, p. 6). At the core of cultural knowledge is:

> . . . a set of assumptions shared by the group of people. The set is distinctive to the group. The assumptions serve as guides to acceptable perception, thought, feeling, and behavior, and they are manifested in the group's values, norms, and artifacts. The assumptions are tacit among members, [are developed through and evolve from experience], and are learned by and passed on to each new member of the group. (Phillips 1990, p. 10)

Thus, the set of cultural assumptions is an "ideational order" that is the property of the group's members (Goodenough 1964, p. 11). More colloquially, it is a dynamic, shared *mindset* (Fisher 1988), a term which will be used interchangeably with "culture" in the following discussion.

Shared mindsets directly underpin perception, thought, feeling, and behavior of people who are members of a group in ways that are not directly obvious to either themselves or observers. Therefore, researchers have sought to identify the assumptions of groups in organizational settings to gain insight into human activity within the organizational context. While not predictive of individual behavior, assumptions delineate the "central tendencies" (Hofstede 1991, p. 253) of a group. Thus, awareness of these assumptions is a starting point from which both organization researchers and group participants can anticipate and interpret activities within the organization setting such as decision making, identification of threats and opportunities, intra- and inter-group interaction, adoption of organization structures and processes, and socialization of new members.

Traditionally, the mindset believed to be of greatest relevance in the organizational arena has been the *national* culture of each individual organization member (e.g., Adler 1991, Harris and Moran 1991, Hofstede 1980, Lane and DiStefano 1988, Nath 1988). In the past decade, monolithic *organization-wide* cultures have become a prominent focus for research on mindsets shared by organization members (e.g., Frost, Moore, Louis, Lundberg, and Martin 1985, 1991, Jones, Moore, and Snyder 1988, Schein 1985, Schneider 1990).

More recently, it has been posited that a multiplicity of mindsets may exist within and around an organization (Phillips 1990, Phillips, Goodman, and Sackmann 1992, Sackmann 1991, 1992). These mindsets may emanate from a variety of different contexts whose boundaries may or may not coincide with national or organizational boundaries. The salience of any of these mindsets at any point in time, in any particular circumstances, and as an influence on any specific type of individual or organizational behavior is considered an empirical question.

Giving credence to this notion that multiple mindsets exist within and around organizations is the growing number of empirical investigations that identify distinct cultures in organizational settings at levels of analysis beyond nations and organizations. This research has surfaced *intra-organizational* cultures based in locations, functions, and/or hierarchical levels (e.g., Bushe 1988, Martin and Siehl 1983, Martin, Sitkin, and Boehm 1985, Sackmann 1991, 1992), mindsets *crosscutting* organizations such as professional cultures (e.g., Barley 1983, 1986, Dubinskas 1988, Everett, Stening, and Longton 1982, Gregory 1983, Van Maanen and Barley 1984), and *nonnational* cultural *overlays* upon sets of organizations such as regional cultures (e.g., Weiss and Delbecq 1987). In this research, externally oriented and internally oriented cultural assumptions (Davis 1984) shared by a cross-section of group members have been uncovered. The identification of these multiple cultural levels illustrates the existence, scope, and impact of a wider variety of mindsets upon organizational life.

Industry mindsets are potentially a fruitful field for similar empirical inquiry. If cultural knowledge is shared at this level of analysis, an understanding of the core set of assumptions should certainly allow insight into an industry's perception of its environment, internal interpersonal relationships, and intra-industry structures and processes. In addition, it should provide organization researchers and participants with a basis from which to interpret and anticipate characteristics of cross-industry interactions. Thus, activities that potentially pose cultural disjunctures (e.g., mergers, acquisitions, joint ventures, managing conglomerate organizations, communicating with or assimilating employees from other industries) could be facilitated.

This chapter describes a systematic attempt to identify and map industry mindsets. First, previous explorations of the notion of industry mindsets are reviewed. This includes a discussion of theoretical arguments for the existence of cultural commonalities within industries and prior attempts to surface industry-based cognitive constructs. Potential elements of industry assumption sets are then identified. The inductive data collection and interpretation process developed for this investigation is described. Subsequently, the dominant cultural assumptions of two industries explored using this investigative process are summarized. Finally, implications of this research for organizational scholars and for managers are suggested.

PREVIOUS EXPLORATIONS OF THE NOTION OF INDUSTRY MINDSETS

Theoretical support for the existence of industry-based mindsets is found in the literatures of institutional theory, industrial economics, marketing, organization behavior, and strategy. Some initial empirical investigations have also emanated from several of these fields.

Institutional theorists appear to support the idea in their discussions of "industry systems" (Hirsch 1972), "societal sectors" (Scott and Meyer 1983), and coercive, mimetic, and normative processes leading to homogeneity in form and behavior among organizations within the same "organizational field" (DiMaggio and Powell 1983). A strong *industrial-economics*-based rationale for the notion of evolutionary industry cultures is offered in Dosi's (1982) proposition that economic, institutional, and social factors drive the development of technological paradigms within industries. *Marketing* theory argues that global commonalities in perceptions exist within certain industries and are developed and maintained through shared experiences (Levitt 1983).

Organization behavior theorists describe industry as one of several possible "transorganizational loci of culture" (Louis 1985, p. 79) and assert that assumptions shared within an industry (i.e., regarding the competitive environment, customer requirements, and societal expectations) shape the corporate cultures of organizations within that industry (Gordon 1991). Gordon (1985) attempted an empirical investigation of cultural commonalities across industries. However, he grouped organizations into industries at a very high level of abstraction, inconsistent with generally accepted definitions of industry (Porter 1980, p. 5). A lower level of aggregation is desirable if the emergent cultural commonalities are to be attributed to "industry" rather than to other, unspecified qualities of the aggregation.

Strategy theorists, who traditionally focus on the industry level of analysis, propose that commonly held mindsets exist across firms within industries and drive strategic decision making by individuals within those firms. For example, Huff (1982) and Rumelt (1979) contend that shared "strategic frames" for the structuring of uncertainty develop and are used within industries. Porter (1980) argues that shared assumptions about a selected set of strategic variables are the basis for the competitive grouping of firms. Fombrun and Shanley (1990) suggest that cognitive constructs are shared by both internal and external constituents of firms within a given industry.

Grinyer and Spender (1979a) and Spender (1989) assert that an "industry recipe" provides the context for strategic decisions and is used by senior managers across firms within an industry to resolve their individual firms' strategic uncertainties. Spender describes an industry recipe as "the business-specific world-view of a definable 'tribe' of industry experts," "much . . . like a *local culture*" (1989, p. 7, emphasis added).

Several strategy researchers have undertaken empirical investigations into cognitive constructs shared by industry members. Fombrun and Shanley (1990) examined the collective judgment of industry executives, outside directors, and analysts in their attempt to understand stratification within industries. Grinyer and Spencer (1979b) attempted to operationalize their concept of "industry recipes" in a study of top managers in several organizational units of a single conglomerate firm. Porac, Thomas, and Baden-Fuller (1989) uncovered the mental models of key decision makers in 17 U.K. knitwear firms with regard to competitive boundaries and competitive conditions. Spencer (1989) compared strategic constructs held by senior managers of firms in three British industries (iron foundries, dairies, and industrial fork-lift rental firms).

Although the results of the empirical studies are promising, researchers have made various methodological choices that limit the generalizability of their findings. They have aggregated organizations into broadly conceived groups that transcend the notion of "industry." Their studies have attempted to identify externally oriented cultural assumptions (i.e., those shared cognitions related to the competitive positioning of firms), ignoring internally oriented constructs. They have largely concentrated on discerning the mental models of narrow sets of industry participants, specifically, industry executives and subunits of a single organization. Therefore, it has not yet been determined if a shared culture exists among the wider set of participants in a well-defined industry, nor has the broad content of such a mindset been delineated.

THE DATA COLLECTION AND INTERPRETATION PROCESS

When this investigation was first envisioned in 1984, little empirically based knowledge about cultures in organizational settings was available to frame the study theoretically and to guide the research process. However, anthropological experience advises that any investigation into an alien culture requires surfacing characteristics of that culture with minimal imposition of the investigator's own culture. Therefore, an *inductive methodology* was deemed necessary.

It was then necessary to balance the requirements of an inductive methodology with the logistics of doing research in settings as broad in scope as "industry" and into issues as possibly transitory as "culture in modern organizations." Inductive anthropological methods tend to be time-consuming, costly, and intrusive upon all parties involved in the research. Cultural research in organizational settings that are broad in scope is constrained by several factors: (1) the need for a relatively large sample of informants drawn, in the case of industries, from a variety of organizations to represent a broad cross-section of industry participants; (2) the desire to complete the study within a realistic time frame so the findings that are captured and disseminated will largely reflect a culture that still exists; and (3) the importance of minimizing intrusion upon participating organizations for the benefit of both the research and the organizations. Additionally, culture in modern organizational settings is potentially more transitory than culture in traditional anthropological settings (e.g., isolated tribes) because organizations are more open networks with more rapid member turnover and, therefore, more susceptible to change. Since this study undertook to provide a basis for the understanding of and for action in currently existing cultural contexts (rather than just offering historical description), traditionally prolonged inductive methods needed to be adapted to a shorter time frame. Therefore, a three-step process for the collection and interpretation of the data was devised to achieve the requisite balance.

Step 1. Definition of the Sample

Step 1 consisted of a preliminary study to define the sample. This involved the identification of industries, organizations, and informants that would serve as appropriate data sources for the study.

Identification of Industries. Two conditions governed the selection of the industries to be investigated to enhance the possibility that generalizations about the nature of industry-based cultural assumptions and comparisons and contrasts of industry-specific findings could be made at the study's conclusion. These two conditions were: (1) more than one industry must be studied and (2) the probability of finding a common culture across informants and organizations within each industry must be maximized. To meet the first condition, *two* industries were selected. To meet the second condition, a variety of selection criteria were established. The criteria for industry selection are summarized in Table 15.1.

Of primary importance were the first two criteria noted in Table 15.1: (1) these two industries exhibit some degree of *between-industry heterogeneity,*

TABLE 15.1 Criteria for Industry Selection

1. Between-industry heterogeneity
   (a) contrasting environments
      (1) service/manufacturing
      (2) capital-intensive/labor-intensive
      (3) for profit/not-for-profit
      (4) private sector/public sector
   (b) no overlap in product or service
2. Within-industry prima facie homogeneity (from DiMaggio and Powell 1983, p. 153)
   (a) highly centralized suppliers and/or resources
   (b) high rate of interaction with regulatory agencies
   (c) small number of visible models of organization
   (d) high degree of technological uncertainty and/or goal ambiguity
   (e) high degree of professionalization
   (f) high degree of structuration
3. Accessible (local)
4. Replicable (e.g., regional/national/societal)
5. Not over-researched
6. Boundable
   (a) at least four-digit SIC level
   (b) single business units
7. Personal interest

and (2) the industries display a strong measure of *within industry* prima facie *homogeneity.*

Maximization of *between-industry heterogeneity* would increase the probability of finding distinct industry-based cultures. This would ensure that comparisons, contrasts and generalizations might be made from any industry-specific findings that did emerge. Such maximization could be achieved by seeking industries from contrasting environments, i.e., service and manufacturing, capital-intensive and labor-intensive, for profit and not-for-profit, and private sector and public sector. Selecting two industries with no overlap in product or service would also maximize between-industry heterogeneity.

Maximization of *within-industry* prima facie *homogeneity* would increase the likelihood that commonalities in industry culture might exist and that an industry culture might be more observable in greater detail and complexity. If a mindset shared across organizations within such an industry cannot be found, then the notion of industry culture may not be worth pursuing. Prima facie within-industry homogeneity could be determined by assessing each industry in terms of the coercive, mimetic, and normative forces that DiMaggio and Powell (1983) argue promote "institutional isomorphism and collective rationality"—that is, homogeneity in character among organizations within the same "organizational field." Key indicators of these forces, as specified by DiMaggio and Powell (1983, 153), are summarized under Criterion 2 of Table 15.1.

In addition, as shown in Table 15.1, other selection criteria were established. Specifically, a heterogeneous sample of organizations from each industry should be geographically *accessible* to the researcher on a long-term basis. The sample should be *replicable* in other regions of the U.S. and in other nations of the world so that regional and national cultural effects could be teased out in future research. The industries should *not have been over-researched* (Spender 1989, p. 76). The industries should be *"boundable"* in the sense that organizations are either members of that industry or they are not. To this end, the industries should be identifiable at the four-digit SIC level at least (thus attending to Gordon's (1985) methodological limitation of level of aggregation) and primarily composed of single-business-unit organizations. Finally, the industries should be *personally interesting* to the researcher, a criterion necessary to sustain the long-term intensive investigation required.

Initial industry assessment in terms of these established criteria was accomplished through an extensive review of published data on a variety of industries and through directed-in-depth interviews with leaders, educators, and analysts (Fombrun and Shanley 1990) in these industries.[1] Two industries—*the museum industry* and *the wine industry*—appeared particularly promising because of their fit with many of the established criteria. This assessment, coupled with the assessment in terms of *within-industry* prima facie *homogeneity,* supported the narrowing of the focus of the study to the *fine arts museum* and the *California wine* industries. In terms of DiMaggio and Powell's (1983) key indicators, both industries displayed strong prima facie within-industry homogeneity,[2] thus enhancing the possibility of finding cultural commonalities among members within each industry.

Identification of Organizations. In order to claim identification of an industry-wide culture, a variety of organizations from each industry would be needed as field sites for the study. Because industries are segmented and the sets of organizations within these segments differ in some respects, knowledge of the critical variables that differentiate these segments would allow a stratified sample of organizations to be identified. However, industry participants often see their industry segmented differently from the manner used by those presenting data in statistical or economic descriptions of the industry (Porac and Thomas 1987). In order to ascertain this "native view"

(Gregory 1983), during the industry specialist interviews and the review of published data, special attention was paid to how various segments of the industry were referenced and to how organizations were categorized into these segments.

From these interviews and other conversations with industry specialists, it was discovered that three organizational variables are critical in segmenting the fine arts museum industry: *size, governing authority,* and *type of collection.* Four organizational variables were found to be critical in segmenting the California wine industry: *size* (i.e., annual case shipments)/*wine type/location,* which are interacting variables, and *ownership. Age* of the firm and the *range of activities* performed by the organization were additional organizational variables found to be important for detailing full membership within the wine industry.

Organizations representative of each segment of each industry were then identified using recommendations from the industry specialists and data from trade association directories. Table 15.2 lists the six fine arts museums that were included in the study and highlights the variables deemed most critical in selecting each particular organization. The six participating wineries are similarly presented in Table 15.3.

Identification of Informants. Informants from the participating organizations who would serve as a stratified sample of the membership of each industry were then identified. It was recognized that culture research requires a broader sample of informants than that selected by others who have investigated industry-based cognitive constructs (i.e., Grinyer and Spender 1979b, Porac et al. 1989, Spender 1989). However, it was necessary to consider the potential complications of breadth. Although previous research on culture in organizational settings suggested the advantages of selecting a cross-section of informants across functional, divisional, hierarchical, and occupation boundaries (e.g., Everett et al. 1982, Gregory 1983, Martin et al. 1985, Sackmann 1991, 1992), the logistics of including informants representative of all of these various suborganizational groupings across 12 different organizations were daunting. Therefore, a mid-range strategy was pursued. It was decided to first identify the primary activities of each industry and then to identify work roles within the set of primary activities that met two criteria: (1) they were commonly found in some form in all organizations within the industry, and (2) they offered opportunities for interaction (directly or indirectly) across organizations within the industry (per Levitt 1983).

The review of industry publications and the interviews with industry specialists allowed identification of the primary activities of each industry. For fine arts museums, these were found to include administration, curato-

TABLE 15.2 Fine Arts Museum Field Sites with Critical Variables for Selection

Fine Arts Museum	*Location*	*Size*	*Governing Authority*	*Collection Type*
Santa Barbara Museum of Art	Santa Barbara	*coll = medium $ = medium/large	private np-fdtn	general
Crocker Art Museum	Sacramento	medium	*muni/ np-bpso	general
Los Angeles County Museum of Art	Los Angeles	*large/Big 8	county/ np-bpso	general
Newport Harbor Art Museum	Newport Beach	small/medium	private np-fdtn	*contemporary
University Art Museum Calif. State Univ. Long Beach	Long Beach	small	*public university/ np-fdtn	contemporary
Severin Wunderman Museum	Irvine	*very small	private fp-fdtn	*boutique

*Variable(s) considered most critical in selecting the organization

Abbreviations:

coll = collection
$ = budget
muni = municipality
np-fdtn = nonprofit foundation
np-bpso = nonprofit broadly, publicly supported organization

rial, education, operations, and support. For wineries, these were found to include administration, vineyard operations, production-operations, production-winemaking, and marketing, sales, and distribution. A further review of extant trade associations and networks, trade association subgroups and committees, collaborations and joint programs, and commonly pursued career paths, as well as conversations with industry-based personnel officers, narrowed the list of potentially appropriate work roles. Pilot interviews were conducted in part to refine this selection of work roles.

Thirteen informant work roles were targeted in fine arts museums; nine informant work roles were targeted for wineries, which have fewer and more broadly specified job categories than do museums. These work roles are summarized in Table 15.4. Guided by Spradley's suggestions for selecting individual informants for inductive research (e.g., length of membership in group, not analytical of own responses and behaviors) (1979, pp. 45-54),

TABLE 15.3 California Winery Field Sites with Critical Variables for Selection

Winery	*Location*	*Size*	*Ownership*	*Wine Type*
Robert Mondavi	*Napa Valley San Joaquin Valley	medium-large	*family	premium/ superpremium/ popular
Sarah's Vineyard	*Monterey area	very small boutique	*limited partnership —active	superpremium
Chateau Souverain	*Sonoma	medium	*foreign conglomerate	premium/ superpremium
Guild	San Joaquin Valley	*large	*cooperative	champagne/ popular
Santa Ynez Valley	*Santa Barbara County	small	*limited partnership —passive	premium/ superpremium
Cilurzo	*Temecula	small	*owner-operated	premium/ superpremium

*Variable(s) considered most critical in selecting the site.

TABLE 15.4 Informant Work Roles by Industry

California Wineries	*Fine Arts Museums*
1. President/owner/partner	1. Director
2. Senior administrative officer (e.g., finance)	2. Board of trustees member or chair
3. Vineyard worker	3. Administrative director
4. Grower relations worker	4. Curator
5. Production operations worker (e.g., cellar-master, — "rat")	5. Registrar
6. Winemaker or enologist	6. Exhibition designer or preparator
7. Public relations or marketing worker	7. Educator
8. Sales worker	8. Publications worker
9. Hospitality worker (e.g., tour guide)	9. Development worker
	10. Public relations worker
	11. Volunteer director or docent
	12. Operations officer or facilities manager
	13. Conservator

informants occupying these work roles in the participating organizations were targeted: 56 in fine arts museums and 40 in wineries. The number of informants selected from each organization varied in relation to the organization size because, in smaller organizations, a single person often has multiple areas of responsibility, and some activities either do not exist or are contracted out.

Thus, a stratified sample of informant roles was defined for each industry and a cross-section of informants from each participating organization was identified. It is believed that by following this rigorous process each industry was represented by a cross-section of its membership in the data collection phase of this study.

Step 2. Field Data Collection

The central activity for data collection was an individual ethnographic interview (Spradley 1979) with each of the targeted informants. These interviews were "guided" by a set of "grand tour" and "experience" questions, followed by a series of "triggering questions" (Spradley 1979, pp. 85-91). The questions raised a range of issues in an open-ended manner, allowing informants to cover the topics to the extent and at the level of intensity that *they* deemed appropriate. "Grand tour" questions allowed rapport to be established, an open-ended tone to be set, "native" terms to be collected, and an overview of the organization from the perspective of the informant to be acquired. "Experience" questions assisted in increasing rapport, expanding understanding of native terminology, and learning the background of the informant.

The "triggering questions" were specific to the surfacing of industry-based cultural assumptions. The design of these questions proved to be the most challenging task, because at the root of such questions lies probably the most vexing problem in cultural research: *what to identify as ostensibly "cultural" characteristics.* Delacroix (1987) noted that

> . . . each culture forms an integrated whole; its parts hang together with some degree of coherence, like the furniture in a tasteful home. The lay observer senses the coherence before he recognizes the parts. [Yet, ordinarily] . . . we don't know enough about contemporary modern cultures to avoid arbitrariness in selecting what is essential to this coherence. (Delacroix, 1987, p. 7)

The theoretical and empirical contributions previously cited, as well as findings of previous research on culture in organizational settings, offer guidance in this regard. This collection of work suggested that assumptions regarding *strategic issues, interpersonal work relationship issues,* and *social issues* were potentially the essential elements of a "coherent" industry culture.

Strategic issues around which shared assumptions have been thought to form within industries include: the identification of the competitive boundaries of an industry and definitions of competition (Porac et al. 1989); specialization, financial leverage, price policy, and technological leadership (Porter 1980, pp. 127-129); and the relevant elements of the market segment for which the industry produces, the input and output mechanisms employed, and the methods for recognizing and dealing with the uncertainties inherent in the particular market and in these input/output mechanisms (Grinyer and Spender 1979b, Spender 1989).

Interpersonal work relationship issues also have been shown to be an important focus for uncovering a group's mindset (Davis 1984, Gordon 1985, Gordon and Cummins 1979) and are particularly relevant for uncovering assumptions attributed to cultural overlays upon organizational settings (Hofstede 1980). Shared assumptions have been found to form around interpersonal work relationship issues such as vertical and horizontal interdependence, clarity of performance expectations, performance emphasis, conflict resolution, and individual initiative (Gordon 1985, Gordon and Cummins 1979), as well as superior-subordinate relationships, the level of anxiety in the employee-company relationship, individual dependence on the organization, and the relative importance of a more assertive versus a more nurturing work environment (Hofstede 1980).

The notion that assumptions regarding *"social issues"* are possible elements of an industry cultural assumption set was extrapolated from Levitt's (1983) argument regarding the development and maintenance of commonly exhibited artifacts, norms, and values in "global industries." Levitt contends that these global commonalities within industries are developed and maintained through shared experiences, such as managerial training at common universities or institutes and attendance at international conference (Westreich 1983). University or institute training programs (managerial and technical), the use of the same consultants (Capon, Farley, and Hulbert 1980), industry conferences, trade shows, international trade journals, and trade associations are also channels of direct and indirect communication within industries. They provide opportunities for industry members to jointly approach and define new situations, to experiment with or report the results of potential solutions to common problems and "generic situations" (Porter 1980), and to engage in discussion that leads to a consensus on appropriate and/or efficient resolutions (Becker 1982). In this way, these common communication channels serve as the mechanisms by which industry-based assumptions are formed, learned, and passed on. Important strategic and work relationship issues are certain to be discussed in these forums (Huff 1982), and the content and outcome of these discussions is expected to affect the way one conceptualizes the competitive business environment and one's work situation. However, these ever more numerous opportunities for interaction and joint problem solving also provide opportunities for establishing common assumptions related to issues *beyond* the strategic or work-related issues at hand. Such issues might include the source of control over one's life, central life interests (work/family/leisure/other activities), what constitutes work versus play, social responsibilities, political leanings, definition of the role of industry in society, and delineation of the relative importance of personal growth. Thus, the not necessarily intended consequence of the formal communication activities may be the establishment of informal channels of communication (e.g., friendships, personal networks) through which assumptions about *"social"* issues—those *outside* the realm of work—are derived, selected, and undergo review and revision.

Schein (1983, 1985) and Kluckhohn and Strodtbeck (1961) provided additional inspiration to identify potential elements of an industry cultural assumption set. Their work illustrated that a series of categories of cultural assumption appears to be generic in societal and organizational context (e.g., Adler 1991, Dyer 1985, 1986, Lane and DiStefano 1988, Nath 1988). Schein's categorization scheme offered direction regarding issues that could be pursued to elicit insights into the cultural assumptions of a group. This typology, with Schein's suggestions of issues that may uncover assumptions in each category, is contained in Table 15.5.

When Schein's typology was overlapped with the three issue categories (strategic, interpersonal work relationship, and social) generated from previous theoretical contentions and empirical research regarding industry cultures, a picture emerged that mapped the range of specific topics useful as focal points for surfacing elements of an industry-based cultural assumption set. Table 15.6 illustrates the matrixing of these two sets of categories and the resultant suggestions of topics for inquiry. As an example, Table 15.6 shows that the first category of the Schein typology—the relationship between the group and the environment—suggests that assumptions regarding strategic issues might be surfaced by inquiry into such topics as definitions and estimations of competitors, stakeholders, and other internal and external environmental elements. This same category also suggests that inquiry into the perceived role of the industry in the society is needed to uncovered assumptions regarding social issues.

Thus, the topics for inquiry outlined in Table 15.6 offered direct guidance concerning what might be essential elements of a "coherent" industry culture. Their range expanded the frame of attention of the researcher, broadening the focus for data collection beyond the single class of strategic issues explored in other research on industry mindsets (Fombrun and Shanley 1990,

TABLE 15.5 Schein's Typology of Cultural Assumptions with Issues for Uncovering Elements of the Assumption Set

---

Category 1: The relationship between the group and the environment
Assumptions that fall into this category are concerned with the group's perception of itself as either (1) dominating, (2) in harmony with, or (3) subjugated by its environment. Important clues to commonly held assumptions of this type come from knowledge of a group's perception of the composition of its environment, the relative importance of elements in its environment, its identity, its perception of its boundaries, and its role or function within its environment.

Category 2: The nature of reality and truth
Assumptions in this category are concerned with what is "real," what is "true." Conceptions of time and space help to define this reality. Therefore, elements of the assumption set pertinent to this category might be gleaned from knowledge of how reality and truth are determined by the group (specifically, the group's bases for decision making), from insight into the group's temporal focus (past, present, or future), from an understanding of how the group structures time, and from information about the group's perception of the availability and use of its physical environment.

Category 3: The nature of innate human nature
Assumptions in this category are concerned with the group's perception of human beings as inherently good, evil, a mixture of good and evil, or neutral. Of subsequent concern is whether the inherent quality is alterable or unalterable. Evidence of the group's perception of what constitutes a "good" group member versus a "bad" group member (if such categories even exist) and of what mechanisms, if any, can promote change in performance provides knowledge as to the character of assumptions of this type.

Category 4: The nature of human activity
Assumptions in this category concern the group's perception of human activity as: (1) proactive, purposive, aimed toward accomplishment of external goals, oriented toward "doing"; (2) controlled by fate, the spontaneous expression of a "given" personality, oriented toward "being"; or (3) self-development in-progress, focused on the perfection of oneself, oriented toward "being-in-becoming." Clues to the character of assumptions of this type come from knowledge of the group's perception of humans as active pursuers of external goals, as passive beings, or as seekers of opportunities for growth and self-perfection.

Category 5: The nature of human relationships
Assumptions in this category are concerned with the group's perception of the appropriate basis for structuring human relationships for the purposes of distributing power and influence and of experiencing love and intimacy. Schein describes the appropriate focus of the structuring as either on the individual ("individualistic"), on the group ("collateral"), or on lines of direct descent/succession ("lineal"). Knowledge of how the group structures work, how the group resolves conflict, and whether the group emphasizes (1) individual rights and welfare, (2) group consensus and welfare, or (3) hierarchy, tradition, continuity, and/or family offers clues to existing assumptions of this type.

SOURCE: Adapted from Schein (1985, pp. 128-135).

TABLE 15.6 Topics for Inquiry into Industry-Based Cultural Assumptions

	Issue		
Category from Schein Typology	*Strategic*	*Work Relationship*	*Social*
1. Relationship between the group and the environment	Competitors and stakeholders		Role of the industry in society
2. Nature of reality and truth	Planning resources and horizons	Decision-making styles; space allocation	
3. Nature of innate human nature	Evaluation of stakeholder motivation	Standards for selection and promotion	
4. Nature of human activity	Personal motivation		Central life interest; job choice rationale
5. Nature of human relationships		Patterns of communication and authority	Social responsibility

SOURCE: Generated from matrixing the Schein (1985) typology and the issues drawn from the literature-based arguments.

Grinyer and Spender 1979b, Porac et al. 1989, Spender 1989). Most importantly, these topics for inquiry gave rise to a series of direct questions that could be asked and specific activities that could be observed in attempting to uncover the cultural assumption sets of industries. These questions/activities were adapted into "triggering questions" for the interview.

"Grand tour," "experience," and "triggering questions" were collected and sequenced in a General Interview Guide,[3] which specified the *minimum* range of topics to be covered with each informant. Ethnographic interviews with the 96 informants were conducted solely by the researcher between June 1987 and May 1988, ranging from 45 minutes to 7 hours and averaging about 100 minutes each. Pilot interviews were conducted in one identified "model" organization in each industry in part to test the language, flow, and generic nature of the guided interview.

Supplementary data was also collected by document review, observation, and participation. Specifically, published data and documents by and about both industries and the individual organizations within them were read. Intra-industry interactions (e.g., trade association meetings, conferences, a "harvest festival") and intra-organization activities (e.g., formal and informal company and laboratory tours, staff meetings, the 1988 grape "crush," the physical mounting of exhibitions, staff analytical wine tastings, museum members activities) allowed opportunities for observation and, at times, participation.

The set of 96 interviews yielded the interview tapes and notes that served as the basic data for analysis. The supplementary activities of document review, observation, participation, and the preparation of a verbal journal allowed internal validation of the interview data.

Step 3. Thematic Content Analysis

In Step 3 of the process, thematic content analysis (Carney 1972, Holsti 1969) was performed on the data collected to identify individual informant's themes. This process requires that "categories" that capture the essence of the research focus be initially and tentatively identified as part of a "unitizing" scheme for classifying the various data (Carney 1972, pp. 38-40, Holsti 1969, pp. 94-126). Therefore, themes surfaced from informant interviews were initially classified using the Kuckhohn and Strodtbeck (1961) and Schein (1985) typologies as basic guides. As the classification process progressed, an inductively derived modification of the Kluckhohn and Strodtbeck (society-specific) and the Schein (organization-specific) categories of cultural assumptions evolved for these industry settings (Phillips 1990, pp. 119-128, 205-224). This evolution is illustrated in Table 15.7.

TABLE 15.7 Evolution of the Basic Categories of Cultural Assumptions: Categorizations for Societies. Organizations, and Industries

Categories of Cultural Assumptions in Societies[a]	*Categories of Cultural Assumptions in Organizations*[b]	*Categories of Cultural Assumptions in Industries*[c]
1. Man-nature orientation	1. Relationship between the group and the environment	1. Relationship between the group and the environment
2. Time orientation	2. Nature of reality and truth	2. Origins of truth
		3. Nature of time and space
3. Human nature orientation	3. Nature of innate human nature	4. Nature of innate human nature
4. Activity orientation	4. Nature of human activity	5. Purpose of work
5. Relational orientation	5. Nature of human relationships	6. Nature of work relationships

a. Kluckhohn and Strodtbeck (1961).
b. Schein (1985).
c. Phillips (1990).

Using these modified categories, the themes of each individual informant were then reclassified to identify individually held assumptions. Finally, these individually held assumptions were collated across subgroups (e.g., organization, profession, work role, tenure, division, hierarchy) to identify those dominant assumptions shared by the majority of informants within each industry—the "central tendencies" (Hofstede 1991, p. 253) of each macro-organizational group. Feedback from a variety of participants in Steps 1 and 2 of the data collection process was then employed to assure that the assumptions surfaced from the analysis *reflected,* rather than *invented,* the industry cultures.

CULTURAL ASSUMPTIONS IN THE FINE ARTS MUSEUM AND CALIFORNIA WINE INDUSTRIES

Although the mindset of any group is a richly textured "gestalt," its parts must be unwoven to be tersely conveyed in the linear format of the written word. Therefore, the mindsets of the two industries studied will be conveyed by specifying the dominant assumptions that were surfaced during the research process. Table 15.8 presents a summary of the dominant assumptions found to be shared within each industry. The assumption sets are organized for our presentation using as a framework the above-mentioned inductively derived typology of cultural assumptions for industry settings. The italicized elements in Table 15.8 are the categories and subcategories of this typology.

Despite each culture's holistic nature, distinct differences between the mindsets of the fine arts museum and the California wine industries can be concisely illustrated in a most effective manner by contrasting the assumptions of each industry within each category of the typology (Phillips, 1990, pp. 141-224). Several points of greatest contrast between these assumption sets will be considered.

Relationship Between the Group and the Environment: Identification of "The Group"

Fine arts museum industry members identify themselves and other group members in terms of *why their industry exists.* "Museum people" speak primarily of their shared responsibility to convey their passion for visual arts and to fulfill an educational mission to their immediate communities and to the public at large. They express a permanent allegiance to the institution of the fine arts museum and to its educational mission. This mission is described

TABLE 15.8 Cultural Assumption Sets Found in Two Industries: Fine Arts Museums and Wineries

Assumptions in Fine Arts Museums	*Assumptions in Wineries*
1. *Relationship between the group and the environment*	1. *Relationship between the group and the environment*
a. *identification of group* membership based on degree of allegiance to educational mission; "**why** we exist"; internal status structure	a. *identification of group* membership at several levels; firm and geographic regions; "**where** we are"
b. *critical elements*	b. *critical elements*
1) *constraining:* $ resource suppliers; time	1) *constraining,* but can be modified: grape supply; regulators; physical environment
2) *freeing:* positive image	2) *enabling/enhancing:* quality product; appropriate image; educated public
3) *seek harmony with:* primary/direct $ resource suppliers; public at large	3) *seek harmony with:* consuming public; firms in region; industry at large
c. *competition* friendly interdependence; identified by resource	c. *competition* within regions, between industries; ever-expanding market
2. *Origins of truth* expertise through education and, secondarily, experience	2. *Origins of truth* expertise through experience gained from experimentation; expertise revealed by hierarchy
3. *Nature of time and space*	3. *Nature of time and space*
a. *time* polychronic exhibition cycles; orientation to present; time = constraining element	a. *time* annual cycle = vineyard year; sequential improvement in quality/reputation/knowledge; 1 yr. planning horizon
b. *space* private offices not for privacy; light & space = precious commodities	b. *space* reflect small, family-owned image
4. *Nature of innate human nature*	4. *Nature of innate human nature*
variable by individual; *mutable?:* staff—no audience yes	variable by individual; *mutable?:* staff—no re: attitude yes re: skills consumers—yes re: skills
5. *Purpose of work*	5. *Purpose of work*
fulfill mission, evangelistic; feed personal passion for art	work = "a job"; done for rewards (tangible & intangible)
6. *Nature of work relationships*	6. *Nature of work relationships*
collective/collaborative; hierarchical overlay	hierarchical; open communication along chain of command

as follows: "to narrow the distance between a work of art and the visitor" {educator}[4] by increasing exposure to and knowledge about specific art objects, certain eras of art, and art history in general; to provide a "continually enriching experience" {educator} through ongoing exposure to "significant work that [has the potential to] impact peoples' lives [by] providing new perspectives and stimulating new ideas" {publications officer}; to "use the educational potential of artworks to engage [people] in the search for the great 'ah-ha!' " {educator}. They feel they must continually "bring people [into the museum] to have experiences [because they] never know when [the museum visit might] become a significant event for a person" {administrative director}; "for 1%, something clicks and changes their lives" {curator}. Accordingly, the industry's mission is not felt to be a "charter," as in the normal corporate use of the term "mission." Rather, it is believed to be a true "mission," in the religious sense of the term. Indeed, it is felt that "all of us in art museums are working for a higher purpose" {registrar}.

In contrast to museum workers' strong identification with the industry at large and with its educational mission, winery workers tend to identify who they are and who are the members of their "group" in terms of the company for whom they currently work and the California wine-growing region in which that company is located. The primary group with which they personally identify is their *firm.* Secondarily, winery workers have a *regional* sense of "group," seeing themselves as a part of a specific intra-state geographic region, which they define in a variety of ways. For example, Napa Valley-based winery workers may identify specifically with the Napa Valley or more generally with "Napa-Sonoma," and winery workers in the Santa Ynez Valley may identify specifically with the Santa Ynez Valley or with the larger Santa Barbara County or with the even broader "Central Coast." Often, California is referred to as an ancillary geographic region of identification. However, this does not imply that winery workers perceive the statewide industry to be their cultural reference group. Rather, they consider California to be only a geographical reference group that can be exploited for attributes such as its marketing benefits. By no means does the sense of group identification among winery workers (at any of the multiple levels at which they define group boundaries) carry the same connotation of permanency, loyalty, dedication, and self-sacrificing, missionary-like zeal characteristic of the group of fine arts museum workers.

The Relationship Between the Group and the Environment: Competition

In conversation with fine arts museum workers, any reference to the term "competition" is usually met with a preliminary expression of chagrin, as if the term were embarrassing or offensive. Quickly following is the explanation that "it is not like being Procter and Gamble versus Lever Brothers" {development officer}, rather more like "the 'two-gas-stations-on-the-corner' theory" {director}. The relationship among museums in particular and cultural institutions in general is professed to be a "fraternity of interests" {director}, even a collaborative effort, rather than competitive.

Paradoxically, this belief in friendly interdependency exists in parallel with beliefs that belie the existence of a competition-free environment. Fine arts museum workers map their competitors in terms of critical resources for which they compete: *audience, money,* and *art.* They can readily enumerate distinctly different sets of organization or industry competitors for each of these resources.

Competition for *audience* is felt to emanate from art museums with a similar collection focus, from all types of museums within the same geographical region, and, primarily, from all forms of local leisure activities (e.g., the outdoors, amusement parks).

> When you go to New York as a tourist, you go to the Met, the Modern, the Guggenheim, and the Natural History Museum, as well as the Statue of Liberty. In Los Angeles, museums are in competition with Disneyland, Universal Studios, and Farmer's Market. {publications officer}

This illustrates the shared belief that a large part of the art museum audience views the museum as an alternative form of entertainment or recreation. This belief coexists with, yet stands in marked contrast to, the art museum community's perception of itself as a source of education and enlightenment—a scholarly institution.

In the competition for *money,* fine arts museums distinguish two sources of financial support: local donors (e.g., individuals, charitable foundations, corporations) and government funding. For support from the civic-minded local donor, art museums compete with other cultural institutions and not-for-profit organizations. However, substantial and sustaining support is relied upon from those donors believed to be passionate about art, because

> . . . the arts are different. People care passionately about them. In my conversations with donors about [such inducements/deterrents to financial contributions as] the tax code, they don't give these reasons for supporting the museum. {trustee}

Because of their more recent development, West Coast museums are not heavily endowed, as are their Eastern relatives. Heretofore, they have depended greatly on local and/or federal government funds for even their basic operating expenses. With these funds steadily declining, museum people are feeling stronger competition for government support among art museums, with other cultural institutions, and with government's other programmatic responsibilities. At the same time, paradoxically, this situation is promoting expanded *collaboration* among the competitors to urge increased government spending.

Competition for *art,* both for exhibition and for acquisition, is perceived to exist between the informant's organization and other art museums with a similar collection type *and* of greater size or reputation. Success in obtaining traveling exhibitions is determined by "who's where, the [exhibition organizers'] commitment to [exhibit the show in] the area, and the museum's reach to [the show's] audience" {curator}. Increasingly, competition with private collectors (individuals and corporations) for acquisitions is being felt by the industry as it contends with the effects of rapidly escalating prices and the rise in the establishment of the "boutique" museums of private collections.

Unlike the resource-based delineation of competitors in fine arts museums, winery workers have a multi-leveled conception of their competitive environment. The first level is composed of competitors to their individual firm; the second level is that sustained by the industry at large. Firm-specific competition is narrowly defined in geographical terms, with other wineries within the same geographic region seen as primary competitors for wine quality and the consumer dollar (despite the fact that any winery's product shares retail shelf space with wines from a variety of different regions).

The wine industry at large is perceived as experiencing its primary competition from other alcoholic beverage industries (e.g., beer, distilled spirits). But this perception is not based in winery workers' beliefs about their product. In fact, winery workers take great pains to distinguish their industry from other alcoholic beverage producers because of wine's food-product basis, its natural (versus chemical-like) production process, and the fact that it is believed to be a healthful "beverage of sophistication and moderation" {president}. Instead, the shared belief that other alcoholic beverage industries are the wine industry's primary competitor is based in winery workers' beliefs that consumers and the general public hold misconceptions about wine due to their lack of education about the product.

> Our industry is in competition with the liquor and beer industries. But we need to change consumers' ideas regarding alcohol. We need to help them understand that you drink good wine to complement food. We make wine to give sensory satisfaction to people. Wine is not for guzzling, rather for a celebration. We need to change people to make them not think of alcohol [in the form of wine] as a vice. {winemaker}

Winery workers believe that as the public becomes more educated about wine, the market for their product will expand in an analogous fashion. Even as they admit that consumption is currently declining, regulation is tightening, and the voices of the neo-prohibitionists are rising, winery workers hold to the belief that most members of the general public are potential consumers. They see themselves in competition for a portion of an ever-expanding, increasingly educated market for quality wine.

Origins of Truth

The art museum community looks to experts for answers. These experts may be on a museum's board, on its paid or volunteer staff, within the museum community, or within an individual's personal professional network. Expertise is gained from a combination of education and experience, with the emphasis primarily on the former, and is manifested in knowledge and competence on the job. Most valued in art museums is the aesthetic education that, at its most advanced level, is illustrated by the curator with an "eye." An "eye" is not to be confused with inherent taste or talent. Although it is a set of aesthetic standards and a vision of what is or will be important in the history of art, it is believed to be a *trained* ability, the success of the training being enhanced by a passion for art.

Wineries also rely on truth being revealed or determined by experts. However, expertise is believed to be gained largely through experience. The belief that one can "learn everything by doing it" {winemaker} is evidenced in the dominant role of experimentation within the industry.

> We have a common philosophy because we have explored and learned together. We are always trying new vineyards. We will sacrifice a percent of the harvest to always try something new, to learn something new. The willingness to experiment leads to improvement in the future. {grower relations officer}

Experimentation most often takes the form of controlled variation, such as in vineyard research or studies of batches, or "lots," of wine. From this type of research it is believed that objective facts about the environment can be gleaned. When expertise is sought from outside the firm, persons with practical experience in industry processes and experimentation are usually consulted. But, while experimentation is seen as an underpinning for experience, intuition and the confidence to use it are considered valuable byproducts.

Winery workers believe that the degree of expertise is revealed in the position in the chain of command, or the level of the hierarchy. Despite their penchant for experience-based information, winery employees consistently turn to higher-ups for answers and view these "authorities" as having superior knowledge and experienced-based instincts. To members of this industry, the degree of a person's legitimate authority is assumed to be indicative of (and usable as a surrogate for) their degree of wisdom.

Purpose of Work

As previously expressed in the discussion of group identification, fine arts museum workers are driven in their work by their "missionary mentality" {director}. This spirit of evangelism usually flows from a significant experience with art sometime in their life, often at an early age.

> I am from a middle class, non-visually oriented family. We never went to a museum. But in the fourth grade, my class took a field trip to the [city] art museum. I remember a painting—it was a Renaissance painting—of a figure with red robe. I vividly remember standing there looking at it. And I remember thinking to myself, "I don't like it, but it's there for some reason!". {administrative director}

> I always loved art. As a child I used to watch my mother draw and paint. I thought it was "magic." I still think it is magic. {exhibition designer}

They are attracted and attached to art museums because the context allows them to feed their personal passion for art.

> I have always been art oriented—drawing, painting. It is as much a part of me as any physical feature. It is a passion. And it gives me a sense of home, though there is nothing particularly artistic in my background. I started majoring in studio art in college, but I ran out of the creative-side drive. I thought of studying art history to recreate the passion, but the passion shifted to art history. I [am drawn to] art museums because they are an educational and archival tool and [they allow me to be] close to art and to others with a passion for it. {registrar}

> I can feel the pull toward art history in my bones and in my soul. I get a sense of beauty, a sense of life, a sense of the past—it encompasses so much of life. It is a field that draws people in, in a quest for information and knowledge. {educator}

Because of their intense experience and interaction with the art and the museum, museum workers want to give others the opportunity to see the same light, to experience the same revelation, to sense the same "sense of soul and self." {facilities manager}

In direct contrast, most winery employees feel "the wine business is a job, not a passion" {winemaker}. They perform their jobs for the rewards that they receive, many of which are tangible, such as those identified by a grower relations officer:

> . . . the lifestyle—the tasting, the salaries, the fun, the sense of family, the opportunity to interact with growers and university people.

Other tangible rewards include the variety of activities and the fact that the work intensifies only at certain times of the year. Some rewards are intangible, such as "getting respect for my knowledge and opinion" {operations officer}, "the romance of the wine industry" {partner}, and "the pride and satisfaction that you get from the idea that somewhere someone is enjoying the fruits of your labor" {owner}. Although there is an expectation that learning will take place on the job, it does not contain any strong inference of the occurrence of personal development. Rather, this expectation is framed more in terms of skill acquisition or the learning of practical matters for practical purposes.

Nature of Work Relationships

"Team," "teamwork," and "team effort" are oft-used phrases in conversations with fine arts museum workers about the conduct of their work. The structure of museum organizations is essentially flat and the staff small, yet contributions from all functional areas are usually needed to produce the tangible work product (i.e., the exhibition with its related programs). Therefore, work is by nature, collaborative. The collaborative quality of relationships is manifested in the communications practices among individuals within and across organizations in this industry, including large professional networks often tapped on a daily basis for information and ideas. This information and these ideas flow freely and openly.

> To generate new ideas I contact my friends at [local museums] to interact with and to check on how programs went. Either my assistant or I go to the meetings of the Museum Educators of Southern California. It's refreshing to meet with others, to get new ideas and to contribute ideas. I have their roster and can call upon certain people in this group. I also attend the Los Angeles Chapter of the Art Table, a national organization of women professionals in the arts—museums, galleries, consultants, artists. They publish a newsletter. I also value the opinions of members of the curatorial staff. They have a good sense of what a good program is, and they sometimes like to talk about new approaches, so I get new perspectives. I also value the Docent Board members' opinions. They are very committed and knowledgeable, therefore I bounce ideas off them. {educator}

But, despite the collective, collaborative nature of communications and task-related activities, there exists a perceived hierarchical overlay upon individual museums. This stems from the formal organizational structure of museums—the common corporate functional form (Chandler 1977)—with formal reporting responsibilities flowing through the functional head up to the director, who then formally reports to the board of trustees. Because of these formal structural relationships and formal reporting relationships, the functional form is perceived as the mechanism for both *reporting* and *control,* as it usually is in business organizations. However, the assumption of collaborative interpersonal relationships belies any nonritualistic need for formal lines of reporting. Additionally, the assumption that workers are primarily motivated by a missionary zeal balanced by attributes such as competence, interpersonal skills, productivity, and resourcefulness, belies the need for a formal hierarchically based control mechanism. The result is much chafing against the hierarchical overlay, as illustrated in remarks about "the tension between the amateurs [on the board of trustees] and the professionals [on the staff]" {trustee} and in comments such as the following:

> When [the director] came to this institution, we needed more structure. We needed a greater awareness of staff versus board responsibilities and of staff jobs. Much has been accomplished in this regard. But we are still a small institution and, given the size of the institution, there is too much compartmentalization. As a result, there is not enough communication. [The director] is a control freak. [S/he] wants all information passing through [her/him]. Control [should come from a] feeling within an institution of a unity of beliefs, a joy of work. People do better not only when they are well paid and respected, but when their hearts are in it. From this comes a sense of belonging, a sense of family. [But with our director] we have more of an autocratic rule than is needed. {curator}

Interpersonal work relationships among winery workers are structured in a hierarchical manner both formally and informally. Consistent with their belief that the position in the hierarchy is an indicator of experienced-based expertise, winery employees look to their superiors for guidance and directives and are "reactive to instructions and priorities" {marketing officer}. Communication is open, but along the chain of command. Winery workers express a strong feeling of being influenced by their conceptions of their superiors' standards in any individual decision making, especially by the standards of their firm's founder or current leader. For example, when reflecting on what most influences decisions with broad impact for which s/he is responsible, a sales officer revealed:

When I am by myself, it's [the founder]. I think of [founder]. But when my boss is around, it's him; I request his input. I would never go over my immediate supervisor unless there is a problem. It's not polite. I go up the chain of command.

IMPLICATIONS AND CONCLUSIONS

The descriptions of the cultural assumptions of the fine arts museum and the California wine industries presented provide evidence of the existence of industry cultures. Several explicit elements of the inductively derived cultural assumption sets of the two industries have been shown to differ substantially, thus illustrating that the mindsets are distinct. In direct contrast with the notion of monolithic organization cultures as the primary context for cognition in organizational settings, these mindsets each individually transcend suborganizational, transorganizational, and organizational boundaries to be held in common by members of discrete industries. In contrast to the same belief about the primacy of national cultures, these discrete industry mindsets exist in parallel within the same geographic region (i.e., the State of California) of a single nation.

It is also evident from the findings that the current focus in the cognitive literature on industry constructs, which is exclusively strategic in nature, can be productively broadened using this approach. Commonalities in assumptions within industries and differences between industries certainly can be observed with regard to such *strategic* issues as competitor definition and establishment of group boundaries. However, industry cultural assumption sets also include elements related to *interpersonal work relationship* issues, such as patterns of communication and authority, and to *social* issues, such as the purpose of work. Therefore, a broader array of issues can be effectively and constructively explored at this level of analysis.

Additionally, the findings reveal that commonalities in assumptions are shared quite broadly among diverse members of the industry at large. Rather than concentrating only on those members of the industry who are responsible for positioning their individual organizations in relation to their competitors, as have most recent explorations into industry mindsets in the cognitive literature, a focus on the broader spectrum of industry participants is both possible and advised. The effect of the pervasiveness of the industry mindset might be investigated in terms of both its positive and negative potential effects. For example, strategists may wish to consider the finding of the existence of industry culture as the uncovering of a new type of mobility barrier, possibly impeding an organization's or an individual's entry into and exit from an industry. On the positive side, industrial relations specialists may consider surfacing assumptions shared across hierarchical levels and across organizations to facilitate communication in multi-firm union-management negotiations.

For management scholars, the findings reinforce the idea that a multiplicity of cultures exist in an organization's environment, and they provide a new, alternative cognitive lens. They direct the attention of researchers in the field of managerial and organizational cognition to issues of cultural context. They invite further investigation into industries as a single level of cultural analysis and in combination with other levels, and they imply the necessity of sorting out overlaid industry-based influences prior to asserting that a culture is uniquely organizational or suborganizationally based.

The surfacing of industry-based cultural assumptions such as those found in this study, along with this delineation of methods for accomplishing this task, should lead management scholars to pursue an ensuing set of questions: (1) "what is the source of extant cultural assumptions in particular industries?" and (2) "what effect do particular cultural assumptions shared by members of an industry have upon the evolution of that industry?" Using awareness of currently held cultural assumptions as a starting point, researchers are challenged to explore in two directions. First, they might *move backwards* in a historical analysis of the cultural evolution of industries. In this direction, one must take care to attend to problems of reconstructed logic in the analysis of data from informants' recollections and from archival materials. A second direction, one more in keeping with the logic of inductive methodology requiring "real-time" surfacing and verifying of assumptions, is to *move forward* in longitudinal study of new and/or rapidly evolving industries. Multiple efforts in both directions might lead to sufficient comparative data to allow the development of a causal model of cultural variations between industries. Institutional theorists may use such data to verify and further specify the relative influence of the forces that DiMaggio and Powell (1983) have hypothesized promote homogeneity in organizational fields.

The findings of this study also have direct implications for management practitioners. Managers have long been attentive to national cultural differences. Of late, they have become aware of possible organizational cultural differences. More recently, managers have been advised to pay attention to cultural distinctions between, for example, suborganizational groupings and professions. For these managers, the findings of this study add complexity to an already complex world by bringing to light another cultural level that must be attended to—that of industry. This study suggests to managers dealing across industry boundaries not to assume that those with whom they interact are using the same mindset as they are. Yet, simultaneously the findings advise that presumed cultural differences attributed by managers to those with whom they interact based on, for example, the others' national or ethnic culture, might be irrelevant in the face of the industry-based commonalities in assumptions shared by both parties.

A second practical outcome of this research is that basic knowledge of the existence and content of industry mindsets should help facilitate cross-industry communications and assimilation. This information may be particularly relevant to the manager engaging in such cross-industry activity as planning and implementing mergers, acquisitions, or joint ventures, working in conglomerate organizations, starting new lines of business in substantially different industries, hiring and socializing employees from other industries, and working in sales, marketing, or other functional areas that require a high degree of cross-industry contact. Individuals with cross-industry career paths will also benefit from an awareness of industry cultures.

Perhaps the most important contribution of this study for all who work in the field of management, whether as researcher, educator, consultant, or practicing manager, is that it underscores the need to have available a variety of cognitive lenses through which to view organizational life. We must now further broaden our perception of relevant cognitive frames and our conceptualization of culture in organizational settings to include industry-based cultures. Finally, we must consider the existence, the range of influence, and the pervasiveness of industry mindsets in any analysis of cognition in and of organizations.

ACKNOWLEDGMENTS

I wish to acknowledge the substantial contributions to the accomplishment of this research made by Richard A. Goodman, Sonja Sackmann, Mario Gerla, Anthony P. Raia, and the many members of the museum and wine industries who participated in this study. I also wish to thank Michele Kremen Bolton, Bill McKelvey, Ann Feyerherm, three anonymous reviewers, and, especially, the editors of this special issue for their helpful suggestions and support in the preparation of this chapter for publication.

NOTES

1. In-depth interviews with these industry specialists assessed within-industry homogeneity using a set of questions designed around DiMaggio and Powell's (1983) key indicators of forces toward institutional isomorphism and collective rationality. These questions are specified in Appendix A of a set of appendixes to this chapter available upon request from the TIMS Editorial Office, 290 Westminster Street, Providence, RI 02903.

2. Early understandings of *prima facie* homogeneity within the fine arts museum and the California wine industries are specified in Appendixes B and C, respectively, of a set of appendices to this chapter available upon request from TIMS (see endnote 1 above for address).

3. The General Interview Guide is Appendix D of a set of appendixes to this chapter available upon request from TIMS (see endnote 1 above for address).

4. Quoted passages are exemplars of how themes were expressed by informants and were drawn from informant interviews. The {bracketed} job title following each quote indicates the informant's organizational role. Organizational affiliation is not identified to avoid any breach of confidentiality.

REFERENCES

Adler, N. J. (1991), *International Dimensions of Organizational Behavior* (2nd ed.), Boston: PWS-Kent.

Barley, S. R. (1983), "Semiotics and the Study of Occupational and Organizational Cultures," *Administrative Science Quarterly,* 28, 3, 393-413.

——— (1986), "Technology as an Occasion for Structuring: Evidence from Observations of CT Scanners and the Social Order of Radiology Departments," *Administrative Science Quarterly,* 31, 78-108.

Becker, H. S. (1982), "Culture: A Sociological View," *The Yale Review,* 71, 4, 513-527.

Bushe, G. R. (1988), "Cultural Contradictions of Statistical Process Control in American Manufacturing Organizations," *Journal of Management,* 14, 1, 19-31.

Capon, N., J. U. Farley, and J. Hulbert (1980), "International Diffusion of Corporate and Strategic Planning Practices," *Columbia Journal of World Business,* 15, 3, 5-13.

Carney, T. F. (1972), *Content Analysis: A Technique for Systematic Inference from Communications,* Winnipeg, Canada: University of Manitoba Press.

Chandler, A. D., Jr. (1977), *The Visible Hand: The Managerial Revolution in American Business.* Cambridge, MA: Belknap.

Davis, S. M. (1984), *Managing Corporate Culture,* Cambridge, MA: Ballinger.

Deal, T. E. and A. A. Kennedy (1982), *Corporate Cultures,* Reading, MA: Addison-Wesley.

Delacroix, J. (1987), *Cultural Differences in International Business: A Minimalist Proposal,* paper presented at the Western Academy of Management Annual Meeting, Universal City, California. (Available upon request from Professor Jacques Delacroix, Organizational Analysis and Management Department, Leadey School of Business Administration, Santa Clara University, Santa Clara, CA 95053.)

DiMaggio, P. J. and W. W. Powell (1983), "The Iron Cage Revisited: Institutional Isomorphism and Collective Rationality in Organizational Fields," *American Sociological Review,* 48, 2, 147-160.

Dosi, G. (1982), "Technological Paradigms and Technological Trajectories," *Research Policy,* 11, 3, 147-162.

Dubinskas, F. A. (1988), "Janus Organizations: Scientists and Managers in Genetic Engineering Firms," in F. A. Dubinskas (Ed.), *Making Time: Ethnographies of High-Technology Organizations,* Philadelphia: Temple University Press, 170-232.

Dyer, W. G., Jr. (1986), *Cultural Change in Family Firms,* San Francisco: Jossey-Bass.

——— (1985), "The Cycle of Cultural Evolution in Organizations," in R. H. Kilmann, M. J. Saxton, and R. Serpa (Eds.), *Gaining Control of the Corporate Culture,* San Francisco: Jossey-Bass, 200-229.

Everett, J. E., B. W. Stening, and P. A. Longton (1982), "Some Evidence for an International Managerial Culture," *Journal of Management Studies,* 19, 2, 153-162.

Fisher, G. (1988), *Mindsets: The Role of Culture and Perception in International Relations,* Yarmouth, ME: Intercultural Press.

Fombrun, C. and M. Shanley (1990), "What's in a Name? Reputation Building and Corporate Strategy," *Academy of Management Journal,* 33, 2, 233-258.

Frost, P. J., L. F. Moore, M. R. Louis, C. C. Lundberg, and J. Martin (1985), *Organizational Culture,* Beverly Hills, CA: Sage.

———, ———, ———, ———, and ——— (1991), *Reframing Organizational Culture,* Newbury Park, CA: Sage.

Goodenough, W. H. (1957), "Cultural Anthropology and Linguistics," in P. L. Garvin (Ed.), *Report of the Seventh Annual Round Table Meeting on Linguistics and Language Study,* Washington, DC: Georgetown University Monograph Series on Languages and Linguistics No. 9.

——— (1964), "Introduction," in W. H. Goodenough (Ed.), *Explorations in Cultural Anthropology,* New York: McGraw-Hill, 1-24.

Gordon, G. G. (1991), "Industry Determinants of Organizational Culture," *Academy of Management Review,* 16, 2, 396-415.

——— (1985), "The Relationship of Corporate Culture to Industry Sector and Corporate Performance," in R. H. Kilmann, M. J. Saxton, and R. Serpa (Eds.), *Gaining Control of the Corporate Culture,* San Francisco: Jossey-Bass, 103-125.

——— and W. M. Cummins (1979), *Managing Management Climate,* Lexington, MA: Lexington Books.

Gregory, K. L. (1983), "Native-View Paradigms: Multiple Cultures and Culture Conflicts in Organizations," *Administrative Science Quarterly,* 28, 3, 359-376.

Grinyer, P. H. and J.-C. Spender (1979a), "Recipes, Crises, and Adaptation in Mature Businesses," *International Studies of Management and Organization,* 9, 3, 113-133.

——— and ——— (1979b), *Turnaround: Managerial Recipes for Strategic Success,* London: Associated Business Press.

Harris, P. R. and R. T. Moran (1991), *Managing Cultural Differences* (3rd ed.), Houston, TX: Gulf.

Hirsch, P. M. (1972), "Processing Fads and Fashions: An Organization Set Analysis of Cultural Industry Systems," *American Journal of Sociology,* 77, 4, 639-659.

Hofstede, G. (1991), *Cultures and Organizations: Software of the Mind,* London: McGraw-Hill.

——— (1980), *Culture's Consequences: International Differences in Work-Related Values,* Beverly Hills, CA: Sage.

Holsti, O. R. (1969), *Content Analysis for the Social Sciences and Humanities,* Reading, MA: Addison-Wesley.

Huff, A. S. (1982), "Industry Influences on Strategy Reformulation," *Strategic Management Journal,* 3, 2, 119-131.

Jones, M. O., M. D. Moore, and R. C. Snyder (1988), *Inside Organizations: Understanding the Human Dimension,* Newbury Park, CA: Sage.

Kluckhohn, F. R. and F. L. Strodtbeck (1961), *Variations in Value Orientations,* Evanston, IL: Row, Peterson.

Kroeber, A. and T. Parsons (1958), "The Concept of Culture and of Social System," *American Sociological Review,* 23, 582-583.

Lane, H. W. and J. J. DiStefano (1988), *International Management Behavior: From Policy to Practice,* Scarborough, Ontario: Nelson Canada.

Levitt, T. (1983), *The Marketing Imagination,* New York: Free Press.

Louis, M. (1985), "An Investigator's Guide to Workplace Culture," in P. J. Frost, L. F. Moore, M. R. Louis, C. C. Lundberg, and J. Martin (Eds.), *Organizational Culture,* Beverly Hills, CA: Sage, 73-93.

Martin, J. and C. Siehl (1983), "Organizational Culture and Counterculture: An Uneasy Symbiosis," *Organizational Dynamics,* 12, 2, 52-64.

———, S. B. Sitkin, and M. Boehm (1985), "Founders and the Elusiveness of a Cultural Legacy," in P. J. Frost, L. F. Moore, M. R. Louis, C. C. Lundberg, and J. Martin (Eds.), *Organizational Culture,* Beverly Hills, CA: Sage, 99-124.

Nath, R. (Ed.) (1988), *Comparative Management: A Regional View,* Cambridge, MA: Ballinger.

Phillips, M. E. (1990), *Industry as a Cultural Grouping,* doctoral dissertation, Los Angeles: Anderson Graduate School of Management, University of California, Los Angeles. (Ann Arbor, MI: University Microfilms International, No. 9017663.)

———, R. A. Goodman, and S. A. Sackmann (1992), "Exploring the Complex Cultural Milieu of Project Teams," *pmNETwork—Professional Magazine of the Project Management Institute,* 6, 8, 20-26.

Porac, J. F. and H. Thomas (1987), *Strategic Groups and Cognitive Taxonomies,* paper presented at the Academy of Management Annual Meeting, New Orleans, LA.

———, ———, and C. Baden-Fuller (1989), "Competitive Groups as Cognitive Communities: The Case of Scottish Knitwear Manufacturers," *Journal of Management Studies,* 26, 4, 397-416.

Porter, M. (1980), *Competitive Strategy,* New York: Free Press.

Rumelt, R. P. (1979), "Evaluation of Strategy: Theory and Models," in D. E. Schendel and C. W. Hofer (Eds.), *Strategic Management,* Boston: Little, Brown, 196-217.

Sackmann, S. A. (1991), *Cultural Knowledge in Organizations: Exploring the Collective Mind,* Newbury Park, CA: Sage.

——— (1992), "Cultures and Subcultures: An Analysis of Organizational Knowledge," *Administrative Science Quarterly,* 37, 1, 140-161.

Schein, E. H. (1985), *Organizational Culture and Leadership,* San Francisco: Jossey-Bass.

——— (1983), "The Role of the Founder in Creating Organizational Culture," *Organizational Dynamics,* 12, 1, 13-28.

Schneider, B. (Ed.) (1990), *Organizational Climate and Culture,* San Francisco: Jossey-Bass.

Scott, W. R. and J. W. Meyer (1983), "The Organization of Societal Sectors," in J. W. Meyer and W. R. Scott, *Organizational Environments: Ritual and Rationality,* Beverly Hills, CA: Sage, 129-153.

Spender, J.-C. (1989), *Industry Recipes: An Enquiry into the Nature and Sources of Managerial Judgement,* Cambridge, MA: Basil Blackwell.

Spradley, J. P. (1972), "Foundations of Cultural Knowledge," in J. P. Spradley (Ed.), *Culture and Cognition: Rules, Maps, and Plans,* San Francisco: Chandler, 3-38.

——— (1979), *The Ethnographic Interview,* New York: Holt, Rinehart, & Winston.

Van Maanen, J. and S. R. Barley (1984), "Occupational Communities: Culture and Control in Organizations," in B. M. Staw and L. L. Cummings (Eds.), *Research in Organizational Behavior* (Vol. 6), Greenwich, CT: JAI, 287-365.

Weiss, J. and A. Delbecq (1987), "High-Technology Cultures and Management: Silicon Valley and Route 128," *Group and Organization Studies,* 12, 1, 39-54.

Westreich, J. (1983), "Thinking of the World as One Market: An Interview with Theodore Levitt," *Newsweek* (International Edition), September 19, 56.

Index

About the Editors

James R. Meindl is Professor of Organization, and Director of the Center for International Leadership, School of Management, State University of New York at Buffalo. He received his PhD in social psychology from the University of Waterloo. His research interests are in the area of social construction processes as they affect organizing and managing. Recent work focuses on cognitive and social network models of leadership.

Joseph F. Porac received a PhD in social psychology from the University of Rochester. For the past several years, he has been on the faculty of the University of Illinois at Urbana-Champaign, where he has taught organizational science. From 1991 to 1992 he was a visiting faculty member in the Department of Management at New York University. His research interests concern the social psychology of industrial communities. He has recently completed studies in the grocery and knitwear industries concerning the competitive structure among firms and how this structure is shaped by various social and cognitive processes. He has served on the editorial boards of the *Academy of Management Review* and the *Administrative Science Quarterly*.

Charles Stubbart is currently Associate Professor and Interim Chairperson at Southern Illinois University in Carbondale. He took a PhD in Strategic Planning from Pittsburgh University in 1983. Since then he has taught at McGill University, Rochester Institute of Technology, and University of Massachusetts-Amherst, prior to his present assignment. He has long been active in the Managerial Cognition movement. He attended the early meeting at Boston University in 1978 and he was one of the active organizers of the

1989 Conference in Washington, D.C. He also played a role in the general movement to establish managerial cognition as an Academy Interest Group. He has recently published in *Journal of Management Studies, Academy of Management Review, Columbia Journal of World Business, Organization Science,* and *Accounting Management and Information Technology.*

About the Contributors

Paul Bacdayan ("Organizational Routines Are Stored as Procedural Memory: Evidence from a Laboratory Study") is a doctoral candidate in Organizational Behavior at the U-M School of Business, and received his MBA from the Amos Tuck School at Dartmouth. His thesis extends production-system-based learning theories to the study of managerial skill acquisition among leaders of quality improvement teams. The thesis develops a procedural-memory-oriented individual-level model of skill in dynamic environments and is intended to further explore the psychological basis of organizational routines. He is also coauthor (with Robert E. Cole and Joseph White) of "Quality, Participation, and Competitiveness," which appeared in the *California Management Review* in 1993.

Richard J. Boland, Jr. ("Designing Information Technology to Support Distributed Cognition") is Professor of Information and Decision Systems and Professor of Accounting, Weatherhead School of Management, Case Western Reserve University. His research over the last 15 years has emphasized interpretive studies of how individuals experience the process of designing, implementing, and using information systems in organizations. Some representative publications have appeared in *Management Science, Accounting, Organizations and Society*, and *Scandinavian Management Review*.

Robert A. Burgelman ("Intraorganizational Ecology of Strategy Making and Organizational Adaptation: Theory and Field Research") is Professor of Management and Director of the Stanford Executive Program (SEP), Graduate School of Business, Stanford University. He has been at Stanford since 1981 and teaches courses in the areas of Strategic Management and Strategic Management of Technology and Innovation. He obtained a Licenciate Degree in Applied Economics from Antwerp University, Belgium (1969). He also obtained an MA in Sociology (1978) and a PhD in Management of Organizations (1980) from Columbia University. He was the recipient of CIM (Belgium) and Ford Foundation (USA) Doctoral Fellowships. He received a Certificate of Distinction for his doctoral dissertation from the Division of Business Policy and Strategy of the Academy of Management and the General Electric Company in 1980. He also received the 1984 Outstanding Paper Award from the Division of Business Policy and Strategy. He has twice received the "Honorable Mention for Distinguished Teaching" from Stanford's MBA students (1986, 1988).

Kumar Chittipeddi ("Symbolism and Strategic Change in Academia: The Dynamics of Sensemaking and Influence") is Associate Professor of Management at Bryant College in Smithfield, Rhode Island. He received his PhD in Business Administration in 1986 at Pennsylvania State University. His research and teaching interests are primarily in the area of strategic management process issues, and the role of the CEO in managing strategic change. His work has been published in various journals including *Strategic Management Journal*. He has served on the boards of the Eastern Academy of Management, the Entrepreneurship Division of the Academy of Management, and the U.S. Association for Small Business and Entrepreneurship.

Shawn M. Clark ("Symbolism and Strategic Change in Academia: The Dynamics of Sensemaking and Influence") received an MA in Organizational Behavior from Brigham Young University in 1989. He is currently a doctoral candidate in the Department of Management and Organization, Pennsylvania State University. His research interests include strategic sensemaking, the relationship between business strategy and information technology, and organizational learning.

Michael D. Cohen ("Organizational Routines Are Stored as Procedural Memory: Evidence from a Laboratory Study") is Professor of Political Science and Public Policy at the University of Michigan and an External Faculty member of the Santa Fe Institute. His current work centers on field and laboratory research on organizational learning and on computer simulation models of organization.

Deborah Dougherty ("Interpretive Barriers to Successful Product Innovation in Large Firms") received a PhD in management from MIT in 1987. Before that she worked as a Head Start teacher, a social worker, and a university administrator. Her research considers problems understanding customer needs, how and why organizational barriers inhibit effective product innovation, and how these underlying barriers can be overcome, especially in large, established organizations. She has published articles in *Organiza-*

tion Science, Strategic Management Journal, Creativity and Innovation Management, California Management Review, and other journals, along with a number of book chapters. After teaching at the Wharton School, she is now Associate Professor of Policy at McGill University, Faculty of Management.

Patricia Doyle Corner ("Integrating Organizational and Individual Information Processing Perspectives on Choice") is Lecturer (Assistant Professor) in strategic management at the University of Waikato. She received her PhD from Arizona State University. Her research interests include strategic decision processes and top management teams (TMTs). In particular, she is interested in TMT characteristics, information processing, and the quality of decisions made by teams.

C. Marlene Fiol ("Consensus, Diversity, and Learning in Organizations") is Associate Professor of Management at the College of Business at the University of Colorado-Denver. She received her PhD in Strategic Management from the University of Illinois, Urbana-Champaign. Her research focuses on cognitive processes in organizations, particularly as these relate to change, learning, and innovation.

Raghu Garud ("A Socio-Cognitive Model of Technology Evolution: The Case of Cochlear Implants") is Associate Professor of Management at New York University, Stern School of Business. He received his PhD from the University of Minnesota. His research interests lie at the interface of technology and strategy. He teaches a course on the management and assessment of technologies at New York University.

Dennis A. Gioia ("Symbolism and Strategic Change in Academia: The Dynamics of Sensemaking and Influence") is Professor of Organizational Behavior in the Department of Management and Organization, Smeal College of Business Administration, Pennsylvania State University. His primary research and writing concern the nature and uses of cognitive processes by organization members and the ways these processes affect sensemaking, influence, and organizational change. Prior to his ivory-tower career, he worked for Boeing Aerospace at Kennedy Space Center and as recall coordinator for Ford Motor in Dearborn, Michigan.

Stanley G. Harris ("Organizational Culture and Individual Sensemaking: A Schema-Based Perspective") is Associate Professor of Management at the College of Business at Auburn University. He received his PhD in Organizational Psychology from The University of Michigan. His research interests revolve around the domains created by the overlap of several topics: organizational change and transformation, organizational culture, strategic human resource management practices, and individual sensemaking. He is an active member of the Academy of Management and also currently serves on the editorial review board of *Human Resource Management.*

Edwin Hutchins ("Organizing Work by Adaptation") is Professor in the Cognitive Science Department at the University of California at San Diego. He received his PhD in cultural anthropology at UCSD in 1978. Before joining the department of Cognitive Science in 1988, he held postdoctoral and research faculty appointments in the Institute for Cognitive Science at UCSD. From 1980 to 1986 he worked as a civilian scientist for the U.S. Navy designing computer-based instruction systems and doing a cognitive ethnography of ship navigation. His primary interests are in the study of cognition in naturally occurring, culturally constituted settings. He received the prestigious John D. and Catherine T. MacArthur Foundation fellowship in 1985.

Barbara W. Keats ("Integrating Organizational and Individual Information Processing Perspectives on Choice") is Associate Professor of Management in the College of Business at Arizona State University. She received her PhD from Oklahoma State University. Her current research interests include organizational downsizing and restructuring, intra- and inter-organizational strategic networks and strategic leadership. Her publications have appeared in such journals as *Academy of Management Journal, Strategic Management Journal, Journal of Management.* She has served on the Executive Committee of the Business Policy and Strategy Division of the Academy of Management, and is a member of the editorial review board of the *Academy of Management Journal.*

Angelo J. Kinicki ("Integrating Organizational and Individual Information Processing Perspectives on Choice") is Professor of Management at Arizona State University. He received his DBA from Kent State University. His research on coping with involuntary unemployment and work stress, performance appraisal, employee selection, and measurement has been published in more than 50 articles. He also is the coauthor of a textbook on organizational behavior. He has worked with management teams from large and small organizations to implement performance management systems. He is the recipient of two teaching awards and a research award from Arizona State University.

Mauri Laukkanen ("Comparative Cause Mapping of Organizational Cognitions") D.Sc. (Econ.), is currently Associate Professor with the Department of Management and Organization, University of Vaasa, Finland. Before that he was with the Helsinki School of Economics, where he also received his doctorate in 1989, having previously worked several years as an SME-CEO.

Nancy Paule Melone ("Reasoning in the Executive Suite: The Influence of Role/Experience-Based Expertise on Decision Processes of Corporate Executives") is Associate Professor of Management at the University of Oregon's Lundquist College of Business. She received her BA, MAIR, and MLIS from the University of Iowa and her MBA (MIS) and PhD from the Carlson School of Management at the University of Minnesota, where she was an IBM Doctoral Fellow and elected to research affiliate status in the Center for Research in Human Learning (Department of Psychology). Her research is eclectic and interdisciplinary, ranging from studies of managerial cognition to analyses of the economic impacts of professionalization of software engineering. She was recently awarded a 3-year appointment as affiliate staff scientist with Pacific Northwest National Labortatory, a U.S. national laboratory. Her work has appeared in *Organization Science, Behavioral and Brain Sciences, Management Science, Organizational Behavior and Human Decision Processes, Journal of Health and Social Behavior, Accounting, Management and Information Technology, Journal of Systems and Software* and several edited volumes, one of which has been translated into Japanese. Her experience as a corporate strategy analyst inspired the study that appears in this volume.

Paul C. Nutt ("The Formulation Processes and Tactics Used in Organizational Decision Making") is Professor of Management Sciences, Management and Human Resources, and Public Policy and Management in the College of Business at Ohio State University. He received his BS and MS degrees from the University of Michigan and his PhD from the University of Wisconsin-Madison in Industrial Engineering. He has over 100 articles to his credit that have received awards from the Academy of Management, Decision Sciences, TIMS, AAMC, ACHCE, and others. His more recent work has been devoted to strategic management, decision making, and leadership. He has written six books. The more recent include: in 1992 (with Robert W. Backoff) *The Strategic Management of Public and Third Sector Organizations* (1992) and *Making Tough Decisions* (1990) and *Managing Planned Change*. The strategic management book received the best book award from the Academy of Management's public and non-profit division in 1994. He serves on several editorial review boards, including that of *The Strategic Management Journal.*

Margaret E. Phillips ("Industry Mindsets: Exploring the Cultures of Two Macro-Organizational Settings") is Assistant Professor of Organization and Management at the School of Business and Management, Pepperdine University. She received her PhD in Management from the University of California, Los Angeles, in 1990. Her research interests include cultural influences on behavior in and of organizations, management development in multicultural contexts, qualitative methods, and arts management.

Richard L. Priem ("Executive Judgment, Organizational Congruence, and Firm Performance") is Associate Professor at the University of Texas at Arlington, where he received his PhD in Strategic Management in 1990. His research on executive judgment, consensus, group decision making, and marketing theory has appeared in the *Strategic Management Journal, Journal of Management, Group and Organization Studies,* and *Journal of the Academy of Marketing Science.*

Michael A. Rappa "A Socio-Cognitive Model of Technology Evolution: The Case of Cochlear Implants") is Associate Professor of Management at the Massachusetts Institute of Technology, Sloan School of Management. He received his PhD from the University of Minnesota. His current research examines the sociology of research communities and the emergence of new technologies. At MIT, he teaches courses in technology assessment and managing R&D.

Dov Te'eni ("Designing Information Technology to Support Distributed Cognition") is Associate Professor of Management Information Systems at Case Western Reserve University. He received his PhD in Managerial Studies from Tel Aviv University. He studies human-computer interaction for managerial work (e.g., the design of feedback in DSS and GDSS). He is also interested in behavioral and organizational aspects of information systems and organizes voluntary computer support for nonprofits.

Ramkrishnan Tenkasi ("Designing Information Technology to Support Distributed Cognition") received his PhD from Case Western Reserve University. His research examines organizational learning in complex and nonroutine task environments such as new product development. Recent publications have appeared in *Journal of Engineering and Technology Management* and *Research in Organizational Change and Development, Volume 7.*

James B. Thomas ("Symbolism and Strategic Change in Academia: The Dynamics of Sensemaking and Influence") is Associate Professor in the Department of Management and Organization, Smeal College of Business Administration, Pennsylvania State University. He received his PhD degree from the University of Texas at Austin in 1988. His current research interests include strategic issue interpretation, top management team information processing, and strategic alignment of business and information technology domains.

Cognition Within and Between Organizations

James R. Meindl
Charles Stubbart
Joseph F. Porac
Editors

Organization Science

SAGE Publications
International Educational and Professional Publisher
Thousand Oaks London New Delhi

For information address:

SAGE Publications, Inc.
2455 Teller Road
Thousand Oaks, California 91320
E-mail: order@sagepub.com

SAGE Publications Ltd.
6 Bonhill Street
London EC2A 4PU
United Kingdom

SAGE Publications India Pvt. Ltd.
M-32 Market
Greater Kailash I
New Delhi 110 048 India

Printed in the United States of America

Library of Congress Cataloging-in-Publication Data

Cognition within and between organizations / editor[s], James R. Meindl, Charles Stubbart, Joseph F. Porac.
p.. cm. — (Organizational science)
Includes bibliographical references and index.
ISBN 0-7619-0113-2 (cloth: acid-free paper) —
ISBN 0-7619-0114-0 (pbk.: acid-free paper)
1. Organizational behavior. 2. Management—Psychological aspects. 3. Human information processing. 4. Cognitive learning. 5. Organizational learning. I. Meindl, James R. II. Stubbart, Charles. III. Porac, Joseph Francis Allen, 1952- . IV. Series: Organizational science.
HD58.8.C62 1996
302.3′5—dc20 96-4525

96 97 98 99 00 10 9 8 7 6 5 6 5 4 3 2 1

Sage Production Editor: Michèle Lingre
Sage Typesetter: Janelle LeMaster

Contents

Part IV: COGNITION BETWEEN ORGANIZATIONS

Introduction

JOSEPH F. PORAC
JAMES R. MEINDL
CHARLES STUBBART

One of the most important developments in organizational science during the past 20 years has been the growing interest in how organizational members conceptualize and make sense of their organizational worlds. This interest is consistent with the general cognitive emphasis of the social sciences during the past three decades as researchers in many disciplines have turned their attention to the epistemic, representational, and constructed aspects of social life. More specifically, however, the cognitive turn within organizational science can be traced to two theoretical developments. One stems from the work of Herbert Simon and his associates (e.g., March and Simon 1958, Simon 1946). Simon's early theories of administrative practice encouraged a bracketing of overly rational theories of organizational action by viewing the quality of managerial decisions as contingent on the psychology of the managerial mind. Simon's work opened the *black box* of organizations and stimulated research on how organizations actually process information about uncertain environments and on how managers make decisions when such information is costly to acquire. The influence of these ideas can be seen very clearly in early research on decision processes (e.g., Mintzberg, Raisinghani and Theoret 1976) and organizational problem solving and learning (e.g., March and Olsen 1976). In addition, Simon's later work on computer models of human thought helped to incite general cognitive theory by encouraging research on artificial intelligence, problem solving, and symbolic representation. Much of modern cognitive science has evolved out of this work and has subsequently provided powerful orienting constructs and a theoretical vocabulary for studying cognitive phenomena across a variety of disciplines. Organizational science has been one of these disciplines.

Second, developments in epistemology (e.g., Rorty 1979), the sociology of science (e.g., Knorr-Cetina 1980), the sociology of knowledge (e.g., Lukes 1982), psychology (e.g., Medin 1989), and organizational science itself (e.g., Weick 1979, 1995) have called into question a strictly realist view of the world in which the environment imposes itself on passive perceivers. Instead, scholars now recognize that people actively construct their environments by combining existing knowledge structures with external information through acts of interpretation (e.g., Weick 1995). As a general approach to knowledge and perception, constructionism breaks down a strict distinction between person and environment by making *the environment* at least partially contingent on the person or group who perceives it, a contingency that makes truth claims relative to a community of believers. This relativity calls into question universal standards of judgment and focuses attention on the local rationalities that predominate at the point of a decision or action. Because local rationalities are embedded in systems of meaning, partly shared and partly idiosyncratic, an understanding of choice and action requires an interpretative stance toward social situations. Much of the interest in how organizational actors think about and frame events and actions has developed out of the acceptance of a constructionist logic by many organizational scholars. That is, if one assumes that organizational actions, at whatever level of abstraction, are driven by local rationalities embedded in larger systems of meaning, it is necessary to unpack these rationalities to explain organizational choice. The growing interest in cognition, both within and between organizations, has coincided (not accidentally) with the increasing legitimacy of a constructionist point of view among organizational scholars.

This volume brings together a series of chapters that exemplifies the research trajectories that have been spawned by these theoretical developments. The topical foci of the chapters vary widely, from cognitive coordination on the bridge of a ship to cultural belief systems in the California wine industry, from strategy formulation at a major university to the evolution of cochlear implant technologies. Despite this variation, however, the contributions to this volume are more similar than they are different in that all are attempts to apply the insights of modern cognitive science to the problems of sense making and decision making in organizations. This commonality creates the book's coherence while simultaneously marking the contributions as being at the cutting edge of cognitive research within and between organizations. In the remainder of this introduction, we will elaborate on this theme by showing how the chapters differ from other strands of related organizational research. We will also address several critical questions in the study of mind and organization.

CONTRASTS AND COMPARISONS WITH OTHER RESEARCH

Historically, the study of organizations in many disciplines—for example, sociology, political science, economics, psychology, and so on—has centered around constructs heavily laced with cognitive connotations. Industrial economists, for example, have for at least a century based their arguments about firm and industry behavior on assumptions about the way the managerial mind uses and combines information on costs, demands, competitors, and profits (e.g., Scherer and Ross 1990). Sociologists have for some time attributed great importance to normative and taken-for-granted beliefs in shaping organizational practices (e.g., Scott 1994); and psychologists have studied the cognitive bases of motivation, employee performance, and leadership for years. The research on organizational cognition represented in this volume must be understood from within this historical context in that it shares with much of its interdisciplinary history a focus on beliefs, perceptions, and decision making. At the same time, however, the confluence of cognitive science and constructionism has brought with it certain theoretical emphases that distinguish more recent cognitive research from its progenitors.

Foremost is an emphasis on meaning and knowledge representation. Early research on and assumptions about cognition within organizations essentially ignored the problem of *meaning* by concentrating on cognitive *processes,* such as the formation of expectations and the calculation of probabilities, or by analyzing cognitive structures, such as beliefs and norms, without the benefit of an explicit theory of knowledge organization. One of the major contributions of modern cognitive research has been a growing sophistication in the use of various systems and nomenclatures for representing managerial and organizational knowledge. Seminal work in organizational science—such as Axelrod's (1976) study of the belief systems of political elites or Bougon, Weick and Binkhorst's (1977) research on collective cognition within a jazz orchestra—suggested two decades ago that the explicit description of knowledge structures in everyday organizational settings was not only possible but very informative in regard to how organizational members construe their world. More recent research has been inspired by these insights, but it has also benefited from developments within general cognitive science that have provided organizational researchers with powerful symbol systems and logics for describing knowledge. Many of these developments had their origins in artificial intelligence research, in which scholars were unable to simply assume the existence of knowledge and meaning but had to build working algorithms to replicate them. The contributions to this volume make heavy use of these tools. Concepts such as schemas, scripts, knowledge structures, causal maps, routines, and semantic networks are used liberally in the following pages to describe the structures of knowledge underlying organizational cognition. These systematic nomenclatures for knowledge representation are one distinguishing feature of modern cognitive research in organizations.

A second distinguishing feature is a focus on *sense making,* as opposed to *calculation.* Historically, a great deal of cognitive research in organizations has examined how managers and other actors make decisions in either certain or uncertain environments. The underlying metaphor of mind on which much of this research is based is one of computation—that is, calculating the benefits and costs of certain actions and maximizing, or at least satisfying, one's utility through behavioral choices. Calculative approaches to managerial thinking are usually associated with the use of mathematical probability models as a universal benchmark with which the quality of managerial judgment can be compared. The research that we have selected for the present volume is based on a very different metaphor of mind. Because the research is embedded in a constructionist view of the world, the issue of whether a choice is correct or incorrect in some abstract mathematical sense is not meaningful. Probability theory is often useful in determining the quality of a managerial choice, but in a constructed world it represents only one of many plausible judgmental benchmarks—one that is itself embedded in a history of scholarship, argument, and theoretical conjecture. Indeed, in a constructed world, the correctness of a particular decision is contingent on the point of view that is being used to evaluate it. Different points of view may result in different opinions about whether a choice was good or bad. This contingency means that the important theoretical substance of managerial cognition is not in the *downstream* choice (or calculation) process but in the *upstream* sense-making process that extracts a pattern of meaning from an inherently ambiguous environment. Thus, the contributions in this volume are much more concerned with sense making than with calculation—that is, with meaning construction and pattern matching rather than with choice.

The focus on meaning construction in the present volume is associated with yet a third distinguishing property of modern cognitive research—a clear emphasis on the social context of organizational and managerial knowledge, on *inter*psychic as opposed to *intra*psychic cognitive phenomena (e.g., Weick 1995). This interest goes beyond the mere recognition that actors think about and make sense of social collectivities, such as industries, organizations, or work groups, to a strong interest in how such collectivities act as *cognitive communities* to shape both the contents and processes of thought itself. Of course, this interest has deep historical roots in the study of collective thought (e.g., Douglas 1986, Moscovici 1983) and is a keystone of modern social constructionism (e.g., Berger and Luckmann, 1967). What makes recent research on organizational cognition distinct, however, is the depth and detail with which scholars probe the collective mind. Just as important is the starting point for these probes. Whereas most traditional cognitive research in organizations started from the perspective of individual minds and asked how individual thinking aggregates into collective cognitive phenomena, more recent research begins with the assumption that all thought is inherently social and asks how individual thinking is derived from the collective cognitive order.

Finally, more recent cognitive research in organizations shows much greater eclecticism in the choice of research methods than has historically been the case. The chapters included within this volume, for example, use methods as divergent as text analysis, ethnography, artificially constructed quasi experiments, questionnaire surveys, and in-depth interviews to capture managerial and organizational cognition. One could argue that methodological breadth is a sign of poor paradigm development and a lack of consensus in regard to which important phenomena to study. With respect to recent cognitive research, however, in our view methodological breadth indicates more that no single method is sufficient to capture the full range of sense making within and between organizations. Indeed, we see methodological eclecticism as a general willingness on the part of cognitive researchers not to become method-bound in their definition of the theoretical problems at hand. For example, to the extent that meaning is proximally contextualized within a particular work group, organization, or industry, it is necessary to embed the study of meaning within the same context. Ethnographic investigation becomes essential. At the same time, any given social aggregate is itself embedded within historical trajectories that play a large role in shaping collective thought and controlling human agency. Therefore, it is important to frame microlevel meaning construction within a wider temporal perspective. In-depth historical and archival data help to do this. An important aspect of the modern attitude toward cognitive research in organizations is the willingness of researchers to explore multiple methods to triangulate the complexity of sense-making processes and structures.

Taken together, these four distinguishing characteristics of modern cognitive research in organizations create the space of theoretical problems that is the subject for this volume. By and large, the volume focuses on meaning, representation, and sense making rather than on calculation and choice, on the social context of thought rather than on individual mental processes. To capture these phenomena, the authors use the wide-angled lens of multiple methods and divergent temporal units. In doing so, they provide an eclectic portrait of the modern sensibility of studying cognition within organizational settings. Embedded within this portrait are a number of key background issues that have been shaping much of the scholarly discourse and research agenda in this area. In the next section, we will examine these issues in detail and show how the contributions to this volume make different choices and trade-offs in dealing with them.

KEY ISSUES IN THE STUDY OF COGNITION WITHIN AND BETWEEN ORGANIZATIONS

Although there seems to be substantial consensus among organizational researchers studying cognition in regard to the core problems of the area and the general approach to addressing these problems, there is nonetheless a good deal of variety in the nuances of particular projects and studies. This variety is important because it suggests that subtle differences of opinion exist with respect to underlying constructs, theoretical foci within the broad sense-making paradigm, and levels of analysis in methodological discourse. These differences seem to revolve around five key issues.

1. What is an appropriate construct system for describing managerial and organizational cognition? It is one thing to emphasize the importance of how managers and organizations make sense of situations and events and quite another to actually describe the *sense* that results from the processes of learning and communication. The latter requires the researcher to develop a nomenclature for describing thought and meaning. Historically, this has been a nontrivial task. Most organizational researchers agree that *interpretations, frames, schemas, assumptions,* and *routines* are part of the sense-making process. The current literature reveals many different frameworks for *mapping* and operationalizing these very imprecise terms. Moreover, there has yet to emerge a consensus about which frameworks are useful for particular types of descriptions.

This diversity is very apparent in the contributions to this volume. The theoretical chapters by Corner, Kinicki, and Keats and by Harris take a very micropsychological approach to sense making within organizations. In keeping with the language of modern cognitive science, both chapters make heavy use of concepts such as schemas and beliefs to describe the knowledge structures inherent in organizational cognition. Implicit in this shared nomenclature is an expectation that cognitive theory has progressed far enough to provide a basis for a consistent theoretical nomenclature. When one goes beyond theory, however, to the actual empirical articulations in some of the other special-issue chapters, it becomes clear that such consistency is more illusory than real. For Laukkanen, cognitive structures are networks of nodes and links that can be operationalized and mapped very precisely. For Garud and Rappa; Gioia, Thomas, Clark and Chittipeddi; and Phillips, the operationalization of thought requires more flexible interpretive methods, whereby the emphasis is less on developing a precise measurement system and more on showing how broadly conceived thought patterns become intertwined with the social circumstances of organizational activities. For Cohen and Bacdayan, knowledge is a set of organizational routines that are coordinating the actions of multiple actors. Fiol measures cognitive structures by coding the verbalizations of organizational actors into broad themes relevant to her research question. Priem measures thought by assessing managerial responses to a questionnaire. Each of these methods has strengths and weaknesses. Their very diversity, however, raises important questions about how far the cognitivist agenda can progress if the operational definitions of apparently similar constructs are so different. One of the greatest challenges facing research on managerial and organizational sense making is the development of consistent standards for defining and measuring cognitive phenomena. In this regard, the chapters in the present volume demonstrate the spectrum of definitional alternatives that must be included in any cognitive systematics.

Compounding the problem of defining and mapping cognitive structures is the fact that such structures are themselves of multiple types. For at least two decades, there has been general recognition in the cognitive science community that the mind is a collection of modular subsystems, each consisting of its own representational logic and process dynamics. Taking Tulving's (1985) work as a starting point, at least three memory subsystems can be distinguished: *semantic* memory, which is the basis for language and conceptual representations; *episodic* memory, which is bound to visual cues and is the basis for specific experiences and event memories; and *procedural* memory, which is heavily action oriented and tacit and which controls skilled behavior. Although the knowledge subserved by each of these systems is partially overlapping (e.g., when a procedural routine is semantically coded in language and labeled with a word or phrase), each system can be analytically separated and treated as a distinct memory domain. In everyday organizational settings, however, the systems converge into integrated knowledge applied to problems at hand. In practice, this makes it difficult to separate the various types of knowledge that are involved in a given organizational setting. The more *macro* the perspective, the more difficult it is to untangle the three types of knowledge. So, for example, the causal knowledge explored by Laukkanen is a relatively pristine case of semantic memory in action. Cohen and Bacdayan's and Hutchins's studies of organizational routines hone in on procedural memories. As we move to higher organizational units, however, this separation begins to break down. Clearly, Dougherty's notion of functional *thought worlds* encompasses semantic, episodic, and procedural knowledge representations. This is true of Phillips's conceptualization of industry culture and Garud and Rappa's technological enactment cycle. The attractiveness of these latter chapters rests on the robustness and integration of their cognitive viewpoint, but it is exactly this robustness that makes it difficult to untangle and represent the underlying cognitive systems involved. Precisely mapping and classifying integrated knowledge in organizational settings represents a major challenge for organizational cognition researchers.

2. *What is an appropriate level of analysis for cognitive research?* The choice of level of analysis (i.e., individual, group, organization, industry, etc.) is an issue confronting most areas of organizational science. It is not surprising, then, that the level of an analysis problem arises in cognitive research as well (e.g., Schneider and Angelmar 1993). The important tension here is very old: Are more aggregated forms of cognition (e.g., group, organization, etc.) derived from cognitive processes at the level of individual persons, or is cognition at the level of persons merely a reflection and articulation of collective-level processes?

The chapters included within this volume demonstrate how critical this question is for shaping the character of cognitive research. For example, Laukkanen necessarily takes a micro-to-macro stance on the matter by mapping the belief structures of individual managers. Laukkanen's detailed individual cognitive measures are noteworthy for their precision and operational validity. However, Laukkanen wants to go beyond the beliefs of managers to say something about collective beliefs at an industry level of analysis. To do this, he is forced to operationalize collective beliefs as an agreement among individual managers. Such consensuality may be a sufficient condition for assuming the existence of collective cognition, but it is hardly a necessary condition. Indeed, to a true collectivist, Laukkanen's analysis would be considered overly reductionistic.

Phillips's interesting study of the California wine and museum industries illustrates some of the opposite problems that are entailed in starting from an explicitly collective level of analysis. She sets out to show that industries are characterized by cultural systems of belief that create "mindsets" shaping the worldviews of industry members. There has been increasing interest among organizational scholars in the cognitive and cultural factors embedded within interorganizational communities (e.g., Powell and DiMaggio 1991). Phillips's comparative method is very informative because it calls into relief the contrasting belief systems of two very different industrial communities. Ethnographic methods allow her to probe different levels of meaning within these two industries and to penetrate very basic assumptions that seem to control the activities of wineries and museums respectively. At the same time, however, her study lacks the precise operationalizations of Laukkanen's. Consequently, the specific linkages between collective level assumptions and individual and organizational level perceptions and attitudes are not well specified. Where Laukkanen's operationalization allows him to begin at an individual level of analysis and define collective level thought patterns precisely and empirically (i.e., intermanager agreement), Phillips's more interpretive methods take the collectivity of thought as given and leave individual level beliefs unspecified and unmeasured. One is left to speculate about the possible *downward* influence of collective belief systems on individual minds.

It is tempting to conclude from these observations that the relationship between individual and collective level beliefs is an intractable philosophical problem rather than an empirical question. Depending on one's epistemological stance, one assumes that thought moves from individual minds to collective minds or vice versa. However, some of the other chapters raise the possibility that the levels-of-analysis question might be reframed more productively as an issue of temporal dynamics. This idea is apparent in the theoretical discussion of Corner et al. but is empirically fleshed out in some detail by Fiol and by Garud and Rappa. Fiol's study, for example, nicely shows how agreements and disagreements about an issue evolve over time within a decision-making group. Rather than simple consensus versus diversity, Fiol's results suggest that it is the temporal, dynamic, linking consensus with diversity that shapes the collective decision environment. Similarly, in Garud and Rappa's study, it is the interplay of two distinct interpretations of efficacy and safety that shape the cognitive evolution of cochlear implant technology. Rather than agreement or disagreement per se, Garud and Rappa's results call attention to the enactment of a belief system over time in which the strength of specific beliefs waxes and wanes as interest groups vie for *interpretive dominance.*

The notion of interpretive dominance holds promise for overcoming some of the intractability of the levels-of-analysis problem. In effect, it injects human agency into the character of belief systems by recognizing that beliefs are actively developed, manipulated, and diffused. Rather than viewing belief systems as being held by individuals, groups, organizations, or industries, the notion of interpretive dominance conceptualizes a belief system as an arena of interest groups (of whatever level of aggregation) vying to impose their preferred psychological order onto nonbelievers. In this sense, the level of aggregation is not particularly important. What is important is who believes what and the power that believers have to impose their assumptions onto others.

Hutchins's study of navigation on a ship represents another approach to this same problem. In Hutchins's view, collective cognition as embodied in organizational routines is a set of interlocked activities defined across a group of actors engaged in goal-directed behavior. The activities and outputs of one actor provide cues triggering appropriate actions by other actors, and this interlocking of modular and local routines characterizes coordinated work in organizational settings. Perhaps because Hutchins is dealing with procedural knowledge, the questions of collective *belief* and collective *representation* are not so obvious. At the procedural level, the issue is one of collective *behavior*, and Hutchins shows how coordinated action can occur within collective settings even though the local routines of individuals are quite distinct. The cognitive glue in Hutchins's Navy ship is a normative order that evolves to coordinate individual action by creating expectations that are triggered by the stimulus properties and constraints of the task setting. As with the case of interpretive dominance, the level of aggregation is not particularly important in Hutchins's analysis. What *is* important is the normative order that creates expectations and coordinates action across interlocked behavioral systems.

3. What is the relationship between cognitive structure and cognitive process? Historically, studies exploring cognition within organizations have tended to emphasize either the processes of thought (individual or collective) or the structures of thought (knowledge representations). Emphasizing the former has meant studying how information and beliefs are combined and used in forming judgments and making decisions. Emphasizing the latter has meant describing knowledge and its inherent organization. There have been few attempts to study both of these aspects of thought simultaneously. Studying one has meant de-emphasizing or assuming away the other. Thus, there are few theoretical frameworks for linking structure and process together in a meaningful and useful way.

This schism is apparent in the present collection of chapters. Phillips, Laukkanen, and Garud and Rappa emphasize the content of managerial thought by mapping specific belief systems and their social effects. Corner et al., Harris, and Nutt are much more process oriented. However, some of the chapters demonstrate that studying process and content are not mutually exclusive. For example, Melone's study of the effects of functional expertise on information usage shows that functionally based expertise leads to different patterns of information usage. Melone finds that corporate development executives place less weight on financial considerations than do chief financial officers in their evaluation of possible acquisition targets. Melone's study shows that by combining a process tracing method with information about functional background, cognitive process and structure can be usefully integrated in a study on individual decision making. This sort of integration, albeit at different levels of analysis, can also be seen in the studies by Fiol, Gioia et al., and Burgelman. These studies demonstrate process-structure integration by showing how collective beliefs evolve over time within the process of strategic problem identification, resolution, and adaptation.

4. What is the relationship between managerial cognition and organizational outcomes? There are strong pressures within the organizational cognition literature to link cognitive processes and structures to important organizational outcomes, such as profitability, innovativeness, and adaptability to change. An underlying theme to this pressure is that cognitive constructs are not very interesting theoretically unless they have measurable effects on organizational performance. Whether or not one agrees with this view, it is easy to understand the motivation to seek out these outcome-related effects. Not only do such linkages legitimize the study of managerial and organizational cognition, but there are also strong anecdotal reasons for believing that the way managers conceptualize and understand their business environment is important for what organizations do and how they perform.

Unfortunately, cognitive constructs are difficult to measure in the field. Even when they are measured, cognition is so intertwined with other organizational variables that it is difficult to isolate their causal impact on behavior and outcomes. The inertial effects of organizational structures, the disruptive effects of uncontrollable and unforeseeable environmental jolts, and myriad other noncognitive factors are all plausible alternative explanations for any supposed influence of cognition on organizational outcomes. Given the complexity of factors affecting organizational outcomes, how is it possible to assess the specific impact of difficult-to-measure cognitive variables?

One research strategy that has shown some success has been to use the demographic characteristics of managerial actors and teams as proxies for specific cognitive constructs. Thus, for example, if one argues that top management cognitive heterogeneity is important in responding to uncertain environments, then one can use heterogeneity of managerial background characteristics as an indicator of cognitive differences as well. Although this strategy is reasonable as far as it goes, clearly it is preferable to measure cognitive structure and processes directly and relate these direct measures to organizational outcome variables.

In this volume, the chapters by Priem, Burgelman, Dougherty, and Hutchins come closest to examining the relationship between cognition and organizational outcomes. Priem's research is an interesting and important addition to the cognitive literature. In his study, CEOs of manufacturing firms were asked to complete a judgment task that required them to reveal their beliefs about the linkages between strategy, structure, and environment. Priem then compared these beliefs to the prescriptions of organizational-environment fit in the organizational literature. Priem's results suggest that firms whose CEOs have beliefs that are more consistent with theoretical prescriptions outperform those firms whose CEOs have less consistent beliefs. What is particularly important about these results is Priem's careful direct assessment of managerial judgment policies and the explicit linkages he builds between these policies and organizational performance. This work goes far in showing how researchers can tease apart, in theoretically useful ways, the cognition-behavior-performance nexus.

Burgelman's case study of strategic adaptation at Intel is a counterpoint to Priem's emphasis on top management cognition in showing that strategic change depends on widely dispersed and routinized decision criteria that winnow out arguments and narrow a firm's strategic focus. It is clear from Burgelman's arguments that strategic decisions at Intel are shaped by organization-wide administrative selection systems that have become part of the company's planning process. These selection mechanisms have their effect by shaping managerial incentives even in the absence of shared beliefs. In fact, selection systems are designed to forge consensus of action even when consensus of belief may not exist. Burgelman argues that selection mechanisms provide the strategic stability around which Intel has built its business. At the same time, however, these selection mechanisms tend to narrow the strategic focus of the company, making strategic change difficult. Adaptation to new business realities comes about through what Burgelman calls "autonomous strategic processes" that operate outside routine selection systems to create new options for the company. Crucial to these autonomous processes are the efforts of issue entrepreneurs who build their own resource pools and are eventually persuasive enough to convince others of the viability of a course of action. In showing how key strategic decisions flow in and around the nooks and crannies of Intel, Burgelman's study demonstrates that organizational choice and action is hardly the exclusive province of the top management team. Burgelman's study embeds strategic change in dispersed organizational processes, thus complicating any attempt to directly link top management beliefs to what organizations actually do and accomplish.

Dougherty's investigation of new product introductions shows how these complications can be used to good effect in the study of cognition-action relationships lower down in organizational hierarchies. After studying 18 new product introductions at five different firms, Dougherty concludes that functional differentiation within organizations creates distinct *thought worlds* that are oriented toward specific problems and cultures of each functional group. These thought worlds influence what people anticipate about the future, their individual priorities in the product development process, and the way they make sense of the product development process itself. Manufacturing personnel are short-term oriented, whereas product planners are oriented toward long-term trends. Technologists are focused on technical issues, whereas field personnel are customer driven. According to Dougherty, these divergent cognitive sets create barriers to coordinated action if organizations fail to provide appropriate and powerful integration mechanisms that can meld the different perspectives together in a unified approach to developing, building, and selling new products. In Dougherty's research, successful product introductions were associated with good functional integration, whereas unsuccessful products were not. In some sense, Dougherty's conclusion harkens back to Hutchins's results in recognizing the importance of a higher-level normative order that can serve to coordinate divergent cognitive subsystems. In many ways, this is the same conclusion that Burgelman reached in his study of Intel.

5. What role should cognitive aids *have in shaping managerial and organizational cognition?* To the extent that there is some relationship between the way managers and organizations think and important organizational outcomes, it makes sense to ask whether such thinking can be *improved* with appropriately designed *cognitive aids,* such as decision and executive support systems or management information systems. If certain thought structures and processes are associated with more desirable organizational outcomes than others, should it not be possible to enhance the former and make the latter less likely through appropriate thinking technologies? If cognitive research is to have any managerial significance, should not the design of such technologies be a prime directive?

The role of cognitive aids in shaping managerial thought raises many thorny epistemological issues concerning rationality and the criteria used in evaluating the quality of, for example, a CEO's thinking. These issues are much too complex to treat adequately in this introduction. Philosophy aside, however, there are very practical questions involved in the use of cognitive aids that lie squarely within the province of research and theory in managerial cognition. Many of these questions are covered in a very creative way by Boland, Tenkasi, and Te'eni's chapter on supporting distributed cognition within organizations. These authors take issue with much of the current literature on cognitive aids by suggesting that too much emphasis has been placed on individual decision making and not enough attention has been given to collective problem formulation and problem solving. Drawing extensively from the literature on managerial thinking, Boland et al. suggest that managerial and organization cognition is open-ended and exploratory, whereas most current cognitive aids are built around closed systems of rules or models that have been derived either statistically or through expert knowledge engineering. To overcome these constraints, Boland et al. outline a set of principles for designing hermeneutic inquiry systems to support distributed cognition within organizations. Their own SPIDER system is based on these design guidelines and shows promise as an alternative to overly mechanistic cognitive aids that are motivated more by engineering principles than by research on the managerial mind. If successful, inquiry technologies such as SPIDER will fundamentally alter the form of cognitive aids in organizations. Perhaps it is not too much to expect that such support systems will be useful spinoffs from the burgeoning literature on managerial and organizational cognition.

SUMMARY

As might be expected, the five questions we have outlined above are so fundamental that it is unreasonable to expect easy answers within the boundaries of a single volume. Nonetheless, collectively, the 15 chapters that follow represent a good cross section of recent scholarship in this area of research. Each addresses one or more of the above questions in a unique and thoughtful way, and each provides the reader with a look into a particular corner of the research literature. We feel that this volume can legitimately be viewed as state of the art because it highlights some of the promises and challenges for future research. We also see examples of how some critical issues can be resolved, overcome, or skirted by good conceptual fundamentals and solid research designs.

REFERENCES

Axelrod, R. (1976), *Structure of decision,* Princeton, NJ: Princeton University Press.

Berger, P. L. and Luckmann, T. (1967), *The social construction of reality,* New York: Doubleday Anchor.

Bougon, M. G., Weick, K. E., and Binkhorst, D. (1977), "Cognition in organizations: An Analysis of the Utrecht Jazz Orchestra," *Administrative Science Quarterly,* 22, 606-639.

Douglas, M. (1986), *How institutions think,* New York: Syracuse University Press.

Knorr-Cetina, K. (1980), *The manufacture of knowledge: An essay on the constructionist and contextual nature of science,* Elmsford, NY: Pergamon.

Lukes, S. (1982), *Rationality and relativism.* Cambridge: MIT Press.

March, J. G. and Olsen, J. P. (1976), *Ambiguity and choice in organizations,* Bergen, Norway: Universitetsforlaget.

March, J. G. and Simon, H. A. (1958), *Organizations,* New York: John Wiley.

Medin, D. L. (1989), "Concepts and conceptual structure," *American Psychologist, 44,* 1469-1481.

Mintzberg, H., Raisinghani, D., and Theoret, A. (1976), "The Structure of 'Unstructured' Decision Process," *Administrative Science Quarterly, 21,* 2.

Moscovici, S. (1983), "The Phenomenon of Social Representations," in R. M. Farr & S. Moscovici (Eds.), *Social Representations* (pp. 1-83), Cambridge, UK: Cambridge University Press.

Powell, W. W. and DiMaggio, P. J. (1991), *The new institutionalism in organizational analysis.* Chicago: University of Chicago Press.

Rorty, R. (1979), *Philosophy and the Mirror of Nature,* Princeton, NJ: Princeton University Press.

Scherer, F. M. and Ross, D. (1990), *Industrial Market Structure and Economic Performance* (3rd ed.), Boston: Houghton Mifflin.

Schneider, S. C. and Angelmar, R. (1993), "Cognition in Organizational Analysis: Who's Minding the Store?" *Organizational Studies, 14*(3), 347-365.

Scott, R. W. (1994), *Institutions and Organizations,* Thousand Oaks, CA: Sage.

Simon, H. A. (1946), *Administrative Behavior,* New York: Macmillan.

Tulving, E. (1985), "How Many Memory Systems are There?" *American Psychologist, 40*(4), 385-398.

Weick, K. E. (1979), *The Social Psychology of Organizing* (2nd ed.), Reading, MA: Addison-Wesley.

Weick, K. E. (1995), *Sensemaking in Organizations,* Thousand Oaks, CA: Sage.

Part I

INDIVIDUAL COGNITION WITHIN ORGANIZATIONS

1

Comparative Cause Mapping of Organizational Cognitions

MAURI LAUKKANEN

Increasingly, thoughtful managers recognize the role of knowledge and learning in corporate action and performance. Concurrently, a new field, management and organization cognition (MOC), has emerged producing useful insights and findings. Thus far, empirical studies have largely focused on single cases or actors, using often archival data and sometimes ambiguous methods. To advance the field will require pragmatic tools for eliciting data on thinking in real organizations and for conducting rigorous and more comparative studies of management and organization cognitions.

This chapter describes a method for comparatively studying real-life managerial thinking, defined here as the respective manager's beliefs about key phenomena and their efficacy links in their strategic and operative situations. The applicability of such a definition will depend on the requirements of research at hand. The payoff is that, thus defined, key elements in managerial and organizational cognitions can be usefully captured by cognitive mapping, an established approach in MOC research.

The approach contains, first, a method for eliciting comparison- enabling interview data of several subjects. Then, using researcher-based, interpretive standardization of the individual natural discourses, databases of standard concepts and causal links, constituting the cause map elements, are distilled. This facilitates a text-oriented description of the thinking patterns of single actors like managers or organizational groups, which can be used in traditional-type mapping studies, which typically assume unitary or quasiunitary actors. However, the method is

This chapter originally appeared in *Organization Science,* Vol. 5, No. 3, August 1994.

intended for comparative analyses, e.g., for pinpointing the cognitive differences or similarities across organizational actors or for constructing and comparing groups, assumed cognitively homogeneous. Also, it is applicable for longitudinal studies or aggregated, e.g., industry-level, descriptions of MOC. A PC application is available for the technique, although many of the processing tasks are amenable to general-purpose relational database software.

The chapter presents a study case comparing the cognitive structures of managers in two interrelated industries in terms of their concept bases and causal beliefs. The objective was to understand the substance of management thinking, as well as the formative logic behind how managers come to think in shared ways. It is shown that patterns of industry-typical core causal thinking, manifestations of a dominant logic or recipe, can be located, operationalized, and comparatively analyzed with this method. Substantively, the contents of management thinking are typically products of complex long-term mechanisms. These consist, first, of organizational problem-solving, recurrently facing a specific, adequately stable constellation of strategic tasks and environment elements, similar within industries and systematically different across them, and, second, of various social processes, which directly transfer and influence management thinking. The chapter concludes with discussing the cause mapping method and suggests some options for further studies.

(COGNITIVE MAPPING; CAUSE MAPPING;
COMPARATIVE COGNITIVE ANALYSIS;
INDUSTRY COGNITION; MANAGEMENT COGNITION;
ORGANIZATION COGNITION; COMPUTERIZED
SOCIAL RESEARCH METHODS; CMAP)

INTRODUCTION

Scientific and pragmatic interest in management organization cognition (MOC) has increased markedly in recent years, as manifested in key books (Axelrod 1976, Eden et al. 1979, Huff 1990, Sims and Gioia 1986), special issues of journals (deGeus 1992, Porac and Thomas 1989, Eden 1992) and in specialized workshops and seminars. Propelling the movement is a shared vision of cognition as a key factor underlying social action and performance in organizations. By cognition the field refers broadly to various individual- and organization-level phenomena, related to the acquisition, kinds, uses, and implications of knowledge, beliefs, or intelligence.

The MOC field has proved a meeting ground for many paradigms, producing considerable diversity. Most salient among the contributors are those with an individualistic cognitive psychology base, with links to the Artificial Intelligence community, and those with sociological and interpretivist backgrounds. Thus, there may exist rather divergent ideas about proper research objectives, and of how organizational cognitions are best studied, interpreted, and differentiated vis-à-vis cognitions at the individual level. On the other hand, there are interests, problems, and constraints which may be shared, at least among empirically oriented researchers.

First, empirical research needs tools to help process and analyze raw data so that the study object, organizational cognitions, whatever the definition employed, can be described in a stable manner. So far a typical approach has been to use, in a hermeneutic tradition, texts as the description vehicle, based on the researcher's interpretation of the raw data and their thematic contents. Often most adequate, such methods can impose difficulties in comparing and aggregating the cognitions of several subjects, intended to track the differences, sharedness, or evolution of cognitions.

Second, MOC research often uses raw data that originates at the individual level; e.g., CEOs or a management team may be interviewed and a secondary text derived of the raw data to serve as a proxy for the organizational cognitions, argued to represent what the organization thinks. However, it is useful to have additional tools to help construct aggregated models of organizational cognitions.

Third, there are pragmatic data-acquisition and data-analysis constraints, most salient if one contrasts typical MOC studies with the highly detailed knowledge acquisition and representation modes of Expert Systems (cf. e.g., Cooke 1992). They may take hundreds of interview and programming hours, seldom feasible in real-life MOC studies. Besides, for all their sophistication, ES tools are not meant for comparative analyses, which is what many MOC studies need.

The cumulative effects of such influences are conspicuous: MOC studies so far typically gravitate towards single cases, use archival data instead of interview- or observation-based data, and employ sometimes rather nonrigorous methods for data processing and analysis. Also, the constraints can hamper important MOC research, e.g., studies of small and medium-size enterprises (SMEs) or intraorganizational and comparative-design studies, which all are dependent on locally acquired data.

This chapter presents an approach that deals with some of the above problems. It defines and describes organization and management cognitions in terms of *cause maps,* which are constructed of interview data and analyzed using accessible *database* techniques,[1] which facilitate the critical comparison and *aggregation* operations. Thus, we can describe the subjective concepts and causal ideas of a manager, a manager team; or any group in an organization or an industry. Specifically, the method facilitates comparative analyses, which are a precondition for examining the cognitive differences or similarities and for creating and comparing cognitively unitary groups. Also, it can support longitudinal studies or aggregated descriptions of MOC at several levels of analysis.

The chapter consists of four sections. First, there is a brief discussion of cognitive mapping especially in MOC studies. Next, the CMAP approach for comparative cause mapping is described. The third section presents excerpts of a study to illustrate the method. Lastly, cognitive methods and some possibilities for substantive and method-related research projects are discussed.

Mapping Organizational Cognitions

MOC research must conceptualize[2] what exists or goes on in human minds at individual or organizational level of analysis (Evans 1988, Gordon 1992, Laukkanen 1990, Regoczei and Hirst 1992). The obvious difficulty is that such phenomena, whether linked to individuals or some social unit, are not directly observable. Their study builds on what can be experienced, e.g., as oral communication. In addition, we need representation tools, media, or formalisms to model the unseen cognitive structures and/or processes. They help capture and analyze the information embedded in raw data about the substance assumed to hide in the Ss' [subjects'] minds.

There is nothing unusual about the processes. Every day we infer people's thinking, beliefs, or knowledge and inform others of our thoughts, using the medium of language. Moreover, we rarely doubt the validity of such epistemological operations, although there is plenty of reason for that (Evans 1987, Hogarth 1985). However, in cognitive MOC studies, we need empirical methods that are more rigorous, yet feasible in terms of typical real-life resources.

Cause Mapping

Originally, *cause*[3]*maps* refer to directed graphs (e.g., Hage and Harary 1983) which consist of *nodes* (terms) and *arrows* that link them. The nodes stand for concepts, phenomena which their owners, such as managers, subjectively seem to perceive in their domains. The arrows represent their beliefs about efficacy (causal) relationships among the phenomena. A configuration of such interlinked concepts and beliefs can thus model the patterns of causal thinking of a person or a group.

The notion that cognitive/cause mapping is a device for representing or mapping some phenomena into another system of description has some *implications*. First, the information, which is traditionally presented visually as graphical maps, can have other overt formats. These include natural language-like text or a matrix often used in mapping studies (Axelrod 1976, Eden et al. 1979, Ramaprasad and Poon 1985, Roos and Hall 1980, Stubbart and Ramaprasad 1988). Another option introduced in this approach are *databases* that contain the information about the Ss' cognitions. There, the causal node-arrow-node elements (or matrix entries) will correspond to databases records (table rows). As will be shown, this has considerable advantages for the comparison and aggregation of individual cognitions.

Second, the mapping of cognitions must usually be based on human *communication* collected by interviewing or found in documents such as corporate reports or memos. We are looking there for expressions having the general type: "Phenomenon/entity *A* leads to /causes/is followed by/ influences/etc./phenomenon/entity *B*," or "*B* is an outcome of /caused/ effected/preceded/influenced /etc./ by *A*." These are *causal assertions*, which are taken to indicate that the Ss (a) possess and in some sense use *concepts* (*A*, *B*) to refer to some phenomena in their domain, and (b) think (believe, know, assume, argue, etc.) that there are certain *efficacy relationships* between the phenomena. These may be called the subjects' phenomenological and causal beliefs (Sproull 1981), or manifestations of their subjective ontologies (Schutz 1962, Sowa 1984).

Everyday Cognition: Implications for Mapping

Management and organization cognitive mapping is influenced by general human cognitive tendencies. These include, first, that people are *limited* in their epistemological capabilities (e.g., Hogarth 1985). They are skillful but also fallible and systematically biased in perception and inference. They may exhibit tendencies towards cognitive economizing, favoring tried or quick-and-dirty solutions, and social copying instead of direct learning. Second, human intelligence and thinking have a task-oriented and domain-bound and thus a *localized* quality. In management, knowledge is pursued, not for art's sake, but to be used functionally for survival and other less distant, practical ends (Evans 1987, Scribner 1986). Third, the *memory* of, say, a manager, is not a filing system with a linear structure and a transparent interface. Memory access and processing (i.e., decisions, solutions, or answers to an interviewer's questions) are association- and stimulus-dependent and linked with the cognitive task and domain at hand (Evans 1987, 1988; Lord 1991).

Fourth, in organizations, various *contextual* factors, such as those modeled in *groupthink*-phenomena (Janis 1982), influence what will happen.

The research implications of such findings are complex and difficult to generalize. However, it seems safe to assume that we generally need to tap those elements and aspects of managers' cognition that are most likely to "count," i.e., are probably in play when corporate action is contemplated and decided. This logic should be manifest in the modes of raw data acquisition and their subsequent analysis.

To elaborate, *data acquisition* in MOC studies should probably ideally use more long-term local observation and/or researcher involvement with management and the organization. This is, of course, seldom feasible, but we may at least be able to design the acquisition so that it approximates real-life situations and elicits probably authentic thinking procedures and operative knowledge/beliefs. The probing and the format of our questions and interviewing should "localize," "domainize," and multiply the Ss' cognitive response processes during the interviewing (cf. Klein 1992). With documentary data, analogically, we might prioritize action-concurrent material, if possible.

Similarly, *mapping analysis,* if it is about studying actual cognitions and their implications, should build on cognitive representations, e.g., types of cause maps, that approximate the "real thing," i.e., pertain to memory contents and/or relatively stable traces of processing, which have a high probability of being accessed or to occur. Thus, when analyzing natural map systems (databases), we should prefer locally meaningful, "humanly possible" subareas of thc total map configuration and not treat everything in the full map database on an equal basis. The grounds for this seem obvious. Map systems based on natural data can contain hundreds of concepts and thousands of causal units. Although they did originate with the Ss, this is not equivalent with the same Ss also being able or likely to access them as similar interlinked systems of knowledge. Raw-data elicitation and real-life problem solving involve partially different processes and contexts. Cognitive limitations and problems of memory access play a role, too. Thus, when processing large map configurations we may inadvertently create and link phenomena which are not normally linked at all, although a path, even a short one, may formally exist in the database. Accordingly, such linkages could be artificial and the conclusions based on such findings possibly problematic.

Organizational cognitions involve additional problems. A relevant issue for mapping studies concerns the weight given to *shared* cognitions, e.g., the dominant or common patterns in thinking (Langfield-Smith 1992, Prahalad and Bettis 1986) versus something else.

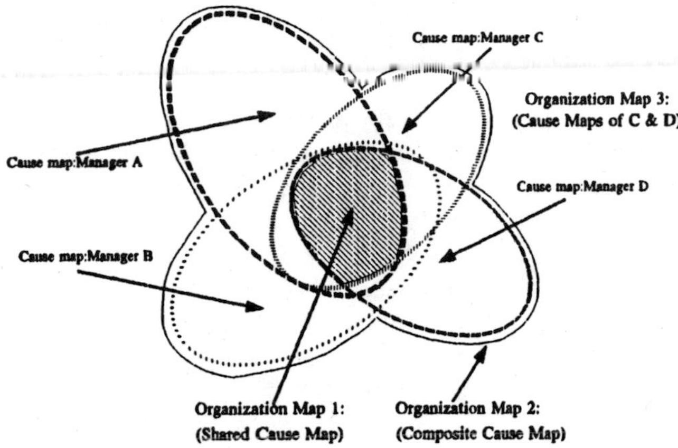

Figure 1.1. Cause Map Definition Options for Organization Cognition

Organizations can and do function, indeed it is their *raison d'être,* without the right hand knowing what the left is doing. The actual division of labor varies over organizations, persons, tasks, and contexts, even within otherwise homogeneous groups of firms. The internal balance of power can evolve, too (Hall 1984).

The organizational context can be described in mapset terms (Figure 1.1). The circles represent cause maps of the manager team in a firm for a key action domain. The intersection would depict the fully shared causal elements. It seems that the meaningful definition will be relative and depends on the task and the context. Sometimes, the consensual thinking could be important, e.g., if local decision making makes it so. Sometimes OC should be defined, instead, as the full area, irrespective of sharedness, or as some single actor's map or sometimes as something in-between. This would match the common situation, where the responsibilities are informally divided and the team members learn to rely on each other's judgment. Thus, the issue can be decided *in casu,* using knowledge of local practices, tasks, and research interests. The researcher must try to find out what is probable and relevant in his/her context. This implies, e.g., the inclusion of the right persons into the informant set and a good grasp of the probable processes of interaction. The present approach flexibly supports different combinations of cause maps, once the data are there.

CMAP—COMPARATIVE CAUSE MAPPING

Let us assume a study project, which involves the description and comparison of organizational cognitions (OC) in two sets of firms. We will define OC as the core patterns of natural managerial thinking of the CEOs, known to us through their responses during interviews, and consider it adequate to focus specifically on the *phenomena* the CEOs/organizations perceive in their worlds, enact (Weick 1977, Smircich and Stubbart 1985), and the *efficacy* or causal links they believe exist among those entities. For the expository purpose it is not critical if this is, indeed, an optimal way to define OC. However, it is not an unusual interpretation, and, specifically for SMEs, often controlled by individual entrepreneur-managers, it may be the logical definition (cf. Cossette and Audet 1992).

This kind of research would face two tasks. First, the acquired data must eventually support the construction of valid and *comparative* operationalizations of the organizational cognitions. Second, the raw data must be distilled into a format that enables the description and comparison of the OC in a study-relevant manner. Such problems are not, of course, totally novel. An interpretively oriented researcher (or consultant) would interview the CEOs and produce a secondary text, which in his/her judgment contains the gist of the CEOs' thinking, as interpreted within the research framework (cf. Donaldson and Lorsch 1983, Spender 1989). A researcher with a quantitative bent would put the transcripts through a variant of-content analysis, assessing the occurrence, timing, and relative weight of various concepts, or locate and compare the underlying discourse themes (cf. Huff 1990, Potter and Wetherell 1990, Tesch 1989). However, the tasks would also be manageable by *comparative cause mapping*. The main phases of such an approach (Figure 1.2) will be discussed next, after which we examine a study case, which did utilize such an approach.

Acquiring Raw Data for Comparing Cognitions

To be usable as a basis for *comparable* cause maps (or equivalent) of *many* subjects (Ss), an elementary requirement is that our probing and the produced data pertain to identical topics, issues, or domains of action, uniform over the Ss. However, the difficulty may be that we do not know, a priori, what those domains or topics are and what local terminology is relevant and effective as probes. Moreover, we should get this right during our first pass of the field. Therefore, a *two-phased approach* is used by the present approach for data elicitation (cf. Bougon 1983; Bougon et al. 1977, 1990):

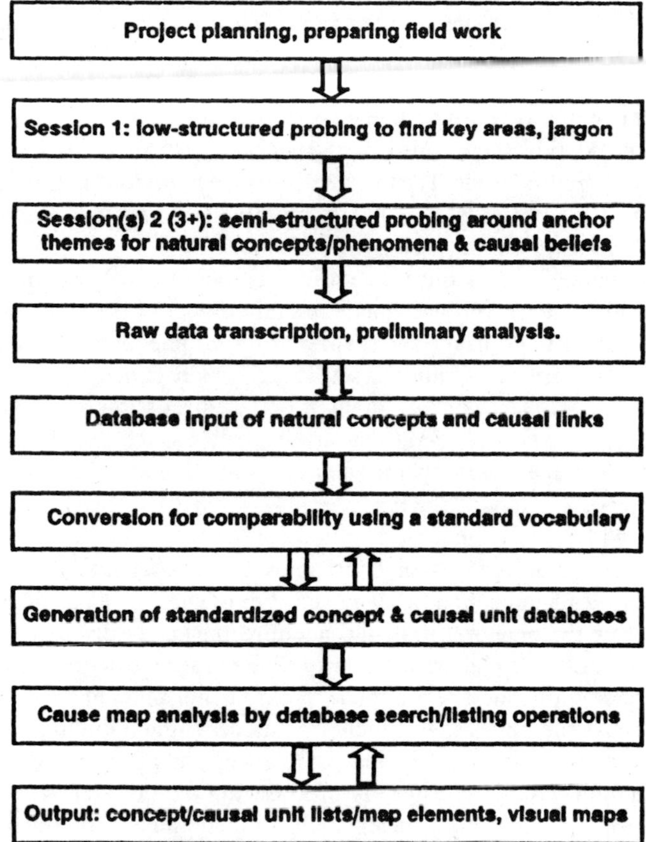

Figure 1.2. Phases of a CMAP Process

- 1st interview session (S1): targeted towards collecting background information and, specifically, locating of domain key issues and jargon to serve in S2-3 as "anchor" concepts.

- 2nd interview sessions (S2-3): eliciting the Ss' subjective concepts and causal beliefs ("causes"/"effects" of the anchor concepts) using successive subdiscussions around a set of common anchors.

In *S1*, the respondents' thinking for key areas of the business, or whatever the research task demands, is covered without strict prestructuring to minimize the risk that the researcher's preconceptions inadvertently determine the responses. For example, an approach is to use open-ended discussions around general, yet domain-relevant topics, such as descriptions of the business or its key success or crisis factors. When the Ss discuss and explain them, they eventually resort to domain-specific jargon, which should also be encouraged. At this stage, sensitive issues are best avoided, keeping the discourse on a neutral basis. The talks will surface numerous key action areas and topics of the business or industry, manifested in typical shared, often recurring local expressions used by the subjects.

The discourses in S1s must be uniformly noted and transcribed afterwards. Besides the background data, the main object of the analysis are the terminology and word-usage for the key referent phenomena, as it occurs over the Ss. The target is to choose a set (15-25) of key concepts (phenomena) to be used as so-called *"anchor" themes,* i.e., as discussion hubs, during the next interview stage (S2, S3). The criteria are especially their research relevance, coverage of key operative or strategic domains, and their unambiguous sharedness among the respondents.

In *S2* (and S3, etc.), the logic is to induce the Ss to talk, for each anchor concept, about its antecedents and outcomes, i.e., the "causes" and "effects" of the referent phenomenon, as *they* see them. The same probing style is repeated over the anchors: first, the anchor concept is discussed and the respondent is asked to elaborate it briefly. The purpose is to understand what each respondent includes within the referent anchor phenomenon. Thereafter, the discussion moves to the anchor's antecedent and outcome phenomena, first simply asking the Ss what the "causes and effects" are in *his/her* mind. The interviewer can carefully prod during the production, by asking the Ss to provide additional concepts and to elaborate on the linkages (see below). When the autonomous flow of the subjective cause or effect phenomena clearly dries up, the "other side" is taken up similarly. Often ideas will turn out and will be added to the earlier subdiscussion context.

We seek valid, reliable data, within feasible limits. *Validity* may be understood here as *authenticity* and *sincerity* of the elicited causal assertions, and *reliability* as a high level of response *consistency, uniformity* over the Ss (cf. Axelrod 1976, Huff 1990). No simple magic can produce data quality. Some of the things to observe include careful management of atmospheric issues; preparation and use of instructions, possibly with neutral examples; uniform probing; productive, positive questioning modes (indirect, nonpersonal), and finally, adequate attention to the Ss' response uniformity and their state of vigilance. Most of these things are obvious but deserve attention all the same. For instance, it is important but sometimes difficult to start the interviews properly. There is also a paradox in mapping research: sophisticated, busy managers should feel genuinely committed to talk about things, which for them are trivial, although for the researcher *everything,* not only the esoteric or innovative, may be critical to hear in order to validly capture the real-life, everyday thinking base. Therefore, it is important to alert the Ss about the trap and pay continuous attention to it along the road, too.

When probing for cognitive mapping, it is essential to observe how human memory normally works. Raw data volume and quality depend on the number and format of probing, in this case, the anchors and the actual probing around them. The Ss will transform them into successive memory search and/or ad hoc production processes (Gordon 1992). Because thinking and memory have a local, situation- and domain-bound character, and an association-based entry, we should create multiple occasions for the access; e.g., it is helpful to provide the Ss multiple and localized probes, accomplished, first by the anchor-approach of S2-S3 and second by inducing Ss to think about the phenomena using several viewpoints instead of asking for linear lists of "causes and effects." Thus, the Ss might consider cases where the anchors, e.g., the firm's liquidity or market share, assume a high or a low value or exhibit highly critical or very desirable situations. Often the thinking emerges best when Ss[4] elaborate their methods for controlling or adapting to the phenomena.

In a comparative study, *consistency and relevance,* i.e., reliability, over the interviews is important. This is also partly accomplished by the uniform anchor themes. Further, the Ss should be allocated uniform airtime with some allowance for differences in fluency or vigilance. The subtopics, anchors, can be taken up in uniform or a random order, but, if optimum memory access is preferred, they could be arranged so that logically or operatively related domains are close. There are, of course, more mundane considerations, as well. For instance, faced with risks of losing respondents during a long series of interviews, it is prudent to pack into S2 the anchors that at least salvage most of the project.

This kind of *"semi-structured"* interviewing usually produces a lot of raw data, partly redundant. To maintain flow and a productive atmosphere, it is suggested that we should, within limits, just *capture all data* and defer the processing, compression, pruning, etc. to be taken care of later in a separate stage. To handle the data mass, effective capturing tools are needed. A workable technique for the S2 notes is to use a prepared *form,* which resembles a cause map format with the anchor concept in the middle, with slots for the "causes and effects" around it, and with room for comments. Of course, a recording device would be very useful as a backup tool, if agreed upon.

The result of the S2-S3 interviews are the notes, possibly recordings, too. They contain large numbers of the Ss' expressions having the general type: *A affects B* or *C is affected by D.* This constitutes the raw data, and, if we have several Ss, there will be many such data sets. With a lot of such material, it is advisable to first *distill* of the notes and tapes the elicited natural terms (A, B) and the causal assertions (A->) using *intermediate forms.*[5] Such transcripts are necessary if computer input is needed. and they can make auditing and tracking work more rigorously and fast.

For brevity, we will use the acronym *NLU* (= natural language units) to refer to the acquired terms or words (A, B), and *NCU* (= natural causal unit) for the causal assertions (A causes/leads to/etc. B). Most NLUs refer to the (subjective) causes or effects of the anchors, used as discussion hubs. Often the probing also elicits script-like event paths or scenarios, which adds to the elicited NLU and NCU number. Some NLUs and NCUs, especially those referring to some central issue like profitability or market share, come up more than once. This is normal, especially if there is time between S2 and S3.

Creating and Using Standard Vocabularies

To compare individual actors' cognitive maps, the natural language expressions (NLUs) underlying them must usually be first *standardized.* The intuitive reason is the *redundancy* caused by synonyms, common in mapping data, especially elicited for established domains of domain professionals. A rich language, jargon, typically develops for the local conceptualization and communication tasks. In MOC mapping, however, we must penetrate through this to the actual referent phenomena.

Figure 1.3 clarifies standardizing. The upper array consists of *natural terms (NLUs)* used by the respondents to express their knowledge/beliefs about the causal links. The lower part displays three *standard terms (STs),* interpreted to represent the referent phenomena to which the richer natural language pertains. Thus, the NLUs, considered synonymous, are figuratively put into the same meaning baskets. In the subsequent data processing, this means that the NLUs will be replaced by their standard terms, e.g., *liquidity.* As a consequence, also the *natural causal assertions (NCUs)* will be converted into a set of *standardized causal units (SCUs).* Importantly, the database method can also generate information about the *ownership,* i.e., the user distribution, of each *used* ST and SCU.

Using a database, the standardizing can be done elegantly by linking the NLUs with the respective standard term vocabulary database by entering to the NLU database the correct ST code. The essential task, however, is to locate the *referent phenomena* behind the natural expressions of the Ss, embedded in the captured discourse. Ideally, each standard concept should refer to a *unique* phenomenon or entity. This implies a thorough understanding, even empathizing, so as to comprehend the *cognitive base* of the

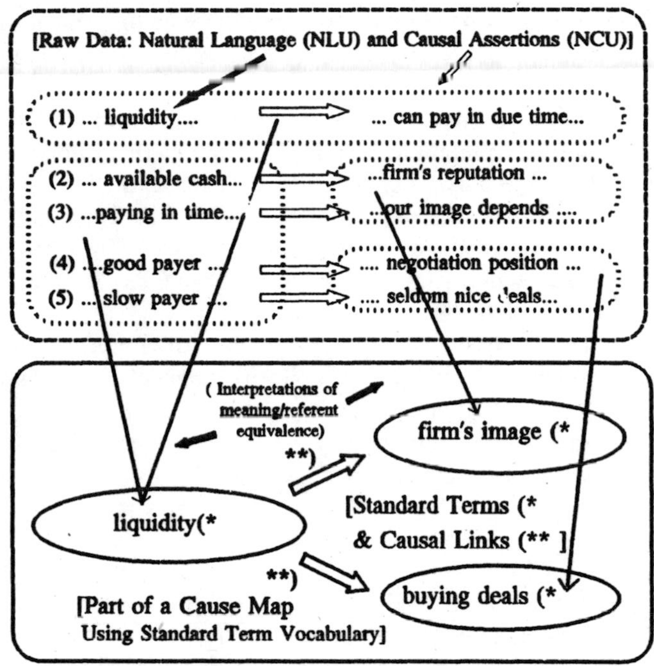

Figure 1.3. Standardizing Raw Terms and Causal Assertions for Cause Maps

respective actors about their domain. The result of the work is a system of *standard terms,* a *vocabulary.* It consists of descriptive plain language terms, which also have a shorthand code, standard term tag (STAG), such as D01 in Table 1. In a database approach, the vocabulary occupies its own independent database file. It is technically possible and often advantageous that this database can contain more standard terms than are finally needed in a given project. Their actual use will be decided in the linking, when the NLUs are tagged with standard codes.

It is clear that such a mapping from one vocabulary system to another is critical. On one hand, for meaningful, functional comparison, it may be unavoidable to convert the idiosyncratic, synonymous responses into a common vocabulary. On the other, sloppy work weakens the preconditions of valid representation and analysis of the underlying cognitions. The solutions depend on the researcher's field knowledge, interpretation acumen, and meticulousness. It can involve tedious, iterative work. Usually one would first examine the full NLU base and produce a *first pass grouping* into tentative broad categories of related meaning. Then, we may need several successive rounds of regrouping into ever smaller meaning categories, until a solution is found, which is an acceptable *compromise* in terms of *internal homogeneity* and the *level of compression* necessary. For each such pass, the interim result may be printed, if we use some computerized method.

The ST-coding/interpretation should be explicit so that interested others can understand and evaluate our judgments, at least for the most critical areas. Also, the interpretations of the researcher can be augmented by independent *validation.* The respondents themselves may be asked to assess the coding (i.e., the categorizing of their NLUs to our ST groups) or we could use a panel of informed judges.

The redundancy removal is only a special case of compressing raw data by successively collapsing the previous level's concepts into larger meaningful categories at a higher level or by mapping them "sideways" into a meaning system based on a different viewpoint. In comparative cause mapping, the main reason for standardizing, of course, is the comparability in terms of the underlying referents instead of the overt terms and language used to refer to them. However, it is important to notice that the data can indeed be converted into several *parallel* or *successive* vocabulary systems. The original NLUs *or* the standard terms—which remain available as reusable databases—can be remapped using different levels of analysis or conceptual frameworks; e.g., the data can be examined in terms of their linguistic properties in addition to the cognitive main perspective. Another example would be to group the first-level standard concepts into a secondary category system based on operative key functions or task areas in the business. This would enable a comparative analysis in terms of the respondents' *cognitive grip* of those domains or functions. In the study example below, the secondary system is a tightly aggregated, artificial concept space, which compresses the near-natural primary-level maps into a compact *overview* of industry thinking.

In comparative mapping studies, one of the standard vocabularies should usually be roughly identical with the original jargon, the NLU base located in the raw data. Its main function is to remove the interpretively unproblematic redundancy caused by normal richness in local jargon. Such a primary ST-set is not difficult to create, and its validation, e.g., by feedback, is easy if it is needed at all. This facilitates analyses and maps which are very close to the originally communicated level and yet not too cluttered. Also, it provides a fallback position for the subsequent ST systems. Such *secondary* vocabulary options are almost limitless, provided there is a rationale, e.g., a theoretical framework linked with them. However, a rigorous *audit trail* to the original observation should be preserved.

Processing Interview Data for Cause Maps

In principle, raw mapping data could be processed manually, at least if the data volume is small. With several sets of natural data for comparative mapping—unless we are prepared to accept a restricted and clumsy analysis—computerized techniques will be necessary. We assume, therefore, at least a general purpose database program or the *CMAP2* program, which was designed specifically for comparative cause mapping processing tasks.

Using a database application, raw data are best entered in *two phases.* First, the natural words/terms (NLUs) of the Ss are input. This updates a *database file,* which will contain every single NLU occurrence in the original interviews. Next, the NCUs (causal links) are input into another database file. Both classes of data are entered in their natural order of occurrence, as defined by the interviews notes or the intermediate transcripts forms. No screening is done here, which means that the databases will have the same content as the raw data sheets/transcripts (cf. note 5).

The natural language used by the respondents for the same referents must usually be *standardized.* As explained above, this means simply that one expression, usually some typical term, will be chosen to represent the synonymous terms. If such a standard vocabulary exists, even in a tentative form, before the NLU-entry, the standard codes are usually best input together with the NLUs. More often, the vocabulary can be created only later. In that case, the NLUs will be "tagged" by inputting their standard term codes separately.

The next operation is to generate the *analyzable databases,* which use the standard vocabulary instead of the original NLUs. Because the raw terms are replaced by the respective standard terms, a kind of a compression takes place, reducing the number of unique units. This is visible in the number of records in the ST-and SCU-databases, which need only one entry (record) for each *unique* standard term or causal unit, used by at least one respondent, because they carry also the *user information.* The present approach uses two analyzable databases:

- A database containing the *standard terms (STs) used* by the respondents, including the incidence information (= *standard term use file,* not to be mixed with the standard vocabulary file), and

- A database file which contains all *standard causal unit types (SCUs)* which were located in the data, also with incidence information for each used unit (= *standard causal unit file*).

The two files form the basis for the comparative mapping analysis of this approach. If the CMAP2 application is used, the two databases are generated by an automatic process, which uses as *source files* the previously created three databases that contain, respectively, the raw data's NLUs, NCUs, and the standard term vocabulary. The generation process can be rerun to test different standardization vocabulary or coding solutions, respondent grouping combinations, or simply to correct an error. If a generic database program is used, the computer operations are analogical. However, the user will now issue successive commands, or, preferably, learn to create small programs in the database application's language, to make it perform the repetitive operations by itself.

Comparative Analysis of Cause Map Elements

The objective of the previous effort is to facilitate the study of natural cognitions within the research framework. The present approach emphasizes two main areas for the comparative analyses:

- The *concept bases* of the respondents can be analyzed and the differences and similarities of term usage studied, including the incidence patterns of terms over groups/clusters of respondents.[6]

- The *causal thinking* patterns are the traditional focal object of analysis. This method emphasizes studying the domain- and problem-related cognitions using the device of focal and domain maps.

The first area, *concept-usage,* has been neglected in cognitive mapping studies. Managerial and organization thinking is action-oriented and functional. Therefore, especially in studies of organization performance, a critical factor to understand is the *interface* of key actors like managers in relation to the context, where the action takes place and which is both an object and a determinant of action. The expressions embedded in the raw data, later standardized, serve as an indication of this interface and the ontology of the respondents (Regoczei and Plantinga 1987, Rouse and Morris 1986, Sowa 1984). As stressed above, the database approach creates information about the standard concepts' ownership, which tells about the *referents* to which the respective actors do (or do not) heed, and of their differences and similarities along this dimension. Thus, the user incidence informs us about the reach and quality of the interface and of the *cognitive grip* the Ss seem to possess relative to their domains of action. It also informs about the prevalent levels and types of thinking among the Ss or their groups.

The *standardized causal units (SCU)* database contains all the SCUs found in the raw data with *incidence* information about which of the respondents own which SCU; all of them, only one of them, or something in between.[7] The database can be subjected to various analyses, depending on whether we use the *CMAP2*-application or a general-purpose database program. In both cases, the analysis is grounded on doing selective listings of SCUs, using a relevant criterion. Examples of technically possible searches are the following:

- Display/list all SCUs that are owned by a certain (individual) respondent.
- As above, with the restriction that the SCUs are idiosyncratic, i.e., belong only to one respondent.
- Display/list all SCUs that are owned by a defined set of respondents.
- As above, but again with the idiosyncrasy restriction.

The queries will access the full SCU database, which may be what is needed. However, sometimes the resulting SCU number can be too high, leading to cumbersome lists. A comparative analysis is often more pointed and meaningful if it is focused on local, action-domain-related thinking about issues like the market position or liquidity maintenance in firms. This follows the concept/interface-logic mentioned earlier, but makes it more dynamic and simulative, which is a unique strength of cause mapping methods as compared with text-based analysis.

Technically, analyses of the requested type are relatively simple using a database program. In *CMAP2*, the following types of SCU-/cause map sets are available as automatic, preprogrammed entities:

- *Focal Map,* which is a set of SCUs generated around a *seed ST-concept,* defined by the researcher, containing the standard concepts that are either causes or effects of the seed term.
- *Domain Map 1,* which contains the focal map SCUs, but adds to this set standard terms that are in a cause or effect position relative to the focal map's *cause* terms.
- *Domain Map 2,* which is similar to the previous one, but contains standard terms that are in a cause or effect position relative to the focal map's *effect* terms.

- *Domain Map 3,* which contains all the above elements.

The principle underlying focal and domain map analysis is to create focused, comparable views of action-domain-related thinking, which is idiosyncratic or shared by a group of actors. In this respect, a database approach is flexible and neutral. For instance, the researcher can use any available seed standard term (ST) he/she sees fit. experiment with different combinations, or trace various paths in the total SCU-set, thereby using constraining criteria that seem relevant. By studying either the cause side (DM1) or the effect side (DM2), the analysis can emphasize, respectively, the control or adaptation or the subjective consequences and utilities aspects in the local thinking. Because of the availability of ownership information for search criteria, it is simple to compare that thinking over Ss or create cognitively homogeneous subgroups and/or locate typical or core thinking patterns.

The majority of PC-database-programs, also the *CMAP2* application, are text-based. Their output are therefore screen or paper listings of the databases, e.g., the focal and domain map sets. If found useful, graphical maps can be drawn using the SCUs as modules. Database programs, including CMAP2, can also create ASCII *text files,* which can then be imported by a word processor for editable reporting.

COMPARING MANAGERIAL CORE THINKING: A STUDY CASE

This section describes an application of the comparative cognitive mapping approach.[8] We will first discuss the study's background and design, which help evaluate the steps taken and how they fit into the approach and its methods solutions.

Study Background and Mechanics

At the outset, the goal was to *understand* the *common substance* in everyday managerial thinking: why and how do managers in established industries come to think in a shared way? That such patterns exist has been shown and was not at issue (e.g., Fahey and Narayanan 1989, Grant 1988, Hall 1984, Porac et al. 1989, Prahalad and Bettis 1986, Spender 1989), although it has been suggested that their operationalization could be more rigorous (Lenz and Engledow 1986, Pfeffer 1981, Prahalad and Bettis 1986, Sproull 1981). However, it is also important to understand their *substantive* or *content* dimension, not just redescribe them or find that they are, indeed, more or less shared. This calls for research targeted to problems of *formation* and to finding explanatory patterns for why and how the specific cognitive contents can be born and, consequently, also a logic why there are those consistent differences, when we compare managers' beliefs over industries. Of course, the *actual* formative processes, i.e., some managerial learning or transfer experiences, can seldom be observed or validly reconstructed retrospectively. Instead, we can expect hypotheses or models of the formative mechanisms in play, at least in their *outline*. However, this will be tentative and general, as they must largely be inferred using the logic of elimination (cf. Allison 1971, Mintzberg 1983, Yin 1991).

In the study, managerial thinking was described in terms of *cause maps.* This provides a new and efficient operationalizing platform for the inherent comparative element of the study. The research was given three interrelated tasks:

- First, a *method* had to be devised to handle the incoming large, natural-language-based raw data and facilitate the comparative cause mapping. The outcome of this work was described above.

- Second, it was necessary to gather the *raw data* and derive and describe the core patterns in the causal thinking, using the new tools.

- The third, substantive, task was to suggest a general *tentative logic* that could account for the found core patterns of managerial thinking, operationalized as cause maps.

In the literature, the *formation* of management thinking has traditionally been explained in terms of organizational learning involving experiential feedback-processes and/or various forms of social transfer and knowledge diffusion (cf. Bandura 1986, Brehmer 1980, Collins and Gentner 1987, Fiol and Lyles 1985, Hedberg 1981, Read 1987). Barring metaphysical phenomena, this is what overtly must happen, but this is inadequate as a general explanation for the *contents* in local thinking.

At the outset, it was assumed that managerial thinking is characteristically functional, pragmatic, i.e., its rationale is to be useful for local managerial functions, notably the firms' survival (Douglas 1986, Schön 1983, Schutz 1962, Scribner 1986, Stubbart 1989). As a corollary, we should expect to find a *correspondence* of local thinking, on one hand, and of at least the most critical demands of survival and the strategic context facing the firms or the industry, on the other. A logical first test of this notion is, of course, if *any shared* patterns of thinking can be found with managers in an industry, because their elicitation presupposes a high level of commonality. To elaborate the formative notion, we must show that such a pattern of thinking/context-isomorphism is consistent, when more industries and their operative subdomains are examined (Yin 1991).

Consequently, the driving logic of the study was largely one of creating observational opportunities regarding the existence or the lack of the cognition/context-isomorphism, hypothesized to constitute an *underlying force* that energizes and directs the manifest processes of organizational learning. In view of the study's scope, novel tasks, and inherent risks, it was decided that a careful comparative analysis of *two* industries would be adequate. Accordingly, the study focused on two established, non-complicated industries: a *special goods retailing* (home electronics and appliance dealers) and the respective *importer-distributor* industry.

The two target industries have different strategic contexts, yet face also identical elements, such as a dependence on the end-consumer and on the munificence of the economy. Interestingly, they share an interface because they cooperate in an importer-distributor-dealer relationship. The training background of the CEOs was varied to highlight the transfer processes of managerial thinking: the distributor CEOs had MBA-level degrees, whereas their dealer counterparts had little formal education. In both groups, four ($n = 4$) medium-sized, comparable firms in terms of size and operations were accessed. The managers—all with over 20 years of industry experience—were *interviewed* for their business-domain thinking patterns in a series of intensive (three 3-4 hrs/manager) interviews, as described earlier. Their work practices and personal histories were examined for possible formative experiences. The strategic tasks and contexts and major modes of operation in both industries were described and analyzed in detail, using outside industry experts as additional informants and judges.

Raw Data and Data Processing

The study's raw data were comprised of the natural language assertions of the Ss representing the local ontology and causal thinking. They were transcribed and processed (see above) using database methods. The standardized concept and causal unit *databases* of the study employed *two levels* of standard vocabularies:

- A *primary level* set of concepts (*PLCs*) that were roughly corresponding to the natural language terms used by the respondents, for synonym redundancy and comparability, and

TABLE 1.1 Primary (PLC) and Aggregate Level (A) Standard Terms

CEOs's Local NLU Expressions	*Collapsed into Primary-level Term*
Dealer's Ability to Play Dealer's Liquidity Dealer's Collateral status Dealer's Financial Situation Dealer's Financial Quality Dealer's Solidity Dealer's Payment History Dealer's Quality/Liquidity Dealer's Prospects/Finances	→ Dealer's Liquidity Financial Status (D01)
Standard Dealer-related Terms	*Collapsed into Aggregate Level Term*
D01: Dealer's Liquidity/Financial Status D03: Dealer's Activity Level D06: Distribution Outlet D10: Dealer Relations D15: Dealer's Know-How D17: Dealer's Inventory Level D27: Dealer Loyalty/Grip	→ Dealer/Distribution (A18)

- A secondary, highly compressed set of *aggregate level* (A) terms, for a summary view of the causal thinking in both industries and for their comparison.

Table 1.1 gives an example of the vocabulary levels, including the raw data level. The first array contains natural language expression (NLUs), used by the distributor CEOs to describe their dealer firms' cash position and ability to meet their financial obligations: in plain language, to pay their bills in time. The NLUs were first collapsed (standardized) using a vocabulary of *primary level concept* (PLC), e.g., *dealer's liquidity/financial status* (D01). This merging was soft. In addition, the PLC vocabulary was also standardized, by merging them *hard,* as can be seen in the lower array, where all PLCs, including the D01, that pertain to dealers and the distribution system, as used by the distributor CEOs, were now collapsed into a single *aggregate-level standard term* (A18).

The study's raw data comprised of 1418 + 2120 original expressions (NLUs) in the dealer and distributor CEO clusters, respectively. The first-level standardizing resulted in a standard term use database (= PLCs in use) of 240 terms for the dealer group and 257 terms for the distributor group. The net PLC number was 352, because 145 of the PLC terms were owned by at least one respondent in both clusters. Most PLCs were, of course, shared by several respondents.

Analysis of the Concept Bases

As noted, the standard term use database contains information about each term's *user incidence.* In the study, we used this facility to explore two concept-related issues:

- What is the *logic of the concept use,* i.e., why do managers use exactly those concepts, enact (Weick 1977) those referents, and not something else and

- What *mechanisms* could have produced exactly those concepts and their underlying NLUs as the managers' memory *traces* to be now encountered by the study's data acquisition process?

To demonstrate a database analysis, we can examine a high-profiled case produced by a restrictive search. Array A in Table 1.2 lists PLCs that were shared by *everyone* among the eight interviewed managers, dealers, and distributors alike, thus indicating phenomena that are shared in *both* industries. Array B, on the other hand, contains PLCs used by everybody in the *dealer* set, but by none of the distributor managers. Finally, C's PLCs were used by all *distributor* CEOs, but not by any dealer.

Substantively, we can observe that the found concept-ownership incidence follows the expected logic of pragmatics and contextual isomorphism. The managers' situations contain phenomena they encounter frequently and must conceptualize and label for comprehension and communication. The contexts provide differentially the phenomena to be labeled and the functional needs as the motive to do so. Both forces are adequately similar within the groups but dissimilar across them. Moreover, they were salient enough to be shared and to turn up in these sets, despite the high threshold of the search.

Focal Maps of Interrelationships

The raw data contained a very large number of natural causal assertions (NCUs). The standardization fused some of them, when both end-NLU nodes collapsed into a single PLC. The PLC-level database of standardized causal units contained finally 1932 + 2957 SCUs for the dealer and distributor

TABLE 1.2 Industry-common and Industry-typical Standard Terms

A: Standard Primary Level (PLC)	*Terms Used by All Respondents*
Profitability	"Product Tails"
Gross Margin	Industry Demand
Margin Level	Personnel Motivation
Volume/Sales	SP-campaign(s)
Sales Promotion-support	Firm's Market Position
Inventory	Firm's Image
B: Exclusive Terms/Dealers	*C: Exclusive Terms/Distributors*
Entrepreneur Role/Risk	Dealer Purchases
Overdue Interest	Dealer Targets
Store Location	Dealer Number/Market Area
Dealer Colleagues	Slow-moving Products
"Inventory Heaps"	Competitor(s)
Customer Traffic	Brand Advertising
"Natural Demand"	Dealer Liquidity/Finan. Status
Brand's Competitiveness	Dealer Loyalty/Grip on Dealer

groups, respectively. The reason for the still high number was the soft approach used in PLC-level standardizing, which avoided collapsing together NLUs that could not be shown to have the same referent content. The analysis used SCUs that were shared by at least half of the respondents in either industry group. There were 372 + 665 such SCUs, for the dealers and distributors respectively.

The SCU-database analysis was analogical with that for the standard terms. We perform selective searches based on the user information and links in the databases, using mainly two sets of criteria:

- *Owner-related criteria:* Who or which groups among the respondents use which SCU, either alone or shared with others.

- *Action-domains:* Focal and Domain-map analysis (see above) by cutting off subsets of SCUs of the total set to represent causal thinking patterns relative to an important topic or action area.

The direct outcome of the database operations are (paper or screen) *lists* of SCUs. Using them, we can create matrices or draw visual cause maps, whatever is useful. The real work is in the analysis, making the distilled data illuminate relevant areas and provide answers to research questions.

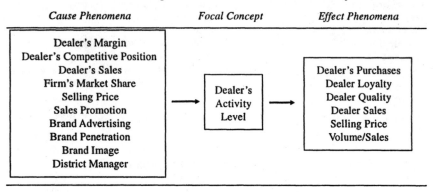

TABLE 1.3 Focal Maps of Dealer- and Distributor-manager's Reciprocal Causal Beliefs

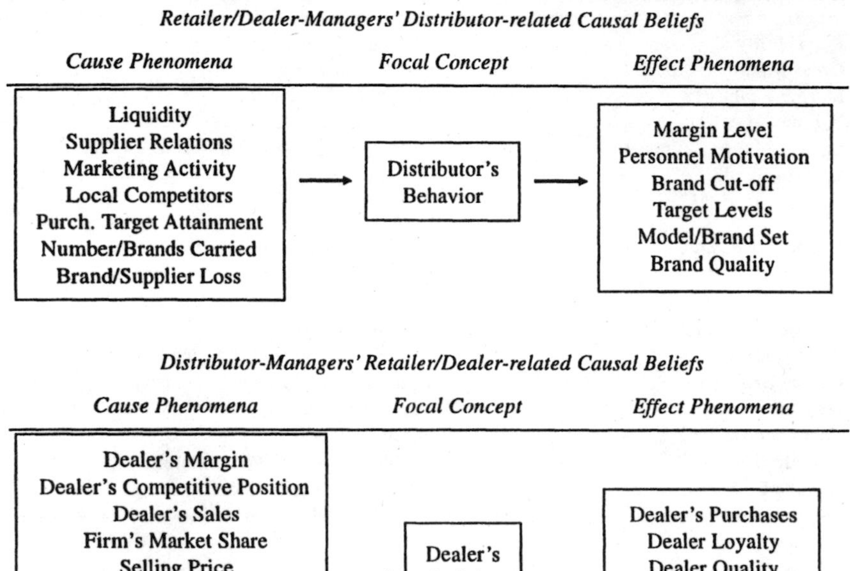

One of the promising areas to examine was how the two industries *collaborate* to fulfill important strategic needs and view the other party as a social player to be influenced, even manipulated, to ensure the flow of the necessities. Illuminative views of the patterns can created by using Focal Maps, an example of which is shown in Table 1.3.

The upper array lists the phenomena that most *dealers* believe affect their suppliers, i.e., distributor firms, and the things they feel the distributors respectively influence on in a dealer firm. Some of the phenomena are controllable by the dealer, some are not, and serve mainly to explain (attribute) the distributor's behavior towards dealers. Respectively, the *distributors* —who critically need dealers to reach the end consumer—see the dealers' level of activity and cooperation as affecting important outcomes. They also have notions of what controls the level of dealer interest. Should we trace the influence paths *behind* the shown elements using Domain Maps or sequential Focal Maps, we would find further indications of subjective, industry-typical processes, which the CEOs have learned.

For the study, the simple Focal Map analysis highlights some of the generic formative tendencies which underlie managerial thinking. Stable outside constituencies, controlling key resources or contingencies, will be influential in the context and thus also in the thinking about it, leaving their marks in the cognitive maps of the counterplayers. Here, such imprinting processes were obvious, e.g., the ongoing communication during negotiations at different levels will continuously teach the interests, often also their explanations, of one party to the other.

Cause Mapping Strategic Domains

To focus the analysis of cause maps on locally relevant areas of action, we use Domain Maps, i.e., sets of SCUs selectively filtered of the total SCU-database as described. Thus, we can study how the respondents and the industry groups structure important strategic and operative problems, such as:

- How to *control a key phenomenon,* i.e., what are the typical situation elements that affect it and what can be done to tackle them?

- What are the *contextual elements* that affect valued phenomena, but to which we must adapt, perhaps taking some counter-measures?

- What seem to be the *key criteria* that are heeded to when controlling a phenomenon or when adapting to an environmental factor change?

Technically (see above), the domains or phenomena studied are defined by a seed concept (PLC), when the Domain Map's SCU-set generation is started. At the same time, we choose the respondents or groups to be analyzed and the type of the maps, depending on whether we need to look at the cause or the effect side, i.e., to stress the problems of influence, control, and attributions, or those of prediction and evaluation. The lists of SCUs can be converted into a graphical format for visual comparison.

For the study, domain analysis was important. To illustrate, Figure 1.4 gives a partial view of a Domain Map 1. It remains the *distributor* CEOs' thinking about how their company *sales,* obviously a key phenomenon *non plus ultra,* are affected and controlled. Also, the immediate consequences of the phenomenon "sales" are visible in this map.

To facilitate a comparison, Figure 1.5 is the counterpart of the distributor managers' view, mapping the sales control problem from the *dealers'* viewpoint. For them, too, sales is a critical *sine qua non.* The point—in methods

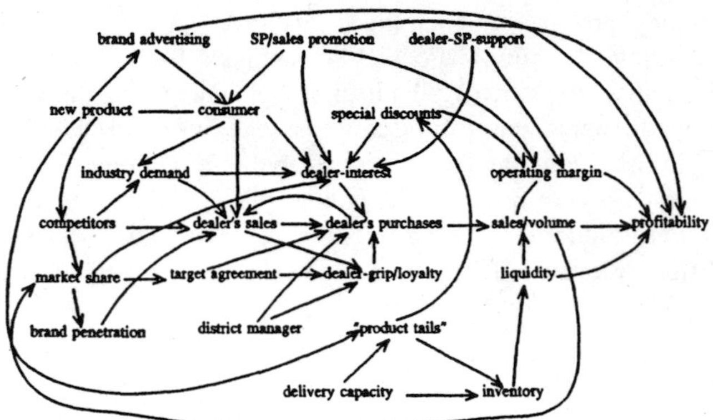

Figure 1.4. Sales Control Domain Map 1 of Distributor Managers

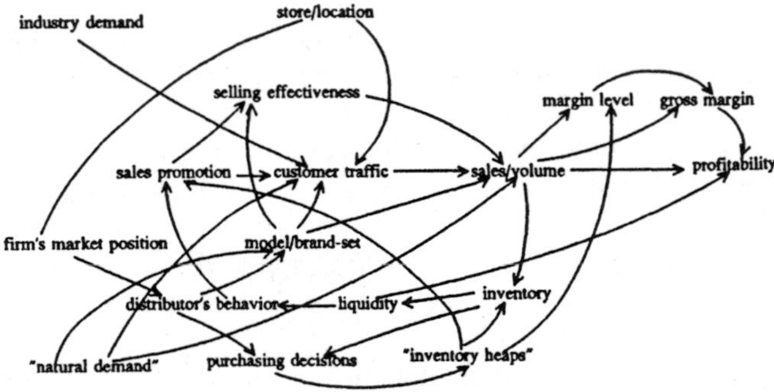

Figure 1.5. Sales Control Domain Map 1 of Dealer Managers

terms—is that, using the two cause maps, we can *compare,* how the *same* strategic task, i.e., sustaining sales, is represented in the minds of the two manager groups. It is consistently dissimilar over the groups whereas, within them, the thinking, for its core features, is very similar. Note again that unless this were not so, we could not have elicited any such shared map systems.

At first glance, the cause maps seem complicated despite the fact that they are in the standard PLC language instead of the natural terms and that only a quite limited set of available standard causal belief units is included. However, the maps represent the managers' real-life thinking about a key area and are results of years of learning. That is seldom simple even for partial domains. The observation is, however, a healthy reminder of the limits of graphical maps' usefulness for cognitive analyses.

The dealer managers' domain map (Figure 1.5) is less dense, indicating a simpler cognitive task/problem or a way of structuring. The operative strategy of a typical dealer is conspicuous. Sales are generated in the store, where customers are drawn by promotions, store location, etc. To sell, one needs tools such as products and effective sales work. These are controlled by one's own decisions and the actions of other parties, notably suppliers and competitors. The same—in *relative* terms—task of sales generation looks quite different from the distributor managers' perspective. In their map (Figure 1.4), the dealers appear as a critical intermediary. Now, the sales equal dealers purchases. which depend on dealers' sales, and, among other things, on the prototypical consumer. The map displays several links that mirror the normal methods of sales control, incorporated in the taxonomics and doctrines of marketing.

For the study, the domain maps illustrate the isomorphism theme. Managerial thinking as we found it is clearly not random but internally and externally logical and consistent in the groups. Why is this? We can see how the relevant *action contexts* must have been learned and *internalized* by the actors, so as to later emerge within the raw data and the cause maps. We can conjecture that this is as if the cause maps were overt traces, "frozen dynamics," of past problem-solving processes, performed many times over, thus providing a tentative explanation for the observed situational isomorphism of the underlying causal link assertions. In addition, besides being experientially learned causal tendencies, they are probably also pieces of industry-wide knowledge, transmitted through various socializing processes (cf. Bandura 1986, Brehmer 1980, Collins and Gentner 1987, DiMaggio and Powell 1983).

In a similar fashion, models for thinking about any strategically or operatively interesting domain can be constructed, assuming data has been collected and duly processed. Using selective SCU listings, underlying the Focal and Domain Maps, analyzing them, drawing interesting cuts into a graphical format, we can perform thorough comparative analyses of managerial cognitions. That was facilitated by the successive processing of the acquired rich natural data into the standardized databases.

Aggregate Level Analysis and Comparisons

As the last type of in the study, we will look at the consequences of further compressing the standard PLC vocabulary (Table 1.2). Its objective was a *summary* view of the thinking patterns in both industries so that they could be directly *compared.* This was accomplished by a second vocabulary, a new meaning space, into which the PLCs in use and the PLC-level SCUs were mapped.

There were only 24 *aggregate (A)* level concepts, which are thus very, broad categories of phenomena. Analogically with the primary level causal units, aggregate-level causal unit sets (A-SCU) were created first for both of the industry groups. In this case, for compactness and calculation, cause *matrices* were used next. They have been customary in cognitive mapping, e.g., in path analysis. Here, the objective was only to compare the two industries by locating the different or identical causal units in the groups. This was done by building, first, an *industry matrix* for both industries with an *identical row/column-structure* using the A-level SCU-lists and a computer spreadsheet program. The distributor matrix was then simply multiplied by factor 2, after which both matrices were added into a *sum matrix.* This contained now active cell entries, whose values range from 1 to 3 to indicate the industry ownership of each A-SCU.

Table 1.4 displays the sum matrix. The cell values 1, 2, and 3 denote, respectively, the dealer or the distributor industry group, or both together, as the origin of each aggregated causal unit. In the study itself, also the Id/Od-values were calculated as column/row-sums, respectively. All three map systems were also drawn for visual inspection.

For the study, the aggregate-level matrix is a representation that models the interviewed managers' thinking in an extremely dense way. Because of the coding and the identical matrix (and map) structures, the causal patterns of the two industry groups can now be easily *compared.* In the matrix form shown, this is seen, e.g., as the *shared* causal units (cell = 3). When we draw this particular set of A-SCUs into a map (Figure 1.6), the common elements, representing the intersection of the maps, have a pattern with a plausible logic.

The mapped *intersection* pattern is interpretable in terms of the basic contingencies of *both* industries. Among the obvious ones, with a correlate trace in the shared aggregate map, is the fact that both are *trading businesses,* dealing with the market by marketing (A14) their products. Integral elements of trading are operations such as purchasing (A10) or carrying inventory (A09)—i.e., merchandise in hand making subsequent sales possible but incurring risks of unsaleability and margin losses (A03, A05) and cost of financing (A05, A03). Second, operating under money and market economy brings along issues of liquidity (A05), financial results (A03), and the existence of antagonistic organizations, called competitors (A11). Lastly, both classes of firms are *social organizations* that consist of people (A12), who implement the business. They must be led/managed (A01) by managers,

TABLE 1.4 Aggregate-Level Causal Links in the Dealer- (1) and Distributor-Managers' (2) Cause Maps with the Shared Links (3) in a Cause Matrix Format

Aggregate Level Terms With Clusters Tag (Code)	*A 01*	*A 02*	*A 03*	*A 04*	*A 05*	*A 06*	*A 07*	*A 08*	*A 09*	*A 10*	*A 11*	*A 12*	*A 13*	*A 14*	*A 15*	*A 16*	*A 17*	*A 18*	*A 19*	*A 20*	*A 21*	*A 22*	*A 23*	*A 24*	*A 25*
A01 Management							2		1	1	2	2				1	2	2	1						1
A02 Firm/Business Unit	1		1		1											1									
A03 Financial Performance	3	3			1		2		2	1		3		2		1	2	2		2				2	
A04 Economic Factors												3													
A05 Financial Position			1													1									
A06 Societal Factors	1										1			2	1										
A07 Firm Strategies		2	1						1	1		1		2	1	1								2	1
A08 Industry											2											2			
A09 Inventory Status			3		3																				
A10 Purchasing/Purchases			1							3															
A11 Market/Consumer		1	3				1			1			3	2	1			2	2						
A12 Organization	2		3											3			2							2	
A13 Competition			3											2	2	1			1					2	
A14 Marketing			3		2					3					2			2						2	1
A15 Product/-set		1	3				1		2		3			2		1		1				2			
A16 Supplier/ Manufacturer					1											3				2		2			
A17 Concern Level	2	2					2													2					
A18 Dealer/Distributor			2				2					2	2	2										2	
A19 Operations	3			2								3		2											
A20 Market Position		2											2	1		1		2							
A21 International Factors											2				2									2	
A22 Constraining Organizations			2											2										2	
A23 Dealer-chain/Concentration																		2							
A24 Brand/-position		2	2										2		1			2	2	2					
A25 Firm's Image																1									

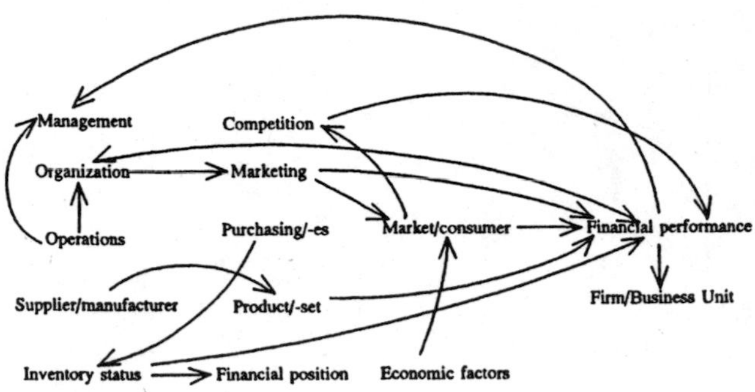

Figure 1.6. Aggregate Level Map of Shared Causal Units

who may have a personal stake in the situation, as is the case with the dealer entrepreneurs.

Methodically, it can be argued that compression of this magnitude creates cognitive representations of problematic validity. We should observe, however, that validity depends partially on the meaning compression, here from the PLC to the A-level. Also, doing something like this has advantages, and, to calm us down, we can note parallels like factor or principal component analysis. They perform some of the interpretive work for the researcher, but this is only a matter of degree. In interpretively oriented research, the degrees of freedom are higher than here. Naturally, one must be careful about what such dense, artificial models of thinking are argued to represent. Certainly they are not natural replicas of the local thinking, but they may be useful as models of its basic elements and core belief patterns.

COGNITIVE MAPPING AND MOC-RESEARCH

This chapter first raises some methodological and methods issues in cause mapping (CM), which are sometimes overlooked. Second, we will sum up the comparative and database-oriented approach to CM, incorporated in the *CMAP2* application. Finally, methods-related projects and examples of substantive MOC research topics for the comparative approach are suggested.

Methodological Issues in Cognitive Mapping

As a research tradition, cognitive mapping has been characteristically *method-driven.* Many practitioners in the field saw the basic CM techniques as a "heaven-sent" for fascinating new research. With some exceptions (cf. Cossette and Audet 1992), ontological and methodological issues have largely been deferred to be addressed later. Although there are not necessarily any definite answers, a discussion may at least sensitize future researchers to some problems and options in the tradition.

Mapping What? Implied by the label *cognitive* mapping, it is normally assumed that we are, of course, in the business of studying cognitions. However, it is possible to loosen at least cause mapping of that premise, positioning it as a generic tool for many representation and analytic tasks. At least five such candidates are possible. Cause maps can be used to (1) analyze a *discourse* itself, especially for the causalistic dimension, or they can (2) model *a domain of reality,* its entities and their interrelationships, as represented in the knowledge/belief base of the respondents or of the researchers themselves (cf. Diffenbach 1982, Roos and Hall 1980). They can also represent (3) interlinked, domain-related *knowledge and/or belief-base,* e.g., an "ideology" or a "worldview" of a group, as manifested in related communication. Traditionally, they are assumed to model (4) the *cognitive structures* of the respondent/s, called, e.g., schemas, cognitive maps, or mental models. At the same time, however, cause maps will also mirror (5) cognitive *processes,* such as generating algorithms or heuristics, which the respondents may use when they produce their oral responses or some text data. As a set of techniques, cognitive/cause mapping is not critically sensitive to what the underlying interpretation or theoretic stance is. Thus, it can serve a wide set of research traditions.

There is a related issue: how specific should MOC studies be about their underlying assumptions, in this case especially about the individual and social cognitive mechanisms, which are necessary to make the research and its results meaningful and plausible. It is apparent that many feel that MOC research can live without such explicit platforms, possibly because its problems, by the academic division of labor, are not about *pure* cognition, but rather about using cognition. However, e.g., studies of cognition-performance links are unconvincing without plausible mechanisms that mediate between the two spheres. Likewise, cognitive mapping could sometimes be more attentive to its underpinnings, at least if it is supposed to represent real-life cognitions. For instance, cause maps sometimes have an artificial character, with a life given by the researcher. Large map systems with hundreds of nodes and links may be analyzed as independent entities, searching for paths, feedback loops, clusters, etc. The map's humble origins appear forgotten, creating instead a virtual reality without a plausible real-life counterpart that could be owned by people with normal cognitive capabilities or located in the context of origin. On the other hand, such an approach is of course, defensible and useful if the objective is idea generation or decision support (Eden et al. 1992, Morecroft 1992, Rosenhead 1989), i.e., various heuristic or "emancipatory" purposes (Cossette and Audet 1992).

Method vs. Data. Using traditional or the more advanced techniques for idiosyncratic and composite cognitive mapping (cf. Cropper et al. 1990, Eden 1989, 1991; Lee et al. 1992) or the present comparative CM method, it is possible to *represent, analyze, and compare* individual or organizational cognitions, of course, in the sense incorporated by each method. This is no small feat, considering the short history of the tradition. However, in terms of the main objectives in MOC research, CM itself, *any* method, is a minor player, although a necessary one.

The critical problem in most MOC studies is their dependence on human communication for raw data, and the validity of data in terms of each task. This issue was implied by Schwenk's (1989) question: "Can we believe what they say?" referring, e.g., to distorted or withheld information about managerial thinking in documents like company reports. Does this render archival data always useless? On the other hand, it has been suggested that direct questioning, such as in the present approach, could introduce biases (Fiol 1990). Should we forget about local eliciting, too?

In MOC studies, the raw data production by our Ss must usually be *retrospective,* post-hoc, as they respond to our probing by simulating events in the "mind's eye" in terms of some virtual, reconstructed subjective reality. Thus, there is another dimension in validity, expressed by asking: "Can they say what they believe?" Some view this pessimistically; e.g., Argyris and Schön (1978) argued that people cannot talk about their *theories-in-use* as differentiated from the *espoused* ones, which we will hear. The former—"real stuff"—should be inferred instead, changing of course the problem into another form.

Today, a cautiously optimistic view has surfaced, suggesting that validity depends largely on the type of cognitive elements acquired, and on the methods' appropriateness. Assuming no filtering, people are now regarded as capable of producing valid data on their declarative knowledge, either by accessing memory or by reconstructing ad hoc the requested explanations (causes) or predictions (effects) (Bandura 1986, Evans 1988, Gordon 1992). These are the raw data we elicit and will present later, e.g., as cause maps. Importantly, if the momentary reconstruction is about the same that would consistently happen anyway, i.e., *"in-use,"* this need not bother us much. Moreover, we seldom could really differentiate between them. Furthermore, it is also possible that effects and prevalence of interview filtering are overdramatized. First, many researchers have experiences now even very sophisticated managers will, assuming rapport and trust, talk astonishingly openly, producing authentic, sincere data. More importantly, filtering, which is probably always present, is often a random thing, whose effects may be assumed to cancel themselves when several Ss are interviewed. Also, they are less important when data are used for locating general, shared patterns (Spender 1989).

Despite such cheery notes, validity problems will stay with us. Instead of extreme views or lamenting over unavoidable problems, however, a more realistic stance and sophisticated methods for data acquisition and assessment are called for. E.g., documentary data may reveal some of the underlying cognitions, using unobtrusive semiotic methods or simple concept analysis (Fiol 1990, p. 240, Huff 1990, p. 17). Especially methods and approaches for eliciting natural data at-site need developing. This work could benefit of the psychological and AI/KE methods (cf. Evans 1988, Gammack and Young 1984, Isenberg 1986, Kidd 1987) and elicitation approaches in cognitive anthropology (Holland and Quinn 1987) and discourse analysis (Potter and Wetherell 1990).

Adequacy of Cause Maps. Cause maps have been *criticized*, e.g., for nonexisting feedback-loops, nonrepresentation of the subjective certainty level of the causal links, or missing time element (Huff 1990, p. 31). At closer look, these problems are caused by their raw (archival) data or they simply reflect a tradition. Thus, they can, if necessary be amended, using, respectively, natural data or by adding to the elicited and mapped detail, e.g., the descriptive notation of cause maps can—technically—be more detailed than is customary.[9] However, there is a trade-off between elicited detail and the cognitive domain covered. In the above study case, e.g., the characteristics of causal links were *not* inquired, because time would have been expended on simple questions whether the links are direct or indirect, etc. Yet, the outcome would have been largely irrelevant in terms of the research questions.

What to include in the visible information base and what should be left out, even uncovered, to produce an adequate cause map obviously will depend on the *task* the map is meant for. Clearly, CM, in its traditional form, is not cranking out answers like an Expert System. It could perhaps be adapted for useful (subjective) system simulation and related hypothesis testing (Nozicka et al. 1976, Bonham et al. 1988). We know that CM can be powerful in DSS and heuristic purposes for individual and group decision making. Also, it can be used for describing and understanding important elements in past strategic thinking, for analyzing its changes (see above) and, importantly, for teaching them.

Underlying the established uses is the notion that cause mapping is a robust tool that helps capture—for overt observation and analysis—covert aspects of individual and social thinking, although certainly not *everything* they may include. More studies are needed to show the strengths and limits of the method and what new dimensions of cognition should be added in the basic toolset we now know.

Comparative Cognitive Mapping with Databases

The critical phases in the approach discussed are *data acquisition* and *standardizing*. To compare people's causal thinking or to locate cognitively homogeneous groups, the first prerequisite are data, produced in a *uniform* acquisition process. Next, the resulting expressions need *standardizing*, which will enable us to find out about the referent phenomena that lie behind the many synonymous words used as their proxies. This will determine how valid the actual comparison and its conclusions will be and how faithful to the original terms the standardized meaning space will be. Only then, using whatever techniques, we can construct the analyzable sets of standardized concepts and causal units, owned by the Ss, to be used as representations of individual or group cognitions.

Although data processing could be done manually, computerizing will considerably extend the limits of data volume and our analytic possibilities. A powerful, yet quite accessible platform is offered by common (relational) *database* programs. This is based on the simple observation that cause maps can be *decomposed* into constituent *units* like concepts and the causal relationships. These are stored in database files (cf. Laukkanen 1992) along with related information, e.g., the units' ownership. Using this information as criteria, we can perform data transformations and various searches and listings of the databases. These constitute an important part of comparative cause mapping operations and analysis. In addition, by creating automatic routines using the command language incorporated in most advanced database programs, we can further enhance our processing power and analytic options.

Database programs are neutral, as far as a researcher's theoretic stance or methodical decisions are concerned. For example, they accept different standard vocabularies, including stupid ones, and do not mind if the interpretation given to the links among the concepts are not causalistic at all but, e.g., connotative or temporal. Also, database platforms provide flexibility by making repeated analysis passes reasonable, e.g., in tests of different vocabulary or criteria systems or when using the database for different subprojects. Databases are useful tools when planted in the cause mapping paradigm.

CMAP2 is a database-oriented program,[10] designed specifically only for the data processing and modes of analysis needs in the comparative cause mapping approach (Laukkanen 1992). It consists of uncomplicated subprograms for the various tasks, such as input of natural concepts (NLUs) and causal assertions (NCUs), creation of the standard vocabulary, the generation of the analyzable files of standard terms (STs) and standard causal units (SCUs), and, finally, tools for analyzing these sets and producing comparative findings about the cognitions. The application can also hold several CMAP projects accessible, including projects that share one or more of the source databases.

Some Future Studies

First, developing *CM methods* offers many options for research. It is clear that the more we use natural data, the more critical are smooth, reliable processing and analytic tools. As shown, traditional methods of CM can benefit considerably, if rather plain databases are used. However, as the power of personal computers grows, there is an impetus to new software for basic data input and analysis, which just process more data at higher speeds. However, this will be most useful for *simulation* software of MOC and for *DSS/EIS*-related applications in organizations, which certainly are fields where we should see exciting new developments. There are more mundane areas, too:

- Exporting of the *CMAP2* facilities into a *graphical user interface* (GUI) environment like Windows, preferably with added capabilities for analysis and output.
- Combining the present comparative database- and text-oriented analysis with *concurrent graphical map* production and analysis in a visual graph format.
- Adding to the coverage or *representative detail* by bringing new dimensions of cognition into the sphere of computerized analysis.
- Methods for *direct raw data acquisition* and input by the actors themselves, possibly coupled with some primary-level standardizing, using the concurrent feedback opportunity.

A subarea in methods' research are mapping-related *quantitative measures*. There is a paradox: if we add to the descriptive grain or broaden the coverage of the cognitive domains, we loosen the broad view and weaken the intuitive comparability. This is harmful in comparative tasks, also underlying explanatory designs. Therefore, we need to develop map-based measures that carry stable, concise information, yet are intuitive and meaningful enough in terms of the actual cognitions.

Second, as to *substantive studies* in the MOC field (cf. Schwenk 1988, Stubbart 1989), cause mapping is probably most useful as a *"blackboard."* It can operationalize parts of located, sometimes evolving or non-evolving, organizational thinking or, if we will, at least the patterns of discourse about the phenomena. Some previous studies exemplify this idea (cf. Fahey and Narayanan 1989, Hall 1984, Sevón 1984, Stubbart and Ramaprasad 1988). This research is not interested in the maps themselves—or whatever the overt format—but instead wants to describe, explain, or predict aspects of the underlying belief configurations, discourse themes, or the referent phenomena found in the context. The comparative methodology introduced here can be employed in further projects along such lines.

As an example, studies could build on the assumption of *core organizational thinking* patterns, operationalizing these with cause maps. It would be interesting to clarify, e.g., how far they really are shared. In *CMAP* terms, shared cognitions in organizations should be observable as overlapping or incongruent elements in the map systems originating with people of different hierarchical or functional positions. Another study might examine cognitive adaptation and learning in management, defined as evolution around such a core or as changes in the core itself. Variations of the theme could study the diffusion processes in industries or the effects of the differential verifiability of the environments.

Another area can be based on the observation that MOC studies are often ultimately concerned with *performance* in organizations. This involves the issue of beliefs/knowledge data's usability for predicting performance (cf. Nystrom and Starbuck 1984, Stubbart 1989). However, threshold problems like the mediation of manager's influence need to be addressed, too. E.g., the cognitive impact implied by ideas like industry recipe (Spender 1989), management's symbolic role (Pfeffer 1981), or the loose-coupling concept within organizations (Orton and Weick 1990), would benefit from being operationalized in more tangible and cognitively meaningful terms, as shown in the study discussed here. In such research, comparative cause mapping can help contrast the substantive and the structural differences, e.g., the cognitive complexity dimension, in the knowledge structures of managers or groups, who perform at different modes or levels.

Although overtly different, the critical tasks in such research projects would be more or less identical: a need to acquire comparable natural data